BYRON THE MAKER

By the same author

The Myth of the Bad Lord Byron (Old Forge Press, 1998)

Bright Darkness: The Poetry of Lord Byron Presented in the Context of his Life and Times (Nottingham Court Press, 1984)

In Search of Byron in England and Scotland (Old Forge Press, 1988)

This Means Mischief (Robert Hale, 1996)

Death and Deconstruction (Robert Hale, 1995)

The Desert and the Marketplace: Writings, Letters, Journals of Ursula Fleming, ed. A Fleming (Gracewing, 1995)

Sophie is Gone (Robert Hale, 1994)

There Goes Charlie: A Rural Murder (Collins Crime Club, 1990)

BYRON THE MAKER

Liberty, Poetry and Love

Part One: Byron in England

Part Two: Byron in Exile

Anne Fleming

Book Guild Publishing
Sussex, England

First published in Great Britain in 2009 by
The Book Guild Ltd
Pavilion View
19 New Road
Brighton, BN1 1UF

Volume One: Byron in England
published by Book Guild Publishing, 2006

Typesetting in Times by
Keyboard Services, Luton, Bedfordshire

Printed in Great Britain by
Antony Rowe, Chippenham, Wiltshire

A catalogue record for this book is available from
The British Library

ISBN 978 1 84624 339 4

BYRON THE MAKER

Maker – one that makes; (archaic) – a poet

If the essence of poetry must be a *Lie* – throw it to the dogs – or banish it from your republic – as Plato would have done – he who can reconcile Poetry with truth and wisdom – is the one true *'Poet'* in its real sense – *'the Maker' 'the Creator'*.

(Byron's Letter to John Murray Esqre, 1821)[1]

In one of the plates of *Los Caprichos*, originally intended as a frontispiece, Goya shows the artist asleep over his drawing-board, while nightmarish bats, owls and huge cats swarm up behind him. It is captioned *El sueño de la razón produce monstruos*. Byron has not a little in common with his great elder contemporary. They recall each other in their real feeling for gaiety and innocence; in their savage indignation against war and tyranny; in their honesty, more shattering than mere contempt, towards little men in great places; in their rejoicing in the sensuous beauty of women. Not least, both were sons of the Enlightenment, who, without denying the claims of the heart, believed passionately that 'the sleep of reason breeds monsters'.

M.K. Joseph, *Byron the Poet*[2]

Byron's years of sexual and geographic exploration made him the great and sympathetic reader of human motives that he was.

Jonathan David Gross, *Byron the Erotic Liberal*[3]

Even sound authors are wrong in stubbornly trying to weave us into one invariable and solid fabric... Whoever would judge a man in his detail, piece by piece, would hit on the truth more often.

Montaigne

CONTENTS

INTRODUCTION

This book is, I believe, at a rough guess, the 204th biography of Byron since his death. I have called it *Byron the Maker* because writing the life of a great poet requires a treatment which regards the works as not wholly other than the life. No-one could write a satisfactory life of Beethoven without understanding, and even perhaps foregrounding, the music.

Professor John Clubbe has asked for such a biography 'so that Byron's words may be as compelling for our time as Beethoven's music and for comparable reasons – because they exalt and challenge the human spirit.'[1]

I do not believe that *Byron the Maker* will achieve what Professor Clubbe is looking for, but it is written in answer to his request and I hope it is a step in the right direction. To those familiar with William Anderson's *Dante the Maker* I should make it clear that in echoing his title I am naturally making no comparison of *Byron the Maker* with that brilliant work, but I do invite comparison of Byron with Dante and this should raise no eyebrows.

Byron the Maker will work from the evidence in order to build (so far as possible) a true image of Byron the Poet just as a forensic scientist builds up the simulacrum of a living face from the bare bones of the skull when the flesh and skin and features have been obliterated. The forensic scientist neither wants, nor expects, a certain sort of face – a beautiful face or an ugly face. He wants the real face. So do I. This requires the reader to expunge all preconceived notions about the subject and be willing to start afresh.

In his book, *Gorky Park*, Martin Cruz Smith describes how the scientist builds the face and arrives at a mid-point which might have been the building of the features by a sculptor or a dissection of them by an anatomist.[2]

The biographer working on his subject may be either, or both, sculptor (artist) or anatomist (scientist) but, more important, he must be passionate in pursuit of the truth we owe the dead, whether the biographer and his readers find it palatable or not.

The story of Byron as man and poet is startling enough. It requires no suppression of evidence, no exaggeration, no distortion, no unfounded speculation, no unnecessary and definitive judgements, no overarching psychological or theoretical explanations. It does, however, need extensive and representative quotations.

Byron's character cannot easily be pinned down, studied and explained. His great friend (and biographer) Thomas Moore judged that his poetry and his life were so intermingled that it was not easy to distinguish the real from the fanciful in either.

It was unfortunate that the young woman Byron chose as his bride was wholly unable to distinguish between the fanciful and the real in Byron's discourse. It is not easy for the biographer. Byron is as changeable as our images of the moon. If he says something outrageous at one time he may say the opposite at another. And both may be true. His comprehension and grasp of a reality as protean as himself is all-encompassing. We should expect a biography to explore as far as possible the bewildering totality of Byron's character and life rather than abide by some master interpretation of it.

In 1822 he listed some comparisons made by his contemporaries:

> ... I have seen myself compared personally or poetically – in English, French, *German* (as interpreted to me), Italian and Portuguese within these nine years – to Rousseau – Goethe – Young – Aretine – Timon of Athens – 'An Alabaster Vase lighted up within', Satan – Shakespeare – Buonaparte – Tiberius – Aeschylus – Sophocles – Euripides – Harlequin – The Clown – Sternhold and Hopkins – to the Phantasmagoria – to Henry the 8th, to Chenier – to Mirabeau – to young R. Dallas (the school boy) to Michael Angelo – to Raphael – to a petit mâitre – to Diogenes, to Childe Harold – to Lara – to the Count in *Beppo* – to Milton – to Pope – to Dryden – to Burns – to Savage – to Chatterton – to 'oft have I heard of thee my Lord Biron' in Shakespeare, to Churchill the poet – to Kean the Actor – to Alfieri &tc. &tc.[3]
>
> (*Detached Thoughts*, 1821)

To produce a clear-cut image of so many-faceted a character may prove impossible. It may be necessary to admit to being completely baffled by the complex nature of the poet who was acclaimed a genius at the age of twenty-four. We may have to settle for no more than a shimmering reflection of the clear-cut image we are trying to build,

This will be something, but it will not be enough. We can hope that the 205th biography will go a little further in pursuit of what Professor Clubbe and all his colleagues in the world of Byron studies require, but which is needed, not by professional Byronists, but by the informed general public to whom, unlike many of his contemporaries, Byron addressed his writing and the judgement on his life.

PREFACE

In telling the story of Byron's life and work my aim is to rely on nothing which is not supported by what appears to be reliable evidence. The sources I have used are the works of writers and scholars of integrity both familiar and recent who have researched Byron's life; of literary critics whose explanations of the poetry and the literary traditions surrounding Byron, have proved most useful to me; of those historians and letter-writers who have cast useful light on the time in which Byron lived; and, above all, the letters and journals, the poetry and the prose of Byron himself.

Where I provide insufficient detail for some readers the best bet remains the three-volume *Byron a Biography* by Leslie A. Marchand (1957), bearing in mind, however, that Professor Marchand was obliged by the rigid decorum of that period to censor his own work. By 1971 when he published the shorter version, *Byron a Portrait* he was able to speak freely on matters which were unmentionable in print in 1957. Marchand's work has the great advantage of scrupulous reliance on declared sources.

By far the most valuable source on Byron is his own words. To paraphrase them would be absurd. But there are pitfalls of which the reader should be made aware throughout. Particularly in his early days Byron is apt to strike dramatic attitudes which did not necessarily represent his true feelings but, confusingly, sometimes do; in common with many other young men in Regency society he often went in for 'bamming and humming', that is, talking nonsense so earnestly as to hoodwink the onlooker into taking seriously what was meant in jest. Another Byronic trait to look out for is his habit of boasting of his own transgressions in such exaggerated language as to constitute a *fanfaron des vices*. His friends and his half-sister knew him well enough to judge how much of this trumpeting to believe. Others, including Lady Byron, did not.

M.K. Joseph starts his book on *Byron the Poet* with a quotation from William J. Calvert – a watchword for the wary biographer:

> It is impossible not to take Byron seriously, and it is disastrous to take him literally.[1]

ACKNOWLEDGEMENTS

I am particularly indebted to one of Britain's most generous, brilliant and well-loved Byronists, Bernard Beatty of the University of Liverpool, Academic Editor of *The Byron Journal*, who kindly found time to read an early draft of *Byron the Maker*, advised, rebuked and made suggestions, thereby re-shaping and honing the text. His encouragement and praise were invaluable. He is, of course, in no way responsible for any shortcomings which may have arisen since then.

I am most grateful to that most amiable and clubbable of bookmen, Derek Wise, for his generosity in opening his collection to me, ferrying books to and fro, drawing my attention to some obscure nineteenth-century publications and tracking down books on the internet.

My thanks go to the staff of the Public Library in Haywards Heath who gave me the impression that I had both an English and an American University Library on my doorstep which could produce recent publications from both sides of the Atlantic at great speed.

I must thank Deborah Fletcher who typed the text from my handwriting, dealt patiently with second thoughts, alterations and lost pages, and said she couldn't wait to turn the page.

I am grateful to Christine Padmore who kindly took over when Deborah had to withdraw, and brought her splendid efficiency and understanding into play.

My thanks go to all the writers and scholars whose works on Byron I have enjoyed and learned from over the years, in particular, to Leslie Marchand and Doris Langley Moore, and to those from whom I have quoted in this volume. Among these are Jerome J. McGann, Michael Cooke, M.K. Joseph, Paul Elledge, G. Wilson

Knight, Jeffery Vail, Jonathan David Gross, Louis Crompton, William St Clair, David Erdman, Ian Gilmour, Peter Gunn, Michael and Melissa Bakewell, Andrew Nicholson, Jane Stabler, Charles Donelan, Iris Oriqo, David Brewer, Peter W. Graham and Jerome Chris Vensen.

I would like to thank the editors of *The Byron Journal*, Liverpool University Press, and the writers of articles in the *Journal* from whom I have quoted, namely William St Clair, C.J. Tyerman, David Woodhouse, Graham Pont and Philip Shaw. The *Journal* is an invaluable resource for Byronists.

My thanks go to several people who have encouraged me over the years; Michael Foot, Doris Langley Moore, Elizabeth Longford, Peter W. Graham, Vincent Newey, William St Clair, Mrs Elma Dangerfield, Michael Rees, J. Drummond Bone and Vivian, Maureen O'Connor, Thérèse Tessier, Malcolm and Mary Kelsall, Barbara and Jim Jackson, Peter Cochran, Val Doulton, Maureen Crisp and Ken Purslow, Ridley Burnett and Michael Sidney (who published my first book on Byron).

Every book ever published on Byron owes a debt to the firm of John Murray, beginning with the original John Murray, who not only allowed the young Byron to criticise important and influential people and institutions in *Childe Harold's Pilgrimage*, but stood by him for most of *Don Juan* and, on learning that the bailiffs had moved in and that Byron was preparing to sell his books, sent him a large cheque and offered to sell the copyrights of the poems for his benefit. Byron refused to accept such generosity, but he never forgot it.

Finally, I am grateful to Isabel Quigly for many kindnesses and for recommending The Book Guild to me. In this independent publisher I have met with unequalled enthusiasm, energy, efficiency and patience, and the employment of discrimination and good judgement on every issue; qualities certainly displayed by Joanna Bentley, the Managing Editor, who dealt with the unexpected external tribulations which beset the preparation of the typescript, and Gareth Vaughan, my dauntless copy-editor. I am most grateful to Carol Biss, the Managing Director, who took on *Byron the Maker* and offered the author both encouragement and guidance.

Part One

Byron in England

1

SCOTLAND

... my heart flies to my head, –
As 'Auld Lang Syne' brings Scotland, one and all,
Scotch plaids, Scotch snoods, the blue hills and clear streams,
All my boy feelings, all my gentler dreams.[1]

Byron is not usually counted among the Scottish poets although he himself claimed to be 'half a Scot by birth and bred/A whole one'.[2] Nor is he thought of as anything but an English poet in England although he was born a Gordon and spent the first ten years of his life in Scotland.

On his father's side Byron was descended from the Norman Byrons or Buruns who came over from France with William the Conqueror and received Newstead Abbey and its lands from Henry VIII some centuries later, after the dissolution of the monasteries. The Byron title is a Civil War title created in 1643. The first Baron, formerly Sir John Byron, died in Paris in 1652 and was succeeded by his brother, Richard.

It was said that the family which accepted the Abbey taken from the monks would suffer only misfortune as a result. The Third Baron lost most of his fortune and the Fifth Baron was tried before his peers for killing a neighbour in a duel. The legend which has been widely accepted until recently is that the fifth Lord Byron, henceforth known as 'The Wicked Lord', became a recluse after the duel and began to lay waste his estate to spite his son and heir, cutting down great oak trees and slaughtering two thousand head of deer. His motives, it appears, were not inimical to his son but the result was the same. His son died young and his grandson

3

was killed at Calvi and when the Wicked Lord died the ten-year-old George Gordon Byron, who was living in Aberdeen, succeeded to the Barony and the despoiled estates.

Colourful as the history of the Byrons might be it could not compare with the goings on of the poet's maternal ancestors, the Gordons of Gight, lairds of Gight Castle which stands in the valley of the River Ythan thirty miles north of Aberdeen.

> [My mother was] precise on points of genealogy like all the Aristocratical Scotch. She had a long list of ancestors like Sir Lucius O'Trigger's – most of whom are to be found in the old Scottish Chronicles ... in arms and doing mischief.[3]
>
> (Byron to John Murray, 25 October 1820)

The first Laird of Gight was the third son of the Earl of Huntley and his second wife, Arabella Stuart, daughter of James I of Scotland. He swapped his lands at Aboyne with his elder brother in return for Gight in 1490. He fell at Flodden. One of his sons and a son-in-law fell at Pinkie. His grandson took part in the murder of Wallenstein and was executed. In 1592 John Gordon of Gight was hanged at Edinburgh for the murder of Lord Moray. The carnage went on – foray, poison, siege and murder – till one Laird drowned in the River Ythan and his son drowned himself in the Bath Canal. In the (unsurprising) absence of a male heir, his daughter, Catherine Gordon, became mistress of Gight. In 1785 she went to Bath to find herself a husband. There she met Captain John Byron, a charming, handsome, French-educated, Guards officer who had recently sold out, had lost his first wife (also an heiress) and who married Catherine Gordon six weeks later.

Catherine Gordon was a lively young woman with a tendency to corpulence (a characteristic inherited by her son), a warm heart and an unbridled temper. She gave her feckless husband unconditional love. All he wanted from her was access to her fortune. Scottish pipers were soon playing this ballad about the heiress of Gight and her Sassenach fortune-hunter:

> Oh whaur are ye ga'en, bonny Miss Gordon?
> Oh whaur are ye ga'en, sae bonny and braw?
> Ye've married, ye've married wi' Johnny Byron
> To squander the lands o' Gight awa'.

4

At the time of her marriage Catherine Gordon owned salmon fisheries, timber and a small fortune in the Bank at Aberdeen as well as the lands and Castle of Gight. Her husband owned nothing but debts and a monumental facility for amassing more and more of them. Catherine's friends and kinsmen and advisors, Captain William Abercromby of Glassaugh, Colonel Duff of Fetteresso, Mr John Leslie, Captain Alexander Davidson, Mr Russell of Aden, were not present in Bath to see that proper marriage settlements were made. The result was that Catherine's fortune was at the mercy of every one of her husband's creditors. It was somewhat ironic that Catherine's kinsmen had plotted to get her to Bath to protect her from possible Scottish fortune hunters.

The young couple came to live at Gight in the summer of 1785. Soon uneasy rumours were circulating as far as Aberdeen. Gight was said to be the scene of wild extravagance: guests every night for the reels and they never left off at midnight even on the eve of the Sabbath; quantities of brandy and wine brought up from the cellars; foreign kickshaws served at table; a French novel (*La Nouvelle Héloise*) lying about for all to see and the needy husband out and about using his wife's funds to buy horses and hounds. Worst of all, Jack Byron was selling off his wife's lands. Advertisements went up: 'To be Sett. The Mains of Gight. Enquiries of Mr John Byron Gordon of Gight.'

On the banks of the River Ythan was the Gight Heronry where herons had nested for hundreds of years in the reeds. An old Gordon saying ran:

> When the herons leave the tree
> The Lairds of Gight will landless be.

The third Earl of Aberdeen was walking with his factor when they saw the herons from Gight come flying in. A year later the earl bought Gight Castle and its lands for the sum of £17,850 most of which went straight to John Byron's creditors.

The adult Byron wrote to his friend and banker, Douglas Kinnaird, before setting off on his last journey to Greece:

Dear Douglas
My mother's estate of Gight was sold to the former Lord Aberdeen many years ago – before I was born I believe – I have always preferred

5

my mother's family – for its royalty – and if I could buy it back – I would consent even at a reduction of income. – It is in Scotland.[4]

(To Douglas Kinnaird, R[avenn]a, 2 February 1821)

Looking back, Byron must have forgotten that he often took issue with his mother over which of the two families was the grander:

> My Mother, who was as haughty as Lucifer with her descent from the Stuarts, and her right line, from the *old Gordons, not the Seton Gordons*, as she disdainfully termed the Ducal branch ... always reminding me how superior *her* Gordons were to the southern Byrons – notwithstanding our Norman, and always masculine descent.[5]

In 1787 Captain William Abercromby wrote from Hampshire to his kinsmen in Scotland that John Byron had hired a vessel and fled to France for debt. Mrs Byron, 'poor unhappy woman', was 'big with bairn' and must soon follow him. For a time the Byrons lived at Chantilly, the town near Paris dominated by the Château of the Condé. There Mrs Byron nursed her little step daughter, Augusta, through a serious illness. Then, knowing that John Byron was unfit to have the care of a child, she took Augusta back with her to England to her maternal grandmother, Lady Holderness, and set to work to find lodgings for herself in London in preparation for her confinement.

George Gordon Byron was born in a back room on 22 January 1788 at no. 16 Holles Street. He was baptised at St Marylebone Church and his kinsmen, Colonel Duff of Fetteresso and the Duke of Gordon, stood sponsors. Within two years Mrs Byron had moved to Scotland. Byron spent most of his first ten years in Aberdeen with forays to Banff and Deeside. John Byron, who had continued sponging on his wife in London, followed her to Scotland to get more money from her. They quarrelled violently and took separate lodgings, meeting only to drink tea with each other. The child was three years old when his father went back to France where he died at Valenciennes in 1791.

The little boy who might have been brought up in feudal grandeur at Gight Castle, neighbour to Lord Aberdeen, served by his own people and pipers, presiding over the yearly Gight Games when the prettiest girl was dubbed the Rose of Gight, lived instead with his mother (her income now reduced to £150 a year) in a flat on Broad Street, Aberdeen. This may have been no bad thing, for Aberdeen provided him with influences which affected his whole life. Aberdeen first formed his ideas on books, politics, war, and love and instilled into him a certain superstition that he never quite lost, a love of the sea, scepticism about medical men, a love of the theatre, a love-hate relationship with religion, and the common touch – an ability to get on with people of all sorts.

Aberdeen was no provincial backwater. It boasted two colleges, one of which, the Marischal, though rebuilt since Byron's day, still stands in the same place, a little further down Broad Street than the house, long gone, where Mrs Byron lived with her 'wee cruikit deevil' Geordie Byron. The boy had been born with a deformed foot which gave him pain when he walked so that he was never easily able to walk far. Efforts were made to cure it by bandaging, special boots, and a wooden contraption which hurt abominably and did no good. He was lame all his life and suffered much anguish over his deformity.

The Professors from the Marischal gave public lectures. There were three circulating libraries and several bookshops, among them Brown at the sign of the Homer's head, and Angus, whose catalogue may still be seen at Aberdeen Central Library. As a small boy Byron was sent to Bodsy Bowers' little school where he had to repeat his lessons by rote. He failed to learn to read by this method. Mrs Byron then put him in the hands of two excellent teachers from the Marischal. Mr Ross, a gentle scholarly clergyman, inspired Byron with a passion for Roman history. Somewhere he acquired an equal passion for the history of Turkey. Once he had learned to read he read voraciously but he was more interested in proving his prowess at sports than in study.

A comment on his education (or lack of it) was confided to his *Journal*:

> I acquired this handwriting, which I can hardly read myself, under the fair copies of Mr Duncan of the same city (Aberdeen); I don't think he could plume himself much upon my progress.[6]

Aberdeen formed his views on politics. *The Aberdeen Journal* was positively cosmopolitan. Local events got scant coverage. Aberdonians were glued to accounts of the stirring happenings in France: first the Revolution and later the rise of Napoleon. Mrs

Byron was brought up by her grandmother, Mrs Duff, cousin to the Earl of Fife, who was known as Lady Gight and was of the Whig persuasion. Mrs Byron read the papers intelligently, thought herself quite a Democrat (a term of opprobrium in that period) and held that the French king would have behaved as cruelly as the Jacobins if he had succeeded in crushing the Revolution.

Something of the commonsense spirit of this verdict was later echoed by her son in *Don Juan* though he was never 'quite a Democrat' like his mother:

> I wish men to be free
> As much from mobs as kings – from you as me.[7]

Byron attended the Grammar School which was founded before 1256 and was the oldest in the British Isles. When they were not involved in the daily grind of Latin, Latin and then more Latin, the boys romped in the playground, playing marbles, hand ball and peg tops, fighting and racing each other. This happy rough and tumble may have given Byron that common touch that made him so beloved of his friends from all walks of life, especially at Cambridge:

> ... this evening a large assortment of *Jockies*, *Gamblers*, *Boxers*, *Authors*, *Parsons* and *Poets* sup with me.[8]

From the grammar school yard the boys used to watch the volunteers marching by in their brave, brightly-coloured uniforms with drums and trumpets. This may have contributed to Byron's enthusiasm for military glory which he never lost, though he later confined it to wars of liberation and, inconsistently, grew to abhor the horrors of war and to blame those who caused others to engage in it, for their stupidity and indifference. Looking back on his childhood he remembered 'My earliest dreams were all martial.' The young Byron told his friends:

> I will, some day or other, ... raise a troop of men which shall be dressed all in black and ride on black horses! They shall be called 'Byron's Blacks' and you will hear of their performing prodigies of valour![9]

Having learned to 'hate licensed murder' the adult Byron would have smiled at the naïvete of his younger self:

8

[There are] ways to benefit mankind as true
Perhaps as shooting them at Waterloo.[10]

Even as a child Byron valued courage highly, but he was not immune from fear. The verse on the Brig o' Balgounie by Thomas the Rhymer is said to have inspired superstitious terror in the boy as he rode over the bridge:

Brig o' Balgounie
Wight is thy wa'
Wi' a wife's ae son
And a mare's ae foal
Down shalt thou fa'

Byron was the only son of his mother and he knew by heart this verse. He was afraid that he and his pony would fall down into the deep pools below the bridge and be drowned. Byron dreaded his thirty sixth year as he had been told that the years 1816 and 1824 would be dangerous for him. The Brig o' Balgounie may still be standing but 1816 was the year of Byron's downfall and 1824 the year of his death. We may smile at these correspondences but Byron would not have done.

It was perhaps at Banff that Byron conceived his distrust of the doctors of his day, later to be increased by the quack in Nottingham who made him suffer by ignorant attempts to cure his lameness. His doctor at Aberdeen, however, was perfectly sensible about the case and corresponded with the famous surgeon Dr John Hunter, who had special boots made for the child. He remained lame.

While staying with the minister and his wife at the manse in Banff Byron climbed a tree in the garden and, reaching for some fine pears hanging over the wall, tumbled to the ground. His mother called in 'the old red-nosed doctor' as Byron described him, and the child was told he was to be bled. Byron had seen the doctor bleed his nurse and he was determined not to submit to the procedure. Scoldings from Mrs Byron had no effect. Kicking and screaming, he told the old man, 'I'll pull your nose.' The doctor departed in high dudgeon, first instructing Mrs Byron to put the boy to bed, give him nothing but water and gruel and administer drops twice a day. Byron threw the medicine out of the window, and his mother (who alternately spoiled and ranted at him, but

9

always adored him) let him get up and gave him a whole plate of bread and butter instead of *brochan*.

Mrs Byron sent her lame son to the dancing class in Peacock Close where, every week, he saw his cousin Mary Duff. He was seven, she eight. Byron fell desperately in love with the little girl and wrote later of his restlessness and sleeplessness and how he tormented his mother's maid into writing to her for him as he was unable to write himself. 'How the deuce could this occur so early? Where could it originate? I certainly had no sexual feelings for years afterwards'.[11] Thomas Moore regards this episode as significant for Byron's development as a poet. In a note he writes, 'Dante we know was but nine years old when, at the May Festival, he saw and fell in love with Beatrice, and Alfieri, himself a precocious lover, considers such early sensibility to be an unerring sign of a soul formed for the fine arts.'[12]

Moore does not consider the scenes of wildness and grandeur (Lachin-y-Gair, Morven, Deeside – where Byron had wandered in his early years) were in any way an influence on his poetry. Experiences such as these 'no more *make* the poet than – to apply an illustration of Byron's own, – the honey can be said to make the bee.'[13] Taken literally, this judgement cannot be denied, but one has only to bear in mind Byron's reaction to similar scenes in Switzerland and even at Malvern to conclude that wandering in the Highlands as a boy must have contributed to the development of the poetic imagination which imbued both *Manfred* and parts of the third Canto of *Childe Harold's Pilgrimage* with the majesty and horror of high mountains.

The husband of Byron's former nurse, Agnes Gray, told Moore, after Byron's death, that the small boy was always inquisitive and puzzling about religion. Byron himself claimed to have been cudgelled to church for the first ten years of his life. Agnes Gray made him recite the psalms and so did her sister May. But May crept into his bed and sexually abused him before he was ten and this gave him a somewhat jaundiced view of both women and religion. He always respected those who were sincerely religious but he loathed hypocrisy. As a child he experienced Calvinistic gloom and this perhaps explains his later preference for Catholicism and his decision to make his illegitimate daughter, Allegra, a Roman Catholic. But he had no patience with squabbling clergymen of any persuasion, deploring the behaviour of '... seventy-two villainous sects tearing each other to pieces for the love of the Lord and hatred of each other'.[14]

His characteristic attitude to religion was:

> ... I deny nothing, but doubt everything.[15]

Wandering round the harbour and along the shores of Aberdeen Bay Byron grew to love the sea. He swam in the Don and found that he was equal to boys with two perfect feet. He learned not to fear the water and this early familiarity with it explains his calmness when in peril at sea. Imagery and descriptions of the sea are to be found throughout the poetry:

> In the wind's eye I have sailed and sail; but for
> The stars I own my telescope is dim.
> But at the least I have shunned the common shore,
> And leaving land far out of sight, would skim
> The Ocean of Eternity.[16]

At the age of nine Byron was taken to the play, the beginning of a long association with the theatre. We know of Byron attending plays and operas in London, Nottingham, Brighton and Venice, where he loved the Fenice Theatre. He joined the management of Drury Lane. He was often moved to tears and sometimes taken ill by a particularly moving or dramatic performance. In Aberdeen he threw himself rather too literally into a performance of *The Taming of the Shrew*:

PETRUCCHIO: Good Lord, how bright and goodly shines the moon!
KATHERINE: The moon! The sun: it is not moonlight now.
PETRUCCHIO: I say it is the moon that shines so bright!
KATHERINE: I know it is the sun that shines so bright!
PETRUCCHIO: Now by my mother's son, and that's myself,
             It shall be moon, or star, or what I list,
             Or ere I journey to your father's house
HORATIO: Say as he says, or we shall never go.
KATHERINE: Forward, I pray, since we have come so far,
             And be it moon, or sun, or what you please,
             And if you please to call it a rush-candle,
             Henceforth I vow it shall be so for me.
PETRUCCHIO: I say it is the moon!
KATHERINE: I know it is the moon!

11

PETRUCCHIO: Nay then, you lie, it is the blessed sun.
KATHERINE: Then, God be praised, it is the blessed sun.

Here the young Byron jumped up from his place crying out in a fury, 'But *I* say it is the *moon*, sir', which caused consternation on stage and in the audience.

Life was to change for Byron. It was only by chance that Mrs Byron learned in 1794 that her son's cousin, heir to the Wicked Lord, had been killed at Calvi. No-one had taken the trouble to inform her that her small boy was now heir to the Barony, to Newstead Abbey and all its lands. Four years later the Wicked Lord was dead.

When the Headmaster of the Grammar School broke the news to him that he was now Sixth Baron Byron of Rochdale, the boy's reaction was 'Must the other boys know?', and when his name was read out at Assembly next morning as Georgius Dominus de Byron he burst into tears. But he was not so upset as to be unable to deal intelligently with the change in his circumstances, agreeing with his mother that although neither of them could see any change in him since he became a Lord everybody behaved very differently to him now, even the Headmaster, who offered him wine and cakes to celebrate his accession to the peerage. For Mrs Byron it was more honourable to be descended from the kings of Scotland than to be an English Lord and own wide lands. All the same, she proceeded to deal briskly with her son's new situation, packing up their belongings and organizing a 'Sale of Furniture Belonging to Genteel Persons who are leaving the Country'. The sale fetched no more than £74 17s 7d and with this, and little more, in her pocket Mrs Byron set out for Nottingham with the ten-year-old Peer of the Realm and his nurse.

Notes

1. *Letters and Journals of Lord Byron with Notices of his Life* by Thomas Moore is the chief source for Byron's early years. Much as he loved Byron, Moore does not hesitate to offer criticism where criticism is due. His biography is no work of hagiography. It is judged by William St Clair 'one of the great biographies of the nineteenth century'.[1] He adds that its success was well deserved: 'He was a careful and thorough researcher – he took the trouble to interview Byron's friends and to borrow and copy as many original documents as he could find.'

Jeffery Vail agrees with St Clair, defending Moore's biography from criticism by Joseph W. Reed for being insufficiently theoretical. Vail demurs: '...the lack of an "organising structure" of the kind Reed expects in a biography is really a triumph of Moore's realism and his respect for the disorderliness of human life, especially in the case of Byron.'[2]

Moore refrained from imposing his own theoretical explanations and patterns on a life as lacking in any imposed structure as *Don Juan*.

2. Until the publication of the researches of John Beckett in his interesting and useful book, *Byron and Newstead Abbey. The Aristocrat and the Abbey*, which treats Byron not as poet but as custodian of Newstead Abbey, it was believed that the fifth Lord Byron stripped his estates of timber and deer to spite his son because the young man had ruined his plans for retrieving his fortunes by refusing to marry the heiress picked out for him by his father. The legend of the so-called 'Wicked Lord' also had him so vilified and traumatised over the unorthodox duel in the course of which he killed his neighbour, William Chaworth, in a dark room at the Star and Garter Inn in London, that he became a recluse, hiding himself away at Newstead.

Beckett shows that if the fifth baron became a recluse it was only in the final years of his life. Until then he continued to plan for his estates, dividing part of his lands into new farms and employing as steward a sensible man called Daws who managed the land efficiently and was on good terms with the tenants, from whom he regularly collected the rents.

When his son left the chosen bride at the altar and ran off to Gretna Green to marry his cousin Juliana, daughter of the John Byron who won fame in the navy as 'Foulweather Jack', and became an admiral, Lord Byron was angry but John Beckett shows that he was reconciled with his son within a few years.

The fifth baron's financial arrangements appear to have vied with those of his successor for recklessness, extravagance and muddle. The result was an estate stripped of many of its assets. This was the condition of Newstead Abbey on his death when, the heir having died in London, his son having been killed at Calvi, the house and lands went to the little boy from Aberdeen.

2

NEWSTEAD ABBEY

'Before the mansion lay a lucid Lake.'[1]

Moore spoke to many who knew and remembered the young Byron in Scotland and from these researches we have some idea of the character of the child who arrived at Newstead Abbey in 1798:

> That as a child his temper was violent, or rather sullenly passionate, is certain. Even when in petticoats, he showed the same uncontrollable spirit with his nurse, which he afterwards exhibited when an author, with his critics. Being angrily reprimanded by her, one day, for having soiled or torn a new frock in which he had just been dressed, he got into one of his 'silent rages' (as he himself has described them) seized the frock in both hands, rent it from top to bottom, and stood in sullen stillness, setting his censurer and her wrath at defiance.

Moore points out that such tantrums were encouraged by the example of his mother 'who frequently, it is said, proceeded to the same extremities with her cap gowns &tc.' (Mrs Byron was volatile, noisy and, on occasion, violent, but Moore ignores her tragic situation and the courage with which she endured it.) Moore goes on: '...there was in his disposition, as appears from the concurrent testimony of nurses, tutors and all who were employed about him, a mixture of affectionate sweetness and playfulness, by which it was impossible not to be attached; and which rendered him then, as in his riper years, easily manageable by those who loved and understood him sufficiently to be at once gentle and firm enough for the task.'[2] From Byron's former schoolfellows in Aberdeen Moore learned that he was:

15

... a lively, warm-hearted, high-spirited boy – passionate and resentful, but affectionate and companionable with his schoolfellows – to a remarkable degree venturous and fearless and, (as one of them significantly) expressed it, 'always more ready to give a blow than to take one.'[3]

Moore felt that the boy came into his inheritance too early:

Had he been left to struggle on for 10 years longer, as plain George Byron, there can be little doubt that his character would have been, in many respects, the better for it.[4]

Byron spent his early years not in aristocratic but in middle class circles. This gave rise to anxiety about his status exemplified by his reply to an Aberdonian who told him she looked forward to hearing his future speeches in the House of Commons. The child showed that he had thought about his future inheritance and was fully aware of its significance. 'I hope not', he told the lady. 'If you read any speeches of mine, it will be in the House of Lords.'[5]

The sudden acquisition of wealth (as he supposed), status, ownership of a great mansion and some of the servants of the fifth baron, the lands and all that went with them, was confusing enough for a boy of ten with an exalted notion of the dignity and honour pertaining to his new rank. The disappointment which followed was heart-rending. It was not long before he would have to reconcile himself to spending the next few years away from his magically beautiful new possession with its lakes and monastic ruins, vast overgrown gardens and pleasure grounds, the two forts built by the Wicked Lord for fake naval manoeuvres on the lakes, and the kindly old servant, Joe Murray, who showed him round his new domain and was dearly loved by Byron for the rest of Joe's life.

The fifth baron had taken no notice of his heir. Mrs Byron received no advice from the Byron family about the future of her son. She dealt with this situation by hiring a London lawyer, John Hanson, to manage the financial affairs and other arrangements which must now be made for the boy. Everything she did was for the future welfare of her son. Without friends, without family, without funds, she gave little or no thought to her own status and welfare and was always ready to sacrifice provision for herself to that of her son.

Mr and Mrs John Hanson travelled from London to meet the new arrivals at Newstead Abbey, treating them with the utmost kindness. Hanson had familiarised himself with the situation of the estate. He explained that repairs were urgently needed (which they could see for themselves, since parts of the roof had collapsed, cattle were stabled in the hall and hay was stored in the monks' refectory) and little money was available to pay for them. The rents had not been raised for years in spite of the marked increase in prosperity of the tenant farmers. This had to be put in hand and as soon as possible. The Abbey and its lands would be let until Byron reached his majority. For the time being Mrs Byron and her son could move into a few rooms, using what sticks of furniture remained.

Byron's lameness prevented him from exploring his new domain on foot so a pony was borrowed from the Parkyns family in Nottingham who were related to the widow of the brother of the fifth Baron. Mrs Parkyns lived with her sister, Byron's great aunt the Hon. Frances Byron, and her own two daughters. Mrs Byron was able to indulge in quiet visits to these ladies – not the most exciting of social lives but probably more congenial than she had expected.

When the weather became colder and the roofs let in the autumn rain Byron and his mother moved to Nottingham where Byron was often left in the care of May Gray while his mother did what she could to deal with the disorder of Newstead. During this time Byron's deformed foot was subjected to unavailing but extremely painful treatment by an unskilled practitioner in Nottingham.

It was at this early age that the boy began to try to take control (as far as was possible for a young child) of his own destiny. He insisted on being allowed to go to lessons with the tutor of the Misses Parkyns, Dummer Rogers. He wrote to his mother:

> I am astonished that you do not acquiesce in this scheme... I recommend this to you because if some plan of this kind is not adopted I shall be called or rather branded with the name of dunce, which you know I could never bear, I beg you will consider this plan seriously and I will lend it all the assistance in my power...[6]
>
> (Nottingham, 13 March 1799)

This new tendency of Byron to think and plan for himself would cause violent disputes with his mother who was often in the right of it but tactless in making her will felt.

In these early days of their long relationship Hanson exerted

17

himself energetically in the management of the affairs of the Byrons and became very fond of the boy. Later he was to become almost criminally negligent and both Catherine Byron and her son were exasperated, tormented and finally deprived of funds as a result of his dilatory handling of their affairs.

Now Hanson went back to London to search for necessary papers connected with Byron's inheritance and, calling on the Earl of Carlisle (who was a kinsman of Byron through the marriage of Isabella, the wayward sister of the fifth baron, to the fourth Earl of Carlisle), he persuaded the somewhat reluctant nobleman to act as joint guardian to the young peer together with himself and Catherine Byron. Lord Carlisle was already playing the part of kindly and hospitable guardian to Byron's half-sister, Augusta Byron, daughter of John Byron by his first wife. Later Hanson took the boy to London to meet his guardian and arrange what was to be done about the deformed foot and whether the boy should be sent to school to prepare him for entrance to Harrow. The Earl was persuaded to agree to a course of treatment for the foot by a distinguished London practitioner, Dr Baillie, and to the plan of sending Byron to Dr Glennie's Academy in Dulwich.

Now the unfortunate effect of Byron's early enoblement became apparent. Moore remarks that '...Lord Byron's high notions of rank were, in his boyish days, so little disguised or softened down as to draw upon him at times the ridicule of his companions.' He was not unpopular at Dr Glennie's but was sometimes mockingly referred to as 'the old English baron.'[7] Mrs Byron took lodgings in London to be near her boy and often insisted on taking him home for visits, interrupting his studies, which were somewhat half-hearted, though he read widely among many of the books in Dr Glennie's study. Remonstrance by Dr Glennie, who disapproved of Mrs Byron's Scottish accent and untidy appearance, brought noisy outbursts of wrath from her which were commented on by Byron's schoolfellows, much to his humiliation.

Mr Hanson invited the boy to spend part of his holidays at his home, a practice that was repeated on several occasions while Byron was at Harrow, and introduced the boy to his four children thus providing him with his first experience of family life. On leaving Harrow Byron wrote a poem entitled 'Childish Recollections' some lines of which express movingly the pleasure the lonely child must have experienced in joining the Hanson household. It is, however, likely that the young poet was thinking not of the Hansons who welcomed him into their family, but of the Howards, who did not:

> ... friendship will be doubly dear
> To one, who thus for kindred hearts must roam,
> And seek abroad, the love denied at home ...
> Stern Death forbade my orphan youth to share
> The tender guidance of a Father's care;
> Can Rank or e'en a Guardian's name supply
> The love, which glistens in a Father's eye?
> For this, can Wealth, or Title's sound atone,
> Made, by a Parent's early loss, my own?
> What Brother springs a Brother's love to seek?
> What Sister's gentle kiss has prest my cheek?[8]
> (From 'Childish Recollections', 1807)

Mrs Byron could have instructed her son in how much 'tender guidance' he might have received from John Byron had 'Stern Death' spared him. Soon after Byron's arrival in London a 'father's tender care' was in fact extended to him by John Hanson. Byron asked Hanson to tell his mother to send May Gray away. She had taken to beating him till his bones ached and bringing undesirable drinking companions into his room in Nottingham and at Newstead. He also told the kindly lawyer (but this was never repeated to Mrs Byron) that May Gray used to get into bed with him and, as Hanson described it, 'play tricks with his person'. Hanson advised Mrs Byron that so able and honourable a boy as her son, should not be allowed to suffer ill-treatment from a servant.

Mrs Byron reluctantly dismissed May Gray before Byron came home for the Christmas holidays. Later Byron wrote of this episode:

My passions were developed very early – so early – that few would believe me – if I were to state the period – and the facts which accompanied it.'[9]

(*Detached Thoughts*, 1821)

Little account has been taken by biographers of this plain statement of Byron's. Yet nowadays the sexual abuse of a boy of nine would result in counselling, psychotherapy, and possibly the intervention of the police. Recent biographers have been more diligent in uncovering charges against Byron than emphasising actions perpetrated against him for which formidable evidence exists.

19

It was soon decided by Lord Carlisle in consultation with Mr Hanson that, as he was not making satisfactory progress at Dr Glennie's establishment, Byron's going to Harrow should no longer be delayed and, at the age of thirteen and a half, he was delivered by Mr Hanson in the spring of 1801 to the care of Dr Joseph Dury who had been a most successful Headmaster there for the last 16 years.

3

HARROW

I have been idle *and I certainly ought not to talk in church. But I have never done a mean action at this school to him or any one.*[1]

The boy who rode up Harrow Hill with Mr Hanson to join his new schoolfellows was described to Thomas Moore by Dr Drury after his death: 'I found that a wild mountain colt had been submitted to my management... But there was mind in his eye ... he might be led by a silken string ... rather than by a cable.'[2] In his extremely useful paper on 'Byron's Harrow' (later developed into a book), C.J. Tyerman (who, as a master at Harrow for many years is steeped in the history of the school) invites his readers to compare what Joseph Drury told Thomas Moore with what he wrote about Byron privately when Byron was at the school. Moore heard nothing of the boy's 'negligence', 'childish pranks', 'idleness and indifference', 'animal spirits' and 'want of judgement'.[3] Nevertheless, Drury was kind to the boy, putting him into the care of his son, Henry, so that he need not go straight into a form where his backwardness would be apparent to his schoolmates.

After various arguments with Henry Drury, Byron wrote to his mother in great distress refusing to have anything more to do with him. (It is typical of Byron that Henry Drury later became a friend he kept up with long after Harrow.)

Had I *stole* ... his language could not have been more outrageous, what must the boys think of me? ... better let him take away my Life than ruin my *character* – I have been *idle* and I certainly ought not to talk

21

in church, But I have never done a mean action at this school to him
or any*one*... If you love me you will now show it.[4]

(Harrow on the Hill, Sunday, 1 May 1803)

Instead of punishing the boy Dr Drury sensibly dealt with the
problem by transferring him to the care of another master.

Henry Drury, we are told by Paul Elledge, was a big man and
a fierce, intimidating figure. It took courage for Byron to oppose
him. Elledge points out that Byron felt that the masters, including
Henry Drury, and some of the boys, despised him for his lameness
and his poverty. This may have been his motivation for attempting
to shine at the Speech Day recitals in his later years at Harrow.
His success in his first appearance at the event, playing the part
of King Latinus in the *Aeneid*, was, according to Elledge, a pivotal
occasion. Dr Drury's praise delighted Byron and seemed to give
his approval to the prospect of a parliamentary career for his
turbulent pupil. Byron had come to regard Dr Drury as a father
figure by this time. But to begin with Byron was bored and rebellious
and was regarded as a difficult and unruly boy.

Tyerman gives an account of:

> ... formal teaching of the classics at Harrow (about all that was taught),
> which was 'monotonous and endlessly repetitive'... Learning was
> something that largely occurred outside the form room... It was as social
> figures, models of behaviour and tone, rather than as pedagogues that
> masters were respected or not... The syllabus was exclusively classical
> and based heavily on the Eton system. Founded on Latin, in particular
> Latin verse, the curriculum, apart from the customary obeisance to Virgil,
> displayed a typically eighteenth-century preference for the convivial,
> speculative and satirical Horace, a preference that, for all his later
> disdain, may be thought to have left a profound influence on Byron's
> poetic style and tone. Harrow was unusual in the prominence it gave to
> Greek... So Byron read Greek tragedies as well as Homer. Throughout,
> the emphasis lay on verse, as an exemplar of grammar and vocabulary
> and a model of how to express thoughts in a disciplined style.[5]

Byron's first year at Harrow was turbulent. He wrote in 1820,
'I always hated Harrow until the last year and a half.'[6] He fought
those who mocked him for his deformity. He fought to protect
younger or weaker boys. He fought later on to protect his bust of
Napoleon. The explanation of this exaggerated pugnacity which
best fits the facts is that boys tend to torment those who suffer

from infirmity and resent those who refuse to conform. Byron's reaction was to fight them. When he came south from Scotland, the English were to him a strange, almost a foreign, race. He was precocious in many ways. An intelligent 13 year old who had been brought up in Aberdeen by a mother who was interested in politics, read the papers and called herself almost a Democrat, was likely to question much that English boys would take for granted. Political discussion in Aberdeen was European in outlook and certainly not prejudiced in favour of the English Establishment. The *Aberdeen Journal* was enthusiastic for the French Revolution; and France, the traditional enemy of England, was the traditional ally of Scotland.

Byron distanced himself from his schoolfellows in other ways. Tyerman has pointed out that Dr Drury had succeeded in more than doubling the size of the school since 1797. Byron felt the need to escape from the crowded buildings. He took to lying for hours on end on the Peachey tomb in the churchyard on Harrow Hill, looking out over the wide countryside below.

Tyerman points out that the real importance of Harrow was that, as a schoolboy, Byron began to write poetry:

> Byron the schoolboy was by no means unique, Byron the poet, it could be argued, was ... Perhaps of more importance than his brawls and pranks, his attempts to prove himself an athlete and a cricketer [he became a fairly competent cricketer and was inordinately proud of having played against Eton] his quicksilver skill at doing the minimum of preparation for form work, or even his famed friendships with glittering young aristocrats, was the present he received, not from a peer or a peer's son, but from the son of a banker, Henry Boldero, who in 1803 gave his friend Byron, then fifteen, a copy of the works of Alexander Pope.[7]

Tyerman believes that the contrast between the frenzied world of school rivalries, arguments, games and friendships, and the tranquillity of the churchyard and the surrounding countryside lent piquancy to some of Byron's early school verse. So did his friendships. His early verse includes poems addressed to the Duke of Dorset, the Earl of Clare, to George, Earl Delawarr and to Edward Noel Long. Another of Byron's young favourites was William Harness who had been lamed in an accident and whom Byron tried to protect. His strong relationship with these boys developed after his passionate love for his pretty neighbour at Newstead was frustrated.

When Byron first arrived at Newstead Hanson took him to be introduced to the Clarks of Annesley Hall and Mrs Clark's daughter by a previous marriage, Mary Chaworth. Byron knew the story of the duel in which William Chaworth had been killed by The Wicked Lord in dubious circumstances. He told Mr Hanson that, for him, meeting the Chaworths seemed like Montagues meeting Capulets.

Byron took to riding over to Annesley to visit Mary. The orderly beauty of Mary's home and the care with which she was looked after by her parents, her old nurse and the groom who followed her whenever she rode out was a painful contrast to his own circumstances at Newstead. Washington Irving describes Annesley Hall. 'You enter a paved court – shrubs and antique flower pots – ruined stone fountain in the centre. It is like the approach to a French chateau.'[8] Under the window of Mary's sitting room was a flower garden; below the house a long terraced walk, heavy stone balustrade, sculpted urns with ivy and evergreens, great flights of steps down to the flower gardens which were laid out in formal plots, unlike the neglected gardens at Newstead.

By the age of fifteen Byron was desperately in love. Mary teased him, flirted with him and treated him as the schoolboy he was. She was already in love with Jack Musters, a handsome young neighbour whose chief pleasure was riding to hounds.

Years later, Mary's old nurse gossiped with Irving about the young poet who had become so notorious and the subject of such hideous rumours that he had to leave the country:

Like him? Bless him that I did. He used to ride over here and stay three days at a time and sleep in the blue room. Ah! poor fellow, he was very much taken with my young mistress. He used to walk about the terrace and gardens with her and seemed to love the very ground she trod on. Ah, sir, and why should I not like him? He was always main good to me when he came over. Well well they say it is a pity he and my young lady did not make a match of it, but it was not to be. He went away to school and then Mr Musters saw her and so things took their course.[9]

By March 1803 Hanson had managed to find a tenant for Newstead, the 23-year-old Lord Grey de Ruthyn. Mrs Byron moved into a house standing on the Green near the edge of the pleasant village of Southwell. Byron later wrote of life in Southwell:

There are very few books of any Kind that are either instructive or amusing, no society but old parsons and old Maids; I shoot a Good deal, but thank God I have not so far lost my reason as to make shooting my only amusement. There are indeed some of my neighbours whose only pleasures consist in field sports, but in other respects they are only one degree removed from the brute creation...[10]

(Burgage Manor, 2 April 1804)

Hanson had engaged a steward for the Newstead estate who had moved into the lodge near the Pilgrim's Oak. This man, Owen Mealey, was a surly unpleasant fellow who tried to make trouble by complaining to Hanson of both Byron and his mother. Byron now insisted on spending the summer holidays in the lodge, waited upon by Mealey. He had the grace to write to his mother 'You know as well as I do that it is not your Company I dislike but the place you reside in.'[11] A more pressing reason was his passion for Mary. When the time came to return to Harrow he wrote his mother an impassioned plea for one day's grace:

I was not wishing to resist your *Commands*, and really seriously intended coming over tomorrow ... I know it is time to go to Harrow. It will make me *unhappy* but I will obey; I only *desire*, *entreat*, this one day and on my *honour* I will be over tomorrow, in the evening or afternoon. I am Sorry you disapprove my Companions, who however are the first this county affords, and my equals in most respects, but I will be permitted to Chuse for myself, I shall never interfere in yours and I desire you will not molest me in mine; if you Grant me this favour, and allow me this one day unmolested you will eternally oblige your unhappy Son, Byron...[12]

(To Mrs Catherine Gordon Byron [15 September 1803])

Mrs Byron could no more resist her son in this vein than she had been able to resist her rapacious husband in another. It was not until the beginning of the next term that he returned to Harrow. She wrote an explanation to Hanson to be passed on to Dr Drury admitting that young Byron was headstrong and was refusing to return to Harrow because he was desperately in love, a condition, in her view, worse than any sickness.

Byron returned to school disillusioned and deeply wounded. He had overheard Mary telling her maid that she could never love that lame boy. His reaction was to lavish affection on his young friends at Harrow. He was quite open about his love for these boys and this

is borne out by a letter to his half-sister, Augusta Byron, with whom
he developed, while at Harrow, a loving and protective relationship:

> You Augusta are the only relation I have who treats me as a friend ...
> if you too desert me, I have nobody I can love but Delawarr. If it was
> not for his sake, Harrow would be a desert.[13]

(Friday, 2 November 1804)

Later he told the whole story of his love for the young chorister
at Cambridge, John Edleston, to his new friend and confidante,
Eliza Pigot, without the slightest embarrassment. Ian Gilmour points
out that when Byron fell in love with Edleston at Cambridge:

> In always stressing that this love was 'pure' he was evidently contrasting
> it with other loves or relationships; he never claimed that his relationships
> at Harrow were 'pure'. Secondly, early in 1807, he wrote a short
> autobiographical poem, 'Damaetas' (whose suppressed title was 'My
> Character'), which began, 'In law an infant and in years a boy / In mind
> a slave to every vicious joy.' ... The transition from Byron's heterosexual,
> though unconsummated, passion, to a series of homosexual ones was
> not unusual. Many adolescent boys, especially if they live in an exclusively
> male society, go through a homosexual phase which does not preclude
> being attracted to women...[14]

This account of the matter is the most persuasive although the
poem 'Damaetas' is an example of a tendency in Byron throughout
his life to present himself as worse than he was – particularly to
the censorious:

> In law an infant, and in years a boy,
> In mind a slave to every vicious joy;
> From every sense of shame and virtue wean'd,
> In lies an adept, in deceit a fiend;
> Vers'd in hypocrisy, while yet a child;
> Fickle as wind, of inclinations wild;
> Woman his dupe, his heedless friend a tool;
> Old in the world, though scarcely broke from school;
> Damætas ran through all the maze of sin,
> And found the goal, when others just begin;
> Ev'n still conflicting passions shake his soul,
> And bid him drain the dregs of Pleasure's bowl;
> But, pall'd with vice, he breaks his former chain,
> And what was once his bliss appears his bane.[15]

This is an early example of Byron's habitual *fanfaron des vices* and at least some items in this list of vice can be seen as a literary exercise since deceit, lies and hypocrisy were absolutely foreign to Byron's nature. His openness, especially about his own misdemeanours, and supposed misdemeanours, was so exaggerated as to be almost in itself a misdemeanour.

At Harrow Byron's interest was in boys younger than himself but there is no evidence of any interest in pre-sexual eight-year-old boys, just as we know of no interest in pre-sexual girls at any time in his life.

Whether Byron considered, at this age, unlicensed sexual congress with women a 'vicious joy' is unclear, but years later he teased Thomas Moore by claiming that his book of erotic verse, published anonymously in 1801 under the title *Poetical Works of the Late Thomas Little*, was responsible for all his sexual peccadilloes:

> I have just been turning over Little, which I knew by heart in 1803, being then in my fifteenth summer. Heigho! I believe all the mischief I have ever done, or sung, has been owing to that confounded book of yours...[16]
>
> (Ravenna, 9 June 1820)

When the first cantos of *Don Juan* were met with an outcry of indecency Byron repeatedly protested, often citing Thomas Little as an example of a really immoral production:

> D[on] Juan will be known by and bye for what it is intended a *satire* on *abuses* of the present *states* of Society – and not an eulogy of vice; – it may be now and then voluptuous – I can't help that – Ariosto is worse – Smollett ... ten times worse – and Fielding no better. – No Girl will ever be seduced by reading D[on] Juan – no – no – she will go to Little's poems – & Rousseau's romans – for that – or even to the immaculate De Stael – they will encourage her – & not the Don – who laughs at that – and – and – most other things.[17]
>
> (To John Murray, Genoa 25 October 1822)

Paul Elledge is persuasive in his discussion of the relation of Byron's boyish sexual engagements at Harrow to the episode at Newstead in November 1803 when Byron's tenant, Lord Grey de Ruthyn, is generally believed to have made a sexual overture to the fifteen-year-old boy which Byron rejected, either with disgust, distress or at the least some form of disquiet which caused him to

27

leave Newstead and put an end to his friendship with the older man. Elledge writes:

> Now, amorous experimentation with one's school bedmate or dormitory neighbour is a very different order of engagement from the sort historically assumed to have been proposed by Grey. My hunch, however, is that Byron was less neutrally experimental or playful than sentimentally romantic in his Harrow sexual adventures: his poetry of adolescent boy-love is warm but earnest, guileless, almost painfully sincere, without a trace of the carnal nonchalance often imputed to the later Byron, whose love poetry nevertheless, as long as he composed in the genre, continued to show this tender, sentimental bent.[18]

Jerome Christensen takes a very different view:

> Lord Byron learned his homosexuality from books – old books. One of the most impressionable students of the classics the English public schools have ever formed, Byron invested sexual desire only in Greek boys. For Byron – classical in his tastes, anthropological in his desires – *Greek love* meant love of Greeks.[19]

Others have seen Byron not as bisexual but as exclusively homosexual and have claimed that, in making love to women, he was going against his nature, which caused him to treat them with cruelty. It would be interesting to see evidence of this alleged cruelty to women apart from Lady Byron's allegations and insinuations, which were never tested in court.

I do not believe it possible to make any definitive judgement between Christensen and Gilmour on this question but I do not believe the sweeping judgement that Byron was exclusively homosexual allows for all the known facts. To look simply at this supposition as applied to Byron's life at Harrow it must be borne in mind that he was pouring out poetry, most of it concerned with love. Roughly a quarter of these poems are either addressed to boys or concerned with love or friendship with boys, and some are quite impassioned. But the same is true of some of the poems addressed to girls – particularly the ones concerned with his lost love, Mary Chaworth. Some of the poems addressed to girls may be using girls' names to disguise the fact that those addressed are boys, but many of the poems addressed to named girls we know of at Southwell or Newstead or London display that 'tender, sentimental bent' described by Elledge. If Byron was engaged in homosexual love affairs or experimentation it was certainly not an exclusive interest.

I believe it possible that the family affection he was beginning to feel for his half-sister, Augusta Byron, may have been as important to him (though at this stage less thrillingly exciting) as his love for his Harrow favourites. He longed for a family and his pride of lineage made him particularly intrigued by the meeting with a young woman who was so clearly a Byron, so like him and yet so different in her background and her experience of life which gave her a glamour he delighted in. She was six years older than her brother and the love he felt for her at this time had nothing of *eros* in it but was purely friendship and love of family and, gradually, the hope that through her he might be accepted by the Howards, the Osbornes and other great families.

Much as Byron loved, and was loved by, his mother, the years of putting up with her volatility and the violence of her sudden rages were beginning to alienate him. The poem quoted earlier on his 'Childish Recollections' shows how he felt the lack of a father and of brothers and sisters. Now for the first time he saw his half-sister and began writing to her the affectionate letters which usually begin with 'My Dearest Augusta'. This new sister was tall, elegant, fashionable, though 'shy as an antelope' with strangers, full of fun and ready to love, and be loved by, the young brother she had originally known as 'Baby Byron'. Both were Byrons; both mourned the loss of a father they would never admit to have been a worthless character.

Byron wrote to her on 22 March 1804:

... for the Future I hope you will consider me not only as a *Brother* but as your warmest and most affectionate *Friend*, and if ever Circumstances should require it as your *protector*.[20]

(Burgage Manor)

It seemed unlikely at that time that circumstances would ever warrant Augusta's seeking her brother's protection. She was brought up for the most part in the London house of her grandmother, Lady Holderness, on familiar terms with royalty, and was frequently invited to Castle Howard where she was on the closest terms with the young Howards. Her mother had been Baroness Conyers in her own right and was married to the Marquess of Camarthen by whom she had two sons and a daughter. When she ran away to Paris with John Byron (who thus ensured himself an income of at least four thousand a year) she left her children behind. Their father, now Duke of Leeds, welcomed Augusta into the family after her mother's death and his children were her friends. Those who knew her best loved her dearly and the inference is that she was a charming and lovable young woman. Byron was later to write 'there is not a more angelic being on earth.'[21]

Now he treated her as his confidante and she took to confiding in Mr Hanson whenever she felt her brother needed help or advice or a refuge from his mother's vagaries which, Augusta told the lawyer, would have a damaging effect on any boy's character.

Augusta was already in love with her dashing and handsome cousin, George Leigh, son of John Byron's sister, Frances. The Leighs were firmly opposed to the match since George had joined the army and needed a rich wife to support his extravagant lifestyle. Augusta had a minuscule income left her by her grandmother. In Regency times young women with small incomes had a hard time in the marriage market. Augusta was willing to wait for her George. Byron sympathised with her impatience, as we see in a letter from Southwell:

As to your Future prospects, my Dear Girl, *may they be happy*. I am sure *you* deserve Happiness and if *you* do not meet with it I shall begin to think it is 'a bad world we live in'.[22]

(26 March 1804)

Byron told her he would be a friend to anyone she loved but he wrote with brotherly advice:

Can't you drive this Cousin of ours out of your pretty little head ... [or] give old L'Harpagon ... the slip, and take a trip to Scotland?[23]

(Harrow on the Hill, 25 October 1804)

Byron never showed the slightest trace of envy over the contrast between Augusta's upbringing in the grandest of circles and his own provincial childhood. He had no claim on Augusta's step-family but he was secretly wounded by the lack of interest shown by Lord Carlisle in his new ward. His letters to Augusta show that he could be touchy and distant towards his guardian but it is evident that he longed to meet, and be accepted by, all Augusta's grand relations.

> If you see Lord Sidney Godolphin, I beg you will remember me to him, I fancy he has almost forgot me by now as it is rather more than a year since I had the pleasure of seeing him.[24]
>
> (Burgage Manor, 22 March 1804)

> Be sure to Remember me to my formal Guardy Lord Carlisle, whose magisterial presence I have not been into for some years, nor have I any ambition to attain so great an honour...[25]
>
> (Harrow on the Hill, 25 October 1804)

> You mistake me if you think I dislike Lord Carlisle, I respect him and might like him did I know him better.[26]
>
> (Harrow on the Hill, 11 November 1804)

Then, after Lord Carlisle had helped to persuade Mrs Byron to allow her son to spend a vacation with the Hansons:

> To Lord Carlisle make my warmest acknowledgements. I feel more gratitude, than my feelings can well express, I am truly obliged to him for his endeavours, and am perfectly satisfied with your explanation of his reserve, though I was hitherto afraid it might proceed from personal dislike.[27]
>
> (Harrow on the Hill, 21 November 1804)

Augusta was trying to reconcile Byron with the guardian she loved and Byron writes in January 1805 of dining with his family:

> I on Saturday, dined with Lord Carlisle, and on further acquaintance I like them all very much ... I think your friend Lady G[ertrude] is a sweet girl... Her Ladyship I always liked, but of the Junior part of the family, Frederick is my favourite...[28]
>
> (6 Chancery Lane, 3 January 1805)

These meetings did not develop into the friendly relationship Byron had hoped for when he wrote to Augusta, 2 November 1804

> ...I should like to know your Lady Gertrude, as you and her are so great friends. Adieu, my pretty sister. Write soon...[29]

By 1805 Byron was writing to Augusta:

31

My Dearest Augusta...

I hope, however, to have the pleasure of seeing you on the day appointed, but if you could contrive any way that I may avoid being asked to dinner by Ld. C[arlisle] I would be obliged to you, as I hate strangers.

Adieu, my Beloved Sister.[30]

(Burgage Manor, 23 April 1805)

Once he got into the higher forms at Harrow Byron was taught by Dr Drury who, though not particularly gifted academically, had a predilection for 'illustrating the sentiments of classical authors, especially Greek tragedians, by reference to modern English poets. Furthermore, he encouraged his pupils to write free translations of classical poets into English Verse.'[31] Tyerman concludes that 'Byron's education, relentlessly repetitive and boring as much of it may have been, provided him, not merely with material, but with models of form and expression for his early verse.'[32] Byron was still filled with generous idealism which conflicted with a growing scepticism. The opposition between these aspects of his character illustrates the 'mobility' which he himself recognised as a salient feature in his personality. Both characteristics appear in the poem 'Childish Recollections' which was written in late 1806 and revised later.

> Hours of my youth! when nurtur'd in my breast,
> To Love a stranger, Friendship made me blest, –
> Friendship, the dear peculiar bond of youth,
> When every artless bosom throbs with truth;
> Untaught by worldly wisdom how to feign,
> And check each impulse with prudential rein;
> When, all we feel, our honest souls disclose,
> In love to friends, in open hate to foes;
> No varnish'd tales the lips of youth repeat,
> No dear-bought knowledge purchased by deceit;
> Hypocrisy, the gift of lengthen'd years,
> Matured by age, the garb of Prudence wears:
> When, now the Boy is ripen'd into Man,
> His careful Sire chalks forth some wary plan;
> Instructs his Son from Candour's path to shrink,
> Smoothly to speak, and cautiously to think;
> Still to assent, and never to deny –
> A patron's praise can well reward the lie:
> And who, when Fortune's warning voice is heard,
> Would lose his opening prospects for a word?

Although, against that word, his heart rebel,
And Truth, indignant, all his bosom swell.[33]

In his last years at Harrow Byron covered himself with glory
by his skill at declamation, which delighted Dr Drury. But he
retained his reputation as an unruly pupil, becoming almost as
angry with the headmaster's brother, Mark Drury, as he had earlier
been with Henry. The master twitted him on his lack of fortune,
which seems a strange thing for a schoolmaster to do and one
must suspect that Byron offered him provocation, perhaps in the
form of some piece of adolescent pretension. He raged to his mother
in a letter: 'If my fortune is narrow, it is my misfortune not my
fault.'[34] During the early nineteenth century and the Regency wealth
may not have been openly worshipped but those without it were
deprived of what was described as 'consequence', and 'consequence'
was absolutely necessary for commanding respect. Later, Byron
was to write, 'riches are power, and poverty is slavery all over the
earth.'[35] On the same subject Sydney Smith remarked, 'It was
always considered an impertinence in England if a man of less
than two or three thousand a year had any opinion at all on
important subjects.'[36]

A letter to Augusta shows Byron's fondness for Dr Drury:

...this very morning I had a thundering Jobation from our Good Doctor,
which deranged my *nervous system* for a least five minutes. But
notwithstanding He and I now and then disagree, yet upon the whole
we are very good friends, for there is so much of the Gentleman, so
much mildness, and nothing of pedantry in his character, that I cannot
help liking him and will remember his instructions with gratitude as
long as I live...[37]

(Friday, 2 November 1804)

Byron felt no such admiration for George Butler, the new
Headmaster who replaced Dr Drury shortly before Byron was due
to leave the school. Byron had narrowly escaped being expelled
under Drury. His behaviour to Doctor Butler was outrageous. He
made a nuisance of himself partly because he was unhappy at the
departure of Dr Drury and partly through a snobbish feeling of
superiority, customarily felt by the upper classes of the period
towards the schoolmaster or 'usher'. He was reconciled with Butler
in February 1808, which demonstrates a forgiving nature in the

33

Headmaster who was pilloried by Byron in his verses on 'Pomposus'. These were subversive of school discipline though even 'Pomposus' himself must have thought they were quite well-turned:

Portrait of Pomposus

... Just half a Pedagogue, and half a Fop,
Not formed to grace the pulpit, but the Shop;
The *Counter*, not the *Desk*, should be his place,
Who deals out precepts, as if dealing Lace;[38]

Dr Butler invited all the older boys to dinner. Byron rejected the invitation, an unheard of rebuff to a Headmaster. When Butler taxed him with it and asked for an explanation Byron replied that, should Dr Butler ever find himself near Newstead, he would certainly not be invited to dinner there. Byron was therefore unable to accept an invitation from his Headmaster to dinner at Harrow.

Soon after this Byron left the school to go on to the University of Cambridge. There he would continue for some time to present to the world such an apparently vain and unendearing attitude that John Cam Hobhouse (who was to become his lifelong friend) detested him on sight.

Byron was desolated at having to leave Harrow, although he was prone to indulging in self-pity over his loneliness there. A couplet from 'Childish Recollections' foretells a theme which would appear in many of his early poems – the lonely hero shunned by his kind – and this developed further into the Satanic heroes of his Oriental Tales.

A Hermit, midst of crowds, I fain must stray,
Alone, though thousand pilgrims fill the way;[39]

Lying on the Peachey tomb, his favourite spot in the churchyard on the hill, it was possible to feel himself a Hermit, but he was nothing of the kind when bellowing out ribald songs at Mother Barnard's tuck shop with his friends or roistering around London with them after losing the cricket match against Eton.

It is interesting to notice a significant point made by C.J. Tyerman who remarks how odd it was that in a school staffed entirely by clerics there was a total lack of religious instruction. It is possible that this seemed odd to the boys too and may have added to

Byron's growing scepticism about supposedly pious people. By 1807 his experience of life led him to write, 'I abhor Religion, though I reverence and love my God, without the blasphemous notions of Sectaries, or a belief in their absurd and damnable Heresies, mysteries and thirty nine articles.'[40]

4

SOUTHWELL AND CAMBRIDGE

'At fifteen I began to think myself a very fine gentleman.' [1]

When Mrs Byron moved into Burgage Manor she brought with her the family portraits from Newstead Abbey but not her son. He flatly refused to settle into the provincial life of Southwell and after a short time in the Lodge with Owen Mealey as his servant accepted the invitation of Lord Grey de Ruthyn to stay with him at Newstead. This did not last long. He returned home abruptly and refused to discuss his reason for leaving the Abbey with either his mother or Augusta, though he assured them both that he would never again have anything to do with Lord Grey. In view of Byron's subsequent behaviour the generally accepted view is that Lord Grey made a sexual advance which shocked the young Byron.

This led to impassioned arguments with Catherine Byron who had enjoyed her acquaintance with Lord Grey and resented the embarrassment caused by her son's contemptuous attitude to his tenant. Byron's relationship with his mother was further soured by his growing suspicion that she was a little in love with the sophisticated young man who was so much more entertaining than the rest of her circle of acquaintances. However, much as she enjoyed the company of Lord Grey Mrs Byron did not lose her head over him. She hoped he would be a good tenant but was determined to make it impossible for him to be a bad one.

At the age of fifteen Byron was five feet eight and a half inches tall, which was tall for his time, and weighed over fourteen stone. He was very shy and quite capable of climbing out of the window and decamping if strangers came to call. His mother tried hard to introduce him into Southwell society, throwing a party for him and introducing him to the Pigot family who lived on the other side of the Green. Tongue-tied at first, he became enchanted with Elizabeth Pigot when she made a literary joke referring cleverly but kindly to his awkward behaviour. He immediately sought her friendship. She was older than Byron by six years, was engaged to a subaltern who was in India, and had no intention of flirting with Byron. She became a confidante and mentor, encouraging him to sing to her playing, to join in the parties, assemblies and amateur theatricals put on for the entertainment of the young people of Southwell and, when she discovered that he had written several poems, encouraging him to go into print. Byron and John Pigot, her brother, who was a medical student at Edinburgh, became close friends.

Contrary to his expectations Byron enjoyed himself at Southwell, played a great deal of cricket and wrote several poems addressed to various of Southwell's young women in a sentimental strain: 'To Emma', 'To Caroline', 'To a Lady with the poems of Camoens', 'On the Death of a Young Lady', 'To Mary', 'To Lesbia', 'To Marian', 'To a Beautiful Quaker'. But some of the titles show that the young troubadour was not incapable of regarding his own productions with an ironic eye: 'To a Young Lady who Presented to the author a lock of hair braided with his own and appointed a night in December to Meet Him in the Garden'.

John Pigot was to tell Thomas Moore, after Byron's death, 'Few people understood Byron but I knew that he had naturally a kind and feeling heart, and that there was not a single spark of malice in his composition.'[2] It was Byron's lack of conceit and open-hearted friendliness at this time which earned Pigot's praise. Pigot felt great sympathy for the shy younger man. He writes later of a visit with Byron to Harrogate: 'He was naturally shy, *very* shy; which people who did not know him mistook for pride.'[3] Pigot tells how delighted Byron was at seeing a professor from Cambridge on the street. He sent his carriage to bring the professor to the theatre and later to a ball at the Granby.

In October 1805 Byron went up to Trinity College Cambridge and from now on his arguments with his mother became more bitter. He began to call her 'Mrs Byron Furiosa' when talking to the Pigots and related how she once threw the fire irons at him and laid him flat. The Pigots offered him refuge and even, on one

38

occasion, helped him to escape from Southwell without her knowledge.

One can only sympathise with Catherine Byron. Instead of becoming more sensible Byron's behaviour became more adolescent and more rebellious after he left Harrow and he even began to put on airs, in direct contrast to his conduct in the past and, indeed, by and large during the rest of his life. Elizabeth and John Pigot saw nothing of this phase in Byron's development though they remained his confidants. If John Pigot had read some of Byron's letters to his mother at this period the rosy picture he gave to Thomas Moore might have undergone some modification.

On going up to Cambridge Byron was afraid that those used to grander acquaintances and higher incomes would despise him. To stave off any humiliating rebuff he determined to take a high tone even with Hanson and his mother. There was no father to depress his pretensions and give him good advice. He was fond of Hanson but Hanson was not of the *haute monde*. Lord Carlisle was too distant a figure to be of any help. The boy had to learn his lesson from experience. In the meantime his mother bore the brunt of his disdain.

Byron compensated for his feeling of inadequacy and the always visible evidence of deformity in his lameness by spending money with wild extravagance: fitting up his rooms at Trinity College with some splendour, ordering down a dozen each of wine, brandy, port, sherry, claret and madeira and buying a horse called Oateater. He planned to cut a dash in Cambridge with a servant, a horse and a white hat (which latter annoyed Hobhouse more than any other of his affectations).

Catherine Byron was alarmed at her son's extravagance. Hanson had managed to organize a grant of £500 a year (paid quarterly to Mrs Byron) for Byron's education when he went to Harrow. Mrs Byron foolishly turned the whole of this sum over to Byron when he went up to Trinity. He was seventeen and a half and the son of a spendthrift. Catherine applied for a grant of £200 for herself. This was refused and her Civil List pension was reduced to £200. She was hard put to it to exist without some addition to her income, which was composed of this £200 and another sum of £200 of Scottish income, and was obliged to live very frugally. Her son obstinately refused to recognise the sacrifices his mother made for him until after her death when it was too late to show his gratitude. He told Augusta that he had one of the best allowances in Cambridge:

I need scarcely inform you that I am not in the least obliged to Mrs B. for it, as it comes off my property, and She refused to fit out a single thing for me from her own pocket, my Furniture is paid for & she has moreover a handsome addition made to her own income, which I do not in the least regret, as I would wish her to be happy...[4]

(Trinity College, 6 November 1805)

He wrote to Hanson, '... study is the last pursuit of the Society; the Master eats, drinks and Sleeps, the Fellows *drink*, *dispute* and *pun*; the employments of the under Graduates you will probably conjecture...'[5] (Trinity College Cambridge, 23 November 1805)

Arguments over money caused a coolness between Byron and Hanson. The lawyer who had been so kind to the boy and whose family had welcomed him into their household, became 'that fool, Hanson, in his vulgar idiom', and 'that chattering puppy, Hanson'.

By the time Byron went to London for the Christmas vacation he was so short of money that he asked Augusta to guarantee a loan for him. This she sensibly refused to do, offering instead, to lend him the money. His sense of honour (somewhat inconsistent at this stage in his life) precluded his accepting money from her and he persuaded his landlady at 16 Piccadilly, Mrs Massingberd and her daughter, to act as security for the loan. From this time on, Byron was in the hands of the moneylenders, Mrs Massingberd acting as go-between. By the time he left Cambridge his debts amounted to £5000. The explanation of this foolishly extravagant behaviour is that, during this time and for many years to come, Byron believed – and was encouraged by Hanson in this belief – that his Rochdale lands (which had been illegally sold by the Wicked Lord) would fetch in the region of £60,000 when a lawsuit conducted under Hanson's guidance came to a successful conclusion. More than once Byron was told that he had won the lawsuit but, shortly before his death, he learned that all hope of retrieving the bulk of the money was at an end.

Byron enjoyed himself in London, taking fencing lessons with Henry Angelo and boxing lessons from Gentleman Jackson, and airily announcing to his mother new plans for going abroad. Mrs Byron began to suspect that her beloved son had got into the hands of moneylenders. Augusta was vexed at seeing her brother at the theatre in London when he should have been pursuing his studies at Cambridge. Byron went back to Cambridge but not before the next term was well underway. He wrote later that he was disgusted by 'the commonplace libertinism of the place' – but still took part in it.

Byron finally returned to Southwell bringing with him a manservant and a coach and horses to the consternation of his mother who was expected to house them. He had sent her from London an insufferably patronising letter:

> ...I intend remaining in Town a month longer, when perhaps I shall bring my Horses and myself down to your residence in that *execrable* kennel. I hope you have engaged a Man Servant – else it will be impossible for me to visit you since my Servant must attend chiefly to his horses, at the same Time you must cut an Indifferent Figure with only maids, in your habitation.[6]
> (To Mrs Catherine Gordon Byron, 16 Piccadilly, 26 February 1806)

In fact he returned to Southwell only briefly and not until the Summer vacation, escaping again to London after a scene with Mrs Byron led to his leaving the house in the middle of the night. In September he returned to Southwell and enjoyed himself by taking part in private theatricals, playing Penruddock in Cumberland's *The Wheel of Fortune* and Tristram Fickle in Allingham's *The Weathercock*. Paul Elledge describes *The Wheel of Fortune* as a 'spineless mawkish affair'; nevertheless, it was 'as well-regarded in its day as "Death of a Salesman" in ours'. Elledge regards Allingham's as a much better play from which Byron 'learned something of satiric representation.' Tristram Fickle 'is a colourfully silly fellow.' He becomes 'by turns an actor, a musician, a philosopher, a soldier, a gardener, a Quaker, and ultimately "a buck".' 'He is convinced that "I possess great powers of oratory"' and 'he has summoned his barber to shave half of his head in imitation of "Demosthenes, the Athenian orator".'[7]

In early 1807 a change occurred in Byron's life which was almost as significant as the taking up of his inheritance in 1799. He embarked on a régime for losing weight and the overweight youth was transformed into a 'regular Apollo'. He wrote to Hanson from Southwell:

> ...you will be surprised to hear that I am grown *very thin* ... I have lost 18LB in my weight ... by violent exercise and Fasting ... I wear *seven* Waistcoats & a great Coat, run & play at Cricket in this Dress ... use the hot Bath daily, eat only a quarter of a pound of Butcher's

41

meat in 24 hours, no Suppers or Breakfast ... drink no malt liquor, little Wine.[8]

(To John Hanson, Southwell, 2 April 1807)

Byron succeeded in getting his weight down to eleven stone. From now on his beauty became legendary and, as a result, he was pursued, even hunted down, by women for the rest of his life. The more famous he became the more devastating was his effect. Women fell desperately in love with him on gazing at him from the far side of a room. Harriette Wilson, the famous courtesan whose beauty was fading by the time she caught sight of the poet, wrote to inform him that while watching his very beautiful face she had imagined his lips pressed to hers, as wild and eager as his poetry.

Coleridge later went into raptures about Byron's eyes, filled with light, and declared his face among the most beautiful he ever saw.

This beauty, combined with his musical speaking voice, his reputation for wild deeds and mysterious love affairs and for having experienced and suffered more than most of his age, enhanced the fame which changed his life on the publication of *Childe Harold's Pilgrimage*.

Byron always had to fight his tendency to put on weight, and for the most part he was successful. His motives for fasting were not simply an obsession with the desirability of a slender figure. He liked to fast because he believed that heavy meals, especially if they contained meat, increased the passions. He did not want to be a slave of passion. Starving himself and then eating vast meals when his hunger became too much for him, had a deleterious effect on his digestion. He once wrote to Samuel Rogers, who had invited the young poet to dinner, 'Will you allow me to come in *after* dinner tomorrow instead of before – for I have so bedevilled my digestion – that your *light* supper – the other night – half killed me.'[9]

An advantage of his loss of weight was that there was much less for his lame foot to carry about. At Harrow he had to hire a pony to go to the bathing place because it was too far for him to walk on his lame leg. In 1815 he would scramble up a steep hill near the beach at Seaham, racing Annabella Milbanke to the top. He remained deeply sensitive about his lameness and this was the cause of his remarking as a young man that no woman could ever love 'such a thing as I am.' (He proceeded to try to give the lie to this statement by consorting with 'lewd loves' in London when he escaped from Southwell). It was only a few years later that he wrote in his Journal:

[Four or Five Reasons in Favour of a Change]
1st At twenty three the best of life is over and its bitters double. 2ndly I have seen mankind in various Countries and find them equally despicable, if anything the Balance is rather in favour of the Turks, 3dly I am sick at heart...
4thly A man who is lame of one leg is in a state of bodily inferiority which increases with years and must render his old age more peevish & intolerable. Besides in another existence I expect to have *two* if not *four* legs by way of compensation.[10]

(Malta, 22 May 1811)

Though Byron often suffered from melancholy he was easily made happy by friendship and love. During his first term at Cambridge he spent much of his time with Edward Noel Long who had been at Harrow and was now at Trinity College with him. They would ride and swim together and Long would play the flute and violoncello for Byron in the evenings.

Byron was dismayed when, in May 1807, Long left Cambridge for the army and wrote to tell him he was going to war:

...I am truly sorry the duties of your profession call you to combat, for what? Can you tell me? The ambition of Despotism or the caprice of men placed by chance in the Situation of Governors, & probably inferior to yourself ... I am no *coward*, nor would I shrink from Danger on a proper occasion, indeed Life has too little valuable for me, to make Death horrible; I am not insensible to Glory, and even hope before I am at *Rest*, to see some service in a military Capacity, yet I cannot conquer my repugnance to a Life absolutely and exclusively devoted to Carnage...[11]

(To Edward Noel Long, Southwell, 1 May 1807)

Byron had moved some way from the child who contemplated the glorious future career of 'Byron's Blacks'. Edward Noel Long's military career lasted no more than eighteen months. He was drowned at sea in early 1809 when the transport ship in which he was travelling went down with all hands. Byron was grief-stricken. He wrote later that at Cambridge Edward Long's friendship and a 'violent, though *pure*, love and passion' ... 'were the then romance of the most romantic period of my life.'[12] The 'pure' passion was for a seventeen-year-old chorister who sang in the chapel at Trinity College. Byron included in 'Fugitive Pieces' (his first privately printed book of verse) a poem, 'The Cornelian', which refers to a cornelian ring which was a present from this young man, John Edleston.

G. Wilson Knight explains the idealism of Byron's youthful male loves, contrasting his physical experience later in Greece with Nicolo Giraud with the idealism of his experience with Edleston:

> To Byron youth ... always remained in his mind the age of unsullied insight and valuation. Though in himself and others the early perfection was destined, in various ways and from various causes, to be desecrated, he throughout remained true to this world of ardent friendship, self-sacrifice, and heroism. It was a world of classic, Greek tone. As good an expression of it as any is Vergil's story of Nisus and Euryalus in the *Aeneid* (IX); a translation of it is among Byron's youthful poems.[13]

Jerome Christensen seems to agree with this interpretation of Byron's attitude to love for young males:

> Among the ancient Greeks, according to Dover, the legitimacy that was conferred on a philanthropic relationship between an *erastes* and his youthful *eromenos* was sharply contrasted with 'gross misbehaviour for monetary payment [which] is the act of a *hubristes* and uneducated man' – a vice aptly described by Byron's phrase – (he had in mind his friend Francis Hodgson's penchant for falling in love with prostitutes) 'romantic attachments for things marketable for a dollar.'[14]

Byron wrote of his love for Edleston after his death:

> Ours too the glance none saw beside;
>   The smile none else might understand;
> The whispered thought of hearts allied,
>   The pressure of the thrilling hand;
> The kiss so guiltless and refined,
>   That Love each warmer wish forbore;
> Those eyes proclaimed so pure a mind,
>   Ev'n Passion blushed to plead for more.[15]

Only a hypocrite could have written these lines from the *Thyrza* cycle if the relationship with Edleston was in fact physical.

For many years it has been believed that while Byron was away on his travels with Hobhouse Edleston was accused of indecency in London. The conviction arose from a mistaken reading of an entry in Hobhouse's Journal to the effect that 'The Collection has been accused of indecency.' This refers to his collection of poems. The word 'Collection' was mistakenly read as 'Edleston' at least thirty years ago and Edleston has been supposed to have indulged in behaviour which resulted in a charge of indecency. This has undoubtedly led to a misreading of Byron's relationship with the boy and of his sexual affiliations in general and may have convinced readers of the above stanza that Byron was indeed a hypocrite. This valuable piece of clarification we owe to Phyllis Grosskurth who pointed out the mistake to Paul Elledge by whom her discovery has been verified.[16] Whether or not Jonathan Gross was aware of this mistake in the year 2000 when his book *Byron the Erotic Liberal* appeared, his view of Byron's *eros* seems to chime with that of G. Wilson Knight and that of Jerome Christensen:

> Byron's *eros* has little in common with libertinism. This is an important distinction. Where those driven by *eros* become dissatisfied with themselves and strive for self-improvement, libertines regard each new conquest as proof of their intellectual superiority. Erotic lovers are overwhelmed by passion, which they struggle in vain to control; libertines control others by controlling themselves. Plato explains how *eros* leads the lover from loving beautiful bodies to loving beautiful acts. – The libertine's progress is toward hell and damnation ... Byron conformed to Plato's definition of *eros*, to an erotic ladder rather than a libertine descent.[17]

When Edleston left Cambridge Byron was determined to leave it too. He toyed with the idea of living with his protegé and confided in Elizabeth Pigot:

> ... [I] quit Cambridge forever, with little regret, because our *Set* are *vanished*, and my *musical* protegé ... has left the Choir, & is to be stationed in a mercantile house ... in the Metropolis. You may have heard me observe he is exactly to an hour, 2 years younger than myself, I found him grown considerably; & as you will suppose, very glad to see his former *patron*. – He is nearly my height, very thin, very fair complexion, dark eyes, & light locks...[18]
>
> (Cambridge, 30 June 1807)

A few days later he wrote:

45

...at this moment I write with a *bottle* of *Claret* in my *Head* and *tears* in my *eyes*, for I have just parted from 'my *Cornelian*' ... my mind is a *Chaos* of *hope* and *Sorrow* ... I certainly *love* him more than any human being... In short, we shall put *Lady E. Butler, & Miss Ponsonby* [the ladies of Llangollen] to the *Blush, Pylades* and *Orestes* out of countenance.[19]

(To Elizabeth Pigot, Trinity College, Cambridge, 5 July 1807)

While he was at Southwell Byron almost succeeded in putting most of its female population out of countenance by collecting his early verse into a volume called *Fugitive Pieces* which he took to be printed by John Ridge, at Newark. Elizabeth had persuaded him to take this step but she must have been astonished at the verses 'To Mary' – a much naughtier Mary than Mary Chaworth – and surprised at the other poems on love and sex (an unmentionable subject in front of ladies since the middle of the eighteenth century). The Reverend John J. Becher, who was a friend of the young poet, took him gently to task and they agreed that the volume was 'unfit for the perusal of ladies'. Byron destroyed the whole print-run but the Revd. Mr Becher kept his own copy, presumably in the conviction that it was quite fit for the perusal of parsons. The 'Lines to Mary' present a marked contrast to the idealistic poems addressed to Edleston, describing, as they do, the delights of 'love's ecstatic posture' which would have both shocked and intrigued the elderly gossips of Southwell.

Byron was more distressed than he seemed by this débacle. He gave in to the pressure of public opinion but defied his critics on paper – much as he had defied his nurse at the age of four:

TO A KNOT OF UNGENEROUS CRITICS
RAIL on, rail on, ye heartless crew!
My strains were never meant for you;
Remorseless Rancour still reveal,
And damn the verse you cannot feel...
Your efforts on yourselves recoil;
Then Glory still for me you raise,
Yours is the Censure, mine the Praise.[20]

Byron produced a second privately printed collection, *Poems on Various Occasions* which he described as 'miraculously chaste'. His friends were kind enough to praise these poems and Byron determined to produce a third volume printed not privately but for the public. He called it *Hours of Idleness*. Byron spent the summer

46

vacation in London and could not resist boasting to Elizabeth Pigot about the mild success of *Hours of Idleness*:

My dear Elizabeth

...My Cousin, Lord Alexander Gordon, ... told me his Mother, her *Grace* of *Gordon*, requested he would introduce my *poetical* Lordship, to her *highness*, as she had bought my volume, admired it extremely, in common with the Rest of the fashionable world, & wished to claim her relationship with the Author ... So much for *Egotism*, my *Laurels* have turned my Brain, but the *cooling acids* of forthcoming criticisms, will probably restore me to Modesty ... Southwell, I agree with your Brother, is a *damned* place, I have done with it & shall see it no more ... excepting yourself, I esteem no-one ... you were my only *rational* companion, & in plain truth I had more respect for you, than the whole *Bevy*, with whose foibles I *amused* myself ... you gave yourself more trouble with me & my *manuscripts*, than a thousand *dolls* would have done, believe me, I have not forgotten your good nature, ... As for the village '*Lasses*' of *every description*, my *Gratitude* is also unbounded, to be equalled only by my *contempt*, I saw the *designs* of all *parties* while they imagined me *everything they wished*.[21]

(Byron to Elizabeth Bridget Pigot)

Byron is referring in this last sentence chiefly to the family of Julia Leacroft, who tried to force him into a proposal of marriage by accusing him of compromising the 'Lesbia' of one or two of his poems. Byron's reply to the lady's brother was that the only remedy was to decline all further intercourse with 'those whom my acquaintance has unintentionally injured ... however careful I am of your Sister's honour, I am equally tenacious of my own.'[22]

Byron's letter to Elizabeth from London was a farewell. Fond as he was of both the Pigots, they belonged to a narrow world he was leaving forever. London and literary fame were intoxicating for a budding poet but he was contemplating further, far-flung and exotic destinations. First, he must complete the work he had conceived as retaliation for the harsh words directed by the *Edinburgh Review* and the *Satirist* against his first published volume.

Note

1. *Hours of Idleness* has been described in the Dictionary of National Biography as 'probably the worst first book ever written by a considerable

poet' and it was savagely reviewed in the *Edinburgh Review*. Modern criticism takes a different view. Brian Nellist writes: 'the whole volume is a digression around the subject of poetry itself, an *eclogue* of potential Byronic voices, appropriate to a first offering in verse.'[1] Michael G. Cooke found Byron's early lyrics worthy of close scrutiny:

...they can be shown to encase in a plain, cryptic exterior finely wrought personal positions on time, memory, nature, will, culture, knowledge, and essential being... Many of Byron's lyrical positions turn out to bear comparison with those of Wordsworth, who it may be recalled, was not unsympathetic to *Hours of Idleness*.

'On a Distant View of the Village and School of Harrow on the Hill' ... looks forward with Wordsworth – Coleridge rather than back to Gray ... the crucial point, however, is that the eighteen-year-old Byron, with no great finesse or feeling as a poet, correctly and sensitively carries out a romantic exercise, and concocts a Wordsworthian flavour. This gives a peculiar extension to a verdict he later passed on himself: 'My earlier poems are the thoughts of one at least ten years older than the age at which they were written: I don't mean for their solidity, but their Experience.[2]

5

THE NEWLY PUBLISHED POET

'The cry is up, and scribblers are my game;'[1]

When Byron went back to Cambridge in June 1807 he intended to pay his College dues, take his leave of John Edleston and leave Cambridge for good. In the event he decided to return to University in the autumn. He could no longer be regarded as the fop he had seemed on his first appearance at Cambridge since he was now a published poet. Charles Skinner Matthews, a brilliant young intellectual whom he had met briefly at Trinity College, introduced him to John Cam Hobhouse, author of an 'Imitation of Juvenal' and son of Benjamin Hobhouse MP. Their lively conversation, mordant wit, interest in literature and politics and membership of the Whig Club (which they had founded themselves) promised a more stimulating time ahead, and Byron was not disappointed.

He returned to Trinity in the autumn, bringing with him a tame bear to annoy the college authorities who had pronounced that Statutes forbade the keeping of dogs in College by the undergraduates. There was nothing in the Statutes about a tame bear.

His new friends made Byron known to Douglas Kinnaird who would become his banker and to Scrope Berdmore Davies, fellow of King's College, a wit, a gambler and a friend of Beau Brummell. Years later when Davies was forced into exile by his gambling debts Byron wrote to Hobhouse from his own exile in Ravenna:

So – Scrope is gone – down – *diddled* – as Doug. K. writes it – the said Doug being like the Man who when he lost a friend went to the St James's Coffee House and took a new one – but to you and me – the loss of Scrope is irreparable – we could have 'better spared' not

49

just 'a better man' but 'the best of Men.' – Gone to Bruges – where he will get tipsy with Dutch beer and shoot himself the first foggy morning – Brummell – at *Calais* – Scrope at Bruges – Buonaparte at St Helena – you in – your new apartments – and I at Ravenna – only think so many great men! – there has been nothing like it since Themistocles at Magnesia – and Marius at Carthage.[2]

(To Hobhouse, Ravenna, 3 March 1820)

Another new friend at Cambridge was Francis Hodgson, a tutor at King's College who intended to take Holy Orders, was easily shocked by Byron's racy conversation and nursed hopes of converting him to a more conventional attitude towards religion. In spite of continuing wide divergences in their outlook they remained close friends until Byron's death.

This last year at Cambridge was a turning-point in Byron's life. Edleston had gone. Long had gone. His younger friends from Harrow days were separated from him by distance or their own avocations. Now he had found the friends who would love him and be loved by him all his life. After his death Hobhouse claimed that no man ever had such devoted friends as Lord Byron.

In spite of his decision to spend another year at Cambridge he spent the Christmas vacation in London and stayed on there in January 1808, returning to Cambridge only for visits to his new cronies and, in July, to take the degree of MA reluctantly awarded to him by the University in spite of his far too frequent and lengthy absences.

Byron was now on the fringes of the literary world of the reviews and magazines which were setting up at the beginning of the nineteenth century as critics of literature and commentators on politics. This was a battle field on which he would first be an eager participant and later an interested onlooker.

In 1802 Francis Jeffrey, Henry Brougham and Sydney Smith had founded the *Edinburgh Review*. By 1812 it had a circulation of 10,000. This alarmed Sir Walter Scott for, as a Tory, he felt that the Whig partisanship of the *Edinburgh Review*'s political commentaries was unedifying. To combat this horrifying tendency he joined John Murray and William Gifford in founding the rival *Quarterly Review*. Supporters of the *Edinburgh* took just as partisan an attitude to the Tory *Quarterly* as Scott took to the *Edinburgh*; Hazlitt wrote of the *Quarterly* that in it nothing was regarded but the political creed or external circumstances of a writer, whereas

50

the *Edinburgh* adverted to nothing but his literary merits. He claimed that the *Quarterly* presents 'one foul blotch of servility, intolerance, falsehood, spite and ill-manners'.[3]

Feelings ran so high that angry literary men challenged each other and Sydney Smith told Lady Holland in a letter of 1809, 'Wordsworth vows personal vengeance upon Jeffrey for his last critique, and blood will flow.'[4]

Hours of Idleness was reviewed briefly in the *Monthly Review*, November 1807:

> ...the poems exhibit strong proofs of genius, accompanied by a lively but chastened imagination, a classical taste and a benevolent heart.[5]

From now on Mrs Byron, at home in Southwell and later in Newstead Abbey, collected all the reviews of Byron's works. There is no doubt that the reference here to his 'tenderness and feeling' must have given her great pleasure. She would have been affronted by the critical review in *The Satirist* in January 1808 and would have shared Byron's fury when a critic pronounced his poems no more than 'school exercises' and suggested that if Byron escaped whipping for them the masters at Harrow must have 'an undue respect for Lords' bottoms.'

Byron now showed a new solicitude for his mother, writing from London to the Revd John Becher:

> ...a most violent attack is preparing for me in the next number of the *Edinburgh Review*... Tell *Mrs Byron* not to be out of humour with them, and to prepare her mind for the greatest hostility on their part, it will do no injury however, and I trust her mind will not be ruffled – They defeat their object by indiscriminate abuse, and they never praise except the partizans of Ld. Holland & Co.[6]
>
> (Dorant's, 26 February 1808)

(This conviction was the ground of Byron's attack on Lord and Lady Holland in his projected satire.)

Later he wrote to Becher:

> You have seen the *Edinburgh Review*, of course. I regret that Mrs Byron is so much annoyed. For my own part, these 'paper bullets of the brain' have only taught me to stand fire.[7]
>
> (Dorant's, 28 March 1808)

51

John Cam Hobhouse, now Byron's closest friend, told a different story – of extreme distress. Byron believed Jeffrey was the author of the review and he harboured great resentment against him for many years. The writer was in fact Henry Brougham who mocked the young poet unmercifully as much for his nobility as for any literary shortcomings. The *Eclectic Review* sneered at *Hours of Idleness* on the same grounds: 'The book is a collection of juvenile pieces, some of very moderate merit, of very questionable morality; but the author is a nobleman.'[8] Wordsworth objected to such unfair criticism of a young writer. H. Crabb Robinson related that:

> I was sitting with Charles Lamb, when Wordsworth came in with fume in his countenance and the *Edinburgh Review* in his hand. 'I have no patience with these Reviewers,' he said; 'here is a young man, a lord and a minor, it appears, who publishes a little volume of poetry; and these fellows attack him as if no-one may write poetry unless he lives in a garret. The young man will do something if he goes on.'[9]

The young man was about to do something surprising. He wrote a satire attacking most of the writers of the day. Moore's is the best account of this crucial moment in Byron's life, the publication of his first important work, of which a second edition was to follow fast upon the first:

> It was not long, however, before he was summoned back to town by the success of his Satire, – the quick sale of which already rendered the preparation of a new edition necessary. His zealous agent, Mr Dallas, had taken care to transmit to him, in his retirement, all the favourable opinions of the work he could collect; and it is not unamusing, as showing the sort of steps by which Fame at first mounts, to find the approbation of such authorities as Pratt and the magazine writers put forward among the first rewards and encouragements of a Byron.
>
> You are already (he says) pretty generally known to be the author. So Cawthorne tells me, and a proof occurred to myself at Hatchard's, the Queen's bookseller. On enquiring for the latest Satire, he told me that he had sold a great many, and had none left, and was going to send for more ... I asked who was the author? He said it was believed to be Lord Byron's. Did *he* believe it? Yes, he did. On asking the ground of his belief, he told me that a Lady of distinction had, without hesitation, asked for it as Lord Byron's satire. He likewise informed me that he had enquired of Mr Gifford, who frequents his shop, if it was yours. Mr Gifford denied any knowledge of the author, but spoke very highly of it, and said a copy had been sent to him. Hatchard assured me that all who came to his

reading-room admired it. Cawthorne tells me it is universally well spoken of, not only among his own customers, but generally at all the booksellers. I heard it highly praised at my own publisher's, where I have lately called several times. At Philip's it was read aloud by Pratt to a circle of literary guests, who were unanimous in their applause: The *Antijacobin*, as well as the *Gentlemen's Magazine*, has already blown the trump of fame for you. We shall see it in the other Reviews next month, and probably in some severely handled, according to the connection of the proprietors and editors with those whom it lashes.[10]

English Bards and Scotch Reviewers was an astonishing achievement for so young an author. Byron is setting himself up, powerfully, though imperfectly, as continuing in the tradition of Pope who was always to be the poet he most admired, perhaps from as early as 1803 when his friend Henry Boldero gave him the complete works of Pope at Harrow.

The theme of the Satire was praise of Pope, Congreve and Otway as a préamble to a series of hearty attacks on some of the leading and some of the minor poets of the day. In *English Bards and Scotch Reviewers* Byron is extremely scathing about some who later became friends. One can only admire the forgiving nature of Walter Scott, Moore and Lord and Lady Holland. Byron accuses Scott of racking his brains for lucre, not fame and condemns the 'prostituted Muse' of this 'hireling bard'. Lord Holland is accused of bribing scribblers by inviting them to the famous banquets at Holland House which makes them his 'hirelings'. As for Lady Holland:

> My lady skims the cream off each critique;
> Breathes o'er the page her purity of soul,
> Reforms each error, and refines the whole.[11]

He accuses Strangford of plagiarism in a brilliant metaphor:

> Think'st thou to gain thy verse a higher place,
> By dressing Camoëns in a suit of lace?[12]

His diatribe against Amos Cottle is that of a formidable 'enfant terrible' in full cry:

> Bœotian COTTLE, rich Bristowa's boast,
> Imports old stories from the Cambrian coast,
> And sends his goods to market – all alive!

Lines forty thousand, Cantos twenty-five!
Fresh fish from Hippocrene! who'll buy? who'll buy?
The precious bargain's cheap – in faith, not I.[13]

Wordsworth,

('Who, both by precept and example, shows
That prose is verse, and verse is merely prose')[14]

was briskly dealt with. It is unlikely that the great poet ever forgave Byron for this, and Brougham (although it was he who had written the cruel review of *Hours of Idleness* in the *Edinburgh Review*) certainly never forgave him for these lines:

Beware lest blundering Brougham destroy the sale,
Turns Beef to Bannocks, Cauliflowers to Kail.[15]

If anyone deserved retaliation it was Brougham and this was no more than a glancing blow, though Byron at this time was unaware that Brougham was author of the review which had distressed him. Brougham, however, waited for the appropriate moment and took a damaging, but secret, revenge.

Some readers who resented the hegemony of the *Edinburgh Review* over English letters may have enjoyed the lines:

For long as Albion's heedless sons submit,
Or Scottish taste decides on English wit.[16]

Many more must have enjoyed the sheer gusto and lèse-majesté of the whole performance. Others may have been mollified by the self-deprecation which was a novel attitude for an audience used to poets who tended to place themselves on a pedestal, above the ordinary run of mankind:

E'en I – least thinking of a thoughtless throng,
Just skilled to know the right and choose the wrong,
Freed at that age when Reason's shield is lost,
To fight my course through Passion's countless host,
Whom every path of Pleasure's flow'ry way
Has lured in turn, and all have led astray –
E'en I must raise my voice, e'en I must feel
Such scenes, such men, destroy the public weal:

Altho' some kind, censorious friend will say,
'What art thou better, meddling fool, than they?'
And every Brother Rake will smile to see
That miracle, a Moralist in me.[17]

In these lines Byron shows that he is well aware that he cannot set himself up as a moralist and perhaps he is conceding that his own earlier efforts at verse are no better than some of those he is criticising.

It was not long before he began to repent of the whole satire and in particular of the lines on Carlisle. In the original version he had some lines in praise of his guardian. After having been snubbed by Carlisle on his first appearance in the House of Lords he was so resentful that he replaced them with some outrageous verse referring to Carlisle's attempts at verse as 'the paralytic puling of Carlisle?'[18] This caused a rift with Augusta.

Moore describes Byron's attitude to the Satire on re-reading it during his stay at the Villa Diodati on the Lake of Geneva in the summer of 1816:

But, whatever may have been the faults or indiscretions of this Satire, there are few who would now sit in judgment upon it so severely as did the author himself, on reading it over nine years after, when he had quitted England, never to return. The copy which he then perused is now in possession of Mr Murray, and the remarks which he has scribbled over its pages are well worth transcribing. On the first leaf we find –
'The binding of this volume is considerably too valuable for it contents.
'Nothing but the consideration of its being the property of another prevents me from consigning this miserable record of misplaced anger and indiscriminate acrimony to the flames.

Opposite the passage,

'to be misled
By Jeffrey's heart, or Lamb's Boeotian Head,'

is written, 'This was not just. Neither the heart nor the head of these gentlemen are at all what they are here represented.' Along the whole of the severe verses against Mr Wordsworth he has scrawled 'Unjust,' – and the same verdict is affixed to those against Mr Coleridge. On his unmeasured attack upon Mr Bowles, the comment is, – 'Too savage all this on Bowles;' and down the margin of the page containing the lines 'Health to immortal Jeffrey,' &c. he writes, – 'Too ferocious – this is mere insanity;' – adding, on the verses that follow ('Can none remember that eventful day?' &c.), 'All this is bad, because personal.'

Sometimes, however, he shows a disposition to stand by his original decisions. Thus, on the passage relating to a writer of certain obscure Epics (v. 793), he says, – 'All right;' adding, of the same person, 'I saw some letters of this fellow to an unfortunate poetess, whose productions (which the poor woman by no means thought vainly of) he attacked so roughly and bitterly, that I could hardly regret assailing him; – even were it unjust, which it is not; for, verily, he *is* an ass.' – On the strong lines, too (v. 953), upon Clarke (a writer in a magazine called the Satirist), he remarks, – 'Right enough, – this was well deserved and well laid on.'

To the whole paragraph, beginning 'Illustrious Holland,' are affixed the words 'Bad enough; – and on mistaken grounds besides.' The bitter verses against Lord Carlisle he pronounces 'Wrong also: – the provocation was not sufficient to justify such acerbity;' – and of a subsequent note respecting the same nobleman, he says, 'Much too savage, whatever the foundation may be...'

Opposite the paragraph in praise of Mr Crabbe he has written; 'I consider Crabbe and Coleridge as the first of these times in point of power and genius.' On his own line, in a subsequent paragraph, 'And glory, like the phoenix mid her fires,' he says, comically, 'The devil take that phoenix – how came it there?' and his concluding remark on the whole poem is a follows:

The greater part of this Satire I most sincerely wish had never been written; not only on account of the injustice of much of the critical and some of the personal part of it, but the tone and temper are such as I cannot approve.[19]

Byron was exceedingly rude to Jeffrey in the postcript to the second edition of the satire and he later repented of it when he discovered that the review of *Hours of Idleness* had been written not by Jeffrey but by Brougham. He was delighted when he heard that Jeffrey had compared his *Manfred* to the *Prometheus* of Aeschylus.

Once he became an habitué of Holland House and friend of Walter Scott and Thomas Moore he refused to allow any further editions of *English Bards and Scotch Reviewers* to be published and in 1813 he wrote of his repentance:

To-night I went with young Henry Fox to see 'Nourjahad,' – a drama, which the Morning Post hath laid to my charge, but of which I cannot even guess the author. I wonder what they will next inflict upon me. They cannot well sink below a Melodrama; but that is better than a

Satire, (at least, a personal one,) with which I stand truly arraigned, and in atonement of which I am resolved to bear silently all criticisms, abuses, and even praises, for bad pantomimes never composed by me, without even a contradictory aspect. I suppose the root of this report is my loan to the manager of my Turkish drawings for his dresses, to which he was more welcome than to my name. I suppose the real author will soon own it, as it has succeeded; if not, Job be my model, and Lethe my beverage![20]

(Journal, 27 November 1813)

A year later Byron gave some good advice to a novice writer, telling him not to be discouraged or enraged by the attacks of the critics. He then went on to ensure that the young man would not be as roughly handled as he himself has been. At this time Byron was twenty six but he writes like a sage, firstly to the writer, John Hamilton Reynolds and then to Francis Hodgson:

The first thing a young writer must expect, and yet can least of all suffer, is *criticism* – I did not bear it – a few years, and many changes, have since passed over my head, and my reflections on that subject are attended with regret. I find, on dispassionate comparison, my own revenge more than the provocation warranted ... the best reply to all objections is to write better – and if your enemies will not then do you justice, the world will. On the other hand, you should not be discouraged – to be opposed, is not to be vanquished, though a timid mind is apt to mistake every scratch for a mortal wound.[21]

(To John Hamilton Reynolds, 20 February 1816)

There is a youngster – and a clever one, named Reynolds, who has just published a poem called 'Safie', published by Cawthorne. He is in the most natural and fearful apprehension of the Reviewers – and as you and I both know by experience the effect of such things upon a *young* mind, I wish *you* would take his production into dissection and do it *gently*. *I* cannot, because it is inscribed to me; but I assure you this is not my motive for wishing him to be tenderly entreated, but because I know the misery, at his time of life, of untoward remarks upon first appearance.[22]

(To Francis Hodgson, 28 February 1814)

These letters show that Byron was far from being the cold, selfish, egotistical young man so often portrayed by writers who appear to ignore the bulk of the twelve volumes of letters.

The satire was well received by most critics. Hazlitt's criticism was in general opposed to the tradition of satirical verse from Pope onwards so it was to be expected that he would slate *English Bards and Scotch Reviewers* on literary grounds, as an attempt to continue in this tradition. He is even more scathing on the nobility of the young poet:

> We must say we think little of our author's turn for satire. His *English Bards and Scotch Reviewers* is dogmatical and insolent but without refinement... This is the satire of a lord, who is accustomed to have all his whims or dislikes taken for gospel and who cannot be at the pains to do more than signify his contempt or displeasure.[23]

Hazlitt continually refers in his criticism to Byron's being a lord and this clouds his judgement, reducing him to the pettiness we find in Leigh Hunt's references to Byron after he had accepted his hospitality in Italy. Hunt seems to have resented his generosity and Hazlitt his aristocracy. Byron was later well aware of all such nuances in the hatred that was borne him by so many of his compatriots and soon after his exile he began to take it lightly, sending back to England 'A sigh to those who love me / And a smile to those who hate.'[24]

6

RETURN TO NEWSTEAD

Newstead! what saddening change of scene is thine!
Thy yawning arch betokens slow decay;
The last and youngest of a noble line,
Now holds thy mouldering turrets in his sway.[1]

In October 1807 Byron's chief worry was his enormous burden of debt. He asked Hanson to remit his quarterly allowance as soon as possible:

> ...for I am at this moment contemplating with a *woeful* visage, one *solitary Guinea*, *two bad sixpences* and a *shilling*, being all the *Cash* at present in possession of
> Yours very truly
Byron[2]
(Dorant's Hotel, 19 October 1807)

On leaving Cambridge his debts amounted to £5,000. By the time he set out on his travels in June 1809 they had increased to over £12,000. He described his way of life in London as 'an abyss of sensuality'.[3] He gambled, and he led the life of a man about Town with Scrope Davies, resorting through Mrs Massingberd to the money-lenders to finance his excesses.

He had written of his London life to Elizabeth Pigot:

> The Intelligence of London cannot be interesting to you who *have rusticated* all your life, the annals of Routs, Riots, Balls & Boxing matches, Dowagers & demireps, Cards & Crim-Con, Parliamentary Discussion, Political details, Masquerades, Mechanics, Argyle Street

Institution & Aquatic races, Love & Lotteries, Brookes's and Buonaparte, Exhibitions of pictures with Drapery, & *women without*, Statues with more *decent dresses* than their *originals*, Opera-singers & Orators, Wine, Women, Waxworks and Weathercocks, cannot accord with your *insulated* ideas of decorum.[4]

(Gordon's Hotel, 13 July 1807)

Byron naturally made no mention to Elizabeth of the deterioration in his health caused by excessive love-making with his 'blue-eyed Caroline'. This damsel claimed to be pregnant and, from some remark he made to them, Byron's friends were afraid he would feel obliged to marry her, but no more was heard of such a plan although he addressed some tender verses to her:

> But Breeze of night again forbear,
>   In softest murmurs only sigh:
> Let not a Zephyr's pinion dare
>   To lift those auburn locks on high.[5]

In the summer of 1808 Byron spent some weeks recuperating in Brighton with Hobhouse and Scrope Davies and various visitors including Gentleman Jackson and a Miss Cameron who was dressed in boy's clothes and may have been Byron's 'blue-eyed Caroline'. Nanny Smith later revealed that Byron had once brought a girl to Newstead who was dressed as a boy. These masquerades may have been concerned with disguise for practical purposes, with sexual arousal at the sight of a girl dressed as a boy or simply with the fun of hoodwinking all the onlookers.

In Brighton the three young men lodged on the seafront and would plunge into the sea at all hours of the day or night, visit the new theatre, perhaps attend assemblies at the Ship Hotel and even visit the Pavilion. Byron wrote to Augusta (now married and settled at a country house near Newmarket with her handsome Colonel and a baby girl) that he had seen George Leigh in Brighton. George's regiment, the tenth Hussars, was stationed at Brighton and he was in the service of the Prince Regent.

In September 1808 Lord Grey's lease of Newstead Abbey expired and Byron returned to his ancestral home with old Joe Murray (who had been Byron's pensioner most of the time since they had left Newstead) and William Fletcher, his groom, who was now promoted to valet and was to stay with Byron until his death at Missolonghi.

Byron now began spending lavishly on putting several apartments in order and told his mother, when she remonstrated, that it must be done and that she was to live in the renovated part of the Abbey when he went on his travels. Byron omitted to have the roof repaired so the new decorations were soon ruined by damp and rain. In the meantime he invited his friends to visit him. Hobhouse, Matthews, Scrope Davies, were surprised at being greeted not only by Byron's dogs but by the tame bear which his unfortunate mother was to take care of while he was away. Charles Skinner Matthews describes one such visit:

> Our party consisted of Lord Byron and four others, and was, now and then, increased by the presence of a neighbouring parson ... the order of the day was generally this;- for breakfast we had no set hour ... everything remaining on the table till the whole party had done; though had one wished to breakfast at the early hour of ten one would have been rather lucky to find any of the servants up. Our average hour of rising was one... It was frequently past two before the breakfast party broke up. Then, for the amusements of the morning there was reading, fencing, single-stick, or shuttle-cock in the great room; practising with pistols in the hall; walking – riding – cricket – sailing on the lake, playing with the bear, or teasing the wolf. Between seven and eight we dined [arrayed in the monkish robes and beads supplied by Byron]; and our evening lasted from that time till one, two, or three in the morning. The evening diversions may easily be conceived.[6]

Jonathan Gross comments on the self-conscious play-acting of this performance which included the passing round the table of wine in a goblet formed from a human skull:

> Byron's antics at Newstead Abbey and his references to Laurence Sterne, the Medmenham monks and *Choderlos de Laclos* show him emulating a version of eighteenth century libertinism long after it was unfashionable, even politically dangerous, to do so.[7]

The result was rumours of wickedness which spread round the world once Byron became famous and which helped to build up the false image which has influenced biographers and reviewers, and which Byron's friends would never have recognised. In France it was reported that Byron had murdered one of his mistresses and habitually drank wine out of her skull. When George Ticknor called on him in London in 1815 Byron reported with some amusement that the young American was expecting to meet 'a misanthropical gentleman in wolf-skin breeches'.[8] When Byron arrived in Rome after leaving England in 1816 Lady Lidell caught sight of him at St Peter's and ordered her daughter to avert her eyes for it was dangerous to look at him. Teresa Guiccioli's brother, Pietro Gamba, warned his sister to have nothing to do with this dangerous English lord who had shut up his wife for several years in one of his castles.

Nanny Smith, the housekeeper at Newstead, told Washington Irving after Byron's death that he and his friends had 'played some mad pranks but nothing but what young gentlemen do and no harm done.'[9] She explained that with his lame leg Byron was often unable to keep up with the gentlemen and then the only comfort he had was to be with the ladies a little. It is remarkable how much more censorious many modern biographers have been in comparison with this simple, kind-hearted elderly female servant with all the prejudices of her kind and the strictest notions of what constituted decorous and acceptable behaviour in a nineteenth century household. When old Joe Murray began singing lewd songs in front of the housemaids she would read him a lecture and flounce off to bed in a rage. But she was moved to compassion by the obvious suffering and frustration his deformity caused her young master, and made allowances for his need of comfort.

Although Byron was posturing as an eighteenth century libertine the goings-on described by Nanny Smith and Charles Skinner Matthews appear more reminiscent of typical undergraduate misbehaviour than anything more sinister. Sexual congress with willing housemaids may have been reprehensible but it was not unusual. When the youngest of the housemaids, Lucy, became pregnant Byron provided £100 a year for her, later altered to £50 for her and £50 for the boy. This may be compared with the income of £150 a year on which Mrs Byron and her son had lived in Aberdeen.

Wordsworth came to regard Byron as a moral pariah but the younger man was more honest than Wordsworth in admitting his moral failings and, in taking care of his illegitimate offspring, displayed both moral responsibility and kindness.

The suspicion has been aired that Byron and his Cambridge friends were a coterie of homosexuals and that the diversions of the evenings at Newstead were homo-erotic. This may indeed have been the case but it is most unlikely. Romping with the housemaids was one thing but it is hard to imagine the young men indulging in homosexual practices in Byron's ancestral home (which was inhabited by giggling girls, a young page who was the son of one of Byron's tenants, Fletcher, Joe Murray and Nanny Smith) and inviting the local parson to join them on several occasions.

Modern biographers often assume that Byron went in for every form of sexual excess but to imagine the staid Hobhouse (who was so painfully shy that he was unable to approach women of education and social standing and was obliged to resort to prostitutes) making sexual overtures to Byron, or vice versa, appears somewhat ludicrous. There is no hint of erotic tension in their correspondence over many years. As for Matthews, he appears to have set himself up as their professor in matters to do with Greek love. His letters spur his friends on to ever greater interest in the classic relationship of the older man with the younger boy, but there is no hint of erotic intentions towards his correspondents of his own age.

Jonathan Gross warns, in a different context, against the danger of confusing 'licentious language with licentious deeds'. It is not possible here to rule out licentious deeds of this nature but neither can one pronounce with any degree of certainty that such deeds were done.

Hobhouse sets out the ground of the close and loving friendship which linked Byron, himself, Scrope Davies and Douglas Kinnaird over the years as he deals with Lady Byron's prejudice against her husband's friends:

> Her Ladyship had formed an incorrect judgement not only on his Lordship but on his Lordship's friends, who, from not exactly bearing that cast of character which she might have been accustomed to regard as necessary for the communion of married men, she was induced to look upon as the associates of wickedness rather than as the votaries and encouragers of a steady and honourable attachment to the companion of many years.[10]

Byron started planning his travels in earnest, assuring Hanson that living out of England for a year or two would save him much expense. In the meantime Hanson could sell the Rochdale property to pay off his debts and, in particular, to relieve Scrope Davies who had guaranteed a loan for him and was afraid the creditors might come down on him in Byron's absence. This was an excellent plan but Hanson's failure to dispose of the Rochdale property left Scrope in dismal uncertainty for several years; the fact that Hanson did not write to him for long periods during his travels left Byron fuming with anxiety over the outcome.

The money for expenses abroad had to be raised by loans and proved difficult, especially as it was necessary to raise double the amount required since Hobhouse was on bad terms with his father and the quixotic but heedless young debtor offered to raise the money for him too. At this time Mrs Byron was worrying about Byron's creditors in Nottingham, who would be ruined if he failed to pay his bills. Raising the necessary funds took so long that their departure was put off time and again.

While waiting for a passage Byron was thrown once more into melancholy by a meeting at the Infirmary Ball in Nottingham with Mary and Jack Chaworth-Musters, as they were now known. Byron brought Hobhouse with him to the Ball and arranged for Mrs Byron to meet them there, a rare occasion for his mother to bask in the mild success and new-found beauty of her beloved son. It was the first time Mary saw her formerly fat, school-boy admirer in the persona of a divinely beautiful young poet. As a result Byron and Hobhouse were invited to dinner at Annesley Hall, a distressing experience for both Byron and Mary:

> ... [I] was determined to be valiant, and converse with 'sang froid', but instead I forgot my valour and my nonchalance, and never opened my lips even to laugh, far less to speak, and the Lady was almost as absurd as myself, which made both the object of more observation, than if we had conducted ourselves with easy indifference.[11]
>
> (To Francis Hodgson, Newstead Abbey, Notts, 3 March 1808)

Byron's love for Mary inspired several poems one of which described Byron's trysts with Mary on the hill known as Diadem hill because it was crowned with a diadem of trees. When Byron became famous the poem was read all over Europe. Jack Musters had all the trees cut down. His jealousy may well have originated with the strange behaviour of his wife and her guest when Byron and Hobhouse came to dine.

Soon after this episode Byron was writing, 'My dear Hodgson, Boatswain is dead! ... I have lost everybody except Old Murray.'[12] Byron was always besotted by his animals and Boatswain, a huge and amiable Newfoundland, was his particular favourite. He nursed him through the rabies attack which killed him, wiping the slaver from his jaws with his bare hands. Boatswain was buried in a vault near the nave of the ruined Priory Church and Byron decreed that he himself, together with old Joe Murray, would be buried beside him. Old Joe demurred saying he would not mind so long as his Lordship lay there with him, 'But I should not like to lie there alone with the dog.'

Before Byron left England he wanted to see the publication of his satire, now entitled *English Bards and Scotch Reviewers*. He was assisted in this object by Charles Dallas who claimed distant kinship with Byron in 1807, had written some minor novels, and now offered to find him a publisher, fixing on James Cawthorne.

Many who met Byron briefly and were regarded by him with a sceptical eye, made haste to produce accounts of their relationship with him after his death. Dallas was no exception. In his book he relates how he called on Byron one day to find him on the point of setting out for the House of Lords to undergo the ceremony of taking his seat for the first time. Byron was in a state of nervousness and melancholy, the explanation being that when he wrote to tell his guardian that he was planning to take his seat, expecting Carlisle to accompany him to the House and introduce him there, Lord Carlisle wrote a letter explaining what steps he must take and describing the ceremony. All Byron's doubts about Carlisle's coldness towards his ward and the reason for it (strong dislike) arose once again. To Byron this rebuff was tantamount to a blow in the face. As a result he was obliged to set about the irksome business of proving his right of succession to the barony and then to proceed alone in his robes to the House of Lords. Byron welcomed Dallas's offer to accompany him to the House. His seat taken, he was ready to leave England as soon as possible after the publication of his satire.

Byron left England with his affairs in a state of confusion. Hanson begged him to postpone his departure until they could be brought into some sort of order. Now was the time for him to take an interest in his estates. He failed to do so and set off on his travels leaving some large debts for work on the Abbey unsettled and instructing Hanson airily to sell the Rochdale property in order to settle them.

Byron had not been brought up as heir to the estate or taught, as were most heirs, to regard his inheritance as a sacred trust.

More importantly, he was so extravagant as a young man that the sale of Newstead became almost inevitable. Just as the fifth baron relied on the marriage of his son to an heiress to save the day, Byron relied on the sale of Rochdale to make him rich. It never did.

John Murray, Byron's publisher, visited Newstead on 5 October 1814 and wrote a description of what he found:

> Not a tree is left standing ... the hall of entrance has about eighteen large niches, which had been filled with statues, and the side walls covered with family portraits and armour. All these have been mercilessly torn down, as well as the magnificent fireplace, and sold. No sum short of £100,000 would make the place habitable ... the whole place is crumbling into dust ... I am far more surprised that Lord Byron should ever have lived at Newstead, than that he should be inclined to part with it ... I came away with an aching heart.[13]

7

THE PILGRIMAGE

'London and the world is the only place to take the conceit out of a man'[1]

Thomas Moore was convinced that Byron suffered from a deep melancholy at this point in his life and he explains away the evidence of sheer youthful energy and high spirits as isolated incidents which concealed a wounded spirit. G.K. Chesterton took the view that this melancholy was a youthful affectation. Byron took pleasure in dramatic storms and stricken peaks because he was very young and very happy.

Byron planned to take with him on his travels old Joe, William Fletcher and his page, Robert Rushton. Shortly before they left England Byron angrily changed his mind about bringing Robert and Fletcher abroad with him. Fletcher, who was supposed to be looking after the boy in London, had actually introduced him to a prostitute. Byron wrote to Mrs Byron from London:

I have sent the lad to his father; before this occurrence he was good hearted, honest, and all I could wish him, and would have been so still, but for the machinations of the scoundrel who has not only been guilty of adultery; but of depraving the mind of an innocent stripling ... for his wife's sake he shall have a farm or other provision of some kind, but he quits me... Break this business to his wife, who will probably hear it from the boy's relatives in another manner.[2]
(To Mrs Catherine Gordon Byron, 8 St James's Street, 19 May 1809)

Then Byron, who was incorrigibly soft-hearted, wrote to his mother from Falmouth, the first stop on his journey:

Fletcher begged so hard that I have continued him in my service...
Pray tell Mr Rushton his son is well, and *doing* well...'[3]
(To Mrs Catherine Gordon Byron, Falmouth, 22 June 1809)

Many authorities have believed the assertion of Lady Caroline Lamb (at a period when she had told Byron, 'You will see how an Englishwoman can revenge.'[4]) that Byron told her he had corrupted Robert Rushton. If this were so, Byron's letter to his mother on the subject of Fletcher's behaviour must have been sheer hypocrisy. The most sensible account of the matter is given by Ian Gilmour:

> [Byron's] rage at Fletcher having taken his page to a whore has been attributed to his having made Rushton his catamite. Rushton was a good-looking lad, who slept in a bedroom next to his master's; and Byron was fond of him – in a will he made before he went abroad he left Rushton £25 a year for life. According to Lady Byron, Lady Caroline Lamb later alleged that Byron had admitted to her that he had 'corrupted' the boy. And there is a remark by Hobhouse which may be stronger evidence.
>
> Even so, it is on the whole unlikely that Byron ever 'corrupted' Rushton. For him to have done that to the son of a tenant would have been far more dangerous than any of his other homosexual escapades. Tongues would surely have been busy, and he would have faced exile like William Beckford, Lord Leicester and other homosexuals involved in scandal. Indeed both his own and Rushton's lives would have been in danger. While other countries were becoming more liberal over homosexuality, England was becoming more draconian; the number of executions for sodomy was growing...

Gilmour also adds that sending Rushton back to his father as Byron did after the incident with the prostitute 'would have been crazily imprudent had he really corrupted the boy.'[5]

Treating the allegation on the subject of Rushton with some scepticism does not entail a belief that Byron was uninterested in Greek love. Both he and Hobhouse discussed with Matthews their intention of experimenting with this fascinating and, to them, romantic subject when they reached Greece. Those who disagree with this analysis and believe that Byron took Rushton with him as his catamite are faced with the question why he should do so on a journey to Greece with the expectation he and Hobhouse harboured of sexual freedom with Greek boys there. Nor can one easily imagine Byron corrupting the boy with Fletcher in his entourage after the angry remonstrances over the visit to the London prostitute.

From Falmouth Byron wrote a lively description of the town to Francis Hodgson, omitting the *bonne bouche* he saved for Charles Skinner Matthews: 'We are surrounded by Hyacinths and other flowers of the most fragrant [na]ture, & I have some intention of culling a handsome Bouquet to compare with the exotics we expect to meet in Asia.'[6] Hodgson, and even Hobhouse were more inhibited or disapproving on this subject than Matthews, and Byron was always tactful in suiting the tone of his letters to their recipients. With Matthews he employed a code derived from the *Satyricon* of Petronius for the achievement of sexual gratification. But, as Jonathan Gross warns, 'licentious language' does not necessarily mean 'licentious deeds.'[7] It may be that Henry Drury was not the most suitable recipient of the joke about Hobhouse which Byron confided to him in yet another letter from Falmouth – 'Hobhouse further hopes to indemnify himself in Turkey for a life of exemplary chastity at home by letting out his "fair bodye" to the whole Divan.'[8]

On 25 June 1809 Byron and Hobhouse sailed from Falmouth in the Lisbon packet with 'two officers' wives, three children, two waiting maids, ditto subalterns for the troops, three Portuguese esquires, and domestics, in all nineteen souls.'[9]

He wrote to Hodgson from Lisbon:

I am very happy here, because I loves oranges, and talk bad Latin to the monks, who understand it, as it is like their own, – and I goes into society (with my pocket-pistols), and I swims in the Tagus all across at once, and I rides on an ass or a mule, and swears Portuguese, and have got a diarrhoea and bites from the mosquitoes. But what of that? Comfort must not be expected by folks that go a pleasuring.***

When the Portuguese are pertinacious, I say, 'Carracho!' – the great oath of the grandees, that very well supplies the place of 'Damme,' – and, when dissatisfied with my neighbor, I pronounce him 'Ambra di merdo.' With these two phrases, and a third, 'Avra Bouro,' which signifieth 'Get an ass,' I am universally understood to be a person of degree and a master of languages. How merrily we lives that travellers be! ... To-morrow we start to ride post near 400 miles as far as Gibraltar, where we embark for Melita [Malta?] and Byzantium. A letter to Malta will find me, or to be forwarded, if I am absent ... Hodgson! send me the news, and the deaths and defeats and capital crimes and the misfortunes of one's friends; and let us hear of literary matters, and the controversies and the criticisms.[10]

(To Frances Hodgson, Lisbon, 16 July 1809)

He wrote a long account of his travels to Mrs Byron from Gibraltar. Now that they were separated he ignored their former differences. His letters to her from Greece are unusually friendly and direct:

I find that reserve is not the characteristic of the Spanish belles, who are in general very handsome, with large black eyes, and very fine forms... Intrigue here is the business of life, when a woman marries she throws off all restraint, but I believe their conduct is chaste enough before. – If you make a proposal which in England would bring a box on the ear from the meekest of virgins, to a Spanish girl, she thanks you for the honour you intend her and replies 'wait till I am married and I shall be too happy...' I am going over to Africa tomorrow, it is only six miles from this Fortress. – My next stage is Cagliari in Sardinia where I shall be presented to his S[ardinian] Majesty. I have a most superb uniform as a court dress, indispensable in travelling...

(To Mrs Catherine Gordon Byron, Gibraltar, 11 August 1809)

15 August
... I cannot go to Barbary; the Malta packet sails tomorrow & myself in it... Joe Murray delivers this. I have sent him and the boy back, pray shew the lad any kindness as he is my great favourite, I would have taken him on (but you *know boys* are not *safe* amongst the Turks –) say this to his father who may otherwise think he has behaved ill.[11]

(To Mrs Catherine Gordon Byron, 13 August 1809)

In Malta Byron was introduced to a pretty and sophisticated young married woman called Constance Spenser Smith who lived in Vienna and had been through adventures which gave her an intriguing glamour. They fell in love but not deeply enough on Byron's side to cause him to postpone his departure. They planned to meet again the following year and Byron wrote several poems about her during his travels, the last of which spoke of a passion that was waning:

xxx
Sweet Florence! could another ever share
This wayward, loveless heart, it would be thine:[12]

70

They did meet again when Byron returned briefly to Malta, and he went through the embarrassing business of convincing the lady that the undying love they had sworn two years ago was in reality no more than a fleeting romance. In thus writing of his 'loveless heart' Byron did himself less than justice. 'Wayward' it was, but certainly not 'loveless'. Moore rightly characterised his life as a series of 'the most passionate attachments'[13] and he himself later wrote 'I cannot exist without some object of love.'[14]

CHILDE HAROLD'S PILGRIMAGE

Itinerary of Lord Byron and J.C. Hobhouse
(Originally published in E.H. Coleridge's edition of 1905)

1809	CANTO I
July 2	Sail from Falmouth in Lisbon packet. (Stanza 12)
July 6	Arrive Lisbon. (Stanzas 16, 17)
	Visit Cintra. (Stanzas 18–26)
	Visit Mafra. (Stanza 29)
July 17	Leave Lisbon. (Stanza 28)
	Ride through Portugal and Spain to Seville. (Stanzas 28–42)
	Visit Albuera. (Stanza 43)
July 21	Arrive Seville. (Stanzas 14, 46)
July 25	Leave Seville.
	Ride to Cadiz, across the Sierra Morena. (Stanza 51)
	Cadiz. (Stanzas 65–84)

	CANTO II
Aug. 6	Arrive Gibraltar.
Aug. 16	Sail from Gibraltar in Malta packet. (Stanzas 17–28)
	Malta. (Stanzas 29–35)
Sept. 19	Sail from Malta in brig-of-war *Spider*.
Sept. 23	Between Cephalonia and Zante.
Sept. 26	Anchor off Patras.
Sept. 27	In the channel between Ithaca and the mainland. (Stanzas 39–42)
Sept. 28	Anchor off Prevesa (7 p.m.). (Stanza 14)
Oct. 1	Leave Prevesa, arrive Salakhora (Salagoura).
Oct. 3	Leave Salakhora, arrive Arta.
Oct. 4.	Leave Arta, arrive, han St Demetre (H. Dhimittrios).
Oct. 5	Arrive Janina. (Stanza 47)
Oct. 8	Ride into the country. First day of Ramazan.
Oct. 11	Leave Janina, arrive Zitza ('Lines written during a Thunderstorm'). (Stanzas 48–51)

Oct. 13	Leave Zitza, arrive Mossiani (Móseri).
Oct. 14	Leave Mossiani, arrive Delvinaki (Dhelvinaki). (Stanza 54)
Oct. 15	Leave Delvinaki, arrive Libokhovo.
Oct. 17	Leave Libokhovo, arrive Cesarades (Kestourataes).
Oct. 18	Leave Cesarades, arrive Ereeneed (Irindi).
Oct. 19	Leave Ereeneed, arrive Tepeleni. (Stanzas 55–61)
Oct. 20	Reception by Ali Pacha. (Stanzas 62–64)
Oct. 23	Leave Tepeleni, arrive Locavo (Lacovon).
Oct. 24	Leave Locavo, arrive Delvinaki.
Oct. 25	Leave Delvinaki, arrive Zitza.
Oct. 26	Leave Zitza, arrive Janina.
Oct. 31	Byron begins the First Canto of *Childe Harold*.
Nov. 3	Leave Janina, arrive han St Demetre.
Nov. 4	Leave han St Demetre, arrive Arta.
Nov. 5	Leave Arta, arrive Salakhora.
Nov. 7	Leave Salakhora, arrive Prevesa.
Nov. 8	Sail from Prevesa, anchor off mainland near Parga. (Stanzas 67, 68)
Nov. 9	Leave Parga, and, returning by land arrive Volondorako (Valanidórakhon). (Stanza 69)
Nov. 10	Leave Volondórako, arrive Castrosikia (Kastrosykia).
Nov. 11	Leave Castrosikia, arrive Prevesa.
Nov. 13	Sail from Prevesa, anchor off Vonitsa.
Nov. 14	Sail from Vonitsa, arrive Lutraki (Loutráki). (Stanzas 70, 72, Song 'Tambourgi, Tambourgi'; Stanza written in passing the Ambracian Gulph.)
Nov. 15	Leave Lutraki, arrive Katúna.
Nov. 16	Leave Katúna, arrive Makalá (? Machalas).
Nov. 18	Leave Makalá, arrive Guriá.
Nov. 19	Leave Guriá, arrive Ætolikon.
Nov. 20	Leave Ætolikon, arrive Mesolonghi.
Nov. 23	Sail from Mesolonghi, arrive Patras.
Dec. 4	Leave Patras, sleep at *Han* on shore.
Dec. 5	Leave *Han*, arrive Vostitsa (Œgion).
Dec. 14	Sail from Vostitsa, arrive Larnáki (? Itea).
Dec. 15	Leave Larnáki (? Itera), arrive Chrysó.
Dec. 16	Visit Delphi, the Pythian Cave, and stream of Castaly. (Canto I. Stanza 1)
Dec. 17	Leave Chrysó, arrive Arakhova (Rhakova).
Dec. 18	Leave Arakhova, arrive Livadia (Livadhia).
Dec. 21	Leave Livadia, arrive Mazee (Mazi).
Dec. 22	Leave Mazee, arrive Thebes.
Dec. 24	Leave Thebes, arrive Skurta.
Dec. 25	Leave Skurta, pass Phyle, arrive Athens. (Stanzas 1–15; stanza 74)
Dec. 30	Byron finishes the First Canto of *Childe Harold*.

1810

Jan. 13	Visit Eleusis.
Jan. 16	Visit Mendeli (Pentelicus). (Stanza 87)
Jan. 18	Walk round the peninsula of Munychia.
Jan. 19	Leave Athens, arrive Vari.
Jan. 20	Leave Vari, arrive Keratéa.
Jan. 23	Visit temple of Athene at Sunium. (Stanza 86)
Jan. 24	Leave Keratéa, arrive plain of Marathon.
Jan. 25	Visit plain of Marathon. (Stanzas 89, 90)
Jan. 26	Leave Marathon, arrive Athens.
Mar. 5	Leave Athens, embark on board the *Pylades*.
Mar. 7	Arrive Smyrna.
Mar. 13	Leave Smyrna, sleep at *Han*, near the river Halesus.
Mar. 14	Leave *Han*, arrive Aiasaluk (near Ephesus).
Mar. 15	Visit site of temple of Artemis at Ephesus.
Mar. 16	Leave Ephesus, return to Smyrna
Mar. 28	Byron finishes the Second Canto of *Childe Harold*.[15]

Byron wrote to Hanson from Prevesa in Albania:

The Consul has gotten me a house here... The bay where we now lie
was the scene of the famous battle of Actium. – I have seen Ithaca &
touched in the Morea at Patras, where I found the Greeks polite &
hospitable... Remember me to all your family, particularly to Mrs
Hanson, but do not expect to see me soon, I am now above three
thousand miles from Chancery Lane.[16]

(To John Hanson, Prevesa in Albania, 29 September 1809)

Byron wrote also at some length to his mother:

Prevesa, 12 November 1809

My dear Mother –
I have now been some time in Turkey; ... When I reached Yanina the
capital after a journey of three days over the mountains through a
country of the most picturesque beauty I found that Ali Pacha was with
his army in Illyricum besieging Ibraham Pacha in the castle of Berat –
He had heard that an Englishman of rank was in his dominions & had
left orders in Yanina with the Commandant to provide a house & supply
me with every kind of necessary, *gratis* ... though I have been allowed
to make presents to the slaves etc.

Byron then travelled over the mountains through Zitza 'a village
with a monastery where I slept on my return', reaching Tepelene

nine days later where he was introduced to Ali Pacha. He describes the scene on entering Tepaleen (as he calls it):

The Albanians in their dresses ... (a long *white kilt*, gold worked cloak, crimson velvet gold laced jacket and waistcoat, silver mounted pistols and daggers) ... the Tartars with their high caps, the Turks in their vast pelises and turbans, the soldiers & black slaves with the horses ... two hundred steeds ready caparisoned to move in a moment, couriers entering or passing out with dispatches, the kettle drums beating, boys calling the hour from the minaret of the mosque...

[Ali Pacha] told me to consider him as a father whilst I was in Turkey ... – Indeed he treated me like a child, sending me almonds and sugared sherbet, fruit and sweetmeats 20 times a day ... his manner is very kind and at the same time he possess that dignity which I find universal among the Turks. He has the appearance of anything but his true character, for he is a remorseless tyrant, guilty of the most horrible cruelties, very brave & so good a general that they call him the Mahometan Buonaparte...

Two days ago I was nearly lost in a Turkish ship ... – Fletcher yelled after his wife, the Greeks called on all the Saints, the Mussulmen on Alla, the Captain burst into tears & ran below deck telling us to call on God, the sails were split, the mainyard shivered, the wind blowing fresh, the night setting in ... I did what I could to console Fletcher but finding him incorrigible wrapped myself up in my Albanian capote (an immense cloak) and lay down on deck to await the worst ... – Luckily the wind abated...

Fletcher's next epistle will be full of marvels, we were one night lost for <u>nine</u> hours in the mountains in a *thunder* storm.[17]

(To Mrs Catherine Gordon Byron, Prevesa, 12 November 1809)

In Athens the young men took lodgings in the house of Theodora Macri, widow of the late English Vice Consul. These consisted of a sitting room and two bedrooms opening onto a courtyard where there were five or six lemon trees, from which Hobhouse wrote, '...during our residence in the place, was plucked the fruit that seasoned the pilaf and other national dishes served up at our frugal table.'[18] Their landlady had three pretty daughters and Byron fell in love with the youngest of them, Teresa. On leaving Athens to visit Constantinople Byron wrote to his mother from Smyrna:

I have traversed the greatest part of Greece besides Epirus & resided ten weeks at Athens, and am now on the Asiatic side on my way to Constantinople ... Greece, particularly in the vicinity of Athens, is

74

delightful, cloudless skies, and lovely landscapes ... I keep no journal, but my friend Hobhouse scribbles incessantly.[19]
(To Mrs Catherine Gordon Byron, Smyrna, 19 March 1810)

Byron failed to mention that he had almost completed Cantos I and II of *Childe Harold's Pilgrimage*, a poem of a wholly different kind and scale than anything he had yet attempted.

Byron and Hobhouse set off from Smyrna to Constantinople in the naval frigate sent to pick up the retiring Ambassador, Robert Adair. When they anchored off Abydos Byron imitated the feat of Leander in swimming from Sestos to Abydos, lamenting that there was no Hero to greet him as he came up out of the water. He was very proud of this performance, boasting of it in letters to several friends. Now he wrote to Henry Drury describing his adventures:

I have been with Generals and Admirals, Princes and Pachas, Governors and Ungovernables, ... I wish to let you know that I live with a friendly remembrance of you and a hope to meet you again ... I see not much difference between us & the Turks, save that we have foreskins and they none, that they have long dresses and we short, and that we talk much and they little. – In England the vices in fashion are whoring and drinking, in Turkey, Sodomy and smoking, we prefer a girl and a bottle, they a pipe and pathic... Tell Dr Butler I am now writing with the gold pen he gave me before I left England.[20]
(To Henry Drury, Salsette Frigate, 3 May 1810
in the Dardanelles off Abyssinia)

When they arrived in Constantinople Byron proceeded to make himself unpopular by an ill-mannered insistence on his right to precedence as a man of rank. The two young men were treated with immense courtesy by the departing Ambassador to the Porte, Robert Adair, who invited them regularly to dine and then to join the ceremonial procession which accompanied his leavetaking of the Turkish representative of the absent Grand Vizier. Byron was offended at being required to walk behind the first Secretary, Stratford Canning, and stormed off in a fury. Even so the Ambassador invited him to the ceremonial leavetaking from the Sultan. Byron consulted the powers-that-be on protocol and, finding that an English peer was not in these circumstances entitled to precedence, accepted the invitation with an apology for his former discourtesy. It was a discreditable episode which can have done his reputation no good

75

in the English community of the city. When Byron felt at a disadvantage he tended, at this age, to become haughty and belligerent. He refers later to the fact that travel in the world takes 'the conceit out of a man'.[21]

In July 1810 he had received news which depressed him deeply. He heard that Augusta was annoyed at his attack on Lord Carlisle in *English Bards and Scotch Reviewers*. He wrote, '...had I been aware that she would have laid it to heart, I would have cast my pen and poem both into the flames... But the mischief is done, Lord forgive me! this it is to have tender hearted she-relations.'[22] (To Edward Ellice, Constantinople, 4 July 1810)

He also learned that Hanson had been unable to pay off his creditors and that the Nottingham upholsterer who had refurbished Byron's apartments at Newstead had presented his bill for £1,600 and was threatening an execution. On 30 July he wrote to Mrs Byron from Patras, 'I suppose some arrangement has been made with regard to Wymondham [his Norfolk property] and Rochdale.'[23]

He wrote to Hobhouse:

[I have had] two billets from Hanson, he wants me to sell Newstead, but I wont. ... My affairs are greatly embarrassed ... Tell Davies, in a very few months I shall be at home to relieve him from his responsibility which he would never have incurred so long, had I been aware 'of the law's delay.'[24]

(To Hobhouse, Athens, 26 November 1810)

Byron had written to Hodgson from the Salsette frigate:

... I hope you will find me an altered personage, I do not mean in body, but in manner, for I begin to find out that nothing but virtue will do in this damned world. I am tolerably sick of vice which I have tried in its agreeable varieties, and mean on my return to cut all my dissolute acquaintance, leave off wine and 'carnal company', and betake myself to politics and Decorum. – I am very serious and cynical, and a good deal disposed to moralize, but fortunately for you the coming homily is cut off by default of pen, and defection of paper.[25]

(To Francis Hodgson, Salsette Frigate,
in the Dardanelles off Abydos, 5 May 1810)

This frame of mind is reflected in Canto I of *Childe Harold* where he echoes Shakespeare's 'expense of spirit in a waste of shame' theme:

XXXV

The paltry prize is hardly worth the cost:
   Youth wasted – Minds degraded – Honour lost –
These are thy fruits, successful Passion! these![26]

He looks back to Mary Chaworth:

V

For he through Sin's long labyrinth had run,
Nor made atonement when he did amiss,
Had sighed to many though he loved but one,
And that loved one, alas! could ne'er be his.
Ah, happy she! to 'scape from him whose kiss
Had been pollution unto aught so chaste;[27]

When Byron learned later that Mary had left Jack Musters (who had always been an inveterate womaniser both before and during the marriage) he may have concluded that his own kiss was no more polluted than that of the man she married and to whom she had borne five children.

Byron and Hobhouse left Constantinople with Robert Adair and his suite on the Salsette Frigate. At Zea Hobhouse parted from Byron and went on to England while Byron headed back to Athens. Byron had told Hobhouse not to worry about the sum (in excess of £800) which he was owed for the expenses of the journey, but Hobhouse, more sensible about money matters than his friend, decided that he could not allow the debt to increase any further. When he reached home his father refused to settle his debts unless he would agree to join the Militia. When Byron received the letter with this news he tried hard to dissuade Hobhouse, as a few years ago he had tried to dissuade Long from joining the military:

You talk of the Militia, – Santissimi Coglioni! the Militia at five and twenty, Boys over your head, & brutes under you, Mess, Country quarters, Courts martial, and quelling of Riots. – If you will be mad or martial ('tis the same thing) go to Portugal again & I'll go with you.[28]
   (To John Cam Hobhouse, Volage Frigate, at sea, 19 June 1811)

Having said farewell to Hobhouse Byron returned to Athens. He had fallen in love with the city during his earlier stay there with Hobhouse and had written a famous poem to the youngest daughter of Mrs Macri:

I

Maid of Athens, ere we part,
Give, oh, give me back my heart![29]

On his return Byron would have been happy to resume his love affair with Teresa Macri but Mrs Macri was greedy and wanted to sell her daughter to him. Uneasy and embarrassed, he moved into the Capuchin monastery near the Acropolis which combined a school for the children of foreigners, or Franks, with an inn for Frankish travellers.

Byron made some excursions from Athens during this time, joining Lord Sligo with his vast train of servants and horses in a journey into the Morea and then visiting Veli Pasha at Tripolitzia. He was embarrassed by the young man's sexual overtures but accepted from him the gift of 'a very pretty horse'. Veli Pasha might have saved himself the cost of the horse. He was not a charming Greek youth and there was no lack of beautiful and willing boys in Athens. Byron had been accompanied on an earlier trip by a handsome boy called Eustathius Gregorious who joined him again, much to the scorn of Fletcher who laughed at the boy's holding up a parasol to protect himself from the sun while on horseback. Eustathius was demanding and capricious and, after a parting which entailed much kissing and embracing, he was sent home.

Byron spent several happy weeks in Athens foregathering with the distinguished, intellectual, or simply agreeable Franks of all nationalities who were wintering there. He told his mother:

Here I see and have conversed with French, Italians, Germans, Danes, Greeks, Turks, Americans &tc. &tc., &tc., and without losing sight of my own, I can judge of the countries and manners of others – Where I see the superiority of England (which by the bye we are a good deal mistaken about in many things) I am pleased and where I find her inferior I am at least enlightened.[30]

On his way back one day from swimming Byron was involved in a bizarre incident which he used later as the basis for his Oriental Tale, *The Giaour*, and which was also the ground for what Byron referred to as 'Old Goethe's husband-killing story'.[31] Goethe believed that Byron had killed the husband of a woman with whom he became involved in Greece or Turkey. This conviction does not seem to have altered the reverence in which he held the younger man: 'When you have an opportunity to give news of yourself to that remarkable man tell him also about me and mine and the exhaustible reverence, admiration and love which we feel for him.'[32] Byron and his party came upon a group of men near the banks of the Bosphorus. A Turkish girl had been sewn up in a sack and they were about to throw her into the river. The incident is mysterious. Byron rescued the girl. He is thought to have had some connection with her plight. No evidence of this has been forthcoming and it is unlikely that we will ever learn more about the incident. Lord Sligo gave an account of it, claiming that Byron forced the men to release the girl by producing a pistol which persuaded them to resort to higher authority for arbitration.

The plan of reformation Byron had described to Francis Hodgson was put on hold once he got to Athens where he disported himself with both Greek and Turkish women as well as romping with the six boys at the Capuchin monastery. He would take his favourite, Nicolo Giraud aged fifteen, to swim with him and Nicolo became his amico and swore undying love. Byron decided to pay for his education and in fact dropped him off at Malta for this purpose on his way home. This is the period during which he went in for Greek love with Greek boys. These boys were sexually experienced but full of fun and mischief. Such practices were regarded as no great aberration in Greece so they were free from guilt and anxiety. They were romantic experiences in a romantic landscape bathed in sunshine, its beaches washed by the blue Mediterranean waters. Byron told Hobhouse to inform the Citoyen (Matthews), '...that I have obtained above two hundred pl & opt Cs and am almost tired of them, for the history of these he must wait for my return', and later, in a letter: 'Mention to M[atthews] that I have found so many of his antiques on this classical soil, that I am tired of pl & opt Cs, the last thing I could be tired of, I wish I could find some of Socrates's Hemlock, but Lusieri tells me it don't poison people nowadays.'[33] The expression pl & opt Cs is the code Byron used for buggery. It derives from Petronius: *coitum plenum et optabilem*.

Byron's boast about his sexual prowess may be accurate but he had time for other diversions:

Since your departure from the Cyclades, I have been principally in Attica... Here be many English, and there have been more, with all of

79

whom I have been and *am* on dining terms, & we have had balls and a variety of fooleries with the females of Athens.[34]

(To John Cam Hobhouse, Capuchin Convent, Athens, 10 January 1811)

In March he wrote to Hobhouse:

My fantastical adventures I reserve for you and Matthieu and a bottle of Champagne, I parted as I lived friends with all the English & French in Attica and we had balls, dinners, and amours without number.[35]

(To John Cam Hobhouse, Athens, 18 May 1811)

During his travels Byron had misgivings about Hanson's management of his affairs, but for much of the time of his absence from England he was unaware that Rochdale had not been sold. Throughout his time in Albania and in Greece Byron constantly wrote asking Hanson for news of his financial affairs and Hanson constantly failed to reply. A letter from Byron to Hanson from Prevesa, shows that he was unaware then that his optimistic plans for dealing with his debts had come to nothing:

Now for my affairs, – I have received not a single letter since I left England, – my copyholds I presume are sold, & my debts in some train, what surplus may be of Rochdale, I should wish to convert into annuities for my own life on good security, & tolerable interest, or on good mortgages, if nothing remains, sorry as I should be and much as I should regret it Newstead must go for the sake of justice to all parties...[36]

(Prevesa, 12 November 1809)

In May 1810 he had still received no news from Hanson and writes from Constantinople:

...if Mrs Byron requires any supply, pray let her have it at my expence, and at all events whatever becomes of me, do not allow her to suffer any unpleasant privation. – I believe I mentioned in my last that I had visited the plains of Troy, and swam from Sestos to Abydos in the Dardanelles ... I came up in an English Frigate, but we were detained in the Hellespont ten days for a wind. Here I am at last, ... I am anxiously expecting intelligence from your quarter, I suppose you are now at Rochdale.[37]

(Constantinople, 23 May 1810)

Byron was reluctant to be too business-like with Hanson and wrote with kind messages for his family:

Commend me to your family, I perceive Hargreaves is your partner, he always promised to turn out well and Charles I am sure is a very fine fellow. – As for the others I can't pretend to prophesy. I present my respects to all the ladies, and I suppose I may *kiss* Harriet as you or Mrs Hanson will be my proxy, provided she is not grown too tall for such a token of remembrance. – I must not forget Mrs Hanson who has often been a mother to me as you have always been a friend.[38]

(To John Hanson, Athens, 11 November 1810)

Because he was so eager to communicate with people of every class and nation he happened to meet Byron was studying modern Greek and reported that he could gabble Levant Italian, was tolerably fluent in Lingua Franca, middling at Romaic (modern Greek) and could command several Ottoman oaths. Fletcher was less adaptable. Byron gave his mother an amusing account of his principal servant's shortcomings as a traveller:

Besides the perpetual lamentations after beef & beer, the stupid bigotted contempt for everything foreign, and insurmountable incapacity of acquiring even a few words of any language, rendered him like all other English servants, an incumbrance. – I do assure you the plague of speaking for him, the comforts he required (more than myself by far) the pilaws ... he could not eat, the wines which he could not drink, the beds where he could not sleep, & the long list of calamities such as stumbling horses, want of tea!!! &tc., which assailed him.[39]

(To Catherine Gordon Byron, Athens, 14 January 1811)

Byron sent Fletcher home with papers for Hanson and, characteristically, felt rather lonely without either friend or servant from home to keep him company. His Albanian servants had become attached to him and wept at his decision to return home.

Reluctantly Byron tore himself away from his beloved Greece. On his voyage home he wrote to Hanson when off the Bay of Biscay assuring him that, worried as he was over the plight of his creditors, he would join the Army rather than sell Newstead Abbey:

In the mean time I am compelled to draw on you for 20 or 30 pounds to enable me to proceed from the Port to London & pay the customs house duties. – There is a Bill of Miller's in Albemarle's which also

81

must be paid immediately, on my arrival; I do not mean to reproach you, but I certainly thought there were funds to answer so small a draft when I left London, however it has remained in his hands *dishonoured* more than two years, – However when I consider the sums I owe you professionally, I have nothing further to observe, I have made up my mind to bear the ills of Poverty, Two years travel has tolerably seasoned me to privations. – I have one question which must be resolved, is Rochdale mine, or not? Can I not sell it? and why, if it will bring a sum to clear my debts is it not sold![40]

(To John Hanson, Volage Frigate, 4 July 1811, Bay of Biscay)

He was obliged to write again on 31 July from Reddish's Hotel, London:

Dear Sir, – I have called on you with Mr Miller's bill and I do again (as I repeatedly have done) beg you to enable me to settle it, I have used him so ill (God knows unintentionally) pray let him have the whole and speedily, & do not involve me in fresh disgrace in this instance.[41]

(To John Hanson, 31 July 1811)

Byron had written to his mother to announce his return to England:

I have just been two years ... absent from England, and I return to it with ... indifference, but within that apathy I certainly do not comprise yourself, as I will prove by every means in my power. – You will be good enough to get my apartments ready at Newstead ... for a long time I have been restricted to an entire vegetable diet neither fish nor flesh coming within my regimen, so I expect a powerful stock of potatoes, greens, and biscuit, I drink no wine ... I have brought you a shawl & a quantity of Ottar of Roses.[42]

(To Mrs Catherine Gordon Byron, Volage Frigate, at sea, 25 June 1811)

Byron assured his mother that Newstead was her home and she was to regard him simply as a visitor.

Before he could settle his affairs in London Byron was summoned to Newstead Abbey with the news that his mother had fallen ill. Borrowing from Hanson he hastened up to Nottingham but by the time he arrived there she was dead. He was too late to give her the shawl and the attar of roses and to prove his regard for her as he had promised, by every means in his power. Byron was stunned

82

and devastated by the loss of the mother he had so long taken for granted. One of the reasons he had lingered in London was to set up a libel action against *The Scourge* for scurrilous allegations against her. She was described as passing her days in drunkenness. Byron sprang to her defence: '... with a very large portion of foibles and irritability, she was without a Vice.'[43] He instructed Hanson that this case must go ahead. He would allow no slur on his mother's good name.

Now came the news that Charles Skinner Matthews had drowned in the river at Cambridge. Byron was shocked – '... to him all Men I ever knew were pigmies, he was an Intellectual Giant.'[44] Jonathan Gross points out that a poem appeared in the *Morning Chronicle* in 1811 accusing Byron of having failed to write elegiac verse for Matthews because Matthews was not of his own social class.[45] Yet he spoke openly of his love for Edleston, Delawarr and others, confiding his deepest feelings, pouring out poetry and indulging his compulsion for naming the loved one. After Matthew's death Byron wrote to Scrope Davies: 'To me he was much ... to Hobhouse everything ... I did not love quite so much as I honoured him.'[46] 'Byron surely wrote no elegiac verse for Matthews because he was not in love with him. Had he loved Matthews as he loved Edleston he would have written of his love, just as he composed the *Thyrza* cycle of poems for Edleston who was of considerably lower social standing than Matthews. The poems to the 'Citoyen' could have been disguised in the same way as those addressed to Edleston, with a female pseudonym.

Before long came news that his friend Wingfield had died of a fever in the Peninsula.

He wrote to Scrope Davies:

> My Dearest Davies, – Some curse hangs over me and mine. My mother lies a corpse in this house, one of my best friends is drowned in a ditch ... My dear Scrope, if you can spare a moment, do come down to me, I want a friend.[47]

He wrote to John Pigot thanking him for his condolences and hoping to meet him.

Now the death of his mother and no fewer than four young friends led Byron to rewrite Cantos I and II of *Childe Harold* in such a way that the poem was transformed. From being a travelogue with a series of vignettes it became an account of his own development through grief and tribulation – a more philosophic, perhaps a sadder but wiser, work.

Note

1. Looking back on his younger self Byron declared that, at fifteen, he began to think himself a very fine gentleman. In writing later about James Hogg, the Ettrick Shepherd, he praises the salutary effect of travel and the experience of a wider world:

> ... Hogg is a strange being, but of great, though uncouth, powers. I think very highly of him, as a poet; but he, and half of these Scotch and Lake troubadours, are spoilt by living in little circles and petty societies. London and the world is the only place to take the conceit out of a man.[1]
>
> (To Thomas Moore, Hastings, 3 August 1814)

8

THE MAIDEN SPEECH

'Twelve Butchers for a Jury and a Jeffries for a Judge.'

The air of Greece, Byron said, had made him a poet. His travels changed him in more ways than this, as Ian Gilmour points out:

> ...he had become genuinely broad and cosmopolitan in his outlook. If his prejudices had ever been narrow, they were so no longer; as he was himself, they were fully mature. His weeks in Spain and Portugal and his proximity to the war had strengthened his 'detestation of *licensed Murder*' and what he had seen there and in Greece had intensified his love of Freedom and his hatred of oppression. He had become a philhelline and felt himself 'a citizen of the world.'[1]

His plans on returning home were first to deliver his maiden speech in the House of Lords and second to arrange for the publication of *Hints from Horace* (an imitation of the poet he had hated so at Harrow) which he felt to be the best work he had done during his travels. When he showed it to Dallas he was told this was not likely to please a publisher. He was persuaded to hand over *Childe Harold's Pilgrimage*, in which he had little faith. Dallas was enthusiastic and so was John Murray when it was offered to him.

Soon after his mother's death Augusta sent her brother a letter of condolence which ended the long silence between them. The future prospects of the Leighs were bleak. George had been dismissed by the Prince Regent for having cheated him over the sale of a horse. Discovery of impropriety in the handling of the regimental funds forced him to resign his commission. Augusta, who loved him dearly, petted him, commiserated with him and wrote to Colonel McMahon, the Prince Regent's secretary, in defence of his indefensible behaviour. George was by now an inveterate gambler and continued to spend most of his time at the races, leaving Augusta to deal with their household, their children and his debts. Byron assured her, '... you have a brother in me, & a home here.'[2]

He visited Scrope Davies but learned just before setting out for Cambridge that John Edleston had died while he was in Greece. Cambridge was haunted by memories of the boy and of Charles Skinner Matthews dying horribly, entangled in weeds at the bottom of the Cam. He wrote some elegiac poems for Edleston concealing the fact that their subject was a boy by addressing them 'To Thyrza'. This became for some time an enigma to future readers of the poet though the clues to Edleston's identity are clear enough, particularly in the poem 'Away, away, ye notes of woe!' which was inspired by hearing a familiar song.

He went back to Newstead and invited Francis Hodgson and William Harness to join him there. Both were sober companions who would not prevent him from working. For love he turned to a pretty Welsh housemaid called Susan Vaughan with whom he fell sufficiently in love to suffer great distress when she proved unfaithful: 'I do not blame her,' he wrote, 'but my own vanity in fancying that such a thing as I am could ever be beloved.'[3] He wrote some lachrymose lines about this episode. The year before, he had lamented the marriage of Mary Chaworth with histrionic threats. Byron had the sense not to publish this melodramatic tirade. After his death Francis Hodgson, to whom the poem was addressed, crossed out the most menacing lines and wrote on the manuscript to the effect that poor dear Byron had not meant a word of it. It is hard to reconcile this poem with the virtues, originality and energy of the first two Cantos of *Childe Harold* and there is a great chasm between this outpouring of self-pitying rage and the frame of mind in which he was working on the publication of *Childe Harold* and planning his maiden speech in the House of Lords. John Mortimer gives an explanation of what it was in his character which saved him again and again when he might have succumbed to lethargy and self-pity:

It's the contradictions in Byron's nature that provide its endless fascination. Surely there was never a more puritanical libertine, a more down-to-earth romantic, a more conservative libertarian, a more self-deriding exhibitionist, a more disillusioned freedom fighter. And beneath it all, keeping him as sane and balanced in the mosquito swamps of Missolonghi as he was among the fighting women and dogs and monkeys of his Palazzo on the Grand Canal, in aristocratic London ballrooms or at the gaming tables of Piccadilly, was his invulnerable, his superb common sense.[4]

It was this common sense which prompted his maiden speech on the Bill to impose the death penalty on the frame-breakers. During 1811 and 1812 there were widespread Luddite riots in Nottinghamshire. Starving workers took to storming into factories at night to break up the recently invented knitting frames, use of which by harsh and greedy employers was putting them out of work. The government reaction was repression. Nottinghamshire was full of army encampments, militia, and Bow Street Runners. Byron did not approve of the violent action taken by the frame workers but he had seen their suffering and believed they were driven to violence by employers and politicians who were indifferent to their plight.

On 27 February 1812, he delivered his maiden speech in the House of Lords, attacking the government proposal to bring in the death penalty for breaking stocking frames. Two days before his appearance before the House Byron wrote to Lord Holland to explain his views on the subject:

For my own part, I consider the manufacturers as a much injured body of men sacrificed to ye views of certain individuals who have enriched themselves by those practices which have deprived the frame workers of employment. – For instance; – by the adoption of a certain kind of frame 1 man performs the work of 7 – 6 are thus thrown out of business. – But it is to be observed that ye. work thus done is far inferior in quality, hardly marketable at home, & hurried over with a view to exportation. – Surely, my Lord, however we may rejoice in any improvement in ye. arts which may be beneficial to mankind; we must not allow mankind to be sacrificed to improvements in Mechanism. The maintenance & well doing of ye. industrious poor is an object of greater consequence to ye. community than ye. enrichment of a few monopolists by any improvement in ye. implements of trade, which deprives ye. workman of his bread, & renders ye. labourer 'unworthy of his hire'. – My own motive for opposing ye. bill is founded on it's palpable injustice, & it's certain inefficacy. – I have seen the state of these miserable men, & it is a disgrace to a civilised country. – Their excesses may be condemned, but cannot be the subject of wonder. – The effect of ye. present bill would be to drive them into actual rebellion.[5]

(To Lord Holland, 8 St James's Street, 25 February 1812)

Having consulted Lord Holland in this letter, Byron went rather further than Lord Holland would have done, declaring in his speech that:

...the framers of such a Bill must be content to inherit the honours of that Athenian lawgiver whose edicts were said to be written not in ink but in blood ... suppose one of these men ... dragged into court, to be tried for this new offence, by this new law; still, there are two things wanting to convict and condemn him; and these are, in my opinion, – twelve Butchers for a Jury, and a Jeffries for a Judge![6]

'The poetry of this young aristocrat,' wrote John Mortimer, 'was always at the service of the common people.'[7] His attitude to the common people was made clear in the course of the speech and so was his strong objection to the contemptuous attitude of some of the ruling classes towards 'the mob':

You call these men a mob... Are we aware of our obligations to a *Mob*? – It is the Mob that labour in your fields and serve in your houses, that man your navy, and recruit your army, – that have enabled you to defy all the world, and can also defy you, when Neglect and Calamity have driven them to despair.[8]

The Tories (who were in government) were infuriated by these Radical sentiments uttered by a novice peer with a beautiful voice in a theatrical manner. The Whigs were delighted with him, though Lord Holland was not enchanted with either the speech or the manner in which it was delivered. All the same, he soon called on the young man (an unprecedented honour for a twenty-four-year-old novice peer) and Lady Holland reported how much Lord Holland was growing to like Lord Byron in all his dealings with him. Byron wrote of his experience in Parliament:

The Impression of Parliament upon me – was that its members are not formidable as *Speakers* – but very much so as an *audience* – because in so numerous a body there may be little Eloquence (after all there were but *two* thorough Orators in all Antiquity – and I suspect still *fewer* in modern times) but must be a leaven of thought and good sense sufficient to make them *know* what is right – though they can't express it nobly.[9]

(*Detached Thoughts*, 1821)

and of his own feeling during his performance:

Whatever diffidence or nervousness I felt – (& I felt both in a great degree) arose from the number than the quality of the assemblage, and I thought rather of the *public without* than the persons within – knowing (as all know) that Cicero himself – and probably the Messiah could never have altered the vote of a single Lord of the Bed Chamber or Bishop.[10]

(*Detached Thoughts*, 1821)

Byron was congratulated by many of the Whigs and was invited to sit on a committee for working on amendments to the Bill – a waste of time as the House of Commons threw out all the amendments.

On 2 March 1812 the following poem appeared anonymously in the *Morning Chronicle*. (To publish openly would have jeopardised Byron's political career and the poem did not appear over his name until 1880.)

AN ODE TO THE FRAMERS OF THE FRAME BILL

1.

Oh well done Lord E———n! and better Lord R———r!
    Britannia must prosper with councils like yours;
Hawkesbury, Harrowby, help you to guide her,
    Whose remedy only must *kill* ere it cures:
Those villains; the Weavers, are all grown refractory,
    Asking some succour for Charity's sake –
So hang them in clusters round each Manufactory,
    That will at once put an end to *mistake*.

2.

The rascals, perhaps, may betake them to robbing,
    The dogs to be sure have got nothing to eat –
So if we can hang them for breaking a bobbin,
    'T will save all the Government's money and meat:
Men are more easily made than machinery –
    Stockings fetch better prices than lives –
Gibbets on Sherwood will heighten the scenery,
    Shewing how Commerce, how Liberty thrives!

3.

Justice is now in pursuit of the wretches,
    Grenadiers, Volunteers, Bow-street Police,
Twenty-two Regiments, a score of Jack Ketches,
    Three of the Quorum and two of the Peace;
Some Lords, to be sure, would have summoned the Judges,
    To take their opinion, but that they ne'er shall,
For LIVERPOOL such a concession begrudges,
    So now they're condemned by *no Judges* at all.

4.

Some folks for certain have thought it was shocking,
    When Famine appeals, and when Poverty groans,
That Life should be valued at less than a stocking,
    And breaking of frames lead to breaking of bones.
If it should prove so, I trust, by this token,
    (And who will refuse to partake in the hope?)
That the frames of the fools may be the first to be *broken*,
    Who, when asked for a *remedy*, sent down a *rope*.[11]

Now Byron was part of the political world in London. He had already been initiated into the literary world by his introduction to John Murray who made him known to William Gifford, his colleague in running the *Quarterly Review*, a man of whom Byron had so high an opinion that he had praised him in *English Bards and Scotch Reviewers*. Hazlitt's view of Gifford was, 'In general, his observations are petty, ill-concocted, and discover as little *tact*, as they do a habit of connected reasoning.'[12] Byron's opinion of Gifford was this: 'As Gifford has been ever my "Magnus Apollo", any approbation, such as you mention [from Gifford], would, of course, be more welcome than "all Bokara's vaunted gold, than all the gems of Samarkand".'[13]

Byron was in a better position to judge the abilities of his mentor than Hazlitt. Gifford perceived the strength and originality of Byron's poetry from the beginning and seemed to have no difficulty with the fact that he was a nobleman.

As one of Murray's authors Byron now had the run of the fine front room on the first floor of 50 Albemarle Street where he could consort with some of the most distinguished literary figures of the time such as Walter Scott and look at the latest newspapers and reviews.

In June 1813 he wrote to Murray:

Dear Sir –

I presented a petition to the house yesterday – which gave rise to some debate – & I wish you to favour me for a few minutes with the *Times* and *Herald* to look on their *hostile* report – you will find if you like to look at my *prose* – all my words nearly verbatim in the *Morning Chronicle*.[14]

(To John Murray, 2 June 1813)

Englishmen (and not only the aristocrats and the intelligentsia) were already fixated on their daily newspapers. The general availability of political comment dismayed the government, and in order to stop the spread of Radical ideas and Jacobinism they imposed taxes and stamp duties on newspapers. Those who then found the newspapers too dear promptly resorted to the taverns and coffee houses where they could read them for the price of a mug of ale. Workers' Reform Clubs set up newsrooms where papers were available free. When Byron was in London there were more than ten daily newspapers in the capital, including the *Times*, the *Courier*, the *Sun*, the *Oracle*, the *Morning Post*, the *Morning Herald* and the *Morning Chronicle*. The Government paid subsidies to some of the papers in which it was, accordingly, fulsomely praised. In others it was as enthusiastically blackguarded. Byron must have missed the English papers when he was in Switzerland and Italy.

Samuel Rogers and Thomas Moore were among those who frequented 50 Albemarle Street. Byron had already dined with them at Rogers's house. Moore had taken offence at some mocking lines in *English Bards and Scotch Reviewers* about his abortive duel with Jeffrey of the *Edinburgh Review*, and had sent Byron a challenge before he left England which Francis Hodgson, guessing its purpose, had managed to suppress. On Byron's return Moore wrote again in a more conciliatory tone. Byron replied. Honour on both sides was satisfied and both were invited to dine with Rogers and his friends. Byron was delighted to meet Samuel Rogers whose 'Pleasures of Memory' he admired. Thomas Campbell (another of the writers Byron had praised in his satire) was also present. Hazlitt wrote of the three poets that Campbell '...may be said to hold a place ... between Lord Byron and Mr Rogers... Mr Rogers, as a writer, is too effeminate, Lord Byron is too extravagant: Mr Campbell is neither.'[15]

Byron offered both these poets his admiration and homage. With

Moore, who was nearer his own age (Rogers was 49) there was a different level of understanding and liking. They became intimate almost on the spot, laughing together, teasing each other, confiding, grumbling, arguing. This was a friendship that would last without any diminution until death. It was not surprising that Moore and Hobhouse resented each other. Byron loved Hobhouse perhaps more than his new friend but he had more fun with Thomas Moore. Looking back some years later in Italy he wrote:

> In general I do not draw well with Literary men – not that I dislike them but – I never know what to say to them after I have praised their last publication. – There are several exceptions to be sure – but they have either been men of the world – such as Scott – & Moore, &tc., or visionaries out of it – such as Shelley ... I do not remember a man amongst them – whom I ever wished to see twice.[16]
>
> (*Detached Thoughts*, 1820)

He was enthusiastic about some of the famous men he met at this time:

> Curran! – Curran's the Man who struck me most – such Imagination! – ... I did not see a great deal of Curran – only in 1813 – but I met him at home (for he used to call on me) and in society – at Macintosh's – Holland House &tc. &tc. &tc. And he was wonderful even to me – who had seen many remarkable men of the time.[17]
>
> (*Detached Thoughts*, 1821)

Byron's second speech in the House of Lords was in favour of Catholic Emancipation. On one of his visits to London from Southwell he had listened to the debates in Parliament on this subject in order to inform himself on the wrongs of the Catholics. He later gave to funds for the Irish peasantry and wrote 'The Irish Avator' criticising the Irish in Dublin for the welcome they gave to their 'oppressor', George IV, when he visited Ireland in 1822. He mocks the King in this poem and praises Curran, Sheridan and Grattan:

10

Ever glorious Grattan! the blest of the good!
So simple in heart, so sublime in the rest!
With all which Demosthenes wanted endued,
And his rival, or victor, in all he possess'd.[18]

The speech on Catholic Emancipation was calculated to infuriate most of Byron's fellow-peers:

> It might well be said that the Negroes did not desire to be emancipated; but ... you have already delivered them out of bondage ... I pity the Catholic peasantry for not having had the good fortune to be born black. But the Catholics are contented, or at least ought to be, we are told: I shall therefore proceed to touch on a few of those circumstances which so marvellously contribute to their contentment.[19]

He went on to ask:

> Some persons have compared the Catholics to the beggar in *Gil Blas*: who made them beggars? Who are enriched by the spoils of their ancestors?[20]

He then enlarged on the loss to England of the energies and talents of the Irish people:

> Ireland has done much and will do more. At this moment the only triumph obtained through long years of Continental disaster has been achieved by an Irish general: it is true he is not a Catholic: had he been so, we should have been deprived of his exertions.[21]

His description of the union with England, which had made Lord Castlereagh loathed by his countrymen (including friends of Byron like Thomas Moore, and statesmen he admired like Henry Grattan), was devastating:

> If it must be called a Union it is the union of the shark with his prey; the spoiler swallows up his victim and thus they become indivisible. Thus has Great Britain swallowed up the Parliament, the constitution, the independence of Ireland.[22]

He prophesied the Troubles, expatiating on the consequences of not acceding to the claims of the petitioners:

> You know them, you will feel them, and your children's children when you are passed away.[23]

9

CHILDE HAROLD'S PILGRIMAGE

'*Childe Harold is perhaps the most original work in the English Language*'[1]

Edinburgh Review

'*Humbug like Childe Harold*' (J.G. Lockhart)[2]

When he burst upon the London scene in March 1812 with an electrifying maiden speech in the House of Lords and two Cantos of a poem which was to make him famous overnight little was known of the young Lord Byron except for *English Bards and Scotch Reviewers*. The satire ends with a challenge to the entire literary establishment and those who had read this challenge must have been astonished at the temerity of the young author who had put a new publication before them without even the protection of anonymity:

> Who conquers me shall find a stubborn foe.
> The time hath been, when no harsh sound would fall
> From lips that now may seem imbued with gall;
> Nor fools nor follies tempt me to despise
> The meanest thing that crawled beneath my eyes:
> But now, so callous grown, so changed since youth,
> I've learned to think, and sternly speak the truth;
> Learned to deride the critic's stern decree,
> And break him on the wheel he meant for me;
> To spurn the rod a scribbler bids me kiss,
> Nor care if courts and crowds applaud or hiss:[3]

In the event the success of the two Cantos was such that the young poet was burdened with great fame at the age of twenty-four. The Cantos have been criticised as affected in style and insincere in content. Byron was himself open to criticism on the first count and assured his publisher, John Murray, '... if there are any alterations in the structure of the versification you would wish to be made, I will tag rhymes, & turn Stanzas, as much as you please,'[4] – but he flatly refused to alter anything in order to conciliate the pious or reactionary among John Murray's customers.

This was bold in a young writer who was already nervous about the reception the poem might expect from those who had been satirised in *English Bards and Scotch Reviewers*:

'... you must be aware,' he had written to Charles Dallas, 'that my plaguy Satire will bring the North & South Grubstreets down on the "Pilgrimage", but nevertheless if Murray makes a point of it, & you coincide with him, I will do it daringly, so let it be entitled by "the *Author of* E[ngli]sh *Bards* & S[cot]ch *R[eviewer]s*" ... I much wish to avoid identifying Childe Harold's character with mine, & that in sooth is my second objection to my name on the T[itle] Page ... After all I fear Murray will be in a Scrape with the Orthodox, but I cannot help it, though I wish him well through it.'[5]

(To Robert Charles Dallas, Newstead Abbey, 21 August 1811)

Accordingly, when Murray asked for the changes to conciliate his customers Byron replied:

With regard to the political & metaphysical parts, I am afraid I can alter nothing, but I have high authority for my Errors on that point, for even the *Aeneid* was a *political* poem & written for a *political* purpose, and as to my unlucky opinions on Subjects of more importance, I am too sincere in them for recantation ... As for the '*Orthodox*', let us hope they will buy on purpose to abuse, you will forgive the one if they will do the other.[6]

(To John Murray, Newstead Abbey, Notts., 5 September 1811)

Six months before the Cantos appeared he wrote to Dallas, who was handling negotiations with Murray:

I also feel that I am sincere, and that if I am only to write '*ad capitandum vulgus*,' I might as well edite a magazine at once, or spin canzonettas for Vauxhall ... My work must make its way as well as it can; I know I have every thing against me, angry poets and prejudices; but if the poem is a *poem* it will surmount these obstacles, and if *not*, it deserves its fate.[7]

(To Robert Charles Dallas, Newstead Abbey, 7 September 1811)

Was it a poem? Jeffrey, some years later, referred to the unprecedented effect produced by the Cantos as 'the sudden blazing forth of his genius'. On the whole the reviewers agreed with this verdict and it was enhanced rather than diminished by the succeeding Cantos when they appeared. There were dissentient voices. J.G. Lockhart wrote in 1821 of '...humbug like Childe Harold,' and Hazlitt declared, '...it would be hard to persuade ourselves that the author of *Childe Harold* and *Don Juan* is not a coxcomb, though a provoking and sublime one.'[8]

The reviewers discussed exhaustively the style, the politics, the philosophy and the morals of the author. One reviewer claimed to have found the secret of the power of the verse:

> The principal of *chiaroscuro* will account for much of the strong effect of his pieces. A sombre thought or image is introduced to give high relief to a lovely description: this is often done with too much show of design, – but it is also sometimes done with consummate skill and feeling.[9]
>
> (John Scott, *The London Magazine*, January 1821)

Ever since the day of publication, there has been constant discussion and disagreement about the value and sincerity of the poem. Byron calls on the Greeks to throw off their bondage:

LXXVI

Hereditary Bondsmen! know ye not
Who would be free *themselves* must strike the blow?
By their right arms the conquest must be wrought?
Will Gaul or Muscovite redress ye? No!
True – they may lay your proud despoilers low,
But not for you will Freedom's Altars flame.
Shades of the Helots! triumph o'er your foe!
Greece! change thy lords, thy state is still the same;
Thy glorious day is o'er, but not thine years of shame.[10]

George Finlay, who had many conversations with Byron shortly before his death in Greece, judged that, although he admired military glory in the abstract, he detested the actuality of war. This hatred of war was not something the young man who admired and sought military glory learned as he grew older and wiser. It was there from the start and appears in Canto I of *Childe Harold*, passionate, denunciatory and inconsistent:

Three hosts combine to offer sacrifice;
 Three tongues prefer strange orisons on high;
 Three gaudy standards flout the pale blue skies;
 The shouts are France, Spain, Albion, Victory!
 The Foe, the Victim, and the fond Ally
 That fights for all, but ever fights in vain,
 Are met – as if at home they could not die –
 To feed the crow on Talavera's plain,
And fertilize the field that each pretends to gain.

XLII

There shall they rot – Ambition's honoured fools!
 Yes, Honour decks the turf that wraps their clay!
 Vain Sophistry! in these behold the tools,
 The broken tools, that Tyrants cast away
 By myriads, when they dare to pave their way
With human hearts – to what? – a dream alone.[11]

The anti-war stanzas quoted above (Canto II stanzas 41–43) are preceded by a powerful image of war – the bloody Giant which Jerome Christensen describes as 'Lord Byron's chief essay in sublime war reportage ... By focusing the Peninsular War into a single, mythically charged battle scene, the image of the Giant stretches chivalric motifs toward obscene, Goya-esque caricature.'[12]

XXXVIII

Hark! – heard you not those hoofs of dreadful note?
 Sounds not the clang of conflict on the heath?
 Saw ye not whom the reeking sabre smote;
 Nor saved your brethren ere they sank beneath
 Tyrants and Tyrants' slaves? – the fires of Death,
 The Bale-fires flash on high; – from rock to rock
 Each volley tells that thousands cease to breathe;
 Death rides upon the sulphury Siroc,
Red Battle stamps his foot, and Nations feel the shock.

XXXIX

Lo! where the Giant on the mountain stands,
 His blood-red tresses deepening in the Sun,
 With death-shot glowing in his fiery hands,
 And eye that scorcheth all it glares upon;
 Restless it rolls, now fixed and now anon
 Flashing afar, – and at his iron feet

Destruction cowers, to mark what deeds are done;
For on this morn three potent Nations meet,
To shed before his Shrine the blood he deems most sweet.[13]

Byron had something to say about the fate of freedom in Spain, having first dealt sharply with the perpetrators of the Convention of Cintra:

XXV
Convention is the dwarfish demon styled
That foiled the knights in Marialva's dome:
Of brains (if brains they had) he them beguiled,
And turned a nation's shallow joy to gloom.[14]

It was not surprising that Murray wanted to water all this down, particularly the stanzas where Byron claimed that any class but the nobility would have saved Spain:

LXXXV
Adieu, fair Cadiz! yea, a long adieu!
Who may forget how well thy walls have stood?
When all were changing thou alone wert true,
First to be free and last to be subdued:
And if amidst a scene, a shock so rude,
Some native blood was seen thy street to dye,
A Traitor only fell beneath the feud:
Here all were noble, save Nobility;
None hugged a Conqueror's chain, save fallen Chivalry!

LXXXVI
Such be the sons of Spain, and strange her Fate!
They fight for Freedom who were never free,
A Kingless people for a nerveless state;
Her vassals combat when their Chieftains flee,
True to the veriest slaves of Treachery:
Fond of a land which gave them nought but life,
Pride points the path that leads to Liberty;
Back to the struggle, baffled in the strife,
War, war is still the cry, 'War even to the knife!'[15]

He was not alone in his scepticism on the subject of the Spanish nobility. In 1808 Sydney Smith had written to Lady Holland who was visiting Spain:

99

Why, my dear Lady Holland do you not come home? It is all over, it has been all over this month; except in the Holland family there has not been a man of sense for some weeks who has thought otherwise... If the Spaniards would murder the nobility and clergy there might be some chance. Linendrapers and shoemakers might save Spain, in the hands of Dukes and Bishops it is infallibly gone.[16]

The stanzas castigating Lord Elgin for removing the marbles from the Parthenon must have been deeply embarrassing to Murray. The more closely one reads the Cantos the more must one admire him for having gone ahead with publication:

XV

Cold is the heart, fair Greece! that looks on Thee,
   Nor feels as Lovers o'er the dust they loved;
   Dull is the eye that will not weep to see
   Thy walls defaced, thy mouldering shrines removed
   By British hands, which it had best behoved
   To guard those relics ne'er to be restored: –
   Curst be the hour when from their isle they roved,
   And once again thy hapless bosom gored,
And snatched thy shrinking Gods to Northern climes abhorred![17]

In his notes to *Childe Harold* Byron expresses his outrage at the behaviour of Signor Lusieri, the agent of Lord Elgin, in the removal of the marbles:

While he and his patron confine themselves to tasting medals, appreciating cameos, sketching columns and cheapening gems, their little absurdities are as harmless as insect or fox hunting, maiden speechifying, barouche-driving, or any such pastime: but when they carry away three or four shiploads of the most valuable and massy relics that time and barbarism have left to the most injured and celebrated of cities ... I know of no motive which can excuse ... the perpetrators of this dastardly devastation.[18]

Hobhouse believed that transporting the marbles to London would benefit an infinitely greater number of rising architects and sculptors.[19] Byron's reply to this was: 'I oppose and will ever oppose, the robbery of ruins from Athens, to instruct the English in sculpture (who are as capable of sculpture as the Egyptians are of skating).'[20]

It was not as a political poem that *Childe Harold* found its way into the hands of most of the ladies and many of the men in the

Polite World of the Regency. The passages of description were read aloud and passed from hand to hand.

The farewell song to his native land was a favourite:

I

'ADIEU, adieu! my native shore
   Fades o'er the waters blue;
The night-winds sigh, the breakers roar,
   And shrieks the wild sea-mew.
Yon Sun that sets upon the sea
   We follow in his flight;
Farewell awhile to him and thee,
   My native Land – Good Night![21]

So were the evocations of the Grecian landscape:

LXXXV

And yet how lovely in thine age of woe,
   Land of lost Gods and godlike men, art thou!
   Thy vales of evergreen, thy hills of snow,
   Proclaim thee Nature's varied favourite now:
   Thy fanes, thy temples to thy surface bow,
   Commingling slowly with heroic earth,
   Broke by the share of every rustic plough:
   So perish monuments of mortal birth,
So perish all in turn, save well-recorded *Worth*:

LXXXVI

Save where some solitary column mourns
   Above its prostrate brethren of the cave;
   Save where Tritonia's airy shrine adorns
   Colonna's cliff, and gleams along the wave;
   Save o'er some warrior's half-forgotten grave,
   Where the grey stones and unmolested grass
   Ages, but not Oblivion, feebly brave;
   While strangers, only, not regardless pass,
Lingering like me, perchance, to gaze, and sigh 'Alas!'

LXXXVII

Yet are thy skies as blue, thy crags as wild;
   Sweet are thy groves, and verdant are thy fields,
   Thine olive ripe as when Minerva smiled,
   And still his honied wealth Hymettus yields;
   There the blithe Bee his fragrant fortress builds,

The free-born wanderer of thy mountain-air;
Apollo still thy long, long summer gilds,
Still in his beam Mendeli's marbles glare:
Art, Glory, Freedom fail, but Nature still is fair.[22]

The following description is placed near the monastery at Zitza where Byron and Hobhouse spent the night on their way back from the journey to meet Ali Pasha:

LI
Dusky and huge, enlarging on the sight,
   Nature's volcanic Amphitheatre,
   Chimaera's Alps extend from left to right:
Beneath, a living valley seems to stir;
Flocks play, trees wave, streams flow, the mountain-fir
Nodding above...[23]

Many in safe and civilised Britain were fascinated at the wild scenes the young nobleman had experienced in the land of 'The wild Albanian kirtled to his knee':

XLII
Morn dawns; and with it stern Albania's hills,
Dark Suli's rocks, and Pindus' inland peak,
Robed half in mist, bedew'd with snowy rills,
Arrayed in many a dun and purple streak,
Arise; and, as the clouds among them break,
Disclose the dwelling of the mountaineer:
Here roams the wolf – the eagle whets his beak –
Birds – beasts of prey – and wilder men appear,
And gathering storms around convulse the closing year.[24]

The descriptions of old battles and acts of heroism in 'the bright clime of battle and of song,' were also full of glamour and fierce action and ended in a nostalgic backward look:

LXXXIX
As on the morn to distant Glory dear,
When Marathon became a magic word;
Which uttered, to the hearer's eye appear
The camp, the host, the fight, the Conqueror's career,

102

XC

The flying Mede, his shaftless broken bow –
  The fiery Greek, his red pursuing spear;
  Mountains above – Earth's, Ocean's plain below –
  Death in the front, Destruction in the rear!
  Such was the scene – what now remaineth here?
  What sacred Trophy marks the hallowed ground,
  Recording Freedom's smile and Asia's tear?
  The rifled urn, the violated mound,
The dust thy courser's hoof, rude stranger! spurns around.[25]

In Cantos I and II of *Childe Harold* the young poet had taken a familiar mode and transformed it. The energy and blazing sincerity of his musings were something new in this sort of topographical poetry. So was the imposition on the poem of the strange and original persona of the poet. It is not surprising that it became a *succès fou*. A letter from a Cambridge professor tends to show that Byron's contemporary readers were intensely moved by the passionate grief he expressed in these verses.

Edward Daniel Clarke, a Professor of Mineralogy at Cambridge with whom Byron had compared notes on their travels in Greece, wrote to him on the publication of the Cantos to tell him that he had asked a friend, 'Surely Lord Byron at this time of life, cannot have experienced such keen anguish as these exquisite allusions to what older men *may* have felt, seem to denote.' This was his answer: 'I fear he has – he could not else have written such a poem.'

Professor Clark goes on, '...the eighth stanza [of the second Canto], "Yet if as holiest men," etc., has never been surpassed.'[26]

VII

Well didst thou speak, Athena's wisest son!
  'All that we know is, nothing can be known.'
  Why should we shrink from what we cannot shun?
  Each has its pang, but feeble sufferers groan
  With brain-born dreams of Evil all their own.
  Pursue what Chance or Fate proclaimeth best;
  Peace waits us on the shores of Acheron:
  There no forced banquet claims the sated guest,
But Silence spreads the couch of ever welcome Rest.

Yet if, as holiest men have deemed, there be
  A land of Souls beyond that sable shore,
  To shame the Doctrine of the Sadducee
  And Sophists, madly vain of dubious lore;
  How sweet it were in concert to adore
  With those who made our mortal labours light!
  To hear each voice we feared to hear no more!
  Behold each mighty shade revealed to sight,
The Bactrian, Samian sage, and all who taught the Right.

IX

There, Thou! – whose Love and Life together fled,
  Have left me here to love and live in vain –
  Twined with my heart, and can I deem thee dead,
  When busy Memory flashes on my brain?
  Well – I will dream that we may meet again,
  And woo the vision to my vacant breast:
  If aught of young Remembrance then remain,
  Be as it may Futurity's behest,
For me 'twere bliss enough to know thy spirit blest![27]

Notes

1. M.K. Joseph writes of *Childe Harold*:

One of the themes of the poem – the central theme, as it finally discloses itself – is the traditional one of lament for lost empire and for the decay of love, and of the triumph of time over human mortality, redeemed only by that quasi-immortality which the human spirit achieves when it 'bodies forth' the forms of art and literature. The scenes of *Childe Harold* are used, in various ways, as developing points for this theme. And, in case we think of this as a method more associated with a certain kind of Augustan didactic poem, it is worth recalling that it is also the essential method of poems like 'The Wild Swans at Coole' or the *Four Quartets*.[1]

As we have seen, Michael G. Cooke discovered a Wordsworthian tinge in Byron's poetry as early as *Hours of Idleness* and the following stanza from Canto II seems as Wordsworthian as anything Byron ever wrote:

XXV

To sit on rocks – to muse o'er flood and fell –
  To slowly trace the forest's shady scene,
  Where things that own not Man's dominion dwell,
  And mortal foot hath ne'er or rarely been;

To climb the trackless mountain all unseen,
With the wild flock that never needs a fold;
Alone o'er steeps and foaming falls to lean;
This is not Solitude – 'tis but to hold
Converse with Nature's charms, and view her stores unrolled.[2]

Byron might have been proud of the comparison since he admitted Wordsworth's power 'to do about any thing'. When he met Wordsworth in 1812 he felt for him nothing but reverence: 'I still think his capacity warrants all you say of *it* only – but that his performances since *Lyrical Ballads* – are miserably inadequate to the ability which lurks within him.'[3]

In later years Byron mocked Wordsworth without mercy. Having welcomed the French Revolution with 'Bliss was it in that dawn to be alive!', Wordsworth had, in Byron's view, become a 'lost leader' who approved the suspension of habeas corpus and behaved like a reactionary. Wordsworth returned Byron's distaste with interest: 'Let me only say one word upon Lord Byron. The man is insane; and will probably end his career in a madhouse.'[4]

In the poem 'Churchill's Grave', commemorating a visit on the eve of his exile from England to the churchyard at Dover where the neglected eighteenth century satirist was buried, Byron paid Wordsworth the (somewhat dubious) compliment of an imitation of his poetry in both style and content, including both its felicities and its failings.

In England Byron's poetry has, over the years, been underrated in comparison with that of Wordsworth but Philip Shaw holds that modern critics tend, on the whole, to prefer 'the unerring honesty of Byron to the uncertain equipoise of Wordsworth'.[5] Jerome McGann repudiates the opinion of Ernest J. Lovell Jr. that Byron's poetry is crippled by its inability to offer us 'a consistent attitude towards life', as Wordsworth's does. McGann believes that 'Byron, like his beloved Montaigne, deliberately sought to avoid the kind of ethical consistency that Wordsworth sought. In the end his poetry embraces alienation, scepticism, constant change, as it were by necessity.'[6]

2. Byron felt so strongly about Lord Elgin's removal of the marbles from Athens that in March 1811, when he was living at the Capuchin convent in Athens, he began to write *The Curse of Minerva*, a tirade against Elgin, in the course of which he dubs the Scotland he had loved so well 'a land of meanness, sophistry and mist.'

The Curse of Minerva is a graceless piece berating Elgin for his 'plunder', likening him to Alaric the Goth and, shockingly, wishing a curse upon his seed so that all his sons might be 'as senseless as their sire'. Should one of them prove otherwise, 'Believe him bastard of a brighter race.'

Since no more than eight copies of this production were printed by Murray for private circulation during Byron's lifetime one can hope that he repented this vitriolic attack. There are occasions when fierce resentment results in the display by Byron of deplorable and sometimes cruel antagonism. In this case he was unfair to Elgin who paid for his 'plunder' and was ruined by it. Evidently John Galt remonstrated with Byron for his treatment of Elgin. Byron replied: 'If you will prove to me that Ld. E[lgin]'s "*is* the error of a liberal mind" the "Muse' shall forthwith eat her own words although they choak her – & me into the bargain.'[7] He did suppress *The Curse of Minerva* on meeting Edward Everett, a friend of Elgin's, in June 1815.[8]

10

WHIG LADIES

LVII
...he had that kind of fame
which sometimes plays the deuce with Womankind.[1]

The fame of '*Childe Harold*' opened every door to its author and he stepped into the limelight both a literary and a social lion for, whatever his upbringing might have been, he had the entrée to the Polite World bestowed by high lineage. Even so, it was a precarious position. Captain Gronow describes the vogue of the social lion in Regency London:

> [Alvanley said that] Brummell was the only *Dande*lion that flourished year after year in the hotbed of the fashionable world: he had taken root. Lions were generally annual, but Brummell was perennial, and he quoted a letter from Walter Scott [to the Earl of Dalkeith]: 'If you are celebrated for writing verses, or for slicing cucumbers, for being two feet taller, or two feet less, than any other biped ... your notoriety becomes a talisman, an "open sesame" which gives way to everything, till you are voted a bore, and discarded for a new plaything.'[2]

Byron was probably aware of this from the outset but it did not prevent him from being ravished by the delights of High Society, the charm and courtesy, the dress as exquisite as the manners, the wit and erudition, the political sophistication of both men and women in this milieu.

There is no more entertaining chronicler of the life led by the great ladies of Regency Society than Harriet Cavendish (known to her friends and family as Hary-O) daughter of Georgiana, Duchess

107

of Devonshire and the fifth Duke. Hary-O is lively, witty, well-read and merciless. Born at the very pinnacle of Society she refers constantly to the luxury, elegance and comfort of her surroundings and the brilliance of the intellectual and artistic pursuits in which she revels. She dwells so consistently on her perfect happiness that one senses a faint note of desperation which may derive from the circumstance that her family married her off to Granville Leweson-Gower, later Lord Granville, who had been the lover of her beautiful aunt, Lady Bessborough, for the past seventeen years. Lady Bessborough kept the portrait of her handsome lover in her closet so that she could gaze at 'Those eyes where I have looked my life away.'[3] (Such arrangements were not unusual in Regency and eighteenth century England. Many of the most aristocratic nurseries contained more than one child born to one or other of the parents out of wedlock).

Hary-O wrote praises of her houses and gardens:

My new room ... is so pretty and comfortable and quiet ... It hangs out in the sun like a great green and gold cage. It is as full of *ormolu* and Sèvres china as if it belonged to Lady Jersey and I see all the dandy men and women redouble their regard for me when they find me in a room with four looking glasses and clocks that sing...[4]

You have no idea how comfortable we are. We read German, write verses, play at chess and hazard and sometimes sing for very joy.[5]

Her flower garden is sweeter and more beautiful than 'anything but some of the descriptions in Ariosto or *The Faerie Queene*'.[6]

At four o'clock we all meet. Lady Harrowby drives me in a low coach. Granville, when he is here walks with us and Lord Harrowby and Susan ride.[7]

These idyllic transports are punctuated by sharp comments on other people in the *Haute Monde*:

Princess Esterhazy is coquette, ... ugly and quite foolish, ... sings pretty, odd Tyrolese airs with no voice, ... talks the veriest German nonsense and ... has a lover or two *par ci par là*.[8]

The *Duc de Berri* [one of the emigrés from France] is clever, sings well, but is *difficile à vivre* and tries Lady Stafford by finding fault. Today the eggs at breakfast were abominable – '*Ma foi, Madame, mesdames vos poules ne s'acquittent pas bien.*'[9]

This sort of gossip was amusing and Hary-O and other ladies would throw off a telling comment on a literary figure. Hary-O wrote of Rousseau that he had too much of looking up at the sky, '*larmes dans les yeux*'.[10]

The headquarters of the Whig party was Holland House, Lord Holland's great red-brick Jacobean mansion in Kensington – a short country ride from Mayfair. The Hollands forgave Byron the rude remarks in his satire about Lady Holland's dinners and Lord Holland's hirelings and he became a welcome visitor. 'Dined at Holland House with Whigs and lawyers,'[11] Hary-O once wrote. But at Lady Holland's table you were as likely to find foreign ambassadors, refugee noblemen, Sheridan, Sydney Smith, Lord Grey, the Melbournes and the Bessboroughs. The conversation was lively and everything enjoyable for those guests who did not object to being bullied by Lady Holland. She had been a great beauty in her youth, had divorced her first husband for the young Henry Fox and technically should not have been received in society, but the Hollands were wealthy and powerful enough to escape ostracism. Hary-O described Lady Holland as 'The only undisputed monarchy in Europe, sitting in a corner, throne and footstool, lords and counsellors-in-waiting, countesses and *dames d'honneur*, all *dans les règles*.'[12]

Sydney Smith would tell nervous people setting off for the first time to attend a dinner at Holland House that there was a chemist in Kensington who made up special pills for people who had been frightened by Lady Holland. Lord Holland himself appeared to be in thrall to his strong-minded wife. Hary-O described him one evening at Holland House, '...as merry as a grig though begging in vain for just one glass of Johannisberg.'[13] She ordered her guests about unmercifully, directing one to move from a comfortable to a more distant place, forcing Madame Lieven to pick up the reticule she had dropped on the floor. Byron was never among those bullied or frightened by his hostess. Asked after his death whether Lady Byron had ever loved him Lady Holland retorted that she could not have failed to love him as '...he was so lovable. I can see him now sitting under that lamp looking so beautiful.'[14]

Another great lady who might have been ostracised by society (not for her transgressions but for being found out in them) was Lady Melbourne. She was saved by her close friendship with the Duchess of Devonshire and other great ladies as well as the admiration and protection of the Prince Regent. She was also an assiduous hostess whose dinners were exquisite and attended by all the *ton*. It was well known that her second son, William Lamb, was fathered by Lord Egremont. (The rule was that the heir must not be born out of wedlock. In this case Peniston Lamb, Lord Melbourne's son, died young and William became the heir, a tremendous *faux pas* on the part of a lady who seldom made a false move.) Another son, George, was fathered by the Prince Regent but Lord Melbourne would be hard put to it to resent his wife's infidelity in this case as it was by these means she had helped him to his title.

Lady Melbourne's charm, tact and discretion were such that she was received everywhere. Byron may have been thinking of her (the object of his heartfelt admiration and affection although she was over sixty and he twenty-four when they met) when he wrote these lines years later in *Don Juan*:

LXVI
A little genial sparkling of hypocrisy
Has saved the fame of thousand splendid sinners,
The loveliest oligarchs of our Gynocracy:
You may see such at all the balls and dinners
Among the proudest of our aristocracy
So gentle, charming, charitable, chaste –
And all by having *tact* as well as taste.[15]

Lady Melbourne spent her life planning for the advancement of her family. Both Lady Holland and her sister-in-law, Judith Milbanke, compared her with Madame de Merteuil in *Les Liaisons Dangereuses*. Others declared that everyone liked her and she could be exceedingly kind. She wrote to Lord Melbourne's agent in the country (at Melbourne Hall) instructing him in modern methods of husbandry (for which she was highly praised by Arthur Young) always signing herself 'Your friend, E.M.' and going to the trouble of sending him down the 'Trafalgar Gazette'. She sent her son Frederick at the Embassy in Germany a recipe for 84 mince pies. Frederick reciprocated with a gift of Russian sables for her to wear going to the Opera in the winter.[16] After her death William Lamb, now Lord Melbourne, pointed to her portrait, indicating what a wonderful woman she was, 'But not chaste, not chaste.'[17] He might have added that she was by no means unique in this respect. Lord

110

Egremont wrote that 'There was hardly a woman of fashion who did not think it almost a stain on her reputation if she was not known to have cuckolded her husband.'[18] Byron nursed no illusions about these lovely ladies:

> Went to my box at Covent-garden tonight; and my delicacy felt a little shocked ... It was as if the house had been divided between your public and your *understood* courtesans:- but the Intrigeantes much outnumbered the regular mercenaries ... Now, where lay the difference between [Pauline and her Mama] ... and Lady XXX and daughter? except that the two last may enter Carlton and any *other house*, and the two first are limited to the opera and b——- House.[19]
>
> (*Journal*, 17, 18 December 1813)

He was also aware of the effect of his sudden fame on all those who sought novelty and diversion. His fame had an aphrodisiac effect which caused him some embarrassment. He was pursued by Lady Falkland, who was so astonished at his gift of £500 on her husband's sudden death in a duel that she decided he was in love with her.

LVII
– for he had that kind of fame
Which sometimes plays the deuce with Womankind,
A heterogeneous mass of glorious blame,
Half virtues and whole vices being combined;
Faults which attract because they are not tame;
Follies tricked out so brightly that they blind:[20]

Byron became known to society through his verse but because he was a nobleman he belonged in the grandest circles, as others, however brilliant and famous, never could. Those who did not belong, but were admitted for their talent or some quality which made them unique, were sometimes treated with cruelty and disdain. Hary-O wrote of the actress Miss O'Neill:

> We had a visit from Miss O'Neill, who is odious. She snubbed us all, which is not prepossessing, struts about and throws out sentences in a low tragedy tone, looks short, thick and vulgar, and coolly receives any conversation bearing upon her art.[21]

Hazlitt writes (perhaps a little enviously) of Thomas Moore who, though the son of a Dublin grocer, won his way into every grand drawing room in London by his charm, his verse and the sweet voice in which he sang his own songs. Hazlitt seems yet again to be obsessed with differences in social class:

He [Moore] ought to write with a crystal pen on silver paper ... Mr Moore has a little mistaken the art of poetry for the cosmetic art ... it is not the style of Parnassus...; but it is the style of our English Anacreon and it is (or was) the fashion of the day! ... He has been so long accustomed to the society of Whig Lords, and so enchanted with the smile of beauty and fashion, that he really fancies himself one of the *set* to which he is admitted on sufferance, and tries very unnecessarily to keep others out of it.[22]

Another in high society on sufferance was Henry Brougham. He had lost his seat in Parliament and was contemplating revenge on his friends and colleagues who had not exerted themselves to get him another. Having been great friends with the Hollands he had withdrawn for several years from Holland House and was now allowed back only to find the young poet he had demolished in the *Edinburgh Review* for a complete lack of talent, the centre of attention among his old friends, always surrounded by 'a circle of stargazers'.[23] Although he was accepted everywhere and admired for his extraordinary mind and talents he was aware that he did not belong as Byron belonged, in such circles. Like Thomas Moore – and even Sydney Smith, who was much loved by the Hollands – he had to sing for his supper.

An episode he must have found humiliating is described by Ward, his colleague on the *Edinburgh Review*:

We Edinburgh gents ought not to meddle with field sports. Brougham tried it a few weeks ago at Lord Robert's. But he set fire to the powder horn and burnt off his own eyelashes. He tried to explain it on philosophical principles but the more he did so the more the Duke of Argyle and Lord Ponsonby, who are no philosophers, laughed.

Hary-O is often disparaging – 'Sally Jersey thinks he [Brougham] is sometimes quite beautiful, but with his hair and eyebrows grown so long he looks to me like nothing so much as an orang outang.'[24] Lord Holland regarded him as a brilliant colleague and a friend but Brougham would have been beside himself with injured pride if he had read the rhyme Lord Holland made about him:

> There's a wild man at large doth roam,
> A giant wit, they call him Brougham,
> And well methinks they may.
> He deals whene'er he speaks or acts
> With friends and foes and laws and facts
> In such a sweeping way.

Even his friends did not quite trust Brougham. He eventually got back into Parliament but it was galling to him that Byron had inherited his seat in the Lords without the slightest exertion and then proceeded to speak there on the sort of liberal questions – the treatment of the frame breakers, Catholic Emancipation and Parliamentary Reform – which Brougham would have liked to be seen championing in the Commons himself.

As time went on Byron became more and more disillusioned with the life that he was leading. Captain Gronow, whose battalion was stationed in Portman Street Barracks in 1814, remarked that 'good society' at this period was 'wonderfully select'.[25] Sir Arthur Quiller Couch saw it from a rather different point of view: 'The Mayfair of the Prince Regent's day – a tawdry society of war-profiteers swollen upon the miseries of a bowed and ruined population – a society to my mind even more hateful, because falser, in its smug godliness than in its vices.'[26] This is a description of the sort of hypocrisy at which Byron was to tilt for the rest of his life. He took up the theme of the war-profiteers a few years later in a splendidly fierce tirade in the *Age of Bronze*:

> Alas, the country! how shall tongue or pen
> Bewail her now *un*country gentlemen?
> The last to bid the cry of warfare cease,
> The first to make a malady of peace.
> For what were all these country patriots born?
> To hunt – and vote – and raise the price of corn?
> But corn, like every mortal thing, must fall,
> Kings – Conquerors – and markets most of all.
> And must ye fall with every ear of grain?
> Why would you trouble Buonaparte's reign?
> He was your great Triptolemus; his vices
> Destroyed but realms, and still maintained your prices;
> He amplified to every lord's content
> The grand agrarian alchymy, high *rent*.
> Why did the tyrant stumble on the Tartars,

And lower wheat to such desponding quarters?
Why did you chain him on yon Isle so lone?
The man was worth much more upon his throne.
True, blood and treasure boundlessly were spilt,
But what of that? the Gaul may bear the guilt;
But bread was high, the farmer paid his way,
And acres told upon the appointed day.
But where is now the goodly audit ale?
The purse-proud tenant, never known to fail?
The farm which never yet was left on hand?
The marsh reclaimed to most improving land?
The impatient hope of the expiring lease?
The doubling rental? What an evil's peace!
In vain the prize excites the ploughman's skill,
In vain the Commons pass their patriot bill;
The *Landed Interest* – (you may understand
The phrase much better leaving out the *land*) –
The land self-interest groans from shore to shore,
For fear that plenty should attain the poor.
Up, up again, ye rents, exalt your notes,
Or else the Ministry will lose their votes,
And patriotism, so delicately nice,
Her loaves will lower to the market price;
For ah! 'the loaves and fishes', once so high,
Are gone – their oven closed, their ocean dry,
And nought remains of all the millions spent,
Excepting to grow moderate and content.
They who are not so, *had* their turn – and turn
About still flows from Fortune's equal urn;
Now let their virtue be its own reward,
And share the blessings which themselves prepared.
See these inglorious Cincinnati swarm.
Farmers of war, dictators of the farm;
Their ploughshare was the sword in hireling hands,
Their fields manured by gore of other lands;
Safe in their barns, these Sabine tillers sent
Their brethren out to battle – why? for rent!
Year after year they voted cent. per cent.
Blood, sweat, and tear-wrung millions – why? for rent!
They roared, they dined, they drank, they swore they meant
To die for England – why then live? – for rent!
The peace has made one general malcontent
Of these high-market patriots; war was rent!
Their love of country, millions all mis-spent,
How reconcile? by reconciling rent!

And will they not repay the treasures lent?
No: down with everything, and up with rent!
Their good, ill, health, wealth, joy, or discontent,
Being, end, aim, religion – *rent – rent – rent!*[27]

Byron already saw through the gracious social façade, writing from Bath, 'Bedfords – Jerseys – Ossulstones – Greys & the like ... the women ... hating each other and talking. ... Rogers fell to my share – & we abused everybody ... I never saw anything like it but a print from a scene in Dante's *Inferno*.'[28]

All the same Byron thoroughly enjoyed the adulation of the women and the company of the men. He liked the dandies, and for a time frequented the gaming tables, becoming a member of Watier's where the play was very high:

> I was very fond of it [gambling] when young – that is to say 'Hazard' for I hate all *Card* Games even Faro – When Macco (or whatever they spell it) was introduced I gave up the whole thing – for I loved and missed the *rattle* and *dash* of the box and dice ... I have thrown as many as fourteen mains running – and carried off all the cash upon the table occasionally – but I had no coolness or judgement or calculation ... Upon the whole I left off in time without being much a winner or loser.[29]
>
> (*Detached Thoughts*, 1821–22)

This was as well since Gronow tells of 'Watier's in the days of Brummell and the dandies' when 'Charles Fox, George Selwyn, Lord Carlisle, Fitzpatrick, Horace Walpole, the Duke of Queensbury, and others, lost whole fortunes at faro, macao, and hazard...'[30]

Byron was clearly liked by his male companions and was happy in male company. But surrounded as he was in the ballrooms and drawing rooms by a 'circle of [female] stargazers' it was likely that so beautiful a young man would be pounced upon by one or other of a host of admiring females and borne off as a sacrifice to her vanity.

Lady Caroline Lamb was known in the Polite World as 'Sprite' or 'Ariel' or 'The Fairy Queen'. Her voice was childlike and lisping, and she spoke with the Devonshire House drawl she had acquired from her mother, Lady Bessborough (sister of Georgiana, Duchess of Devonshire), and from the time she spent in the Devonshire House nurseries with her cousins Georgiana (later Lady Carlisle), Hary-O and 'Hart' (Lord Hartington, the heir), who dearly loved his cousin and was grief-stricken when she married William Lamb. Her early letters show that she was a delightful young woman who might well have developed into Byron's 'mutual mind' if she had not lacked a certain balance. Her vanity was inordinate and because she was so funny and charming she was petted into an obsessive need to be the centre of the stage on every occasion. As a young bride she wrote affectionate letters to Lord Hartington, which are evidence of the charm which had enchanted him over the years as they grew up together.

Caroline's letters are delightful. She scolds her cousin, Hartington (later the sixth Duke of Devonshire) light-heartedly, teases him unmercifully, tells him he is provoking and demands that he should write to her without delay. Her letters are full of rhymes, drawings, threats, promises and the occasional 'God bless you!'. Her warm, loving, lively, inconsequential letters to her mother, Lady Bessborough, are very different from the pert, critical and prosy letters of Byron's future bride, Annabella Milbanke, to her mother, Lady Milbanke.

Ominously, however, Lady Bessborough and her mother, Lady Spencer, confided to each other their anxiety about Caroline's ill-health, strange manners and 'sauvagerie' before her marriage, and her headstrong behaviour as a young married woman. Lady Spencer's conclusion was that Caroline would bring great misery upon herself and her family, not from wickedness, but from inordinate vanity.

The marriage with William Lamb was not a brilliant match for Caroline. Until the death of his brother made him heir William would not have dared to offer for her, though he was eventually to become Viscount Melbourne and Queen Victoria's first Prime Minister. However, William was able to calm her down and for some years they were extremely happy together. She bore him a son, Augustus. This boy, her only child, was an epileptic and his development was later found to be retarded.

No husband could have satisfied Caroline's emotional demands and by the time she met Byron they were leading separate lives, he involved with politics and she inventing dramas with the role of heroine reserved for herself. The most uncomfortable of these for her husband was the flirtation she engineered with Sir Godfrey Webster, Lady Holland's son by her first marriage, a man of dubious reputation but handsome appearance. Caroline made sure that she was seen everywhere with Sir Godfrey and seemed to be intimating to society that she was involved in a passionate affair. William remained calm. He was confident that Caro would never run away with Sir Godfrey and patiently waited until, after a few months, she came to her senses.

In March 1812 Caroline read *Childe Harold's Pilgrimage* and told Samuel Rogers she was determined to meet the new poet. David Cecil, in his illuminating account of the background to all these amours and scandals, points out that Caroline was everything Byron least liked in women:

> ...stormy, clever and unfashionably thin... But he had not the strength to withstand her; and he never could refuse the chance of a conquest. Moreover, young as he was, and dazzled by the new and glittering world into which his fame had so suddenly flung him, the prospect of an amour with one of its reigning queens flattered him in a way he was unable to resist.[31]

Byron has been portrayed as the heartless seducer of Lady Caroline. This was not the case. M.K. Joseph rightly pointed out that 'One thing is common to the experience of both Don Juan and his creator – that for both of them it is woman who is the predator, not the prey.'[32] In Italy, years later, Byron wrote to Richard Hoppner, 'I should like to know *who* has been carried off – except poor dear *me* – I have been more ravished myself than anybody since the Trojan war.'[33]

Early in 1812 Byron wrote lines to Caroline Lamb describing a frame of mind which is either a posture of some sort or which lasted so short a time that they were contradicted within a few months. Byron felt an urgent desire to name the loved one in his amorous verse (indirectly via the cornelian the boy had given him, in the case of Edleston). Yet even at the outset he declares in the poem that he wants to resist her spell. All the same, he tells her that the chain she has cast on him will last forever.

It was a potent spell. Her background was impressive to a young man who had been brought up in far less sophisticated circles than Melbourne House and Devonshire House. At first Byron found her irresistible but as early as April he was telling her, 'I never knew a woman with greater or more pleasing talents, *general* as in a woman they should be, something of everything & too much of nothing, but these are unfortunately coupled with a total want of common conduct.'[34] Here Byron discloses his sense of decorum, which was as strong as his contrary need to publicise his own transgressions.

Byron wrote to Caroline before the end of April offering to leave London:

M[oore] is in great distress about us, & indeed people talk as if there were no other pair of absurdities in London. – It is hard to bear all this without cause, but worse to give cause for it. – Our folly has had the effect of a fault. – I conformed & could conform, if you would lend your aid, but I can't bear to see you look unhappy, & am always on the watch to observe if you are trying to make me so. – We must make an effort, this dream this delirium of two months must pass away, we in fact do not know one another, a month's absence would make us rational, you do not think so, I know it, we have both had 1000 previous fancies of the same kind, & shall get the better of this & be as ashamed of it according to the maxim of Rochefoucalt. – But it is better that I should leave town than you, & I will make a tour, or go to Cambridge or Edinburgh. – Now don't abuse me, or think me altered, it is because I am not, cannot alter, that I shall do this, and cease to make fools talk, friends grieve, and the wise, pity. – Ever most affectionately & sincerely yours.[35]

Byron liked the risk-taking that Caro offered, as he later half revelled in and half shuddered at the risk of his affair with his half-sister. But Caroline was incapable of carrying on her affair with Byron with the discretion that would have prevented it from becoming an open scandal and Byron was forced either to run away with her or to end their liaison. His friends became alarmed at the growing scandal caused by the folly of her behaviour. Byron himself was shocked and embarrassed when she invaded his lodgings dressed in page's clothing. When she ran away from Melbourne House it was Byron who searched for her, found her and restored her to her embarrassed family, thus displaying the contradictory elements in his character.

Lady Bessborough and William Lamb succeeded in whisking Caroline off to Ireland. Caroline wrote frenzied letters to Byron boasting of her conquests there. He wrote to Lady Melbourne who had become his adviser and confidante, 'I cannot write, I would not seem jealous, and it would be ... improper to appear indifferent.'[36] He admitted generously, '... she never did nor can deserve a single reproach which must not fall with double justice & truth upon myself.'[37]

Byron felt that if Caroline ran away from her husband for his sake he was in honour bound to marry her. '[If after all] I *must* be hers, she shall be *mine* as long as it pleases her ... wretched as it would render me, she should never know it.'[38] This is what he *says* and doubtless he *felt* it in the act of writing it. There is no evidence that he was insincere. But whether he felt it in some stronger sense is hard to determine. This ambiguity is what makes the task of the biographer, who is anxious to explain, pin down and fit into some explanation or theory, all the more difficult.

He was relieved to find that Caroline had no firm intention of leaving her husband. He told Lady Melbourne, ... 'I am much more unwilling to hurt her feelings now than ever, ... [She] has a claim on *me* ... for every respect that she may not feel her own degradation.'[39] But he longed to be free of her – '...if I can *honourably* be off?'[40] Lady Melbourne thought he could. Since Caroline's pursuit of him showed no sign of flagging, Byron determined to escape either by going abroad or by getting married. In March 1812 he had noticed among the young women gathered at Melbourne House for lessons in the new art of waltzing, Annabella Milbanke, a demure and modest-looking girl from the north of England who happened to be a niece of Lady Melbourne. He asked her to sound out his chances with Annabella and later told Medwin that 'there was a simplicity, a retired modesty about her which ... formed a happy contrast to the cold artificial formality and studied stiffness, which is called fashion. She interested me exceedingly.'[41]

Annabella rejected him and this rejection coincided with an invitation to Eywood, the country house of Lord and Lady Oxford in Herefordshire. Lady Melbourne had scolded Caroline when she took to foregathering with ladies of somewhat tarnished reputation, among whom was Lady Oxford. Some of Lady Oxford's tribe of beautiful children were said to be the progeny of various fathers other than Lord Oxford and, the Oxford family name being Harley, they were known by society as 'The Harleian Miscellany.' One of Lady Oxford's lovers was the famous Radical, Sir Francis Burdett. Under his influence Lady Oxford had become a Radical herself and it was at the Hampden Club that she first met Byron who respected Sir Francis so highly as a fair and honourable man that he appointed him some years after he had left London, to be arbiter over the division of the Wentworth inheritance on Lady Noel's death.

119

Lord Oxford was a conniving husband and Lady Oxford a safe refuge from Caroline. For several months Byron spent much of his time at Eywood or at Kinsham Court, a house he took to be near his 'Armida' without causing 'il sposo' to have 'the crotchets'.

When Caroline returned to London she desperately tried to revive Byron's interest in her, following him, demanding locks of his hair, threatening to stab herself, forging his signature in order to make off with his portrait and forcing her way into his apartments in Albany at all hours. Once when she had entered his rooms in his absence she wrote on the fly leaf of one of his books, 'Remember Me'. Underneath this cry of anguish Byron, driven to fury, wrote the lines:

1.

Remember thee! remember thee!
 Till Lethe quench life's burning stream,
Remorse and Shame shall cling to thee,
 And haunt thee like a feverish dream!

2

Remember thee! Ay, doubt it not.
 Thy husband too shall think of thee:
By neither shalt thou be forgot,
 Thou *false* to him, thou *fiend* to me![42]

Byron and Lady Melbourne had become allies and fast friends, and to her he confided the irritation which had culminated in the writing of *Remember Thee!*: 'Good God – am I to be hunted from place to place like a Russian *bear* or *Emperor*?'[43] Byron was genuinely distressed at being 'stalked' by Lady Caroline Lamb and he certainly felt the desperation displayed in the poem but he was doubtless also delighted to be given the impetus to inhabit so dramatic an attitude. One must remember that in all his experiences of love he was always as much poet as lover – not more so but as much.

Byron wrote a poem addressed not to Lady Oxford but to her eleven-year-old daughter, Lady Charlotte Harley, which was published with the seventh edition of *Childe Harold's Pilgrimage*. It is a very innocent affair which can have caused the child's mother no concern, but it was quoted in Benita Eisler's biography as evidence that Byron was caught by Lady Oxford trying to rape her daughter.

Eisler carefully omits the lines which militate against her theory – lines 3, 4, 5, 12 and 13. Lady Oxford was a particularly devoted mother who would have thrown Byron out of the house if this accusation had been true.

FROM TO IANTHE

Ah! may'st thou ever be what now thou art,
    Nor unbeseem the promise of thy Spring –
    As fair in form, as warm yet pure in heart,
    Love's image upon earth without his wing,
    And guileless beyond Hope's imagining!
    And surely she who now so fondly rears
    Thy youth, in thee, thus hourly brightening,
    Beholds the Rainbow of her future years,
    Before whose heavenly hues all Sorrow disappears.

Young Peri of the West! – 'tis well for me
    My years already doubly number thine;
    My loveless eye unmoved may gaze on thee,
    And safely view thy ripening beauties shine;
    Happy, I ne'er shall see them in decline;
    Happier, that, while all younger hearts shall bleed,
    Mine shall escape the doom thine eyes assign
    To those whose admiration shall succeed,
    But mixed with pangs to Love's even loveliest hours decreed.

Oh! let that eye, which, wild as the Gazelle's,
    Now brightly bold or beautifully shy,
    Wins as it wanders, dazzles where it dwells,
    Glance o'er this page; nor to my verse deny
    That smile –[44]

Byron wrote to Lady Melbourne of his admiration for the little girl whom –

... I should love forever if she could always be only eleven years old – & whom I shall probably marry when she is old enough & bad enough to be made into a modern wife. – We have had as yet very few fine days & these I have passed on the water & in the woods – scrambling and splashing about with the children – or by myself – I always feel happier here or at Newstead than elsewhere – & all my plagues are at least 150 miles off...[45]

(Byron to Lady Melbourne, 5 April 1813)

121

In London he could not escape the worst of his plagues and the Caro Lamb affair remained a scandal of epic proportions.

'*Manage her!*' he protested to Lady Melbourne, '... it is impossible – & as to friendship – no – it must be broken off at once, & all I have left is to take some step which will make her hate me...'[46]

The step he took was the cruel letter – a version of which Caroline made public later in her *roman à clef, Glenarvon*. The letter concluded: '... correct your vanity, which is ridiculous, exert your absurd caprices upon others; and leave me in peace.'[47]

It is inexcusable and so is the unpleasant trick he played on Caroline with the connivance of Lady Oxford. When she asked for a lock of Byron's hair they sent one of Lady Oxford's, which was the same colour. Thus Byron allowed resentment to blot out his better nature.

There is in existence, though she never knew it, a poem written in October 1812 which shows that after their parting and when he was already in the toils of his Enchantress, Lady Oxford, Byron could still refer in romantic terms to his liaison with Caroline. It was addressed to her sister-in-law, Mrs George Lamb. This young woman was also a 'Caroline' – Caroline St Jules, daughter of the fifth Duke of Devonshire and Lady Elizabeth Foster, who had been brought up with the Cavendish children at Devonshire House. Because both Lamb brothers lived in separate apartments in Melbourne House the two Carolines were known, to avoid confusion, as Caro William and Caro George.

For a moment Byron seems to have forgotten the pain and aggravation and he looks back fondly on the love he had felt for Caro William. Byron loved to hear a woman sing and Caro George's singing moved him to write:

TO THE HON^{BLE} M^{RS} GEORGE LAMB

1.
The sacred song that on mine ear
  Yet vibrates from that voice of thine,
I heard, before, from one so dear –
  'T is strange it still appears divine.

2.
But, oh! so sweet that *look* and *tone*
  To her and thee alike is given;
It seemed as if for me alone
  That *both* had been recalled from Heaven!

3.
And though I never can redeem
The vision they endeared to me;
I scarcely can regret my dream,
When realised again by thee.[48]

This was not published during Byron's lifetime. If Caro William had seen it she might have been comforted to know that Byron clung to so romantic a memory of her via song. On the other hand it might have tempted her to scratch Caro George's eyes out. In any case Byron could not let her see it, knowing that even so romantic and dream-like an expression of nostalgia would only serve to set her off again. Her subsequent behaviour proved that he was right not to publish.

After a period during which Byron sat at the feet of his Armida, listening to music, talking about books, being lectured about 'his senatorial duties', Lord Oxford began to cut up rough and seems to have threatened to throw his wife out of the house. Although she was well over forty and he in his mid twenties Byron immediately offered her a '*carte blanche*' whereupon, to Byron's intense relief, Lord Oxford '. . . ate his own words & intentions and now they are to live happy ever after.'[49] Lord Oxford had for some time been contemplating a sea voyage. The love affair ended with great regret on both sides when Lady Oxford went reluctantly abroad with her husband and Byron stayed reluctantly at home.

11

LOVE AND FRIENDSHIP

'By Mahomet! I begin to think I like everybody ... a sort of social gluttony'[1]

After the departure of Lady Oxford, Byron missed the company of his Enchantress but there were plenty of diversions in London to help him forget the months he had passed with her at Eywood like 'the gods in *Lucretius*'.[2] One of the social lions of that summer was Madame de Staël who had left her château at Coppet in Switzerland to enjoy the adulation of those English who, like Byron, admired her latest book, *De l'Allemagne*, which was published by John Murray since Napoleon had had the Paris edition destroyed. She was greatly respected for her courageous opposition to Napoleon's tyranny which had led to her exile from Paris where she had her literary salon and, as the daughter of Necker (late Director General of Finance to Louis XV and XVI) and possessor of a great fortune, she had been a prominent figure.

Byron found her overpowering, '...a very plain woman forcing one to listen & look at her with her pen behind her ear and her mouth full of *ink*.'[3] When they met at Lady Jersey's she congratulated him on the perfect English constitution and listened in amazement to his reply that the English constitution was mired in corruption and that the King and Pitt between them had destroyed the liberties of the English. 'And you count for nothing the liberty to say all that? And in front of the servants too!'[4]

He left her notes unanswered. 'I admire her abilities, but really her society is overwhelming – an avalanche that buries one in glittering nonsense – all snow and sophistry.'[5] Two notes from Madame de Staël to Byron speak for themselves:

Dinez chez moi dimanche avec vos amis – je ne dirai pas vos admirateurs car je n'ai rencontré que cela de touts parts.

A dimanche
De Staël

A few days later she wrote, no doubt in some exasperation:

Je prends le silence pour oui.[6]

Some years later Madame de Staël was to heap coals of fire on his head by treating him with great kindness when he visited her at Coppet, by then an exile himself. He showed his sympathy for her by remarking that though Madame de Staël thought like a man, unfortunately for her, she *felt* like a woman. Her comment a few years later from Switzerland on the 'Farewell Verses' to his wife shows that he had understood her very well – she wrote of these lines that if they had been addressed to her she would have flung herself into Byron's arms: '*Je n'aurais pu m'y tenir un instant!*'[7]

Lady Melbourne, 'the best friend I ever had in my life, and the cleverest of women',[8] remained his confidante and mentor. He found himself obliged to decline her invitations to dinner at Melbourne House: 'I am rather hungry, having lived on tea & bread and butter ever since I left E[ywood] (where I was under the necessity of conforming to a less Eremetical regimen) & should do justice to your viands – Yet I must resist all these.'[9] A few days later he was unable to accept her invitation since 'I have unfortunately dined for the week yesterday.'[10]

Byron has been diagnosed as anorexic and, though such a diagnosis at long distance in time suffers from the disadvantage that the patient is not present for examination, the argument is persuasive. In his diary for 17 November 1813 he wrote:

> I wish to God I had not dined now! – It kills me with heaviness, stupor, and horrible dreams; – and yet it was but a pint of bucellas, and fish. Meat I never touch, – nor much vegetable diet. I wish I were in the country, to take exercise, – instead of being obliged to *cool* by abstinence, in lieu of it. I should not so much mind a little accession of flesh – my bones can well bear it. But the worst is, the devil always came with it, – till I starve him out – and I will *not* be the slave of *any* appetite ... I wonder how Buonaparte's dinner agrees with him.[11]

(*Journal*, 17 November 1813)

Nothing could have pleased him more than the arrival in London of Augusta Leigh coinciding with the departure of Lady Oxford. He invited her to come with him to a reception given by Lady Davy (wife of Sir Humphrey Davy, the great chemist) where she would see Madame de Staël – 'some people whom you know – & *me* whom you do *not* know – and you can talk to which you please – and I will watch over you as if you were unmarried ... Now do as you like – but if you chuse to array yourself before or after half past ten I will call for you.'[12] (Byron to Augusta Leigh, 27 June 1813)

He asked Lady Melbourne for vouchers so he could take Augusta to a masque at Almack's. Later he told her, 'I should have been glad of your advice how to untie two or three *"Gordian* knots" tied round me – I shall cut them ... though some are closely twisted round my *heart*.' ... (He is hinting at his having fallen in love with his half-sister.) 'Perhaps I shall not see you again – if not – forgive my follies & like as much of me as you can.'[13] (Byron to Lady Melbourne, 11 August 1813)

Byron found Augusta utterly beguiling because she looked and behaved like a Byron. She was as shy with strangers as he. He was impressed with the background in which she had been brought up and she was proud of her younger brother's fame and genius. For three weeks they were constantly together and on her return home he went down to Six Mile Bottom, near Newmarket, to visit her. He had been trying to arrange to go abroad again and told Lady Melbourne that his sister was planning to go with him. Byron felt completely at ease with Augusta and told his wife later, 'I only want a woman to laugh... I can make Augusta laugh at anything.'[14] He called her 'Gus' and this soon became 'Goose'. George Leigh neglected Augusta and left her to bear all the burdens of their establishment. Byron understood the inconveniences and humiliations of poverty only too well, and could be unfailingly sympathetic, helpful and generous to her. With Augusta and her children at Six Mile Bottom he found he could enjoy the affectionate domestic life his mother had been unable to provide for him. They could laugh uproariously together and comfort each other in their misfortunes.

Byron was now deeply in love with his half-sister. Her greatest charm for him was her love and affection. She made him no scenes, looked after his comfort and welfare, gave him good advice, continued to love and pity him when he did not take it, laughed him out of his moods and melancholy and made allowances for his failings.

Soon after Augusta's arrival in London Caro Lamb's hysterical behaviour caused the scandal which finally ruined her reputation. Byron wrote to Lady Melbourne the day after Lady Heathcote's ball:

> ... I have heard a strange story of C's scratching herself with glass – and I know not what besides... What I said or did to provoke her – I know not ... She took hold of my hand as I passed & pressed it against some sharp instrument – and said – 'I mean to use this...' had I guessed her to be serious or had I been conscious of offending I should have done everything to pacify or prevent her.[15]

Gossip spread that Caro Lamb had stabbed herself at Lady Heathcote's ball for love of Byron. This incident caused Lady Westmoreland and Lady Ossulstone, who were present, to conclude that Byron must have done something to offend Caroline. They scolded him and gave him 'angry looks' which were repeated by many other of Caroline's train of 'compassionate countesses' when word of the scandal got out. Sydney Smith's comment was 'And then, of course, he is a poet! What a charming thing to be a poet! I preached for many years in London and was rather popular but I never heard of any Lady who did herself the smallest injury on my account.'[16]

Byron was feeling aggrieved. He wrote a few days later to Thomas Moore, 'The Staël last night attacked me most furiously – said that I had "no right to make love – that I had used [Caroline] barbarously – that I had no feeling, and was totally *in*sensible to *la belle passion*, and *had* been all my life." I am very glad to hear it but I did not know it before.'[17]

He was then extremely irritated by a rumour that the purchaser Hanson had found for Newstead, a Mr Claughton, was a young man who had been over-reached and ruined over the transaction. The true story was that Claughton was a lawyer, forty five years old, who had bought the estate at his own offer price – '...he evaded and at last drove me into Chancery...'[18]

Annabella Milbanke now decided that she had made a mistake in rejecting Byron so decidedly and wrote from Seaham offering him her friendship, stipulating that their correspondence must remain a secret 'except for Mamma and Papa'. Annabella knew that it was unusual for a young unmarried woman to solicit letters from a single man – in this case one who had been the lover of her cousin-by-marriage, Caroline Lamb, and caused thereby a resounding scandal. She tried to reassure Byron by inventing a previous but hopeless attachment. This lie had a second advantage in that it would, she hoped, obviate any suspicion that she was trying to ensnare him. Byron believed in the hopeless love for another man but he was otherwise undeceived. 'Friendship,' Thomas Medwin reported him as saying, 'is a dangerous word for young ladies. It is Love full-fledged and waiting for a fine day to fly.'[19]

Annabella wrote to him regularly and by the following spring was hinting at a visit to Seaham. The formal invitation from Sir Ralph would follow at a time when he felt little inclination to accept it, much to Annabella's disappointment. She was puzzled as to how to admit that the previous attachment was a fiction without coming down off what Lady Melbourne called 'her stilts' and admitting to a lie. Byron was not as deeply concerned with Annabella as she would have liked. He had confessed his love for his half-sister to Lady Melbourne who told him he would ruin Augusta. Augusta too was having second thoughts and when he went down to Newmarket and found her immovable he cut short his visit. After this there was no more talk of going abroad together; Lady Melbourne persuaded Byron to pay a visit to his friend, Wedderburn Webster, who had a pretty young wife. Lady Frances was to be the saving of Byron by allowing herself to be seduced by him. Lady Melbourne can be forgiven much for her amiable character but this seems an unforgivable act of cynicism. However, it is entirely possible that the shrewd and subtle older woman had heard rumours of Lady Frances, or perhaps had drawn inferences from her own experience of the young woman, which caused her to rate the girl fair game. Byron, however, was incapable of carrying on the game without falling in love. 'I cannot exist without some object of love.'[20] This was to become, in at least some sense, one of the 'series of passionate attachments' described by Thomas Moore. But it was to be short-lived. He wrote to Lady Melbourne to keep her *au fait* with his progress.

He was regularly receiving letters from Annabella and had replied to her questions about his attitude to religion.

I believe doubtless in God – & should be happy to be convinced of much more – [Annabella was clearly longing to be allowed to convince him] – if I do not at present place implicit faith on tradition & revelation of any human creed I hope it is not from a want of reverence for the Creator but the created ... the *moral* of Christianity is perfectly beautiful – & the very sublime of Virtue – yet even there we find some of its finer precepts in earlier axioms of the Greeks. – particularly 'do unto others as you would they should do unto you'. – the forgiveness of injuries – & more which I do not remember – Good Night.[21]

(To Annabella Milbanke, 26 September 1813)

He was puzzled by Annabella's behaviour and confided to Lady Melbourne:

The epistles of your mathematician ... continue – & the last concludes with a repetition of a desire that none but Papa & Mamma should know it ... but – observe – here is the strictest of St Ursula's 11000 what do you call 'ems? – a wit – a moralist – & religionist – enters into a clandestine correspondence with a personage generally presumed a great Roué – & drags her aged parents into this secret treaty – it is I believe not usual for single ladies to risk such brilliant adventures – but this come of *infallibility* – not that she ever says anything that might not be said by the Town cryer – still it is imprudent – if I were rascal enough to take an unfair advantage. – Alas! poor human nature!...[22]

(Byron to Lady Melbourne, 28 September 1813)

He was to find Lady Frances's behaviour even more puzzling. He wrote from Aston Hall to his confidante:

I am not exactly cut out for the Lady of the mansion – but I think a stray Dandy would have a chance of preferment – she evidently expects to be attacked – & seems prepared for a brilliant defence – my character as a Roué had gone before me – and my careless and quiet behaviour astonished her so much that I believe she began to think herself ugly – or me blind – if not worse.[23]

(Byron to Lady Melbourne, September–1 October 1813)

During a game of billiards Frances asked him '... an odd question – "how a woman who liked a man could inform him of it when he did not peceive it."' He wrote her a note which '... produced an *answer* – a very unequivocal one too – but a little too much about virtue – and indulgence of attachment in some sort of ethereal process in which the soul is principally concerned ... one generally

130

ends and *begins* with Platonism – & as my proselyte is only twenty – there is time enough to materialize...[24]. Byron wrote indignantly of the husband:

> ...if a man is not contented with a pretty woman & not only runs after any little country girl he meets with but absolutely boasts of it – he must not be surprised if others admire that which he knows not how to value...[25]
>
> (Byron to Lady Melbourne, 8 October 1813)

And again:

> She ... managed to give me a note – & to receive another and a ring before [Webster's] very face – and yet she is a thorough devotee – & takes prayers morning and evening – besides being measured for a new bible once a quarter.[26]
>
> (Byron to Lady Melbourne, Newstead Abbey, 10 October 1813)

Now Byron produced one of his extraordinary acts of utterly quixotic generosity. To save Webster from having to apply to the usurers he, though already in the hands of the usurers himself, instructed Hanson to advance a loan of £1000 to James Wedderburn Webster Esquire of Aston Hall, York County.

Matters with Lady Frances became more serious. 'You who know me and my weakness so well – will not be surprised when I say that I am totally absorbed in this passion – that I am even ready to take a *flight* if necessary.'[27] (To Lady Melbourne, 13 October 1813)

He was no longer writing to Augusta. Lady Melbourne's plan seemed to be working. Now came the crisis:

> ... it came to this – 'I am entirely at your *mercy* – I own it – I give myself up to you – I am not *cold* – whatever I seem to others – but I know that I cannot bear the reflection hereafter ... I tell you the truth – now act as you will.' – was I wrong? – I spared her ... There was a something so very peculiar in her manner – a kind of mild decision – no scene – not even a struggle – but still I know not what convinced me she was serious – it was not the mere 'No' which one has heard forty times before ... I love her – if I did not and much too – I should have been more *selfish* ... I have offered to go away with her – & her answer whether sincere or not is 'that on *my account* she declines it' ... she is either the most *artful* or *artless* of her age (20) I ever encountered ... she is so thin and pale ... if she were

131

once my wife ... a warm climate should be the first resort ... for her recovery. – The most perplexing – & yet I can't prevail upon myself to give it up – is the *caressing* system – in her it appears perfectly childish – and I do think innocent – but it really puzzles all the Scipio about me to confine myself to the laudable portion of these endearments...[28]

(Byron to Lady Melbourne, Newstead Abbey, 17 October 1813)

Later he wrote, 'I do detest everything which is not perfectly mutual ... Perhaps after all – I was her dupe – if so – I am the dupe also of the few good feelings I could ever boast of.'[29] (Byron to Lady Melbourne, 21 October 1813)

He assured Lady Melbourne, '... you really *wrong* me too – if you do not suppose that I would sacrifice everything for *Ph* [Frances] – I hate sentiment – and in consequence my epistolary levity makes you believe me as hollow & heartless as my letters are light – Indeed it is not so.'[30] (Byron to Lady Melbourne, Monday – [25 October 1813?])

In 1815 Byron wrote a poem inspired by the scandal arising from the very public love affair Lady Frances was reported to be conducting in Paris with the Duke of Wellington:

1.
WHEN we two parted
    In silence and tears,
Half broken-hearted
    To sever for years,
Pale grew thy cheek and cold,
    Colder thy kiss;
Truly that hour foretold
    Sorrow to this.

2.
The dew of the morning
    Sunk chill on my brow –
It felt like the warning
    Of what I feel now.
Thy vows are all broken,
    And light is thy fame:
I hear thy name spoken,
    And share in its shame.

3.

They name thee before me,
    A knell to mine ear;
A shudder comes o'er me –
    Why wert thou so dear?
They know not I knew thee,
    Who knew thee too well:–
Long, long shall I rue thee,
    Too deeply to tell.

4.

In secret we met –
    In silence I grieve,
That thy heart could forget,
    Thy spirit deceive.
If I should meet thee
    After long years,
How should I greet thee? –
    With silence and tears.[31]

It has been claimed that Byron felt revengeful because Lady Frances had rejected his love. He admitted to Lady Melbourne that he was unhappy at thinking of the 'not'. But Lady Frances did not reject Byron. She admitted that she was ashamed at having confessed to him that she adored him and, having offered herself to him with various face-saving provisos, she, later, thanked him for having 'spared her'.

Thomas Moore met Lady Frances in 1819. His account of the meeting is interesting:

She was (or fancied herself) very much in love with him [Byron] ... I should pronounce her cold-blooded and vain to an excess – and I believe her great aim is to attract people of celebrity – if so, she must have been gratified – as the first Poet [Byron] and first Captain [Wellington] of the age have been her lovers – the latter liaison was at all events not altogether spiritual – her manner to me very flattering and the eyes played off most skilfully.[32]

Lady Melbourne tried hard to persuade Byron that the young woman she described as 'This poor little ignorant girl', was truthful, and sincerely in love with him. But she could not resist admitting that Lady Frances was sometimes childish and tiresome. One cannot help suspecting that Lady Melbourne is less than sincere in the opinion she gives of the girl she hopes will charm Byron away from Augusta.

Though Byron claimed to have no very high opinion of women he delighted in the company of Lady Melbourne, Augusta, and, at first, until she threw over the traces, that of Caroline Lamb. All were intelligent women though Augusta found it amusing to appear more scatterbrained than she really was. She had what is called 'emotional intelligence' in high degree. He describes his susceptibility to women of all sorts and classes:

There is something to me very softening in the presence of a woman, – some strange influence, even if one is not in love with them, – which I cannot at all account for, having no very high opinion of the sex. But yet, – I always feel in better humour with myself and everything else, if there is a woman within ken. Even Mrs Mule, my firelighter, – the most ancient and withered of her kind, – and (except to myself) not the best-tempered – always makes me laugh, –[33]

(*Journal*, 27 February 1814)

Moore writes of Byron's kindness to old Mrs Mule:

This ancient housemaid, of whose gaunt and witch-like appearance it would be impossible to convey any idea but by the pencil, furnished one among the numerous instances of Lord Byron's proneness to attach himself to any thing however homely, that had once enlisted his good nature in its behalf, and become associated with his thoughts. He first found this old woman at his lodgings in Bennet Street, where, for a whole season, she was the perpetual scarecrow of his visitors. When, next year, he took chambers in Albany, one of the greatest advantages which his friends looked to in the change was that they should get rid of this phantom. But no, – there she was again – he had actually brought her with him from Bennet Street. The Following year saw him married and with a regular establishment of servants in Piccadilly; and here, – as Mrs Mule had not made her appearance to any of the visitors, – it was concluded, rashly, that the witch had vanished. One of these friends, however, who had most fondly indulged himself in this persuasion, happening to call one day when all the male part of the establishment were abroad, saw, to his dismay, the door opened by the same gaunt grim personage, improved considerably in point of habiliments since I last saw her, and keeping pace with the increased scale of her master's household, as a new peruke, and other symptoms of promotion testified. When asked how he came to carry this old woman about with him from place to place Lord Byron's only answer was, 'The poor old devil was so kind to me'.[34]

He was equally kind to old Joe Murray:

Old Murray, the servant he mentions ... as the only faithful follower remaining to him, had long been in the service of the former Lord and was regarded by the young poet with a fondness of affection which it has seldom been the lot of age and dependence to inspire. 'I have more than once,' says a gentleman who was at this time a constant visitor at Newstead, 'seen Lord Byron at the dinner table fill out a tumbler of madeira and hand it over his shoulder to Joe Murray, who stood behind his chair, saying, with a cordiality that brightened his whole countenance, "Here, my old Fellow".'[35]

Byron told Annabella Milbanke that she was wrong to believe in his *general despondency*. '[I] may safely appeal to most of my acquaintance (Ly. M. for instance) in proof of my assertion – "Nobody laughs more".'[36] (Byron to Annabella Milbanke, 6 September 1813)

Moore bears witness to the truth of this assertion:

Among the many gay hours we passed together this spring, I remember particularly the wild flow of his spirits one evening, when we had accompanied Mr Rogers home from some early assembly, and when Lord Byron, who, according to his frequent custom, had not dined for the last two days, found his hunger no longer governable, and called aloud for 'something to eat.' Our repast, – of his own choosing, – was simple bread and cheese; and seldom have I partaken of so joyous a supper. It happened that our host had just received a presentation copy of a volume of poems, written professedly in imitation of the old English writers, and containing, like many of these models, a good deal that was striking and beautiful, mixed up with much that was trifling, fantastic, and absurd. In our mood, at the moment, it was only with these latter qualities that either Lord Byron or I felt disposed to indulge ourselves; and, in turning over the pages, we found, it must be owned, abundant matter for mirth. In vain did Mr Rogers, in justice to the author, endeavour to direct our attention to some of the beauties of the work: – it suited better our purpose (as is too often the case with more deliberate critics) to pounce only on such passages as ministered to the laughing humour that possessed us. In this sort of hunt through the volume, we at length lighted on the discovery that our host, in addition to his sincere approbation of some of its contents, had also the motive of gratitude for standing by its author, as one of the poems was a warm and, I need not add, well-deserved panegyric on himself. We were, however, too far gone in nonsense for even this eulogy, in which we both so heartily agreed, to stop us. The opening line of the poem was, as well as I can recollect, 'When Rogers o'er this labour bent,' and Lord Byron undertook to read it aloud; – but he found it impossible to get beyond the first two words. Our laughter had now increased to such a pitch that nothing could restrain it. Two or three times he began; but no sooner had the words 'When Rogers' passed his lips, than our fit burst forth afresh, – till even Mr Rogers himself, with all his feeling of our injustice, found it impossible not to join us; and we were, at last, all three, in such a state of inextinguishable laughter, that, had the author himself been of the party, I question much whether he could have resisted the infection.[37]

A day or two after, Lord Byron sent me the following:

ON LORD THURLOW'S POEMS

1

WHEN Thurlow this damned nonsense sent,
(I hope I am not violent)
Nor men nor gods knew what he meant.

2

And since not even our Rogers's praise
To common sense his thoughts could raise –
Why *would* they let him print his lays?

3

* * * * * * * * * * * * * * * * *

4

* * * * * * * * * * * * * * * * *

5

To me, divine Apollo, grant – O!
Hermilda's first and second canto,
I'm fitting up a new portmanteau;

6

And thus to furnish decent lining,
My own and others' bays I'm twining –
So, gentle Thurlow, throw me thine in.[38]

136

He could, as we have seen, enjoy himself in male company of all kinds and this persisted throughout his life.

> Tuesday I dined with Ward & met Canning and all the Wits – and yesterday I dined with the Patrons of Pugilism & some of the professors – who amused me about as much.[39]
>> (To Lady Melbourne, 25 November 1813)

One of his dearest and most amusing friends was Sheridan who, at this time, was growing maudlin through drink, misfortune and lack of funds. Byron admired Sheridan and looked upon his failings with the most complete understanding and fellow-feeling.

> Poor dear Sherry – I shall never forget the day he and Rogers and Moore and I passed together; when *he* talked and *we* listened without one yawn, from six till one in the morning.[40]
>> (*Journal*, 16 November 1813)

> Poor fellow! he got drunk very thoroughly and very soon. – It occasionally fell to my lot to convey him home – no sinecure – for he was so tipsy that I was obliged to put on his cock'd hat for him – to be sure it tumbled off again and I was not myself so sober as to be able to pick it up again. –[41]
>> (*Detached Thoughts*, 15 October 1821)

In those days of high play and deep drinking when young bloods would drink 'a couple of bottles at least at dinner' and 'there were four or even five bottle men', it was just as well that Byron, whose careless spendthrift behaviour and confessed plunge into an 'abyss of sensuality' on his earlier visits to London, had burdened him with enormous debts, was able to summon up the strength of will to avoid constant heavy drinking and to give up gambling altogether, thus escaping the slow, sad, deterioration which made Sheridan a subject for pity and disdain among many who had envied him at the peak of his powers.

'The Monody on the Death of Sheridan' spoken at Drury Lane Theatre in September, 1816, includes a passage which describes the envy and denigration which gather about those who win extraordinary fame:

> The secret Enemy whose sleepless eye
> Stands sentinel – accuser – judge – and spy,
> The foe, the fool, the jealous, and the vain,
> The envious who but breathe in other's pain –

137

Behold the host! delighting to deprave,
Who track the steps of Glory to the grave,
Watch every fault that daring Genius owes,
Half to the ardour which its birth bestows,
Distort the truth, accumulate the lie,
And pile the Pyramid of Calumny![42]

With *Childe Harold's Pilgrimage* Byron too had won extraordinary fame and he too would suffer from the 'secret enemy' who stands 'accuser – judge – and spy'. He became aware of this as early as 1813:

C[ampbell] last night seemed a little nettled at something or other – I know not what. We were standing in the ante-saloon, when Lord H. brought out of the other room a vessel of some composition similar to that which is used in catholic churches, and, seeing us, he exclaimed, 'Here is some *incense* for you.' C. answered – 'Carry it to Lord Byron, *he is used to it . . .'*

Now, this comes of 'bearing no brother near the throne'. I, who have no throne, nor wish to have one *now* – whatever I may have done – am at perfect peace with all the poetical fraternity; or, at least, if I dislike any, it is not *poetically* but *personally*. Surely the field of thought is infinite; – what does it signify who is before or behind in a race where this is no *goal*?[43]

He wrote to Thomas Moore from Venice defending Sheridan's memory:

As for his creditors, – remember, Sheridan *never had* a shilling, and was thrown, with great powers and passions, into the thick of the world, and placed upon the pinnacle of success, with no other external means to support him in his elevation. Did Fox*** pay his debts? – or did Sheridan take a subscription? Was the Duke of Norfolk's drunkenness more excusable than his? Were his intrigues more notorious than those of all his contemporaries? and is his memory to be blasted, and theirs respected? Don't let yourself be led away by clamour, but compare him with the coalitioner, Fox, and the pensioner, Burke, as a man of principle, and with ten hundred thousand in personal views, and with none in talent, for he beat them all *out* and *out*. Without means, without connexion, without character, (which might be false at first, and make him mad afterwards from desperation) he beat them all, in all he ever attempted. But alas poor human nature! Good night – or rather, morning. It is four, and the dawn gleams over the Grand Canal and unshadows the

Rialto. I must to bed; up all night – but, as George Philpot says, 'It's life, though, damme it's life!'[44]

Byron became more and more disillusioned with both politics and society. He turned down a request to present another Petition to Parliament. 'Had [Lady Oxford] been here she would have *made* me do it. *There* is a woman who, amid all her fascination always urged a man to usefulness or glory.'[45] But he was 'sick of parliamentary mummeries'[46] and persuaded Lord Holland to present the petition. He was longing to go abroad and had toyed with the idea of visiting Holland which was on the brink of Revolution. 'I should like to listen to the shout of a free Dutchman.'[47] Some months later he wrote to Hobhouse with another plan for escaping from England, a letter which shows the warmth of his friendship and, with its expression of a preference for the company of Hobhouse on his travels, must have hurt the feelings of Thomas Moore if he read the letter after Byron's death:

now I would wish to set apart £3000 – for the tour – do you think *that* would enable me to see all *Italy* in a gentlemanly way? – with *as few* servants & luggage (except my aperients) as we can help. – And will you come with me? – you are the only man with whom I could travel an hour except an 'ιατρος' – in short you know my dear H – that with all my bad qualities – (and d––d bad they *are* to be sure) I like you better than any body – and we have travelled together before – and been old friends and all that – and we have a thorough fellow-feeling & contempt for all things of the sublunary sort – and so do let us go & call the 'Pantheon a cockpit' like the learned Smelfungus. – The Cash is the principal point – do you think that will do – viz £3000 clear from embarkation onwards. I have a world of watches and snuffboxes and telescopes – which would do for the Mussulmans if we liked to cross from Otranto & see our friends again. – They are all safe at Hammersleys. – would my *coach* do? – *beds* I have & all canteens &c. from *your* Man of Ludgate Hill – with saddles – pistols – tromboni – & what not. – I shall know tomorrow or next day – whether I can go – or not – and shall be in town next week – where I must see you or hear from you – if we set off – it should be in October and the earlier the better – Now don't engage yourself – but take up your map – and ponder upon this – ever, dear H.[48]

(Byron to Hobhouse, September 1814)

The plan for this journey never came to fruition since, before it could be put into action, Annabella Milbanke decided to regard a

139

tentative letter from Byron about a possible renewal of his courtship as a proposal of marriage. She sent an acceptance by return of post to Albany, with copy to Newstead Abbey to make assurance doubly sure.

She had captured her poet.

12

BYRON, MOORE AND THE ORIENTAL TALES

'Yes, Love indeed is light from heaven;
A spark of that immortal fire
With angels shared, by Alla given,
To lift from earth our low desire.
Devotion wafts the mind above,
But Heaven itself descends in Love;
A feeling from the Godhead caught,
To wean from self each sordid thought;
A ray of Him who formed the whole;
A Glory circling round the soul!'[1]

Annabella Milbanke told her mother that Byron wrote so beautifully of love in *The Giaour* as to almost make her in love. It was published in June 1813 and ran through fourteen editions by 1815. Described as 'A Fragment of a Turkish Tale'[2] it was based on the mysterious incident of the Turkish girl rescued from death beside the Bosphorus when Byron was in Constantinople. This and the later tales were widely thought to be autobiographical and Byron was generally supposed to have experienced wild adventures and to have indulged in exotic crime. He complained about this in his dedication to Thomas Moore of a later tale, *The Corsair*:

I have no particular desire that any but my acquaintance should think the author better than the beings of his imaginings; but I cannot help a little surprise ... when several (far more deserving I allow) poets ... quite exempted from all participation in the faults of those heroes who nevertheless might be found with little more morality than the *Giaour*.[3]

141

Byron writes a note on the passage in the poem beginning, 'He who hath bent him o'er the dead', which he must surely have realised would give rise to suspicions that would make his protests to Thomas Moore somewhat otiose:

I trust that few of my readers have ever had an opportunity of witnessing what is here attempted in description; but those who have will probably retain a painful remembrance of that singular beauty which pervades, with few exceptions, the features of the dead, a few hours, and but a few hours, after 'the spirit is not there.'

So far so good, but it was unnecessary to add:

It is to be remarked in cases of violent death by gun-shot wounds, the expression is always that of languor whatever the natural energy of the sufferer's character; but in death from a stab the countenance preserves its traits of feeling or ferocity, and the mind its bias to the last.[4]

Byron may have had this interesting information from the Suliote warriors with whom he foregathered round their camp fires in Albania. Here, whether intentionally or not, he gives the impression that he might himself have been involved in sinister goings-on in the East. Jerome Christensen describes the piece as 'a passage of daring necrophilia':[5]

> He who hath bent him o'er the dead,
> Ere the first day of Death is fled,
> The first dark day of Nothingness,
> The last of Danger and Distress,
> (Before Decay's effacing fingers
> Have swept the lines where Beauty lingers,)
> And marked the mild angelic air,
> The rapture of Repose that's there,
> The fixed yet tender traits that streak
> The languor of the placid cheek,
> And – but for that sad shrouded eye,
> That fires not, wins not, weeps not, now,
> And but for that chill, changeless brow,
> Where cold Obstruction's apathy
> Appals the gazing mourner's heart...[6]

There is no doubt that Byron was fascinated by the transition from life to death but there is surely no justification for describing

142

a loving gaze at the features of a dead person 'ere the first day of Death is fled' as necrophilia.

Byron wrote of his own poem: '*The Giaour* is certainly a bad character – but not dangerous – & I think his fate and his feelings will meet with few proselytes.'[7] In discussing the episode beside the Bosphorus which inspired the poem Byron for once abandoned his 'hatred of sentiment' and 'epistolary levity' and wrote '...to describe the *feelings* of *that situation* were impossible – it is *icy* even to recollect them.'[8]

Annabella Milbanke was one among many young women who yearned over *The Giaour*. Lady Frances Webster told Byron that *The Giaour* was printed on her heart. Byron was surprised at continued messages from this quarter – 'If people will stop at the first tense of the verb "aimer" they must not be surprised if one finishes the conjugation with somebody else.'[9]

The *Edinburgh Review* pronounced on *The Giaour*, criticising the guilt and worthlessness of *The Giaour* himself, deploring the gloomy and revolting subject but praising the poetic power of the author.[10] The review in *The Satirist* pleased Byron. An author assured that a work of his 'abounds with proofs of genius' could afford to overlook some fair though 'vituperative' remarks.[11]

The Giaour was followed by *The Bride of Abydos* which was highly praised but not on the whole considered as fine as *The Giaour*. The painter, Delacroix, was later delighted with it and wrote in his Journal, 'Poetry is always full of riches; always remember certain passages from Byron, they are an unfailing spur to the imagination ... the end of *The Bride of Abydos* and *The Death of Selim*, his body tossed about by the waves and that hand – especially that hand – held up by the waves as they break and spend themselves upon the shore. This is sublime, and it is his alone. I feel these things as they can be rendered in paint.'[12]

Ten thousand copies of the third Oriental Tale, *The Corsair*, were sold on the day of publication but there were those who disapproved strongly of both subject and manner of all the tales. They reminded Hazlitt of 'flowers strewed over the face of death'.[13] The writer in the *Critical Review* describes the author as the 'poet of sentiment and nature' who should '... despise all affected ornament and elaborate artifice of decoration' ... 'Lord Byron sometimes takes more pains to be *pretty* than a great poet ought to take.'[14]

The *Edinburgh Review* wrote of *The Corsair* that Byron '...had adorned a merciless corsair on a rock in the Mediterranean with every virtue under heaven except common honesty.'[15] The *British Critic* prophesied that '...even female admirers would tire of their querulous villainy and misanthropic sensibility.'[16]

Byron's literary mentor, Gifford, admired the narrative skill displayed in the Tales and wrote later of *The Siege of Corinth*, 'It is a dreadful picture, Caravaggio out done in his own way...', but he also declared, 'I keep my old opinion of Lord Byron. He may be what he will. Why will he not will to be one of the finest of poets and men. I lament to see a great mind run to seed and waste itself in rank growth.'[17]

Byron wrote to Thomas Moore:

> I have lately begun to think my things have been strangely overrated; and, at any rate, whether or not, I have done with them for ever, I may say to you, what I would not say to every body, that the last two were written, *The Bride* in four and *The Corsair* in ten days, – which I take to be a most humiliating confession, as it proves my own want of judgement in publishing, and the public's in reading things, which cannot have stamina for permanent attention.[18]
>
> (To Thomas Moore, 3 March 1814)

Byron was clearly anxious about the worth of the Tales but what he writes here is not his considered opinion and he had by no means done with them forever. *Lara*, *Parisina* and *The Siege of Corinth* were still to come. He was trying to persuade Moore not to give up his own Oriental poems, sending him reference books and assuring him, 'I need not say to you that your fame is dear to me, – I really might say *dearer* than my own.'[19] Denigrating his own work may have played a part in trying to encourage Moore to persevere.

Jeffery Vail explains the pre-eminence of Moore up to this date – exceeded only by the fame of Walter Scott:

> Moore's satires, his political poems, his prose works or the songs that everyone knew and sang, the lyrics ... His influence on his vast readership as well as on the current of Irish nineteenth century nationalism and culture was incalculably great: as Howard Mumford Jones observes, 'Hundreds who turned a deaf ear to Wordsworth, listened, enraptured, to Moore; thousands to whom Shelley was a filthy atheist learned of tyranny and nationalism from the persuasive Irishman.'[20]

When Byron came on the scene Moore was convinced that Scott would be dethroned, and so he was. *Rokeby* (1813) and *The Lord of the Isles* (1815) were considerably less successful than *The Lay of the Last Minstrel*. Scott bore Byron no malice for this change in the fortunes of his poetry and may have concluded that these new poems were inferior to his earlier efforts. He decided to abandon the field and turn to the novels. Moore on the other hand was worried that his own success would pale before that of Byron, though the latter wrote of his admiration for Moore:

[Moore] has wonderful powers, and much variety; besides, he has lived and felt. To write so as to bring home to the heart, the heart must have been tried.[21]

But Moore had no illusions. He knew that in the realms of poetry this young man was Caesar. When *Lalla Rookh* came out some time after Byron had left England it was much admired but, as Moore had feared, it was judged to be an imitation of Byron. On the other hand, *Beppo* was compared with Moore's *Twopenny Post-Bag*.

Harriet Granville's comment on *Lalla Rookh* is probably representative of the general attitude in London to the poetry of Moore and Byron:

I have been reading, that is, hearing L... R... K, Moore's poem and I think some of it quite beautiful. There is so much *radiance* and tenderness. Lord Byron has so much thought and passion that it makes everything flat in comparison, but it is also a repose to escape from crime and read of birds of paradise and innocent loves.[22]

It may be that Hary-O heard only the two shorter and lighter of the four tales which make up *Lalla Rookh* since Jeffery Vail points out that the longer tales, *The Haunted Veil* and *The Fire-Worshippers*, are more violent than any of Byron's tales. This may explain Byron's protest at being saddled as author with all the crimes of the characters in his own poems.

Byron was easily plunged into gloom from time to time during his years in London. His imagination was haunted by the Orient and he found he could escape from reality by losing himself in the composition of dream-like tales set among the exotic scenes he could never forget. The Giaour, Conrad the Corsair, Lara,

Alp, were examples of anti-heroes widely but mistakenly believed by many of his readers to be based on the poet himself. Among these sinister inventions the most popular was probably the Corsair:

> Sun-burnt his cheek, his forehead high and pale
> The sable curls in wild profusion veil;
> And oft perforce his rising lip reveals
> The haughtier thought it curbs, but scarce conceals.
> Though smooth his voice, and calm his general mien,
> Still seems there something he would not have seen:
> His features' deepening lines and varying hue
> At times attracted, yet perplexed the view,
> As if within that murkiness of mind
> Worked feelings fearful, and yet undefined;
> Such might it be – that none could truly tell –
> Too close inquiry his stern glance would quell.
> There breathe but few whose aspect might defy
> The full encounter of his searching eye; ...
> Slight are the outward signs of evil thought,
> Within – within – 'twas there the spirit wrought!
> Love shows all changes – Hate, Ambition, Guile,
> Betray no further than the bitter smile;
> The lips least curl, the lightest paleness thrown
> Along the governed aspect, speak alone.[23]

Nostalgia for the climate and the beauty of Greece resulted in such lines as the famous opening of the third canto of *The Corsair*, originally composed for the *Curse of Minerva*:

> Slow sinks, more lovely ere his race be run,
> Along Morea's hills the setting Sun;
> Not, as in Northern climes, obscurely bright,
> But one unclouded blaze of living light!
> O'er the hush'd deep the yellow beam he throws,
> Gilds the green wave, that trembles as it glows.
> On old Aegina's rock and Idra's isle,
> The god of gladness sheds his parting smile;
> O'er his own regions lingering, loves to shine,
> Though there his altars are no more divine.
> Descending fast the mountain shadows kiss
> Thy glorious gulf, unconquered Salamis!
> Their azure arches through the long expanse

146

> More deeply purpled met, his mellowing glance,
> And tenderest tints, along their summits driven,
> Mark his gay course, and own the hues of heaven;
> Till, darkly shaded from the land and deep,
> Behind his Delphian cliff he sinks to sleep.[24]

'I still sigh for the Aegean,'[25] he told E.D. Clarke, but he was not writing for the pleasure of such memories of the 'living light' of a Grecian sunset but, as he wrote of his state of mind when writing *The Bride of Abydos*, 'to distract my dreams from * *'.[26] In the opening lines to *Lara* he is concerned with the reality which was part cause of all this *angst*:

> When she is gone, the loved, the lost, the one
> Whose smile hath gladdened though perchance undone;
> Whose name, too dearly cherished to impart,
> Dies on the lip, but trembles in the heart;
> Whose sudden mention can almost convulse
> And lighten through the ungovernable pulse,
> Till the heart leaps so keenly to the word
> We fear that throb can hardly beat unheard,
> Then sinks at once beneath that sickly chill
> That follows when we find her absent still;
> When such is gone, too far again to bless,
> Oh God, how slowly comes Forgetfulness!
> Let none complain how faithless and how brief
> The brain's remembrance or the bosom's grief;
> Or, ere they thus forbid us to forget,
> Let Mercy strip the memory of regret,
> Yet – selfish still – we would not be forgot;
> What lip dare say, 'My love – remember not'?
> Oh, best and dearest, thou whose thrilling name
> My heart adores too deeply to proclaim![27]

The 'she' who is lost is Augusta Leigh.

Wilson Knight writes that *Lara* is a study in personal anguish. But the hero is also a political revolutionary. The poor love him. He refuses religious consolation. It is clear that he resembles the poet in many important ways:

> With more capacity for love than Earth
> Bestows on most of mortal mould and birth.[28]

147

Jeffery Vail points out that Byron and Moore shared the same audience and often consulted each other about what their readers wanted: 'This sensibility and responsiveness to their readers' desires often led Byron and Moore to produce poems in a similar genre or style within a year or two or even within months of each other's productions.'[29] With less magnanimity and affection on either side the friendship between the two men might have been destroyed by the interest in Orientalism which they shared, the audience for works inspired by which was divided between them, though some other poets – in particular, Southey – had attempted works of the same genre.

On 10 July 1817 Byron sent Moore the following farewell lyric in a letter:

1.

My boat is on the shore,
   And my bark is on the sea;
But, before I go, Tom Moore,
   Here's a double health to thee!

2.

Here's a sigh to those who love me,
   And a smile to those who hate;
And, whatever sky's above me,
   Here's a heart for every fate.

3.

Though the Ocean roar around me,
   Yet it still shall bear me on;
Though a desert should surround me,
   It hath springs which may be won.

4.

Were't the last drop in the well,
   As I gasped upon the brink,
Ere my fainting spirit fell,
   'T is to thee that I would drink.

5.

With that water, as this wine,
   The libation I would pour
Should be – peace to thine and mine,
   And a health to thee, Tom Moore.[30]

This tribute was set to music by Henry Bishop and became a popular song, often struck up when Moore was present. 'The song fixed the image of Byron and Moore as close comrades even more firmly in the public mind.'[33]

Byron's dedication of *The Corsair* to Moore had also fixed this image and since the 'Lines to a Lady Weeping' were published with *The Corsair* Moore had suffered some of the vituperation earned by Byron for his lèse majesté.

Notes

1. Paul Elledge writes of the *Oriental Tales* in 1968:

Byron writes, therefore, at least at this stage in his career, for catharsis and escape. To elude the conflicting, tormenting, and to some degree stultifying emotions of his own mind, he projects them into fictional protagonists who continually flutter between worlds of past and present, dreams and reality, states of action and ennui, poles of passion and intellect.'[1] Yet Elledge dismissed *The Giaour* and *The Bride of Abydos* as 'even cruder experiments in the genre than *The Corsair*.'[2]

2. Jerome J. McGann rescues Byron's *Oriental Tales* from critics who condemned them.

The Bride of Abydos, *The Corsair*, *Lara* and *Parisina* all deal with the same general motifs that appear in *The Giaour*. Contrary to popular belief, however, the ideas and problems are by no means trivial. The tales are repetitive to a fault, but not so much in the matter of theme as of versification. Byron is still learning the fundamentals of language. They are all notable achievements, and if *The Corsair* and *Lara* contain the most memorable passages, *Parisina* is probably, on the whole, the best tale. Each centres round an exploration of the nature and consequences of life that is Eros-directed. Each tells a story of frustrated love and the war of repression within a context where time and contingency in general are strongly emphasized.[3]

McGann explains the fragmentary structure of *The Giaour*. It is an oral poem – 'The performance of one of those storytellers in one of those coffee-houses "that abound in the Levant". What Byron intends us to apprehend in the poem is its narrated quality. The bard sings his tale and avails himself of the privilege of all oral poets from Homer to the present: to assume as many roles as he needs to tell his story, and to enter into the psychology of his characters and present his tale from their point of view.'[4]

3. M.K. Joseph writes of the Byronic hero:

Behind him lie the titanism of Prometheus and of Milton's Satan; Hamlet, the melancholy dandy in the haunted castle; the sentimental heroes of Rousseau's *Nouvelle Héloise* and of Goethe's *Werther*; the hero-villains of *Otranto* and Gothic melodrama and the Radcliffean tale of terror, as modified by the humanitarianism of Holcroft and Godwin.[5]

4. Some modern critics attribute great significance to the *Oriental Tales*, which might possibly have surprised their author. Eric Daffron observes that:

In these tales, according to some twentieth century critics he [Byron] contributed to the creation of the modern self.[6]

5. Byron's poetry inspired revolutionaries and Philhellenes during his lifetime and throughout the nineteenth century. It still retains its power. Lines from *The Giaour* were spoken at Gdansk and carved on the Three Crosses monument to the workers who died in the shipyard there when the trades union movement, Solidarity, was founded:

> Clime of the unforgotten brave!
> Whose land from plain to mountain-cave
> Was Freedom's home or Glory's grave!
> Shrine of the mighty! can it be,
> That this is all remains of thee?
> Approach, thou craven crouching slave:
>   Say, is not this Thermopylæ?
> These waters blue that round you lave, –
>   Oh servile offspring of the free –
> Pronounce what sea, what shore is this?
> The gulf, the rock of Salamis!
> These scenes, their story not unknown,
> Arise, and make again your own;
> Snatch from the ashes of your Sires
> The embers of their former fires;
>   And he who in the strife expires
>   Will add to theirs a name of fear
>   That Tyranny shall quake to hear,
>   And leave his sons a hope, a fame
>   They too will rather die than shame:

For Freedom's battle once begun,
Bequeathed by bleeding Sire to Son,
Though baffled oft, is ever won.[7]

13

SHOCK-TACTICS

There are those who think that the great events which marked the close of the last century, [the American War of Independence and the French Revolution] by giving a new 'impulse to men's minds, by habituating them to the daring and the free, and allowing full vent to 'the flash and outbreak of fiery spirits' had led naturally to the production of such a poet as Byron, and that he was, in short, as much the child and representative of the Revolution in poetry as another great man of the age, Napoleon, was in politics.[1]

Byron was as liberal in his politics as in his poetry. It was Hobhouse who persuaded him to join the Whig Club in Cambridge but Byron was already an admirer of Charles James Fox, the great liberal Whig known as 'the Man for the People'. (He was so beloved that country people following fox hounds call out 'There goes Charlie!' even today when they catch sight of the fox.)

Fox died when Byron was eighteen. On reading a verse in *The Morning Post* maligning Fox Byron composed a poem in his defence and sent it to *The Morning Chronicle* which declined to publish. The piece then appeared in *Hours of Idleness*. Like Fox, Byron was concerned throughout his life not only with the rights of Englishmen but with the Rights of Man. Like Fox, he ruined his career by advocating liberal principles injudiciously. For years after Fox's death Fox dinners were held annually all over England in his honour. Macaulay said that twenty-five years after his death there were people who could not talk about Charles James Fox for a quarter of an hour without weeping. When Byron died in Greece he was mourned all over the world but there were no annual Byron dinners in England. The French Revolution may have given 'a new

153

impulse' to the minds of some, but the Terror alarmed every one else and government reacted in England with panicky measures of repression. During the long years of war the Secretary of State for home affairs, developed a network of secret agents, spies and informers, the purpose of which was to make sure that any Jacobinical activity in Britain which might lead to revolution would immediately be crushed.

The fears of the government were not totally unfounded. In 1817 the leader of the Derbyshire rising shot dead a servant who refused to get up out of his bed and join the rebels, and in 1820 the plotters of the Cato Street Conspiracy planned to take with them into the room where the Cabinet were dining, several knives and bags for cutting off heads and transporting them to where they could be impaled on pikes.

The spectre of the French Revolution and the Terror had by no means been laid and although Major Cartwright told his followers to 'Stand fast by the laws', it was said that it was safer to be a felon than a Radical. William Cobbett, whose *Weekly Political Register* became available to the poor for twopence in 1816 and sold fifty thousand copies in a week, fled for a time to America in 1817 when habeas corpus was suspended. The government's reaction to the events leading up to the Peterloo Massacre in 1819 was to crush all protest by Gag Acts. When Byron in his maiden speech had told their lordships, 'I have been in some of the most oppressed provinces of Turkey; but never under the most despotic of infidel governments did I behold such squalid wretchedness as I have seen since my return, in the very heart of a Christian country...'[2] government was unmoved, convinced that repression was the only answer to unrest and insurgency because government could do nothing to relieve the misery of the poor. So Gag Acts were followed by Corn Laws and more Enclosure Acts which turned independent small-holders eking out a miserable income by grazing their animals on common land and shooting birds and rabbits for the pot, into poverty-stricken labourers dependent on farmers and landowners for work and thus deprived of independence which made them 'saucy'.

It was not surprising that in such an atmosphere Byron became a marked man – though in spite of attacks on him by the Tory Press this may not have become clear to him until he was visited by an emissary of government shortly before he went into

154

exile in 1816. To be a liberal was suspect but to be so famous a liberal was unacceptable. The publication in 1813 of the first of his Oriental Tales, *The Giaour*, added to his fame. It reached a high point when 'the odious book' [*Childe Harold*] '...attained the *summit* of *fame* by giving a name to a *very slow racehorse*.'[3] If Byron had been an obscure personage his defiance of political decorum might have been ignored but by 1814 he was celebrated all over the world:

> As Moore and I were going to dine with Lord Grey in P[ortman] Square – I pulled out a *Java Gazette* (which Murray had sent to me) in which there was a controversy on our respective merits as poets – it was amusing enough that we should be proceeding peaceably to the same table – while they were squabbling about us in the Indian Seas ... But this is fame, I presume![4]
>
> (*Detached Thoughts*, 1821)

Byron's third speech in the House of Lords outraged both the Whigs and the Tories and put an end to the possibility of a career in Parliament, at least for the time being. It was the presentation of a petition by the famous old Radical, Major Cartwright, for Parliamentary Reform. Byron had no very high opinion of Major Cartwright but supported his right to make the petition.

The old campaigner and his adherents had been forcibly prevented by the military from presenting his petition for Parliamentary reform. Byron told their lordships:

> It is in the cause of the Parliament and people that the rights of this venerable freeman have been violated, and it is, in my opinion, the highest mark of respect that could be paid to the House that to your justice, rather than by appeal to any inferior court, he now commits himself... I have this opportunity of publicly stating the obstruction to which the subject is liable, in the prosecution of the most lawful and imperious of his duties, the obtaining by petition reform in Parliament... Your Lordships will, I hope, adopt some measure fully to protect and redress him, and not him alone, but the whole body of the people, insulted and aggrieved in his person, by the interposition of an abused civil and unlawful military force between them and their right of petition to their own representatives.[5]

This was grasping a very toxic nettle indeed. It was not until 1832 that the first Parliamentary Reform Bill was passed. In 1813

155

the great Whig landowners still controlled most of the rotten boroughs which allowed them to return their own creatures to Parliament. This was a power they would not easily relinquish. They had not yet begun to understand that the development of a new and prosperous middle class was changing politics forever (though not in ways that Byron would necessarily have approved of).

By the 1830s they were ready to make concessions, not because they believed in or welcomed democracy, but in order to protect their own interests and prevent more sweeping reforms which might put an end to their own ascendancy.

If this was the grudging attitude of the Whigs in 1832, how alarming for the Whig party in 1813 must Byron's shock-tactics on Parliamentary Reform have been. The tactical problems within the party were at least as intractable in 1813 as in the 1830s. As a result of almost twenty years of war with France the Whigs were already in turmoil. Fox had believed (and rightly) that Pitt would use the war to justify repression in England which would set back the cause for liberty for years. The Whig party split over Fox's opposition to the war. The Portland Whigs joined Pitt, judging the danger from France should outweigh the Whig concern for protecting the people from the tyranny of the Crown and its ministers. The Foxite Whigs were reduced to a small minority but their principles and their influence were fundamental to the achievements of the party which, led by Grey and Holland, succeeded in bringing about Catholic Emancipation (passed reluctantly by the Tories), the first steps towards Parliamentary Reform and the abolition of slavery in the British Colonies, by the early 1830s. If Byron had lived and returned to England he would have been with them in all these achievements.

But in 1813/14 he was an embarrassment to both parties. He made matters infinitely worse with eight lines of poetry written and published anonymously in 1812 which, when republished in 1814 under the writer's name, caused a furore by insulting the Prince Regent. As a young man George, Prince of Wales, was known as 'Prince Florizel' for his beauty and as the 'First Gentleman of Europe' for his exquisite manners. In the Twelfth Canto of *Don Juan* Byron looked back with regret on the youth whose promise had been unfulfilled:

LXXXIV

There too, he saw (what'er he may be now)
    A Prince, the Prince of Princes at the time,
With fascination in his very bow,
    And full of promise as the spring of prime.
Though Royalty was written on his brow,
    He had *then* the grace, too, rare in every clime,
Of being, without alloy of fop or beau,
    A finished Gentleman from top to toe.[6]

Following the tradition of Hanoverian heirs-apparent, the Prince threw in his lot with the Opposition party, the great Whig earls. He declared in 1811 that it was his glory to have bred up his daughter, Princess Charlotte, in the principles of Fox. In the autumn of 1805 Thomas Creevey had written:

I remember dining with him (the Prince) at George Johnstone's in Brighton – the Duke of Clarence, old Thurlow, Lord and Lady Bessborough and a very large party, of which Suza, the Portuguese Ambassador, was one. After dinner the Prince, addressing himself to Suza, described himself as being the head of the great Whig party in England and then entered at great length upon the merits of Whig principles and the great glory it was to him, the Prince, to be the head of a party who advocated such principles.[7]

The Whig, Creevey, wrote at this auspicious moment: 'God send we have a Regency and then the cards are in our hands.'[8] But when the Prince became Regent he abandoned the Whigs without warning and retained his father's Tory administration. The Whigs were thunder-struck, although the defects in the character of the Prince had been well known – in 1804 Sheridan was already talking of his unsteadiness and by 1811 the Whigs were talking of his folly and villainy. 'The more one sees of the conduct of this most singular man,' wrote Creevey, 'the more one becomes convinced he is doomed, from his personal character alone, to shake his throne.'[9] These remarks were made by Whigs disappointed in their expectation of taking power. They exaggerated the foibles of the Prince Regent. Some authorities have applauded his decision to retain the Tory administration. The Whigs were critical of the government's handling of the Peninsular War and might have brought it to a disastrous conclusion by recalling Wellesley.

157

Byron had met the Prince Regent and was aware of his charm but this did not prevent him from writing 'Lines to a Lady Weeping'. The 'lady' is Princess Charlotte, who was distressed at what she regarded as her father's apostasy. Many people hoped the Princess would be the saving of the monarchy. George Lamb remarked that he would like to put the Prince Regent in a boat and send him out to sea so that Princess Charlotte could be Queen.

> WEEP, daughter of a royal line,
>   A Sire's disgrace, a realm's decay;
> Ah! happy if each tear of thine
>   Could wash a Father's fault away!
> Weep – for thy tears are Virtue's tears –
>   Auspicious to these suffering Isles;
> And be each drop in future years
>   Repaid thee by thy People's smiles![10]

Byron was as unaccountably surprised at the furore caused by these lines as he had been at the predicted reaction of the ladies of Southwell to his lines 'To Mary'. He wrote to Thomas Moore:

You can have no conception of the uproar the eight lines on the little Royalty's weeping in 1812 (now republished) have occasioned. The Regent who had always thought them *yours*, chose – God knows why – on discovering them to be mine, to be *affected* 'in sorrow rather than in anger.' The *Morning Post, Sun, Herald, Courier*, have all been in hysterics ever since. Murray is in a fright and wanted to shuffle – and the abuse against me in all directions is vehement, unceasing, loud, some of it good and all of it hearty. I feel a little compunction as to the R's *regret* – would he had been only angry...[11]

(To Thomas Moore, 10 February 1814)

Byron's compunction for the Regent's sorrow over the 'Lines to a Lady Weeping' led him to make amends some years later. When the Prince (now George IV) repealed the forfeiture imposed on the family of Lord Edward Fitzgerald in consequence of his involvement in the Irish rebellion of 1798, Byron sent a sonnet to John Murray in praise of the King's act:

SONNET TO THE PRINCE REGENT
ON THE REPEAL OF LORD EDWARD
FITZGERALD'S FORFEITURE

To be the father of the fatherless,
    To stretch the hand from the throne's height, and raise
    His offspring, who aspired in other days
To make thy Sire's sway by a kingdom less, –
This is to be a monarch, and repress
    Envy into unutterable praise.
    Dismiss thy guard, and trust thee to such traits,
For who would lift a hand, except to bless?
    Were it not easy, Sir, and is't not sweet
    To make thyself belovéd? and to be
Omnipotent by Mercy's means? for thus
    Thy Sovereignty would grow but more complete,
A despot thou, and yet thy people free,
    And by the heart – not hand – enslaving us.[12]

In 1814 he was amazed at the effect of the lines which had upset the Prince Regent:

Did you ever know anything like this? – at a time when peace and war – and Emperors & Napoleons – and the destinies of the things they have made of mankind are trembling in the balance – the Government Gazettes can devote half their attention and columns day after day to *eight lines* written two years ago – and now *republished only* – (by an individual) and suggest them for consideration of Parliament probably about the same period with the Treaty of Peace – I really begin to think myself a most important personage – what would poor Pope have given to bring this down upon his *'epistle to Augustus'*?[13]

                     (To Lady Melbourne, 11 February 1814)

Byron was distracted from his own difficulties by 'peace and war – and Emperors and Napoleons'. He was distressed by the defeat of Buonaparte by the allies and deeply distressed by the less than heroic role played by the Emperor in his own débacle and by the restoration of the Bourbons which would destroy all the high hopes brought into being by the Revolution.

This distress is made clear by the entries in his *Journal* during this period:

To-day I have boxed one hour – written an ode to Napoleon Buonaparte – copied it – eaten six biscuits – drunk four bottles of soda water –

                              (10 April 1813)

159

I don't know – but I think *I*, even *I* (an insect compared with this creature), have set my life on casts not a millionth part of this man's. But, after all, a crown may be not worth dying for. Yet to outlive *Lodi* for this!!! Oh that Juvenal or Johnson could rise from the dead! 'Expende – quot libras in duce summo invenies?' I knew they were light in the balance of mortality; but I thought their living dust weighed more *carats*. Alas! this imperial diamond hath a flaw in it and is now hardly fit to stick in a glazier's pencil: – the pen of the historian won't rate it worth a ducat.

Psha! 'something too much of this.' But I won't give him up even now; though all his admirers have, 'like the Thanes, fallen from him'.

(14 April 1813)

There is ice at both poles, north and south – all extremes are the same – misery belongs to the highest and the lowest only, – to the emperor and the beggar, when unsixpenced and unthroned. There is, to be sure, a dammed insipid medium – an equinoctial one – no one knows where, except upon maps and measurement.

'And all our *yesterdays* have lighted fools
The way to dusty death,'
I will keep no further journal of that same hesternal torch-light; and, to prevent me from returning, like a dog, to the vomit of memory, I tear out the remaining leaves of this volume, and write, in *Ipecacuanha*, – 'that the Bourbons are restored!!!' – 'Hang up philosophy.' To be sure, I have long despised myself and man, but I never spat in the face of my species before – 'O fool! I shall go mad'.

(19 April 1813)

What strange tidings from the Anakim of anarchy – Buonaparte! Ever since I defended my bust of him at Harrow against the rascally time-servers, when the war broke out in 1803, he has been a 'Héros de Roman' of mine – on the continent; I don't want him here. But I don't like those same flights – leaving of armies, &c. &c. I am sure when I fought for his bust at school, I did not think he would run away from himself. But I should not wonder if he banged them yet. To be beat by men would be something; but by three stupid, legitimate-old-dynasty boobies of regular-bred sovereigns – O-hone-a-rie! – O-hone-a-rie![14]

(17 November 1813)

Byron was not alone in his distress at the idea of the Bourbons once again restored to the throne of France. Charles James Fox had thought that the French and not the English were the proper persons to determine whether the Bourbons ought to reign in France.

From *Ode to Napoleon Buonaparte*, 1814:

I

'Tis done – but yesterday a King!
And armed with Kings to strive –
And now thou art a nameless thing:
So abject – yet alive!
Is this the man of thousand thrones,
Who strewed our earth with hostile bones,
And can he thus survive?
Since he, miscalled the Morning Star,
Nor man nor fiend hath fallen so far.

X

And Earth hath spilt her blood for him,
Who thus can hoard his own!
And Monarchs bowed the trembling limb,
And thanked him for a throne!
Fair Freedom! we may hold thee dear,
When thus thy mightiest foes their fear
In humblest guise have shown.
Oh! ne'er may tyrant leave behind
A brighter name to lure mankind!

XVIII

But thou forsooth must be a King,
And don the purple vest,
As if that foolish robe could wring
Remembrance from thy breast.
Where is that faded garment? where
The gewgaws thou wert fond to wear,
The star, the string, the crest?
Vain froward child of Empire! say,
Are all thy playthings snatch'd away?

XIX

Where may the wearied eye repose
When gazing on the Great;
Where neither guilty glory glows,
Nor despicable state?
Yes – one – the first – the last – the best –
The Cincinnatus of the West,
Whom Envy dared not hate,
Bequeathed the name of Washington,
To make man blush there was but one![15]

161

The Ode brought Byron an angry letter which he passed on to Thomas Moore.

> I enclose you an epistle received this morning from I know not whom, but I think it will amuse you. The writer must be a rare fellow.
>
> (To Thomas Moore, 13 Piccadilly Terrace, 12 June 1815)

Moore includes the enclosure:

> My Lord,
> I have lately purchased a set of your works and am quite vexed that you have not cancelled the *Ode to Bonaparte*. It was certainly prematurely written without thought or reflection. Providence has now brought him to reign over millions again, while the same Providence now keeps as it were in a garrison another potentate, who, in the language of Burke, he 'hurled from this throne.' See if you cannot make amends for your folly and consider that, in almost every respect, human nature is the same, in every clime and in every period, and don't act the part of a foolish boy. Let not Englishmen talk of the stretch of tyrants, while the torrents of blood shed in the East Indies cry aloud to Heaven for retaliation. Learn, good sir, not to cast the first stone.[16]

In 1815 Byron wrote three poems calculated to outrage every patriot in Britain (as well as government and establishment) entitled 'Napoleon's Farewell', 'From the French', and 'The Star of the Legion of Honour', all of which purported to be translated from the French. Each was published anonymously in *The Examiner* and then openly in *Poems, 1816*. One hinted at a return by Napoleon, one was an address to the exiled Emperor by one of his faithful soldiers, another prophesied further bloodshed. In writing such poems as these, Byron is exploring possibilities. These are all possible postures he is occupying. He is not being totally insincere but neither is he totally sincere. Arthur Symons wrote of him: 'Byron's thought embraced Europe as another man's thought might have embraced the village from which he had sprung.'[17] His attitude toward Europe might be considered more admirable in a poet than Sydney Smith's attitude in a clergyman:

> How can any man stop in the midst of the stupendous joy of getting rid of Buonaparte and prophecy the little piddling evils that will result from restoring the Bourbons? ... Nor am I quite certain that I don't wish Paris burnt and France laid waste by the Cossacks for revenge and for security.[18]

162

Those who were outraged by Byron's purported translations might have been mollified if they had known that, as pointed out by Elizabeth Longford:

> ...although Wellington called Napoleon 'the grand disturber', yet he felt that, once peace had been made, the Emperor might still be the best available ruler for France provided he behaved as he promised. Most of the Allied Army, however, took the simpler view of Pakenham that the grand disturber must be 'dethroned and Decapitized [sic]'.[19]

Robert Southey thought Napoleon 'a mean-spirited villain' and the 'Ode to Napoloen Bonaparte' convinced him that Byron had arrived at the same opinion. Southey was reckoning without Byron's self-confessed 'mobility'. He could move from one opinion to another but without cancelling the first. All possibilities were valid in explicating a complicated world.

Byron had praised the young Napoleon as the 'Morning Star' and at Harrow he had fought to protect his bust of the Emperor from angry school fellows. He was obliged to accept, by the time he wrote the *Ode*, that his hero had become a tyrant. Yet he still hoped for better from the great man. Jonathan Gross points out that 'Byron condemned tyranny in his own lifetime, whether incarnated by Lord Castlereagh, George III or Napoleon Bonaparte.'[20] The succinct description by this writer of 'the principles of Whiggery' is a condensation of the basis of all Byron's political endeavours: 'resistance to royal power on the one hand and to mob rule on the other...'[21] though one should add the proviso that Byron objected to royal power not because it was royal but where it was tyrannical. He eventually came to believe a republic was probably the best form of government. His resistance to mob rule has infuriated many left-wing politicians and he has been so thoroughly misunderstood that Bertrand Russell thought him almost a Fascist, an unfortunate, and probably influential, misreading of the whole tenor of Byron's life and work. Bertrand Russell observed on the subject of Byron's politics:

> He wrote in later life much noble verse in praise of freedom, but it must be understood that the freedom he praised was that of a German prince or a Cherokee chief; not the inferior sort that might conceivably be enjoyed by ordinary mortals.[22]

Byron's concern with freedom for the Greeks had nothing to do with princes or aristocrats. William Parry who was with him during his last days at Missolonghi reports his saying, 'No system of government in any part of Greece can be permanent which does not leave in the hands of the peasantry the chief part of the political power. They are warmly attached to their country and they are the best portion of the people.'[23] We have seen how he praised the common people of Spain above their leaders and rebuked the members of the House of Lords for their contemptuous attitude to 'the mob'. Later in life he changed his mind about a plan for starting a new life in Venezuela, when he discovered that its economy was based on slavery:

> The accounts sent from England in consequence of my enquiries – discouraged me ... there is *no* freedom – even for *Masters* – in the midst of slaves ... I sometimes wish that I was the Owner of Africa – to do at once – what Wilberforce will do in time – viz. – sweep Slavery from her deserts – and look on upon the first dance of their Freedom...[24]

Byron was in favour of all oppressed peoples struggling for freedom – the Dutch, the Italians, the Greeks, the South Americans. But he was opposed to lawlessness and wrote of the Radical agitators, Hunt and Cobbett:

> ... I am glad to hear you have nothing to do with those scoundrels – I can understand and enter into the feelings of Mirabeau and Lafayette – but I have no sympathy with Robespierre – and Marat ... I do not think the man who would overthrow all laws – should have the benefit of any.[25]

Byron praised Mirabeau and Lafayette not because they were aristocrats but because they were sensible and moderate in contrast to the cruel tyranny of Marat and Robespierre. He would have applauded the verdict on Cobbett and Hunt of E.P. Thompson:

> The national leaders, Cobbett and Wooler with their pens, Hunt with his voice – were adept at pitching their rhetoric just on the right side of treason: but they laid themselves open to the charge ... of encouraging other men to take illegal or treasonable actions from the consequence of which they themselves escaped...[26]

By October 1819 Byron was writing, 'My taste for revolution is abated – revolutions are not to be made with rosewater – on either side harm must be done before good can come.'[27] But in 1822 he wrote, 'There's nothing left for Mankind but a Republic – and I think that there are hopes of such ... the two Americas (South and North) have it – Spain and Portugal approach it – and all thirst for it – oh! Washington![28]

14

HEBREW MELODIES: BYRON AND SONG

Hark! the note,
The natural music of the mountain reed –
For here the patriarchal days are not
A pastoral fable – pipes in the liberal air,
Mix'd with the sweet bells of the sauntering herd;
My soul would drink those echoes. Oh that I were
The viewless spirit of a lovely sound,
A living voice, a breathing harmony,
A bodiless enjoyment – born and dying
With the blest tone which made me![1]

'Manfred'

Byron loved to listen to women singing and often burst into song himself. When he was staying at Aston his host asked him to refrain from singing in his bedroom as it made his wife, Lady Frances, cry. Graham Pont describes Byron as 'a natural musician, a collector of songs and improviser of "stanzas for music". He was an amateur singer – a classic "bathroom baritone" – who once described Moore's music as his "matins and vespers": "I won't call it singing", he admitted, "for I never attempt that except to myself".'[2] Thomas Moore remembered that he had watched Byron listening to his own *Irish Melodies* with tears in his eyes.

In September 1814 a collaboration initiated by Douglas Kinnaird between Byron and a young Jewish composer called Isaac Nathan was to produce a series of songs set to music by Nathan with the help of a composer and singer called John Braham.

Graham Pont reminds us that *Hebrew Melodies* belong to the era when 'social music-making was still a civilised recreation' and Nathan describes an evening when he was invited to dine with Douglas Kinnaird and his mistress, Maria Keppel: 'When Lord Byron appeared "we talked a little, drank a little, ate a little, sang a little, drank a little more: the beautiful hostess took part in a trio of one of my *Hebrew Melodies* and her Lothario took the bass part".'[3]

The poems were published in April 1815 with a dedication to Princess Charlotte of Wales and 'soon found their way into ladies' albums or commonplace books ... William St Clair has discovered that, although John Murray's edition [which did not include the music] was not one of Byron's best-sellers, the *Hebrew Melodies* were amongst those most commonly copied into private albums. In her commonplace book (Add. 58802) Augusta Leigh copied several including "She Walks in Beauty".'[4]

The songs were sung in public performances as well as in private drawing rooms and Nathan agreed to the suggestion of John Braham that he should be the performer: 'I should be paying a just tribute of respect to the first poet of the age, by having his verses sung by the greatest vocalist of the day.'[5]

Some of the poems were written on subjects suggested by Nathan, others were lyrics by Byron not necessarily on sacred or Hebrew subjects, which were set to music by the composer. It was a true working collaboration. A friendly relationship grew up between composer and poet. Byron invited Nathan to dinner more than once and Nathan was one of the last people to call at Piccadilly Terrace with a farewell gift for Byron before he left for the continent.

One of the songs Byron gave Nathan for *Hebrew Melodies* was a poem he had written earlier in praise of the wife of his cousin, Robert Wilmot, whom he had seen wearing a dark, spangled frock at a party at Lansdowne House. Lady Byron was involved with the production of *Hebrew Melodies* and copied out some of the poems for Nathan. She must have read this poem soon after her marriage. Byron wrote no poems addressed to Annabella until after their parting and both the young bride and her mother were unhappy at his having neglected to do so. One can give Byron no marks whatsoever for tact:

SHE walks in Beauty, like the night
   Of cloudless climes and starry skies;
And all that's best of dark and bright
   Meet in her aspect and her eyes:
Thus mellowed to that tender light
   Which Heaven to gaudy day denies.

II

One shade the more, one ray the less,
   Had half impaired the nameless grace
Which waves in every raven tress,
   Or softly lightens o'er her face;
Where thoughts serenely sweet express,
   How pure, how dear their dwelling place.

III

And on that cheek, and o'er that brow,
   So soft, so calm, yet eloquent,
The smiles that win, the tints that glow,
   But tell of days in goodness spent,
A mind at peace with all below,
   A heart whose love is innocent![6]

One of the most famous of Byron's poems appears in *Hebrew Melodies.* It has been so popular ever since that it has become an 'anthology piece'.

THE DESTRUCTION OF SENNACHERIB

I

The Assyrian came down like the wolf on the fold,
And his cohorts were gleaming in purple and gold;
And the sheen of their spears was like stars on the sea,
When the blue wave rolls nightly on deep Galilee.

II

Like the leaves of the forest when Summer is green,
That host with their banners at sunset were seen:
Like the leaves of the forest when Autumn hath blown,
The host on the morrow lay withered and strown.

For the Angel of Death spread his wings on the blast,
And breathed in the face of the foe as he passed;
And the eyes of the sleepers waxed deadly and chill,
And their hearts but once heaved, and for ever grew still!

IV

And there lay the steed with his nostril all wide;
But through it there rolled not the breath of his pride;
And the foam of his gasping lay white on the turf,
And cold as the spray of the rock-beating surf.

V

And there lay the rider distorted and pale,
With the dew on his brow, and the rust on his mail:
And the tents were all silent – the banners alone –
The lances unlifted – the trumpet unblown.

VI

And the widows of Ashur are loud in their wail,
And the idols are broke in the temple of Baal;
And the might of the Gentile, unsmote by the sword,
Hath melted like snow in the glance of the Lord![7]

G. Wilson Knight shows how much more 'The Destruction of Sennacherib' is than an 'anthology piece' with a piece of criticism which is valuable in alerting the reader to overtones some might well miss without his enthusiastic guidance:

> We are made aware of imperial and military glory, of its flash and ambition, its pride and fall. The Assyrian host challenges the stars and sea, man as against the cosmos, its co-equal and rival. But it is, nevertheless, of earth; subject like leaves to the rhythm of the seasons, summer and autumn, life and death...
> Much of Byron, apart from his humour, is here compacted: his love of the stellar universe, of the sea, of animal vigour; his sense of human endeavour in magnificence and crime; the repudiation of militarism, coupled with the soft feeling in 'dew' and 'brow', the forgiveness (as at *Don Juan*, III, 109, on Nero); his life-long devotion to the Old Testament; and his sense of an overruling – to use his favourite term – 'Deity.'[8]

Nathan was overjoyed at being invited to collaborate with the celebrated young poet, but he was not so overwhelmed that he

170

dared not make suggestions, or even fairly comprehensive criticisms and Byron was always prepared to listen. 'The Harp the Monarch Minstrel Swept' originally ended with the fifth line of the second verse. This made the second verse five lines shorter than the first. Nathan objected to the resulting lack of balance:

I

The Harp the Monarch Minstrel swept,
  The King of men, the loved of Heaven!
Which Music hallowed while she wept
  O'er tones her heart of hearts had given –
Redoubled be her tears, its chords are riven!
It softened men of iron mould,
  It gave them virtues not their own;
No ear so dull, no soul so cold,
  That felt not – fired not to the tone,
Till David's Lyre grew mightier than his Throne!

II

It told the triumphs of our King,
  It wafted glory to our God;
It made our gladdened valleys ring,
  The cedars bow, the mountains nod;
Its sound aspired to Heaven and there abode!

When Nathan asked for a longer second verse Byron protested, 'Why I have sent you to Heaven – it would be difficult to go further.' Nathan relates that 'My attention for a few moments was called away to some other person, and His Lordship whom I had hardly missed, exclaimed – "Here, Nathan, I have brought you down again", and he immediately presented me with the beautiful and sublime lines which conclude the melody':

Since then, though heard on earth no more,
  Devotion and her daughter Love
Still bid the bursting spirit soar
  To sounds that seem as from above,
In dreams that day's broad light cannot remove.[9]

Michael Cooke describes this as 'a near-mystical statement' and adds that 'Even allowing for Byron's usual fluency in composition the prompt and flawless execution of these last five lines of the

171

poem which bring us "down again" from heaven may well betoken the ripeness of the humanistic idea in his mind.'[10]

In allowing his name to be associated with Jewish songs and a Jewish composer Byron showed his lack of prejudice. He would have no truck with anti-semitism. He was extremely kind to Nathan, particularly on an occasion when Douglas Kinnaird (who had initiated the project) offended the musician by hinting that he might cheat Byron over the standard of production of *Hebrew Melodies*. Nathan wrote in praise of Byron's lack of prejudice in matters of race:

> He was entirely free from the prevalent prejudice against that unhappy and oppressed race of men. [the Jews] On this subject he has frequently remarked that he deemed the existence of the Jews as a distinct race of men the wonderful instance of the effects of persecution. Had they been kindly or even honestly dealt with in the early ages of their dispersion they might, in his Lordship's opinion, have amalgamated with society in the same manner as all other sects and parties have done... This liberality of sentiment was not confined to the Jews alone. His Lordship often regretted the truly distressed state of Ireland. Two thirds of that unhappy country, he observed, had laboured for ages to obtain that liberty which was only extended to a third part of its population and he hoped a time would arrive when religious distinctions in political matters would not prove a barrier to preferment in that country, till which period Ireland would never cordially coalesce with Great Britain but continue as it had been the scene of bloodshed, anarchy and confusion.[11]

Jeffery Vail observes that 'By writing songs that purported to express the feelings of the Jews, a people at least as oppressed and defeated as the Irish, Byron was enabled like Moore to indulge his penchants both for melancholy poetry, and for the advocacy of the downtrodden.' He also remarks that the *Hebrew Melodies* were '...a natural result of his admiration for Moore's work.'[12]

G. Wilson Knight writes illuminatingly on Byron's attitude to the Jews:

> In *The Age of Bronze* Byron's attack on international Jewry corresponds to Alcibiades' reference to 'usury that makes the Senate ugly' (III, V, 101). Byron saw banks beginning to rule the world. But his Jewish sympathies were strong. In 1814 he told Isaac Nathan ... that if the occasion presented itself he was prepared to join in action for the liberation of the Holy Lands. The poems themselves [*Hebrew Melodies*],

made for Hebrew tunes, have been welcomed by the chronicler of Zionism, Nahum Sokolov, as authentic Zionist songs: 'There is in his work an intensity of grief and yearning ... a tenderness which makes him comparable only to the sweet Hebrew muse of Jehuda Halevi. Zionist poetry owes more to Byron than to any other Gentile poet.'[13]

Mrs. Byron's turbulent boy: Byron at the time he left Harrow.
(The National Historical Museum, Athens)

Byron in 1814, engraving by Robert Graves, after oil painting by Thomas Phillips.

Newstead Abbey by R Harraden. (Nottingham City Museums and Galleries: Newstead Abbey)
'Newstead and I stand or fall together. I have fixed my heart on it.' Byron

Wordsworth by Edward Nashe, 1818.
(by permission of the Wordsworth Trust)
'The young man will do something if he goes on.'
Wordsworth on *Hours of Idleness*

Lady Caroline Lamb by Mary Anne Knight.
(Nottingham City Museums and Galleries:
Newstead Abbey)
'A month's absence would make us rational.'
Byron

Lady Melbourne by Thomas Lawrence.
(by kind permission of Lord Ralph Kerr,
Melbourne Hall, Derbyshire)
*'She is the cleverest of women and her heart I
know to be of the kindest.'* Byron

Charles James Fox. (National Portrait Gallery)
*'Sheridan and Fox - these are great names. I may
emulate, I can never equal them.'* Byron

The Hon Augusta Leigh by Sir George Hayter.
(© Trustees of the British Museum)
'My Sister! my sweet Sister!' Byron

Lady Byron, engraving by R Page, 1816.
'Every lady could manage my Lord except my Lady' William Fletcher

Napoleon after the Battle of Lodi, 1796, by Appiani. (By permission of the Accademia di Belle Arti di Brera, Milan)
'Since he, miscall'd the Morning Star, Nor man nor fiend hath fall'n so far.'

Holland House. (V & A Images/Victoria and Albert Museum)
'At Holland House I am always convinced that there will be Revolution before breakfast.'
Lady Caroline Lamb

15

AUGUSTA

'There is not a more angelic being upon earth'[1]

Augusta Leigh has received cavalier treatment over the years from many writers on Byron but not from her biographers, Peter Gunn and the Bakewells, who know more about her than most. Those who dismiss her as dull and feather-headed might consider whether Byron could have written such poetry as the opening lines to *Lara* for a feather-headed woman. Augusta's character was firm (albeit gentle). She had a lively humour, an all-embracing kindness and a compelling charm. She was both undemanding and unselfish but she had the courage to defend those she loved and to stand up to those who attacked her where she felt strongly that they were unjust. She had religious principles but did not always live up to them. George's neglect and his frequent absences provided the reason for her need of Byron's love and the opportunity for enjoying the company of her lover. In all else she was a loyal and faithful wife.

Michael and Melissa Bakewell have discovered new facts about her upbringing. For seven years from the age of six she was placed by her grandmother, Lady Holdernesse, in the care of the family chaplain. For this purpose the Reverend and Mrs Alderson were given the living at Eckington in Yorkshire – a remote village where Jack Byron would be unlikely to visit his daughter. It was hoped that the elopement of her mother might be forgotten if Augusta was not in London to remind all Lady Holdernesse's friends of the scandal. The Aldersons, it was felt, would instil in the child moral principles to combat any tendency to emulate her mother.

Brought up with the Alderson children she would have a more natural childhood than alone with her grandmother in Holdernesse House. Mrs Alderson was a motherly woman and Augusta became fond of her daughter Mary. The Bakewells point out that Augusta's life at Eckington must have developed her talent for homemaking and 'her readiness to roll up her sleeves and scrub and scour'.[2] It may also explain the shyness remarked on by her step-sister, Mary Osborne, who, with the rest of her step-family, welcomed her affectionately on her return to London.

When the Prince Regent's gift of the rambling, unpretentious house at Six Mile Bottom, near Newmarket, made it possible for Augusta to marry her George 'she seems to have been blissfully content'. ('She married a fool,' was Byron's comment, 'But she *would* have him...'[3]). George was often absent 'with so many demands on him from the Prince, the regiment, the turf and his friends'.[4] Instead of scolding her husband or repining, Augusta dealt sensibly and intelligently with her unenviable situation. 'She consoled herself ... by writing long letters, sketching and reading; she also began to compile a commonplace book.'[5] Though she was far from the opera, the balls, the milliners and all that constituted the social round she was used to in London her half-brother, Francis Osborne, and his family were within visiting distance at Gogmagog, near Cambridge, and her cousins the Duke and Duchess of Rutland were often at Cheveley, near Newmarket, where the Duke had his racing stables.

The Bakewells describe the love and concern shown Augusta by her step-family. The Chichesters invited her to Stratton Street for her first confinement. Lady Carlisle sent frocks for her little girls. The Duchess of Rutland came to make sure she could manage when George was in the Peninsula during the Corunna Campaign. Augusta consulted her family in every dilemma – a Baby George had arrived, the little girls were unwell, George's debts were mounting and there was not always enough money for paying the servants and the household bills – even discussing with Lady Gertrude Sloane Stanley her early plans for going abroad with Byron. When George was away Augusta was without a carriage. Escape abroad with the brother who adored her must have been tempting indeed. The family were deeply relieved when she decided against the scheme.

In face of all her troubles and privations Augusta did not give way to despondency. It was her serenity, commonsense and playfulness that appealed to Byron. 'One of Augusta's unexpected talents' we are told by the Bakewells, 'was her gift for mimicry and Byron delighted in her irreverent and accurate impersonations, egging her on to do his valet, William Fletcher, Lady Melbourne, Madame de Staël, Lord Carlisle, and, best of all, the heavily accented English of her grandmother, Lady Holdernesse.'[6]

In the spring of 1813 Augusta confessed to Byron that financial problems were destroying her peace of mind. He was mortified at being unable to give her immediate help since Claughton, the prospective purchaser of Newstead Abbey, had not yet paid the deposit on the purchase, let alone the full price. Eventually Claughton disgorged £5000 on account which enabled Byron to clear some of George's debts and to lend Hodgson a sum which would enable him to settle with his creditors and enable him to marry. (Byron had earlier travelled overnight to persuade the mother of Hodgson's beloved to allow her daughter to marry the future Provost of Eton, assuring her that he would pay off Hodgson's debts.)

By November Byron and Augusta found their passion for each other's company growing stronger than their doubts. They used crosses in their letters to convey feelings too strong to be expressed in words. Augusta sent him a lock of her hair. Byron was still confiding in Lady Melbourne, whose hope that Frances Webster or even Mary Chaworth-Musters might succeed in detaching him from Augusta must have been fading fast.

Byron's romantic memories of Mary were being replaced by an embarrassing reality. He wrote to Lady Melbourne:

Now for a confidence – my old love of all loves – Mrs – [Chaworth-Musters] ... has written to me *twice* – no *love* but she wants to see me – and though it will be a melancholy interview I shall go – we have hardly met and never been on any intimate terms since her marriage – *he* has been playing the Devil – with all kinds of *vulgar* mistresses – and behaving ill enough in every respect ... she is *unhappy* – she was a spoilt heiress – but has seen little or nothing of the world – very pretty – & once simple in character and clever – but with no peculiar accomplishments – but endeared to me by a thousand childish and singular recollections...[7]

(Byron to Lady Melbourne, 8 January 1814)

He asks for advice. Should he see her? Then writes again:

I hear ... they are to be reconciled ... I have no feelings beyond esteem ... & she still fewer for me ... – evidently she does not desire *him* to know anything of the matter. – 'Like C[aroline]' no more than I am like *Wm* and as far *her* superior as ... Wm is to me in every good and praiseworthy quality.[8]

(Byron to Lady Melbourne, 10 January 1814)

Mary and her husband were not yet to be reconciled but Byron was obsessed with his present 'love of all loves' and had little to offer his old one though he wrote to her kindly and told Augusta she would see Mary in Nottingham.

In December Augusta came to London again and Byron went back with her to Six Mile Bottom. Lady Frances Shelley and her husband, Sir John, came to call on Augusta and Lady Frances wrote:

He is decidedly handsome and can be agreeable. He seems to be easily put out and at times looks terribly savage. [Byron may have *felt* savage because these unexpected visitors were intruding on his precious time with Augusta]. He was very patient with Mrs Leigh's children, who are not in the least in awe of him. He bore their distracting intrusions into his room [where he was writing *The Corsair*] with imperturbable good humour. Mrs Leigh had evidently great moral influence over her brother, who listens to her occasional admonitions with a sort of playful acquiescence.[9]

Back in London in early January he was busy preparing *The Corsair* for publication, writing to John Murray, 'When published let the *Notes* be at the *end* as in the other tales – I shall send some mottoes from Dante for each Canto – and one for the title page tomorrow.'[10] Soon he was writing to Augusta:

My Dearest Augusta – On Sunday or Monday next with leave of your lord and president – you will be *well* & ready to accompany me to Newstead – which you *should* see & I will endeavour to render as comfortable as I can for both our sakes – as to time of stay there – suit your own convenience I am at your disposal – Claughton is I believe inclined to settle – if so – I shall be able to do something further for *yours* & *you* - which I need not say will give me ye greatest pleasure – More news from Mrs – [Chaworth-Musters] *all friendship* – you shall see her – Excuse haste and evil penmanship.[11]

Ever yours
Byron

(Byron to Augusta Leigh, 12 January 1814)

178

Later he asked her:

Can you tell me ... *how much* G[eorge] *owes* – I trust on C[laughto]n's paying the residue – I shall be able to make some arrangement – for *him* – but at all events you & the Children shall be properly taken care of. – what I did for *him* might be seized &tc. anything done for yourself would be safer and more advantageous to both.[12]

(Byron to Augusta Leigh, January 1814)

Augusta was relieved to find her brother able and willing to help her. She was in no way rapacious or prompted by self-interest in her relationship with him but she felt that, as a Byron, she was entitled to some sort of provision if her brother could spare it. Later she wrote quite sharply about George Anson Byron's ungracious resentment over Byron's will (which left to Augusta and her seven children moneys which George Anson believed should have been left to him as heir to the barony). It was not generally understood that the bulk of the legacy would become available to Augusta only after the death of Lady Byron, an event not likely to occur before Augusta's own death. Nevertheless, Augusta became the target for much unfounded jealousy and resentment.

As they drove north from London in Byron's coach they found the roads were already deep in snow. Augusta first saw Newstead Abbey in a heavy snowfall looking more beautiful and romantic than ever. Byron was still trying to sell the Abbey to Claughton and had he succeeded in doing so Augusta's financial difficulties would have been at an end. But, far from encouraging her brother to sell, Augusta begged him to keep 'the dear old Abbey'.

Byron wrote to Murray: '... the roads are impassable and return impossible – for ye. present – which I do not regret as I am much at my ease and *six* and *twenty* complete this day – a very pretty age if it would always last. – Our coals are excellent – our fireplaces large – my cellar full – and my head empty.'[13] He told Hanson: 'Mrs L[eigh] is with me & being in ye. family way – renders it doubly necessary to remain till the roads are quite safe ... we desire our best remembrances to all.'[14] Eventually he revealed to Murray, 'Mrs Leigh is with me – *much* pleased with the place – and less so with me for parting with it.'[15] He even dared to tell Lady Melbourne 'Augusta is here – which renders it much more pleasant – as we never yawn nor disagree – and laugh much more than is suitable to so solid a mansion – and the family shyness makes us more amusing companions to each other – than we could be to anyone else.'[16]

Neither Byron nor Augusta would ever be as happy again. Byron's remark that 'she was not aware her own peril until it was too late'[17] seems the likeliest explanation of the incest if it did occur. That lovemaking occurred is certain but how far it went will never be known. It was, in any case, not the most culpable of misdemeanours. They were half-brother and sister who had never met in childhood. Both were orphaned and both cherished the memory of the father they had shared and lost.

Byron's habit of flaunting his vices laid him open to the worst possible interpretation of his actions and he would later celebrate in verse a theoretically darker side to their relationship, but some of the critics subscribed to theories of his motives which seem the wildest nonsense. Professor Praz remarks on some who even go so far as to claim that Byron's love affair with his half-sister was a plagiarism because Byron committed in reality the crime (of incest) of which René had only conceived the horrible possibility. In a letter to Thomas Moore Byron referred to his love for Augusta not as a 'horrible possibility' or an 'unthinkable crime' but as 'a scrape',[18] which seems to support the case for a mutual surrender to the delight of the moment rather than the pursuit of shocking crime for its own sake or in order to rival Chateaubriand, author of the immensely popular Romantic novel, *René*, published in 1802.

Byron expressed his feeling of guilt combined with delight in the relationship in a poem which he sent to Thomas Moore. This poem, which was not published until after his death, and several later poems and letters addressed to Augusta after his parting from her, together with the 'Opening lines to *Lara*', are the record of a most passionate and loving relationship. It has been suggested that Byron's sexual orientation was not bisexual (as most authorities believe) but wholly directed towards male love objects, so that he was going against his own nature when he made love to women. To anyone familiar with the poems and letters addressed to Augusta the theory that Byron was entirely homosexual seems mistaken. Even G. Wilson Knight, who finds the homosexual side of Byron's nature the finer, repudiates this view:

Whatever the strength of Byron's homosexual instincts there is no question but that heterosexual love often burned in his imagination as, at least for passion as opposed to idealism, the best. Women could attract him fierily. His actual experience with them may never have drawn level with that that he knew ideally with Edleston and physically with Nicolo Giraud; yet again, Mary Chaworth shone from his youth onwards as a star, and his love for Augusta, whatever its exact nature, was probably his most enduring emotion of all.[19]

STANZAS FOR MUSIC

1
I SPEAK not, I trace not, I breathe not thy name,
There is grief in the sound, there is guilt in the fame;
But the tear which now burns on my cheek may impart
The deep thoughts that dwells in that silence of heart.

2
Too brief for our passion, too long for our peace,
Were those hours – can their joy or their bitterness cease?
We repent, we abjure, we will break from our chain, –
We must part, we will fly to – unite it again!

3
Oh! thine be the gladness, and mine be the guilt!
Forgive me, adored one! – forsake, if thou wilt; –
But the heart which I bear shall expire undebased
And *man* shall not break it – whatever *thou* mayst.

4
And stern to the haughty, but humble to thee,
This soul, in its bitterest blackness, shall be;
And our days seem as swift, and our moments more sweet,
With thee by my side, than with worlds at our feet.

5
One sigh of thy sorrow, one look of thy love,
Shall turn me or fix, shall reward or reprove;
And the heartless may wonder at all we resign –
Thy lip shall reply, not to them, but to *mine*.[20]

Once the thaw came they were obliged to end their idyll. They spent a last night together at the Haycock Inn, Wansford, then Augusta went home to Six Mile Bottom and Byron continued on to London.

Bad weather, lack of inclination and a sudden illness suffered

181

by Mary Chaworth-Musters had prevented Byron from meeting her, though Augusta had urged him to go. Mary had been writing to him, obviously unhappy, obviously in need of comfort. Experienced by now in judging the probable effect of his fame on women to whom he was completely unknown he must have suspected that, in spite of her protestations and her indecision over whether to return to her husband or not, a meeting with the famous poet who had once loved her passionately and unavailingly might result in an embarrassing show of feelings he was unable to return. She wrote, in all, as many as fifty letters to him.

Back in London he wrote to Leigh Hunt whom he had visited in Surrey gaol (imprisoned for a libel on the Prince Regent) in April 1813 at the instigation of Thomas Moore:

My dear Sir, I have been snow-bound and thaw-swamped ... in Newstead Abbey ... & have not been four hours returned to London. – Nearly the first use I make of my benumbed fingers is to thank you for yr. very handsome note in the volume you have just put forth [*The Feast of the Poets*] ... you must think me strangely spoiled – or perversely peevish – ever to suspect that any remarks of yours in the spirit of candid criticism could possibly prove unpalatable. – Had they been harsh – instead of being written as they are in the most indelible ink of good Sense & friendly admonition ... as I ... know that you are above any personal bias at least *against* your fellow bards – believe me – they would not have caused a word of remonstrance ... I have always thought the Italians the *only* poetical *moderns*: – our Milton & Spenser & Shakespeare ... are very Tuscan and surely it is far superior to the French School ... I have been regaled at every Inn on the road by lampoons ... in the ministerial gazettes [this was the furore caused by the 'Lines on a Lady Weeping'] ... *The Morning P[ost]* has one copy of devices upon my deformity ... another upon my Atheism ... and another very down-rightly says I am the Devil (*boiteux* they might have added) and a rebel and what not.'[21]

(Byron to Leigh Hunt, 9 February 1814)

To Lady Melbourne he wrote, 'Murray took fright and shuffled in my absence ... but I made him instantly replace the lines as before – it was no time to shrink now...'[22] A few days later he wrote on another subject – again refusing to 'shuffle' or 'shrink'. Having told Lady Melbourne that she was wrong in thinking that Augusta had tried to persuade him to put an end to his visits to Melbourne House, he added, '... you will easily suppose – that –

182

twined as she is round my heart in every possible manner – dearest & deepest in my hope & my memory – still I am not easy.' But he went on: 'I have not lost all self-command... I am here – and here I *will* remain [London] – but it cost me some struggles.'[23] (Byron to Lady Melbourne, 21 February 1814)

Annabella had asked his opinion of Lady Melbourne and he had replied, 'I am not ... an impartial judge of Lady M – but she is doubtless in talent a superior – a *supreme* woman – & her heart I know to be of the kindest ... Her defects I never could perceive as her society makes me forget them & everything else for the time – I do love that woman (*filially* or *fraternally*) better than any being on earth.'[24] (Byron to Annabella Milbanke, 12 February 1814)

Annabella cannot have been pleased with this reply.

At the same time Byron was doing his best to recommend Hobhouse to Lady Holland:

I can I think venture to prophesy that the more you allow my friend Hobhouse to become acquainted with you the more you will like him ... he is sincere active & unalterable in his friendships – God knows – I have but too often tried his patience very severely. – Nothing can give me greater pleasure than your partiality in his favour?[25]
(Byron to Lady Holland, 12 February 1814)

In March he was writing to James Hogg, the Ettrick Shepherd: 'You seem to be a plain-spoken man, Mr Hogg, and I really do not like you the worse for it. I can't write verses, and yet you want a bit of my poetry for your book ... You shall have the verses ... Poetry must always exist, like drink, where there is a demand for it ... You love Southey, forsooth – I am sure Southey loves nobody but himself...'[26] (Byron to James Hogg, Albany, 24 March [1814])

Byron was surprised at the virulence of the continuing attacks on him over the 'Lines to a Lady Weeping'. He told Lady Melbourne, 'I have that within me that bounds against opposition'[27] and expressed to Samuel Rogers his angry determination:

All the sayings and doings in the world shall not make me utter another word of reconciliation to any thing that breathes. I shall bear what I can and what I cannot I shall resist. The worst thing they could do is to exclude me from society. I have never courted it, nor, I may add, in the general sense of the word, enjoyed it – and 'there is a world elsewhere.'[28]
(To Samuel Rogers, 16 February 1814)

He would not make any attempt to suppress the attacks on him, having earlier written to Lady Melbourne, '*Prosecute?* ... Oh No – I am a great friend to liberty of the press – even at the expense of myself – besides – do I not deserve all this? and am I not in reality much worse...[29]

Claughton having now relinquished the deposit on Newstead and given up the purchase, Byron was able to forward to Scrope Davies the final repayment on his loan. At the same time he was sending heartfelt condolences to the Hanson family on the death of the kindly Mrs Hanson. In April he was lamenting the fall of Napoleon and '...the utter wreck of a mind which I thought superior even to Fortune.'[30] He adds a comment which has some bearing on his later reaction to the break-up of his own marriage:

> It is said the Empress had refused to follow him [to Elba] – this is not well – men will always fall away from men – but it may generally be observed that no change of Fortune – no degradation of rank or even character will detach a woman who has truly loved – unless there has been some provocation or misconduct towards herself on the part of the man.[31]
>
> (To Annabella Milbanke, Albany, 20 April 1814)

George Leigh now went off to Yorkshire and Augusta summoned Byron to her side. He had just moved into his new apartments in Albany but he went to Six Mile Bottom and stayed five days with her. Soon after this Augusta gave birth to another daughter who was christened Elizabeth Medora.

Byron, however, was trying to make up his mind whether to visit the Milbankes at Seaham. In May and June he was writing *Lara*. Then Moore arrived in London and together they enjoyed the excitement and the revelry of the 'Summer of the Sovereigns' when the Czar, the King of Prussia, Metternich, Marshal Blücher and lesser dignitaries from Europe converged on London to celebrate the banishment of Bonaparte to Elba. Byron liked going to the theatre with Moore and was enthusiastic over the acting of Kean.

In May he sent the Leighs another £3000, which Augusta found embarrassing. He wrote to her:

> I did it on your account – & that I would do for anyone I know in a similar situation – he need not consider himself under the least obligation – ... I must ... get *you* out of debt – and in the mean time ... let him

184

think well of some plan for regulating his expenditure – I will have
no interest – no bond – no repayment – unless his father left him so
rich as to make it easy & pleasant to himself – he can then repay it
or not as he likes – I am sure I don't care – if any accident happened
to George – I am more deeply interested ... I am also unconnected &
less incumbered ... and then, consider the *children* – & my Georgiana
in particular.[32]

(To Augusta Leigh, 24 June 1814)

He makes no mention of Elizabeth Medora who was then nearly
two months old and it was not until 3 July when he returned to
Six Mile Bottom and saw Augusta's baby daughter for the first
time. There they discussed arrangements for a three week holiday
at Hastings with all the children. Francis Hodgson, who was in
Hastings with his bride-to-be, found them a house by the sea to
rent and they were joined there by George Anson Byron, heir to
the title. In the course of a happy seaside interlude Byron and
Augusta came to the conclusion that he must marry. For Augusta
this was the only course which would bring 'redemption' for them
both. She wanted him to choose a shy young friend of hers, Lady
Charlotte Leveson-Gower, who dithered charmingly for a while,
then announced that her family had other plans for her.

Augusta and the children accompanied him back to Newstead
and it was there that he composed his tentative proposal to Annabella
and received her very determined acceptance. Augusta tried to
persuade him to travel straight up to Seaham but he was determined
to see Hanson first and settle his financial affairs. He did not
despair of Claughton's renewing his offer for Newstead the sale
of which was necessary to produce the basis for a generous settle-
ment for Annabella and her children. He and Augusta spent
their last hours together at Newstead regretting the loss of the
'dear old Abbey' and the imminent parting from each other. They
carved their names on an ancient elm in the park. From now on
Augusta did everything she could to persuade Byron to throw
himself wholeheartedly into preparations for his marriage. She
wanted her beloved brother to be happy, and so Annabella must
be happy too.

Note

1. It has often been assumed that the child Augusta bore that spring was Byron's daughter. Byron never behaved to Augusta's little girl, Elizabeth Medora, as if he knew himself to be her father. He showed no more interest in her than in the rest of Augusta's children. At the time when she was born he adored Augusta. It is likely that if he had believed the child was his he would have stayed with her for the birth and would have asked for news of the child and taken an interest in her health and her education as he did later with his other daughters. And surely Augusta would have rejoiced with him over the birth of the little girl and later sent him bulletins about her progress.

   George Leigh never questioned that the child was his, absolutely discounted the rumours about Augusta and Byron, and made no difficulties about his wife's staying at Piccadilly Terrace to look after Byron when he was ill after Lady Byron had left for Seaham. It is not impossible that he was prepared to barter his wife in return for financial help from Byron but Byron was still in debt and the failure of the sale of Newstead Abbey made the benefits to be obtained from him in the future quite uncertain.

   The only evidence that Elizabeth Medora might have been Byron's daughter is the letter from Byron to Lady Melbourne: 'Oh! but it is "worth while" – I can't tell you why – and it is *not* an *Ape* and if it is – that must be my fault – however, I will positively reform'.[1]

   This has been read as a reference to the superstition that the child of incest would be a monster. It could also apply to another superstition – that the appearance and character of an unborn child could be influenced by the experiences of the mother during her pregnancy.

   Hary-O tells a story (which illustrates how terrified pregnant women of that period were of evil influences on their babies) about Lady Stuart, wife of the British Ambassador in Vienna, running away from an extremely ugly Austrian count for fear her unborn child would resemble him. She sent for a famous Austrian beauty, Marie Branner, and paid to be allowed to gaze at her for an hour to banish the image of Count Trauttsmandorf from her mind.

   The Bakewells' comment on the paternity of Elizabeth Medora is practical and to the point:

   > The widely held belief that Byron was unquestionably the father of her fourth child is based on the chivalrous assumption that Augusta, out of romantic consideration for Byron, would not have let George make love to her; but this was not the case. Augusta did not, as Annabella later put it, suffer from 'moral idiocy from birth', but took life as it came and was generally inclined to settle for the easy way out. She had slept with both Byron and George. She would, in any case, have regarded it as her conjugal duty not to deny herself to George, and to do so would only have provoked an unnecessary scene.[2]

186

16

CHILDE HAROLD AND THE PRINCESS OF PARALLELOGRAMS

She is a very superior woman, and very little spoiled, which is strange in an heiress – a girl of twenty – a peeress that is to be, in her own right – an only child and a savante, who has always had her own way. She is a poetess – a mathematician – and yet withal, very kind, and generous, and gentle, with very little pretension.[1]

In most respects Byron held to this opinion of Annabella throughout the marriage. In March 1816 he defended his wife from the criticisms of his friends, writing to Thomas Moore:

> I must set you right in one point, however. The fault was *not* – no, nor even the misfortune – in my 'choice' (unless in *choosing at all*) – for I do not believe – and I must say it, in the very dregs of all this bitter business – that there ever was a better, or even a brighter, a kinder, or a more aimiable and agreeable being than Lady B. I never had, nor can have, any reproach to make her, while with me. Where there is blame, it belongs to myself, and, if I cannot redeem, I must bear it.[2]
>
> (Byron to Thomas Moore, 8 March 1816)

This testimony by Byron must be accepted. Lady Byron bears little guilt for what happened during the marriage. Byron takes full blame for its collapse. This is not to say that he believed her perfect. Before he asked her to marry him the second time he had realised that he was wrong in thinking her unspoiled:

> ... she seems to have been spoiled – not as children usually are – but systematically Clarissa Harlowed into an awkward kind of correctness.[3]

187

This was perceptive. Annabella had been treated like a little queen by her elderly and adoring parents. Judith Milbanke encouraged what she described as Annabella's 'very natural manners' and allowed her daughter to criticise the people around her and to write 'characters' of friends in her journal.

Annabella was very fond of her father who could be swayed into giving her her own way by affectionate cajolery. Her mother was naturally dictatorial and Annabella reacted by telling her she was old-fashioned and addressing her disparagingly as 'Old Lady' or even 'Old Woman'.

An upbringing such as that of the orphaned Augusta at Eckington might have dispelled some of Annabella's complacency but the constant praise she received from family, friends and servants at Seaham could only increase it. Before she was despatched to London for her first season on the marriage market, an older cousin wrote of her prospects: 'It is not every day that she is likely to meet with a *Mind* which ought to claim kindred with one so superior as hers.'[4] Later, Lady Milbanke told her daughter: 'Your character is like *Proof-Spirits* – not fit for common use. I could almost wish the tone of it lowered nearer the level of us every-day people.'[5]

It was hardly surprising after years of such adulation that by the end of her fourth season in London Annabella had rejected no fewer than five eligible suitors, including Lord Byron. Her only remaining *prétendant* at that time was Hugh Montgomery, brother of one of her dearest friends, but no very eligible parti compared with 'the first poet of the age'.

If she was in love with Byron at this stage she was not prepared to admit it. Her ambition was to save his soul and she saw herself as his guide and mentor.

This is not reprehensible. She was young and inexperienced and failed to understand what she was taking on in trying to influence so complex a character as Byron. Her tragedy was her inability to admit a weakness in herself or even a mistake. She was capable of changing neither her attitude nor her behaviour.

By now Byron had become aware of her strong belief in her own infallibility and prophesied that this belief '... will, or may, lead her into some egregious blunder.'[6] The 'egregious blunder' of her life was her acceptance of his proposal. It is hard to understand why, with his eyes open, Byron allowed himself his own 'egregious blunder' in offering to marry a girl with whom he had so little in common. He 'could love anything on earth that appeared to wish it'[7] (a quality not shared by his wife-to-be) and he did develop a sort of love for Annabella, but his early encomium on her spoke not of love but of esteem – 'I never saw a woman whom I *esteemed* so much'[8]). In renewing his addresses to her after his rejection he was ignoring what he had earlier seen clearly – that Annabella required 'all the cardinal virtues'[9] (some of which he might claim, but certainly not all). Annabella was more concerned with esteem than with love. If she had remained with Byron this might conceivably have changed. The separation fixed her on a path towards piety and virtue rather than love.

It is surprising that they ever became engaged. Their reluctance to commit themselves is striking. In August 1814 Annabella informed Byron quite firmly that she ought not to choose him as her companion in life. 'Very well,' he replied, 'now we can talk of something else'. By September she was ready to snap up a tentative renewal of his courtship, treating it as a direct offer of marriage.

The Milbankes were pleased because Annabella seemed happy but they were apprehensive, as well they might be. Their daughter's unrealistic attitude to her conquest appears in a letter she wrote in November to her friend and confidante, Lady Gosford:

After having had nearly 'the world before me where to choose' I have fixed with mature judgement on the person most calculated to support me in the journey to immortality ... for the blessings we have both received ... we will offer our gratitude to Heaven *together*, during as many years as may be spared to us.'[10]

In making this astonishing forecast of Byron's conversion to her own brand of piety Annabella was busy investing him with the qualities she required in a husband instead of examining with a clear regard the real man with whom she proposed to spend her life.

The real man was busy trying to resolve the question of his debts. He was determined to arrange a proper settlement for Annabella and her children but this depended entirely on the sale of Newstead Abbey. Hanson, as usual, was dilatory. But the Milbankes expected Byron's visit and made it known that they had hoped he would arrive before the departure of Lord Wentworth, Annabella's uncle, who had travelled to Seaham on purpose to meet her future husband. Byron knew the Milbankes hoped Lord Wentworth would leave his fortune to Annabella (who would eventually inherit the title) but he had no intention of dashing up to Seaham before he had organised his own affairs. He was finally obliged to set off to visit his bride-to-be. 'It was very foolish dragging me out of town before my lawyer had arrived.'[11]

Seaham was a village on the bleak east coast where the Milbankes led a cosy provincial existence full of private family jokes, teasing each other about food and visits to the lavatory, taking part in local politics, and parading their strict views on piety and religion. It was no very fit milieu for Annabella's wayward genius of a lover. On one of his visits he wrote to Thomas Moore, 'I must go to tea. – damn tea! I wish it was Kinnaird's brandy.'[12] He wrote more ominously to Lady Melbourne:

Do you know I have great doubts – if this will be a marriage now. – her disposition is the very reverse of *our* imaginings – she is overrun with fine feelings – scruples about herself & *her* disposition (I suppose in fact she means mine) and to crown all is taken ill once every 3 days with I know not what – but the day before and the day after she seems well – looks & eats well & is cheerful & confiding & in short like any other person in good health & spirits. – A few days ago she made one *scene* – not altogether out of C[aroline]'s style – it was too long and too trifling in fact for me to transcribe – but it did me no good – in the article of conversation however she has improved with a vengeance – but I don't much admire these same agitations upon slight occasions. – I don't know – but I think it by no means impossible you will see me in town soon – I can only interpret these things one way – & merely wait to be certain to make my obeisances and 'exit singly.' I hear of nothing but 'feeling' from morning till night – except from Sir Ralph with whom I go on to admiration – Ly. M[ilbanke] too is pretty well – but I am never sure of A[nnabella] – for a moment – the least word – and you know I rattle on through thick & thin (always however avoiding anything I think can offend her favourite notions) if only to prevent me from yawning – the least word – or alteration of tone – has some inference drawn from it – sometimes we are too much alike – & then again too unlike – this comes of *system* – & squaring her notions to the Devil knows what – for my part I have lately had recourse to the eloquence of *action* (which Demosthenes calls the first part of oratory) & find it succeeds very well & makes her very quiet which gives me some hopes of the efficacy of the 'calming process' so renowned in '*our* philosophy.' – In fact and entre nous it is really amusing – she is like a child in that respect – and quite *caressable* into kindness and

190

good humour – though I don't think her temper *bad* at any time – but very *self*-tormenting – and anxious – and romantic. ————— In short – it is impossible to foresee how this will end *now* – anymore than 2 years ago – if there is a break – it shall be *her* doing not mine.

ever yrs. truly

B

(Byron to Lady Melbourne, 14 November 1814)[13]

The 'calming process' led Annabella to send her lover away, cutting short his visit because she feared his presence in the house before the wedding ceremony might result in some dangerous impropriety. Before being sent away Byron seems to have got on very well with Annabella's parents.

The engaged couple wrote each other affectionate letters: 'My Heart – We are thus far separated – but after all one mile is as bad as a thousand.'[14] (16 November 1814). 'Well but – sweet Heart – do write & love me – and regard me as thine'.[15] (23 November 1814). Annabella was equally loving in her replies.

But Byron felt himself 'Cold and comfortless as Charity', as he called at Six Mile Bottom on his way back to London from Seaham and even contemplated withdrawing from the engagement. For the next few weeks Annabella, terrified that he might abandon her, wrote repentant letters to him begging him to forgive her and assuring him that she would be all he could wish in a bride. Unfortunately for her, all he could wish as his companion in life was Augusta, Annabella's antithesis in almost every respect.

Hobhouse held that part of Byron's fascination could doubtless be ascribed to '... the entire self-abandonment, the incautious, it may be said, the dangerous sincerity of his private conversation.' Lady Blessington wrote of him: 'The more I see of Byron the more I am convinced that all he says and does should be judged more leniently than the sayings and doings of others – as his proceed from the impulse of the moment and never from premeditated malice. He cannot resist expressing whatever comes into his mind.'[16] His friends agreed that he was 'true-spoken' but deplored his complete lack of discretion. Such a man should never have married one of Shakespeare's 'lords and owners of their faces'. It was fortunate for Lady Byron that she possessed a charm which surrounded her for the rest of her life, after the separation, with a circle of admiring 'stewards of her excellence'.

Byron became fond of Annabella and was often playful with

191

her. They were even reported to be an affectionate couple. But in the end even Hobhouse came to believe that Byron had behaved very badly to his wife.

On reaching London Byron began to hustle Mr Hanson into preparing the marriage settlements. Sir Ralph was in financial difficulties. Byron wrote:

> I know nothing of her fortune, & I am told that her father is ruined, but my own will, when my Rochdale arrangements are closed, be sufficient for us both, my debts are not £25,000 p[oun]ds & the deuce is in it, if with R[ochdale] & the surplus of N[ewstead] [which he still hoped to sell] I could not contrive to be as independent as half the peerage.[17]

Hanson delayed matters so long that Byron was afraid the marriage would fall through. He proposed to settle £60,000 (or £3,500 a year) on Annabella and her children, the sale of Newstead to supply the requisite capital. Hanson thought £2,500 a year would be perfectly adequate but Byron insisted that it must be done generously. Hanson told him he found the Milbankes grasping. When the sale of Newstead fell through once again, Byron offered to release Annabella from the engagement or to postpone the marriage. For Annabella and her parents such a postponement was out of the question and Byron felt obliged to fulfil their expectations. Byron knew that Annabella would eventually inherit her uncle's fortune, in all probability, and he needed to marry a 'Golden Dolly'. In the short run Annabella was no such thing.

When Annabella told him the bells in Durham had rung a peal for their marriage in the belief that it had already taken place, he replied that the bells were in a pestilent hurry. Annabella was distraught, for she saw that her parents were becoming tight-lipped at the bridegroom's delay. The wedding cake went mouldy and a new one had to be baked before Byron and Hobhouse finally arrived at Seaham after a loitering journey taking in Six Mile Bottom and Cambridge – 'Never,' wrote Hobhouse, 'was lover less in haste.'[18] After the marriage ceremony his words were more ominous: 'I felt as if I had buried a friend.'[19]

Byron had wanted to wait two years – during which time he would have considered himself an engaged man. If the Milbankes had agreed to a postponement until both Rochdale and Newstead (or, at least, Newstead) could be sold, the feeling both at Seaham and in the carriage bearing Hobhouse and Byron to the North might have been happier. Travelling to be married in the knowledge that Hanson had completed the marriage settlements and that the sale of Newstead had provided 'a surplus for necessities' Byron might have felt the rejoicing and the pealing of the bells to be appropriate.

17

THE MARRIAGE

'...*I mean to reform most thoroughly & become "a good man and true" ... I will endeavour to make your niece happy...*'[1]

If one excludes the practical problems which wrecked the Byron marriage one is still left with the incompatibility which would have made its success unlikely even if everything had gone smoothly. Byron was unpleasantly surprised when Annabella informed him in a letter from Seaham that she had engaged a cook for them. Byron had no intention of sitting down to regular meals with his wife and though he enjoyed dining with his friends he did not go in for formal social events at home and did not invite ladies. He had no desire to change his ways in this respect.

Both of them had an abnormal attitude towards food and hers would end after the separation in what sounds very like bulimia. Edith Mayne comments on Annabella's love of certain foods:

> Her letters are pervaded by a theme which so often reappears – even in the after-stages of the Separation-Drama – that it is worth dwelling on for a moment. That theme is mutton-chops. From Wetherby, in this February, she told Sir Ralph that she had dined on 'Fleecy mutton-chops'. Enough, one would think, to make her order anything else when she got to Grantham next day. But no. She ordered mutton-chops, ate 'twice two and frightened the waiters'. And afterwards mutton chops are so often reported on for praise or blame that we cannot but recall Byron's fantastic dislike to seeing a woman eat, and remember too that (as he wrote to Lady Melbourne during his first stay at Seaham as Annabella's betrothed) she 'was never well for two days together'. It does emerge from her letters that she was inclined to be greedy. We

195

read of her eating too many peaches (with her own commentary of 'Beast!') of a goose-pie being clamoured for both by her and 'B' ... All through Annabella's correspondence with her parents, especially after the separation, food plays a large part, with a frequent corollary of 'biliousness' and its varying remedies.[2]

To find that she was not to dine regularly with her husband must have been insulting to her pride and produced a feeling of loneliness and rejection. She was used to the pleasant meal times in her parents' house. Nor was she perceptive enough to work out for herself that, having married a genius she ought perhaps to try to adapt herself to his ways and not to repine. It is interesting to learn that Lady Noel was more tolerant than her daughter of Byron's odd behaviour – at Seaham she would always arrange for him to eat alone if he wished.

Again, if Annabella had allowed him the freedom to go to London or to Six Mile Bottom on his own after the honeymoon at Halnaby and then let him consort with his friends quite freely as he had done before the marriage, he would probably have changed his ways and invited her to join him. But this would have required superhuman wisdom and self-sacrifice on the part of the young bride.

He introduced his friends to her and she expected him to meet her own, who were for the most part pious middle-aged ladies. He claimed to have sometimes returned home to find his wife sitting with '...half a dozen Old Blues who thought a man damned if he made a joke.'[3] Annabella had been worried, as a girl, about being in the same room as Lady Holland even though she was determined to reject any introduction. Now she was actually introduced to that lady and expected to be friends with her. She detested Lady Melbourne who was one of Byron's dearest friends.

With goodwill and forbearance they might have dealt successfully with these problems but the financial difficulties in which Byron found himself as a result of marrying before his financial affairs were satisfactorily arranged, proved disastrous.

When Byron and his bride moved into the grand house at 13 Piccadilly Terrace his creditors thought he had married money and descended on him with writs. In April Lord Wentworth died and the creditors assumed that Lady Byron had inherited. Instead, every penny went to Lady Milbanke for her lifetime. The Milbankes (from now on to be known as the Noels) could offer no immediate

196

financial aid as the legacy was tied up and it would be some time before it became available. Sir Ralph did not manage to pay the agreed £6000 advance on the modest dowry agreed by the lawyers until after the terrible year of financial disasters, and the arrival of the bailiffs. Distraught with shame, Byron tried to dispel the feeling of disgrace by drinking heavily and taking laudanum. Perhaps as a result of these excesses he fell ill with some sort of neurological complaint possibly connected with his lameness, the symptoms of which were headaches and bouts of uncontrollable irritation. Augusta remarked how one eye appeared much smaller than the other.

Augusta tried to soothe him and Annabella made little of their financial problems. This was admirable in her, but irritating for Byron who felt the marriage responsible for all his tribulations. He wanted sympathy, not stoicism. All the same, they were reported to be an affectionate couple and some of Byron's friends thought they were too inseparable. This changed when Annabella became pregnant and when Byron took on responsibilities at Drury Lane Theatre. Annabella objected to Byron's interest in the theatre and took to referring to him disparagingly as 'The Manager'. Her objections were proved to have some weight when Byron confessed to her that he had had a brief affair with one of the actresses, for which she forgave him.

The attempt at disposing of Rochdale and Newstead in July 1815 fell through when neither property reached the reserve price. By November a bailiff was sleeping in the house. Byron told Annabella he must break up the establishment and threatened to go abroad alone. Augusta-Ada was born in late December and the Noels offered them refuge at Kirkby Mallory or at Seaham. Byron suggested to Annabella that she should settle on a date for her departure with the child as soon as convenient to her. This was communicated to Annabella in a note and caused angry remonstrance from her. However, Byron believed this difference was resolved and he reported later that he and his wife had lived together on conjugal terms up to the day of her departure. This is borne out by the two playful and loving letters Annabella sent to him, one during the journey and one from Kirkby Mallory. Byron said he would join her there in the near future. Before he could do so a letter arrived from Sir Ralph Noel announcing that his daughter wanted a separation.

These are the bare bones of the story of the marriage. Over the years a superstructure of comment and assertion has been built on this basis, most of which is supported solely by the testimony of Lady Byron and her confidants (of whom there were many). Byron's *Memoirs* were burned in the fireplace at 50 Albemarle Street, unread by most of the perpetrators of this action. Thus Byron's side of the story was not only suppressed but destroyed. Relating the story of the marriage which has been told and re-told over the years is equivalent to accepting the evidence of the injured party in a divorce case without hearing the evidence for the defence, which is unjust.

[Extracts from Harriet Beecher Stowe's *Vindication of Lady Byron*: an account of the marriage conveyed to her by Lady Byron in 1851, will be found in the appendix.]

18

ANNABELLA THROUGH THE LOOKING GLASS

'Augusta ... speaks of my conduct as that of an Angel.'[1]

One cannot avoid the impression that throughout the marriage Annabella was a kind of Alice in Wonderland, lost in a world she was unable to understand, and lacking the common sense that enabled Alice to deal with all the anomalies and the wonders she encountered. Annabella completely misunderstood her husband:

> ...founding her opinions on sundry playful paradoxes of which a total inapprehension of irony and humour of any kind prevented her from appreciating the true value. It is true that Lord Byron upon discovering that his new companion did not understand him so entirely as his old friends, should have desisted from those extravagances of expression and manner which were set down to the account of a depraved mind rejoicing in the contemplation of every enormity.[2]

Byron's friend, William Harness, explains Byron's moods. Talking of Byron as he behaved in normal circumstances he says, 'He had a childish weakness for dramatic effect and excitement and indulged in fantastic rhapsodies full of tragic extravagance. If paid no attention he soon stopped.'[3] Augusta knew how to handle her brother's wild flights. She simply laughed at them and thus teased him into a better frame of mind. Annabella came to the conclusion that her huband was depraved. It is difficult to imagine how she got through the year of marriage with its loving as well as its difficulties if this is the conviction she was forming while she was with Byron. One can only wonder how she later interpreted his going to Greece.

Hobhouse explained how mistaken she was:

His friends had long been acquainted with his singular love of the marvellous in morals which Lord Byron evinced in his conversation and his compositions, but which he was so far from carrying into his own conduct that no man was ever more commonplace than himself in an habitual display of kindness, generosity, and all the every-day virtues of civilised life. He had the habit of marking in his books traits of depravity, and poor Lady Byron mistook these marks for notes of admiration ... they came to the conclusion that Lord Byron had not been guilty of any enormity. They added that his offences might be regretted as subversive of matrimonial felicity but would not render him amenable to the laws of any court, whether of justice or equity.[4]

Hanson, as reported by Hobhouse, relates how Annabella came to see him just before leaving London and told him she believed her husband was mad and, to his amazement and horror, even talked of the possibility of having him put under restraint. This was not rational behaviour. Annabella knew that Byron was drinking heavily and taking laudanum to assuage his despair over the arrival of bailiffs in the house. It would surely occur to a common sense onlooker that his alarming moods were caused by alcohol and drugs rather than by insanity. His behaviour must have been distressing for an inexperienced young woman, though she was supported by maids and nurses and serving men, and Augusta brought in George Byron to help keep her brother in order. But there is no evidence of any act of violence against Annabella or anybody else during this whole period, though Annabella told the lawyers she had a strong conviction of danger while she was with Byron. It would be interesting to know how defending counsel would have dealt with this vague conviction.

Annabella drew up a paper of questions for Augusta and George Byron seeking an admission that they believed she would be in danger of her life if left alone with Byron at Piccadilly Terrace, and *had* been in danger from him both before, during and after, the birth of their child. Lady Noel positively stated to her daughter that Augusta and George Byron had testifed that her life was in danger.

If we are to believe Hobhouse's account, Lady Noel was lying. Hobhouse questioned George Byron and Augusta about this accusation against Byron and he gives their account of the matter:

200

Mrs Leigh avowed that there was occasionally something in his Lordship's manner, when talking of his embarrassments as a married man, which terrified her, and might terrify Lady Byron. She mentioned particularly one instance when Lord Byron desired his wife to walk out of the room with him when his air and tone were such as to make her glad when she saw them come back again. Captain Byron had a general impression that Lady Byron believed Lord Byron hated her, but neither Captain Byron nor Mrs Leigh was aware of any individual act tending to prove the least violence.[5]

Such behaviour to a pregnant woman is inexcusable but it is of a different order from physical violence. Since the matter was never brought before a court it is impossible to establish the truth of the matter. If Lady Noel was not lying in stating that Captain Byron and Augusta said Annabella was in danger then we must believe that Augusta and George Byron, in answering Hobhouse, lied to protect Byron. This is unlikely. Augusta wanted to help Annabella to prove Byron mad in the hope that her sense of duty would induce her to pity him and forgive him rather than cast him off. So she would not have denied any act of violence she had witnessed. George Byron's sympathies tended towards Lady Byron.

Annabella's maid, Ann Rood, spent a few months at Piccadilly Terrace and was now married to Byron's valet. She travelled to Kirkby Mallory with her mistress and the baby when they left London. Her deposition is recorded in Hobhouse's account of the separation. Hobhouse is firmly in the Byron camp, but his account is extremely fair and includes material which is not to Byron's credit. The new Mrs Fletcher accuses the Noels of dishonesty in building their case against Byron. She describes how Lady Noel said to her, 'You know you told Mrs Clermont that her Ladyship was in danger of her life while she remained in the house with Lord Byron.' Ann Fletcher replied that she had said no such thing but that Mrs Clermont had said it to her. Lady Noel thereupon flew into a rage and kept repeating, 'You know it was so.'[6]

Hobhouse relates how, soon after this, from motives of policy, Lady Noel began to pay great attention to the girl, sending her to the coach station in her own carriage and arranging to provide a dinner for her when she travelled to London.

Lady Byron may have felt that in these circumstances the Clermont testimony was not sufficiently convincing on the danger in which she claimed to stand from Byron. She produced a statement claiming that her maternity nurse used to lock the doors leading to her room at night. 'It was decidedly her opinion that my life was in danger.'[7] Then, possibly aware that the nurse might give a conflicting account, she covered herself by adding, 'On the other hand she would probably say that she has seen Lord Byron appear personally fond of me during the few minutes she has seen us together.'[8] In spite of the lurid tales about Byron's cruelty to her during her confinement Lady Byron had told Lady Melbourne that her confinement had been so comfortable, owing to Augusta's care for her, that she had no desire to leave Piccaddily Terrace.

The testimony alleged to be that of the maternity nurse, Mrs Shackleton, is to be found among the Lovelace Papers, the hoard of documents concerning the marriage and the separation collected by Lady Byron and preserved by her grandson, Lord Lovelace. Among these documents is a paper purporting to be a statement by the nurse, which is neither signed nor witnessed and contains alterations and interpolations in a different hand, none of them to Byron's credit.

The last word on whether Lady Byron thought herself to be in danger of her life rests with Lady Byron herself. When she visited Mr Hanson, shortly before she left Piccadilly Terrace with her child, to tell him she thought Byron was mad, Hanson, as reported by Hobhouse, asked her whether she laboured under any personal fear for herself, to which she instantly replied, 'Oh no! My eye can always put down his.'[9]

Byron answered these allegations very clearly in a letter to Lady Byron of 10 April 1816. To omit Byron's defence while printing Lady Byron's allegations would amount to misrepresentation. The letter helps to explain Byron's anger against 'the genial spy', Mrs Clermont. (He refers to Ann Fletcher as Mrs R.):

Enclosed is an extract from Rood's deposition or examination – or whatever it is technically to be called: – from this it will appear that Mrs C[lermo]nt did misstate to Lady Noel what Mrs R. had said – or rather attributed to Mrs R. words which she did not say – but which Mrs Cl[ermo]nt herself had used: – words of doubled falsehood – false as attributed to Mrs R. – false in point of fact whoever asserted them. You – Lady Byron – know – & I know – that you never were in 'peril of your life' from me – that in the extremest withering of mind which distemper of body – distress of circumstances – and exasperation of stimulus singly or united struck through me – you never thought so –

never were so: – no violence was ever even contemplated by me –
from the first day of our connection to that of your desertion – towards
you or anyone near to you – except myself...[10]

There is no doubt that Lady Byron and her supporters were now
intent on giving the impression that the separation was caused by
great wickedness on the part of Lord Byron. Considering that they
were blackening the reputation of Ada's father it seems extraordinary
that this seemed to them necessary. Perhaps the answer is simple.
Annabella was afraid that Byron would take the child away from
her, as the laws of the period might have allowed him to do. Lady
Noel went so far as to take precautions against any attempt to
kidnap the baby from Kirkby Mallory. Byron never made any
attempt to abduct the child but Augusta unwisely told Annabella
that he meant to have her in the end (possibly to frighten Annabella
into coming back to Byron with the baby). Annabella believed in
the threat and conceived it her duty to destroy her husband in
order to protect her child. When Augusta told her she was afraid
Byron would take his own life she replied she could not help it.
She must do her duty. She then told her father, 'I'm told he is
threatening his friends with suicide. A *professed* intention of that
sort is rather amusing'[11] and, 'My mother says that if he does take
laudanum so much the better. It is not fit such men should live.'[12]

The most potent method of blackening Byron's name was the
withholding of the reason why Annabella had sought a separation.
It was well known, by whatever means, that Dr Lushington had
recommended a reconciliation until Lady Byron travelled to London
and told him something which caused him to change his mind.
Since no one was ever to be allowed to find out what this was, it
was widely believed that Byron had committed some enormity so
appalling that it could not be mentioned. This naturally caused avid
speculation. Even today there is no agreement on what this terrible
secret could have been. Jerome Christensen writes, 'What awful
secret did Lady Byron tell? Speculation first produced the rumour
of a murder; it then hunted out incest; it has since settled comfortably
on the suspicion of homosexuality. None of those explanations, as
G. Wilson Knight was the first to show, is satisfactory.'[13]

'[Byron] is more jealous of his character than anyone in the
world,' wrote Lady Byron to her mother. 'How far may he therefore
be brought to terms?'[14] 'I am sure few have been libelled as I

have been,' Byron wrote from Italy years later. 'Time sets things to rights.'[15] Time has never done so. Lady Byron could instantly have set things to rights in March 1816 when she wrote, 'The silence of my friends has been very *dis*advantageous to Lord Byron ... since worse than the true causes are supposed.'[16] But she took no steps to contradict these false suppositions because she was intent on destroying Byron's reputation for her own purposes.

Though the lawyers were silent on the charge of something so horrible that it could not be talked about, the silence of Lady Byron's friends was in fact a myth. She chose confidantes who would join her in covert character assassination – mostly single women who found Byron's behaviour deeply shocking.

A letter containing extravagant charges of brutality against Byron, written by Selina Doyle, a close friend of Annabella's who was staying with the Noels at the time, was read out at a party in London with the consent of Miss Doyle who stipulated only that her name should not be mentioned as its writer.

Some of the damaging charges spread abroad by such methods concerned Annabella's version of the honeymoon journey [see Appendix – Harriet Beecher Stowe] on which Byron's comment, according to Medwin, was: 'If I had made so cavalier, not to say so brutal a speech, I am convinced that Lady Byron would instantly have left the carriage to me and the maid.'[17] Alfred Austin claimed that '... anyone who rejected this statement by Byron and believed one of Lady Byron's contradictory accounts must be constitutionally incapable of weighing evidence or be of the settled opinion that accusation of guilt is equivalent to proof of it.'[18]

The mention of the maid is puzzling. It is virtually incredible that Byron would have behaved as Lady Byron claimed he did, with the maid in the carriage. The butler at Halnaby claimed that Lady Byron was a pitiable sight of unhappiness when she got out of the carriage. The maid, Mrs Minns, testified years later that Lady Byron was buoyant and cheerful as any bride should be. The butler was dependent on the Milbanke family and, as we have seen, Lady Noel was not above bullying the servants in order to get from them the testimony she required. Of the differing versions of these events given by Lady Byron Alfred Austin wrote:

I should very much have liked to see either Sir Samuel Romilly or Dr Lushington [Annabella's lawyers] who both so readily believed whatever it may be that Lady Byron told them, with a witness under cross-examination who had given two such contradictory accounts of the same transaction ... Why, such evidence, if brought against a pick pocket, would ensure his acquittal.[19]

Lady Byron's is the only account we have of the visit to Augusta at Six Mile Bottom on the way back to London after the honeymoon. If we are to believe her, Byron was cruel both to her and to Augusta, flaunted his passion for his half-sister and taunted his wife with his preference for Augusta. If Byron's behaviour was as outrageous as it appears in this account it is quite incomprehensible that his young bride did not immediately return to her parents. (She claims to have already suspected that incest had occurred.) Instead she accompanied Byron to the newly rented house on Piccadilly Terrace and invited Augusta to come and visit them there for several weeks. Yet the melodramatic account given by Annabella of the stay at Six Mile Bottom – with its description of her fear of hearing Byron's 'terrible step' as he left Augusta and came up to her in bed, and her statement that he swore at Fletcher so that she feared for his life, just as the 'testimony' of the maternity nurse claimed that she feared for Lady Byron's life when Byron came to her room – has been accepted by many biographers as if it were statement of fact or sworn testimony proven in court. Few of these writers have mentioned what is pointed out by Malcolm Elwin, that all such accounts of the marriage were written by Lady Byron after the event either with litigation in view, or to justify her own actions. This is not to suggest that Byron's behaviour was acceptable. The correspondence between Augusta and Annabella as well as Augusta's letter to Francis Hodgson immediately after the visit to Six Mile Bottom shows that both women were deeply concerned about Byron's state of mind which was clearly far removed from that of a newly and happily married bridegroom.

Various accusations were made about Byron's wishing his baby dead, trying to disturb the baby's sleep, declaring that in her he had acquired an instrument for torture of Lady Byron. As Hobhouse reports, they are refuted by Mrs Clermont herself who said, soon after Ada's birth, that she never saw a father so proud and so fond of his child as Lord Byron.[20] Annabella echoed this when she suggested that Byron was fonder of the child than she was – even

205

fonder of it than he was of her.[21] Mrs Fletcher, as reported by Hobhouse, claimed to have seen no disagreements between Lord and Lady Byron at Piccadilly Terrace. She would not, however, have seen them together often, or for long periods.[22]

Lady Byron gives various accounts of her reason for leaving Piccadilly Terrace. In one she leaves because Byron turns her out of the house. In another she leaves on the recommendation of the doctors who believe her presence exacerbates Byron's nervous condition. The attempt to give the impression that she was in danger of her life is intended to insinuate a third version – that she fled to her parents from Byron's violence – and this is the version that was generally believed in 1816.

Her belief in her husband's depravity upheld her in the conviction that she was doing right. She was unable to see that her campaign against him was changing her into an obsessive and deluded woman. Byron saw clearly what was happening to his wife – a tragic deterioration. In the poem 'Lines on hearing that Lady Byron was Ill' (written in 1816 in Switzerland and first published in 1831, after his death) Byron gives his changed view of her 'veracity':

> But of thy virtues didst thou make a vice,
>   Trafficking with them in a purpose cold,
>   For present anger, and for future gold –
> And buying other's grief at any price.
> And thus once entered into crooked ways,
> The early truth, which was thy proper praise,
> Did not still walk beside thee – but at times,
> And with a breast unknowing its own crimes,
> Deceit, averments incompatible,
> Equivocations, and the thoughts which dwell
>   In Janus-spirits – the significant eye
> Which learns to lie with silence – the pretext
> Of prudence, with advantages annexed –
> The acquiescence in all things which tend,
> No matter how, to the desired end –
>   All found a place in thy philosophy.
> The means were worthy, and the end is won –
> I would not do by thee as thou hast done![23]

This strikes home dead centre. It describes with devastating accuracy the way Lady Byron had conducted herself during the separation and how she was to conduct herself over the long and lonely years to come. Witness to this is a letter to the editor of the *Pall Mall Gazette* in 1869. The writer, John Robertson, was a friend of Lady Byron who was so shocked by the publication of Mrs Beecher Stowe's revelations that he decided to make public his doubts about Lady Byron's veracity. He revealed that Lady Byron confided details of two separate crimes to six or seven of her friends, three of whom were Americans. One of these crimes had never been mentioned by her before. She told her listeners that these revelations were not to be treated as secrets but to be used to defend her conduct.

Annabella's attitude to her husband had changed completely after she returned home to her parents. In October 1815 she had written to her mother, who had suggested she should come home for her confinement and bring Byron with her:

> He is in great anxiety about me and would have me go by myself which I *will* not. [Byron could not go with her at that time since, the moment he left London, executions in the house which were being held back, would immediately go into effect.] As long as I am with him I am comparatively comfortable.[24]

Later she wrote that although she would be sorry to see Byron's books go she didn't care about it for herself. Then came the playful and loving letters sent during her journey to the north and on her arrival at Seaham.

It is not easy to reconcile her loving behaviour during the marriage with the unfeeling attitude exhibited towards Byron a few months later. On considering the matter carefully, in combination with accounts of her later history, one is led to the conclusion that Byron was being punished. So was Hobhouse. So were other of his friends. Looking back at her earlier history, her upbringing, the deep conviction of infallibility, one can surmise that anyone who seriously criticised her or seemed to oppose her will, however unconsciously, merited punishment in her eyes. This is later quite clear in the case of her son-in-law and Ada. It started with Ann Fletcher, who was dismissed and then denied a reference because she refused to be suborned by Lady Noel into giving the evidence Annabella needed.

In 1819 Byron wrote to his wife on her behalf:

> Fletcher has complained to me of your declining to give his wife a character
> – on account of your 'doubts of her veracity in some circumstances a

short time before she left you, – if your doubts allude to her testimony in your case during the then discussion, *you* must or at least ought to be the best judge how far she spoke the truth or not; – I can only say that She never had directly or indirectly – through me or mine – the slightest inducement to the contrary – nor am I indeed perfectly aware of what her Evidence was ... I presume that you will weigh well your justice before you deprive the woman of the means of obtaining her bread – no one can be more fully aware than I am of the utter inefficacy of any words of mine to you on this or on any other subject, – but I have discharged my duty to Truth in stating the above – and now do yours.[25]

(Byron to Lady Byron, Ravenna, 20 July 1819)

Annabella had built up a picture of herself as the martyred wife, her conduct that of an angel – 'It is my happiness to think that in some degree I live for others.'[26] She could not forgive Byron for calling her 'unforgiving' in the *Separation Poems*. Hobhouse showed only too plainly what he thought of Annabella. He dared to write remonstrating with her and advising her to go back to Byron.

At some stage during the marriage, or possibly not until after the separation, her imagination began to lose all touch with reality on the subject of her husband and his friends. She believed that Byron had committed some crime – probably murder – during his travels with Hobhouse. During the separation crisis she wrote that she had been aware for some time that '... under the guise of friendship Hobhouse was endeavouring Byron's ruin.'[27] Hobhouse, Kinnaird and Frances Hodgson became 'the Piccadilly crew of blackguards'.[28]

One must consider the possibility of some degree of personality disorder here, or at least a breakdown in proper perception of reality (which does not necessarily entail the presence of mental illness).

Obsessed with the breakdown of her marriage and a compulsion to absolve herself of all blame and establish the wrongdoing of everyone else, Lady Byron ignored her own statement to the effect that Augusta was not the cause of the separation. By 1818 she was vehement in declaring that Augusta had tried to engineer the separation for love of money and that she had pretended to reject Byron's love-making during the marriage while secretly giving in to him. By then Annabella had convinced herself that 'there was no secret good' even 'at the bottom of his [Byron's] heart'.[29]

All this was motivated by her pressing need to prove to the

world that in leaving her husband she had done right, and to prove to herself that she had never departed from her own standard of perfection.

As time went on, she developed a surprising ability to present extremely dubious actions in a favourable light. After Byron's death she was even able to assert that she had been his only true friend.

The brooding vindictiveness Annabella developed over the years may have been in her stars, but Byron bears a heavy responsibility for the ruin of her life. He should never have offered to marry her to save himself and Augusta. Having married her he should have concentrated on trying to make her happy, as he had promised Lady Melbourne he would do – and especially so during her pregnancy. Though there are strong mitigating circumstances to be taken into account there is no doubt that Byron was the guilty, and Annabella the injured, party in the shipwreck of their marriage.

However, there is one extremely significant letter from Augusta to Hodgson, written during Annabella's visit to London, two months after she had left Byron:

> I never can describe Lady Byron's appearance to you but by comparing it to what I should imagine a being of another world. She is positively reduced to a skeleton, pale as *ashes*, a deep hollow tone of voice and a *calm* in her manner quite supernatural. She received *me* kindly, but that really appeared the only SURVIVING feeling – all else was *death-like* calm. I can never forget it, never.[30]

No one ever described Annabella in such terms during the marriage. She appeared well and even happy, with a face 'round and rosy as a pippin'. It was the leaving Byron forever that changed her to 'a being from another world', not whatever happened during the marriage.

19

BYRON FOR HIS OWN DEFENCE

'I have seen the Blackwood: but I still think it a pity to prosecute ... yet am sure few have been so libelled as myself. – Time sets things to rights.'[1]

Byron tried hard to win Annabella back:

Dearest Bell – No answer from you yet – perhaps it is as well – but do recollect – that all is at stake – the present – the future – & even the colouring of the past: – The whole of my errors – or what harsher name you choose to give them – you know – but I loved you – & will not part from you without your *own* most express & *expressed* refusal to return to or receive me. – Only say the word – that you are still mine in your heart – and 'Kate! – I will buckler thee against a million' –
ever yours dearest most
B
(To Lady Byron, 5 February 1816)[2]

On the 15th he wrote to her what must, since his memoirs were burned immediately after news of his death arrived in London, be regarded as his answer to the accusations about him circulating in London at the time of the separation – at a moment when, as he later wrote to John Murray, '... my health was declining – my fortune embarrassed – and my Mind had been shaken by many kinds of disappointment – while I was yet young and might have reformed what might be wrong in my conduct – and retrieved what was perplexing in my affairs.:[3]

How far your conduct is reconcileable to your duties & affections as a wife and a mother – must be a question for your own reflection – the trial has not been very long – a year – I grant you – of distress – distemper – and misfortune – but these fall chiefly on me – & bitter as the recollection is to me of what I have felt – it is much more so to have made you a partaker in my desolation. – On the charges to be preferred against me – I have *twice* been refused any information by your father & his advisers: – it is now a fortnight – which has been passed in suspense – in humiliation – in obloquy – exposed to the most black and blighting calumnies of every kind: – without even the power of contradicting conjecture & vulgar assertion as to the accusations – because I am denied the knowledge of all or any particulars, from the only quarter that can afford them – in the mean time I hope your ears are gratified by the general rumours. – I have invited your return – it has been refused – I have entreated to see you – it is refused – I have requested to know with what I am charged – it is refused – is this mercy – or justice? – We shall see. – And now – Bell – dearest Bell – whatever may be the event of this calamitous difference – whether you are restored to – or torn from me – I can only say in the truth of affliction – & without hope – motive – or end in again saying what I have lately but vainly repeated – that I love you: – bad or good – mad or rational – miserable or content – I love you – & shall do to the dregs of my memory & existence.[4]

Lady Byron was not unmoved by Byron's repeated appeals. Her maid, Ann, who was now married to Byron's Fletcher, wrote to her husband that Lady Byron was 'rolling on the floor in a paroxysm of grief'. All the same, with a tenacity, inflexibility and obstinacy, extraordinary in so young a woman and so new a bride and mother, she stuck to her guns, thereby destroying her own chance of happiness and depriving Byron of his wife, his child, his lands and his country.

On 12 February 1816 Hobhouse talked to George Byron who told him of Byron's neglect and bad behaviour towards his wife. He persuaded his friend to admit to some of the accusations and soon after this Byron prepared a statement:

Lady Byron may have had cause to complain of my temper. My manner may have been harsh and rude, perhaps occasionally insulting. My pecuniary distresses and my ill state of body, increased by no very infrequent excesses resorted to for the sake of oblivion, may have made me appear half frantic, but my violence was never directed towards my wife. I made no secret of my hating marriage, but was equally explicit in avowing my love for her. If she can prove that each day I said or did something to give her pain, I can prove that not a day passed without my appearing at least to afford her satisfaction. She may have

212

seen me sullen, silent or morose but she has often been herself surprised sitting on my knee with her arm around my neck. If I was often neglectful I was more often fond. I may have been indiscreet – perhaps too much so. I poured out all my confessions into her ear, told her of all my failings, never committed a fault without making her my confidante. Even those errors which must have been most offensive to herself, whether in word or deed, were communicated with an unreserve which may have been mistaken for insult but which was not meant for such. The allegations at which she hints, my respect for her character and confidence in her veracity, almost make me think must have some foundation and I am therefore inclined at times to believe that at some periods of my married life I might have been deprived of reason for I solemnly protest that I am unconscious of the commission of any enormity which can have prompted Lady Byron to desert me thus suddenly, thus cruelly.[5]

Later Byron changed his mind about his wife's veracity:

I have been, and am now, utterly ignorant of what description her allegations ... are; and am as little aware for what purpose they have been kept back – unless it was to sanction the most infamous calumnies by silence.[6]

Hobhouse writes:

A horrid story of Lord Byron having asked his wife when in labour whether the child was dead, having become common, his friends put the question to him and his sister. He answered that he was content to rest the whole merits of his case upon Lady Byron's simple assertion in that respect, 'She will not say so,' he frequently repeated, 'though, God knows, poor thing – it seems now she will say anything: but she would not say that.'[7]

Of some of the rumours, Byron wrote to his wife that they '... imply a treatment which I am incapable of inflicting – & you of imputing to me.'[8] He was incapable of conceiving how far Annabella would go in her efforts to blacken his character in the belief that it was her duty to do so for the sake of her child. In these endeavours she was supported by Brougham.

In 1814 Byron had written of the Westminster election: 'Brougham is a candidate. I fear for poor dear Sherry. Both have talents of the highest order, but the youngster has *yet* a character. We shall see, if he lives to Sherry's age, how he will pass over the red hot ploughshares of public life.'[9] (Brougham had defended Leigh Hunt on the question of his criticisms of the practice of flogging in the army. Byron still knew nothing of Brougham's authorship of the review of *Hours of Idleness* in *The Edinburgh Review*.)

In 1817 he wrote from Venice, 'She is surrounded by people who detest me – Brougham the lawyer – who never forgave me for saying Mrs G[eorg]e Lamb was a damned fool (by the way I did not then know he was in love with her) in 1814 – & for a former savage note in my foolish satire;'[10] – and, 'I was not till lately aware of *all the things* he B[rougha]m has *said & done* ... he shall answer it – not as Lady B[yron]'s advocate – for to all as such she has a right – but for his conduct & assertions ... he has gone out of his character as an advocate – & been guilty of very improper language.'[11] The lawyer eventually became 'that blackguard Brougham.'

Stories were carefully spread about by Annabella's friends and Byron's enemies – among whom were two of Lady Byron's legal advisers, Dr Lushington as well as Brougham, who did not scruple to reveal scandalous details from the case they were preparing – They succeeded in winning over people who had at first taken a more commonsense view of the matter. In March 1816 the Dowager Duchess of Devonshire wrote from Rome:

> We are all astonished at the separation of Lord and Lady Byron. No one knew the cause when my last letters from England were written but everybody seems to pity her. So do I but I think that if I had married a profligate man knowing him to be so and I had a child and I was not ill treated by him I would not part from him.[12]

Soon after this she heard some of the rumours from London and changed her mind: '...he must be a Caligula. Caro [Mrs George Lamb, who was romantically attached to Henry Brougham] will have told you some of the stories. It is too shocking and her life seems to have been in danger whilst with him from his cruelty.'[13]

Byron himself wrote of the 'black and blighting calumnies' circulating in early 1816: '...my name has been as completely blasted as if it were branded on my forehead.'[14] Almost all the newspapers and magazines joined in the vilification and when a single editor tried to defend him Lady Byron's father called at his office to remonstrate with him.

Byron's reputation was destroyed by accusations of a crime whose

214

nature is still unknown and always will be. Hobhouse's verdict was that Lady Byron's supporters kept silent on the nature of the crime because they knew that conjecture and curiosity would destroy Byron. Hobhouse questioned them about every possible crime a human being could commit and they replied that it was none of these.

The ruin of Byron's reputation for all time was finally achieved by the destruction (with the connivance of Lady Byron) of his *Memoirs*.

The decision of some of Byron's friends, including Hobhouse, Moore and Augusta, to agree to the destruction of his memoirs unread, soon after his death, was more damaging to his reputation than anything perpetrated by his enemies. Witness to this is the conclusion of the *New Monthly Magazine*, October 1824, that the memoirs had not been expurgated because they must obviously be utterly unfit for publication. The opinon of those who had read the memoirs was directly opposed to this conclusion.

Not everyone was prepared to condemn Byron unheard. Many nineteenth century commentators pointed out that his almost universal condemnation was supported by evidence on Lady Byron's side alone. The matter never went to court so the evidence of Byron's friends and supporters never came before the public. A piece published in *Blackwoods* in 1869 sets out the anomalies in Byron's condemnation by the righteous on the sole grounds of Lady Byron's secret testimony:

She lives with her husband for more than a year without communicating to her own parents or to anyone else any cause for discomfort. She leaves him without the slightest indication of displeasure. She tries to prove him mad; failing that, she declares her determination never to return to him. Through her mother she lays before Dr Lushington a statement of her case. He (no doubt very wisely) advises a reconciliation. Failing with Dr Lushington as she had with Dr Baillie, she seeks a personal interview, and then, in the secrecy of his Chambers under the seal of a confidence stricter than that of the confessional, she imparts to him something which he is bound to assume on her sole assurance to be true – which he was, without investigation or inquiry, to accept as the basis of his opinion – which he was, under no circumstances whatever, without her express authority (an authority which death has now put it out of her power to give) to divulge, upon which she obtains his opinion that a reconciliation was impossible. What that something was we shall probably never know but, save in the case of the victims

215

who were sent to the guillotine on suspicion of being suspected, we know of no condemnation so monstrous, so revolting to every principle of justice and common sense as that which has been passed on Lord Byron.[15]

The occasion for publication of various defences of Byron in the mid-nineteenth century was the publication by Mrs Harriet Beecher Stowe in 1869 of a *Vindication of Lady Byron* based on confidences made to her by Lady Byron several years earlier. This book demonised Byron and canonised his wife on no evidence but the word of the injured wife. Nineteenth century editors were shocked and pointed to the lack of reliable evidence. They were much less credulous than present day writers, many of whom appear to accept the wildest unfounded allegations by writers on Byron as statements of fact.

Macmillan's magazine deplored the 'blasting of the reputation of one of the three or four most gifted men England has produced for centuries' and went on to ask, 'Did it never occur to Mrs Beecher Stowe that very strong language may be applied to people who, when reputation is at stake, are guilty of inaccuracy upon inaccuracy which moderate attention would prevent. There is an amount of negligence which English law holds tantamount to fraud.'[16]

In *Tinsley's Magazine*, 1869, a reviewer of Harriet Beecher Stowe wrote: 'At worst Lord Byron's detractors can only array probabilities against him and his defenders may comfort themselves that as imposing an array can be made on his side.'[17] In the *Vindication of Lord Byron* Alfred Austin used stronger terms, 'The uncharitable, the inexperienced and the prurient attributed to Lord Byron unutterable things, sensible men of the world came to the conclusion that there was nothing to solve, that what is called incompatibility, an imperfect fidelity on the part of the husband and an exacting jealousy on the part of the wife had conspired to put asunder a couple who ought never to have been joined together.' He adds a comment with which no sensible person could disagree – 'Great compassion was felt for the lady for no one could pretend that Lord Byron was likely to make an exemplary husband.'[18]

This last sentence is the key to a sensible attitude to the controversies about the marriage. Byron himself stated that he had no one to blame but himself. But for what happened during and after the separation some compassion must be spared for Byron.

216

Some years later Byron commented sadly on the loss of his daughter. In July 1821 he received a letter from a dying girl in England:

> ...[who] could not go out of the world without thanking me for the delight which my poesy for several years &tc. ... [She begged] me to *burn* her *letter* which ... I can *not* do, as I look upon such a letter, in such circumstances, as better than a diploma from Gottingen. I once had a letter from Norway... These are the things which make one at times believe oneself a poet.[19]

Later in that year he commented:

> What a strange thing is life and man? Were I to present myself at the door of the house where my daughter now is – the door would be shut in my face ... and if I had gone ... to Drontheim, (the furthest town in Norway) ... I should have been received with open arms into the mansions of strangers and foreigners.[20]

20

THE SEPARATION POEMS

'All words are idle'.

In March 1816 Byron asked Murray to print 50 copies of the 'Farewell Verses' and of the 'Sketch' (on Mrs Clermont) for private distribution. Byron's poem on Mrs Clermont was inspired by the anger Byron felt when he discovered the part she had played during the marriage and separation. Hobhouse, in his account of the separation, relates that Hanson decided to test the strength of Byron's case by trying to induce the servants at 13 Piccadilly Terrace to reveal facts which might be unfavourable to Byron. All of them replied, 'What! Is my Lady not coming back? Is anything the matter?' and Hobhouse emphasises that Mrs Milward, who was the wife of Sir Ralph Noel's butler, an old family retainer of the Milbankes, agreed with the servants that it was all caused by Mrs Clermont. Mrs Milward remained with Byron until his last day in London. Dr le Mann expressed his belief that Mrs Clermont was introduced into Byron's household to watch him. Byron himself wrote of her to Lady Byron:

Of the woman alluded to – you recollect that she came into this house uninvited by me – that she was neither relative – nor domestic – nor had any business here – except what appears to have been the business of her life. – But she was *your* guest – & as such treated by me with every attention & proper consideration – she was *your* stranger – and I made her our inmate – she came as a guest – she remained as a spy – she departed as an informer – & reappeared as an evidence – if false – she belied – if true – she betrayed me – the worst of treacheries – a 'bread and salt traitress' she ate & drank & slept and awoke to sting me – the curse of my Soul light upon her & hers forever!...[1]

219

This was the frame of mind in which he wrote 'The Sketch', which was much praised as a skilful satire but deplored as a violent attack on a female servant.

FROM A SKETCH

'Honest – honest Iago!
If that thou be'st a devil, I cannot kill thee.'
                                                    SHAKESPEARE

BORN in the garret, in the kitchen bred,
Promoted thence to deck her mistress' head;
Next – for some gracious service unexpressed,
And from its wages only to be guessed –
Raised from the toilet to the table, – where
Her wondering betters wait behind her chair.
With eye unmoved, and forehead unabashed,
She dines from off the plate she lately washed.
Quick with the tale, and ready with the lie,
The genial confidante, and general spy –
Who could, ye gods! her next employment guess –
An only infant's earliest governess!
She taught the child to read, and taught so well,
That she herself, by teaching, learned to spell,
An adept next in penmanship she grows,
As many a nameless slander deftly shows:
What she had made the pupil of her art,
None know – but that high Soul secured the heart,
And panted for the truth it could not hear,
With longing breast and undeluded ear.
Foiled was perversion by that youthful mind,
Which Flattery fooled not, Baseness could not blind,
Deceit infect not, nor Contagion soil,
Indulgence weaken, nor Example spoil,
Nor mastered Science tempt her to look down
On humbler talents with a pitying frown,
Nor Genius swell, nor Beauty render vain,
Nor Envy ruffle to retaliate pain,
Nor Fortune change, Pride raise, nor Passion bow,
Nor Virtue teach austerity – till now.
Serenely purest of her sex that live,
But wanting one sweet weakness – to forgive; ...[2]

It was only when Annabella had left him that Byron was moved to write about her in verse. The verses he composed for her are of a different order from the passionate poems addressed to Augusta:

Dearest Bell – I send you the first verses that ever I attempted to write upon you, and perhaps the last that I may ever write at all. This at such a moment may look like affectation, but it is not so. The language of all nations nearest to a state of nature is said to be Poetry. I know not how this may be; but this I know.

You know that the lover, the lunatic, and the poet are 'of imagination all compact.' I am afraid you have hitherto seen me only as the two first, but I would fain hope there is nothing in the last to add to any grievances you may have against the former.

> FARE thee well! and if for ever,
>   Still for ever, fare *thee well:*
> Even though unforgiving, never
>   'Gainst thee shall my heart rebel.
> Would that breast were bared before thee
>   Where thy head so oft hath lain,
> While that placid sleep came o'er thee
>   Which thou ne'er canst know again:
> Would that breast, by thee glanced over,
>   Every inmost thought could show!
> Then, thou would'st at last discover
>   'Twas not well to spurn it so.
> Though the world for this commend thee –
>   Though it smile upon the blow,
> Even its praises must offend thee,
>   Founded on another's woe:
> Though my many faults defaced me,
>   Could no other arm be found,
> Than the one which once embraced me,
>   To inflict a cureless wound?
> Yet, oh, yet, thyself deceive not –
>   Love may sink by slow decay,
> But by sudden wrench, believe not,
>   Hearts can thus be torn away;
> Still thine own its life retaineth –
>   Still must mine – though bleeding – beat;
> And the undying thought which paineth
>   Is – that we no more may meet.
> These are words of deeper sorrow
>   Than the wail above the dead;
> Both shall live – but every morrow
>   Wake us from a widowed bed.

And when thou would'st solace gather –
  When our child's first accents flow –
Wilt thou teach her to say 'Father!'
  Though his care she must forego?
When her little hands shall press thee –
  When her lip to thine is pressed –
Think of him whose prayer shall bless thee –
  Think of him thy love *had* blessed!
Should her lineaments resemble
  Those thou never more may'st see,
Then thy heart will softly tremble
  With a pulse yet true to me.
All my faults perchance thou knowest –
  All my madness – none can know;
All my hopes – where'er thou goest –
  Wither – yet with *thee* they go.
Every feeling hath been shaken;
  Pride – which not a world could bow –
Bows to thee – by thee forsaken,
  Even my soul forsakes me now.
But 'tis done – all words are idle –
  Words from me are vainer still;
But the thoughts we cannot bridle
  Force their way without the will.
Fare thee well! thus disunited –
  Torn from every nearer tie –
Seared in heart – and lone – and blighted –
  More than this I scarce can die.[3]

Jerome Christensen writes of the farewell verses and 'The Sketch':
'Lord Byron never goes to court, but his impulse to vindication is
acted upon in the greatly wicked poems of farewell.'[4] This is a
surprising judgement.

We shall see why Byron reluctantly refrained from going to
court. In any case, it seems clear that the rumours and accusations
already circulating had so ruined his reputation that he had nothing
to lose by an appeal to the courts. In view of the vilification he
was experiencing he was entitled to appeal to Lady Byron in the
'Fare Thee Well' poem. The worst he does in these verses is to
call her 'unforgiving'. He tries to convince his wife that she should
not lightly deprive their child of a father. Since his wife had slept
with him and enjoyed full conjugal relations up to the very day
on which she set off for Kirkby Mallory on the understanding that

222

he was soon to join her there, it was perfectly reasonable to ask her not to spurn the breast on which she had laid her head. The 'Fare Thee Well' verse may not be a very good poem – it is over-sentimental – but it is not wicked.

Christensen describes what he sees as Byron's motives for writing 'The Sketch'. They seem perfectly reasonable. Indeed, I am not sure that Christensen is not being too charitable in his reading of Byron's motives:

> ... Byron works himself up into a frenzy of antithesis as he attempts to divide Lady Byron from her bad angel, Mrs Clermont, and to retrieve his influence, if not her love.[5]

As for Mrs Clermont, she was clearly a bad angel to both of them in the build-up to the separation. He was not being wicked in trying to drive a wedge between the mischief-maker and the girl he still regarded as an innocent.

The verses met with a mixed reception. Wordsworth wrote of them that they were disgusting in sentiment and contemptible in execution. Pushkin cannot have agreed with Wordsworth for he placed the first two lines of 'Fare Thee Well' at the beginning of Book Seven of *Eugen Onegin*. Thomas Moore discussed the poem with Byron:

> It was about the middle of April that his two celebrated copies of verses, 'Fare thee well,' and 'A Sketch,' made their appearance in the newspapers: – and while the latter poem was generally and, it must be owned, justly condemned, as a sort of literary assault on an obscure female, whose situation ought to have placed her as much *beneath* his satire as the undignified mode of his attack certainly raised her *above* it, with regard to the other poem, opinions were a good deal more divided. To many it appeared a strain of true conjugal tenderness, a kind of appeal, which no woman with a heart could resist: while by others, on the contrary, it was considered to be a mere showy effusion of sentiment, as difficult for real feeling to have produced as it was easy for fancy and art, and altogether unworthy of the deep interests involved in the subject. To this latter opinion, I confess my own to have, at first, strongly inclined; and suspicious as I could not help regarding the sentiment that could, at such a moment, indulge in such verses, the taste that prompted or sanctioned their publication appeared to me even still more questionable. On reading, however, his own account of all the circumstances in the Memoranda, I found that on both points I had, in common with a large portion of the public, done

him injustice. He there described, and in a manner whose sincerity there was no doubting the swell of tender recollections under the influence of which, as he sat one night musing in his study, these stanzas were produced – the tears, as he said, falling fast over the paper as he wrote them. Neither, from that account, did it appear to have been from any wish or intention of his own, but through the injudicious zeal of a friend whom he had suffered to take a copy, that the verses met the public eye.[6]

Moore was mistaken. The agent who made sure the poems met the public eye was no friend of Byron. The man was Brougham who persuaded his friend, John Scott, editor of *The Champion*, to publish the 'Fare Thee Well' and 'A Sketch' although Bryon had printed only a limited number of copies intended for private circulation only. Brougham, as one of Lady Byron's legal advisers, dined with her the day before publication '... obtaining her approval of the publication only when it was rather too late for her to interfere if she had wished to.'[7]

The writer (David Erdman of the Carl H. Pforzheimer Library in *Shelley and his Circle*), goes on:

> The well-kept secret of Brougham's connection with *The Champion* had only recently been discovered by biographers of Byron, and it has not been perfectly assimilated, since it conflicts with the traditional attribution of *The Champion's* attack to Tory politics. Journalistic necessity led to the swift and extensive reprinting of both poems in the rest of the London papers, and it is true that, (except for fair treatment in the Tory *Courier*) vituperation accompanies them in the Tory papers and defensive comment in the Whig *Morning Chronicle* and *Sunday News* and in the independent *Examiner.*[8]

The publication of the verses in *The Champion* was accompanied by an editorial piece accusing Byron of using the poems to 'turn the whole current of public reproach and displeasure against his wife' and attacking him violently on the same lines as earlier attacks in *The Champion* on 'The Prince or Poet who plays the ruffian with his wife or the rogue with his neighbours'.[9]

Later the editor of *The Champion* admitted that 'extraordinary means' had been used to induce him to publish the campaign against Byron. Brougham's malice against Byron was not satisfied by these means. He was heard maligning Byron for his deformity at Brook's Club and he told Perry, editor of the *Chronicle* that

Byron had cheated the Duchess of Devonshire out of £500 by failing to pay the rent of 13 Piccadilly Terrace.

Years later Teresa Guiccioli scolded Byron for 'Fare Thee Well' which she told him was not worthy of him.

Not long after leaving England he wrote a poem about his wife which describes the tragic consequences of their parting for both of them, but particularly for her:

LINES ON HEARING THAT LADY BYRON WAS ILL

AND thou wert sad – yet I was not with thee;
　　And thou wert sick, and yet I was not near;
Methought that Joy and Health alone could be
　　Where I was *not* – and pain and sorrow here!
And is it thus? – it is as I foretold,
　　And shall be more so; for the mind recoils
Upon itself, and the wrecked heart lies cold,
　　While Heaviness collects the shattered spoils.
It is not in the storm nor in the strife
　　We feel benumbed and wish to be no more,
　　But in the after-silence on the shore,
When all is lost, except a little life...

Mercy is for the merciful! – if thou
Hast been of such, 'twill be accorded now.
Thy nights are banished from the realms of sleep: –
　　Yes! they may flatter thee, but thou shalt feel
　　A hollow agony which will not heal,
For thou art pillowed on a curse too deep;
Thou hast sown in my sorrow, and must reap
　　The bitter harvest in a woe as real!
I have had many foes, but none like thee;
　　For 'gainst the rest myself I could defend,
　　And be avenged, or turn them into friend;
But thou in safe implacability
Hadst nought to dread – in thy own weakness shielded,
And in my love, which hath but too much yielded,
　　And spared, for thy sake, some I should not spare;
And thus upon the world – trust in thy truth
And the wild fame of my ungoverned youth –
　　On things that were not, and on things that are –
Even upon such a basis hast thou built
A monument, whose cement hath been guilt!
　　The moral Clytemnestra of thy lord,

225

And hewed down, with an unsuspected sword,
Fame, peace, and hope – and all the better life
Which, but for this cold treason of thy heart,
Might still have risen from out the grave of strife,
And found a nobler duty than to part.[10]

In 1818 Lady Byron went to Newstead. Byron had never taken her there because he knew that it must be sold and feared she might become attached to the place. The account of the visit in Annabella's Journal shows that Byron's words in 'Lines on Hearing that Lady Byron was Ill' were prophetic.

Annabella describes the hall at Newstead where she saw Byron's fencing sword and single sticks. Nothing seemed to have changed and she felt as if he might have walked in. Before leaving she spent some time gossiping with the housekeeper.

It is remarkable that Judith Milbanke failed to teach her daughter such elementary rules of honourable behaviour at the time as the absolute embargo on discussing with servants the private affairs of their employers. If Byron had known that Lady Byron had gone uninvited to his old home, had allowed one of his former servants to talk about his relationship with Augusta Leigh and to make comments about the amounts he gave to charity, he would probably have said what he had written to Augusta when he discovered that Lady Byron had secretly opened his letter trunks before she left Town: 'Upon such conduct I am utterly at a loss to make a single comment – beyond every expression of astonishment. I am past indignation.'[11]

Some lines from Canto IV of *Childe Harold's Pilgrimage* may refer to Byron's sadness and disillusion over the marriage and the separation:

CXX

Alas! our young affections run to waste,
Or water but the desert; whence arise
But weeds of dark luxuriance, tares of haste,
Rank at the core, though tempting to the eyes,
Flowers whose wild odours breathe but agonies,
And trees whose gums are poison; such the plants
Which spring beneath her steps as Passion flies
O'er the World's wilderness, and vainly pants
For some celestial fruit forbidden to our wants.

226

Oh. Love! no habitant of earth thou art –
An unseen Seraph, we believe in thee,
A faith whose martyrs are the broken heart, –
But never yet hath seen, nor e'er shall see
The naked eye, thy form, as it should be;
The mind hath made thee, as it peopled heaven,
Even with its own desiring phantasy,
And to a thought such shape and image given,
As haunts the unquench'd soul – parched,
    wearied, wrung – and riven.

CXXV
Few – none – find what they love or could have loved
Though accident, blind contact, and the strong
Necessity of loving, have removed
Antipathies – but to recur, ere long,
Envenomed with irrevocable wrong;[12]

After Annabella's departure Augusta's presence was necessary for Byron's welfare and Annabella – having invited her to join them at 13 Piccadilly Terrace with Georgiana for an open-ended visit and then repented of it – found herself obliged to ask Augusta to stay on and to send her daily bulletins about Byron's health. This was not easy for Augusta. George Leigh wanted her to come home. Her children needed her. The Duchess of Leeds wrote to her that she must leave at once for the sake of her reputation. These considerations were set aside. Byron needed her and Annabella had asked for her help.

Peter Gunn gives Augusta unstinting praise:

On the morning Annabella left Piccadilly Terrace for Kirkby, Augusta accompanied by George Byron [who, it will be remembered, had been invited to join the household to help deal with Byron's wild moods] paid a visit to the solicitor, Hanson. That afternoon she began a series of almost daily bulletins that kept Annabella in touch with all that was going on in London. Never once did she falter in her absolute loyalty to both Byron and Annabella. It is in these intimate, truthful, amazingly perceptive and tactful letters, at times revealing her despair, at all times her perfect naturalness and balance – written at intervals of running the household, ordering Byron nourishing meals, seeing that he moderated his drinking and followed his medical regimen, interviewing doctors and solicitors, attending to his correspondence as well as her own, and looking after Georgiana – that we see the full measure of the woman, and understand something of the reason why she was Byron's unfailing love.[13]

At first Augusta was influenced by Lady Byron's resentment against Hobhouse who tended to drink heavily with Byron when Augusta was trying to keep him on a healthy and moderate regime. But it was not long before she began to appreciate what a faithful friend he was, and when Byron was at his lowest ebb she wrote poignantly to Hobhouse:

> Do not forsake your most unfortunate friend – if you do he is lost – he has so few *sincere* friends and well judging ones. I can never express what I feel about him, but believe me, I am grateful from my heart for your friendship and friendly forbearance towards his infirmities, of whatever kind they may be. His *mind* makes him the most unhappy of human beings. Let us hope it may not always be so. God bless you. I thank you for all your kindness.[14]

She had always been on the best of terms with Francis Hodgson and often wrote to consult him about Byron's welfare – thus remaining a friend to the group of loyal friends of Byron named 'The Piccadilly crew of blackguards' by Lady Byron.

Before he left England Byron gave Augusta some verses meant only for her eyes:

FROM STANZAS TO AUGUSTA

WHEN all around grew drear and dark,
   And reason half withheld her ray –
And Hope but shed a dying spark
   Which more misled my lonely way;
In that deep midnight of the mind,
   And that internal strife of heart,
When dreading to be deemed too kind,
   The weak despair – the cold depart;
When Fortune changed – and Love fled far,
   And Hatred's shafts flew thick and fast,
Thou wert the solitary star
   Which rose and set not to the last.
Oh! blest be thine unbroken light!
   That watched me as a Seraph's eye,
And stood between me and the night,

228

For ever shining sweetly nigh.
And when the cloud upon us came,
    Which strove to blacken o'er thy ray –
Then purer spread its gentle flame
    And dashed the darkness all away.[15]

Note

'Parisina' was published during the separation crises and did nothing to calm speculation about Byron's iniquities. Jerome McGann's commentary to the *Complete Poetical Works* explains its application to current affairs at the time of publication:

> Byron used *Parisina* to treat current social and political affairs in a veiled way – Byron habitually used older historical situations – and especially people and events from the Italian Renaissance – to highlight analogous circumstances in the contemporary English and European political scene. *Parisina* exposes the moral conflict involved in the 'justice' of Niccolo III of Ferrara (1393–1441) towards his wife and son. Byron's generic terms for such acts was 'cant'. The crux of the tale hangs on the character of Niccolo whose personal life was notoriously profligate, ... Byron probably imagined the work personally in terms of his own life on the one hand and the social world of the Regency on the other, which he saw as badly corrupt though full of a canting morality.[1]

21

LAST DAYS IN LONDON

After the departure of Annabella and Ada, Augusta wrote almost daily to her 'Dear Sis', keeping her informed about events at Piccadilly Terrace and trying to awaken in her some feeling for Byron's distress, and concern for his illness.

The squint and prominence of the left eye, together with the painful headaches described by Augusta may indicate some type of neurological disease. There is, however, no record of Byron's experiencing double vision at the time and, so far as we know, there was no recurrence of the severe headaches, fits of irritation and intolerable thirst described by Byron himself and Augusta, until many years later. It is possible that the stress caused by the trials of the preceding months, the brandy and laudanum resorted to either for relief or oblivion, together with the severe anxiety caused by the sudden (and, to him, inexplicable) demand for a separation, may have brought on the symptoms described. Byron seems to have been free of them once he decided on action and began planning for his future life abroad – 'There is a world elsewhere.'[1]

In January Augusta wrote to Annabella with wry amusement covering deep concern:

> B returned between 12 and 1 this Mng with Hobhouse – both drunk – sent me and George to bed & call'd for Brandy! Fletcher says H drank none but B. replied to his declarations to that effect 'So much the better – there will be more for me' – and drank two glasses – would not take his Calomel & in short so far so bad! One comfort is H looks really dying – God forgive me, I hope he will take him to a better world – but however B. frown'd to such a degree at me to go away that this dear friend (I mean fiend) either was or pretended to be quite shock'd

231

– said he w'd go – & when B pursued me out of the room to apologise for his frowns (when by the bye he tumbled flat on his face up the staircase) H said to George all sorts of *tendresses* of course to be repeated to me – I was *all the Angels* in ye world and fortunate for him I was married! Fletcher has just informed me he left the house door open at 3 o'clock in ye morn'g and 'lucky we had not all our throats cut!'[2]

This letter cannot have pleased Annabella – Augusta usurping her own preferred role of angel. Augusta may have been exaggerating her dislike of Hobhouse in sympathy with Annabella for she soon became convinced of his true worth as a loyal friend both to herself and to her brother. To her dismay Byron continued to dine out and visit the theatre, all his friends rallying round him, anxious about the rumours and puzzled about the abrupt departure of Annabella.

Byron's friends, like George Leigh, completely discounted the suggestion that he had committed incest with Augusta.

It was perhaps with a feeling of relief that Byron continued with his London avocations, business and pleasure, though the rumour that the beautiful actress, Mrs Mardyn, had been his mistress, obliged him to stay away from Drury Lane to protect her reputation. The unfortunate woman had been hissed off the stage though she had met Byron only once and there had been no impropriety between them.

On 20 January he had written to Samuel Rogers about a plan suggested by Sir James Mackintosh. Byron was still refusing to accept payment for his poems and had rejected a cheque for over £1000 from John Murray for *The Siege of Corinth* and *Parisina*. Mackintosh suggested that Byron might donate the money to William Godwin, the philosopher, who was in great financial difficulties. Byron stipulated that the matter should be handled with tact (which was unnecessary since Godwin felt no shame whatsoever about sponging on the young Shelley, or anyone else) and wrote to Rogers, 'I shall feel very glad if it can be of any use to Godwin – only don't let him be plagued – nor think himself obliged & all that – which makes people hate one another.'[3] Murray refused to produce the money for such a purpose, thereby infuriating his most lucrative author who angrily demanded the return of the manuscripts before relenting and allowing them to be published. He wrote of Murray to Leigh Hunt:

...he is really a very good fellow – & his faults are merely the leaven of his 'trade' ... I feel sure that he will give your work a fair or a fairer chance in every way than your late publishers...[4]

In February Leigh Hunt's *Rimini* came out with a fulsome and over-familiar dedication to Byron who wrote to him:

Your prefatory letter to 'Rimini' I accepted as it was meant as a public compliment & a private kindness – I am only sorry that it may perhaps operate against you – as an inducement and with some a pretext – for attack – on the part of the political & personal enemies of both.[5]

He answered a kind letter from Thomas Moore:

I don't know that in the course of a hair-breadth existence I was ever, at home or abroad, in a situation so completely uprooting of present pleasure, or rational hope for the future, as this same ... But I shall not sink under it ... By the way, however, you must not believe all you hear on the subject; and don't attempt to defend me ... Leigh Hunt's poem is a devilish good one – quaint, here and there, but with the substratum of originality, and with poetry about it, that will stand the test ... I have not the most distant idea what I am going to do myself ... I had, a few weeks ago, some things to say, that would have made you laugh; but they tell me now that I must not laugh...[6]

(To Thomas Moore, 29 February 1816)

There was little to make him laugh in the failure of all attempts to placate Annabella and her parents. He had written to Lord Holland, 'They think to drive me by menacing with legal measures – let them go into court – they shall be met there – After what has been already said – they cannot be more anxious for investigation than myself ...' but he added, 'I can attach no blame to *her*.'[7] (To Lord Holland, 23 February 1816)

He tried to persuade Annabella to consent to an interview but she remained adamant. When he received no immediate reply to Lord Holland's attempt at mediation he wrote, 'I will now not only sign no separation – but agree to none – not even to a verbal permission for Lady B[yron]'s absence.'[8] (To Lord Holland, 2 March 1816)

Annabella decided to offer Byron a bribe of half her inheritance when her mother died and all but £200 a year from the income payable as part of the marriage settlement. Byron saw this offer as the greatest insult he had received from Annabella's family:

If you or yours conceive that I am actuated by mercenary motives – I
appeal to the tenor of my past life in such respects – I appeal to my
conduct with regard to settlements previous to our marriage – I appeal
to all who know me – or who ever will know –.[9]

(Byron to Lady Byron, 4 March 1816)

In early March Byron and Hobhouse discussed with Hanson the
possibility of prosecuting the Milbankes for conspiracy or detainer.
But now the situation changed. Annabella and her advisers had
threatened legal measures in order to induce Byron to agree to a
private arrangement. Once they realised that Byron was prepared
to meet them in court they changed tack and accused Byron of
cruelty in insisting on dragging Lady Byron through the courts.
She wrote to him and reminded him that he had promised to agree
to a separation if convinced that she was acting of her own accord
and not under the influence of her parents. She went to see Augusta
and convinced her that she would never go back to Byron. In
consequence of this appeal from Annabella Byron consented in
principle to a separation. He suggested turning over the entire
income of the marriage settlement to her but stipulated that he
would not be bound by any agreement over the Wentworth inheritance
but would act justly on the matter when it came in.

Hobhouse had suggested that Byron should demand a disavowal of
the rumours by Lady Byron. This was not to be a part of the agreement
as it would seem as if it was being demanded in return for the settlement.
Much argument ensued over this disavowal and its text, Lady Byron
at first declaring that she would never sign it. In the end Annabella
herself drafted a disavowal which was torn up when the negotiations
fell through. Byron's cousin, Robert Wilmot (husband of the girl who
'walked in beauty like the night') had been chosen to mediate the
agreement. It was an unfortunate choice since both he and George
Byron were to go over to Lady Byron. After some discussion Wilmot
was under the impression that Byron had agreed on a formula for the
agreement and took offence when Byron told him he was mistaken.
He had agreed it only as a basis for negotiation. The matter came close
to causing a duel between the cousins.

Byron now heard that Lady Byron had complained that he was
abusing her to his friends. He went to great trouble to produce
letters from Lord Holland, Samuel Rogers and others stating that
he had never said a word against her in their presence.

Byron's advisers were in disarray, arguing among themselves. In the end Byron agreed to accept legal arbitration over the Wentworth inheritance and the separation papers were finally signed on 21 April. Lady Byron was now asked to reinstate her disavowal and produced a document which avowed that she and her friends had nothing to do with the rumours but carefully refrained from stating that they were untrue.

Byron's friends were so horrified by the general rumours that they had advised him not to come to a private arrangement '... which might compromise his character, by the supposition that he was *afraid* of the disclosures of a public court of law.'[10] By mid-January Caroline Lamb's accusations of incest had been spread abroad. Incest was a shocking, but not a criminal, offence and was a theme prominent in the literature of the day. By the end of February Caroline had added hints of homosexuality to her campaign. This was an even more serious allegation. In 1808 the Earl of Leicester had won his case in court when accused of homosexual acts but the scandal forced him to leave the country. When Byron and Hobhouse were in Greece a military man and the drummer boy with whom he had been discovered *in flagrante delicto* were both executed.

Byron was the victim not only of Caroline Lamb's revelations but of political machinations which built on these accusations. In 1816 John Wilson Croker wrote, 'Party is in England stronger than love, avarice or ambition.'[11] Byron had angered both the Tory and the Whig parties. He had praised Napoleon and was regarded as unpatriotic. His fame and success, together with his support for Whig policies, had alienated the Tories; the allegations against him were alienating the Whigs and everyone else. Now that the scandal had destroyed his reputation his political opponents gathered to bring about his downfall. Enemies like Brougham fanned the flames.

There was little his friends could do. He would neither conform nor apologise. He made no attempt to conceal his contempt for many of the politicians. He kept company openly with the Princess of Wales, who was anathema in both court and government circles. The Princess was delighted with him:

He was all 'couleur de rose' last evening ... he sat beside me at supper and we were very merry. I always tell him there are two Lord Byrons and when I invite him I say I ask the agreeable Lord, not the disagreeable one. He takes my *plaisanterie* all in good part.[12]

235

A bond between them may have been their dislike of Brougham, whom she had misguidedly chosen as her advocate against the Prince Regent. She wrote, 'If my head ends up on Temple Bar Brougham will be to blame.'[13]

When Byron went to the House of Lords most of the peers shunned him. Lord Holland kept an open mind but while the rumours circulated and the outcome was uncertain the Hollands felt it prudent to distance themselves from him for the time being, without going to the length of cutting him. Lord Holland did what he could to offer mediation between the parties over the separation.

On 19 March Brougham spoke in the Commons on the repeal of the income tax, which was regarded generally as an iniquitous imposition, acceptable only in time of war and which should have been repealed immediately once the peace was signed. The Whigs won the day with a huge majority and expected to form a new ministry forthwith. (It was said that the roads were blocked with coaches from all over the country bringing petitions against the income tax and the Commons was stuffed to the ceiling with parchment.) The Tory ministry was reeling and in need of whatever help it could get. According to the account of Teresa Guiccioli (written in 1869) '...an influential person, not belonging to the peerage, came to visit him [Byron] and told him that if he wished to see how far the folly of men went, he had only to give orders for having it shown that nothing said against him was true, but that he must change politics and come over to the Tory party.'

David Erdman speculates that this influential Tory might have been Canning, who had joined the 'shaky Liverpool – Castlereagh government' a few days before 19 March. 'The Tories were fighting for dear life ... Canning might well have proposed something to Byron when the Whigs began to desert him; as for changing the tune of the government papers, Canning was accustomed to use such tactics.' Guiccioli relates that Byron rejected the proposal and was told that '...he must suffer the consequences, which would be heavy, since his [Byron's] colleagues were determined on his ruin, out of party spirit and political hatred.'[14]

The Tories were rescued when Brougham, two days later, made an attack on the Prince Regent in the Commons so intemperate that the Whig majority crumbled away. From being the much-fêted saviour of his party Brougham became the villain of the piece. His disappointment

236

and anger may have put him in a mood to take the extreme measures he initiated in April for destroying Byron's reputation.

Byron was not sick of politics but he *was* sick of this sort of politics. Going abroad would lead him into utterly different political paths.

At the end of March he received a letter from a young woman who was unknown to him, asking for an interview. Claire Clairmont was an eighteen-year-old girl whose step-sister, Mary Godwin, daughter of Godwin and his first wife, Mary Wollstonecraft, had run away with the poet, Shelley. Hoping to catch for herself a more famous poet than her sister, Claire offered herself to Byron, suggesting that they should travel about ten miles outside London and spend the night together. Byron disliked this sort of behaviour intensely but in the end he succumbed. It was a brief distraction from his troubles but he was to regret it. Claire made a point of preaching about the views of her family on the degradation of marriage and the beauty of free love, believing that this would please Byron. She was wrong.

Claire Clairmont sang so beautifully that Shelley wrote a poem about her called 'To Constantia Singing.' These 'Stanzas for Music' were thought to have been addressed to Claire but it is hard to imagine Byron writing in such romantic terms of 'that odd-headed girl'.[15]

STANZAS FOR MUSIC

1

THERE be none of Beauty's daughters
   With a magic like thee;
And like music on the waters
   Is thy sweet voice to me:
When, as if its sound were causing
The charmed Ocean's pausing
The waves lie still and gleaming,
And the lulled winds seem dreaming;

2

And the midnight moon is weaving
   Her bright chain o'er the deep;
Whose breast is gently heaving,
   As an infant's asleep:
So the spirit bows before thee,

To listen and adore thee;
With a full but soft emotion,
Like the swell of Summer's ocean.[16]

He once wrote that he had heard one of Lord Grey's daughters play upon the harp so modestly that she '*looked* music'.[17] Of Claire his opinion was different. She had blatantly pursued him and he gave in reluctantly to her importunities. She wrote to him humbly: 'I shall ever remember the gentleness of your manners and the wild originality of your countenance.'[18] She brought her sister Mary to meet him and hinted that they should all three meet again. She was planning to persuade Mary and Shelley to travel with her to Switzerland, there to await the arrival of Byron when he left England.

To understand why Byron could not tolerate the company of Claire Clairmont it is only necessary to read such entries in her journal as the 'Caricatures for Albé', one of which is described in the entry for 8 November, Florence, 1820:

Another to be called Lord Byron's receipt for writing pathetic Poetry. He sitting drinking spirits playing with his white mustachios. His mistress the Fornara opposite him Drinking coffee. Fumes coming from her mouth, over which is written garlich; these curling direct themselves towards his English footman who is knocked backward – Lord Byron is writing he says, Imprimis to be a great pathetic poet. 1ˢᵗ Prepare a small colony, then dispatch the mother by worrying and cruelty to her grave afterwards to neglect and ill treat the children – to have as many and as dirty mistresses as can be found: ... from their embraces to catch horrible diseases.[19]

Hobhouse was now a constant visitor at 13 Piccadilly Terrace. When he felt he was needed he came up from the country to join Scrope Davies in his lodgings. One day he found Augusta in tears, because she must leave for Six Mile Bottom. She had stayed long enough to discredit the rumours and ought to return to her husband and children. Hobhouse promised to move in with Byron if it proved necessary (and he did in fact do so on 13 April). Augusta's return home was delayed by her appointment as lady-in-waiting to the Queen, which necessitated a move into rooms in St James's Palace. This place she never lost and it was assumed that the court discredited the rumours too. The small salary from this appointment and the grace and favour apartments later granted to the Leighs at St James's were to save them from complete financial ruin.

On 8 April Augusta had bravely accompanied Byron and Hobhouse to a party at Lady Jersey's. When they came into the room many of those present left and Mrs George Lamb gave Augusta the cut direct. Byron never forgot the kindness of Lady Jersey and of the heiress, Mercer Elphinstone – with whom he had once had a brief flirtation.

Byron was determined to go abroad as soon as the separation papers were signed. He had been longing for blue skies and seas at intervals ever since his return from Greece. More important, he was still being dunned by creditors and he knew that everything at 13 Piccadilly Terrace would soon be commandeered by the bailiffs. As the time of his departure grew near his friends gathered about him. He himself alternated between light-hearted moments and moods of deep depression. Sir Walter Scott wrote of a happy occasion when they had joined friends for an early dinner at Long's in September 1815: 'I never saw Byron so full of fun, frolic and wit and whim. He was as playful as a kitten. Well, I never saw him again.'[20]

During the years of exile Byron missed Scott. 'Wonderful man! I long to get drunk with him.'[21] He wrote to him from Italy 'The Gods be with your dreams'.[22]

Samuel Rogers wrote to Thomas Moore describing Byron in a sadder mood shortly before he left England:

He goes to Italy in a few days. I see him now as he looked when I was leaving him one day and he cried out after me with a gay face and a melancholy accent 'Moore is coming and you and he will be together and I shall not be with you.' It went to my heart for he loves you dearly.[23]

Byron wrote to Moore from Venice: 'Remember me in your "smiles and wine".'[24]

He was planning for his departure and had ordered a large Napoleonic carriage for the journey. He appointed a young doctor, John Polidori, as his personal physician. John Murray offered this young man a substantial sum for any diary he might keep during his travels with Byron.

On 14 April Byron wrote to Samuel Rogers excusing himself from a planned meeting with Sheridan: 'My sister is now with me and leaves town tomorrow; we shall not meet again for some time, at all events – if ever.'[25] He then wrote to Lady Byron:

I have just parted from Augusta – almost the last being you had left me to part with – and the only unshattered tie of my existence – wherever I may go – and I am going far – you and I can never meet again – let this content and atone. – If any accident occurs to me – be kind to *her*. – if she is then nothing – to her children. – some time ago – I informed you that with the knowledge that any child of ours was already provided for by other and better means – I had made my will in favour of her and her children – as prior to my marriage: this was not done in prejudice to you for we had not then differed – & even this is useless during your life by the settlements ... she has ever been your friend ... She is gone – I need hardly add that of this request she knows nothing.[26]

(Byron to Lady Byron, Sunday, [14] April 1816)

On 15 April he wrote to Augusta:

I trust you got home *safe* – & are well – I am sadly without you – but I won't complain ... ever thine – dearest A
     Most truly
          B
turn over –
P.S. – I can't bear to send you a short letter – & my heart is too full for a long one – don't think me unkind or ungrateful – dearest A – & tell me how is Georgey & *Do* – & you & *tip* – & all the *tips* on four *legs* or *two* – ever & again – & for ever
     P.P. Clerk of this parish[27]

(Byron to Augusta Leigh, 15 April 1816)

On the 16th he wrote to James Wedderburn Webster, husband of Lady Frances, reminding him of the loan he had made three years earlier. Hearing that his friend was buying lands and tenements he thought he might be able to settle, but added '...if inconvenient to you – I will say no more on the subject.'[28]

On 22 April Byron gave all his papers up to Hobhouse. Mr and Mrs Kinnaird called that night with a cake and two bottles of champagne.

On the 23rd Polidori and Hobhouse set off at 9.30 in the morning in Scrope Davies's chaise, Byron and Scrope in the Napoleonic carriage. 'There was a crowd about the door ... Arrived at Dover by half past 8 – dined at the Ship.'[29]

On the 24th Byron wrote to Hanson from Dover:

Dear Sir – Denen has distrained on the effects left at the house in Piccadilly Terrace for the half year's rent: ... there is one trunk of wood with papers – letters &tc – also some *shoes* ... I could wish redeemed from the wreck – They have seized all the *servants' things*, Fletcher's & his wife's &tc – I hope you will see to these poor creatures having *their* property secured – as for *mine* it must be sold ... I sail tonight for Ostend ... I wish you for yourself & family every possible good ...[30]

(Byron to John Hanson, Dover, 24 April 1816)

On the same day he sent some news to Augusta for passing on to Lord Carlisle, whose youngest son had been killed at Waterloo:

I met last night with an old school fellow (Wildman by name) a Waterloo aide de camp of Lord Uxbridge's. He tells me poor Fred Howard was *not* mangled, nor in the hands of the French; he was shot through the body charging a party of infantry and died (*not* on the field) half an hour afterwards at some house not far off, and in no great pain. I thought this might make his friends easier as they had heard he was a sufferer by falling into the enemy's hands.[31]

(Byron to Augusta Leigh, 24 April 1816)

In his last letter to Hanson before departure Byron had reminded him '... to seize an early opportunity of bringing Rochdale and Newstead to the hammer – or private contract.'[32] Wildman was the man who bought Newstead Abbey in 1818.

On the 24th the winds were contrary. That evening they walked to the church to see Churchill's tomb. 'Byron lay down on his grave and gave the man a crown to fresh turf it.'[33]

On the 25 April Hobhouse wrote:

Up at 8. breakfasted, all on board except the company. The Captain said he could not wait, and B could not get up a moment sooner – even the serenity of Scrope was perturbed. – however after some bustle out comes Byron and, taking my arm, walked down to the quay ... the bustle kept B in spirits, – but he looked affected when the packet glided off.[34]

241

Note

During the first summer of his exile Byron wrote a most extraordinary poem about his visit to the grave of Churchill, the eighteenth century satirist. In a note he explained that he is attempting 'a serious imitation in the style of a great poet – its beauties and its defects.'[1] The great poet was Wordsworth.

Byron's attitude to Wordsworth here is somewhat equivocal and one cannot imagine that the older poet regarded the poem as anything other than an insult. David Woodhouse points out some biographical references. The description of Churchill as 'him who blazed/The comet of a season' could be applied to Byron's own 'sudden change of fortunes.'[2]

CHURCHILL'S GRAVE

A FACT LITERALLY RENDERED

I stood beside the grave of him who blazed
    The Comet of a season, and I saw
The humblest of all sepulchres, and gazed
    With not the less of sorrow and of awe
On that neglected turf and quiet stone,
With name no clearer than the names unknown,
Which lay unread around it; and I asked
    The Gardener of that ground, why it might be
That for this plant strangers his memory tasked,
    Through the thick deaths of half a century;
And thus he answered – 'Well, I do not know
Why frequent travellers turn to pilgrims so;
He died before my day of Sextonship,
    And I had not the digging of this grave.'
And is this all? I thought, – and do we rip
    The veil of Immortality? and crave
I know not what of honour and of light
Through unborn ages, to endure this blight?
So soon, and so successless? As I said,
The Architect of all on which we tread,
For Earth is but a tombstone, did essay
To extricate remembrance from the clay,
Whose minglings might confuse a Newton's thought
    Were it not that all life must end in one,
Of which we are but dreamers; – as he caught
    As 'twere the twilight of a former Sun,
Thus spoke he, – 'I believe the man of whom
You wot, who lies in this selected tomb,
Was a most famous writer in his day,
And therefore travellers stop from out their way

To pay him honour, – and myself whate'er
  Your honour pleases:' – then most pleased I shook
  From out my pocket's avaricious nook
Some certain coins of silver, which as 'twere
Perforce I gave this man, though I could spare
So much but inconveniently; – Ye smile,
I see ye, ye profane ones! all the while,
Because my homely phrase the truth would tell.
You are the fools, not I – for I did dwell
With a deep thought, and with a softened eye,
On that Old Sexton's natural homily,
In which there was Obscurity and Fame, –
The Glory and the Nothing of a Name.[3]

David Woodhouse points out that:

...the poet's graveside musings on 'The Glory and Nothing of a Name'
(line 42) place more emphasis on the 'Nothing' than the 'Glory', as if
Byron were laying his own good name to rest on the eve of his departure
from England.[4]

22

POET INTO EXILE

'There is a world beyond Rome'.

When Byron embarked on the Lisbon packet in 1809 he was a comparatively insouciant and unknown young man. He embarked at Dover in 1816 a famous literary figure. Wherever he went he was recognised. Society women dressed up as chambermaids to watch him walk from the Ship Inn at Dover to the quayside. When he reached Switzerland and moved into the Villa Diodati near Geneva, English tourists would spy on him with telescopes from the other side of Lac Léman. The fame was derived from his poetry. Yet most of his finest work was yet to come.

Goethe had already written of him in 1815, 'I have taken cognisance of the English poet Lord Byron who deserves to interest us. His strange nature shines out in his poems which find much favour because of his wild yet controlled talent.'[1] The 'wild yet controlled talent' was to develop though suffering into something much deeper. Michael Cooke writes of '...the austere sense of responsibility to be principled and humane in action, to acknowledge without collapse the normal complexities and corruptions of existence, to profit and be honoured by the opportunity of confronting the self and the universe through suffering.'[2]

G. Wilson Knight calls Byron '...a great tragic poet, directing us to a sense of (1) human magnificence; (2) its inevitable tragedy; and to (3) a supervening acceptance.'[3]

These are the aims of the highest philosophy and these were the directions in which the poet was heading as he embarked, 'Once more upon the waters! yet once more!'[4]

It has been suggested that it is only by reading the lives and letters of his astonished contemporaries that you are able to form some estimate of the powers of Byron. A better way to estimate his powers would be to read his poetry. But this remark demonstrates the extraordinary fame of the young man who was now to oblige his readers with a third and fourth canto of *Childe Harold*.

It was as a great poet that he was known in Europe, not, as in England, an object of scandal. But, strongly as he felt at this time that England was not fit for him, in little more than a year he was to write, with affectionate amusement: 'England! with all thy faults I love thee still.'[5]

Working men in England did not join in the general vilification. They even hoped that Byron would return to England and lead a revolution. As late as 1872 Charles Harney, the Chartist, spoke of Byron's poetry as an inspiration, and its influence was already at work soon after he left England:

> He was being toasted, along with Burns and Shelley, at secret Tom Paine dinners around 1820, and his works, like Shelley's, were much reprinted in cheap (mostly pirated) editions. Louis James notes twenty five such editions for working class readers before 1844.[6]

The very reasons which made Byron popular with the poor ensured that he would not be loved by the English Establishment. Sydney Smith describes the hatred felt for a reformer in early nineteenth century England:

> ...he was sure to be assailed with all the Billingsgate of the French Revolution. Jacobin, leveller, atheist, Socinian, incendiary, regicide, were the gentlest of appellations used, and anyone who breathed a syllable against the senseless bigotry of the two Georges, or hinted at the abominable tyranny and persecution against Catholic Ireland, was shunned as unfit for the relations of social life. To say a word against ... the delays of the Court of Chancery, or the cruel punishments of the Game-laws [or, one might add, the death penalty for the framebreakers] or against any abuse which a rich man inflicted and a poor man suffered, was treason against the plutocracy, and was bitterly and steadily resented.[7]

Byron had made himself a target for all this hatred by his outspokenness against all such evils. Some of the English came to regard the poet himself as the embodiment of evil. In February 1822 the Reverend John Styles preached in Holland Chapel, Kensington,

246

describing Byron as 'A denaturalised human being who, having drained the cup of sin to its bitterest dregs, is resolved to show that he is no longer human, even in his frailties, but a cool, unconcerned fiend.'[8]

His European contemporaries were to take a different view.

PROMETHEUS

I

TITAN! to whose immortal eyes
   The sufferings of mortality,
   Seen in their sad reality,
Were not as things that gods despise;
What was thy pity's recompense?
A silent suffering, and intense;
The rock, the vulture, and the chain,
All that the proud can feel of pain,
The agony they do not show,
The suffocating sense of woe,
   Which speaks but in its loneliness,
And then is jealous lest the sky
Should have a listener, nor will sigh
   Until its voice is echoless.

II

Titan! to thee the strife was given
   Between the suffering and the will,
   Which torture where they cannot kill;
And the inexorable Heaven,
And the deaf tyranny of Fate,
The ruling principle of Hate,
Which for its pleasure doth create
The things it may annihilate,
Refused thee even the boon to die:
The wretched gift Eternity
Was thine – and thou hast borne it well.
All that the Thunderer wrung from thee
Was but the menace which flung back
On him the torments of thy rack;
The fate thou didst so well foresee,
But would not to appease him tell;
And in thy Silence was his Sentence,
And in his Soul a vain repentence,
And evil dread so ill dissembled,
That in his hand the lightnings trembled.

247

III

Thy Godlike crime was to be kind,
　To render with thy precepts less
　The sum of human wretchedness,
And strengthen Man with his own mind;
But baffled as thou wert from high,
Still in thy patient energy,
In the endurance, and repulse
　Of thine impenetrable Spirit,
Which Earth and Heaven could not convulse,
　A mighty lesson we inherit;
Thou art a symbol and a sign
　To Mortals of their fate and force;
Like thee, Man is in part divine,
　A troubled stream from a pure source;
And Man in portions can foresee
His own funereal destiny;
His wretchedness, and his resistance,
And his sad unallied existence:
To which his Spirit may oppose
Itself – and equal to all woes –
　And a firm will, and a deep sense,
Which even in torture can descry
　Its own concentered recompense,
Triumphant where it dares defy,
And making Death a Victory.[9]

APPENDIX

Lady Byron and Harriet Beecher Stowe

The account of her marriage given to Mrs Harriet Beecher Stowe in 1857 produced the melodramatic *Vindication of Lady Byron* published by Mrs Stowe in 1869. The influence of this version is to be found at second or third hand in many modern accounts of the marriage.

Mrs Stowe had met Lady Byron only briefly and had never set eyes on Lord Byron. She knew nothing of the background to the events of the separation and accepted everything Annabella told her. She relates that Byron's debts were paid off by Lady Byron with her own money when they came in – that she had 'thrown a princely fortune at his feet' when she married him and that Byron kept this money when she left him. Lady Byron is even described as having a keener reason than her husband.

Extracts from the *Vindication of Lady Byron*

The result of Byron's intimacy with Miss Milbanke and the enkindling of his nobler feelings was an offer of marriage, which she, though at the time deeply interested in him, declined with many expressions of friendship and interest. In fact, she already loved him, but had that doubt of her power to be to him all that a wife should be which would be likely to arise in a mind so sensitively constituted and so unworldly. They, however, continued a correspondence as friends; on her part, the interest continually increased; on his, the transient rise of better feelings was choked and overgrown by the thorns of base unworthy passions.

From the height at which he might have been happy as the husband of a noble woman, he fell into the depths of a secret adulterous intrigue

249

with a blood relation, so near in consanguinity, that discovery must have been utter ruin and expulsion from civilised society.

From henceforth, this damning guilty secret became the ruling force in his life; holding him with a morbid fascination, yet filling him with remorse and anguish, and insane dread of detection. Two years after his refusal by Miss Milbanke, his various friends, seeing that for some cause he was wretched, pressed marriage upon him...

Her answer was a frank, outspoken avowal of her love for him, giving herself to him heart and hand. The good in Lord Byron was not so utterly obliterated that he could receive such a letter without emotion, or practise such unfairness on a loving, trusting heart without pangs of remorse. He had sent the letter in mere recklessness; he had not seriously expected to be accepted; and the discovery of the treasure of affection which he had secured was like a vision of lost heaven to a soul in hell.

But, nevertheless, in his letters written about the engagement, there are sufficient evidences that his self-love was flattered at the preference accorded him by so superior a woman, and one who had been so much sought. He mentions with an air of complacency that she has employed the last two years in refusing five or six of his acquaintance; that he had no idea she loved him, admitting that it was an old attachment on his part. He dwells on her virtues with a sort of pride of ownership. There is a sort of childish levity about the frankness of these letters, very characteristic of the man who skimmed over the deepest abysses with the lightest jests. Before the world, and to his intimates, he was acting the part of the successful *fiancé*, conscious all the while of his deadly secret that lay cold at the bottom of his heart.

When he went to visit Miss Milbanke's parents as her accepted lover, she was struck with his manner and appearance: she saw him moody and gloomy, evidently wrestling with dark and desperate thoughts, and anything but what a happy and accepted lover should be. She sought an interview with him alone, and told him that she had observed that he was not happy in the engagement; and magnanimously added, that, if on review, he found he had been mistaken in the nature of his feelings, she would immediately release him, and they should remain only friends.

Overcome with the conflict of his feelings, Lord Byron fainted away. Miss Milbanke was convinced that his heart must really be deeply involved in an attachment with reference to which he showed such strength of emotion, and she spoke no more of a dissolution of the engagement...

The moment the carriage-doors were shut upon the bridegroom and the bride, the paroxysm of remorse and despair – unrepentant remorse and angry despair – broke forth upon her gentle head:

'You might have saved me from this, madam! You had all in your own power when I offered myself to you first. Then you might have made me what you pleased; but now you will find that you have married a *devil*!'

In Miss Martineau's Sketches, recently published, is an account of the termination of this wedding-journey, which brought them to one of Lady Byron's ancestral country seats, where they were to spend the honeymoon.

Miss Martineau says, –

'At the altar she did not know that she was a sacrifice; but before sunset of that winter day she knew it, if a judgment may be formed from her face, and attitude of despair, when she alighted from the carriage on the afternoon of her marriage-day. It was not the traces of tears which won the sympathy of the old butler who stood at the open door. The bridegroom jumped out of the carriage and walked away. The bride alighted, and came up the steps alone, with a countenance and frame agonized and listless with evident horror and despair. The old servant longed to offer his arm to the young, lonely creature, as an assurance of sympathy and protection. From this shock she certainly rallied, and soon. The pecuniary difficulties of her new home were exactly what a devoted spirit like hers was fitted to encounter. Her husband bore testimony, after the catastrophe, that a brighter being, a more sympathising and agreeable companion, never blessed any man's home. When he afterwards called her cold and mathematical, and over-pious, and so forth, it was when public opinion had gone against him, and when he had discovered that her fidelity and mercy, her silence and magnanimity, might be relied on, so that he was at full liberty to make his part good, as far as she was concerned.

'Silent she was even to her own parents, whose feelings she magnanimously spared. She did not act rashly in leaving him, though she had been most rash in marrying him.'

Not all at once did the full knowledge of the dreadful reality into which she had entered come upon the young wife. She knew vaguely, from the wild avowals of the first hours of their marriage, that there was a dreadful secret of guilt; that Byron's soul was torn with agonies of remorse, and that he had no love to give to her in return for a love which was ready to do and dare all for him. Yet bravely she addressed herself to the task of soothing and pleasing and calming the man whom she had taken 'for better or for worse.'

Young and gifted; with a peculiar air of refined and spiritual beauty; graceful in every movement; possessed of exquisite taste; a perfect companion to his mind in all the higher walks of literary culture; and with that infinite pliability to all his varying, capricious moods which true love alone can give; bearing in her hand a princely fortune, which, with a woman's uncalculating generosity, was thrown at his feet, – there is no wonder that she might feel for a while as if she could enter the lists with the very Devil himself, and fight with a woman's weapons for the heart of her husband. . . .

251

But there came an hour of revelation, – an hour when, in a manner which left no kind of room for doubt, Lady Byron saw the full depth of the abyss of infamy which her marriage was expected to cover, and understood that she was expected to be the cloak and the accomplice of this infamy.

Many women would have been utterly crushed by such a disclosure; some would have fled from him immediately, and exposed and denounced the crime. Lady Byron did neither. When all the hope of womanhood died out of her heart, there arose within her, stronger, purer, and brighter, that immortal kind of love such as God feels for the sinner, – the love of which Jesus spoke, and which holds the one wanderer of more account than the ninety and nine that went not astray. She would neither leave her husband nor betray him, nor yet would she for one moment justify his sin; and hence came two years [*sic*] of convulsive struggle, in which sometimes, for a while, the good angel seemed to gain ground, and then the evil one returned with sevenfold vehemence.

Lord Byron argued his case with himself and with her with all the sophistries of his powerful mind. He repudiated Christianity as authority; asserted the right of every human being to follow out what he called 'the impulse of nature.' Subsequently he introduced into one of his dramas the reasoning by which he justified himself in incest...

Lady Byron, though slight and almost infantine in her bodily presence, had the soul, not only of an angelic woman, but of a strong reasoning man. It was the writer's lot to know her at a period when she formed the personal acquaintance of many of the very first minds of England; but, among all with whom this experience brought her in connection, there was none who impressed her so strongly as Lady Byron. There was an almost supernatural power of moral divination, a grasp of the very highest and most comprehensive things, that made her lightest opinions singularly impressive. No doubt, this result was wrought out in a great degree from the anguish and conflict of these two years, when, with no one to help or counsel her but Almighty God, she wrestled and struggled with fiends of darkness for the redemption of her husband's soul....

During this time, such was the disordered and desperate state of his worldly affairs, that there were ten executions for debt levied on their family establishment; and it was Lady Byron's fortune each time which settled the account.

Toward the last, she and her husband saw less and less of each other; and he came more and more decidedly under evil influences, and seemed to acquire a sort of hatred of her.

She followed him through all his sophistical reasonings with a keener reason. She besought and implored, in the name of his better nature, and by all the glorious things that he was capable of being and doing; and she had just power enough to convulse and shake and agonise, but not power enough to subdue....

252

When Lord Byron found that he had to do with one who would not yield, who knew him fully, who could not be blinded and could not be deceived, he determined to rid himself of her altogether.

It was when the state of affairs between herself and her husband seemed darkest and most hopeless, that the only child of this union was born. Lord Byron's treatment of his wife during the sensitive period that preceded the birth of this child, and during her confinement, was marked by paroxysms of unmanly brutality, for which the only possible charity on her part was the supposition of insanity. Moore sheds a significant light on this period, by telling us that, about this time, Byron was often drunk, day after day, with Sheridan. There had been insanity in the family; and this was the plea which Lady Byron's love put in for him. She regarded him as, if not insane, at least so nearly approaching the boundaries of insanity as to be a subject of forbearance and tender pity; and she loved him with that love resembling a mother's, which good wives often feel when they have lost all faith in their husband's principles, and all hopes of their affections. Still, she was in heart and soul his best friend; true to him with a truth which he himself could not shake.

In the verses addressed to his daughter, Lord Byron speaks of her as

'The child of love, though born in bitterness,
And nurtured in convulsion.'

A day or two after the birth of this child, Lord Byron came suddenly into Lady Byron's room and told her that her mother was dead. It was an utter falsehood; but it was only one of the many nameless injuries and cruelties by which he expressed his hatred of her. A short time after her confinement, she was informed by him, in a note, that, as soon as she was able to travel, she must go; that he could not and would not longer have her about him; and, when her child was only five weeks old, he carried this threat of expulsion into effect....

The re-action of society against him at the time of the separation from his wife was something which he had not expected, and for which, it appears, he was entirely unprepared. It broke up the guilty intrigue and drove him from England. He had not courage to meet or endure it. The world, to be sure, was very far from suspecting what the truth was: but the time was setting against him with such vehemence as to make him tremble every hour lest the whole should be known; and henceforth, it became a warfare of desperation to make his story good, no matter at whose expense.

This account is deeply false and was judged to be so by many of the nineteenth century commentators cited in the chapter on Byron's Defence.

253

Part Two

Byron in Exile

'I saw him on horseback today,' said a young lady [in Ravenna] – 'Oh God! How beautiful he was!' 'Is he married?' asked her younger sister.

Teresa Guiccioli

He was more a mental being, if I may use this phrase, than any man I ever saw. He lived on thought more than on food.

William Parry

And if I laugh at any mortal thing,
'Tis that I may not weep.

Byron

INTRODUCTION TO PART 2

When Byron left England in April 1816 he was so traumatised by the events of the separation from his wife and child and the 'black and blighting rumours' which, he said, were 'branded on his forehead', that he was uncertain whether he would ever write another poem.

In the event, the poems he wrote in exile were a culmination and led up to his decision to go to the help of the Greeks in their War of Independence. A contemporary magazine wrote of Canto IV of *Childe Harold's Pilgrimage*, 'He has trod in the highest sphere of his art, and with a majesty and a glory which have eclipsed the splendour of all contemporary genius.' The verdict of Jerome McGann is that, 'Even Wordsworth at his most sublime has not eclipsed the grand conclusion of Byron's poem, with its comprehensive presentation of the glory and the insignificance of man, his works and his days.' *Blackwood's Magazine* predicted that, 'If he continues to write Byron will be placed by universal acclamation far above Pope ... and form a fourth star of a glorious constellation with Shakespeare, Milton and Dryden.'

These verdicts have, on the whole, failed to convince Byron's countrymen that here we have one of the greatest of English poets, and they have been equally sceptical of his virtues as a man. In Greece, 'Byron is revered as no other foreigner and very few Greeks, and, like a Homeric hero, is accorded an honorific standard epithet, *megálos kai kalós*, a great and good man.'

Evidence will be presented in these pages which may help the reader to come to a conclusion.

1

JOURNEY TO GENEVA

Since my young days of passion – joy, or pain,
Perchance my heart and harp have lost a string,
And both may jar: it may be, that in vain
I would assay as I have sung to sing.[1]

Byron set off for Brussels in the great Napoleonic coach which had been rushed on board at Dover for fear it might be impounded by the bailiffs. There he hired a caleche for his three servants, William Fletcher, a Swiss courier called Berger and Robert Rushton. His companion in the coach was William John Polidori, a clever but vain and quarrelsome young physician he had engaged to accompany him on his travels. Polidori was envious of Byron, jealous of his friends and so deeply sensitive that he imagined slights where none was intended. So intense was the interest in Byron's affairs that John Murray had offered the young man £500 for any diary he might keep during the journey.

Like any modern celebrity, Byron was irritated by English tourists who spied on him. When he left Piccadilly Terrace there were crowds about the door. The way to the quayside at Dover was lined with spectators, including women who had dressed as chambermaids in order to spy on him at the Ship Inn.

Embarking for Ostend he was heading in the same direction as hordes of English tourists who '... availed themselves of the regular services from Dover to Calais (a guinea a head) or from Southampton to Le Havre (two guineas).[2] Such travellers had been cut off from Europe since the beginning of the Revolutionary Wars, with the exception of the short truce of the Peace of Amiens.

Travellers to the continent in 1814, as described by Professor Ernest Giddey, had included:

> ...Caroline, Princess of Wales; the Duke of Wellington; Sir David Brewster, the natural philosopher; Stratford Canning, the diplomat; Sir Humphrey Davy, who a few months later, was to invent his famous lamp; Michael Faraday, the physicist; John Mayne, the Scottish poet; Edward Coplestone, the future Bishop of Llandaff; Sir James Mackinstosh, who was soon to publish his study *On the State of France*; John Milford, who wrote a book on his conducted tour; Samuel Rogers, the banker-poet; Claire Clairmont ... and, of course, Percy Bysshe Shelley.[3]

But now that the Napoleonic Wars were over and the continent was at last re-opened to the English, travel was no longer confined to the prominent and the wealthy. Travellers from England now included 'merchants, medical doctors, teachers, lawyers, civil servants, artists, students...'.[4] When Napoleon escaped from Elba they all ran for home, but, to Byron's dismay, they poured back in even greater numbers once peace was restored, and those who spotted him in Switzerland and later, in Italy, would follow him about with blatant curiosity. He postponed his visit to Rome with Hobhouse to avoid the crowds: '...a parcel of staring boobies who go about gaping and wishing to be at once cheap and magnificent.'[5]

But he was delighted to meet old friends. In Brussels (where he was delayed for two days, having been forced to return there for repairs to the Napoleonic coach which had been made for him by Baxter in London) he ran across Pryse Lockhart Gordon, a friend of his mother's family whom he had known as a boy. Pryse Gordon offered his services as guide round the field of Waterloo. He reported that Byron appeared to be silently musing when they arrived at Mont St Jean. They then enjoyed a gallop over the battlefield.

The first of the Waterloo stanzas of *Childe Harold* Canto III were composed for Pryse Gordon's wife. Prothero reports the story told by Gordon:

> Mrs Gordon asked Byron to write some lines in her scrapbook. He readily consented saying 'If she would trust him with her book he would insert a verse in it before he slept. He marched off with it under his arm, and next morning returned with the two beautiful verses which were soon after published in his third canto of *Childe Harold*.
> "A few weeks after he had written them" continues Gordon "the well-known artist, R.R. Reinagle, a friend of mine, arrived in Brussels,

when I invited him to dine with me, and showed him the lines, requesting him to embellish them with an appropriate vignette to the following passage:

'Here his last flight the haughty eagle flew,
Then tore, with bloody beak, the fatal plain' etc etc

Mr Reinagle sketched with a pencil a spirited chained eagle, grasping the earth with his talons.

I had occasion to write to his Lordship and mentioned having got this clever artist to draw a vignette to his beautiful lines, and the liberty he had taken by altering the action of the eagle. In reply to this he wrote to me 'Reinagle is a better poet and a better ornithologist than I am; eagles and all birds of prey attack with their talons and not with their beaks and I have altered the line thus -

'Then tore, with bloody talon the rent plain'..."[6]

Mrs Gordon's two stanzas then read as follows (becoming stanzas 17 and 18 of Canto III):

XVII.

Stop! – for thy tread is on an Empire's dust!
  An earthquake's spoil is sepulchred below!
  Is the spot marked with no colossal bust?
  Nor column trophied for triumphal show?
  None; but *the moral's truth* tells simpler so, –
  As the ground was before, thus let it be; –
  How that red rain hath made the harvest grow!
  And is this all the world has gained by thee,
Thou first and last of Fields! king-making Victory?

XVIII.

And Harold stands upon this place of skulls,
  The grave of France, the deadly Waterloo!
  How in an hour the Power which gave annuls
  Its gifts, transferring fame as fleeting too! –
  In 'pride of place' here last the Eagle flew,
  Then tore with bloody talon the rent plain,
  Pierced by the shaft of banded nations through;
  Ambition's life and labours all were vain –
He wears the shattered links of the World's broken chain.

XIX.

Fit retribution! Gaul may champ the bit
  And foam in fetters; – but is Earth more free?[7]

263

The musings on the battlefield produced the dramatic lines on the Duchess of Richmond's ball and the first ominous sound of the distant cannonade on the eve of Waterloo:

XXI.

There was a sound of revelry by night,
And Belgium's Capital had gathered then
Her Beauty and her Chivalry – and bright
The lamps shone o'er fair women and brave men;
A thousand hearts beat happily; and when
Music arose with its voluptuous swell,
Soft eyes looked love to eyes which spake again,
And all went merry as a marriage bell;
But hush! hark! a deep sound strikes like a rising knell!

XXII.

Did ye not hear it? – No. – 'twas but the Wind,
Or the car rattling o'er the stony street;
On with the dance! let joy be unconfined;
No sleep till morn, when Youth and Pleasure meet
To chase the glowing Hours with flying feet –
But hark! – that heavy sound breaks in once more,
As if the clouds its echo would repeat;
And nearer-clearer-deadlier than before;
Arm! Arm! it is – it is – the cannon's opening roar!

XXIV.

Ah! then and there was hurrying to and fro –
And gathering tears, and tremblings of distress,
And cheeks all pale, which but an hour ago
Blushed at the praise of their own loveliness –
And there were sudden partings, such as press
The life from out young hearts, and choking sighs
Which ne'er might be repeated; who could guess
If ever more should meet those mutual eyes,
Since upon night so sweet such awful morn could rise!

XXV.

And there was mounting in hot haste – the steed,
The mustering squadron, and the clattering car,
Went pouring forward with impetuous speed,
And swiftly forming in the ranks of war –
And the deep thunder peal on peal afar;
And near, the beat of the alarming drum
Roused up the soldier ere the Morning Star;

264

While thronged the citizens with terror dumb,
Or whispering, with white lips – 'The foe! They come!
they come!'[8]

The horror of the carnage and the unending sadness of the mourners is made evident in Byron's stanzas on the death of Frederick Howard, Lord Carlisle's youngest son, whom Byron had liked best of the Howard family when he had dined years ago in Grosvenor Square:

XXIX.

Their praise is hymned by loftier harps than mine;
    Yet one I would select from that proud throng,
    Partly because they blend me with his line,
    And partly that I did his Sire some wrong,
    And partly that bright names will hallow song;
    And his was of the bravest, and when showered
    The death-bolts deadliest the thinned files along,
    Even where the thickest of War's tempest lowered,
They reached no nobler breast than thine, young, gallant
    Howard!

XXX.

There have been tears and breaking hearts for thee,
    And mine were nothing, had I such to give;
    But when I stood beneath the fresh green tree,
    Which living waves where thou didst cease to live,
    And saw around me the wide field revive
    With fruits and fertile promise, and the Spring
    Come forth her work of gladness to contrive,
    With all her reckless birds upon the wing,
She turned from all she brought to those she could not
    bring.[9]

Sir Arthur Quiller-Couch describes stanza 30 thus:

... the exquisite stanza to young Howard, Byron's kinsman – who fell in the swoop of Vivian's cavalry upon the dying final attack of the French Guard. If any man deny that for poetry – deny to that last line, with its dragging monosyllables the informing touch of high poesy – let us not argue with him – let us content ourselves with telling him.[10]

Once the Napoleonic carriage was repaired, Byron resumed his journey. He crossed the Rhine at Coblenz and quixotically sent a bunch of lilies-of-the-valley to Augusta although they would die long before reaching either Six Mile Bottom or St James's. His longing for her company was expressed in the lines on the Drachenfels which were to appear between stanzas 55 and 56 of Canto III:

LV.

And there was one soft breast, as hath been said,
   Which unto his was bound by stronger ties
   Than the church links withal; and – though unwed,
That love was pure – and, far above disguise,
   Had stood the test of mortal enmities
   Still undivided, and cemented more
   By peril, dreaded most in female eyes;
   But this was firm, and from a foreign shore
Well to that heart might his these absent greetings
   pour!

1.

The castled Crag of Drachenfels
Frowns o'er the wide and winding Rhine,
Whose breast of waters broadly swells
Between the banks which bear the vine,
And hills all rich with blossomed trees,
And fields which promise corn and wine,
And scattered cities crowning these,
Whose far white walls along them shine,
Have strewed a scene, which I should see
With double joy wert *thou* with me.

2.

And peasant girls, with deep blue eyes,
And hands which offer early flowers,
Walk smiling o'er this Paradise;
Above, the frequent feudal towers
Through green leaves lift their walls of gray;
And many a rock which steeply lowers,
And noble arch in proud decay,
Look o'er this vale of vintage-bowers;
But one thing want these banks of Rhine, –
Thy gentle hand to clasp in mine!

3.

I send the lilies given to me –
Though long before thy hand they touch.
I know that they must withered be,

266

But yet reject them not as such;
For I have cherished them as dear,
Because they yet may meet thine eye,
And guide thy soul to mine even here,
When thou behold'st them drooping nigh,
And know'st them gathered by the Rhine,
And offered from my heart to thine![11]

At this stage of his journey Byron's thoughts were still with Augusta and his friends in England. He wrote to them all and continued to do so throughout his years of exile. Even from the beginning he was disappointed at their lack of response.

But he knew that he could rely on Hobhouse to help him with all the small practical problems he could not, at a distance, deal with himself. He wrote of his fury at the breakdown of the expensive travelling coach: 'Mr Baxter's wheels and springs have not done their duty, for which I hope you will abuse him like a pickpocket ... and say that I expect a deduction.'[12]

Apologetically he asked Hobhouse to rectify his own omission in forgetting to give a character '... to my late Coachman & footman [he gives their names] ... they lived with me more than four years & discharged their duties honestly & faithfully ... I hope they will get places – or at any rate not be left out of them owing to my forgetfulness.'[13] (Byron to John Cam Hobhouse, Brussels, 20 May 1816)

When Byron arrived at Sécheron near Geneva on 25 May he wrote to Hobhouse (to whom he had already addressed three letters): 'I have not had a line since we parted ... I shall stay here for some time in the expectation of seeing or hearing from you.'[14] (Byron to John Cam Hobhouse, Geneva, 27 May 1816)

Perhaps of all Byron's correspondents during, and especially in the early years, of his exile John Murray was the kindest, Readers of the splendid new edition of *The Letters of John Murray to Lord Byron* (published in 2007 by Liverpool University Press and edited by Andrew Nicholson) could come to no other conclusion. Murray tries to assure the young man that he is not, and will never be, forgotten by his friends and admirers in England, Andrew Nicholson remarks on how touching some of these letters are.

The first was written before Byron left England. Murray borrows from the 'Farewell Verses':

Letter 87, Monday 22 April, 1816
My Lord
I have just received the inclosed letter from Mrs Maria Graham – to whom I had sent the Verses – it will shew you that you are thought of in the remotest corners, and furnishes me with an excuse for repeating that *I* shall not forget you – God bless your Lordship
Fare <u>Thee</u> well
J. Murray.[15]

The arrival of Hobhouse would soon give Byron both pleasure and reassurance. In the meantime he was delighted when a book of poetry by the Italian poet, Casti, arrived for him from Pryse Gordon and he replied:

I cannot tell you what a treat your gift of Casti has been to me; I have almost got him by heart. I had read his 'Animali Parlanti', but I think these 'Novelle' much better. I long to go to Venice to see the manners so admirably described...[16]

(Byron to Pryse Gordon, Geneva, June 1816)

But for the time being he intended to remain where he was, telling Hobhouse:

I have taken a very pretty villa in a vineyard – with the Alps behind – and Mt. Jura and the lake before – it is called Diodati ... when you come out – don't go to an Inn – but come on to head-quarters – where I have rooms ready for you – and Scrope – and 'all appliances and means to boot.' – Bring with you also for me some bottle of *Calcined magnesia* – a new *Sword* cane ... procured by Jackson ... (my last tumbled into this lake) – some of Waite's *red* tooth-powder – and toothbrushes.[17]

(Byron to John Cam Hobhouse, Evian, 23 June 1816)

2

A SUNLESS SUMMER

Then the mortal coldness of the soul like death itself comes
   down;
It cannot feel for others' woes, it dare not dream its own.[1]

March, 1815

The 'mortal coldness of the soul' felt by Byron early in 1815, has an ominous ring. But Byron maintained his mental balance even when he was beset by the 'black and blighting rumours' of the Separation crisis, ostracised at the House of Lords, cut at Lady Jersey's party, his books put up for sale, his possessions, and those of his servants, impounded by bailiffs.

His distress found expression in his poetry. 'My springs of life were poisoned'[1] he wrote in Canto III of *Childe Harold*. This is echoed in another stanza of the same poem:

There is a very life in our despair,
Vitality of poison...[3]

And later in that summer, in 'The Dream', he returns to the image of poison:

He fed on poisons, and they had no power,
But were a kind of nutriment.[4]

In July he wrote the poem 'Could I Remount the River of My Years' in which the 'mortal coldness' Byron had attributed to himself is transferred to his absent friends: Moore, Hobhouse, Hodgson, Kinnaird, Davies, Augusta. These are his friends and

269

they are 'the dead' because they are not present. They are cold and comfortless, 'And they are changed and cheerless.'[5] On 10 June 1816 the summer itself became 'changed and cheerless'. From that day on it was unseasonably cold and stormy. Professor John Clubbe describes the climatic conditions of the summer months in Switzerland that year:

> The sun on its few appearances was a pale disk ... In the spring astronomers had sighted mysterious sunspots in their telescopes. During May and June these blemishes became large enough to be visible to the naked eye. People squinted at them through shaded glasses. Superstitious folk, even some less so, concluded that the sun was dying: others thought a chunk of the sun would break off and destroy the world...
>
> ... The Lake of Geneva and the Rhone swelled monstrously, not from melting snow but from the perpetual rain. Low-lying areas of Geneva were flooded. In certain quarters people could only circulate by boat ... 'Bridges were washed away, roads became impassable ... Dead animals were seen floating on the river... It was chilly in the homes and fires were lit to keep warm.' The summer remains the coldest and dampest in Geneva's history since weather records began in 1753, colder even than the bitterly cold summer of 1628...
>
> Conditions in some areas of Switzerland approached famine ... cargoes of grain from Russia, which had had an abundant harvest, began to arrive by sea by 20 November in time to prevent actual famine.[6]

Byron's poem 'Darkness' was written during these extraordinary conditions.

DARKNESS.

I HAD a dream, which was not all a dream.
The bright sun was extinguished, and the stars
Did wander darkling in the eternal space,
Rayless, and pathless, and the icy Earth
Swung blind and blackening in the moonless air;
Morn came and went – and came, and brought no day,
And men forgot their passions in the dread
Of this their desolation; and all hearts
Were chilled into a selfish prayer for light:
And they did live by watchfires – and the thrones,
The palaces of crownéd kings – the huts,
The habitations of all things which dwell,
Were burnt for beacons; cities were consumed,
And men were gathered round their blazing homes

To look once more into each other's face;
Happy were those who dwelt within the eye
Of the volcanos, and their mountain-torch:
A fearful hope was all the World contained;
Forests were set on fire – but hour by hour
They fell and faded – and the crackling trunks
Extinguished with a crash – and all was black.
The brows of men by the despairing light
Wore an unearthly aspect, as by fits
The flashes fell upon them; some lay down
And hid their eyes and wept; and some did rest
Their chins upon their clenchéd hands, and smiled
And others hurried to and fro, and fed
Their funeral piles with fuel, and looked up.
With mad disquietude on the dull sky,
The pall of a past World; and then again
With curses cast them down upon the dust,
And gnashed their teeth and howled: the wild birds shrieked,
And, terrified, did flutter on the ground,
And flap their useless wings; the wildest brutes
Came tame and tremulous; and vipers crawled
And twined themselves among the multitude,
Hissing, but stingless – they were slain for food:
And War, which for a moment was no more,
Did glut himself again: – a meal was bought
With blood, and each sate sullenly apart
Gorging himself in gloom: – no Love was left;
All earth was but one thought – and that was Death
Immediate and inglorious; and the pang
Of famine fed upon all entrails – men
Died, and their bones were tombless as their flesh;
The meagre by the meagre were devoured,
Even dogs assailed their masters, all save one,
And he was faithful to a corse, and kept
The birds and beasts and famished men at bay,
Till hunger clung them, or the dropping dead
Lured their lank jaws; himself sought out no food;
But with a piteous and perpetual moan,
And a quick desolate cry, licking the hand
Which answered not with a caress – he died.
The crowd was famished by degrees; but two
Of an enormous city did survive,
And they were enemies: they met beside
The dying embers of an altar-place
Where had been heaped a mass of holy things

271

For an unholy usage; they raked up,
And shivering scraped with their cold skeleton hands
The feeble ashes, and their feeble breath
Blew for a little life, and made a flame
Which was a mockery; then they lifted up
Their eyes as it grew lighter, and beheld
Each other's aspects – saw, and shrieked, and died –
Even of their mutual hideousness they died,
Unknowing who he was upon whose brow
Famine had written Fiend. The World was void,
The populous and the powerful was a lump,
Seasonless, herbless, treeless, manless, lifeless –
A lump of death – a chaos of hard clay.
The rivers, lakes, and ocean all stood still,
And nothing stirred within their silent depths;
Ships sailorless lay rotting on the sea,
And their masts fell down piecemeal: as they dropp'd
They slept on the abyss without a surge –
The waves were dead; the tides were in their grave,
The Moon, their mistress, had expired before;
The winds were withered in the stagnant air,
And the clouds perished; Darkness had no need
Of aid from them – She was the Universe.[7]

In the stanzas which Byron gave to Augusta before leaving England he had stated that he was half mad during the separation:

When all around grew drear and dark,
And reason half withheld her ray[8]

This line and the horror-story gloom of 'Darkness' together with the familiar case-history – the beautiful boy born lame, deserted by his father, sexually assaulted by a nursemaid, hinting in later life at ineradicable guilt – might point to a period of deep depression which could be taken as evidence, by those who hold the view, that Byron was a manic-depressive.

But there are notes of hope even in 1816. In *Childe Harold* Canto III, he '... remounts with a fresh pinion... / Spurning the clay-cold bonds which round our being cling.'[9]

By September 1817 he was writing the light-hearted *Beppo*. And although he sinks into the despair of grief and loss on many occasions during the summer of 1816 and after, there is no dearth of energy or inspiration. Canto III is completed within two months of leaving England. He is able to renew old friendships and to revel in a new friendship, with Shelley. He sings wild Albanian songs on the lake to astonish the girls (Mary Shelley and Claire Clairmont), teases the troublesome Polidori, deals efficiently with Douglas Kinnaird over his financial affairs and, like any modern traveller, arranges for his friend to bring or send him products which he cannot get abroad.

When Byron arrived at the Hotel d'Angleterre at Sécheron he found the Shelleys there with their little boy, William, and, to his dismay, Claire Clairmont.

He was delighted with Shelley and this was the beginning of a friendship which would stimulate, amuse, console and, occasionally, irritate him for the next six years. He disapproved of Shelley's 'out of the way notions about religion'[10] (and erased the entry in the hotel register of the word 'atheist' beside Shelley's name, for fear it might cause scandal and do the young man harm) but they got on tremendously well and talked for hours about politics and literature:

'Alas! poor Shelley!' he wrote later from Genoa – 'how he would have laughed – had he lived, and how we used to laugh now & then – at various things – which are grave in the Suburbs.'[11]

When Shelley went back to London carrying with him the manuscript of Canto III for delivery to John Murray, Byron wrote to Kinnaird:

Pray continue to like Shelley – he is a very good – very clever – but a very singular man – he was a great comfort to me here by his intelligence & good nature.[12]
(Byron to Douglas Kinnaird, Diodati, 29 September 1816)

Byron found both the young women tiresome. The two men escaped from them in a small sailing boat they had bought for excursions on the lake, undertaking a literary pilgrimage to the haunts of 'Rousseau – Voltaire – our Gibbon and De Staël.'[13]

After a dramatic storm during which Byron discovered, at a moment when it seemed likely that the boat might sink, that Shelley could not swim (he assured his friend that he could save, him but Shelley firmly forbade him to make any such attempt) they visited the Castle of Chillon which inspired Byron to write a poem on the subject of Bonivard who was imprisoned there for many years.

It was typical of Byron's devotion to fact rather than fiction that when he discovered the poem did not reflect the heroism the prisoner had in fact displayed, he wrote a sonnet on Chillon which includes the famous line: 'And Freedom's Fame finds wings on every wind,'[14] and states that the marks of Bonivard's pacing footsteps on the stone floor of his dungeon must never be effaced: 'For they appeal from tyranny to God.'[15]

In reviewing *The Prisoner of Chillon* for the *Quarterly Review* Walter Scott pointed out that Byron had transformed a story of endurance for the sake of conscience into a study of captivity in the abstract and its mental and physical effects.[16]

From Chillon Byron and Shelley went on to Vevay, Clarens and Lausanne where they visited the summerhouse in which Gibbon had completed *The Decline and Fall of the Roman Empire.* Byron picked acacia leaves in Gibbon's garden and sent them to Murray. They must have arrived in much the same state as Augusta's lilies from Coblenz.

During that summer by the lake an extraordinary literary work was produced by the nineteen-year-old Mary Shelley. When days of storm and ceaseless rain succeeded each other the Shelleys and Claire would foregather with Byron and Polidori at the Villa Diodati. One evening Byron challenged them each to write a ghost story and produced a fragment of one himself which he called 'The Vampyre'. Mary's effort was the story of *Frankenstein* which has been widely read ever since and associated with countless imitations and modern plays and films.

An unfortunate result of that evening's diversions was Polidori's later attempt to finish Byron's 'Vampyre'. The publisher Colburn put it out as the work of Byron without Polidori's sanction. Goethe believed that it was Byron's and praised it highly. The result was an association of Byron with vampirism which has been so widely accepted that a writer recently entitled his chapter on Byron's marriage 'Sleeping with the Vampire'. The same author claimed that Polidori's nonsense had created 'a harmless' association of Byron and vampirism. Byron would not have considered it harmless.

During this time Claire invited herself into Byron's bed as often as she dared. At this stage the Shelleys were unaware of the liaison with Byron, and although Claire herself regarded the seduction of the great poet as a triumph she could not be sure that Mary and Shelley would approve of it.

Byron eventually asked Shelley to keep Claire away from Diodati and this may have influenced Shelley in his decision to return to London with the two girls.

Byron later wrote to Augusta:

> ... as to all these 'mistresses' – Lord help me – I have had but one – Now – don't scold – but what could I do? – a foolish girl – in spite of all I could say or do – would come after me – or rather went before me – for I found her here – and I have had all the plague possible to persuade her to go back again but at last she went ... I am not in love ... but I could not exactly play the Stoic with a woman – who had scrambled eight hundred miles to unphilosophize me.[17]
>
> (Byron to Augusta Leigh, Diodati, Geneva, 8 September 1816)

During all this time Byron went often to visit Mme de Staël at Coppet, her château near Geneva. He wrote to John Murray, trying to persuade him to publish a poem by Coleridge:

> I won't have you sneer at *Christabel*. It is a fine, wild poem ... Mme de Staël wishes to see The Antiquary and I am going to take it to her tomorrow; she has made Coppet as agreeable as society and talent can make any place on earth.[18]
>
> (Byron to John Murray, Diodati, 30 September 1816)

By October 1817 Byron had become disillusioned with Coleridge. Andrew Nicholson notes that, 'Coleridge's *Biographia Literaria* was published by Rest Fenner in 2 volumes in 1817. B had read it by 12 October, on which date he told JM he thought Coleridge's "attack upon the then Committee of D[rur]y L[ane] Theatre – "for acting Bertram" and "attack upon Mathurin's Bertram for being acted" were "not very grateful nor graceful on the part of the worthy auto-biographer," and he added: "He is a shabby fellow and I wash my hands of and after him." '[19] [BLJ, Vol. 5, p. 267]

In 1825, the year after Byron's death, Coleridge wrote, less than generously, of the man who had given him money when he was in need and recommended his plays to the management of Drury Lane that he dared predict that Byron would not be remembered at all except as a wicked lord who, from morbid and restless vanity, pretended to be ten times more wicked than he was.

Byron often mentions in his letters at this period the pleasure he takes in his visits to Mme de Staël at Coppet. There he met

275

the Swiss man of letters, Charles Bonstetten – 'a fine & very lively old man – and much esteemed by his Compatriots...'[20]

Mme de Staël's daughter, Albertine, was there with her husband, the *Duc de Broglie*. 'Schlegel is in high force – and Madame as brilliant as ever...'[21] he told Samuel Rogers. He wrote to Augusta:

> I go out very little – except into the air – and on journeys – and on the water – and to Coppet – where Mme de Staël has been particularly kind and friendly towards me – & (I hear) fought battles without number in my very indifferent cause.[22]
> (Byron to Augusta Leigh, Diodati, Geneva, 8 September 1816)

Mme de Staël initiated a fruitless attempt to persuade Lady Byron to be reconciled with her husband. Its failure convinced Byron that his marriage was at an end and from now on he suppressed any hankerings after Annabella. By the time he arrived in Venice he would be ready to succumb once more to the *besoin d'aimer*. His hopes of Augusta, as we shall see, were gradually being extinguished. Her letters were few and unsatisfactory. He was distressed by their inadequacy but had no idea that she was being tormented and bullied into a lack of spontaneous warmth towards her beloved brother.

On 14 August Byron was delighted at receiving his first visitor from England, Monk Lewis, who stayed only briefly but long enough to translate to him (orally) some passages from Goethe's *Faust* and to accompany him to Voltaire's château at Ferney.

Hobhouse and Scrope Davies arrived two days before the departure of the Shelleys and Claire Clairmont for London and the three men set off on a tour of Chamonix and Mont Blanc. Scrope Davies went back to England with Robert Rushton on 5 September laden with trinkets for Augusta's children and Ada. In early September Byron and Polidori parted amicably and on the 17th he and Hobhouse set off for the Bernese Oberland, travelling by country carriage and on mule or horseback, leaving their mounts with the servants in order to reach the higher slopes. Byron's Alpine journal was written for Augusta and sent to her in England with the assurance that:

> – I was disposed to be pleased – I am a lover of Nature – and an Admirer of Beauty – I can bear fatigue – & welcome privation – and have seen some of the noblest views in the world. – But in all this –

276

the recollections of bitterness – & more especially of recent & more home desolation – which must accompany me through life – have preyed upon me here – and neither the music of the Shepherd – the crashing of the Avalanche – nor the torrent – the mountain – the Glacier – the Forest – nor the Cloud – have for one moment – lightened the weight upon my heart – nor enabled me to lose my own wretched identity in the majesty & power and the Glory – around – above – & beneath me. – I am past reproaches – and there is a time for all things – I am past the wish of vengeance – and I know of none like for what I have suffered – but the hour will come – when what I feel must be felt – & the – – but enough. – – To you – dearest Augusta – I send – and *for* you – I have kept this record of what I have seen & felt. – Love me as you are beloved by me. – –[23]

(Byron, Alpine Journal, 29 September 1816)

Notes

Jerome McGann and others have pointed out that when *The Prisoner of Chillon* first appeared the sonnet on Chillon appeared on the page before *The Prisoner.*

> Editors have generally followed this procedure ever since. As a result readers have sometimes been misled to think that the Promethean defiance of the sonnet carries over into the tale.[1]

This is not the case. Paul Elledge observes that though the poem is '...to a limited degree about growth through suffering, spiritual insight induced by physical pain; it is chiefly about stunted growth, astigmatic vision and abortive re-birth.[2]

In a note to the poem Byron himself said, 'I was not sufficiently aware of the history of Bonivard, as I should have endeavoured to dignify the subject by an attempt to celebrate his courage...[3]

And so he did in the sonnet.

William St Clair points out that '...the invocation of the "Eternal Spirit of the chainless mind" [in the 'Sonnet on Chillon'] is often regarded as the free spirit of romanticism, and we know much about the attitudes of those readers, real and fictional, who learned the poem by heart. Most contemporary readers were, however, probably more in sympathy with the prison authorities of Chillon than with the undefeated Bonivard, and the book sold badly.'[4]

Perhaps the book would have been more popular if Byron had treated Bonivard as a hero in *The Prisoner of Chillon*. Bernard Beatty discusses the problem of the attitude Byron takes up to liberty in this poem:

> The nameless prisoner does not sound like any mythical or historical

Bonivard nor like one of the 'sons' of Liberty who, the sonnet confidently tells us, when they, like Beethoven's Florestan, 'to fetters are consign'd', extend 'Freedom's fame ... on every wind'. Manifestly *The Prisoner of Chillon* tells a very different tale from Beethoven's *Fidelio*. The sensibility of Byron's prisoner seems closer to that of Monsieur Manette in Dickens's *A Tale of Two Cities* who, whenever asked whether he was pleased to be 'recalled to life' after his eighteen years of imprisonment, invariably answered: 'I can't say'. Liberty is clearly not always 'Brightest in dungeons'. Should we conclude that Byron falters in his belief in Liberty? Or would it be better to hazard that only someone passionately attached to Liberty would be so interested in tracking its failure to be real to a consciousness ostensibly devoted to it?[5]

3

ADA

Ada, sole daughter of my house and heart.[1]

Perhaps the saddest loss for Byron when he left his own country was his baby girl. He addresses his daughter at the beginning and end of Canto III of *Childe Harold*:

I.

Is thy face like thy mother's, my fair child!
   ADA! sole daughter of my house and heart?
   When last I saw thy young blue eyes they smiled,
   And then we parted, – not as now we part,
   But with a hope. – [2]

           *   *   *

CXV.

My daughter! with thy name this song begun!
   My daughter! with thy name thus much shall end! –
   I see thee not – I hear thee not – but none
   Can be so wrapt in thee; Thou art the Friend
   To whom the shadows of far years extend:
   Albeit my brow thou never should'st behold,
   My voice shall with thy future visions blend,
   And reach into thy heart, – when mine is cold, –
A token and a tone, even from thy father's mould.

CXVI.

To aid thy mind's development, – to watch
   Thy dawn of little joys, – to sit and see
   Almost thy very growth, – to view thee catch
   Knowledge of objects, – wonders yet to thee!
   To hold thee lightly on a gentle knee,

And print on thy soft cheek a parent's kiss, –
This, it should seem, was not reserved for me –
Yet this was in my nature: – as it is,
I know not what is there, yet something like to this,

CXVII.

Yet, though dull Hate as duty should be taught,
  I know that thou wilt love me: though my name
  Should be shut from thee, as a spell still fraught
  With desolation, and a broken claim:
  Though the grave closed between us, – 'twere the same,
  I know that thou wilt love me – though to drain
  My blood from out thy being were an aim,
  And an attainment, – all would be in vain, –
Still thou would'st love me, still that more than life retain

CXVIII.

The child of Love! though born in bitterness,
  And nurtured in Convulsion! Of thy sire
  These were the elements, – and thine no less.
  As yet such are around thee, – but thy fire
  Shall be more tempered, and thy hope far higher!
  Sweet be thy cradled slumbers! O'er the sea
  And from the mountains where I now respire,
  Fain would I waft such blessing upon thee,
As – with a sigh – I deem thou might'st have been to me.[3]

Mme de Staël later wrote to the Duchess of Devonshire that Byron's lines to his daughter were very charming. Others believed, with Matthew Arnold, that he was using his daughter to flaunt his 'bleeding heart' through Europe.

Byron had not intended to publish the lines but changed his mind, writing to John Murray:

> ... & recollect also that the concluding stanzas of C[hilde] H[arold] – (those to my *daughter*) which I had not made up my mind whether to publish or not when they were *first* written (as you will see marked in the margin of ye 1st Copy) I had (& have) fully determined to publish with the rest of the Canto – as in the copy which you received by Mr Shelley – before I sent it to England.[4]
>
> (Byron to John Murray, Martigny, 9 October 1816)

This decision may have been the result of a rumour that Lady Byron proposed spending the winter on the continent with Ada.

He wrote to Augusta:

— Since my return here — I have heard by an indirect Channel — that Lady B[yron] is better — or well. — It is also said that she has some intention of passing the winter on the Continent. Upon this subject I must [say?] a word or two — and as you are — I understand — on terms of acquaintance with her again — you will be the properest channel of communication from me to her. — It regards my child. — It is far from my intention now or at any future period — (without misconduct on her part which I should be grieved to anticipate) to attempt to withdraw my child from it's mother — I think it would be harsh — & though it is a very deep privation to me to be withdrawn from the contemplation & company of my little girl — still I would not purchase even this so very dearly; — but I must strongly protest against my daughter's leaving England — to be taken over the Continent at so early a time of life — & subjected to many unavoidable risks of health & comfort; — more especially in so unsettled a state as we know the greater part of Europe to be in at this moment — I do not choose that my girl should be educated like Lord Yarmouth's son — (or run the chance of it which a war would produce) and I make it my personal & particular request to Lady Byron — that — in the event of her quitting England — the child should be left in the care of proper persons — I have no objection to it's remaining with Lady Noel — & Sir Ralph — (who would naturally be fond of it) but my distress of mind would be very much augmented if my daughter quitted England — without my consent or approbation. — — I beg that you will lose no time in making this known to Lady B[yron] — and I hope you will say something to enforce my request, — I have no wish to trouble her more than can be helped. — — My whole hope — and prospect of a quiet evening (if I reach it) are wrapt up in that little creature Ada — and you must forgive my anxiety in all which regards her even to minuteness. — [5]

(Byron to Augusta Leigh, Diodati, 1 October 1816)

Discussion of this request went on for months. Byron became agitated and threatened legal action through Mr Hanson. In March 1817 he discovered to his great distress that Sir Ralph Noel had secretly filed a bill in Chancery against him, the previous spring. He wrote to Lady Byron:

The object is evident — it is to deprive me of my paternal right over my child — which I have the less merited as I neither abused nor intended to abuse it. You & yours might have been satisfied with the outrages I have already suffered ... conduct — which you may yet live to condemn in your own heart ... it would be as well if even you at

281

times recollected – that the man who has been sacrificed in fame – in feelings – in every thing ... to the convenience of your family – was he whom you once loved...[6]

(Byron to Lady Byron, Venice, 5 March 1817)

Later, Byron became very alarmed at the possibility that disclosure that he was the author of *Don Juan* would deprive him of his parental rights.

In December 1819 he wrote to Douglas Kinnaird, who helped him with his business affairs and in his dealing with John Murray:

Murray it seems wishes to try a question of copyright of Don Juan – and bring *in my* name – I would rather pay him back the money; ... Murray should recollect one thing – if he tries his copy question and loses it - on the ground of the work being called licentious or irreligious – I lose all right legal & paternal to the guardianship or a portion of the guardianship of my legitimate daughter Ada. – I would rather refund his purchase – as is fair ... Pray write.[7]

(Byron to Douglas Kinnaird, Venice, 10 December 1819)

In October 1820 Byron detailed his worries over Ada to Murray:

Recollect that if you put my name to '[Don] Juan' in these canting days – any lawyer might oppose my Guardian rights of my daughter in Chancery – on the plea of its containing the parody [of the Ten Commandments] – such are the perils of a foolish jest: ... and you may be sure that the Noels would not let it slip – Now I prefer my child to a poem at any time – and so should you as having half a dozen.[8]

(Byron to John Murray, Ravenna, 12 December 1820)

Lockhart in his anonymous 'Letter to Lord Byron' in *John Bull* (April 1821) accuses Byron of humbug over Ada:

The object of that stanza (Ada sole daughter...) was of course to humbug women and children into an idea that you were very much distressed with being separated from the sweet little *Ada*! But *men* knew, even then, that you might have rocked her cradle to pieces had you had a mind, – and we all know that you have been enjoying yourself very heartily for four or five years among ladies and misses of quite another kind.[9]

282

Byron praised the 'fun and ferocity' of Lockhart's 'Letter to Lord Byron' and declared that he 'must forgive the dog, whoever he is.'[10] He had perhaps become hardened by now to speculation about his marriage and separation.

4

CHILDE HAROLD'S PILGRIMAGE,
CANTO III

*'Did you ever read anything so exquisite as the new Canto
of Childe Harold?' writes Susan Ferrier in 1816 when the
third Canto was published. 'It is enough to make any woman
fly into the arms of a tyger!*[1]

(William St Clair)

Byron wrote of the new Canto:

> I care not much about opinions at this time of day, and I am certain
> in my mind that this Canto is the *best* which I have ever written; there
> is depth of thought in it throughout and a strength of repressed passion
> which you must feel before you find; but it requires reading more than
> once, because it is in part *metaphysical*, and of a kind of metaphysics
> which every body will not understand. I never thought it would be
> *popular* & should not think well of it if it were.[2]

Murray must have expected the Canto to be both popular and
successful for he told Byron he was delighted with it and reported
the reaction of Gifford who was suffering from jaundice. Gifford
judged Canto III the most interesting and original as well as the
most finished of Byron's poems.

Byron was startled by the enthusiasm shown in London:

> I tremble for the 'magnificence' which you attribute to the new Childe
> Harold. I am glad you like it; it is a fine indistinct piece of poetical
> desolation, and my favourite. I was half mad during the time of
> its composition, between metaphysics, mountains, lakes, love

285

unextinguishable, thoughts unutterable, and the nightmare of my own delinquencies, I should, many a good day, have blown my brains out, but for the recollection that it would have given pleasure to my mother-in-law.[3]

(Byron to Thomas Moore, Venice, 28 January 1817)

Hobhouse was puzzled:

Byron has given me another Canto of Childe Harold to read – It is very fine in parts, but I don't know whether I like it as much as his first cantos. There is an air of mystery and metaphysics about it.[4]

Jerome McGann observes that, 'Byron welcomes the prospect of a new activity and announces the therapeutic end of his renewed pilgrimage, to create "a being more intense".'[5]

(From *Childe Harold's Pilgrimage*, Canto III)

Awaking with a start,
The waters heave around me; and on high
The winds lift up their voices: I depart,
Whither I know not; but the hour's gone by,
When Albion's lessening shores could grieve or glad mine eye.

II.

Once more upon the waters! yet once more!
And the waves bound beneath me as a steed
That knows his rider. Welcome to their roar!
Swift be their guidance, wheresoe'er it lead!
Though the strained mast should quiver as a reed,
And the rent canvas fluttering strew the gale,
Still must I on; for I am as a weed,
Flung from the rock, on Ocean's foam, to sail
Where'er the surge may sweep, the tempest's breath prevail.

*   *   *

V.

He, who grown agèd in this world of woe,
In deeds, not years, piercing the depths of life,
So that no wonder waits him – nor below
Can Love or Sorrow, Fame, Ambition, Strife,
Cut to his heart again with the keen knife
Of silent, sharp endurance – he can tell

Why Thought seeks refuge in lone caves, yet rife
With airy images, and shapes which dwell
Still unimpaired, though old, in the Soul's haunted cell.

VI.

'Tis to create, and in creating live
  A being more intense that we endow
  With form our fancy, gaining as we give
  The life we image, even as I do now –
  What am I? Nothing: but not so art thou,
  Soul of my thought! with whom I traverse earth,
  Invisible but gazing, as I glow
  Mixed with thy spirit, blended with thy birth,
And feeling still with thee in my crushed feelings' dearth.[6]

Moore found traces of both Shelley and Wordsworth in Canto III:

Here and there among those fine bursts of passion and description that
abound in the third Canto of *Childe Harold*, may be discovered traces
of that mysticism of meaning, – that sublimity, losing itself in its own
vagueness, – which so much characterised the writings of his extraordinary
friend ... [He also perceived] the tinge, if not something deeper, of the
manner and cast of thinking of Mr Wordsworth, which is traceable
through so many of his most beautiful stanzas. Being naturally, from
his love of the abstract and the imaginative, an admirer of the great
poet of the Lakes, Mr Shelley omitted no opportunity of bringing the
beauties of his favourite writer under the notice of Lord Byron; and it
is not surprising that, once persuaded into a fair perusal, the mind of
the noble poet should – in spite of some personal and political prejudices,
which unluckily survived this short access of admiration – not only feel
the influence but, in some degree, even reflect the hues of one of the
very few real and original poets that this age (fertile as it is in rhymers
quales ego et Clusenius) has had the glory of producing.[7]

Byron himself admitted that Shelley used to dose him with
'Wordsworth physic' in Switzerland – even to nausea.
Some of the stanzas of Canto III were written under this influence:

LXXII.

I live not in myself, but I become
  Portion of that around me; and to me
  High mountains are a feeling, but the hum
  Of human cities torture: I can see
  Nothing to loathe in Nature, save to be

287

A link reluctant in a fleshly chain,
Classed among creatures, when the soul can flee,
And with the sky – the peak – the heaving plain
Of Ocean, or the stars, mingle – and not in vain.

LXXIII.

And thus I am absorbed, and this is life: –
I look upon the peopled desert past,
As on a place of agony and strife,
Where, for some sin, to Sorrow I was cast,
To act and suffer, but remount at last
With a fresh pinion; which I feel to spring,
Though young, yet waxing vigorous as the Blast
Which it would cope with, on delighted wing,
Spurning the clay-cold bonds which round our being
cling.

LXXIV.

And when, at length, the mind shall be all free
From what it hates in this degraded form,
Reft of its carnal life, save what shall be
Existent happier in the fly and worm, –
When Elements to Elements conform,
And dust is as it should be, shall I not
Feel all I see less dazzling but more warm?
The bodiless thought? the Spirit of each spot?
Of which, even now, I share at times the immortal lot?

LXXV.

Are not the mountains, waves, and skies, a part
Of me and of my Soul, as I of them?
Is not the love of these deep in my heart
With a pure passion? should I not contemn
All objects, if compared with these? and stem
A tide of suffering, rather than forego
Such feelings for the hard and worldly phlegm
Of those whose eyes are only turned below,
Gazing upon the ground, with thoughts which dare not
glow?[8]

In stanzas like these Byron writes in such uncharacteristically pantheistic terms that Wordsworth was to proclaim he was 'poaching upon my manor' in Canto III of *Childe Harold*.[9]

Byron was not being insincere. Paul Elledge points out that

Ernest J. Lovell Jr suggests that the Wordsworthian note 'is an expression of Byron's *mobilité*, acted upon by others and reflecting views wholly foreign to his more usual thoughts and feelings.'[10]

This discussion is so crucial that modern critics must be called in here and not relegated to the Notes at the end of the chapter. Paul Elledge claims that Byron's

> ...skepticism was rather more increased than diminished by the uncompromising certitude with which Shelley propounded Wordworth's doctrines of natural harmony and benevolent necessity... Certainly Wordsworth and Shelley are clearly visible in the poems of this period ... but at the same time Byron shrinks from the belief that Wordsworth's and Shelley's truth is the *final* truth ... his skepticism gets momentarily clouded by what at first glance appears to be pantheistic deifications of Nature. But Byron always thumps himself back soundly to a recognition of the futility and even the danger of such self-deluding dreams.[11]

Samuel Chew, writing fifty years ago or more, remarked on the fundamentally Byronic point of view of nature summed up by Lord Morley: 'Nature in her most dazzling aspects or stupendous parts, is but the background and the theatre of the tragedy of man', and Chew points out that such a scene as the sunset described by Byron at the beginning of Canto III of *The Corsair* inspires in Byron '...no pantheistic fervor, but recalls to him the death of Socrates.'[12]

M.K. Joseph observes that, 'As Byron moved away from Shelley and the Rousseau-haunted lake, his own sense of reality reasserted itself.'[13]

Byron appears to find peace in the calm beauty of the Lake at night:

> LXXXVI.
> It is the hush of night, and all between
>   Thy margin and the mountains, dusk, yet clear,
>   Mellowed and mingling, yet distinctly seen,
>   Save darkened Jura, whose capt heights appear
>   Precipitously steep; and drawing near,
>   There breathes a living fragrance from the shore,
>   Of flowers yet fresh with childhood; on the ear,
>   Drops the light drip of the suspended oar,
> Or chirps the grasshopper one good-night carol more.[14]

Then comes the storm:

XCII.

The sky is changed – and such a change! Oh Night,'
  And Storm, and Darkness, ye are wondrous strong,
  Yet lovely in your strength, as is the light
  Of a dark eye in Woman! Far along,
  From peak to peak, the rattling crags among
  Leaps the live thunder! Not from one lone cloud,
  But every mountain now hath found a tongue,
  And Jura answers, through her misty shroud,
Back to the joyous Alps, who call to her aloud![15]

M.K. Joseph comments that:

The last part of the Canto is dominated by the image of the 'contrasted
lake'; and other natural objects – mountains and stars – appear as
mirrored in it. At night, in calm, the scene becomes 'the fit and unwalled
temple' of a natural worship; in storm, it rouses him to an incoherent
fury of identification with the wilder elements.[16]

Jerome McGann informs us that:

The storm sequence, then, has two important effects: first it foreshadows
the psychological instability of the poet set forth at the end of the canto;
second, it raises the question of whether pilgrims can ever find complete
rest or conclusive self realization ... In Canto IV the poet tells us
explicitly that they cannot, but in Canto III he leaves the question
unanswered.[17]

Notes

1. When Sir Arthur Quiller-Couch writes of Byron his tone is often polemical
   since he sees (as few other critics of his period saw) that Byron was
   astonishingly underrated in England at that time, both as man and Poet.
   Quiller-Couch's judgements, however, are measured and sensible – though
   for all his perspicacity I believe he underrates the sincerity of the first
   cantos.
      He writes of Cantos III and IV of *Childe Harold's Pilgrimage*:

   Using April, 1816, for a book marker, divide the first two cantos of
   Childe Harold from the remainder, begun in early May of that year.
   Who can fail to perceive the sudden deepening of the voice to
   sincerity, the as sudden lift to music and imagination. Who can fail
   to feel that out of Vanity Fair we have passed at one stride into a

290

region of moral earnestness, into acquaintance with a grand manner, into a presence.[1]

2. Michael Cooke agrees with this analysis:

> ...Byron's writing, his singing, had undergone a change since the morning when he awoke and found himself famous. It had become substantially richer in thought, feeling, and style. In his handling of the persons met with in *Childe Harold III*, for example, we find none of the high-handed partiality of the beginner satires, none of the straitening, feverish brooding of the tales, and, most notably, none of the spectral abstraction of the first two cantos.[2]

3. M.K. Joseph puts the Canto in the context of Byron's later writings:

> Recollections of Rousseau dominate Byron's feeling for the Lake, yet his last impression of it is different again. It is with a salute to the protean Voltaire and to Gibbon, 'the lord of irony', that he turns away from Leman towards the hinterland of the Alps and towards Rome... The pessimism of *Manfred* owed much to Voltaire [whose pessimism was earlier characterised by Joseph when he describes *Candide* as 'that great gesture of derision at the idea of a benevolent universe']. The rejection of benevolism was to lead Byron later to the cosmic pessimism of *Cain*, which was in turn to be partly conquered, partly absorbed in the tragi-comic humanism of *Don Juan*.[3]

5

MANFRED

I have no tragedy, nor tragedies – but a sort of metaphysical drama which I sent to Murray the other day – it is all in the Alps and the other world – and as mad as Bedlam.[1]

Byron knew perfectly well that *Manfred* was not 'as mad as Bedlam', but it was a new departure for him and he was not at all sure how it would be received. It was written in the second half of September, 1816, and was inspired by the tour of the Bernese Alps which he undertook with Hobhouse in August and recorded in an Alpine Journal addressed to Augusta:

Ascended the Wengren [*sic*] Mountain ... heard the Avalanches falling every five minutes nearby – as if God was pelting the Devil down from Heaven with snowballs ... the clouds rose up from the opposite valley, curling up perpendicular precipices – like the foam of the Ocean of Hell ... on arriving at the summit we looked down the other side upon a boiling sea of cloud – dashing against the crags on which we stood.[2]

On reading the opening lines of *Manfred* we can picture Byron sleepless at Diodati with a dying lamp:

> *Man.* THE lamp must be replenished, but even then
> It will not burn so long as I must watch:
> My slumbers – if I slumber – are not sleep,
> But a continuance of enduring thought,
> Which then I can resist not: in my heart
> There is a vigil, and these eyes but close
> To look within[3]

293

Though Manfred is not evil he is not wholly differentiated from the spirit described in terms which call to mind the Satan of Milton:

> ...on his brow
> The Thunder scars are graven; from his eye
> Glares forth the immortality of Hell – [4]

He characterises himself as differing from ordinary mortals:

> My joy was in the wilderness, – to breathe
> The difficult air of the iced mountain's top,
> Where the birds dare not build – [5]

His proud spirit is revealed when, in the hall of the ruler of the evil spirits, he refuses to bow down to Arimanes, calling out:

> *Man.* Bid *him* bow down to that which is
> The overruling Infinite – the Maker
> Who made him not for worship – let him kneel,
> And we will kneel together.[6]

Almost with the first line of the play we learn of Manfred's despair in knowing that 'The Tree of Knowledge is not that of Life',[7] and we find that he is tormented by guilt whose consequence is that 'My solitude is solitude no more / But peopled with the Furies.'[8]

When Manfred summons the Spirits to his aid we learn that the boon he craves is Forgetfulness. This the spirits have no power to grant him.

In the scene on the Jungfrau Manfred describes Man as half-dust, half-deity. He compares himself to the withered pines Byron had seen in the Alps and described for Augusta. Preparing to fling himself from the precipice he is saved by a simple chamois-hunter, who encourages him with kindliness and praise to come with him to his cottage: '– Come, 'tis bravely done – / You should have been a hunter – Follow me.'[9]

Manfred admires the simple kindness of this man but knows that he himself is of a higher order and must pursue higher aims.

In Act II the figure of Astarte is connected with hints of incest which were to add to the rumours about Byron's relations with Augusta. Jerome McGann discusses Astarte in his commentary to the play:

The fullest treatment of the work's biographical dimension is in *Astarte*. That work emphasizes the relation of the theme of guilt to B's incestuous relationship with his sister, but although he expressed concern for her and her reputation, I do not think the evidence reveals a sense of guilt (see his letters to his sister written in 1816–18, especially). What they show is a bitter resentment directed at his wife, concern for Augusta and her worries, and a self-disgust born of wounded pride. His 'guilt', it seems to the editor, is directed at himself, for he felt that he was his own destroyer, that he had 'filed [his] mind' (CHP 111, st. 113) by trafficking with contemptible people during his 'Years of Fame'. All of the 1816 poems emphasize B's sense that he was 'the careful pilot of my proper woe...' To the extent that this is the case, the Astarte of the play is not Augusta, it is Manfred's/Byron's 'star' which presides over so much of the play's action (see 1.i.44 and the stage direction after 49): that is, Astarte is Manfred's Fate understood as his destined and inmost Self, his epipsyche.[10]

In this McGann departs from the explanations most widely accepted in the past, but his view is shared by Paul Elledge:

Although [E.H.] Coleridge did not find (or did not admit to finding) an illicit love motif in the drama, nearly everyone since has insisted that the Byron-Augusta Leigh affair is unnervingly imaged in the Manfred-Astarte relationship, and has axiomatically assumed that Manfred's guilt is rooted in incest. The incest theme cannot be blinked away; but a biographical reading of the play fails to answer large and troublesome questions. Hence, to my mind, the motivation behind Manfred's search for 'self-oblivion' is not so much a guilt over illicit love as it is a more generalised remorse over an unfulfilled potentiality: frustrated attempts to realise within himself the perfectibility embodied in the imagined ideal have bred in him paranoic self-reproach.[11]

It is difficult to believe that Byron would have published *Manfred* if he intended Astarte to be seen as Augusta. He would not knowingly have harmed his beloved sister. 'When we were in our youth, and had one heart, / And loved each other as we should not love,'[12] is not an accurate description of the Byron-Augusta relationship. Nor can the description of Astarte (with the exception of the first few lines) be applied to Augusta:

> *Man.* She was like me in lineaments – her eyes –
> Her hair – her features – all, to the very tone
> Even of her voice, they said were like to mine;
> But softened all, and tempered into beauty:

> She had the same lone thoughts and wanderings,
> The quest of hidden knowledge, and a mind
> To comprehend the Universe.[13]

Byron must have felt that no one who knew his beloved 'Goose' (as he often called his lively, loving and sometimes scatterbrained sister) could possibly have taken this description as intended for her. 'I loved her, and destroy'd her!'[14] That he loved Augusta is true but it is not true that he destroyed her. She remained with her husband and children and retained her place at court. The rumours would die down. Augusta was destroyed not by Byron but by George Leigh's debts and the resulting financial ruin from which Byron tried unavailingly to save her.

It is unlikely that this controversy will ever be resolved.

Nemesis calls up the figure of Astarte in answer to Manfred's demand. He begs her for forgiveness and love but all she can vouchsafe to him is the knowledge of his imminent death.

The spirits are amazed at Manfred's proud independence in dealing with his anguish:

> *Another Spirit.* Yet, see, he mastereth himself, and makes
> His torture tributary to his will.
> Had he been one of us, he would have made
> An awful Spirit.[15]

The Abbot of a nearby monastery comes to visit Manfred and tells him the time has come for repentance. He speaks of Manfred with mingled admiration and compassion:

> *Abbot.* This should have been a noble creature – he
> Hath all the energy which would have made
> A goodly frame of glorious elements,
> Had they been wisely mingled; as it is,
> It is an awful chaos – Light and Darkness –
> And mind and dust – and passions and pure thoughts
> Mixed, and contending without end or order, – [16]

To the end Manfred defies both the holy Abbot who would save his soul and the evil spirits:

> I stand
> Upon my strength – I do defy – deny –
> Spurn back, and scorn ye![17]

296

The Abbot is with him as the prophecy of the phantom of Astarte is fulfilled: 'Old man! 'tis not so difficult to die.'[18]

Manfred was published on 16 June 1817 and translated into German. It was reviewed by Goethe who praised it highly. Many reviewers pointed out its similarity to *Faust*.

In August 1817 Francis Jeffrey in the *Edinburgh Review* described *Manfred* as '... undoubtedly a work of great genius and originality but very strange and not very pleasing.'[19]

On the whole the verdict of the public on Byron's plays has been similar to Jeffrey's verdict on *Manfred*. They are highly philosophical works, the fruit of deep thought, and the writer makes greater demands on his audience than, even in the more reflective nineteenth century, most of them were willing to give.

Byron's fellow-countrymen were puzzled by *Manfred*. Their chief reaction was an intrigued curiosity about the hints they perceived of an incestuous relationship between Manfred and Astarte, which was widely assumed to mirror Byron's relationship with Augusta Leigh. Both Jerome McGann and Paul Elledge strongly dispute this reading of the play.

With *Manfred* Byron embarked on a process of thought and endeavour which would culminate in his sailing for Greece to join the Greeks in their struggle for Independence. This process began soon after Byron left England and lasted throughout his years of exile. As we shall see, it can be traced through all the plays.

Byron insisted that his dramas were never to be performed in the theatre. In spite of this there have been many performances, and these are discussed in Margaret Howell's interesting book *Byron Tonight*, details of which are provided in the Bibliography.

Notes

Jerome McGann writes that the best introduction to *Manfred* is still Professor Chew's *Dramas of Lord Byron*.

Manfred was, as might be expected, compared with Goethe's *Faust*. Professor Chew observes, however:

> ... Manfred's rejection of the pact with the spirits of evil is Byron's great alteration of the Faust idea. Manfred retains his independence ... Byron in *Manfred* and throughout his poetry, points to an idea truer

and nobler than Goethe's just because it is impossible of accomplishment. Such a doctrine is indeterminate, enormous, but it is full of inspiration.

It is no doctrine of mere negation, such as Carlyle attributes to Byron, and the reader who finds *Manfred* only a poem of revolt has not reached its full meaning. For the final message of the poem is very positive ... In *Lara*, for example, there are expressions of a distinctly fatalistic nature ... In *Manfred* ... 'Man is man and master of his fate' ... *Manfred* is ... the fullest expression of a doctrine that recurs constantly throughout Byron's poetry – the doctrine of the authoritative and reflective principle of conscience, the Categorical Imperative... It is a declaration of moral and spiritual responsibility ... its chief message is one of encouragement and hope. It tells of the triumph of mind over matter, of soul over body, in that conflict which a dualistic conception of the universe implies. Here again it is one of the great Byronic 'notes', for his poetry and philosophy are shot through with the idea of this struggle. In *Manfred*, despite the sense of the clod of clay which clogs the soul, the final victory is felt to remain with the forces of good![1]

Michael Cooke points out that

... [Manfred] typifies the perfectionist and iconoclast in collision with reality, and ordained to recover strength and sanity through acceptance rather than action and aggression... It is crucial to see that Manfred rises above the things he rejects.[2]

6

AUGUSTA LOST

When she is gone – the loved – the lost – the one...[1]

A letter from Augusta to John Murray (1 November 1816) throws light on the distress she felt and the conflicting pressures which prevented her from writing to her brother openly, warmly and without constraint:

> When you were so good as to call upon me at St James's and told me of the arrival of the Canto, and *some lines addressed to me, which were to be published or not as I liked*, I answered, instinctively almost – 'Whatever is addressed to me do not publish'. I felt most forcibly that such things could only serve to *me faire valoir aux dépens de sa Femme* – besides 1000 other reasons, which I can better explain whenever I have the pleasure of seeing you ... You must know how I have suffered in the late melancholy proceedings. I have, I can truly say, felt for *both*, and done my utmost and, to the best of my judgement, all I could, and such reflections must be my only consolations. Yet I am so afraid of *his* being hurt!

Then, on 8 November, she wrote again to tell Murray, '... upon reflection, perhaps the lines should be published since he might be provoked into something wrong, – representing me as a *Victim of Slander* and *bitterness* to the *other party* and in short I hope I decide for the best.'[2]

The stanzas sent to Murray ('Though the day of my destiny's over') praised Augusta who had never betrayed Byron and therefore deserved to be dearest of all:

> From the wreck of the past, which hath perished,
> Thus much I at least may recall,

299

It hath taught me that what I most cherished
    Deserved to be dearest of all:
In the Desert a fountain is springing,
    In the wide waste there still is a tree,
And a bird in the solitude singing,
    Which speaks to my spirit of *Thee*.[3]

In her letter to Murray Augusta shows her emotional intelligence. She is not deceived by Lady Byron's angelic poses. She immediately perceives that any poem addressing Augusta with praise will raise a fury of jealousy in her sister-in-law. But, just as she goes on loving Byron, whatever he does, her strongest motivation is her reluctance to wound either of them.

Lady Byron showed no such consideration for Augusta, who was recovering from the birth of a son and suffering from the loss of her brother. Annabella had broken off all communication with her sister-in-law in April. Driven by a compulsive need to get Augusta to confess to an incestuous relationship with her brother, and convincing herself that Augusta had indeed sinned with Byron during the marriage, Lady Byron now made overtures to her 'dear Sis' which Augusta, terrified of scandal which might lose her place at court, dared not rebuff. Annabella persuaded herself that her motives were unselfish, but the saving of Augusta's soul was secondary to the desire to drive a wedge between brother and sister and make sure that they should never meet again. She used for this purpose a Mrs Villiers, who was a close friend of Augusta.

This woman allowed herself to be persuaded by Lady Byron into betraying her friend. Under the guise of concern for Augusta's spiritual welfare, these two women treated her with shocking cruelty and succeeded in destroying the perfect confidence between brother and sister which had been of great comfort to both.

Unable to understand why August's letters were so infrequent and inadequate Byron grew jealous. On 17 September he wrote to her from Ouchy where he was showing Hobhouse around:

You have been in London, too, lately, & H[obhouse] tells me that at your leveé he generally found Ld Frederick Bentinck – pray why is that fool so often a visitor? Is he in love with you?[4]
    (Byron to Augusta Leigh, Ouchy, 17 September 1816)

He had noticed that she was *distraite* and believed her distress was caused by the publication of Caroline Lamb's *roman à clef*, *Glenarvon*, which caricatured Byron as the wicked hero of a romantic farrago picturing Caroline herself as the innocent Calantha. He tried to reassure her:

Your confidential letter is safe, and all the others. This one has cut me to the heart because I have made you uneasy. Still I think all these apprehensions – very groundless. Who can care for such a wretch as C[arolin]e, or believe such a seventy times convicted liar? and in the next place, whatever she may suppose or assert – I never 'committed' any one to her but *myself*. And as to her fancies – she fancies any thing – and every body – Lady M[elbourne] &c. &c. Really this is starting at shadows. You distress me with – no – it is not *you*. But I have heard that Lady B[yron] is ill, & am so sorry – but it's of no use – do not mention her again – but I shall not forget her kindness to you...
...do not be uneasy – and do not 'hate yourself' if you hate either let it be *me* – but do not – it would kill me; we are the last persons in the world – who ought – or could cease to love one another.

Ever dearest thine
+ B

P.S. – I send a note to Georgiana. I do not understand all your mysteries about 'the verses' & the Asterisks; but if the name is not put asterisks always are, & I see nothing remarkable in this. I have heard nothing but praises of those lines.[5]

(Byron to Augusta Leigh, Diodati, 27 August 1816)

In September he suggested that she might come to him for a visit in the spring of 1817, bringing one or two of the children, to make a tour in France or Italy at his expense:

The great obstacle would be that you are so admirably yoked – and necessary as a housekeeper – and a letter writer – & a place-hunter to that very helpless gentleman your Cousin, that I suppose the usual self-love of an elderly person would interfere between you & any scheme of recreation or relaxation, for however short a period.
What a fool I was to marry – and *you* not very wise – my dear – we might have lived so single and so happy – as old maids and bachelors; I shall never find any one like you – nor you (vain as it may seem) like me. We are just formed to pass our lives together, and therefore – we – at least – I – am by a crowd of circumstances removed from the only being who could ever have loved me, or whom I can unmixedly feel attached to...

Had you been a Nun – and I a Monk – that we might have talked through a grate instead of across the sea – no matter – my voice and my heart are[6]

ever thine –

B

(Byron to Augusta Leigh, Ouchy, 17 September 1816)

In August Byron had already sent Murray another poem of which Augusta was obliged to forbid the publication. She copied 'Epistle to Augusta' into her Commonplace Book and it may have comforted her when Byron's letters were unkind or not forthcoming:

EPISTLE TO AUGUSTA.

I.

My Sister! my sweet Sister! if a name
Dearer and purer were, it should be thine.
Mountains and seas divide us, but I claim
No tears, but tenderness to answer mine:
Go where I will, to me thou art the same –
A loved regret which I would not resign.
There yet are two things in my destiny, –
A world to roam through, and a home with thee.

II

The first were nothing – had I still the last,
It were the haven of my happiness;
But other claims and other ties thou hast,
And mine is not the wish to make them less.
A strange doom is thy father's son's, and past
Recalling, as it lies beyond redress;
Reversed for him our grandsire's fate of yore, –
He had no rest at sea, nor I on shore.

III.

If my inheritance of storms hath been
In other elements, and on the rocks
Of perils, overlooked or unforeseen,
I have sustained my share of worldly shocks,
The fault was mine; nor do I seek to screen
My errors with defensive paradox;
I have been cunning in mine overthrow,
The careful pilot of my proper woe.

IV.

Mine were my faults, and mine be their reward.
My whole life was a contest, since the day
That gave me being, gave me that which marred
The gift – a fate, or will, that walked astray;
And I at times have found the struggle hard,
And thought of shaking off my bonds of clay:
But now I fain would for a time survive,
If but to see what next can well arrive.

V.

Kingdoms and Empires in my little day
I have outlived, and yet I am not old;
And when I look on this, the petty spray
Of my own years of trouble, which have rolled
Like a wild bay of breakers, melts away:
Something – I know not what – does still uphold
A spirit of slight patience; – not in vain
Even for its own sake, do we purchase pain.

IX.

Oh that thou wert but with me! – but I grow
The fool of my own wishes, and forget
The solitude which I have vaunted so
Has lost its praise in this but one regret;
There may be others which I less may show; –
I am not of the plaintive mood, and yet
I feel an ebb in my philosophy,
And the tide rising in my altered eye.

X.

I did remind thee of our own dear Lake,
By the old Hall which may be mine no more.
Leman's is fair; but think not I forsake
The sweet remembrance of a dearer shore:
Sad havoc Time must with my memory make,
Ere that or thou can fade these eyes before;
Though, like all things which I have loved, they are
Resigned for ever, or divided far.

XI.

The world is all before me; I but ask
Of Nature that with which she will comply –
It is but in her Summer's sun to bask,
To mingle with the quiet of her sky,

303

To see her gentle face without a mask,
And never gaze on it with apathy.
She was my early friend, and now shall be
My sister – till I look again on thee.

XII.

I can reduce all feelings but this one;
And that I would not; – for at length I see
Such scenes as those wherein my life begun –
The earliest even the only paths for me –
Had I but sooner learnt the crowd to shun,
I had been better than I now can be;
The Passions which have torn me would have slept;
I had not suffered, and *thou* hadst not wept.

XIII.

With false Ambition what had I to do?
Little with Love, and least of all with Fame;
And yet they came, unsought, and with me grew,
And made me all which they can make – a Name.
Yet this was not the end I did pursue;
Surely I once beheld a nobler aim.
But all is over – I am one the more
To baffled millions which have gone before.

XVI.

For thee, my own sweet sister, in thy heart
I know myself secure, as thou in mine;
We were and are – I am, even as thou art –
Beings who ne'er each other can resign;
It is the same, together or apart,
From Life's commencement to its slow decline
We are entwined – let Death come slow or fast,
The tie which bound the first endures the last![7]

The phrase in stanza XI: 'The world is all before me;' echoes the closing lines of Milton's *Paradise Lost*:

The World was all before them, where to choose
Their place of rest, and Providence their guide,
They hand in hand with wandering steps and slow
Through Eden took their solitary way.

I believe it is not accidental, but a deliberate reference by Byron,

304

suggesting his sense of loss at being parted from his sister (and implying also the loss of the 'paradise' they once enjoyed in each other's company) as well as suggesting, by implication, that he could better endure his exile were she with him – Eve to his Adam.

By October Byron was in Venice and there, as Shelley later reported, he went in for the wildest dissipation, which Du Bois explained as a natural reaction to the rejection by his strait-laced wife. I believe it equally possible that his disappointment with Augusta may have been the cause. He was stunned by hints that she would be unable to meet him if he came to England. He was not to know that this was one of the peremptory demands made on her by Annabella as part of the concerted effort by herself and Mrs Villiers to reform Augusta and make her humble and repentant:

> My dearest Augusta – Two days ago I wrote you the enclosed but the arrival of your letter of the 12th has revived me a little, so pray forgive the apparent '*humeur*' of the other, which I do not tear up – from laziness – and the hurry of the post as I have hardly time to write another at present.
>
> I really do not & cannot understand all the mysteries & alarms in your letters & more particularly in the last. All I know is – that no human power short of destruction – shall prevent me from seeing you when – where – & how – I may please – according to time & circumstance; that you are the only comfort (except the remote possibility of my daughter's being so) left me in prospect in existence, and that I can bear the rest – so that you remain; but anything which is to divide us would drive me quite out of my senses; Miss Milbanke appears in all respects to have been formed for my destruction; I have thus far – as you know – regarded her without feelings of personal bitterness towards her, but if directly or indirectly – but why do I say this? – You know she is the cause of all – whether intentionally or not is little to the purpose – – You surely do not mean to say that if I come to England in Spring, that you & I shall not meet? If so I will never return to it – though I must for many reasons – business &c &c – But I quit this topic for the present.[8]
>
> (Byron to Augusta Leigh, 28 October 1816)

After this he writes less often and his letters are frequently concerned with Ada.

But as late as 17 May 1819 he wrote to Augusta a letter which Lady Byron would have described as 'an Absolute love letter' (her description of other letters from Byron which she forced Augusta to show her). This letter indicates clearly that none of the diversions he had indulged in through despair could turn his thoughts away from the love he had felt for Augusta – not even the burgeoning love affair with the young Italian Countess, Teresa Guiccioli:

My dearest Love – I have been negligent in not writing, but what can I say[.] Three years absence – & the total change of scene and habit makes such a difference – that we have now nothing in common but our affections & our relationship. – But I have never ceased nor can ever cease to feel for a moment that perfect and boundless attachment which bound & binds me to you – which renders me utterly incapable of *real* love for any other human being – what could they be to me after *you*? ... If ever I return to England – it will be to see you – and recollect that in all time & place – and feelings – I have never ceased to be the same to you in heart – Circumstances may have ruffled my manner – & hardened my spirit – you may have seen me harsh & exasperated with all things around me; grieved and tortured with *your new resolution*, – and the soon after persecution of that infamous fiend who drove me from my Country and conspired against my life – by endeavouring to deprive me of all that could render it precious – but remember that even then *you* were the sole object that cost me a tear? and *what tears!* do you remember *our* parting? ... When you write to me speak to me of yourself – & say that you love me – never mind common-place people and topics – which can be in no degree interesting – to me who see nothing in England but the country which holds *you* ... – They say absence destroys weak passions – and confirms strong ones – Alas! *mine* for you is the union of all passions & of all affections – Has strengthened itself but will destroy me – I do not speak of *physical* destruction – for I have endured & can endure much – but of the annihilation of all thoughts feelings or hopes – which have not more or less a reference to you and to *our recollections*.[9]

(Byron to Augusta Leigh, 17 May 1819)

What could poor Augusta reply to this letter from afar, run ragged as she was by two very present harpies. Her answer was inadequate and elicited the response:

My dearest Augusta – I am at too great a distance to scold you – but I *will* ask you – whether *your* letter of the 1st July *is an answer* to the letter I wrote you before I quitted Venice? – What? is it come to *this*? – Have you no memory? or no heart? – You *had* both – and I *have* both – at least for *you*. – I write this presuming that you received *that* letter – is it that you fear? do not be afraid of the post – the World has its own affairs without thinking of *ours* and you may write safely.[10]

(Byron to Augusta Leigh, Ravenna, 26 July 1819)

On 10 September he concludes, 'You say nothing in favour of my return to England – Very well – I will stay where I am – and you will never see me more.'[11] (Byron to Augusta Leigh, about 10 September 1819)

She never did.

7

VENICE

I.

I STOOD in Venice, on the 'Bridge of Sighs;'
    A Palace and a prison on each hand:
    I saw from out the wave her structures rise
    As from the stroke of the Enchanter's wand:
    A thousand Years their cloudy wings expand
    Around me, and a dying Glory smiles
    O'er the far times, when many a subject land
    Looked to the wingéd Lion's marble piles,
Where Venice sate in state, throned on her hundred isles!

II.

She looks a sea Cybele, fresh from Ocean,
    Rising with her tiara of proud towers
    At airy distance, with majestic motion,
    A Ruler of the waters and their powers:
    And such she was; – her daughters had their dowers
    From spoils of nations, and the exhaustless East
    Poured in her lap all gems in sparkling showers.
    In purple was she robed, and of her feast
Monarchs partook, and deemed their dignity increased.

III.

In Venice Tasso's echoes are no more,
    And silent rows the songless Gondolier;
    Her palaces are crumbling to the shore,
    And Music meets not always now the ear:
    Those days are gone – but Beauty still is here.
    States fall – Arts fade – but Nature doth not die,
    Nor yet forget how Venice once was dear,
    The pleasant place of all festivity,
The Revel of the earth – the Masque of Italy![1]

309

Byron and Hobhouse set off for Italy in early October, travelling over the Simplon Pass and then by way of Lago Maggiore to Milan. They hoped to have done with the vagaries of Dr Polidori as Byron had parted from the young man a few weeks before leaving Diodati. 'He had an alacrity of getting into scrapes – & was too young and heedless.'[2] Polidori, however, had arrived at Milan before them and during their visit, having initiated a quarrel with an Austrian officer (in which he was decidedly in the wrong), had been arrested by the guard. Byron was sent for and dealt with yet another of Polidoni's scrapes, contriving to have him set free on condition that he must leave the country within twenty-four hours. This episode strengthened Byron's detestation of the autocratic Austrian régime which had been imposed on Northern Italy.

In Milan Byron was most delighted with the Ambrosian Library where he was shown love letters of Lucretia Borgia and Cardinal Bembo as well as a lock of the lady's hair: 'the prettiest and finest imaginable.'[3] He managed to extract one strand from the lock and kept it in a paper on which he wrote the quotation from Pope's *Rape of the Lock*: 'And Beauty draws us by a single hair.'

He was welcomed by 'the noble as well as literary classes of society'[4] in Milan and there he met Monti, 'the most famous Italian poet now living.'[5] He told Thomas Moore:

> ... I saw many more of their literati; but none whose names are well known in England except Acerbi. I lived much with the Italians, particularly with the Marquis of Breme's family, who are very able and intelligent men, especially the Abate.[6]

Byron told Augusta, 'the whole tone of Italian society is so different from yours in England ... I am not sure that I do not prefer it.'[7]

Before long he would be quite certain that he did prefer it, at least for the time being. From Milan Byron and Hobhouse travelled on to Verona – 'the ampitheatre is wonderful – beats even Greece' –[8] then to Vicenza and finally to Venice.

Peter Graham perceptively describes Venice as

> ... a place where Byron could evolve a satisfactory here-and-now for himself. Around the monuments life went on – a life very much to his liking – and Venice offered a convenient back-drop against which he could stage the drama or write the poem of his own life.

With comparatively few English in Venice he could explore with some privacy the delights of a new culture. He could form a varied and agreeable routine: study, writing, masquing, salon visiting, 'domestic duties', going about in gondolas, swimming for a stunt.

[But] ... Byron never became truly Venetian in his attitudes ... As he enjoys Venice and its particulars, Byron always anticipates English reaction to his reports or envisions the English standard from which he is deviating.[9]

He writes to Thomas Moore:

My gondola is, at this present, waiting for me on the canal; but I prefer writing to you in the house it being autumn – and rather an English autumn than otherwise. It is my intention to remain at Venice during the winter, probably, as it has always been (next to the East) the greenest island of my imagination. It has not disappointed me; though its evident decay would, perhaps, have that effect upon others. But I have been familiar with ruins too long to dislike desolation. Besides, I have fallen in love, which, next to falling into the canal (which would be of no use, as I can swim), is the best or the worst thing I could do...[10]

(Byron to Thomas Moore, Venice, 17 November 1816)

He liked the Venetians:

XI.
They've pretty faces yet, those same Venetians,
  Black eyes, arched brows, and sweet expressions still
Such as of old were copied from the Grecians,
  In ancient arts by moderns mimicked ill;
And like so many Venuses of Titian's
  (The best's at Florence – see it, if ye will,)
They look when leaning over the balcony,
Or stepped from out a picture by Giorgione.[11]

XLIV.
I love the language, that soft bastard Latin,
  Which melts like kisses from a female mouth,
And sounds as if it should be writ on satin,
  With syllables which breathe of the sweet South.[12]

Paul Trueblood remarks on the change which came over Byron as he settled into Venetian life:

Venice, with its sunny skies, licentiousness, and gaiety, allowed Byron his full personal and mental freedom and, consequently, his artistic

311

freedom as well. Smarting under the ostracism of English society and virtual exile in Italy, and determined to affect indifference to English censure, Byron, for a time, abandoned himself to a career of license, but without allowing this life to absorb him heart and soul. For he saw the comic aspect of his situation. Having put away the sad-hearted anguish, part fact and part affectation, of his youth, he began to see life with a clearer vision; emancipated from his former melancholy and mannerism he began to regard himself less seriously and his foes with ironical amusement.[13]

In December Byron told Moore:

By way of divertisement I am studying daily, at an Armenian monastery, [on the island of San Lazzaro near the Lido] the Armenian language. I found that my mind wanted something craggy to break upon ... It is, to be sure, a Waterloo of an Alphabet.[14]

(Byron to Thomas Moore, Venice, 17 December 1816)

Some months later he was writing a letter of introduction to John Murray for two of the Armenian Friars who were to bring to 50 Albemarle Street some copies of an Armenian grammar which Byron had persuaded Murray to publish. Byron had put up the money for the printing costs.

He told Moore something about the social life of Venice and showed his continuing interest in literary events in London:

Last night I was at the Count Governor's, which, of course, comprises the best society, and is very much like other gregarious meetings in every country, – as in ours, – except that, instead of the Bishop of Winchester, you have the Patriarch of Venice, and a motley crew of Austrians, Germans, noble Venetians, foreigners and, if you see a quiz, you may be sure he is a Consul...

The Contessa Albrizzi, of whom I have made mention, is the De Staël of Venice, – not young, but a very learned, unaffected, good-natured woman; very polite to strangers, and, I believe not at all dissolute, as most of the women are...

When does your Poem of Poems [Lallah Rookh] come out? I hear that the E[dinburgh] R[eview] has cut up Coleridge's Christabel, and declared against me for praising it. I praised it, firstly, because I thought well of it; secondly, because Coleridge was in great distress, and after doing what little I could for him in essentials, I thought that the public avowal of my good opinion might help him further, at least with the booksellers.[15]

(Byron to Thomas Moore, Venice, 24 December 1816)

312

At the end of December he wrote to Murray:

> Yesterday being the Feast of St Stephen – every mouth was put in motion – there was nothing but fiddling and playing on the virginals – and all kinds of conceits and divertisements on every canal of this acquatic city. – I dined with the Countess Albrizzi and a Paduan and Venetian party – and afterwards went to the Opera – at the Fenice theatre (which opens for the Carnival on that day) the finest by the way I have ever seen.[16]
>
> (Byron to John Murray, Venice, 27 December 1816)

He admitted to being content with his life at Venice and the girl he had fallen in love with – 'a handsome woman – who is not a bore'.[17] Marianna Segati was the wife of his landlord in the Via Frezzeria where he had found temporary lodgings. She was twenty-two years old and looked, so he said, like an antelope, with large dark eyes.

He explained to John Murray that by Italian standards this was no misdemeanour:

> The general state of morals here is much the same as in the Doges' time – a woman is virtuous (according to the code) who limits herself to her husband and one lover ... It is only those who are indiscriminately diffuse – and form a low connection – such as the Princess of Wales with her Courier ... There is no convincing a woman here – that she is in the smallest degree deviating from the rule of right or the fitness of things – in having an 'Amoroso'.[18]
>
> (Byron to John Murray, Venice, 2 January 1817)

On one occasion Byron, who was reputed to be so harsh to women, wrote: 'Marianna is not very well today, and I shall stay with her to nurse her this Evening.'[19] (Byron to Augusta Leigh, Venice, 17 January 1817)

In March he was considering leaving Venice which gave rise to problems with Marianna.

> The girl means to go with me, but I do not like this for her own sake ... I am certainly very much attached to her, and I have cause to be so, if you knew all. But she has a child; and though, like all 'the children of the sun', she consults nothing but passion, it is necessary I should think for both.[20]
>
> (Byron to Thomas Moore, Venice, 25 March 1817)

313

Since he remained in Venice after all, Marianna stayed with him. She was lively and amused him with tart comments – 'If you loved me thoroughly [she once told Byron] you would not make so many fine reflections which are only good for *forbirsi i scarpi*'. 'That is [explained Byron] "to clean shoes withal" – a Venetian proverb of appreciation which is applicable to reasoning of all kinds.'[21] (Byron to Thomas Moore, Venice, 25 March 1817)

Byron had written to Augusta as early as December 1816 (having met Marianna in November) to reassure her that he was now relatively content. He asked whether Murray had published the poems sent to him:

> ...Goosey, my love – don't they make you 'put finger in eye'? – You can have no idea of my thorough wretchedness from the day of my parting from you till nearly a month ago ... at present I am better – thank Heaven above – & woman beneath – and will be a very good boy. – – Pray remember me to the babes – and tell me of little *Da* – who by the way – is a year old – and a few days over. – – My love to you all – & to Aunt *Sophy* – pray tell *her* in particular that I have consoled myself.[22]
>
> (Byron to Augusta Leigh, Venice, 18 December 1816)

In February he wrote to ask Augusta's help for Fletcher:

> Fletcher has requested me to remind you that *one* of his *boys* was to be a candidate for the Blue coat School – & as you know the Bentincks (who are governors) he begs by me that you will use your interest to obtain theirs.[23]
>
> ...the Carnival closed last night – and am rather tired or so – it was a fine sight – the theatre illuminated – and all the world buffooning. – I had my box full of visitors ... and ... went down to promenade the pit – which was boarded over level with the stage. – all the Virtue and Vice in Venice was there – there has been the same sort of thing every night these six weeks – besides Operas – Ridottos – parties – & the Devil knows what.[24]
>
> (Byron to Augusta Leigh, Venice, [19?] February 1817)

Carnival was succeeded by Lent and Byron told Thomas Moore, 'This is passion week – and twilight – and all the world are at vespers.'[25]

There was an epidemic of typhus in the city. Byron had just recovered from a fever which had troubled him in March but he had no intention of leaving Venice to escape the disease. 'This malady has sorely discomfited my serving men, who want sadly to be gone away ... But, besides my natural perversity, I was seasoned in Turkey, by the continual whispers of the plague, against apprehensions of contagion.'[26] (Byron to Thomas Moore, Venice, 31 March 1817)

The publication of *Glenarvon* in the late summer of 1816 had contributed to, if not caused, much scandal among the English abroad. In August 1817 Byron told Murray:

An Italian translation of 'Glenarvon' came lately to be printed at Venice – the Censor (Sr Petrotini) refused to sanction the publication till he had seen me upon the subject; – I told him that I did not recognise the slightest relation between that book and myself ... I would never prevent or oppose the publication of *any* book in *any* language – on my own private account; – and desired him (against his inclination) to permit the poor translator to publish his labours. – It is going forward in consequence. – You may say this with my compliments to the Author.[27]

(Byron to John Murray, La Mira, nr Venice, 7 August 1817)

In August Byron tried to do what he could for Dr Polidori, assuring John Murray that he knew of no great harm in the young man and some good:

... he is clever – & accomplished – knows his profession by all accounts well – and is honourable in his dealings – & not at all malevolent – I think with luck he will turn out a useful member of society ... and the college of Physicians – If you can be of any use to him – or know anyone who can – pray be so – as he has his fortune to make.[28]

(Byron to John Murray, Venice, 24 January 1817)

Byron also asked Murray to look at a tragedy Polidori had written. Murray asked Byron to advise him how to reject the play without hurting the young man's feelings.

Byron replied with:

EPISTLE FROM MR MURRAY TO DR POLIDORI.

DEAR Doctor, I have read your play,
Which is a good one in its way, –
Purges the eyes, and moves the bowels,
And drenches handkerchiefs like towels
With tears, that, in a flux of grief,

315

Afford hysterical relief
To shattered nerves and quickened pulses,
Which your catastrophe convulses.
    I like your moral and machinery;
Your plot, too, has such scope for Scenery!
Your dialogue is apt and smart;
The play's concoction full of art;
Your hero raves, your heroine cries,
All stab, and every body dies.
In short, your tragedy would be
The very thing to hear and see:
And for a piece of publication,
If I decline on this occasion,
It is not that I am not sensible
To merits in themselves ostensible,
But – and I grieve to speak it – plays
Are drugs – mere drugs, Sir – now-a-days.
I had a heavy loss by *Manuel* –
Too lucky if it prove not annual, –
And Sotheby, with his *Orestes*,
(Which, by the way, the old Bore's best is),
Has lain so very long on hand,
That I despair of all demand;
I've advertised, but see my books,
Or only watch my Shopman's looks; –
Still *Ivan*, *Ina*, and such lumber,
My back-shop glut, my shelves encumber.
    There's Byron too, who once did better,
Has sent me, folded in a letter,
A sort of – it's no more a drama
Than *Darnley*, *Ivan*, or *Kehama*;
So, altered since last year his pen is,
I think he's lost his wits at Venice.
    *   *   *   *   *   *
    *   *   *   *   *   *
In short, Sir, what with one and t'other,
I dare not venture on another.
I write in haste; excuse each blunder;
The Coaches through the street so thunder!
My room's so full – we've Gifford here
Reading MS., with Hookham Frere,
Pronouncing on the nouns and particles,
Of some of our forthcoming Articles.
    The *Quarterly* – Ah, Sir, if you
Had but the Genius to review! –

316

A smart Critique upon St Helena,
Or if you only would but tell in a
Short compass what – but to resume;
As I was saying, Sir, the Room –
The Room's so full of wits and bards,
Crabbes, Campbells, Crokers, Freres, and Wards
And others, neither bards nor wits:
My humble tenement admits
All persons in the dress of Gent.,
From Mr Hammond to Dog Dent.
  A party dines with me to-day,
All clever men, who make their way:
Crabbe, Malcolm, Hamilton, and Chantrey,
Are all partakers of my pantry. ...

But, to return, Sir, to your play:
Sorry, Sir, but I cannot deal,
Unless 't were acted by O'Neill.
My hands are full – my head so busy,
I'm almost dead – and always dizzy;
And so, with endless truth and hurry,
Dear Doctor, I am yours,
JOHN MURRAY.[29]
21 August 1817

In April he had written to Murray ruefully about the unfortunate result of his attempt to arrange for Leigh Hunt to change publishers:

You & L[eigh] Hunt have quarrelled then, it seems; I introduce him & his poem to you – in the hope that (malgré politics) the union would be beneficial to both – and the end is eternal enmity – & yet I did this with the best intentions – I introduce Coleridge and Christabel & Coleridge runs away with your money ... and I am the innocent Istmhus (damn the word I can't spell it though I have crossed that of Corinth a dozen times) of these enmities.[30]
(Byron to John Murray, Venice, 9 April 1817)

In May 1817 Murray wrote to Byron, 'Your friend Hunt, because I could not give him £500 for his Rimini – has had the baseness to enter upon a series of abuses of me.'[31]

Andrew Nicholson notes that in *The Examiner*, edited by John Hunt, 'JM is cruelly caricatured and denominated "Murrain" throughout.'[32]

In January 1817 Murray again remembered Byron's birthday and assures him that, 'All your old friends chez moi remember you and you are often the subject of their conversation – as their eye catches yours in the Portrait – which I am now facing and which is, I assure you no small happiness to me to possess.'[33]

Later in that year, however, came an unfortunate disagreement between the two men. Murray writes on 29 August:

> I assure your Lordship that I take no umbrage at the spirit of irritability which will occasionally burst from a mind like yours but I sometimes feel a deep regret that in our pretty long intercourse I appear to have failed to shew that a man in my situation, may[be] possess the feelings and principles of a Gentleman – most certainly I do think that from personal attachment I could venture as much in any shape for your service as any of those who have the good fortune to be ranked among your Lordship's friends – and therefore do [sic] cut me up at word as if I were your Taylor.[34]

But this disagreement had no lasting effect. By 1820 Murray was addressing Byron as 'My Dear Lord' and even as 'My Dear Friend'.

In early 1817 Byron produced one of his finest lyrics, perhaps the most widely admired of all his poems. It is gentle and hints of sadness and decline while the Promethean note is absent. The poet was twenty-nine.

SO WE'LL GO NO MORE A-ROVING.

1.

So we'll go no more a-roving
 So late into the night,
Though the heart be still as loving,
 And the moon be still as bright.

2.

For the sword outwears its sheath,
 And the soul wears out the breast,
And the heart must pause to breathe,
 And Love itself have rest.

3.

Though the night was made for loving,
 And the day returns too soon,
Yet we'll go no more a-roving
 By the light of the moon.[35]

8

CHILDE HAROLD'S PILGRIMAGE, CANTO IV

Having just turned nine and twenty I seriously think of giving up altogether – Unless Rome should madden me into a new Canto.[1]

In April 1817 Byron set off to join Hobhouse in Rome by way of Arqua, Ferrara (where he was inspired to write his *Lament of Tasso*) and Florence where:

I went to the two galleries – from which one returns drunk with beauty – the Venus is more for admiration than love – but there are sculpture and painting – which for the first time at all gave me an idea of what people mean by their *cant* and (what Mr Braham calls) 'entusimusy' (i.e. enthusiasm) about these two most artificial of the arts. – What struck me most were the Mistress of Raphael a portrait – the mistress of Titian a portrait – a Venus of Titian in the Medici gallery – *the* Venus – Canova's Venus also in the other gallery – Titian's mistress is also in the other gallery ... the Parcae of Michel Angelo a picture – and the Antinous – the Alexander – & one or two not very decent groups in marble.[2]

(Byron to John Murray, Foligno, 26 April 1817)

After visiting Ariosto's tomb and the cell where Tasso was imprisoned at the Hospital Santa Ana in Ferrara Byron sent to John Murray the *Lament of Tasso*, a poem which seems to have come as a relief to some of the commentators.

John Wilson wrote in November 1817:

In the 'Lament of Tasso' ... Byron has allowed his soul to sink down into gentler and more ordinary feelings. The poem possesses much of the tenderness and pathos of *The Prisoner of Chillon*.[3]

Jerome McGann observes that '... the theme of traduced, imprisoned and persecuted genius dominates Byron's poetry between 1816 and 1819.'[4]

Two lines from *Lament of Tasso* must derive from Byron's experience with Augusta's children. They form a perfect picture of the behaviour of a very small child with a loved adult, and one would think he must have been picturing Allegra, if the poem had not been written soon after she was born:

> But Thou, my young creation! my Soul's child!
> Which ever playing round me came and smiled,[5]

From Rome he wrote to Murray:

> PS. There are few English here – but several of my acquaintance – amongst others, the Marquis of Lansdowne with whom I dine tomorrow – I met the Jerseys on the road at Foligno – all well – Oh – I forgot – the Italians have printed Chillon & a *piracy* a pretty little edition prettier than yours and published as I found to my great astonishment on arriving here & what is odd is, that the English is quite correctly printed – why they did it or who did it I know not – but so it is – I suppose for the English people – I will send you a copy.[6]
> (Byron to John Murray, Rome, 9 May 1817)

In July he told Murray that he had started working up his visit to Rome into a fourth Canto of *Childe Harold*:

> Since this epistle [was] begun – the stanzas of Canto 4th have jumped to 104 – and *Such stanzas*! by St Anthony! (who has a church at my elbow and I like to be neighbourly) some of them are the right thing.[7]
> (Byron to John Murray, La Mira, 15 July 1817)

One stanza was generally thought to be 'the right thing' – a famous call for freedom:

> XCVIII.
> Yet, Freedom! yet thy banner, torn, but flying,
> Streams like the thunder-storm *against* the wind;
> Thy trumpet voice, though broken now and dying,

The loudest still the Tempest leaves behind;
Thy tree hath lost its blossoms, and the rind,
Chopped by the axe, looks rough and little worth,
But the sap lasts, – and still the seed we find
Sown deep, even in the bosom of the North;
So shall a better spring less bitter fruit bring forth.[8]

The stanzas on Rome too were much admired. In May Byron had told John Murray he would not write on Rome:

I am delighted with Rome – as I would be with a bandbox – that is it is a fine thing to see – finer than Greece ... as a *whole – ancient & modern* – it beats Greece – Constantinople – every thing – at least that I have ever seen. – But I can't describe because my first impressions are always strong and confused – & my Memory *selects* & reduces them to order – like distance in the landscape – & blends them better – although they may be less distinct...[9]

(Byron to John Murray, 9 May 1817)

By June he was more enthusiastic about his visit:

– I was delighted with Rome – & was on horseback all round it many hours daily besides in it the rest of my time – bothering over its marvels. – I excursed and skirred the country round to Alba – Tivoli – Frascati – Licenza – &c. &c. besides I visited twice the fall of Terni – which beats everything.[10]

(Byron to John Murray, Venice, 4 June 1817)

M.K. Joseph observes that:

Rome suggested, almost inevitably, the themes of grandeur and decay, of the triumph of time, of the transcendence of human limitations by art, and of art and Nature both opposed and blended in this landscape of mighty ruins. These themes have been present in the earlier cantos and are already being developed in the first section of Canto Four. The key points here are descriptions of the works of man, and, in particular, Byron is concerned with three arts – literature, sculpture and architecture.[11]

LXXVIII.

Oh, Rome! my Country! City of the Soul!
The orphans of the heart must turn to thee,
Lone Mother of dead Empires! and control
In their shut breasts their petty misery.

321

What are our woes and sufferance? Come and see
The cypress – hear the owl – and plod your way
   O'er steps of broken thrones and temples – Ye!
   Whose agonies are evils of a day –
A world is at our feet as fragile as our clay.

LXXIX.

The Niobe of nations! there she stands,
   Childless and crownless, in her voiceless woe;
   An empty urn within her withered hands,
   Whose holy dust was scattered long ago;
   The Scipios' tomb contains no ashes now;
   The very sepulchres lie tenantless
     Of their heroic dwellers: dost thou flow,
     Old Tiber! through a marble wilderness?
Rise, with thy yellow waves, and mantle her distress.

LXXX.

The Goth, the Christian – Time – War – Flood, and
   Fire;
   Have dealt upon the seven-hilled City's pride;
   She saw her glories star by star expire,
   And up the steep barbarian Monarchs ride,
   Where the car climbed the Capitol; far and wide
   Temple and tower went down, nor left a site:
   Chaos of ruins! who shall trace the void,
   O'er the dim fragments cast a lunar light,
And say, 'here was, or is,' where all is doubly night?[12]

According to the *Edinburgh Review*, *Childe Harold* Canto IV was 'one of the most awful records of the agonies of man':

CXX.

Alas! our young affections run to waste,
   Or water but the desert! whence arise
   But weeds of dark luxuriance, tares of haste,
   Rank at the core, though tempting to the eyes
   Flowers whose wild odours breathe but agonies,
   And trees whose gums are poison; such the plants
   Which spring beneath her steps as Passion flies
   O'er the World's wilderness, and vainly pants
For some celestial fruit forbidden to our wants.

Oh, Love! no habitant of earth thou art –
　An unseen Seraph, we believe in thee, –
　A faith whose martyrs are the broken heart, –
　But never yet hath seen, nor e'er shall see
　The naked eye, thy form, as it should be;
　The mind hath made thee, as it peopled Heaven,
　Even with its own desiring phantasy,
　And to a thought such shape and image given,
As haunts the unquenched soul – parched – wearied –
　wrung – and riven.

CXXII.

Of its own beauty is the mind diseased,
　And fevers into false creation: – where,
　Where are the forms the sculptor's soul hath seized?
　In him alone. Can Nature show so fair?
　Where are the charms and virtues which we dare
　Conceive in boyhood and pursue as men,
　The unreached Paradise of our despair,
　Which o'er-informs the pencil and the pen,
And overpowers the page where it would bloom again?

CXXIII.

Who loves raves – 'tis youth's frenzy – but the cure
　Is bitterer still, as charm by charm unwinds
　which robed our idols, and we see too sure
　Nor Worth nor Beauty dwells from out the mind's
　Ideal shape of such; yet still it binds
　The fatal spell, and still it draws us on,
　Reaping the whirlwind from the oft-sown winds;
　The stubborn heart, its alchemy begun,
Seems ever near the prize – wealthiest when most undone.

CXXIV.

We wither from our youth, we gasp away –
　Sick – sick; unfound the boon – unslaked the thirst,
　Though to the last, in verge of our decay,
　Some phantom lures, such as we sought at first –
　But all too late, – so are we doubly curst.
　Love, Fame, Ambition, Avarice – 'tis the same,
　Each idle – and all ill – and none the worst –
　For all are meteors with a different name,
And Death the sable smoke where vanishes the flame.[13]

323

The love of nature and the sea inspired some of the later stanzas:

CLXXVIII.

There is a pleasure in the pathless woods,
  There is a rapture on the lonely shore,
  There is society, where none intrudes,
  By the deep Sea, and Music in its roar:
  I love not Man the less, but Nature more,
  From these our interviews, in which I steal
  From all I may be, or have been before,
  To mingle with the Universe, – and feel
What I can ne'er express – yet can not all conceal.

CLXXIX.

Roll on, thou deep and dark blue Ocean – roll!
  Ten thousand fleets sweep over thee in vain;
  Man marks the earth with ruin – his control
  Stops with the shore; – upon the watery plain
  The wrecks are all thy deed, nor doth remain
  A shadow of man's ravage, save his own,
  When, for a moment, like a drop of rain,
  He sinks into thy depths with bubbling groan –
Without a grave – unknelled, uncoffined, and unknown.

CLXXXIII.

Thou glorious mirror, where the Almighty's form
  Glasses itself in tempests; in all time,
  Calm or convulsed – in breeze, or gale, or storm –
  Icing the Pole, or in the torrid clime
  Dark-heaving – boundless, endless, and sublime –
  The image of Eternity – the throne
  Of the Invisible; even from out thy slime
  The monsters of the deep are made – each Zone
Obeys thee – thou goest forth, dread, fathomless, alone.

CLXXXIV.

And I have loved thee, Ocean! and my joy
  Of youthful sports was on thy breast to be
  Borne, like thy bubbles, onward: from a boy
  I wantoned with thy breakers – they to me
  Were a delight; and if the freshening sea
  Made them a terror – 'twas a pleasing fear,
  For I was as it were a Child of thee,
  And trusted to thy billows far and near,
And laid my hand upon thy mane – as I do here.[14]

324

The Canto ends with a peaceful and modest valediction:

CLXXXV.

My task is done – my song hath ceased – my theme
    Has died into an echo; it is fit
    The spell should break of this protracted dream.
    The torch shall be extinguished which hath lit
    My midnight lamp – and what is writ, is writ, –
    Would it were worthier! but I am not now
    That which I have been – and my visions flit
    Less palpably before me – and the glow
Which in my Spirit dwelt is fluttering, faint, and low.

CLXXXVI.

Farewell! a word that must be, and hath been –
    A sound which makes us linger; yet – farewell!
    Ye, who have traced the Pilgrim to the scene
    Which is his last – if in your memories dwell
    A thought which once was his – if on ye swell
    A single recollection, not in vain
    He wore his sandal-shoon and scallop shell;
    Farewell! with *HIM* alone may rest the pain,
If such there were – with *YOU*, the Moral of his strain.

Constable's Edinburgh Magazine (which was later to review the *Vision of Judgment* with a mixture of horror and contempt) published in May 1818 an almost reverential review:

Trained in the discipline of ardent passion, he has been able to look with a steady eye upon those terrible wonders of our common nature, of which other minds have only had some faint and occasional perceptions; and, gifted at the same time with a courage and an openness, which led him fearlessly to attempt the task assigned to him, he has trod in the highest sphere of his art, with a majesty and a glory which have eclipsed the splendours of all contemporary genius.[16]

Sir Walter Scott earned Byron's enduring gratitude with a generous critique in the *Quarterly Review.*

John Wilson's article in the *Edinburgh Review* was more critical but made what was almost a prophecy of what was to come in *Don Juan*:

Of the Poet himself, the completion of this wonderful performance inspires us with lofty and magnificent hopes. It is most assuredly in his power to build up a work that shall endure among the most august fabrics of the genius of England ... his being has in it all the elements of the highest poetry.[17]

(When *Don Juan* appeared it shocked the English and was not immediately recognised for the work of genius it was. But it amply fulfilled all the hopes expressed by Wilson.)

Byron himself harboured no doubts about the worth of Canto IV. He argued with Murray about the price the publisher had offered for the Canto:

> ... if Mr Eustace was to have had two thousand for a poem on education – if Mr Moore is to have three thousand for Lallah &tc. – if Mr Campbell is to have three thousand for his prose on poetry – I don't mean to disparage these gentlemen ... You will tell me that their productions are considerably *longer* – very true – & when they shorten them – I will lengthen mine, and ask less.[18]
>
> (Byron to John Murray, 4 September 1819)

John Murray sent a copy of Canto IV to Lady Byron. She thought it beautiful and was moved by a stanza which she believed was meant for her.

> CXXXVII.
> But I have lived, and have not lived in vain:
>   My mind may lose its force, my blood its fire,
>   And my frame perish even in conquering pain;
>   But there is that within me which shall tire
>   Torture and Time, and breathe when I expire:
>   Something unearthly, which they deem not of
>   Like the remembered tone of a mute lyre,
>   Shall on their softened spirits sink, and move
> In hearts all rocky now the late remorse of Love.[19]

Hobhouse wrote voluminous and accurate notes for Canto IV which Murray was reluctant to publish. Byron insisted on some of them being published in the text and the rest in a separate volume.

Notes

M.K. Joseph points out that the themes of Canto IV go back to Gibbon and much earlier:

> In the long section on the ruins of Rome, Byron is writing in a well-defined tradition which goes back to the Renaissance, to Petrarch and to Poggio; and the fourth Canto is permeated with the spirit of Gibbon's final chapter, in which so much of its feeling is summed up:
>
> [Gibbon wrote:]
>
> The art of man is able to construct monuments far more permanent than the narrow span of his existence: yet these monuments, like himself, are perishable and frail; and in the boundless annals of time, his life and his labours must equally be measured as a fleeting moment.[1]

Michael Cooke characterises the new Canto:

> *Childe Harold IV* announces and embodies a major new attitude, not a manifesto. Its 'meditative' orientation does not demand solutions, but holds it necessary, proper, and cardinal to 'ponder boldly' (CXXVII) so that the recognition of true problems becomes a substantial value ... *Childe Harold IV* thus takes on a pivotal significance with its unflinching presentation of a mind that sacrifices tidiness to inclusiveness, a mind whose virtue it is to work *ex necessite re*, rather than ex cathedra.[2]

Jerome McGann also points to the sea-change which Canto IV represented:

> Stanzas 128–51 present Byron's accession to a more perfect understanding of the good and evil in himself and his world. In addition, they repeat the method of the whole Canto in which the poet rummages about the museum of Italy for a solution to the problem of human evil. He alternates between periods of hopefulness and expectancy (for example, stanza 47) and spells of terrible despair. In the last thirty-three stanzas of the poem he finds that the truth he has discovered is not The Truth but the way to Truth. Once again we are given a statement of the necessity of constant development and painful growth. In the Coliseum sequence, as elsewhere, the narrator is the prototype of groping, stumbling humanity who is, nevertheless, called to a high and splendid destiny; in the end, by 'pondering boldly' and by preserving always a responsiveness to new sensations and attitudes he is enlightened not to a goal but to the glory of what he is even now engaged in seeking. Gide's famous remark – 'Je ne suis jamais, je deviens' – could not be more appositely applied than to the last Canto of *Childe Harold's Pilgrimage*.[3]

McGann's final verdict on the Canto is this:

> Yet even Wordsworth at his most sublime has not eclipsed the grand
> conclusion of Byron's poem, with its comprehensive presentation of the
> greatness and the littleness, the glory and the insignificance of man, his
> work and his days.[4]

7

BEPPO

But where an English woman sometimes faints,
Italian females don't do so outright;
They only call a little on their saints,[1]

Byron enjoyed a visit from Monk Lewis in early July 1817 and spent a week with him in Venice. But most of that summer and early autumn he spent at La Mira on the left bank of the River Brenta where he rented the ancient palace of the Foscarini for his *villeggiatura*, bringing his horses with him so that he could ride out daily with Hobhouse, who spent the next few months with him there until the chill of winter sent them back to Venice.

Marianna Segati had friends at La Mira whom she could let it be known she was visiting, but she spent most of her time at the Villa Foscarini with Byron. Her husband sometimes called on her there when visiting La Mira in pursuit of another woman.

On one of his visits Pietro Segati related to Byron, Marianna, and Hobhouse, the story of a Venetian missing at sea for several years who returned from captivity in the East dressed as a Mussulman, only to find that his wife had taken a lover during his absence. The awkward situation was resolved without heroics or accusations, the husband resuming his old life and his errant wife, and all three, wife, lover, husband, remaining friends. This story was the inspiration for *Beppo*. Hobhouse, perceiving the similarities between the relationship of the characters in the story and that of Pietro and Marianna Segati with Byron, was somewhat embarrased.

In September Douglas Kinnaird, his brother, Lord Kinnaird, and William Stewart Rose visited Byron at La Mira. They stayed only briefly but brought with them as a gift a copy of Hookham Frere's lively new satirical poem, *Whistlecraft.* This work, an attempt at a revival of the style and stanza of the mediaeval Italian poet, Pulci, was to give Byron a model for the style and stanza of his *Beppo*, based, as has been noted, on Pietro Segati's Venetian story, as well as his lively manner, both of which had been cleverly and comically re-created in Frere's poem.

J. Drummond Bone analyses this new departure for Byron's verse. He works out that of the 99 stanzas of *Beppo* 43 are not strictly necessary to the plot – a taste of what is to come in *Don Juan*. He points out the frequency of references to art in general and the mechanics of writing in particular – '...not far short of half of the poem's stanzas, are in part concerned with the business of the artist'.[2] This reduces the importance of the poem's plot.

As for Byron's attitude in the poem, Michael Cooke observes that Byron shows 'a certain moral and intellectual insouciance or näiveté, and also 'a steady, critical, quasi-religious sense of *honestum.*' He also remarks that although 'indulgent laughter is audible throughout *Beppo*,' it also has 'a continual undertone of sardonic morality.'[3]

This is illustrated by two stanzas from the description of the Venetian women Byron admired for their liveliness, warmth of heart and beauty:

XV.

I said that like a picture by Giorgione
   Venetian women were, and so they *are,*
Particularly seen from a balcony,
   (For beauty's sometimes best set off afar)
And there, just like a heroine of Goldoni,
   They peep from out the blind, or o'er the bar;
And truth to say, they're mostly very pretty,
And rather like to show it, more's the pity!

XVI.

For glances beget ogles, ogles sighs,
   Sighs wishes, wishes words, and words a letter,
Which flies on wings of light-heeled Mercuries,
   Who do such things because they know no better;
And then, God knows what mischief may arise,
   When Love links two young people in one fetter,
Vile assignations, and adulterous beds,
Elopements, broken vows, and hearts, and heads.[4]

330

The main story of the tale might well have concluded in 'broken hearts and heads' but nothing of the kind results from the unexpected return of Beppo, the husband of the Venetian heroine, Laura. The matter is dealt with by commonsense and kindliness:

LXXXIX.
'That Lady is *my wife!*' Much wonder paints
    The lady's changing cheek, as well it might;
But where an Englishwoman sometimes faints,
    Italian females don't do so outright;
They only call a little on their Saints,
    And then come to themselves, almost, or quite;
Which saves much hartshorn, salts, and sprinkling faces
And cutting stays, as usual in such cases.[5]

Although the sight of Beppo in the attire of a Mussulman is rather shocking the Count courteously invites him in and even offers him the loan of some underclothes:

XCI.
They entered, and for coffee called – it came,
    A beverage for Turks and Christians both,
Although the way they make it's not the same.[6]

'Those,' writes Drummond Bone, 'who can marvel at the perception of the lending of underclothes in the idea of tolerance, or can taste another's favourite coffee in the thought of brotherhood, will understand *Beppo*'s radiant sadness.'[7]

Beppo resumes his wife, his friends, his home and his religion and: 'I've heard the Count and he were always friends'.[8]

The 'comic delicacy' Drummond Bone discovers in the story is to be found in such digressions as the discussion of the *cavalier servente* permitted to a married woman in Italy so long as the liaison is carried on with tact and discretion. In the course of this discussion Byron slips in two stanzas comparing the married woman in every society with the naive young girl:

XXXVIII.
However, I still think, with all due deference
    To the fair *single* part of the creation,
That married ladies should preserve the preference
    In *tête à tête* or general conversation –

And this I say without peculiar reference
  To England, France, or any other nation –
Because they know the world, and are at ease,
And being natural, naturally please.

XXXIX.
'Tis true, your budding Miss is very charming,
  But shy and awkward at first coming out,
So much alarmed, that she is quite alarming,
  All Giggle, Blush; half Pertness, and half Pout;
And glancing at *Mamma*, for fear there's harm in
  What you, she, it, or they, may be about:
The Nursery still lisps out in all they utter –
Besides, they always smell of bread and butter.[9]

Another delicately comic digression dwells ironically on Byron's
very real nostalgia for England.

XLVII.
'England! with all thy faults I love thee still,'
  I said at Calais, and have not forgot it;
I like to speak and lucubrate my fill;
  I like the government (but that is not it);
I like the freedom of the press and quill;
  I like the Habeas Corpus (when we've got it);
I like a Parliamentary debate,
Particularly when 'tis not too late;

XLVIII.
I like the taxes, when they're not too many;
  I like a seacoal fire, when not too dear;
I like a beef-steak, too, as well as any;
  Have no objection to a pot of beer;
I like the weather, – when it is not rainy,
  That is, I like two months of every year.
And so God save the Regent, Church, and King!
Which means that I like all and every thing.

XLIX.
Our standing army, and disbanded seamen,
  Poor's rate, Reform, my own, the nation's debt,
Our little riots just to show we're free men,
  Our trifling bankruptcies in the Gazette,
Our cloudy climate, and our chilly women,
  All these I can forgive, and those forget,

And greatly venerate our recent glories,
And wish they were not owing to the Tories.[10]

The Literary Gazette praised *Beppo* highly:

> The dénouement of the 'strange eventless history' the reviewer found 'as comic as the tale is sprightly,' and the poem as a whole 'exquisite of its kind'. It showed 'that the most spiritual touches may be combined with the shrewdest observation of men and manners.' ... As 'a mere jeu d'esprit' it was 'admirable' but it stood 'almost at the top of a style of writing with which England is not the most familiar – that of ingenious and playful satire.'[11]

Jeffrey in *The Edinburgh Review* was also complimentary:

> There is something very engaging in the uniform gayety, politeness and good humour of the author – and something still more striking and admirable is the matchless facility with which he has cast into regular and even difficult versification, the unmingled, unconstrained and unelected language of the most light, familiar, and ordinary conversation.[12]

Others were outraged. William Doherty's notice in the *British Review* was unsigned:

> ... this little poem of *Beppo* which it is said, but we are slow to believe, Lord Byron, an English nobleman, an English husband, and an English father, has sent reeking from the stews of Venice.[13]

Some commentators accused Byron of having plagiarised Hookham Frere's *Whistlecraft* in writing *Beppo*. J.G. Lockhart came briskly to his defence:

> It is also mere humbug to accuse you of having plagiarized it from Mr Frere's pretty and graceful little Whistlecraft. The measure to be sure is the same; but the measure is as old as the hills. But the spirit of the two poets is as different as it can be. Mr Frere writes elegantly, playfully, very like a gentleman, and a scholar and a respectable man, and his poems never sold, nor ever will sell.[14]

333

10

ALLEGRA IN VENICE

I never hear anything of Ada.[1]

On 12 January 1817, Claire Clairmont gave birth to a daughter whom she named, at first, Alba, a feminisation of the nickname, Albé, which she and Mary Shelley had given Byron in Switzerland. Byron accepted that the child was his, although he insisted to Douglas Kinnaird that he had 'never loved, or pretended to love' the mother.

For the first year of her life the child and her mother lived with the Shelleys at Marlowe but this was embarrassing for Shelley who could not afford further scandal. His liaison with Mary would result in his being deprived by the courts of the children of his first marriage and Sir Timothy Shelley might well decide to disinherit the son he regarded as disreputable and immoral.

If it became known that Claire was mother of an illegitimate child and that the father was the wicked Lord Byron, Claire would never succeed in finding a position as a governess and would remain penniless and a burden on the Shelleys, who could not afford to support her. When Byron offered to take the little girl, provide for her, educate her and give her a dowry which would enable her to become a respectable married woman, Claire accepted with alacrity and the Shelleys were able to breathe a sigh of relief. They would never have abandoned Claire and her child.

Claire sent Allegra to Byron with her nurse at fourteen months old. She cherished a hope that, through the child, she might see more of Byron and prevail upon him to renew their unsatisfactory relationship, but Byron, well aware of this, decreed that although

335

Claire could see her child whenever there was 'convenience of access', he would not see Claire himself and all correspondence with her was to be conducted through Shelley. Byron knew his own weakness and was determined to avoid any further 'additions to the family'.

Byron sometimes wrote off-handedly about Allegra to his English friends but his letters to his new friend, Richard Hoppner, British Consul in Venice, and to Augusta, reveal that he was in fact intrigued and delighted with his new daughter, and concerned for her welfare and her health. He wrote to Douglas Kinnaird:

> Shelley (from Marlowe) has written to me about my Daughter (the last bastard one) who it seems is a great beauty – and wants to know what he is to do about sending her ... I shall acknowledge & breed her myself – giving her the name of *Biron* (to distinguish her from little Legitimacy) – and mean to christen her Allegra – which is a Venetian name.[2]
>
> (Byron to Douglas Kinnaird, Venice, 13 January 1818)

Richard Belgrave Hoppner and his Swiss wife had become close friends of Byron by the time the child arrived in Venice and were to take a great interest in Allegra, giving the inexperienced parent good advice and sometimes taking Allegra into their household for prolonged periods.

Hoppner was a son of the celebrated portrait painter. He had studied painting himself and took an intelligent interest in literature which prompted Byron to lend him some of the books he regularly received from England. During the last few days Byron spent with Hobhouse in Venice they dined with the Hoppners and sometimes joined them in their box at the opera. After Hobhouse was gone, Hoppner often joined Byron in his rides at the Lido, sometimes bringing with him a young Englishman, Alexander Scott, and Angelo Mengaldo who had been an officer in Napoleon's army. Byron enjoyed foregathering with these men. His compulsion to compensate for his lameness by performing physical feats to put competitors in the shade resulted in a race with Mengaldo and Scott to establish whose was the greater prowess in long-distance swimming. The contestants were to swim from the Lido to the Grand Canal. Byron won by a large margin and emphasised his triumph by going on to swim the length of the Grand Canal.

On 27 May 1818 Byron wrote to Hobhouse:

My Bastard came a month ago – a very fine child – much admired in the gardens and on the Piazza – and greatly caressed by the Venetians from the Governatrice downwards.[3]

(Byron to John Cam Hobhouse, Venice, 27 May 1818)

In August he told Augusta:

My little girl Allegra (the child I spoke to you of) has been with me these three months; she is very pretty – remarkably intelligent – and a great favourite with every body.[4]

(Byron to Augusta Leigh, Venice, 3 August 1818)

Soon after this the Shelleys arrived in Venice and Percy called on Byron at the Palazzo Mocenigo on the Grand Canal (of which he had taken a three-year lease). Byron was delighted to see Shelley and took him riding on the Lido. They stayed up half the night talking. Shelley turned these conversations into a poem, *Julian and Maddalo*, in which he described the ride on the shore.

In the preface of the poem Shelley described Byron as 'a person of the most consummate genius ... His more serious conversation is a sort of intoxication, men are held by it as by a spell.'[5] Each delighted in the other's company, but while Shelley's influence on Byron was beneficial, foregathering with Byron made Shelley doubt his own powers. He wrote soon after this meeting that he could no longer compose poetry. The sun had extinguished the glow-worm.

But he was enchanted with Allegra and described her in *Julian and Maddalo*:

A lovelier toy sweet nature never made,
A serious, subtle, wild, yet gentle being,
Graceful without design, and unforeseeing –
With eyes – oh, speak not of her eyes – which seem
Twin mirrors of Italian heaven.[6]

Shelley had not told Byron that Claire had come to Venice with him and was now at the Hoppners with Allegra. To his surprise Byron made no difficulty about allowing Claire to see her daughter and offered the Shelleys the use of the villa at Este which he had rented for the summer from the Hoppners. Claire and Allegra could spend several weeks there together. He wrote to Augusta:

337

Allegra is well – but her mother (whom the Devil confound) came prancing the other day over the Appenines – to see her *shild* – which threw my Venetian loves (who are none of the quietest) into great combustion – and I was in a pucker till I got her to the Euganean hills where she & the child now are – for the present...[7]

He goes on to tell Augusta of his new *amour*, Margarita Cogni, who had arrived at the Palazzo Mocenigo uninvited and proposed to stay there. Margarita Cogni was known as the *Fornarina* since her husband was a baker:

> ...she is a very tall and formidable Girl of three and twenty – with the large black eyes and handsome face of a pretty fiend – ... and a carriage as haughty as a Princess ... she keeps my household in rare order – and has already frightened the learned Fletcher out of his remnant of wits more than once ... As the morals of this place are very lax – all the women commend her & say that she has done right – especially her own relations. – You need not be alarmed – I know how to manage her ... She is extremely fond of the child – & is very cheerful & good-natured – when not jealous ... I had known her ... more than a year – but did not anticipate this escapade which was the fault of her booby husband's treatment – who now runs about repenting and roaring like a bull-calf...[8]
>
> (Byron to Augusta Leigh, Venice, 21 September 1818)

Mary and Shelley brought Allegra back to Venice in October and Byron asked the Hoppners to keep her with them for the time being. The household at the Palazzo Mocenigo was not the most suitable environment for a little girl.

Margarita Cogni was eventually sent home to her husband and made Byron several scenes, one involving the brandishing of a knife, another throwing herself into the Canal. Byron wrote ruefully of this episode:

> Moore told me that at Geneva they had made a devil of a story of the Fornaretta – 'young lady seduced – subsequent abandonment – Leap into the Grand Canal – her being in the hospital of *Fous* in consequence' – I should like to know who was nearest being made '*fou*', and be damned to them.[9]
>
> (Byron to Richard Hoppner, 29 October 1819)

Mr Hanson and Newton, his son, arrived at the Palazzo Mocenigo in November with the papers to be signed confirming the sale of

Newstead Abbey to Major Wildman. Byron had been tremendously irritated by Hanson's usual long delays over this journey and was not pleased to discover that they had failed to bring with them most of the books he had asked John Murray to send. But these were the kind friends of his youth and he greeted them with tears in his eyes.

He arranged with Hanson a legacy of £5,000 for Allegra and sent instructions by him to Hobhouse and Kinnaird for paying the rest of his debts.

In June 1819 Byron had told John Murray:

My daughter Allegra ... is growing pretty – her hair is growing darker and her eyes are blue – Her temper and her ways, Mr Hoppner says are like mine – as well as her features – She will make in that case a manageable young lady – I never hear anything of Ada – the little Electra of my Mycenae – the moral Clytemnestra is not very communicative of her tidings.[10]

(Byron to John Murray, Venice, 7 June 1819)

In September he gave Augusta good reports of Allegra:

Allegra is here with me – in good health and very amiable and pretty at least thought so. – She is English – but speaks nothing but Venetian – 'Bon *di* papa' &c. &c. – she is very droll – and has a good deal of the Byron – can't articulate the letter *r* at all – frowns and – pouts quite in our way – blue eyes – light hair growing *darker* daily – and a dimple in the chin – a scowl on the brow – white skin – sweet voice – and a particular liking of Music – and of her *own* way in everything – is not that B. all over?[11]

(Byron to Augusta Leigh, Venice, about 10 September 1819; p.m. 23 September)

339

11

TERESA

LADY! if for the cold and cloudy clime
  Where I was born, but where I would not die,
  Of the great Poet-Sire of Italy
I dare to build the imitative rhyme,
Harsh Runic copy of the South's sublime,
  THOU art the cause; ...[1]

These lines form part of Byron's dedication of *The Prophecy of Dante* to the nineteen-year-old Contessa Teresa Guiccioli who had asked him to write a poem on Dante. They first met briefly in 1818 at the Countess Albrizzi's *conversazione*, three days after the young girl's marriage to the sixty-year-old Count Alessandro Guiccioli. The Count was reputed to be the wittiest and most cultivated man in Ravenna, but he was also rumoured to have poisoned his first wife (an older woman of plain appearance, who had brought him his great wealth) and to have arranged the assassination of more than one business rival.

By the time Teresa met Lord Byron for the second time, in April 1819, at the Countess Benzoni's, she was no longer in love with her husband and was ready to welcome an *amoroso*. Iris Origo, the biographer of Byron's last attachment, came to the conclusion that Guiccioli was a practised seducer who developed an unpleasant hold over his young bride through 'sensualism and violence'. This would explain both her delight in the attentions of a younger, gentler and kinder lover, and Byron's later uneasiness at her continuing relations with her husband.

When they met, at the Benzoni's *conversazione*, Teresa was not more than a year out of her convent school and spoke to Byron with freshness and enthusiasm of Petrarch and Dante. They fell in love and, for the next ten days, met secretly in gondolas, at private suppers, at the theatre, at the *casino* where Byron entertained his lovers (who were barred from the Palazzo Mocenigo by the formidable presence there of his reigning mistress, Margarita Cogni). Fanny Sylvestrini, the mistress of Guiccioli's steward, Lega Zambelli, assisted them as go-between in these assignations.

All this was very discreet but Teresa had no desire to conceal her conquest of the famous English poet and her behaviour reminded Byron momentarily of Caroline Lamb:

> ...[She] has no tact; – answers aloud – when she should whisper ... and this blessed night horrified a correct company at the Benzona's – by calling out to me 'Mio Byron' in an audible key during a dead Silence of pause in the other prattlers, who stared and whispered...[2]
> (Byron to John Cam Hobhouse, 6 April 1819)

In spite of these critical remarks Byron was now thoroughly in love with this girl who seemed to him 'fair as sunrise and warm as noon'.

11.

A stranger loves the Lady of the land,
  Born far beyond the mountains, but his blood
Is all meridian, as if never fanned
  By the black wind that chills the polar flood.

12.

My blood is all meridian; were it not,
  I had not left my clime, nor should I be,
In spite of tortures, ne'er to be forgot,
  A slave again of love, – at least of thee.[3]

Iris Origo comments: 'A year later he said of these verses that they were written in red-hot earnest – and most probably, in spite of all he wrote to Hoppner – it was true.'[4]

The mention of Hoppner refers to Byron's habit of pretending a cool and sardonic attitude towards the objects of his love and passion when he writes about them to his friends. This disloyalty on paper contrasts with the sincerity of his actual love which, at the height of his passion, amounts to near adoration of the loved one.

The conduct of Count Guiccioli, who appears to have turned a blind eye to these the goings-on, would be unaccountable in any but a society accustomed to *serventismo*, the practice whereby a married woman was allowed a male friend or *cavalier* to be her escort when her husband was otherwise engaged. The cavalier was allowed close intimacy with the lady as long as the proprieties appeared to be observed.

After ten days the Count decreed that his wife should join him in visiting two of his estates and then return home with him to Ravenna. Teresa rushed to the theatre and, entering the box where she knew she would find Byron, confronted him dramatically with news of her enforced departure. The box was full of Byron's men-friends so that her entering it was already a flouting of the proprieties and her demeanour was enough to fuel any suspicions already current in that city of gossip and scandal.

Next day Byron bade the Guicciolis farewell, handing Teresa down into their gondola himself and receiving a courteous invitation from her husband to visit them in Ravenna. By the time the Guicciolis arrived in Ravenna Teresa had fallen ill with a fever and was found to be suffering a miscarriage, from which she took a long time to recover.

Byron followed the Guicciolis to Ravenna after a while, stopping at Ferrara on the way to do some sight-seeing. In Venice it was Teresa who had revealed their love affair and she did so on purpose. Byron inadvertently did the same thing in Ravenna. On his arrival at a small inn, the Albergo Imperiale, he sent off a letter of introduction to the Count Alborghetti, Secretary to the Papal Legate, and was invited that very evening to join the Count in his box at the theatre. There he heard the rumour current in Ravenna, that her family despaired of the young Countess Guiccioli's life. He showed such emotion that the situation became clear not only to the Count but to all his companions.

When Count Guiccioli joined the theatre party he invited Byron to call on his sick wife. Teresa immediately began to recover and soon they were driving out together to visit the pine forests between Ravenna and the sea, returning home to the sound of the evening Angelus bell which inspired Byron to write some beautiful stanzas in *Don Juan*:

Ave Maria! blesséd be the hour!
The time, the clime, the spot, where I so oft
Have felt that moment in its fullest power
Sink o'er the earth – so beautiful and soft –
While swung the deep bell in the distant tower,
Or the faint dying day-hymn stole aloft,
And not a breath crept through the rosy air,
And yet the forest leaves seemed stirred with prayer.

CV.

Sweet Hour of Twilight! – in the solitude
Of the pine forest, and the silent shore
Which bounds Ravenna's immemorial wood,
Rooted where once the Adrian wave flowed o'er,
To where the last Caesarean fortress stood,
Evergreen forest! which Boccaccio's lore
And Dryden's lay made haunted ground to me,
How have I loved the twilight hour and thee!

CVIII.

Soft Hour! which wakes the wish and melts the heart
Of those who sail the seas on the first day
When they from their sweet friends are torn apart;
Or fills with love the pilgrim on his way
As the far bell of Vesper makes him start,
Seeming to weep the dying day's decay;
Is this a fancy which our reason scorns?
Ah! surely Nothing dies but Something mourns![5]

Teresa continued weak and Byron asked Guiccioli for permission
(which was freely given) to send for Dr Aglietti from Venice who
prescribed new medicines which seemed to do her good. Dr Aglietti
was interested in literature. Before he left he accompanied Byron
on a ceremonial visit to Dante's tomb on which they laid a copy
of Byron's poems. An observer in Ravenna remarked that he never
saw Byron pass by the tomb of Dante without baring his head.

Teresa describes the interest Byron aroused among Ravenna
society:

'I saw him on horseback today,' said one young lady, 'Oh God! how
beautiful he was! Truly men should agree to exile him' ... 'Is he
married?' asked her young sister, and was answered by a long account
of Byron's past adventures furnshed by another guest who had recently
returned from Milan, and had heard more gossip about the poet there.[6]

Iris Origo remarks that Teresa explained, somewhat superfluously, that, 'It was not Byron's genius that excited public interest about him. It was his rank, his beauty, his fortune, and his mysterious reputation for strange adventures.'[7]

Hobhouse had warned Byron not to become involved with the wife of a nobleman of the Romagna. Hoppner wrote to him from Venice warning him that Teresa would leave him in the lurch and betray him. Byron complained to their friend, Alexander Scott, of Hoppner's 'bile', confessing, 'You will think me a damned fool – but when she was supposed in danger – I was really & truly on the point of poisoning myself...'[8] None of these friends would have believed it, but Teresa was completely disinterested and would not accept any gifts from Byron. After a time she even agreed that she might elope with him, although she had rejected any such suggestions from the beginning. The whole basis of *serventismo* was that the lady stayed with her husband – otherwise she lost her reputation and her right to marital support.

Now the Count spirited his wife off to Bologna, inviting Byron to join them there. Teresa and Byron went to the theatre to see Alfieri's play, *Myrrha*, in the course of which Byron became so distressed by the tragedy that he almost suffered a fit. Teresa caught the infection and sat at his side, sobbing bitterly. But before long Teresa's health gave way once more and Byron persuaded the Count to allow him to escort Teresa to Venice so that she could once again consult Dr Aglietti. The proprieties would be observed. Each would travel in their own coach and Teresa would stay in a separate Palazzo.

On the way they visited Arqua together, remembering Petrarch and looking over his house. At Padua they stayed at an inn whose landlord treated Byron with such deference and respectful affection that Teresa questioned Byron and learned that he had saved the man from destitution a year earlier by lending him money. The grateful innkeeper put on a grand banquet for them with music. Byron was always moved when he met with such gratitude.

On arrival in Venice they decided to move out to La Mira where Teresa ostensibly stayed in a different villa but in fact lived with Byron at the Foscarini. This was an idyllic time for them. They would ride out beside the Brenta and Byron procured a piano so that Teresa could play for him.

Thomas Moore arrived in Venice in October, was introduced to

Teresa and then taken to the Palazzo Mocenigo where he spent the next few days. Byron slept at La Mira during this time but joined Moore each day and showed him the sights of Venice. Moore was in serious financial difficulties (which later culminated in a temporary flight to Paris) and Byron made him a present of the *Memoirs* on which he had been working, to help him out.

This infuriated Hobhouse who was always jealous of Moore's relationship with Byron. In 1821 Byron endeavoured to explain the exact nature of the transaction over the *Memoirs*:

> With regard to 'the Memoirs' I can only say – that Moore acted entirely with *my approbation* in the whole transaction – and that I desire no profit whatever from it – Do you really mean to say that I have not as good a right to leave such an M.S. after my death – as the thousands before me who have done the same? ... Will not my life ... be given in a false and unfair point of view by others? – I mean *false* as to *praise* as well as *censure*? – If you have any *personal* feelings upon it – I can say as far as I recollect that you are mentioned without anything that could annoy you – and if otherwise it shall be cut out ... whatever blame there is attaches to *me* and not to *Moore* ... to whom the papers were left as a kind of legacy ... with the express stipulation of not being published during the writer's lifetime ... and I desired him to sell them *now* – to help him out of his 'Bermuda' scrape.[9]
>
> (Byron to John Cam Hobhouse, Pisa, 23 November 1821)

Byron remarked of Moore's stay in Venice, 'Moore and I do nothing but laugh.'

Moore sold the *Memoirs* to John Murray to be published after Byron's death and received from Murray two thousand pounds for them. These were the *Memoirs* which were burned unread after Byron's death, much against Moore's will, who returned the two thousand pounds to Murray.

When he learned that Teresa was in Venice with Byron, her father, Count Ruggiero Gamba Ghiselli, called on Alessandro Guiccioli and told him he ought not to have allowed his daughter to travel with Byron. He was under the impression that Teresa's friendship with Byron was platonic and was eager to preserve her reputation, if only for the sake of her unmarried younger sisters. He persuaded his son-in-law to fetch his wife home.

When Guiccioli arrived in Venice Byron was at the Palazzo Mocenigo with the Countess and the Count insisted on moving in for two days for appearance's sake. Byron was feeling weak as he had just recovered from so severe a fever that he awoke one night to find Fletcher sobbing on one side of the bed and Teresa on the other. This fever was the excuse for Teresa's presence.

Guiccioli seized the opportunity to lecture Teresa on her duties as his wife. Teresa replied pertly and rebelliously. At one point Guiccioli came weeping to Byron who told him that if he wished to give his wife up he would take her. He later wrote that at twenty he would certainly have taken her. At thirty he did everything possible to persuade her to go back to Ravenna with her husband, and this she reluctantly did.

Now Byron was alone in Venice and his mind turned to England. No invitation came from Augusta who was terrified at the possibility of his return. He considered South America. In November he wrote to Kinnaird:

> I shall bring my little daughter Allegra with me – but I know not where to go – I have nobody to receive me – but my sister – and I must conform to my circumstances – and live accordingly – that is meanly in London & difficultly – on that which affords splendour & ease in Italy – But I hope to get out to America ... I should prefer Spanish America.[10]
>
> (Byron to Douglas Kinnaird, Venice, 16 November 1819)

Later in the month he wrote to Hobhouse:

> There is packing and preparation going on – and I mean to plod through the Tyrol with my little 'shild' – Allegrina – who however is not very well – and half the house have brought the tertian from the Mira – it made me delirious during an attack ... Dr Aglietti has this moment informed me that Allegra has the 'doppia terzano' – a febrile doubloon which it seems renders my departure from hence quite uncertain – (as I will not & can not go without, her) it means the poor child has the fever *daily* – & her nurse has it – besides a cameriere [chambermaid] and barcariola [boatman] – my own has diminished – There are things to say to you – and to Douglas – but Alas! here I am in a gloomy Venetian palace ... all my plans ... are lulled on the feverish pillow of a sick infant.[11]
>
> (Byron to John Cam Hobhouse, Venice, 21 November 1819)

In December he was still making plans for England but abruptly he gave in to Teresa's despairing letters at the prospect of his departure and wrote to Kinnaird: 'My dear Douglas – the Winter has set in hard – & my daughter not being well re-established I

347

have put off my intended voyage till the Spring – or perhaps to the Greek Calends.'[12] (Byron to Douglas Kinnaird, Venice, 10 December 1819)

The Greek Calends it proved to be.

12

THE PROPHECY OF DANTE

> *For what is Poesy but to create*
> *From overfeeling Good or Ill; and aim*
> *At an external life beyond our fate,*
> > *And be the new Prometheus, of new men*
> > *Bestowing fire from Heaven, and then, too late,*
> *Finding the pleasure given repaid with pain,*
> > *And vultures to the heart of the bestower,*
> > *Who, having lavished his high gift in vain,*
> *Lies chained to his lone rock by the sea-shore?*
> *So be it: we can bear.* —[1]

Thus Byron allies himself with Dante. They share the same pain.
As Jerome McGann points out, most of the poems Byron wrote
during the first years of his exile, were concerned with the sufferings
of persecuted genius. There are obvious parallels with Dante in
Byron's own life:

> For all the lack of precise information about his early life and education
> we can imagine the young [poet] as an exceptionally well-endowed boy,
> observant, intellectually curious, open to instruction and gifted with a
> remarkable memory. Allied to his gifts was a driving ambition to excel
> at whatever he touched. This drive, fateful in its effects on him, probably
> owed something of its force to his early life and circumstances; to the
> loss of his mother and his need to demonstrate to his father and
> stepmother that he was still worthy of love. Perhaps from this also
> derive his faults, his pride, his need to justify himself in all his doings,
> the hypersensitivity that made him flare with pain at any criticism, the
> deep capacity for resentment that was to make him so impatient of

349

compromise in any overtures made by Florence for his return when he was in exile...[2]

Change a few words and this could almost have been written of Byron. Yet it is a description of the young Dante from William Anderson's *Dante the Maker.*

Anderson describes the powerful influence of Dante's *Commedia* – [and his words could equally be applied to Byron's *Don Juan*] – 'Art of the order of the *Commedia* may affect history directly ... but it also has a wider and more profound effect in changing and enlarging attitudes of mind and understanding over generations ... his art makes use of all the major social and intellectual currents of his time ... His aim is to remove those living in this life from a state of misery and to bring them to a state of happiness ... the work was conceived not for speculation but with a practical object...[3]

Jerome McGann writes similarly that the concept of *Don Juan* is both intellectual and moral. Like the *Divine Comedy* it has a practical and normative purpose.

Byron's poetry *did* change and enlarge attitudes of mind and understanding over generations. It was declaimed by revolutionaries in Poland in 1980 and later by young dissidents in China during the demonstrations in Tiananmen Square. Mazzini, one of the moving spirits in the Risorgimento, wrote of Byron's influence on the nineteenth century Italian struggle for freedom:

> Byron wished to ... raise us up, to raise us, his brothers ... witnessing the progress of the Restorations and triumph of the principles of the Holy Alliance, he never swerved from his courageous opposition, but maintained in the face of the world, his faith in the rights of the people, in the ultimate triumph of freedom, and in his duty to promote this by every means in his power, and whenever the opportunity offered.[4]

In the preface to *The Prophecy* Byron wrote:

> The reader is requested to suppose that Dante addresses him in the interval between the conclusion of the Divina Commedia and his death, and shortly before the latter event, foretelling the fortunes of Italy in general in the ensuing centuries ... the measure adopted is the terza rima of Dante.[5]

In his commentary Jerome McGann observes that Byron's foremost source was 'Dante's own works and perhaps most especially his epistles.' He was clearly familiar with the older writers on Dante (like Boccaccio and Aretino) as well as modern scholarship. McGann finds that Byron and Shelley made the first extensive and significant efforts to adapt *terza rima* to English verse '... though only Shelley's in the "Ode to the West Wind" and "The Triumph of Life", shows complete mastery of the adapted form.'[6]

In March 1820 Byron sent the manuscript to Murray. In June he told Murray it was 'the best thing I ever wrote' but he was much more diffident about its value than he was over *Childe Harold* Canto IV and added the provision *'if it be not unintelligible'*.[7] He was uneasy about the poem, waiting for others to give their verdict and telling Hobhouse '... for my own part I don't understand a word of the whole four cantos – & was therefore lost in admiration of their sublimity.'[8]

All the same, he was eager for it to be published, telling Murray in August, 'The time for the Dante would be now – ... as Italy is on the Eve of great things.'[9] Byron has Dante declaring '... the Genius of my Country shall arise.'[10]

The Italian police were well aware that Byron was aiming in *The Prophecy* at the Italians. Iris Origo reports that:

A translation of his *Prophecy of Dante* had got as far as Volterra, to fall into the hands of the Commissioner of that small city. Its contents struck him as being extremely dangerous. 'It is decidedly not written in the spirit of our government, nor of any of the Italian governments. To me, indeed, it seems designed to augment popular agitation, which is already sufficiently aroused. Lord Byron makes Dante foresee democracy and independence, as the true *goods* of Italy.' ... The Florentine government replied in some perplexity that it would like to see a copy of this dangerous work (of which the circulation was immediately prohibited) and within ten days the Commissioner forwarded it, quoting the far from complimentary comments of the translator: '... the style of the greater part of living English poets is, in truth, so turgid and extravagant as to deform their ideas even when they are magniloquent or acute.'[11]

Jeffrey reviewed the poem briefly at the end of his review of *Marino Faliero* in the *Edinburgh Review* (July 1820). He gave it some high praise: 'It is a very grand, fervid, turbulent and somewhat mystical composition – full of the highest sentiments, and the highest poetry...' but he went on in a tone not far removed from that of the translator employed by the police at Volterra:

351

'Its great fault with common readers will be that it is not sufficiently intelligible, either in its general drift or in particular passages: – and even those who are qualified to enter into its spirit, and can raise themselves to the height of the temper in which it is conceived, will be entitled to complain of the interminable periods and endless interlacings of the diction, and of the general crudity and imperfect concoction of the bulk of the composition.'[12]

Byron did not write the further cantos he had contemplated and it may be that he agreed with Jeffrey's strictures and paid them more heed than he paid to Shelley's letter of 14 September 1821 which told him:

'The poetry of this piece is indeed sublime; and if it have not general admiration you ought still to be contented; because the subject, no less than the style, is addressed to the few, and, like some passages in Childe Harold, will only be fully appreciated by the select readers of many generations.'[13]

Byron was not interested in select readers. He continually asked for cheap editions of his works to be produced. The audience he aimed at was all mankind.

In his *Life of Shelley* Thomas Medwin purports to quote some contemptuous words spoken by Byron on Dante and the *Divine Comedy*. Medwin remarks (though not on the subject of this passage) that no one mystified so much as Byron – indeed it was impossible to know whether he was in jest or in earnest.[14]

Those who knew Byron better than he had little difficulty in this respect. Teresa Guiccioli tells how Medwin was holding forth on women and love: 'Lord Byron took up the opposite side ... it was easy to see that he was playing a part and that his words, partly in jest, partly ironical, did not express his thoughts.' Seeing that this caused Teresa some distress Byron told her, 'I am very sorry to have grieved you but how could you think that I was talking seriously?'

Teresa did not think it. But she told him Medwin would repeat his words and the world would believe him and think Medwin a man of noble sentiments and Byron a real Don Juan. Byron said, 'I can't help it. I couldn't resist the temptation of punishing Medwin for his vanity. All those eulogiums and sentimentalities about women were to make us believe how charming they had always been towards him...'[15]

William St Clair agrees that Byron often tried to mystify Medwin: 'Byron knew of course that Medwin was writing up his conversations after every meeting, probably with a view to subsequent publication. He was therefore very much a legitimate target.' St Clair dismisses not only Medwin as a reliable source: '[Lady Blessington's] book, to my mind, is highly untrustworthy, more untrustworthy maybe than Trelawny's or even than Medwin's.' St Clair concludes, 'We can, I think, make good guesses at when Byron was being serious and when not. The irony can be subtle and it would be a brave Byronist who would claim to be always able to detect it. But there are times in reading his conversations, when we can confidently shout out what Beau Brummell or Lord Alvanley or Scrope Davies might have shouted at Byron at Watier's. "Byron, that's all my eye and Betty Martin." '[16]

Medwin took Byron literally. We should treat his reports on Byron's conversations with scepticism. It is highly unlikely that Byron ever spoke of Dante and the *Divine Comedy* with serious contempt. In his Ravenna Journal (29 January 1821) he sprang to the defence of Dante against Schlegel:

Read Schlegel. Of Dante he says that 'at no time had the greatest and most national of all Italian poets been much the favourite of his countrymen.' T'is false. There have been more editors and commentators (and imitators) ultimately of Dante than of all their poets put together ... Why, they talk Dante – write Dante – and think and dream Dante at this moment – to an excess, which would be ridiculous but that he deserves it ... This German ... says also that Dante's chief defect is 'want of gentle feelings' – and Francesca of Rimini? – and the father's feelings in Ugolino – ? and Beatrice – ? and 'La Pia'? Why, there is gentleness in Dante beyond all gentleness when he is tender. It is true that treating of the Christian Hades or Hell, there is not much scope or site for gentleness – but who *but* Dante could have introduced any 'gentleness' at all into *Hell*? Is there any in Milton's? No – and Dante's Heaven is all love and glory and majesty.[17]

13

MAZEPPA

'Away! – away! – my steed and I,
  Upon the pinions of the wind!
All human dwellings left behind,
We sped like meteors through the sky,
When with its crackling sound the night
Is chequered with the Northern light.
Town – village – none were on our track,
  But a wild plain of far extent,
And bounded by a forest black;[1]

On 24 September 1818, Byron mentions *Mazeppa* in the same breath as the commencement of *Don Juan*, in a letter from Venice to John Murray: 'I have written the first Canto (180 octave stanzas) of a poem in the style of Beppo and have Mazeppa to finish besides.'[2]

On 9 December he tells Kinnaird '...the purchase of Don Juan – and Mazeppa ... ought to bring a good price – there is more in quantity than my former cargos – and for the quality you will pronounce.'[3]

Mazeppa was finally published by John Murray with the *Ode on Venice* on 28 June 1819.

M.K. Joseph finds that *Mazeppa* 'draws towards the mature poems in its good-humoured tone and vigour of narrative.'[4] He writes of the dramatic ride of the naked hero tied to the back of a wild horse: 'Byron's octosyllables came into their own in the sustained, energetic gallop of Mazeppa's wild ride.'[5]

Jerome McGann agrees that 'the description of that wild ride epitomizes the poetic quality of this neglected masterpiece,' and points out that 'Mazeppa is saved from death when he ceases to struggle against it.'[6]

The poem is based on an incident from Voltaire's *History of Charles XII*.

Mazeppa exerted a notable influence in the world of nineteenth-century music. Liszt wrote a symphonic poem on the theme and his Transcendental Etude No. 4 is called *Mazeppa*; Tchaikovsky wrote an opera. Balfe composed a cantata (1862). It also inspired Victor Hugo's poem of the same name.

The following lines are interesting from a biographical point of view as they display the same passionate sexual tension to be found in the 'Opening Lines to Lara', addressed to Augusta Leigh when Byron was still in England. E.H. Coleridge points out that the use here of 'electric' as a metaphor may be compared with a similar use in *Parisina* (l. 480):

VI.

'We met – we gazed – I saw, and sighed;
She did not speak, and yet replied;
There are ten thousand tones and signs
We hear and see, but none defines –
Involuntary sparks of thought,
Which strike from out the heart o'erwrought,
And form a strange intelligence,
Alike mysterious and intense,
Which link the burning chain that binds,
Without their will, young hearts and minds;
Conveying, as the electric wire,
We know not how, the absorbing fire.
I saw, and sighed – in silence wept,
And still reluctant distance kept, ...[7]

14

RAVENNA AND FILETTO

'Allegrina is flourishing like a pomegranate blossom'

When Byron was summoned back to Ravenna it was Count Ruggiero Gamba, Teresa's father, who insisted on his return. Teresa had staged another apparently near-fatal collapse and gave the impression that the return of Lord Byron alone could save her life. Count Guiccioli was obliged to consent to it and Byron would now be accepted as Teresa's *cavalier servente*, a position he would find irksome. But he was touched at the friendly reception he received from Teresa's large and socially exalted family, some of whom were on terms of close friendship with the Pope, a circumstance which would significantly affect Teresa's welfare.

Living at Albergo Imperiale was uncomfortable and since the weather was bad, Byron had to forego the daily rides which were necessary for his well-being. He grew fractious over fancied slights and the suspicion that Teresa was closer to her sinister and somewhat alarming husband than he liked.

Unlike Annabella, Teresa, immediately aware of the turmoil of his feelings, was able, like Augusta, to manage him by teasing and remonstrating with him affectionately. Sometimes she offered him the stimulus of a lively argument. She even managed to persuade the Count to offer Byron the lease of spacious apartments on the upper floors of the Palazzo Guiccioli and room for his horses in the stables. His ill-humour disappeared at once.

The arrangements for his horses were important to him. Since he was unable to walk far, his health required daily rides and gallops. When he lived in Venice it was said that there were only

357

eight horses in the city – the four bronze horses in the Piazza San Marco and the four live ones in Lord Byron's stables. This was a far cry from the days in Cambridge when Byron had purchased his grey horse, Oateater, to cut a dash.

When the Austrian army was on the march in 1817 they announced that they intended to requisition all horses on their line of march and Byron was informed that his would be among those required. Byron let it be known that he would shoot his horses in the street rather than submit to so unjust an imposition on a stranger and a foreigner.

In Ravenna he rode daily in the pine forests. It was during these rides that he gave so generously to beggars he met in the woods that he became beloved by the poor of the city. He was intrigued one day to find in the forest a woman of ninety-five gathering wood. He questioned her and gave her money. He was enchanted when she approached him a few days later with the gift of a bunch of violets.

Soon after his return to Ravenna he wrote to Richard Hoppner:

My Dear Hoppner – I have not decided anything about remaining in Ravenna – I may stay a day – a week – a year – all my life ... I forgot to thank you and Mrs Hoppner for a whole treasure of toys for Allegra before our departure – it was very kind & we are very grateful.[1]
(Byron to Richard Hoppner, Ravenna, 10 January 1820)

In February he told John Murray:

I write in the greatest haste – it being the hour of the Corso – and I must go and buffoon with the rest – my daughter Allegra is just gone with the Countess G in Count G's coach ... and I must follow with all the rest of the Ravenna world.[2]
(Byron to John Murray, Ravenna, 7 February 1820)

He often wrote to the Hoppners with news of Allegra. Claire was now agitating to have the child sent to her in the Shelley household and Byron explained to them:

'About Allegra – I can only say to Claire – that I so totally disapprove of the mode of Children's treatment in their family – that I should look upon the Child as going into a hospital. – Is it not so? Have they *reared* one? – Her health here has hitherto been excellent – and her temper not bad – she is sometimes vain and obstinate – but always

clean and cheerful – and as in a year or two I shall either send her to England – or put her in a Convent for education – these defects will be remedied as far as they can in human nature. – But the Child shall not quit me again – to perish of Starvation, and green fruit – or be taught to believe that there is no Deity. – Whenever there is convenience of vicinity and access – her Mother can always have her with her – otherwise no. – It was so stipulated from the beginning. – The Girl is not so well off as with *you* – but far better than with them; – the fact is she is spoilt – being a great favourite with every body on account of the fairness of her Skin – which shines among their dusky children like the milky way, but there is no comparison of her situation now – and that under Elise – or with them. – She has grown considerably – is very clean – and lively. – She has plenty of air and exercise at home – and she goes out daily with M[adam]e Guiccioli in her carriage to the Corso. – The paper is finished & so must the letter be –'[3]
(Byron to Richard Hoppner, Ravenna, 22 April 1820)

By now the Palazzo Guiccioli was in turmoil. Byron and Teresa managed to carry on their affair by posting trustworthy servants to alert them when Count Guiccioli appeared on the staircase. His suspicions aroused, he set spies on his wife, broke open her writing-desk and eventually discovered her (in May 1820) in a compromising situation with her lover.

Count Guiccioli told Byron to leave the house, but he refused to go until his lease ran out. However, he went at once to Teresa's father (with whom he was on the best of terms) and assured him that in this crisis he would do whatever Count Gamba considered best for his daughter. He offered to leave Ravenna, but Ruggiero Gamba had developed both respect and affection for his daughter's lover and he applied to the Pope for a separation from her husband for Teresa.

By mid-July the separation was granted. On 18 July Teresa crept out of the Palazzo Guiccioli and fled to her father's country estate at Filetto.

Guiccioli was infuriated by his wife's departure but the whole of Ravenna was on the side of the lovers, finding it illogical for Teresa's husband to object to the relationship at this late stage since he had acquiesced in the presence of Byron for months and had even allowed his wife to go to Venice with him. Count Gamba challenged Guiccioli to a duel over the imbroglio, and no one seems to have felt that it would have been more appropriate to challenge the lover.

359

Aware as he was of Alessandro Guiccioli's reputation for violence by stealth, Byron sent one of his servants as bodyguard for Teresa. He was warned to give up his rides in the forest – a warning he ignored. He stayed on in the Palazzo Guiccioli where now he could write in peace. He had complained of constant interruptions from Teresa when he was writing *Marino Faliero*. This seems to have been the one respect in which Teresa bore any resemblance to Lady Byron.

The Papal judgement laid down that the husband must return the wife's dowry and pay her an allowance. Teresa must live under her father's roof and Byron must keep his distance. Neither of the Guicciolis might marry again until the death of the other. There was no possibility of divorce in Italy.

The heat in Ravenna was intense and Byron looked for a house in the country where Allegra could pass the summer. In August he told the Hoppners, 'Allegra has been ill but is getting better in the country where the air is much purer – the heat has been tremendous. Take care of your little boy.'[4] (Byron to Richard Hoppner, Ravenna, 31 August 1820)

The little girl was installed with her nurse and two maids at the Villa Bacinetta which was near enough to Filetto for Teresa to visit her there. Byron, after a prudent interval, would be able to go secretly to Filetto after visiting Allegra.

The Gambas were accustomed to spending the summer at Filetto '... in patriarchal fashion – a large, cheerful, easy-going family, devoted to each other and to their country pursuits ... they shot duck and snipe in the marshes, rode in the forest and fished in the river; they took an active interest and pride in the management of their estates; they entertained their country neighbours, and ... they came to find this secluded country house a most convenient centre for their conspiratorial activities.'[5]

For Teresa's sake Byron kept away from her for several weeks, much to her dismay. He warned her that if he was known to be visiting Filetto it would harm her reputation and lead to a change in the papal attitude. He also told her that at this time of year he was hardly fit for human contact: 'This season kills me with sadness every year.'[6] A stanza from *Don Juan* seems to describe this feeling:

CXXXIV.

And thus they left him to his lone repose:
  Juan slept like a top, or like the dead,
Who sleep at last, perhaps (God only knows),
  Just for the present: and in his lulled head
Not even a vision of his former woes
    Throbbed in accurséd dreams, which sometimes
      spread
Unwelcome visions of our former years,
Till the eye, cheated, opens thick with tears.[7]

Byron now heard the bad news of the failure of the long drawn out lawsuit for regaining his Rochdale property and wrote to Kinnaird:

Dear Douglas – I have received what you call the 'fatal intelligence' of the Rochdale decision – It is indeed a severe blow after fifteen years of litigation – and almost as many thousand pounds of law expenses with two verdicts in my favour – but ... A man has lived to little purpose – if he cannot sustain such things. – 'Whom the Lord loveth he chasteneth.' – The only thing now is to think what is best to be done. – I (were I on the spot) should immediately order the manor – & whatever rights are mine to be brought to the hammer – and sold to any *bidding* without consideration of price. – This will at least pay the law expenses – and perhaps liquidate some part of the remaining debt – so pray my dear Douglas – let this be done directly ... indeed you must agree with me that the payment of debts must be now my only object.[8]

          (Byron to Douglas Kinnaird, Ravenna, 27 July 1820)

In spite of this disappointment, Byron offered to support Teresa, and wrote to her: 'For my part (if you will) we will live together and send A. [Alessandro] and his alimony to...'[9]

After a period of discretion he began to make frequent visits to Filetto where he thoroughly enjoyed being treated as a member of Teresa's delightful family. He was happy to join with them in shooting at a target but refused to aim at live birds as the Gamba family did. He had made up his mind long ago never to do so again:

I remember in riding from Chrisso to Castri (Delphes) along the side of Parnassus I saw six eagles in the air ... The last bird I ever fired at was an *eaglet*, on the shore of the Gulf of Lepanto, near Vostitza. It was only wounded, and I tried to save it, the eye was so bright; but it pined and died in a few days; and I never did since, and never will, attempt the death of another bird.[10]

In August the Gambas gave an *alfresco* party for witnessing an eclipse of the sun. After watching the sky through smoked glasses the party indulged in a game of bowls in which Byron joined. When they discovered that a rise in the level of the river had brought vast amounts of fish into the stream they all jumped into the water and began fishing with great enthusiasm. Byron had slipped away and gone back to Ravenna but he would not in any case have joined them.

His attitude to fishing is illustrated by a verse in *Don Juan* Canto III (1823):

> And angling, too, that solitary vice.
> Whatever Isaak Walton sings or says,
> The quaint, old, cruel coxcomb, in his gullet
> Should have a hook, and a small trout to pull it.[11]

Now Alessandro Guiccioli accused Teresa of having taken various objects from the Palazzo Guiccioli without permission. His motive was to persuade the Pope to reduce the allowance he was obliged to pay to his wife. In the end, she elected to keep the objects in exchange for agreeing to a lower allowance.

In March 1821 Byron decided that Allegra should be placed in a convent at Bagnacavallo twelve miles outside Ravenna. Claire was beside herself about this decision and Byron wrote to the Hoppners defending himself from her hysterical tirades:

> ...I enclose you also a letter from Pisa – on the usual subject *not* to trouble you as 'umpire' as the person desires – but to enable you to judge whether I do or do not deserve such a piece of objurgation. I have neither spared trouble nor expense in the care of the child – and as she was now four years old complete and quite above the control of the Servants – & as it was not fit that she should remain with them longer in any case – and as a *man* living without a woman at the head of his house – cannot much attend to a nursery, <as is necessary> – I had no resource but to place her for a time (at a high pension too) in the convent of Bagna-Cavalli (twelve miles off) where the air is good and where she will at least have her learning advanced – and her morals and religion inculcated. – I had also another reason – things were and

are in such a state here – that I had no reason to look upon my personal safety as particularly insurable – and I thought the infant best out of harm's way, for the present. – You *know* (perhaps more than I do) that to allow the Child to be with her mother – & with *them* & their principles – would be <like> absolute insanity – if not worse – that even her health would not be attended to properly – to say nothing of the Indecorum. – It is also fit that I should add that I by no means intended nor intend to give a *natural* Child an *English* Education, because with the disadvantages of her birth her after settlement would be doubly difficult. – Abroad – with a fair foreign education – and a portion of five or six thousand pounds – she might and may marry very respectably – in England such a dowry would be a pittance – while <out of it> elsewhere it is a fortune. – It is besides my wish that She should be a R[oma]n *Catholic* – which I look upon as the best religion...[12]

(Byron to Richard Hoppner, Ravenna, 3 April 1821)

The Shelleys supported Byron in his decision though they had to be careful about admitting it to Claire.
Shelley wrote to Byron from Pisa:

I think I mentioned to you before that I never see any of Claire's letters to you – I can easily believe, however, that they are sufficiently provoking, and that her views concerning Allegra are unreasonable. Mary, no less than myself, is perfectly convinced of your conduct towards Allegra having been most irreproachable, and we entirely agree to the necessity, under existing circumstances, of the placing of her in a convent near to you.[13]

Teresa's family took an interest in the little girl, her very correct and deeply religious grandparents even visiting Allegra at her convent.

Byron received reports from Bagnacavallo assuring him that Allegrina had settled down happily among her new playmates. Modern standards of parental behaviour would judge it extraordinary that he did not visit the convent to see for himself that all was well with her. A possible explanation might be that, in view of his lurid reputation, he was terrified of the nuns, and feared they might be terrified of him.

In July he was evidently considering taking Allegra out of the convent on account of the unsettled state of the country, with risings and rumours of risings and acts of violence on the streets. It was Teresa who persuaded him that his little daughter would be safer in her convent during these upheavals.

On 16 July Shelley wrote again from Pisa:

I have this moment received and shall have dispatched by post, the bulletin for Clare. I am delighted to see my little friend's handwriting. I feel more and more strongly, the wisdom of your firmness on the subject, and I applaud it the more because I know how weak I should have been in your case, and I see most clearly all the evils that would have sprung from weakness. Allegra's happiness depends on your remaining firm.[14]

15

THE FIRST VENETIAN PLAY: *MARINO FALIERO*

The black veil which is painted over the place of Marino Faliero amongst the Doges and the Giant's Staircase where he was crowned and discrowned and decapitated struck forcibly upon my imagination.[1]

Samuel Chew produces a four page appendix to his study of Byron's dramas filled with the Shakespearean echoes which can be heard in *Marino Faliero*.

Professor John D. Jump compares Byron's method in *Marino Faliero* with Alfieri:

> What mainly holds our attention as we read is the concentrated, collected fury of Marino Faliero himself. By compressing this within the narrow limits of the three unities Byron achieved effects which bring the tragedies of Vittorio Alfieri to mind ... Again like Alfieri, he loved liberty and hated despotism.[2]

It was in the Venetian plays, *Marino Faliero* and *The Two Foscari*, that Byron experimented with the classical structure of the unities. (The principles of dramatic composition laid down in Aristotle's *Poetics*, which require that each drama should consist of a single plot whose action is confined to a single day and is set in a single place.) In doing so he was protesting against the overblown romanticism and lack of restraint of the London theatre. These, Jerome McGann describes as theatrical ends, and points out that, on the other hand:

365

Poetically, Byron sought – particularly in his Venetian plays – to write about the same kinds of themes we find in his tales, the nature of a sick or doomed society, the dilemma of a man caught in such a milieu. The two purposes merge very nicely however, for his Venetian plays are not concerned with the issue of events but with their meaning. The plays do not aim to arouse surprise about the outcome of a plot development, as melodrama so frequently does, on the contrary, they are intended to make the audience thoughtful and self-conscious, to force an understanding of the nature and causes of the fatality which the plays dramatize.[3]

Byron assured Murray that *Faliero* was not a political play. Jump holds that in a broader sense it is indubitably a political play: 'Can Byron have meant that it was not a verbal attack on the government such as would have scared the Tory publisher?[4]

M.K. Joseph claims that:

Faliero is a heroic figure, with overtones of Brutus, of Othello, and of Otway's Pierre. He is drawn into the conspiracy both by injured pride and by a sense of patriotism; his patriotism to his country is in conflict with his antagonism to its rulers, and his popular sympathies are at odds with his aristocratic contempt for the mob.[5]

He protests to Israel Bertuccio, his fellow-conspirator:

> You are a patriot, a plebeian Gracchus –
> The rebel's oracle, the people's tribune –
> I blame you not – you act in your vocation;
> They smote you, and oppressed you, and despised you;
> So they have *me*: but *you* ne'er spake with them;
> You never broke their bread, nor shared their salt;
> You never had their wine-cup at your lips:
> You grew not up with them, nor laughed, nor wept,
> Nor held a revel in their company;
> Ne'er smiled to see them smile, nor claimed their smile
> In social interchange for yours, nor trusted
> Nor wore them in your heart of hearts, as I have:[6]

Jump observes that it is the vigour and eloquence of some of the speeches which give *Marino Faliero* its lasting appeal. He cites the harangue of Marino:

> I asked no remedy but from the law –
> I sought no vengeance but redress by law –
> I called no judges but those named by law –

As Sovereign, I appealed unto my subjects,
The very subjects who had made me Sovereign,
And gave me thus a double right to be so.
The rights of place and choice, of birth and service,
Honours and years, these scars, these hoary hairs,
The travel – toil – the perils – the fatigues –
The blood and sweat of almost eighty years,
Were weighed i' the balance, 'gainst the foulest stain,
The grossest insult, most contemptuous crime
Of a rank, rash patrician – and found wanting!
And this is to be borne![7]

Jump points out that Byron expresses his own feelings about the longed-for Italian Risorgimento in *Marino Faliero*. He was 'feeling intensely' and 'hoping that 1820 would see a rapid advance by the movement for the liberation of Italy.'[8]

Chew comments that Byron is thoroughly in sympathy with the conspirators: 'Throughout the play there is the impression of the remorseless power of a corrupt aristocracy. The conflict is between the patricians and the people, with all right and justice on the side of the oppressed lower classes.'[9]

Byron has often been compared to Aeschylus. McGann observes that:

'The difference between Byron's Doge and Aeschylus' tragic characters must be measured in terms of consciousness: the latter go to their dooms in ignorance, or with only a fearful, semi-conscious dread, whereas Byron's Doge goes to his demise with clear and terrible understanding of his own helplessness.'[10]

Byron was scrupulous in his attempts at getting the story of his characters right:

'Where did Dr Moore find that Marino Faliero begged his life? I have searched the chroniclers, and find nothing of the kind ... I know no justification ... for calumniating an historical character; surely truth belongs to the dead, and to the unfortunate.[11]

16

HOBHOUSE, BYRON, CATO STREET
AND QUEEN CAROLINE

'Don't diffide in yourself – nor be nervous about your
health –
Leave that to poets and such fellows.'[1]

John Gardner has drawn attention to two theories, about Byron's
motivation for writing *Marino Faliero*, both of which may well be
correct. The first, advanced by David Erdman, Malcolm Kelsall
and Richard Cronin, is that the pretext for *Marino Faliero* was the
Cato Street Conspiracy of 23 February 1820. This is also discussed
by Jerome McGann in his commentary to the poem. The Cato
Street conspirators planned to murder the entire cabinet when they
dined at Lord Harrowby's house (a house Byron had often visited).
They intended to go to Lord Harrowby's with knives for cutting
off heads and bags for carrying them away. There were two
complications. Firstly, the Cabinet did not dine at Lord Harrowby's
on the night in question. Secondly the plot was instigated by the
government. This would not, however, have been known to Byron.
'Reviewing *Marino Faliero*, a critic stated that:

> If Thistlewood and Ings [two of the conspirators] could have delivered
> themselves in blank verse they would have spoken much the same
> words ... as the Doge and his accomplice in the play, Israel Bertuccio.'[2]

Five of the Cato Street conspirators were executed outside Newgate
prison.
John Gardner believes, together with David Erdman and Malcolm

Kelsall, that the Cato Street Conspiracy *was* the pretext for *Marino Faliero*.

The second theory has to do with Byron's long friendship with Hobhouse. Byron was uneasy when he learned that Hobhouse was foregathering with Radicals. To Byron this was reneging on his Whig principles. The truth is Hobhouse was trying to get the Radicals behind him for his second assault on the Parliamentary seat of Westminster. Some inflammatory remarks landed Hobhouse with a three-month jail sentence, much to his friend's dismay. Byron wrote a light-hearted ballad making fun of Hobhouse. The latter was wounded and even considered breaking off his friendship with Byron. Byron apologised. Hobhouse melted.

John Murray was concerned about the consequences of Hobhouse's flirtation with Radicalism, of which he heartily disapproved. Hobhouse was equally disapproving of the conduct of Murray. Andrew Nicholson notes that Hobhouse is severe on Murray in a letter to Byron written from Newgate 18 January 1820:

> ...do not write anything to Albemarle Street you do not wish to be seen by all the public offices – The man does not mean to do you a mischief – but he is vain, Sir, damn'd vain – and for the sake of a paragraph with 'my dear M' in it would betray Christ himself.[3]

It seems likely that Hobhouse was on the look-out for signs of presumption in Byron's publisher whom he regarded as a tradesman. Hobhouse was inclined to jealousy of anyone who presumed a close relationship with Byron and this, rather than personal antipathy, was probably the cause of his disapproval of Thomas Moore. He would have resented Murray's offer on 12 September 1819: 'If you are ill seriously [I] will instantly set out & give you [all] the personal care that I can.'[4]

Byron found this embarrassing. Andrew Nicholson points out that 'Byron's reply was: "You must not mind me when I say I am ill; it merely means low spirits – and folly", but he was "not the less obliged" by JM's "good nature".'[5]

Murray was good-natured enough to visit Hobhouse in Newgate but on 24 January 1820 Murray writes to Byron:

> I am exceedingly vexed at the conduct of Mr Hobhouse for he <is no> has not taken a line in wch there is even the possibility of advantage

370

to him – Sir Francis stands and will stand alone – there is not room for another on the same pedestal – & there he sits in Newgate contenting himself for the loss of liberty by the comfortable reflection that the House of Commons have no *right* to send him there – 'I have often visited him since his confinement & I do most sincerely regard him as a very kind friend – but I am certain that he has no *tact* in politics – no more than I have to be a sculptor...'[6]

Friendly as the relationship with his publisher had become, Byron's love for Hobhouse was paramount and he was eager to atone for his tactlessness.

John Gardner writes that, '*Marino Faliero* can be understood as the poem in which Byron attempts not to castigate but to understand his friend's behaviour., It can even be understood as a splendid apology for that other poem that Hobhouse has so bitterly resented, "My boy Hobby–O".'[7]

'My boy Hobby-O' was tactless, unkind, and seemed a great betrayal, but Hobhouse might have been consoled if he had seen the letter Byron had written to Kinnaird defending his decision to stand for parliament:

'Hobhouse is right to stand at any rate – It will be a great step to have contested Westminster – and if he gains – it is every thing – You may depend upon it that Hobhouse has talents very much beyond his *present rate* – & even beyond his own opinion – he is too *fidgetty* but he has the elements of Greatness if he can but keep his nerves in order – I don't mean *courage but anxiety.*[8]

(Byron to Douglas Kinnaird, Venice, 9 December 1818)

By 1820 Hobhouse had achieved his seat in parliament. He may have forgotten a letter of encouragement he had received from Byron in January 1819:

Take your fortune – take it at the 'flood' – now is your time – & remember that in your very *Start* you have *overtaken* all whom you thought before you – above all don't *diffide* in yourself – nor be nervous about your *health* – leave that to poets and such fellows ... you have already shown yourself fit for very great things –...[9]

(Byron to John Cam Hobhouse, Venice, 19 January 1819)

Hobhouse wrote to Byron fairly often with news from England though Byron complained that none of his English friends replied promptly to his own more frequent letters.

371

If we had none of Byron's letters Hobhouse would be rated a great letter-writer. He tried to keep his friend *au courant* with affairs in England but some of his letters must have given Byron pain, describing as they do, gatherings of friends who had been his own companions, for example:

Hastings, November 6, 1820
I have just been at a jollification at Webster's, Battle Abbey – *Lobsters* ... Champagne – drank like fishes, ate like wolves. D. of Sussex chief performer – I shall write again very soon.[10]

Hobhouse could give Byron news of politics, particularly after he was returned at the Westminster Election:

London, June 19, 1821
The talk of a partial change of administration has died away. Canning, they say, asked too much – The King has been coquetting a good deal with the Whigs lately – dined at Devonshire House – given a ball to Whig children.[11]

Most painful of all was a letter of 15 February 1821:

I hear from Lady Parker that Lady B. is in town. Your daughter is proclaimed on all hands a very lively, good-tempered little girl – Mrs Leigh is looking very well and is very well – seven children have not spoiled her appearance at all.[12]

Hobhouse remonstrated with Byron over *Don Juan* Canto V stanza 61:

London, June 19, 1821
By the way do not cut at poor Queeney in your *Don Juan* about Semiramis and her *courser*, courier – She would feel it very much I assure you – she never sees me without asking after you & desiring to be remembered.[13]

LXI.
That injured Queen, by chroniclers so coarse,
　　Has been accused (I doubt not by conspiracy)
Of an improper friendship for her horse
　　(Love, like Religion, sometimes runs to heresy)
This monstrous tale had probably its source
　　(For such exaggerations here and there I see)
In writing 'Courser' by mistake for 'Courier:'
I wish the case could come before a jury here.[14]

372

In writing such lines about Queen Caroline (whom he liked and against whom George IV was bringing in a Bill of Pains and Penalties in order to divorce her, much to the annoyance of the people, who demonstrated noisily in her favour and against the King) Byron betrayed a coarse and carelessly cruel streak whose occasional appearance shocked his friend. Luckily for Byron, even the 'betrayal', as he saw it, of the lines on 'Hobby-O' could not shake the love and loyalty of Hobhouse.

The stanza on Queen Caroline did not appear until 1833, after Byron's death.

17

THE SECOND VENETIAN PLAY:
THE TWO FOSCARI

So, we are slaves.

Gordon Spence observes that, '*The Two Foscari* is the most modern of the plays of the Romantic period. It speaks to us in the world of the present day, a world in which there have been in recent years countless cases of the detention of prisoners without trial, trials held in secret, the routine torture of political prisoners, executions, disappearances of people, and the intimidation of the populations.'

Yet Spence explains that Byron understood the difference in attitude to law between his own age and the fifteenth century in which he sets his play: 'In all her angry tirades and expressions of what the Doge [her father-in-law] calls her "clamorous grief" (2.132) Marina [the Doge's daughter-in-law, wife of his son Jacopo who has been tortured to death by representatives of the State of Venice] never mentions rights. Her emphasis is on "all human feelings, all/Ties which bind man to man" (1, 262–63). Thus [the author] ... shows her need for a community of affection, rather than the rights of individuals.'[1]

The instigator of the action is Loredano who hates the Doge because he suspects him of having murdered his father and his brother. We are never told whether this is true, though Byron hints that it is not. Jerome McGann describes Loredano as '... a fine example of Byron's ability to invest a completely villainous character with life and secure for him strong dramatic sympathy.'[2] This is perhaps easier to achieve in this play since his victim, the Doge, is not a sympathetic character, at least in the opening stages of the drama. He presides over the judicial murder of his son for reasons of state.

Byron wrote, 'What I seek to show in "the Foscaris" is the suppressed passions rather than the rant of the present day.'[3] Perhaps this is why the Doge appears so passive compared with Marino Faliero. One cannot image Faliero, any more than Manfred, delivering the Doge's speech on the will and then doing nothing to retrieve the situation.

The Doge speaks:

> Our Fame is in men's breath, our lives upon
> Less than their breath; our durance upon days,
> Our days on seasons; our whole being on
> Something which is not *us* / – So, we are slaves,
> The greatest as the meanest – nothing rests
> Upon our will; the will itself no less
> Depends upon a straw than on a storm;
> And when we think we lead, we are most led,[4]

He cries out to Marina:

> I cannot weep – I would I could; but if
> Each white hair on this head were a young life,
> This ducal cap the Diadem of earth,
> This ducal ring with which I wed the waves
> A talisman to still them – I'd give all
> For him.
>   *Mar.* With less he surely might be saved.
>   *Doge.* That answer only shows you know not Venice.
> Alas! how should you? she knows not herself,
> In all her mystery. Hear me – they who aim
> At Foscari, aim no less at his father;
> The sire's destruction would not save the son;
> They work by different means to the same end,[5]

We learn how true this is when Jacopo (the son who has been permitted, after being put to the torture, to go into exile with his wife but without his children) suddenly collapses and dies. Not satisfied with this horror, Loredano then engineers the deposition of the Doge from all his honours. Foscari is told to leave the Ducal Palace by the back stairway to the canal-landing while the great

376

bell begins to sound in celebration of the accession of a new Doge before the old one has departed.

Foscari insists on leaving honourably, in full view of the populace, by the Giant's Staircase, but he is faltering and Marina springs to his side and offers him her arm. This does not suit Loredano and he gives Foscari a poisoned goblet of water. He drinks and dies. The rulers of Venice, disconcerted, declare a state funeral for him but Marina rejects this empty ceremony with scorn. She will use the remains of her dowry to bury her father-in-law quietly without hypocritical ritual and show.

Byron's heroines in the dramas are quite extraordinarily loyal, courageous, and spirited. They are more heroic than the men and spur them on to honour. Byron may have despised the behaviour of many actual women but he had a surprisingly high ideal of womanhood.

Notes

Michael Cooke analyses the motivation of Foscari and describes the drama as '...a story not of heroic action; but of heroic passion, a study of preternatural *principled* endurance of physical as well as emotional and moral torture.'[1]

He writes of the Doge:

Clearly his is no unimaginative or footling sense of duty. He is cruelly cut by having not only to refrain from tying to succor his best-loved and last-surviving Son, but also to sit in inevitable judgment upon him. ... His conduct looks rational, i.e. unemotional. But his reason strikes one as that which, as Santayana has brilliantly observed, springs from the 'passion for consistency and order.' He endures as he does to preserve 'the welfare of the state' which would be imperilled if he were, in his own words, 'disposed to brawl'. He becomes thus the greatest, if not the sole bulwark of the State, and in the terms of the play superior to those whose actions he must decline to revolt against and punish. Foscari, though undergoing and not undertaking in the manner of the heroic protagonist, matches the latter in strength of will. But his will is differently exercised.[2]

18

POLITICS IN RAVENNA

Then battle for freedom wherever you can,
And, if not shot or hanged, you'll get knighted.

The entire Gamba family, together with a large part of the Romagna aristocracy, were involved in secretly fomenting revolt against the Austrians. Byron joined them with a will.

His poem *The Age of Bronze* (written in early December 1822 and published, not by John Murray but by John Hunt, in April 1823), includes lines on the Holy Alliance which illuminate Byron's attitude towards events in Italy in 1821 and 1822. They pour scorn on the sovereigns who were concerned only with maintaining their own power and repressing the aspirations of their people.

At the Congress of Vienna (1814–15) Russia, Austria, Prussia and England formed a Quadruple Alliance to watch over the settlement of European affairs arrived at by the Congress. The Tsar, who had periodic leanings towards liberalism, suggested a Holy Alliance, or pact of Sovereigns, who would pledge themselves to rule in accordance with Christian principles and to outlaw war. Castlereagh described this plan as 'a sublime piece of mysticism and nonsense' since the Congress of Vienna 'was not assembled for the discussion of moral principles but for great practical purposes, to establish effectual provisions for the general security.'

The peoples of Europe had been roused to the desire for the assertion of their rights. The French were fobbed off with the restorations of the legitimate dynasty they had only recently discarded. The Holy Alliance became an instrument for repression of all national and liberal movements in Europe and even in the New World.

The members of the Alliance gathered at the Congress of Verona (October to December 1822) to complete the settlement of the affairs of Europe. The satire in *The Age of Bronze*:

'...shrewdly focuses on the spectacular side of the events widely reported in the newspapers, as a sign of the Congress's political emptiness. Equally impressive is Byron's concentration on the economic interests that shaped the policies of the participants, and his sketch of the financial events that were intimately connected to the entire struggle with the French in both its revolutionary and Napoleonic phases...'[1]

VIII.

But lo! a Congress! What! that hallowed name
Which freed the Atlantic! May we hope the same
For outworn Europe? With the sound arise,
Like Samuel's shade to Saul's monarchic eyes,
The prophets of young Freedom, summoned far
From climes of Washington and Bolivar;
Henry, the forest-born Demosthenes,
Whose thunder shook the Philip of the seas;
And stoic Franklin's energetic shade,
Robed in the lightnings which his hand allayed;
And Washington, the tyrant-tamer, wake,
To bid us blush for these old chains, or break.
But *who* compose this Senate of the few
That should redeem the many? *Who* renew
This consecrated name, till now assigned
To councils held to benefit mankind?
Who now assemble at the holy call?
The blest Alliance, which says three are all!
An earthly Trinity! which wears the shape
Of Heaven's, as man is mimicked by the ape.
A pious Unity! in purpose one –
To melt three fools to a Napoleon,
Why, Egypt's Gods were rational to these;
Their dogs and oxen knew their own degrees,
And, quiet in their kennel or their shed,
Cared little, so that they were duly fed;
But these, more hungry, must have something more –
The power to bark and bite, to toss and gore.
Ah, how much happier were good Æsop's frogs
Than we! for ours are animated logs,
With ponderous malice swaying to and fro,
And crushing nations with a stupid blow;
All dully anxious to leave little work
Unto the revolutionary stork.

Thrice blest Verona! since the holy three
With their imperial presence shine on thee!
Honoured by them, thy treacherous site forgets
The vaunted tomb of 'all the Capulets!'
Would that the royal guests it girds about
Were so far like, as never to get out!
Aye, shout! inscribe! rear monuments of shame,
To tell Oppression that the world is tame!
Crowd to the theatre with loyal rage,
The comedy is not upon the stage;
The show is rich in ribandry and stars,
Then gaze upon it through thy dungeon bars;
Clap thy permitted palms, kind Italy,
For thus much still thy fettered hands are free!

Byron went on to pillory the Tsar of Russia and his half-hearted attachment to Liberalism:

X.

Resplendent sight! Behold the coxcomb Czar
The Autocrat of waltzes and of war!
As eager for a plaudit as a realm,
And just as fit for flirting as the helm;
A Calmuck beauty with a Cossack wit,
And generous spirit, when 'tis not frost-bit;
Now half dissolving to a liberal thaw.
But hardened back whene'er the morning's raw;
With no objection to true Liberty,
Except that it would make the nations free.
How well the imperial dandy prates of peace!
How fain, if Greeks would be his slaves, free Greece!
How nobly gave he back the Poles their Diet,
Then told pugnacious Poland to be quiet![2]

The *Prophecy of Dante* had been regarded by the Police Commissioner at Volterra as a subversive poem. *The Age of Bronze* and *Don Juan* would have taught him what was real subversion and have convinced the police at Bologna and elsewhere (who suspected that the word 'Romantic' signified Roma Antica and must refer to a secret society concerned with fomenting revolution) that they had been right to have Byron shadowed, his visitors listed and spied upon, his letters opened and other police forces warned to be on their guard.

381

In the Dedication to *Don Juan* Byron wrote almost as savagely of Castlereagh as did Shelley in the *Masque of Anarchy*. Castlereagh had been a member of the government which imposed the six Gag Acts after Peterloo. He was responsible for the union of Ireland with England and was known to patriotic Irishmen like Thomas Moore as the assassin of his country. Byron held him responsible for the repressive policies of the Holy Alliance. Yet in 1820 Castlereagh wrote a statement on the principle of one state interfering in the internal affairs of another which could almost have been written by Byron. Byron ought to have approved of Castlereagh's statesmanlike generosity towards defeated France after the Peace of Paris, but Castlereagh got no credit for this from Byron (who may have been unaware of it) or even from Napoleon who was amazed at his restraint in omitting to seize for England every advantage he could lay his hands on and wrote of him jeeringly that England was governed by a lunatic. Yet it was Napoleon who castigated Castlereagh for the repressive policies of the Holy Alliance:

> I shall say nothing of the monstrous inconsistency of a minister who, representing the free nation par excellence, put Italy back under the yoke, maintains Spain in subjection, and helps with all his might to forge chains for the entire Continent. Does he think by any chance that freedom is applicable only to the English?[3]

In the Dedication to *Don Juan* Byron was to write verse which used the same theme as Napoleon – of Castlereagh forging chains for mankind:

XII.

Cold-blooded, smooth-faced, placid miscreant!
 Dabbling its sleek young hands in Erin's gore,
And thus for wider carnage taught to pant,
 Transferred to gorge upon a sister shore,
The vulgarest tool that Tyranny could want,
 With just enough of talent, and no more,
To lengthen fetters by another fixed,
And offer poison long already mixed.

XIII.

An orator of such set trash of phrase
 Ineffably – legitimately vile,

That even its grossest flatterers dare not praise,
   Nor foes – all nations – condescend to smile, –
Nor even a sprightly blunder's spark can blaze
   From that Ixion grindstone's ceaseless toil,
That turns and turns to give the world a notion
Of endless torments and perpetual motion.

XIV.

A bungler even in its disgusting trade,
   And botching, patching, leaving still behind
Something of which its masters are afraid –
   States to be curbed, and thoughts to be confined,
Conspiracy or Congress to be made –
   Cobbling at manacles for all mankind –
A tinkering slave-maker, who mends old chains,
With God and Man's abhorrence for its gains.[4]

Inconsistency does not seem sufficient grounds for so savage an attack, nor for the indefensible reference by Byron elsewhere to Castlereagh's apparent inability to produce an heir.

Castlereagh declared that 'Unpopularity is more convenient and gentlemanlike,' but in 1822, under threat of exposure as an homosexual, he cut his throat.

When Byron's fierce resentment was aroused death proved no protection for his victims. The lawyer, Romilly (who broke his agreement with Byron from whom he had a retainer, and went over to Lady Byron at the time of the separation), committed suicide after the death of his wife. Byron attacked him dead no less savagely than he had attacked him living.

By the time that most subversive and political of poems, *The Age of Bronze*, was published Byron was in Genoa and planning to go to Greece. The authorities at Ravenna and Pisa must have been deeply relieved.

Soon after Teresa's move to Filetto her father brought her younger brother, Pietro, to meet Byron. Pietro was even more ardently revolutionary than his father. Byron described him as 'wild about liberty'. They took to riding, fencing and shooting together and the young man became one of Byron's most loyal admirers. Soon Byron was as fond of him as he was of 'Papa', and Teresa's younger sisters.

Pietro had brought news of a successful Neapolitan rising in July (1820). In August the Gambas initiated Byron into a group of Carbonari called the *Cacciatori Americani*.

In December of that year an event occurred which might have caused Byron great embarrassment with his Carbonari friends, though it had nothing to do with a lack of revolutionary fervour and was merely due to the exercise of compassion for a wounded man – the Commandant of the local troops, who was shot five times outside Byron's door and would have died in the street if Byron had not directed his servants to bring the dying man into the house. He sent a soldier to inform the guard what he had done and a messenger to the Cardinal. Next day several of the officers called to thank him.

War excitement grew as the New Year came in. He noted in his Journal on 29 January 1821:

> Met a company of the sect (a kind of Liberal Club) called the 'Americani' in the forest, all armed, and singing, with all their might in Romagnuole – '*Sem* tutti soldat' per la liberta' ('we are all soldiers for liberty'). They cheered me as I passed – I returned their salute, and rode on. This may show the spirit of Italy at present.[5]

He wrote to Moore on 22 February:

> We are here full of war, and within two days of the seat of it, expecting intelligence momently. We shall now see if our Italian friends are good for any thing but 'a shooting round a corner,' like the Irishman's gun. Excuse haste, – I write with my spurs putting on. My horses are at the door, and an Italian Count waiting to accompany me in my ride.[6]
>
> (Byron to Thomas Moore, Ravenna, 22 February 1821)

The Sovereigns of the Holy Alliance met at Troppau to establish their right and duty to put down all revolutionary movements and uprisings.

In January the Carbonari of the Romagna were indecisively planning revolt and Byron provided them with weapons. The Austrians were on the march towards Naples.

> '*Letters opened*!' to be sure they are – and that's the reason why I always put in my opinion of the German Austrian Scoundrels; – there is not an Italian who loathes them more than I do – and whatever I could do to scour Italy and the earth of their infamous oppression – would be done 'con amore'.[7]
>
> (To John Murray, Ravenna, 16 February 1821)

384

– The Germans are within hail of the Neapolitans by this time. – They will get their Gruel. – They marched ten days sooner than expected – which prevented a general rising. – But they are in a situation that if they do not win their first battle – they will have all Italy upon them. – They are damned rascals and deserve it. – It is however hard upon the poor Pope – in his old age to have all this row in his neighbourhood. –

yrs. ever & truly[8]

(To Hobhouse, Ravenna, 22 February 1821)

Byron noted the progress of the Romagna uprising in his Ravenna Journal:

I advised them to attack in detail, and in different parties, in different *places* (though at the *same* time), so as to divide the attention of the troops, who, though few, yet being disciplined, would beat any body of people (not trained) in a regular fight – unless dispersed in small parties, and distracted with different assaults. Offered to let them assemble here if they choose. It is a strongish post – narrow street, commanded from within – and tenable walls. ******[9]

(8 January 1821)

By the eighteenth of February the Romagna rising was already looking doubtful:

Today I have had no communication with my Carbonari cronies; but in the mean time, my lower apartments are full of their bayonets, fusils, cartridges, and what not. I suppose that they consider me as a depôt, to be sacrificed, in case of accidents. It is no great matter, supposing that Italy could be liberated, who or what is sacrificed. It is a grand object – the very *poetry* of politics. Only think – a free Italy!!! Why, there has been nothing like it since the days of Augustus.[10]

(18 February 1821)

By the twenty-fourth of the month all hope was gone:

Rode, &tc. as usual. The secret intelligence arrived this morning from the frontier to the C[arbonar]i is as bad as possible. The *plan* has missed – the Chiefs are betrayed, military as well as civil – and the Neapolitans not only have *not* moved, but have declared to the P[apal] government, and to the Barbarians, that they know nothing of the matter!!!

Thus the world goes; and thus the Italians are always lost for lack of union among themselves.[11]

(24 February 1821)

By April Byron was writing to Thomas Moore:

> I have no news. As a very pretty woman said to me a few nights ago, with the tears in her eyes, as she sat at the harpsichord, 'Alas! the Italians must now return to making operas'. I fear *that* and maccaroni are their forte, and 'motley their only wear'. However, there are some high spirits among them still.[12]
>
>   (Byron to Thomas Moore, Ravenna, 28 April 1821)

Two interesting letters discovered in the State Archive in Ravenna by Andrea Casadio are useful as proof of '... the growing deterioration of the poet's relationships with the local community [this seems to me to throw entirely new light on Byron's last days in Ravenna] and with the representatives of Papal power.'[13]

The first is a polite reply from Byron to an equally polite letter from the Cardinal (delivered to him by Count Alborghetti) questioning him about his relations with a Neapolitan exile, Giuseppe Giganti, who had been arrested in April 1821. In 1820 Byron had sent this man a message of support for the Neapolitan Liberals. This exchange of letters suggests, according to Casadio, that '... a formal friendly relationship still existed in the late spring of 1821 between Byron and the local authorities.'

The second episode, some weeks later, was to sour these relations. The imbroglio resulted from a squabble between Tita Falcieri and a Lieutenant Pistocchi of the Papal troops. This time the Cardinal sent by Alborghetti a peremptory demand for Tita's immediate dismissal. The second letter discovered by Casadio in the State Archive is Byron's reply to the Cardinal on 25 June 1821, written by Pietro Gamba (who had presumably translated it into perfect Italian) and signed by Byron. It is admirably courteous but, as Casadio points out, 'Byron uses a language typical of a liberal conscience and of the conception of a modern constitutional state which could have been barely understood by the authorities.'[14]

> Most Reverend Eminence...
> When Lieutenant Pistocchi started a quarrel without any sign of a Military Uniform and without provocation, he threatened my Servant with illegal weapons and took offence because of some insults uttered by my ... Servant in anger; hearing his complaints I offered him satisfaction in whatever terms best suited him ... in respect for the rank he holds, in order to remove any idea of protection for my Servants if they transgress the laws ... I did not have full knowledge about the

386

circumstances of the case. As I know everything now, I can at least say that both parties are equally in the wrong.

Byron goes on to complain that Pistocchi, in spite of declaring that he was satisfied with Byron's promise of a reprimand for Tita, had asked the Cardinal to insist on Tita's dismissal which would have resulted in his being sent into exile.

My principles are quite opposed to such a thing and do not allow me to agree! The fortune, life, and especially the Honour of a Man must depend on the Sentence of a Court, we should hear both parties, proceed according to the law, judge accordingly; and then if my Servant is convicted, I will not oppose it.[15]

Byron expresses himself formally and with great respect and humility towards the Cardinal. This may be contrasted to his more downright account of the affair to Count Alborghetti with whom he was on friendly, informal terms:

Dear Sir – It appears to me that there must be some *clerical* intrigue – of the low priests about the Cardinal to render all this nonsense necessary about a squabble in the street of *words only* – between a Soldier and a Servant. If it is directed against *me* – it shan't succeed ... If against the *poor* valet – it is an odious oppression ... if they think to get *rid* of *me* – they shan't ... I will yield to no oppression; but will go in my own good time, when it suits my inclination and affairs.

He suggests that Alborghetti should get the business settled, and it seems that he regarded the Count as venal, for he adds, 'You will not find me less obliged or more ungrateful than you have hitherto found me.'[16]

(Byron to Count Alborghetti, 28 June 1821)

Cardinal Consalvi found a way out – succeeding '... in reconciling both parties by the expediency of a symbolic three-day imprisonment of Tita and Tita's formal apologies to Pistocchi.'[17]

Tita was the mildest of men but he was huge and black-bearded and often armed with knives and pistols. His formidable appearance was to get him into further difficulties before Byron left Italy for Greece, with Tita in his train.

Byron's protest to the Cardinal was courtesy itself but he went on to complain of the most surprising ill-usage by both the authorities and, recently, even some of the populace of Ravenna with whom he had become extremely popular for his generosity. He warns the Cardinal:

> ... But now it is time for Your Eminence to know something ... I have kept silent ... because I didn't want to bother you while concerned with important matters. When the Commanding Officer of 'Del Pinto' square was found dying on the Road, the same servant accused by Mr Pistocchi and I went out to assist him; and we took him into my house (where he died), at a time when no Citizen dared go to his rescue. Without such action He would have died on the public Road...
>
> When I was offended inside the Theatre by a certain Mr Tivoli, because of the respect due to the audience and to Your Eminence I curbed my anger, and You offered me some satisfaction; however, I rejected it, as it did not seem to me that it was worth causing you inconvenience on so small an account.
>
> When the Servants of Monsignor His Excellence the Archbishop tried to overturn my Coach with the utmost insolence, I was satisfied with putting their attempt down in the same way that Mr Pistocchi answered my servant's simple questions, but I didn't try to take the bread out of their mouth by complaining to their Master or even to the Government.
>
> When my life was publicly threatened three months ago in some papers posted on the doors of Your Eminence's Palace, I did not demand any satisfaction from you ... I did not hear that the Authorities took even a single measure for preventing such acts of violence.

Byron assures the Cardinal that he believes him to be both wise and just. He ends:

I profess myself to be
of Your Most Reverend Eminence
Your Obdnt. and very Obliged Servant
Byron
Peer of England[18]

Andrea Casadio describes the aftermath of the failed rising in Ravenna. On 10 July (soon after the exchange of letters between Byron and the Cardinal), 'Pietro Gamba was arrested while he was coming out of the theatre and then forced to leave the State. On that day the Gamba Palace was searched and Teresa's father, Ruggiero, was ordered to leave the town in twenty-four hours. At the same time similar measures were brought in for all those suspected of being members of the Liberal opposition – a large part of the ruling class in Ravenna.'[19]

Teresa's position was now alarming. Much to Byron's dismay she had left Filetto and joined her father in Ravenna. Now that he had gone she was no longer under her father's roof and could, by the Papal decree, be forced to enter a convent. Byron advised her to leave at once and on 25 July she went reluctantly to join her father in Florence. Then anxious plans were considered, the chief of which was for the whole family to emigrate, with Byron, to Switzerland. Byron counselled against it. The country was beautiful but he disliked the Swiss and, even more, the English tourists who would insult and ostracise Teresa and gossip about her and her famous lover. The fiery Pierino should live in a land that was free, Byron told the Gambas. Switzerland was no more free than Italy. Then Shelley came to visit Byron in Ravenna and persuaded him that he should induce the Gambas to come to Pisa. He promised to find Byron a house there.

Byron knew that he must leave Ravenna and follow his Teresa but he always disliked uprooting himself, his household and his horses and menagerie. It was not until 29 October that he left Ravenna.

On the way he would meet unexpectedly with his old Harrow friend, Lord Clare, a brief encounter he would consider one of the most significant hours of his life. He had a rendez-vous with Samuel Rogers in Bologna and wrote to Murray:

> I crossed the Appennines with Rogers as far as Florence ... he is a most agreeable companion in a post-chaise and we slashed away to right and left – cutting up all our acquaintances ... It would have done your heart good to hear us ... I don't think that I heard & uttered so much slander for these last seven years. – But *he* is a clever fellow – that's certain – and said some wonderful things.[20]
>
> (Byron to John Murray, ? November 1821)

Leaving Rogers to continue his journey, Byron made his way to Pisa, where the authorities awaited with some trepidation the arrival of this famous, unpredictable, subversive English aristocrat and poet.

19

THE BOWLES CONTROVERSY

'I hate the word Magnaminity because I have sometimes seen it applied to the grossest imposters by the greatest of fools.'

While Byron was preoccupied with hopes for an Italian Risorgimento he was writing his great play condemning wars of conquest, *Sardanapalus*, and taking up the cudgels against '...those miserable mountebanks of the day – the poets, [who] disgrace themselves – and deny God – in running down Pope – the most *faultless* of Poets, and almost of men.'[1]

The Reverend William Lisle Bowles had produced an edition of Pope's Works in 1806 in which he attacked Pope's character and his poetry. Thomas Campbell defended Pope. Bowles replied. Isaac D'Israeli then castigated Bowles for impugning Pope's moral character. Having read Disraeli's piece in the *Quarterly Review* Byron set about Pope's defence with two letters addressed to John Murray.

Bowles praised Byron for having suppressed *English Bards and Scotch Reviewers* in which Byron had attacked Bowles. This praise cut no ice whatsoever with Byron:

> Mr Bowles does me the honour to talk of 'noble mind' and 'generous magnanimity.' I see no 'nobility of mind' in an act of simple justice; and I hate the word 'Magnanimity', because I have sometimes seen it applied to the grossest imposters by the greatest of fools ... Although I regret having published *English Bards and Scotch Reviewers*, the part which I regret the least is that which regards Mr Bowles with reference to Pope...
>   Pope, who was not a Monk, though a Catholic, may occasionally have sinned in word and deed with a woman in his youth; but is this

391

sufficient ground for ... a sweeping denunciation? Where is the unmarried Englishman of a certain rank of life, who (provided he has not taken orders) has not to reproach himself between the ages of sixteen and thirty with far more licentiousness than has ever yet been traced to Pope? Pope lived in the public eye from his youth upwards; he had all the dunces of his own time for his enemies, and, I am sorry to say, some who have not the apology of dullness for detractors since his death; and yet to what do all these charges amount? To an equivocal *liaison* with Martha Blount, which might arise as much from his infirmities as his passions; to a hopeless flirtation with Lady Mary W. Montague; to a story of Cibber's and to two or three coarse passages in his works. Who could come forth clearer from an invidious inquest on a life of fifty-six years? Why are we to be officiously reminded of such passages in his letters provided that they exist?[2]

Byron describes this process as 'rummaging' for scandal among Pope's letters. His own life and letters have been subject to such officious and inimical 'rummaging', and some modern writers have boasted that the fruits of their own rummaging have augmented the sales of their books. Byron must have been aware that in defending Pope he was defending himself. Pope, he declared, was 'the moral poet of all civilisation'[3] A few months later *Blackwoods Magazine* prophesied of Byron: '... if he continues to write ... he will be placed by universal acclamation far above Pope, the object of his present panegyric, and form a fourth star of a glorious constellation with Shakespeare, Milton and Dryden.'[4]

20

SARDANAPALUS

And how many
Left she behind in India to the Vultures?[1]

This is the rebuke of Sardanapalus, King of Assyria, to those who praised the conquests of his ancestress, Semiramis, in order to spur him on to a similar use of military power. It appears in the play Byron was writing from January to May 1821.

Sardanapalus is Byron's most important anti-war statement. Samuel Chew held that the character of Sardanapalus was Byron's self-portrait, citing:

> ...his love of pleasure, his dislike of war and glory, his energy and perfect fearlessness when aroused, his antagonism towards priests and kings, his wit, pride, scepticism, freedom from illusion, and claim to intellectual liberty...[2]

I believe that Byron was antagonistic only to those priests and kings who were tyrants or who served tyrants and that he was self-absorbed rather than selfish. But Chew is accurate on the '...main point in Byron's character as expressed by Ruskin – "He was the first great Englishman who felt the cruelty of war, and in its cruelty, the shame." '[3]

Chew elaborates on this: 'This brave hostility to war in which Byron voices the modern spirit of international understanding, is combined with a clear-sighted knowledge of the ephemeral nature and pettiness of fame and glory, unless won in the cause of freedom.'[4]

Sardanapalus embodies this distaste for war, and M.K. Joseph points out that '... it is Sardanapalus, not Faliero, who represents his [Byron's] ideal of conduct.'[5]

Marilyn Butler describes *Sardanapalus* as a 'mythological tragedy which is also a pre-Shavian comedy.' She explains:

> Here the monarch concerned is a debauchee and a divorcee who cavorts with his mistress in a newly-built pavilion. He also has the misfortune, as a secularist and pacifist, to be king of a nation seized with belief in a divine mission to conquer India. Sardanapalus is thus both the newly-crowned George IV, unhappily cast as leader of a serious, professional, efficient, middle-class nation, and the equally déraciné Byron, whose role in the public limelight requires him to take up uncongenially responsible positions. A study of a post-religious consciousness, *Sardanapalus* is the most complex and searching of Byron's self-projections. But it is also the most social and political.[6]

Sardanapalus is despised by some of his court for his slothfulness, effeminacy and love of luxury. His enemies call him the 'she-king'. He discovers that two of them are planning a rebellion but refuses to kill or imprison them. With encouragement from Myrrha, the Ionian slave-girl whom he loves, he calls for his armour and (after admiring himself in the mirror) defends the palace with outstanding courage and drives the rebels off.

They attack again and the walls which protect the palace are destroyed by a flood. Sardanapalus chooses death rather than the shame of captivity and Myrrha, who fought splendidly at his side, helps him build a funeral pyre within the palace and joins him there to die in the flames.

Early in the play Sardanapalus condemns the pursuit of glory by war and praises in Bacchus not his conquests but his legacy to mankind, the immortal grape:

> *Re-enter – Cupbearer*
> *Sar.* (*taking the cup from him*). Noble kinsman,
> If these barbarian Greeks of the far shores
> And skirts of these our realms lie not, this Bacchus
> Conquered the whole of India, did he not?
> *Sal.* He did, and thence was deemed a Deity.
> *Sar.* Not so: – of all his conquests a few columns.
> Which may be his, and might be mine, if I
> Thought them worth purchase and conveyance, are
> The landmarks of the seas of gore he shed,

The realms he wasted, and the hearts he broke.
But here – here in this goblet is his title
To immortality – the immortal grape
From which he first expressed the soul, and gave
To gladden that of man, as some atonement
For the victorious mischiefs he had done.
Had it not been for this, he would have been
A mortal still in name as in his grave;
And, like my ancestor Semiramis,
A sort of semi-glorious human monster.
Here's that which deified him – let it now
Humanise thee; my surly, chiding brother...[7]

* * *

I leave such things to conquerors; enough
For me, if I can make my subjects feel
The weight of human misery less, and glide
Ungroaning to the tomb: I take no license
Which I deny to them. We all are men.[8]

He is merciful where commonsense might decree that he should be harsh:

I hate all pain,
Given or received; we have enough within us,
The meanest vassal as the loftiest monarch,
Not to add to each other's natural burthen...[9]

When he conceived the plan of the drama Byron had no intention of providing a love-interest and it was Teresa who told him he must put more love in the play. It was at her request that he created the character of Myrrha, the proud, courageous and selfless Ionian slave-girl who loved Sardanapalus and, because she loved him and his honour, drove him on to defend his throne, prove his kingly courage and die a noble death. Critics have seen Myrrha as Byron's depiction of Teresa, and Teresa did indeed try nobly to influence her lover for good. Like Myrrha, she loved him and was eager for her lover to behave with honour.

When Shelley met Byron in Ravenna some time after his Venice visit, he wrote to Mary:

We ride out in the evening through the pine forests which divide the city from the sea ... Lord Byron is greatly improved in every respect – in genius, in temper, in moral views, in health and in happiness.

395

The connection with La Guicciola has been an inestimable benefit to him ... he says he plunged into libertinism not from taste but from despair.[10]

Teresa was unable to emulate the nobility of the slave-girl when Byron told her he was going to Greece but she did beg to be allowed to go with him, perhaps with the example of Myrrha at the back of her mind.

Harriet Granville found the speeches of Myrrha in *Sardanapalus* extremely moving. If her husband read these aloud to her as he read other plays and poems she must have wept (as she claimed later to have 'roared' over *Cain*) at such lines as these:

> *Myr.*   Frown not upon me: you have smiled
> Too often on me not to make those frowns
> Bitterer to bear than any punishment
> Which they may augur. – King, I am your subject!
> Master, I am your slave! Man, I have loved you!
> Loved you, I know not by what fatal weakness,
> Although a Greek, and born a foe to monarchs –
> A slave, and hating fetters – an Ionian,
> And, therefore, when I love a stranger, more
> Degraded by that passion than by chains!
> Still I have loved you,[11]

Another scene which may have moved the susceptible Harry-O to tears is the meeting of the king with the wife he has long-since deserted for the Ionian slave-girl. He arranges to send Zarina and their children away before the battle to save them from harm. His leave-taking with Zarina is moving and some critics have seen Zarina as Lady Byron. This seems unlikely in view of Byron's strong resentment occasioned by Sir Ralph Noel's secret application to Chancery over Ada and Annabella's refusal to guarantee that she would not take Ada abroad without her husband's permission.

Notes

1. Paul Elledge's discussion of Byron's use of image in the development of *Sardanapalus* shows how important the language and the poetry are for comprehending the full impact of Byron's dramas:

... the evolution of Sardanapalus' psychological stability and his progress toward spiritual triumph are represented throughout the drama in images of light and darkness. Calling Murray's attention to the preservation of classical structure in *Sardanapalus* [i.e. the unities of time, place and theme] Byron wrote 'You will remark that the *Unities* are all *strictly* observed. The time, a *Summer's night*, about nine hours, or less, though it begins before Sunset and ends after Sunrise.' By fixing the time-span of his tragedy between twilight and mid-morning, Byron probably had in mind more than the rules of Greek or Italian dramatic art. Light appears from several sources and in a variety of shades, integrates seemingly disparate themes, and illuminates both the debauchery and the ultimate victory of the king. Light imagery is related variously to the motifs of love, sensualism, war, religious orthodoxy and paganism, historical tradition and, most importantly, to Sardanapalus' spiritual development. But the incoherence which might seem consequent upon so many and paradoxical uses of light is easily clarified by the particularization of sun, star and fire imagery to support the theme of the disparity between man's desires and his limitations. This familiar Byronic motif weaves through the tragedy, supplying motivation for actions and credibility to characters, and endowing the play with a more universal meaning than that contained in Sardanapalus' individual triumph.[1]

2. M.K. Joseph compares *Sardanapalus* with *Marino Faliero*:

Faliero foretells the fall of a society by slow decay; at the end of *Sardanapalus*, the crash of an empire is louder, more remote, more final. Behind both, as in *Childe Harold IV* and in *Don Juan*, is Byron's powerful sense of the transience of civilisations.[2]

3. G. Wilson Knight describes Sardanapalus as one of 'Byron's most powerfully created heroes'[3] (the other being Marino Faliero). He compares Sardanapalus to Shakespeare's Timon of Athens:

Sardanapalus, like Timon, rejects the advice of worldly wisdom until he finds that he has been deceived in taking 'the breath of friends' for 'truth'. Like Timon he endures base ingratitude from those whom he has 'gorged with plenty'.[4]

Wilson-Knight goes on to discuss Byron's own attitude to war:

As for Timon's 'contumelious, beastly, mad-brained war' the Byronic correspondences are too manifold in *Don Juan*, *Sardanapalus* and elsewhere, to need elaboration. Byron could view Wellington as the inferior 'in rational greatness' to a good dentist or hairdresser; and so is any 'bloody blustering booby' who gains a name by breaking heads (Murray, 18 November 1820). And yet he knew also that vicious rule might force opposition. Napoleon had for him just as much, and just as little, justification as Alcibiades had for Timon. When Byron himself took to arms in Italy, he was ironically aware of all the issues; and in Greece he countered generalship with an all but inhuman, and most unwarlike, clemency.[5]

21

PISA

I can walk down into my garden and pluck my own oranges

Iris Origo quotes a student at Pisa University, Francesco Domenico Guerrazzi, on the long-awaited arrival of Byron and his household in Pisa:

> At that time the rumour spread in Pisa that an extraordinary man had arrived there, of whom people told a hundred different tales, all contradictory and many absurd. They said he was of royal blood, of very great wealth, of sanguine temperament, of fierce habits, masterly in knightly exercises, possessing an evil genius, but a more than human intellect. He was said to wander through the world like Job's Satan ... It was George Byron. I wished to see him: he appeared to me like the Vatican Apollo.[1]

Soon after his arrival at Pisa Byron wrote to Thomas Moore: 'At present, owing to the climate &tc. (I can walk down into my garden and pluck my own oranges...) My spirits are much better.'[2] He told John Murray: 'I have got here into a famous old feudal palazzo on the Arno – large enough for a garrison – with dungeons below – and cells in the walls – and so full of *Ghosts* that the learned Fletcher (my Valet) has begged leave to change his room.'[3] Byron was mistaken. The date of the Palazzo Lanfranchi was mid-Renaissance.

Later he ends a letter to Murray about literary squabbles with a description of the view from his window:

> I write to you about all this row of bad passions – and absurdities – with the *Summer* Moon (for here our Winter is clearer than Your Dog

399

days) lighting the winding Arno with all her buildings and bridges –
so quiet & still – what nothings we are! before the least of these Stars![4]
(Byron to John Murray, Pisa, 8 F[ebruar]y 1822)

When Byron was living in Venice Shelley, and others among
his visitors there, were a little shocked to find him so 'Italianate'.
On his first public appearance in Ravenna at a party on New Year's
Eve, in the house of Teresa's uncle, Marchese Cavalli, where he
had been introduced to the best company he had seen in Italy, he
found himself accepted by the whole of Teresa's family as one of
themselves.

At Pisa he behaved, for the first time in Italy, like the majority
of his countrymen abroad, and mingled almost exclusively with
the circle of Englishmen Shelley had gathered about himself. The
Shelleys were living in an apartment on the top floor of the Tre
Palazzi di Chiesa on the opposite side of the Arno from the Casa
Lanfranchi. Among this circle of rather eccentric Englishmen was
'Old Mr Dolby who went about singing at the top of his voice,
his pocket bulging with books',[5] Taaffe who was at work on a
Commentary on Dante, Walter Savage Landor, later, the Leigh
Hunts, 'who could hardly be persuaded to speak to an Italian'. Dr
Nott, a clergyman, and 'that great hawk-like sailor, as dark as an
Arab, with flashing eyes and teeth, loquacious and violent – a
Pirate out of a schoolboy's picturebook, Trelawny.'[6] Close friends
of the Shelleys, and living in the same house, were Edward Williams
and Jane (who went by his name but was not free to re-marry
after separating in India from an uncongenial husband). Thomas
Medwin, a cousin of Shelley, had been eagerly awaiting the arrival
of Lord Byron, the great celebrity, because he planned to record
his conversations and way of life for a book.

Byron returned to his Ravenna custom of working at night,
sleeping until noon, breakfasting on green tea, riding out in the
afternoon to practise shooting with pistols accompanied by some
of the male members of the circle, and spending the evenings with
Teresa, Pietro and Count Gamba. Once a week he gave a dinner
party to which the women were not invited. Shelley declared that,
'Never did Byron display himself to more advantage than on these
occasions; being at once polite and cordial, full of social hilarity
and the most perfect good humour, never diverging into ungracefid
merriment.[7]

Meanwhile Teresa was cut off from Italian society. Now that the conventions of *serventismo* no longer applied she was known to be Byron's mistress and could no longer be received. Young as she was she spent her days living in seclusion with her father and younger brother. She sometimes saw the Shelleys and the Williamses but their ways were foreign to her and she was mortified by Mary Shelley's pretensions to intellect.

Because the Governor of Pisa refused to allow Byron to practise with his pistols in the garden of the Casa Lanfranchi the afternoon ride was often directed towards a farmhouse belonging to friends of Shelley where the horsemen spent some time shooting at a target. Mary and Teresa sometimes went for an outing in Teresa's carriage and appeared at the farmhouse to applaud the skill of the marksmen.

In January 1822 Lady Noel, Annabella's mother, died. Byron instructed Kinnaird and Hanson to ask Sir Francis Burdett to act as arbiter on his behalf over the division of the income from the Wentworth estates between himself and Annabella: 'I have no desire but to act as a Gentleman should do – without any real enmity, or affected generosity towards those who have not set me a very violent example of forbearance.'[8]

By the terms of the will Byron was to take the Noel arms and from now on signed himself Noel Byron. It was said that he took pleasure in the association of the initials N.B. with Napoleon Bonaparte but Professor Marchand observes that this rests solely on the unreliable evidence of Stendhal who met Byron only once, in 1816.

Byron was distressed when he heard that Lady Noel had decreed in her will that his portrait (which had been hanging at Kirkby Mallory all these years concealed behind a curtain) should not be shown to Ada until she reached the age of twenty-one, and then only with the permission of Lady Byron. '...some steps,' he wrote to Hanson, 'must be taken to prevent the Child's mind from being prejudiced against her father...'[9]

Although he had originally refused payment for his poetry Byron now made a habit of boasting of his avarice and his 'exceeding respect for the smallest current coin of any realm'.[10] He told Kinnaird of his eagerness for '...the least sum which, though I may not want it for myself, may at least do something for my children or others who may want it more than me.' He was anxious for his own financial security and was aware that he had not only Allegra to provide for, but also probably Augusta and her chidren. He also felt responsible for the fate of the exiled Gamba family and thought it possible that they too might be obliged to become his pensioners.

He set out for Kinnaird the points for consideration by the referees on the Wentworth income:

> *Firstly*, – the large Settlement (Sixty thousand pounds, i.e. ten thousand pounds more than I was advised to make upon Miss Milbanke) – made by me upon this female; – *secondly*, the comparative smallness of her then fortune – (twenty thousand pounds – and *that* never paid) ... Thirdly – my leaving both her father Sir Ralph, and her Uncle Lord Wentworth (notwithstanding that I was again advised to the contrary), perfectly free to leave their property as they liked – instead of requiring a previous settlement upon her; thereby showing (what was true) that I did not wed her for her expectations, and (for anything I know) I may be as much disappointed in them – as in any comfort which came with her.[11]
>
> (Byron to Douglas Kinnaird, Pisa, 19 F[ebruar]y 1822)

The referees decreed that each of the parties should receive half of the income. After various deductions this would bring Byron £2,500 a year in addition to his income of £6,000 from the funds. He also received income from his writing but this was on the decline.

Byron reminded Kinnaird that while Lady Byron had her father's income in complete reversal to herself, he had only the life interest in her uncle's fortune. He accordingly instructed Hanson to insure Lady Byron's life for ten thousand pounds. He told Kinnaird that in the event of the estate's increasing in value he would have no objection to increasing Lady Byron's allowance.

In December *Sardanapalus*, *The Two Foscari* and *Cain* were published in one volume by Murray. Irritated as he was by Murray's timidity over *Cain* and the first Cantos of *Don Juan*, when the furore over *Cain* gave rise to rumours that Murray might be prosecuted for publishing it, Byron leapt to his defence:

> The attempt to *bully you* – because they think it won't succeed with me seems to me as atrocious an attempt as ever disgraced the times. – What? when Gibbon's – Hume's – Priestley's and Drummond's publishers have been allowed to rest in peace for seventy years – are you to be

singled out for a work of *fiction* not of history or argument? – there must be something at the bottom of this – some private enemy of your own – it is otherwise incredible. – I can only say – 'Me – me adsum qui feci' that any proceedings directed against you I beg may be transferred to me – who am willing & *ought* to endure them all – that if you have lost money by the publication – I will refund – any – or all of the Copyright – that I desire you will say – that both *you* and *Mr Gifford* remonstrated against the publication – as also Mr Hobhouse – that *I* alone occasioned it – & I alone am the person who either legally or otherwise should bear the burthen. – If they prosecute – I will come to England – that is, if by Meeting it in my own person – I can save yours. – Let me know – you shan't suffer.[12]

(To John Murray, Pisa, 8 February 1822)

Byron now wrote to Moore asking him to try to persuade Murray to help his friend, Taaffe, get his Commentary on Dante published:

It will make the man so exuberantly happy. He dines with me and half-a-dozen English today; and I have not the heart to tell him how the bibliopolar world shrink from his Commentary; – and yet it is full of the most orthodox religion and morality. In short, I made it a point that he shall be in print. He is such a good-natured, heavy ** Christian, that we must give him a shove through the Press. He naturally thirsts to be an author, and has been the happiest of men for these two months, printing, correcting, collating, dating, anticipating, and adding to his treasures of learning. Besides, he has had another fall from his horse into a ditch the other day, while riding out with me into the county.[13]

(Byron to Thomas Moore, Pisa, 8 March 1822)

John Murray published Taaffe's *A Comment on The Divine Comedy of Dante Alighieri* in octavo at 18 shillings on 21 December 1822.[14]

Byron and Teresa had both been sitting for the sculptor, Bartolini. He wrote to Murray:

I think it will be allowed that *Her's* is beautiful. – I shall make you a present of them both to show you that I don't bear malice – and as a compensation for the trouble and squabble you had about Thorwaldsen's.[15]

(Byron to John Murray, Pisa, 6 March 1822)

This was an extremely generous gesture but in addition to his desire to please Murray Byron must have taken pleasure in the prospect of his bust and that of his beautiful mistress being displayed at 50 Albermarle Street for all his old friends to see. However, he decided that Bartolini had made him look like a 'superannuated Jesuit' and intended for Murray only the very charming bust of Teresa, assuring him that a copy of the Thorwaldsen bust could be made for him in place of the Bartolini. In the event neither was sent to Murray.

The English circle caused Byron not a few problems with the authorities in Pisa. In December (1821) Medwin had made a stir by reporting to the volatile Shelley that a man had been taken up for sacrilege at Lucca and was to be burned alive. Shelley was for going to Lucca forthwith to rescue the man. Instead Byron sent Taaffe to Lucca to investigate the matter, authorising him 'in my name' to say that Lord Byron '... would do anything, by *money* or *guarantee*, or otherwise – to have this man's sentence commuted – I am willing to make any sacrifice – of money or otherwise – I could never bribe in a better cause than that of humanity.'

He added a postscript:

> Try the *priests* – a little cash to the Church might perhaps save the Man yet?[16]
>
> (Byron to John Taaffe Jr, Pisa, 12 December 1821)

Byron also wrote a joint letter with Shelley to Lord Guilford. The man was sentenced not to the flames but to the galleys, perhaps a very slightly preferable fate.

Now Taaffe was the innocent cause of an incident which damaged Byron's reputation in the city and gave the authorities an excuse to harass Teresa's family who were already under suspicion for their revolutionary sympathies and their friendship with Byron.

This incident occurred on 24 March 1822. An Italian Sergeant-Major of Hussars, in a hurry to return into the city for roll-call just as Byron and his party were making their way towards the city gate on their way back from their usual afternoon ride, galloped past them so close to Taaffe that his horse was startled and Taaffe, a timid horseman never wholly in control of his mount, was disconcerted and felt himself insulted. The whole party (consisting of Shelley, Pietro Gamba, Trelawney and a newcomer to the circle, a Captain Hay, who was an old friend of Byron from London) spurred after the Italian to remonstrate with him. Sergeant-Major Masi replied rudely and Byron, believing him to be an officer, offered him his card as a challenge. In the mêlée Pietro Gamba struck the man with his riding-whip, calling him 'Ignorante!' upon

404

which Masi called upon the guard to arrest the whole party and, placing himself between them and the gate, began to lay about him with his sabre, slashing Captain Hay across the nose and laying Shelley momentarily senseless on the ground. Byron forced his way through the gate, galloped to the Casa Lanfranchi, sent Lega (who had changed masters and was now in his service) to summon the police, and returned with a swordstick. On the way he met Masi and tried to reason with him but Masi galloped on, only to be attacked by one of Byron's servants who rushed out of the Lanfranchi and, stabbing Masi with a long-handled weapon, melted away into the crowd which had gathered outside the house.

An eye-witness takes up the story:

> I saw Masi reeling in the saddle. As he fell to the ground he cried out 'I am killed!'... I also saw – and the impression it made on me was lasting – all the English inhabitants of Pisa, whether they were Byron's friends or not, gather armed to defend the palace of their great national poet. I thought, if he had been Italian, his fellow citizens would have assembled to stone him, and then I began to understand why the English are a great nation and why the Italians are a bundle of rags in the stove of a second-hand dealer – *at all events, up till now.*[17]

Byron tried to mollify the angry crowd of Pisans by distributing alms outside the Lanfranchi but the tumult was such that he set up two field-pieces inside and gathered together all the arms in the house.

Teresa and Mary had been following the riding party in Teresa's carriage and Teresa was hysterical with fear for Byron. Next day he rode out as usual though she begged him not to. He wrote for advice to the British Minister at Florence. A Police Commissioner was sent to take depositions. This officer had read the account of Byron in the French *Lives of Famous Men.* He believed the story that the Englishman had murdered one of his mistresses and was in the habit of drinking wine from her skull. He was astonished to find that the 'Stravagante My Lord' behaved towards him with the utmost mildness and courtesy.

The investigation took several weeks and in the course of it Taaffe, who was reluctant to be involved in the affair, denied to the interrogator that he had been insulted. He became deeply unpopular with the Pisan circle of friends and acquired the nickname Falstaff – 'false Taaffe'.

405

Fortunately Sergeant-Major Masi, having been carried to the Misericordia hospital, survived his wound. But Tita Falcieri, Byron's huge but gentle Venetian gondolier (who had become so attached to him that he remained in Byron's service for the rest of the poet's life) was arrested together with Byron's coachman (who was the real culprit). The coachman was released but Tita was kept in gaol. Byron sent him and his fellow-prisoners an eleven-course meal in prison and wrote on his behalf to the Minister in Florence who was unable to prevent the authorities from banishing Tita from Tuscany. He found refuge with the Shelleys at their rented summer place of *villeggiatura* near Lerici until he could join Byron in Genoa.

Byron's thoughts were now turning to Greece. In early 1821 the resentment of the Greeks against Turkish oppression, and Turkish taxation, broke into revolt. Alexander Ipsilántis led an abortive rising in Moldavia (present-day Roumania). In 1821 and 1822 most of the fortresses of the Peloponnese (the Morea) were captured by the Greeks and the dashing Greek leader, Kolokotronis, inflicted a crushing defeat on a Turkish army. During the same period large numbers of Philhellenes (young men from abroad who travelled to join the Greek fight for independence, many of them with no experience of war) were slaughtered at the Battle of Péta. The Turkish massacre of civilians on the island of Chios was represented dramatically in a painting by Delacroix and aroused widespread sympathy for the Greek cause. From now on it was all but certain that Byron would fight for Greece. He knew, however, that Teresa would be devastated by any such proposal and had to bide his time.

22

CAIN

Why! the yellow fever is not half as mischievous!

Hobhouse was one of the first to read the manuscript of *Cain* and he was horrified. The work was irreligious and would do his friend's reputation great harm. He wrote off to Byron advising him to suppress it.[1]

Moore was more discerning:

> Cain is wonderful – terrible – never to be forgotten. If I am not mistaken it will sink deep into the world's heart: and while many will shudder at its blasphemy, all must fall prostrate before its grandeur.[2]

Walter Scott predicted that Byron's audience would be influenced by cant. He wrote to John Murray, 'Some part of the language is bold and may shock one class of readers whose line will be adopted by others out of affectation or envy.'

He added:

> But then they must condemn the Paradise Lost, if they have a mind to be consistent. The fiend-like reasoning and bold blasphemy of the fiend and his pupil lead exactly to the point which was to be expected, – the commission of the first murder, and the ruin and despair of the perpetrator.[3]

A 'large class of readers' was duly shocked by *Cain*. Harriet Granville knew that the poem was widely condemned as wicked, but having paid lip service to the general opinion she used her own judgement:

Tell dear George that I think 'Cain' most wicked but not without feeling or passion. Parts of it are magnificent and the effect of Granville's reading it out loud to me was that I roared till I could neither hear nor see.[4]

Other readers were more bigoted. Mrs Piozzi [Doctor Johnson's Mrs Thrale], speaking of Richard Carlile's re-publication of Paine's *Age of Reason*, says, 'Lord Byron's book [*Cain*] will do more mischief than his [Paine's]; and you see there is a cheap edition advertised in order to disseminate the poyson. Why, the yellow fever is not half as mischievous.'[5]

Byron described *Cain* to Murray as a 'Mystery', in conscious allusion to the mediaeval mystery plays. He had started writing it on 16 July 1821 and by 9 September had finished it. He told Murray it was a tragedy on a sacred subject in three acts. He had planned to dedicate *The Two Foscari* to Walter Scott but he was so pleased with *Cain* that he instructed Murray to transfer the already-written dedication to this, his new drama.

Scott was delighted. He wrote to Murray of '... the very grand and tremendous drama of Cain. ... I do not know that his Muse has ever taken so lofty a flight amid her former soarings.'[6]

This failed to convince Murray that the subject would not cause offence.

Byron was annoyed at Murray's diffident suggestion that some speeches in the play might be altered. He wrote to Kinnaird:

To me he talks of the *power* – of 'Cain' and that Gifford & Moore &tc. – all place it among the best &tc. as a composition – but he *cants* about its tendency also. – There never was *such cant*.[7]

(Byron to Kinnaird, Pisa, 15 November 1821)

Byron was angry too at the shocked reaction to *Cain* of some of his friends, in particular he resented Hobhouse's letter of remonstrance. Even Kinnaird called *Cain* 'a puzzler' and Byron asked whether he meant 'a puzzler to *understand* – or to answer.'[8]

One can understand Murray's anxiety. He understood only too well the process Walter Scott had predicted – some readers shocked, others influenced by affectation or envy.

Byron's text apparently gave them plenty of armunition:

Souls who dare look the Omnipotent tyrant in
His everlasting face, and tell him that
His evil is not good![9]

*   *   *

            – Perhaps he'll make
One day a Son unto himself – as he
Gave you a father – and if he so doth,
Mark me! that Son wll be a sacrifice![10]

Byron explained the point of *Cain*:

Cain is a proud man – if Lucifer promised him Kingdoms &tc. – it would *elate* him – the object of the demon is to *depress* him still further in his own estimation than he was before – by showing him infinite things – & his own abasement – till he falls into the frame of mind – that leads to the Catastrophe – from mere *internal* irritation – *not* premeditation or envy – of *Abel* – (which would have made him contemptible) but from rage and fury against the inadequacy of his state to his Conceptions.[11]

Lucifer takes Cain on a flight into infinity, and Byron's language makes us aware of the powerful effect on Cain's mind which Lucifer achieved. Cain is drugged with the immensity and beauty of space:

     Cain.   Oh thou beautiful
And unimaginable ether! and
Ye multiplying masses of increased
And still-increasing lights! what are ye? what
Is this blue wilderness of interminable
Air, where ye roll along...[12]

     Cain.
The Immortal – the Unbounded – the omnipotent –
The overpowering mysteries of space –
The innumerable worlds that were and are –
A whirlwind of such overwhelming things,
Suns, moons, and earths, upon their loud-voiced spheres
Singing in thunder round me, as have made me
Unfit for mortal converse; leave me, Abel.[14]

Professor Marchand held that Byron's purpose in *Cain* was to indulge in the farthest realms of metaphysical speculation. Bernard Beatty strongly disagrees with this: 'The speculations in Act II are not the whole point of the play. They are situated within a three act play whose very purpose is to dramatize the bible story on the first, irrational, murder.'[14]

Byron himself writes: 'Cain is nothing more than a drama – not a piece of argument.'[15]

Whatever Byron's contemporaries thought of the speculations in Act II the writers among them were bowled over by the play and its poetry.

Shelley wrote to Gisborne:

What think you of Lord Byron's last volume? In my opinion it contains finer poetry than has appeared in England since the publication of Paradise Regained. Cain is apocalyptic – it is a revelation not before communicated to man.[16]

Scott declared that Byron had matched Milton on his own ground.

Goethe, on the strength of this poem, decreed, 'Byron alone I admit to a place at my side.'[17] In his review of Cain he tells of '... a gifted lady of our acquaintance, akin to us by her great esteem for Byron, [who] expressed the opinion that everything that can be said religiously or morally in the whole world is contained in the last three words of the play.[18]

This might seem a monstrous exaggeration but Bernard Beatty speaks admiringly of those same three words:

Cain goes into exile carrying one of his children followed by his wife Adah carrying the other. Before she leaves the stage Adah bends to kiss the body of Abel.
ADAH   Peace be with him!
CAIN   But with me![19]

Bernard Beatty observes that 'the vowel of the word "me" echoes into an indefinite, open, terrible future. It is a superb ending – just like Manfred's "'tis not so difficult to die".'[20]

Notes

The use of the term 'Satanism' to describe Byron's interest in metaphysical matters to do with God, Man, Lucifer, Cain, can be misleading to those unfamiliar with the literary aspect of the term. A dictionary definition of Satanism gives the generally accepted meaning of the word:

1. Worship of Satan, especially in the form of a travesty of Christian ritual. 2. Evil or Satanic practices or tendencies.

Byron's thought has nothing whatsoever to do with such practices or worship but during his lifetime and after his death Satanism by this definition was attributed to him. Lamartine addressed his fellow-poet in the poem *L'Homme à Lord Byron* from *Méditations Poétiques*:

> Et toi, Byron, semblable à ce brigand des airs, [the eagle]
> Les cris du désespoir sont tes plus doux concerts,
> Le mal est ton autel, et l'homme est ta victim,
> Ton oeil, comme Satan, a mésuré l'abîme.[1]

This could be translated:

> You, Byron, mirror-image of this brigand of the winds,
> For you the sweetest sounds are the wailings of despair,
> Evil is your altar, mankind your sacrifice,
> Your eye, like that of Satan, has measured the abyss.

Byron considered this poem actionable and quoted from it:

> ... Chantre d'enfer! '[threshold of hell] – by ** that's a speech,' and I won't put up with it! A pretty title to give a man for doubting if there be any such place![2]

In a note to the Hachette edition of Lamartine's *Méditations Poétiques* the reader is informed that:

> Byron, like Baudelaire, was famous for his Satanism. [That this 'was no harmless reference to the literary Satanism of a poet such as Milton is evident from the reasons given for this fame] ... Byron's disturbing appearance – he was lame – *boiteux comme Asmodée*; demon of impure delights, and his eye shone with a diabolical brilliance – And then, his entire *oeuvre*, and *Manfred* in particular, is, as it were, positioned beneath the sign of evil by the stirrings of proud revolt which it inspired.[3]

The *Letters and Journals* show that such a description of their writer is superstitious nonsense. But the widespread misreading of the character of the poet was evidently shared by Bertrand Russell who asserted that, while Rousseau admired virtue, provided it was safe, Byron admired sin, provided it was elemental.[4]

411

23

HEAVEN AND EARTH

A bishop might have written it!

Byron described *Heaven and Earth* as '...choral and mystical –
and a sort of Oratorio on a sacred subject'.[1] He intended to write
a second part but never did. He told Murray, 'I wish the first part
to be published before the second – because if it don't succeed –
it is better to stop there – than to go on in a fruitless experiment.'[2]
Later he assured Murray, 'I believe the new Mystery is pious
enough...'[3]

Murray had the play printed but dithered about publishing it,
alarmed at its resemblance to *Cain* which had caused such offence.
His reluctance to publish *Heaven and Earth* almost put an end to
the long connection as sole publisher of Byron's work.

In October 1822 Byron told Murray that he '...clearly wanted
to get out of what you thought perhaps a bad business – either
for fear of the Parsondom – or your Admiralty patrons – or your
Quarter*lyers* – or some other exquisite reason – but why not be
sincere & manly – and for once – say so?' He reminded Murray
that when he [Byron] had '...wished to put an end to the connection
this year – it was at your own especial request to Messrs Moore
and Hobhouse – that I agreed to renew it.'[4] (Byron to John Murray,
31 October 1822)

Eventually the manuscript of *Heaven and Earth* was handed over
to John Hunt and published in the second issue of *The Liberal*, of
which six thousand copies were printed.

Heaven and Earth did not escape the wrath of the critics who
had been appalled at the appearance of *The Vision of Judgment* in
the first issue of *The Liberal*.

The *London Literary Gazette* (4 January 1823) called it 'A bad imitation of the worst Methodist hymns ... but a wretched thing for the Pisan bard to achieve.'[5]

From some critics *Heaven and Earth* came in for high praise: Francis Jeffrey in the *Edinburgh Review* also found more poetry in *Heaven and Earth* than in any of Byron's dramas since *Manfred*, and the February issue of the *Monthly Magazine and British Register* placed the drama in the front rank of Byron's work '... in sublimity, in force, and in pathos, ... conceived in the best style of the greatest masters ... not unworthy of Dante...'[6]

The writer went on to say that '... in our opinion he has far surpassed his competitors.'[7] 'Competitors' may refer to Moore's *Loves of the Angels* which appeared a month after *Heaven and Earth* and with a similar subject. Jerome McGann explains:

> As early as 1813 Byron had entertained the idea of writing about 'the amours of a Peri and a mortal' (28 August 1813 BLJ III 101) but in deference to Moore (whose *Lalla Rookh* included 'Paradise and the Peri') he abandoned the project. Ironically, when he returned to a more Biblical version of the same theme, Moore was engaged in writing *The Loves of the Angels*, and when the works were published within weeks of each other, contemporary reviewers seized the opportunity to compare them. Moore's erotic idylls share little with *Heaven and Earth*, although the maiden's prayer to 'the idol of her dreams' in 'The Second Angel's Story' suggest Anah and Aholibamah's address to their absent lovers in Byron's opening scene.[8]

Moore was nervous about the effect on the public of *The Loves of the Angels* and felt obliged to alter it accordingly, much to the displeasure of Byron who wrote to him in February 1823, 'And you are really recanting, or softening to the clergy? It will do little good for you – it is *you*, not the poem they are at. They will say they frightened you – forbid it, Ireland!';[9] and again in April, 'But why did you change your title? – You will regret this some day. The bigots are not to be conciliated; and, if they were – are they worth it?'[10]

One critic made a cruel comparison between the two poets: 'Moore writes with a crow-quill ... Byron writes with an eagle's plume.'

Crabb Robinson reported in his diary the reaction of Goethe to *Heaven and Earth*:

It was a satisfaction to me to find that Goethe preferred to all the other serious poems of Byron the 'Heaven and Earth', though it seemed almost satire when he exclaimed 'A bishop might have written it.'[11]

Yet Jerome McGann observes that '... in its challenge to divine compassion, and perhaps less powerfully, to divine justice, *Heaven and Earth* continues the argument of *Cain*,' and Cain had horrified the bishops. Although he finds that the two plays have much in common, McGann judges *Heaven and Earth* as much inferior to *Cain*: 'Much of it is superficial and the allegory is flimsy compared with the richness of *Cain*'.[12]

Bernard Beatty gives this explanation of Byron's purpose in the drama *Heaven and Earth*:

> The complexity here is roughly that of classical tragedy. Byron admired this form in self-conscious contradiction to his Romantic contemporaries. He is careful to make the action of both his biblical plays occur within twenty-four hours and he experiments with a chorus of sorts in *Heaven and Earth*. What he is trying to do, as classical tragedy does, is to illuminate the relationship between choice and determination in human affairs. They are determined by God's unexaminable choices and by heredity yet remain capable of choice in some sense. Where classical tragedy uses Fate and the Furies, Byron is much more interested in the parallel, but quite different emphases of the scripture on human responsibility and divine insistences.[13]

The enthusiasm of Goethe for *Heaven and Earth* may possibly have been concerned more with the language than the significance of the play, which was, after all, only half-finished.

The coming of the Deluge which will destroy the descendants of Cain is foreshadowed in the speech of Japhet, a descendant of Seth. He addresses the mountains:

> Ye look eternal! Yet, in a few days,
> Perhaps even hours, ye will be changed, rent, hurled
> Before the mass of waters; and yon cave,
> Which seems to lead into a lower world,
> Shall have its depths searched by the sweeping wave,
> And dolphins gambol in the lion's den!
> And man – Oh, men! my fellow-beings! Who
> Shall weep above your universal grave,
> Save I? Who shall be left to weep?[14]

This first part ends with the stage-direction:

> [*The Waters rise: Men fly in every direction;*
> *many are overtaken by the waves; the chorus*
> *of Mortals disperses in search of safety*
> *up the Mountains; Japhet remains upon a rock,*
> *while the Ark floats towards him*
> *in the distance.*]

This Wagnerian conclusion may be partly responsible for the fact that, so far as I am aware, no-one has yet attempted to mount a production of the play.

24

A MOST LOVABLE CHILD

I shall go to her but she shall not return to me.

Claire had long been pestering Shelley with proposals for stealing Allegra away from the convent. He wrote to her, 'I am shocked at the thoughtless violence of your designs.'[1]

Mary had tried (ironically, in view of later events) to reassure Claire over the child's welfare.

> Your anxiety for Allegra's health is to a great degree unfounded; Venice, its stinking canals and dirty streets, is enough to kill any child; but you ought to know, and anyone will tell you so, that the towns of Romagna situated where Bagnacavallo is, enjoy the best air in Italy.[2]

Claire was not amenable to advice. Her letter to Byron remonstrating over his decision to put Allegra, for the time being, into the convent at Bagnacavallo had been calculated to insult the convent-bred Teresa and cannot have endeared the writer to Teresa's lover:

> Every traveller and writer upon Italy joins in condemning them [convents], which would alone be sufficient testimony, without adverting to the state of ignorance and profligacy of Italian women, all pupils of convents. They are bad wives, most unnatural mothers; licentious and ignorant, they are the dishonour and unhappiness of society.[3]

Thus Claire destroyed any possibility of Byron's listening to her pleas. Neither could have foreseen how cruelly he would be brought to regret it.

News came from Pellegrino Ghigi, Byron's banker at Ravenna,

whose daughter was in the same convent as Allegra, that the little girl was suffering from a fever. Ghigi had gone to visit the child and reported that he '... found her in her little bed in a fine room surrounded by three doctors and all the nuns and asking for some tender cheese. If there is any fault it is of too much care.'[4]

Byron was 'very much agitated' by this news and sent off a courier asking for details and telling the nuns to call in Professor Tommasi of Bologna if necessary. By the fifteenth Allegra was reported to be out of danger but on the twenty-second she died of a convulsive catarrhal attack.

Teresa gently broke the news to Byron and reported that he shed no tears but was overtaken with 'a mortal paleness' and asked to be left alone.

Iris Origo analyses Byron's mixed feelings over Allegra with sensitivity and understanding:

> [His letters] show a complete masculine unawareness of a small child's character or needs – but not deliberate neglect, much less indifference.
> Byron petted the child as long as she was amicable, sent her to scream and kick upstairs with the maids when she was not – or above all, as soon as she reminded him of Claire – and in the end packed her off to her convent-school in a genuine belief that she would receive a wiser upbringing there than under the erratic care of the Shelleys, or exposed to the hysterical affection of her mother.[5]

The Shelleys agreed with him. They had been looking for a house to rent for the summer at Lerici and had fixed on the Casa Magni at the edge of the bay opposite the town. When they heard of Allegra's death they hurried Claire away to the Casa Magni and broke the news to her there. She wrote terrible accusing letters to Byron, and Shelley wrote kind ones: 'I will not describe her grief to you; you have already suffered too much. The portrait and the hair arrived safe – I gave them to Claire ... she now seems bewildered, whether she designs to avail herself of your permission to regulate the funeral I know not. In fact I am so exhausted with the scenes through which I have passed that I do not dare to ask.'[6]

By 16 May he was able to write, 'Claire is much better; after the first shock she has sustained her loss with more fortitude than I had dared to hope.'[7]

Iris Origo relates how the good nuns of Bagnacavallo, one of whom took to her bed with grief after Allegra's death, made a little statue of her 'to preserve the memory of a most lovable child' – and dressed it in her own clothes – '...a chemise, a silken dress, a little fur tippet and a chain of gold round her neck. She had died, they said, because she was too intelligent to live. Never had they had so promising a pupil.'[8]

The nuns were more charitable in remembering the illegitimate child of a foreign nobleman of questionable morality than his countryman, the Rector of the Church at Harrow. Byron sent the body back to England and Murray took charge of the obsequies.

I wish it to be buried in Harrow Church – there is a spot in the Churchyard near the footpath on the brow of the hill looking toward Windsor – and a tomb under a large tree (bearing the name of Peachee – or Peachey) where I used to sit for hours & hours when a boy – this was my favourite spot – but as I wish to erect a tablet to her memory – the body had better be deposited in the Church. – ... – and on the wall – a marble tablet placed with these words:

> In memory of
> Allegra –
> daughter of G.G. Lord Byron –
> who died at Bagnacavallo
> in Italy April 20th, 1822,
> aged five years and three months. –

'I shall go to her, but she shall not return to me. –'
2d. Samuel 12. – 23. –[9]

(To John Murray, Montenero, 26 May 1822)

The Rector protested that this inscription could not be allowed since it was against all taste and morals. The tiny coffin was buried just inside the door of the church and nothing John Murray could say succeeded in persuading the Rector to allow any tablet to be put up in memory of the little girl.

Gossip in England accused Byron of using the dead child to hurt Lady Byron by burying her at Harrow where Lady Byron had taken a house. He wrote to Augusta asking her to explain to Lady Byron:

There has been tell her a stupid story in the papers about the burial of my poor little natural baby – which I directed to be as private as possible; they say that she was to be buried and epitaphed opposite Lady B's pew – now – firstly – God help me! I did not know Lady B had ever been in Harrow Church and should have thought it the very last place she would have chosen – and 2ndly, my *real* instructions are in a letter to Murray of last Summer – and the simplest possible as well as the inscription ... and you see how they have distorted this ... into some story about Lady B – of whom Heaven knows – I have thought much less than perhaps I should have done in these last four of five years.[10]

(Byron to Augusta Leigh, Genoa, 12 December 1822)

Though he had thought little of Annabella during those years Ada was always in his thoughts. Iris Origo writes of his mixed feelings for Allegra and her half-sister:

In the queer mixture of his feelings for Allegra – bravado, affection, impatience, guilt – there was also a feeling of resentment (unjust but not wholly unnatural), on behalf of that other child of his, whom he could never see. Allegra, the little bastard, drove in his carriage, and sat on his knee, but it was Ada's birthday that he noted in his journal; Ada's miniature that stood on his writing desk; Ada's education, her disposition and her future, that were always on his lips.[11]

When Allegra was gone he could only regret that he had not visited her at her convent before it was too late: 'While she lived, her existence did not seem necessary to my happiness, but no sooner did I lose her, than it appeared to me that I could not live without her.'[12]

25

THE END OF A FRIENDSHIP: BYRON AND JOHN MURRAY

When scurrilous stories were circulated in England accusing Byron of having buried his little daughter Allegra in the church at Harrow to insult his wife, who sometimes attended services there, Byron blamed Murray, who tended to flourish Byron's letters about and perhaps boasted of the service with which Byron had entrusted him over Allegra's obsequies. Byron was particularly incensed by these rumours as he did not know that Lady Byron had ever visited Harrow.'

From the *Letters of John Murray* to Byron, and its editor, we learn how relations between poet and publisher deteriorated. It is a sad story. Misunderstandings arose. Byron blamed Murray for his failure to transmit to John Hunt various appendages to the manuscripts Hunt was now to publish. Byron accused Murray of being obstructive. This was unfair as it seems that Kinnaird was probably to blame for the oversight.[2] John Hunt enraged Murray by calling on him unannounced with a companion clearly brought to serve as a witness and demanding the documents in a loud and offensive manner.[3] Murray requested Byron not to ask him to have anything to do with John Hunt.[4]

Eventually Byron wrote an angry letter to Murray which he sent to Kinnaird, instructing him to deliver it to Murray or not as he judged wise. Instead of suppressing the letter Kinnaird passed it on, thereby hastening an end to the relationship. Murray's brief final letter to Byron is dictated to his clerk and ends: 'I am, My Lord, your Obedient Servant (signed) John Murray'.[5] There had been a time when Murray ended his letters: 'With best Compliments

I remain, Dearest Sir, your Lordship's faithful friend and Servant, John Murray.'

Byron's last letter to Murray was sent from Greece two months before his death. Murray had written to Kinnaird to inform Byron that he had heard of a satire against Gifford which had appeared in Italy and was attributed to Byron. Murray did not believe it and suspected Leigh Hunt.[6] Byron told Kinnaird that he could not hurt a hair of Gifford's head and wrote to Murray, '...whoever asserts that I am the author or abettor of anything of the kind on Gifford – he lies in his throat – I always regarded him as my literary father.'[7] Byron, who rarely bore malice for long, then gave Murray news of his doings in Greece.[8]

Note

For a more detailed account of Byron's friendship with John Murray the reader is directed to *The Letters of John Murray to Lord Byron*, Ed. Andrew Nicholson (Liverpool University Press, 2007) – compulsive reading for the light it throws on both men.

26

WERNER

'... the dullest play that ever was written,' Ellen Terry[1]

Werner is the odd-man-out among Byron's plays. Using an illuminating comparison with *Macbeth*, G. Wilson Knight explains why:

> *Werner* reflects that in *Macbeth* which is, or seems, directed by the obvious moral valuations; Byron's other dark dramas reflect that in *Macbeth* which leaves us with the sense that these valuations do not cover the problem. Now because Byron is using the ordinary valuations [in *Werner*] instead of engaging in a thought adventure [as in the other plays] he can employ normal stage technique.[2]

M.K. Joseph agrees that '... in spite of Byron's disclaimers, [*Werner*] comes closest of all the dramas to the acceptable dramatic form of his time.'[3] So much so indeed that it has been suggested Byron wrote it tongue-in-cheek, to show he was capable of producing an actable and successful piece for the contemporary theatre.

In spite of Byron's insistence that none of his plays was intended for performance in the theatre, several were put on stage during the nineteenth century and *Werner* was by far the most successful. However, Margaret Howell points out that this was only after considerable modification, swingeing cuts, and with an actor of the stature of Macready or Henry Irving in the title role.[4]

Werner is based on *Kreutzner or the German's Tale* published in 1801, one of the series of novels by Harriet and Sophia Lee entitled *The Canterbury Tales*. At the age of fifteen Byron was fascinated by this gloomy German melodrama and the version

423

published by John Murray in 1821 was Byron's third attempt at turning the novel into a play.

Jerome McGann points out that Byron's fascination with *Kreutzner* was probably reinforced by his later reading of the equally gloomy plays of Schiller about the Thirty Years War. According to McGann the point of *Werner* is that it 'explores the effect of guilt on the protagonist and those around him'. Specifically it focuses on the title character's double transgression in stealing and then rationalising his theft. It is the latter which has the weightiest consequences. The father's 'situational ethics', to his horror, authorise the son's murder of their common enemy.[5]

The son (Ulrich) tells his father (Werner/Siegendorf) '... we have done with right and wrong.' The play ends with the father's despairing cry, 'The race of Siegendorf is past!'[6]

Many critics have panned the play, Samuel Chew wrote of it: 'Byron followed his original with the utmost closeness and for the most part did little more than to turn the prose of the novel into very inadequate blank verse.' He adds, 'The versification at best is dull, at worst execrable...'[7] and he considers the play both superficial and dependent on incident – very different from the Venetian plays which, as we have seen, were described by Jerome McGann as '... not concerned with the issue of events but with their meaning.'[8]

M.K. Joseph describes the play as an attempt at a *roman policier* but finds it of '... a certain interest ... as a kind of corollary to the theological dramas.'[9]

It is perhaps rather surprising to find other critics praising some aspects of the play with real enthusiasm.

E.H. Coleridge claimed that '... in spite of the ineptness of the blank verse, here and there throughout the play, in scattered lines and passages, he [Byron] outdoes himself. The inspiration is fitful but supreme.'[10]

G. Wilson Knight praises certain aspects of the play wholeheartedly: 'The criminal psychology, the stabs of irony, the tense atmosphere and gripping dialogue, the mysteries and the thrills, are from the hand of a master.'[11]

On the one hand 'inept', 'dull', 'superficial', 'execrable'; on the other 'supreme' and 'from the hand of a master'. On the whole, however, one must agree with those who panned the play. Even Coleridge and Wilson Knight are unable to praise it as a whole, and the flashes of brilliance they claim to perceive other critics have been unable to discern.

Samuel Chew was so critical of the work that he wished the rumour was true that *Werner* had been written not by Byron but by the Duchess of Devonshire.

27

MONTENERO

Sapete qualcosa di Shelley?

The flamboyant figure who had recently joined the English circle at Pisa, Edward John Trelawny, had been persuaded to come to that city by Captain Williams. The Shelleys immediately accepted him as a valued friend. When Byron saw Trelawny he told Teresa, 'I have met today the personification of my Corsair. He sleeps with the poem under his pillow and all his past adventures and present manners, aim at this personification.[1] Byron seems to have been the only sceptic among the Pisa circle who perceived at first sight that Trelawny was a fantasist for whom reality and truth were equally unimportant, with the exception of Mary Shelley who allowed her doubts to be overcome by her liking for this dashing new friend.

Trelawny's arrival at Pisa was to contribute to disaster. Shelley had found a summer refuge for himself and Mary and the Williams in the Casa Magni at the edge of the sea near Lerici and he and Williams decided to build a boat for sailing in the Bay of Spezia. It was Trelawny who found a way of making this possible by introducing them to Captain Daniel Roberts who was able to supervise the construction of a small boat at Genoa which was called by Shelley *The Ariel*. Trelawny then persuaded Byron to commission a schooner for himself which could be skippered by Roberts. This cost far more than the estimate provided by Trelawny and proved of little use to Byron as the authorities at Genoa refused him permission to cruise off the coast – possibly as a result of his calling the schooner *Bolivar* after the Venezuelan revolutionary

427

leader. Byron already had the reputation with the Italian police of being himself a dangerous revolutionary.

Shelley now succeeded in persuading Byron to agree with his plan for starting a political and literary review, eventually to be called *The Liberal*, and to invite Leigh Hunt to come to Italy with his family to join in the project. The three poets would contribute the bulk of the material in the review and they would invite friends in England to send in other items. Byron's friends remonstrated with him over this plan. The Hunt brothers had the reputation of being dangerous Radicals and were regarded as vulgar Cockneys. Even Moore joined in the chorus of disapprobation. As usual such opposition drove Byron to more determined support of the scheme. Shelley's chief aim was to help Hunt out of his financial difficulties. His large family of unruly children could live more cheaply in Italy and the journal, if successful, might provide him with an income. Shelley was delighted when Byron agreed to fit out part of the Casa Lanfranchi to house the Hunts. But was deeply embarrassed when it became clear that Hunt intended to apply to Byron for money for his journey and for the support of himself and his family. Byron sent him £250.

Storms and contrary winds forced the Hunts to postpone their journey. By May 1822 when they arrived, Byron and Teresa had taken a villa at Montenero, south of Leghorn for the summer. The Villa Dupuy stood on a hill looking out on the Mediterranean and the islands of Elba and Corsica. Teresa was delighted with the gardens full of roses and jasmine. In the evenings she would sit with Byron under the orange trees watching the fishing boats to-ing and fro-ing with the lights of Pisa in the distance.

However, the time at Montenero was not a happy interlude. Unlike the vast, cool, Casa Lanfranchi, the Villa Dupuy was stiflingly hot. When the water supply failed the servants had to travel on muleback to distant springs to fetch water. Byron was brooding over the death of Allegra. He still loved Teresa, though no longer with a grand passion, and wrote of the pleasure of solitude with such a woman, but he was beginning to feel himself unable to provide the attention demanded by *serventismo* for the woman he served.

Teresa was no more than twenty-three. To be consigned to such solitude was not the most natural situation for so young a woman but she loved Byron and was willing to put up with whatever tedium he inflicted on her as long as he continued to love her. When Byron first fell in love with her in Venice he had expressed a fear that she would 'plant' him, in which case he would be unable to show his face on the Piazza. Now Teresa was terrified that she would suffer the public humiliation of being 'planted' by her famous lover. Losing him to Greece would be bad enough but it may have been a relief to her that he left her in the end for glory and not for boredom.

Byron was pleased by an invitation to visit the American squadron moored at Leghorn where he was much fêted by the Captain and crew. When he came aboard the *Constitution* on 21 May he told Kinnaird that he was:

> ...received with the greatest kindness, and *rather too much ceremony*. – They have asked me to sit for my picture to an American Artist now in Florence. – As I was taking leave – an American lady took a *rose* (which I wore) from me – as she said she wished to send something which I had about me to America. – ... I also hear that as an author I am in great request in Germany. – All this is some compensation for the brutality of the native English.[2]
> (Byron to Douglas Kinnaird, Villa Dupuy Leghorn, 26 May 1822)

In June Byron experienced the great pleasure of a day in the company of the Earl of Clare who made a detour on his way back to England, to visit his friend. The meeting left Byron unhappily convinced that he and Clare would never meet again.

Ruggiero and Pietro Gamba arrived at Montenero at the end of June after spending some time in Ravenna trying unsuccessfully to save their servant, Maluchielli, from banishment, the penalty for involvement in the Masi affair, of which he was entirely innocent.

Now another unfortunate incident took place which broke up the sojourn at Montenero. One of Byron's servants started an altercation with some of the Gamba servants; it turned violent. Knives were produced. Pietro's arm was grazed as he tried to stop the fight and Byron stormed out onto the balcony and shouted that he would fire upon the combatants if they did not calm down. Eventually the police were called.

This was the opportunity the authorities were waiting for to rid themselves of Byron by threatening to banish the Gambas permanently from Tuscany unless they left voluntarily within three days. Byron wrote to inform the authorities that in these circumstances he too would leave Tuscany. He asked for a few days' delay to enable him to make arrangements for the departure of the whole party.

It was unfortunate that Leigh Hunt walked in to the Villa Dupuy at the moment when the fracas was at its height; Teresa distraught, Pietro hurt, the servant who had started the fight begging forgiveness, Byron dealing with the combatants and then with the police. Byron was unable to welcome Hunt as he would have wished. Shelley was unable to join them until later since Mary was ill. Hunt, whose ship had anchored at Leghorn, had left his family there and walked all the way to Montenero.

On 1 July Shelley arrived, took the Hunts to Pisa and installed them on the ground floor of the Casa Lanfranchi. Byron and Teresa soon followed them and the Gambas moved to Lucca. Hunt had spent all the money advanced to him by Byron and Shelley. Unable to do more for Hunt himself, Shelley persuaded Byron to offer him the copyright of *The Vision of Judgment* which would appear in the first number of *The Liberal*.

At this point another misfortune occurred. Count Guiccioli, claiming that Teresa was no longer living under her father's roof (although Count Gamba was with her at Montenero), succeeded in persuading the Pope to cancel her allowance. There was nothing now to dissuade Teresa and Byron from moving back into the Lanfranchi together.

Byron was irritated by the unruly behaviour of the Hunt children who were allowed to riot all over the ground floor and on the staircase. But, according to Hunt, his host went about the house and gardens singing, laughing and teasing his visitor. Hunt joined in the afternoon rides with Trelawny.

It may be that Byron's good humour was caused by his working on a sixth Canto of *Don Juan* some of which amused him so much that he would run into Teresa's apartments to show her the stanzas.

Shelley had left Pisa for Leghorn on 7 July to join Williams. They found a boy to crew for them as they took the *Ariel* back to Lerici. Captain Roberts watched them taking in their topsails far out to sea as a sudden and violent squall hid them from view. Trelawny brought this news to Pisa and terrible suspicions arose. Hunt dashed off a note to Lerici, hoping that the two men were safely back at the Casa Magni and, on its arrival, Mary and Jane Williams set off for Pisa in great distress, stopping at the Casa Lanfranchi to ask for news, then driving through the night and arriving at Leghorn at 2.00 a.m. Trelawny accompanied them back to the Casa Magni stopping to ask for news along the coast. Byron gave Roberts permission to use the *Bolivar* in the search and joined Trelawny in scouring the coastline over the next days.

On the 19th he wrote to Kinnaird:

Shelley's body has been found and identified ... two days ago – chiefly by a book in his Jacket pocket [Keats' *Lamia*] – the body itself being totally disfigured & in a state of putrefaction. – Another body supposed Capt. Willams's also found ... You may imagine the state of their wives and children – and also Leigh Hunt's – who was but just arrived from England. – Yesterday and the day before I made two journeys to the mouth of the Arno and another river (the Serchio) for purposes of ascertaining the circumstances – and identifications of the bodies – but they were already interred for the present by order of the Sanità or Health Office.[3]

(Byron to Douglas Kinnaird, Pisa, 19 July 1822)

Trelawny took charge of the cremation of the bodies. Byron brought Hunt with him in his carriage to the mouth of the Serchio where Williams was cremated. Next day Shelley's body was burned on the beach at Viareggio. After the ceremony Byron plunged into the water and swam out to sea.

He wrote to Thomas Moore:

You can have no idea what an extraordinary effect such a funeral pile has, on a desolate shore, with mountains in the back-ground and the sea before, and the singular appearance the salt and frankincense gave to the flame.'[4]

(Byron to Thomas Moore, Pisa, 27 August 1822)

Once the gruesome ceremony was over they all drove off to dine and the wine they drank, together with their reaction to the awful events of the day, had them singing and laughing as they returned home in the great Napoleonic coach.

Byron was to suffer for his long swim from the beach at Viareggio in the blazing heat of day. He told Hobhouse that all his skin peeled off and he was violently sick. Trelawny had broken the news of the tragedy to Mary and Jane and brought them to Pisa where Teresa and Byron treated them with great kindness. Mary wrote of her gratitude for this kindness but she read what was sympathy for her bereavement as pleasure in her company and this was to give rise to disillusionment and pain when Byron failed to seek her company in Genoa.

In answer to his enquiries Byron was told that the Gambas would not be given permission for a prolonged stay at Lucca (and police records show that the decision was made not wholly on account of the subversive activities known to have been perpetrated by the Gambas, but chiefly in the hope their expulsion would cause Byron to follow them). The British Resident at Genoa, a Mr Hill, advised Byron that the Gambas would be welcome there. He began to consider moving the whole party to Genoa.

The death of Shelley destroyed the hopes of Leigh Hunt for a successful co-operation with Byron and Shelley on *The Liberal*. The invitation to the Hunts to come to Italy had not been Byron's but Shelley's. Byron would not abandon Hunt but he took little pleasure in his presence. Hunt appeared to assume that it was Byron's duty to support him, his wife and his six children, yet he showed little appreciation of what was done for him. Mrs Hunt was sickly and discontented and made no secret of her disapproval of Byron's relationship with Countess Guiccioli.

Teresa's explanation of the attitude of the Hunts towards their benefactor shows that she was both perceptive and intelligent:

> If Lord Byron appeared to be in good spirits Hunt called him heartless; if he took a bath, a sybarite. If he tried to joke with him, he was guilty of the insufferable liberties that a great nobleman will allow himself with a poor man. If he presented Hunt with numerous copyrights, with the sole intention of helping him, it could only be because he lacked an editor. If he was charitable, it was out of ostentation. If he was adored by the lady who regarded him as superior to the rest of humanity, it was because she had the soul of a slave and a mediocre intelligence. And finally, when he sacrificed everything he cared for, to serve the Greek cause, it was because he was tired of the sentimentality of Mme Guiccioli.[5]

Now Hobhouse arrived for a brief stay at the Casa Lanfranchi. Although he disapproved of the life Byron was leading in Italy Hobhouse was still deeply fond of his friend and Byron was overjoyed at seeing him. When Hobhouse left, Byron embraced him, saying, 'Hobhouse, you should never have come, or you should never go.'[6] He wrote to Kinnaird: '...these glimpses of old friends for a moment are sad remembrancers – ... write to me at Genoa where I am going directly.[7]

On 28 September the large party set off for Genoa. The logistics of the journey were complicated, requiring the transportation of several people with servants, children, horses, carriages, animals and substantial amounts of furniture for fitting up two large houses. Difficulties in the way were mountains, rivers and customs regulations.

They set off in two coaches by land while the servants and goods were put on board a *felucca* at Lerici where the Gambas joined them. Trelawny met them there in the *Bolivar* with Byron's books and papers and various household goods. Byron and Trelawny jumped into the sea and raced each other out to the *Bolivar* with the result that Byron fell ill again from exposure to the sun and spent the next four days confined to bed in a miserable inn.

The whole party then proceeded by sea to Genoa where Mrs Hunt expressed her terror of the perfectly respectable Italian porters who carried them ashore.

The omens for the stay in Genoa were not good.

28

THE VISION OF JUDGMENT

If there is anything obnoxious to the political opinions of a portion of the public in the following poem they may thank Mr Southey.

In the early 1820s Byron's running dogfight with Southey (whom he despised for having, like Wordsworth and Coleridge, reneged on his early enthusiasm for freedom and reform) developed into a pitched battle in the course of which Byron rolled Southey up, horse, foot and guns. Byron had been outraged when, as Poet Laureate, Southey produced a poem on the death of George III which he called *The Vision of Judgment*:

> He might have written hexameters, as he has written everything else, for aught that the writer cared – had they been upon another subject. But to attempt to canonize a monarch who, whatever were his household virtues, was neither a successful nor a patriot king, in as much as several years of his reign passed in war with America and Ireland, to say nothing of the aggression upon France, – like all other exaggeration, necessarily begets opposition. In whatever manner he may be spoken of in this new *Vision* his *public* career will not be more favourably transmitted by history. Of his domestic virtues, though a little expensive to the nation, there can be no doubt.[1]

Byron was not alone in his indignation. Hazlitt entered the fray:

> Does he not dedicate to his present Majesty that extraordinary poem on the death of his father, called *Vision of Judgment*, as a specimen of what might be done in English hexameters? In a court-poem all should be trite and on an approved model. He might as well have presented

himself at the levee in a fancy or masquerade dress. Mr Southey was not to *try conclusions* with majesty – still less on such an occasion. The extreme freedoms with departed greatness, the party-petulence carried to the Throne of Grace, the unchecked indulgence of private humour, the assumption of infallibility and even of the voice of Heaven in this poem, are pointed instances of what I have said.[2]

Byron retaliated with his own *Vision of Judgment* which was published in the first issue of *The Liberal* and held Southey up to ridicule. Byron described it as being 'in my finest, ferocious, Caravaggio style' and it has generally been regarded as a brilliant piece of satire.

In the preface to his poem Southey had described the sojourn of Byron with the Shelleys and Claire Clairmont on the shores of Lac Léman as 'a league of incest' and referred to a 'Satanic School' of poetry which he 'recommended to the notice of the legislature.' In his own preface Byron accused Southey of being an informer and he assured his readers that: 'If there is anything obnoxious to the political opinions of a portion of the public in the following poem, they may thank Mr Southey.'[3]

From *The Vision of Judgment*:

XXXV.

The spirits were in neutral space, before
  The gate of Heaven; like eastern thresholds is
The place where Death's grand cause is argued o'er,
  And souls despatched to that world or to this;
And therefore Michael and the other wore
  A civil aspect: though they did not kiss,
Yet still between his Darkness and his Brightness
There passed a mutual glance of great politeness.

XXXVI.

The Archangel bowed, not like a modern beau,
  But with a graceful oriental bend,
Pressing one radiant arm just where below
  The heart in good men is supposed to tend;
He turned as to an equal, not too low,
  But kindly; Satan met his ancient friend
With more hauteur, as might an old Castilian
Poor Noble meet a mushroom rich civilian.

436

XXXVII.

He merely bent his diabolic brow
  An instant; and then raising it, he stood
In act to assert his right or wrong, and show
  Cause why King George by no means could or should
Make out a case to be exempt from woe
  Eternal, more than other kings, endued
With better sense and hearts, whom History mentions,
Who long have 'paved Hell with their good intentions.'

      *   *   *

LXXXVI.

Confound the renegado! I have sprained
  My left wing, he's so heavy; one would think
Some of his works about his neck were chained.
  But to the point; while hovering o'er the brink
Of Skiddaw (where as usual it still rained),
  I saw a taper, far below me, wink,
And stooping, caught this fellow at a libel —
No less on History — than the Holy Bible.

      *   *   *

XC.

Now the bard, glad to get an audience, which
  By no means often was his case below,
Began to cough, and hawk, and hem, and pitch
  His voice into that awful note of woe
To all unhappy hearers within reach
  Of poets when the tide of rhyme's in flow;
But stuck fast with his first hexameter,
Not one of all whose gouty feet would stir.

XCI.

But ere the spavined dactyls could be spurred
  Into recitative, in great dismay
Both Cherubim and Seraphim were heard
  To murmur loudly through their long array;
And Michael rose ere he could get a word
  Of all his foundered verses under way,
And cried, 'For God's sake stop, my friend! 'twere best —
"*Non Di, non homines*" — you know the rest.'

437

He said – (I only give the heads) – he said,
　He meant no harm in scribbling; 'twas his way
Upon all topics; 'twas, besides, his bread,
　Of which he buttered both sides; 'twould delay
Too long the assembly (he was pleased to dread),
　And take up rather more time than a day,
To name his works – he would but cite a few –
'Wat Tyler' – 'Rhymes on Blenheim' – 'Waterloo.'

He had written praises of a Regicide;
　He had written praises of all kings whatever;
He had written for republics far and wide,
　And then against them bitterer than ever;
For pantisocracy he once had cried
　Aloud, a scheme less moral than 'twas clever;
Then grew a hearty anti-jacobin –
Had turned his coat – and would have turned his skin.

He had sung against all battles, and again
　In their high praise and glory; he had called
Reviewing 'the ungentle craft,' and then
　Became as base a critic as e'er crawled –
Fed, paid, and pampered by the very men
　By whom his muse and morals had been mauled:
He had written much blank verse, and blanker prose,
And more of both than any body knows.

He had written Wesley's life: – here turning round
　To Satan, 'Sir, I'm ready to write yours,
In two octavo volumes, nicely bound,
　With notes and preface, all that most allures
The pious purchaser; and there's no ground
　For fear, for I can choose my own reviewers:
So let me have the proper documents,
That I may add you to my other saints.'

Satan bowed, and was silent. 'Well, if you,
　　With amiable modesty, decline
My offer, what says Michael? There are few
　　Whose memoirs could be rendered more divine.
Mine is a pen of all work; not so new
　　As it was once, but I would make you shine
Like your own trumpet. By the way, my own
Has more of brass in it, and is as well blown.

CI.

'But talking about trumpets, here's my "Vision!"
　　Now you shall judge, all people – yes – you shall
Judge with my judgment! and by my decision
　　Be guided who shall enter heaven or fall.
I settle all these things by intuition,
　　Times present, past, to come – Heaven – Hell – and all,
Like King Alfonso. When I thus see double,
I save the Deity some worlds of trouble.'

CII.

He ceased, and drew forth an MS.; and no
　　Persuasion on the part of Devils, Saints,
Or Angels, now could stop the torrent; so
　　He read the first three lines of the contents;
But at the fourth, the whole spiritual show
　　Had vanished, with variety of scents,
Ambrosial and sulphureous, as they sprang,
Like lightning, off from his 'melodious twang.'

CIII.

Those grand heroics acted as a spell;
　　The Angels stopped their ears and plied their pinions;
The Devils ran howling, deafened, down to Hell
　　The ghosts fled, gibbering, for their own dominions –
(For 'tis not yet decided where they dwell,
　　And I leave every man to his opinions);
Michael took refuge in his trump – but, lo!
His teeth were set on edge, he could not blow!

Saint Peter, who has hitherto been known
  For an impetuous saint, upraised his keys,
And at the fifth line knocked the poet down;
  Who fell like Phaeton, but more at ease,
Into his lake, for there he did not drown;
  A different web being by the Destinies
Woven for the Laureate's final wreath, whene'er
Reform shall happen either here or there.

*   *   *

CVI.

As for the rest, to come to the conclusion
  Of this true dream, the telescope is gone
Which kept my optics free from all delusion,
  And showed me what I in my turn have shown;
All I saw farther, in the last confusion,
  Was, that King George slipped into Heaven for one;
And when the tumult dwindled to a calm,
I left him practising the hundredth psalm.[4]

The poem was published in the first issue of *The Liberal*. Byron knew that there would be difficulty in getting it out in an English edition because of its criticisms of George III.

He wrote to Kinnaird:

My Dear Douglas,

'Try back the deep lane' till we find a publisher for '*The Vision*' – and if none such is to be found – *print* fifty copies (at *my expense*) distribute them amongst my acquaintances – and you will soon see that the booksellers *will* publish them – even if we opposed them. – That they are now afraid – is natural – but I do not see that I ought to give way on that account.[5]

(Byron to Douglas Kinnaird, 6 February 1822)

The *Literary Gazette* described the poem as 'heartless and beastly ribaldry' and *Constable's Edinburgh Magazine* went further:

As to the *Vision of Judgment* by *Quevedo Redivivus* alias Lord Byron, we have some doubts whether we can be justified in polluting our pages by such impious and detestable trash ... *The Vision of Judgment* is one blank, frozen, unvaried, and unvarnished piece of heartless atrocity and cold-blooded ruffianism, in which every generous and honourable feeling of the heart is outraged, – human nature scoffed at, – the memory of an aged Monarch insulted, – the faith of Christians derided, – and the foulest, and, let us add, the lowest abuse flung at the head of a man of amiable manners, great learning and irreproachable life.[6]

The Hunt brothers were prosecuted for having published the poem in *The Liberal*. John Mortimer describes the case:

'His savage, comic satire on the death of George III, *The Vision of Judgment*, caused an indictment to be issued from the King's Bench and the case is a classic example of the use of the libel laws for political censorship.'[7]

As a result of the successful prosecution the version of the poem published by the Hunts in Volume VI of *The Works of Lord Byron* (1824) was heavily censored, but they made sure their readers could see the offending stanzas by publishing them in an appendix giving an account of the court case:

COURT OF KING'S BENCH

Thursday, January 15, 1824

THE KING v. JOHN HUNT.

This was an indictment preferred by the 'Constitutional Association' against the defendant, for publishing in a book called the *Liberal*, a libel on the memory of his late Majesty King George the Third, with intent to hurt the feelings, and destroy the comfort and happiness of our Sovereign Lord the now King, and the other descendants of his late Majesty, and to bring them into public scandal, infamy, hatred, and contempt.

The passages charged as libellous are contained in the poem entitled the *Vision of Judgment*, and were as follows:

VIII

In the first year of freedom's second dawn
   Died George the Third; although no tyrant, one
Who shielded tyrants, till each sense withdrawn
   Left him nor mental nor external sun:
A better farmer ne'er brush'd dew from lawn,
   A worse king never left a realm undone!
He died – but left his subjects still behind,
One half as mad – and t'other no less blind.

441

He came to his sceptre, young; he leaves it, old:
  Look to the state in which he found his realm,
And left it, and his annals too behold,
  How to a minion first he gave the helm,
The beggar's vice which can but overwhelm
The meanest hearts.

'Tis true he was a tool from first to last;
  (I have the workman safe;) but as a tool
So let him be Consum'd! From out the past
  Of ages, since mankind have known the rule
Of monarchs – from the bloody rolls amass'd
  Of sin and slaughter – from the Caesar's school,
Take the worst pupil; and produce a reign
More drench'd with gore, more cumber'd with the slain!

XLV

He ever warr'd with freedom and the free:
  Nations as men, home subjects, foreign foes,
So that they utter'd the word 'Liberty!'
  Found George the Third their first opponent. Whose
History was ever stain'd as his will be
With national and individual woes?

Mr Adolphus addressed the Jury for the prosecution, urged the malignity and falsehood of the slanders in the poem against the memory of a good and pious King, the Father of his People, and contended that the Defendant had published a libel of the most gross, impious and slanderous character.

A man named *Purton* was called to prove the purchase of a copy of the *Liberal* at No. 22, Old Bond Street, and swore he bought it off the Defendant then in court.

Mr Scarlett, for the Defendant expressed his contempt and indignation at a prosecution of so impudent and arbitrary a character. He shewed that fair and impartial history would be at an end, if the characters of deceased monarchs were not allowed to be fully and unrestrictedly discussed, and opinions of all kinds, laudatory or hostile, expressed upon their conduct by their surviving contemporaries. He insisted that the allegation in the indictment, that the alleged libel had wounded the feelings of his present Majesty, was best disproved by the fact, that the AttorneyGeneral had not proceeded against the defendant – and his Majesty's ministers had advised no prosecution. The learned Counsel then took a review of the late reign – its wars, its disasters, its enormous waste of blood and treasure; and contended, that any man might rationally express the opinion of it contained in the poem prosecuted. He further shewed that the alleged libel was principally a satire on a poem of Mr Southey's under the same title, full of gross adulation of George the Third, which the present poem was calculated to expose and counteract.

The CHIEF-JUSTICE (Sir Charles Abbott), in summing up, observed, that human nature was so constituted, that calumny against a father could not be published without wounding the feelings of a son and he left it to the Jury to say, first, whether the publication indicted (of the general tone of which he expressed his abhorrence) was a libel on the late King; secondly, whether it was calculated to destroy the comfort and happiness of his present Majesty and the Royal family.

The Jury retired, and in about half an hour returned with a verdict of *Guilty*.[8]

The day after the court case the entire poem, including the stanzas judged to be libellous, was printed in *The Times*, 16 January, 1824.

In December 1824, eight months after Byron's death, *Blackwood's* published an article on Southey and Byron which came down strongly on the side of Byron:

In Byron ... in one of the greatest of the great poets of England – in a man who never wrote three pages without pouring out some emanation of a soul beautiful, lofty, and glorious, if ever such a soul dwelt within a human bosom – in this great and glorious Poet of England, Southey could see nothing else but a 'pander-general to youthful vice', and the founder of 'a Satanic School.'[9]

Notes

1. M.K. Joseph comments on *The Vision of Judgment*:

   ... the concurrence of a perfected manner and a strongly felt occasion resulted in a brief masterpiece.[1]

2. Bernard Beatty discusses Byron's attitude to trial and imprisonment:

   ... throughout Byron's verse the bleeding heart finds and bears its public pageant or makes a Roman holiday. Public trial or imprisonment, so obvious in *Parisina*, the Venetian plays, *The Prisoner of Chillon*, *The Lament of Tasso*, or the 'Ode to Napoleon Buonaparte', fuse grief and pageant in this way. *The Vision of Judgment* is a kind of trial, too, in

443

which George III finally escapes and Southey forever finds public chastisement. We are always interested in the final verdict and Byron never avoids it.[2]

3. Marilyn Butler defends Southey:

... it is of course a great mistake to accept unexamined Byron's portrayals of Southey in *Don Juan* and *The Vision of Judgment* as merely a paid government hack. Southey was the only one of the trio of 'Lake Poets' to remain a genuine populist, the more troubling because by 1810 he was a Tory populist and Tory populism almost certainly commanded more general British support than 'jacobinism' ever did.[3]

29

GENOA

The English who calumniate me in every direction and on every score; whenever they are in great distress – come to me for assistance.

On arrival at Genoa Byron moved into the Casa Saluzzo and, later, wrote to Hoppner:

> I am staying at Albaro on a hill overlooking Genoa, cold & frosty but airy – only *one chimney* in the whole house, which is spacious enough for twenty... I hope we shall meet again some day and that you will be merry and I be wise.[1]
>
> (Byron to Richard Hoppner, Genoa, 2 January 1823)

Genoa was not the happiest of Byron's Italian sojourns. The house was cold. The intoxicating social life of Venice was absent, and so was the sense of belonging to a large, and congenial Italian family which he had experienced in Ravenna. Shelley had gone, leaving him the legacy of the feckless Leigh Hunt, his difficult and disapproving wife, and his uncontrollable children.

Mary Shelley and the Hunts were installed in the Villa Negroto not far from the Casa Saluzzo. On the day after his arrival in Genoa he wrote to reassure Mary:

> With regard to any difficulties about money I can only repeat that I will be your banker till this state of affairs is cleared up – and you can see what is to be done – so – there is little to trouble you on that score.[2]
>
> (Byron to Mary Shelley, Genoa, 4 October 1822)

445

He wrote to Sir Timothy Shelley on behalf of his son's widow and her child suggesting he might take them under his protection. Sir Timothy replied with a decided negative. Mary appealed to Byron for advice and he promised to put his mind to her problems once he had recovered from a slight illness. He was unwilling to shower largesse on Mary since Shelley had been heir to a considerable fortune and he felt it would be insulting to her to offer anything not described as a loan. However, he rarely expected to receive repayment of the loans he made to his friends and he had assured her that he would pay the cost of her return journey to England with her child when she would presumably join her father.

Now difficulties arose with both Mary and the Hunts. He had told Mary, 'I have a particular dislike to anything of S[helley]'s being within the same walls with Mr Hunt's children. – They are dirtier and more mischievous than Yahoos...'[3] Mr & Mrs Hunt believed that children should not be disciplined and Mrs Hunt professed herself disgusted at Byron's objecting to 'the disfigurement of the walls of a few rooms' at the Casa Lanfranchi by her children.

Shelley had been embarrassed by Hunt's demands on Byron and had written to apologise for his friend's behaviour:

My Dear Lord Byron – I enclose you a letter from Hunt which annoys me very much ... Hunt had urged me more than once to ask you to lend him this money. My answer consisted in sending him all I could spare, which I have now literally done. Your kindness in fitting up a part of your own house for his accommodation I sensibly felt ... believe me without the slightest intention of imposing, or allowing to be imposed, any heavier task on your purse ... I do not think poor Hunt's promise to pay in a given time is worth very much...[4]

Byron was having difficulties with Murray at this time and now he discovered a new reason for dissatisfaction with his publisher.

Murray had shown John Hunt (and, presumably, others) a letter from Byron expressing irritation at the conduct of the Hunts (who accepted his largesse but complained of his attitude to them and their children, and expected him to share with them as much as they felt they needed of what they considered to be his great wealth).

Byron wrote to Hunt admitting that he had told Murray that Mrs Hunt was sick and the children not very tractable '...which is true ... [they] are likely in their present state to be anything but a

446

comfort to you.' ... The rest, he assured Hunt, was only 'what I have said to yourself over and over on the subject of the Journal.'[5]
(Byron to Leigh Hunt, Genoa, 11 November 1822)

Byron told Mary Shelley, who took Hunt's part:

'I presume that you, at least, know enough of me to be sure that I could have no intention to insult Hunt's poverty ... I know what it is, having been as much embarrassed as ever he was, without perceiving aught in it to diminish an honourable man's self-respect ... I engaged in the Journal from good-will towards him, added to respect for his character, literary and personal; and no less for his political courage, as well as regret for his present circumstances.'[6]
(Byron to Mary Shelley, Genoa, 16 November 1822)

Byron called on Mary and the Hunts no more than once a month and Mary was disappointed at being banished from his company. She had always been drawn to him and disliked being housed with the Hunts who were more or less his pensioners. When she was told by Hunt that Byron found her tiresome, she refused to accept money from him and began to talk of his meanness.

In the end he was obliged to write to Hunt:

I have received a note from Mrs S[helley] with a fifth or sixth change of plans – viz. – not to make her journey at all – at least through my assistance on account of what she is pleased to call "estrangement &tc." – On this I have little to say. The readiest mode may be this – which can be settled between you and me without her knowing anything of the matter. – I will advance the money to *you* ... on Monday – you can then say that you have raised it as a loan on your own account – ...and that *you* advance it to *her* ... I have a thing more to state – which is that from this moment – I must decline the office of acting as his executor in any respect, and also all further connection with his family in any of its branches – now or hereafter, – There was something about a legacy of two thousand pounds ... this, of course, I decline.[7]
(Byron to Leigh Hunt, Genoa, 28 June 1823)

Many of Byron's friends were still deploring his connection with Leigh Hunt. He wrote to Moore defending his actions:

'My whole present relation to him arose from Shelley's unexpected wreck. You would not have had me leave him in the street with his family, would you? And as to the other plan you mention, you forget

447

how it would *humiliate* him... Think a moment – he is perhaps the vainest man on earth.'[8]

(Byron to Thomas Moore, Genoa, 20 February 1823)

Byron was forced at this time to economise as far as he could, for he was trying to liquidate his English debts and to collect as much capital as he could for the Greek cause. Having told Kinnaird that his debt to Baxter for the Napoleonic coach must be paid off this year, he had to decide that Baxter must wait for at least another year, though he would of course continue to get his interest on the loan.

James Wedderburn Webster now turned up in Genoa with so little intention of repaying his debt to Byron that he persuaded him to guarantee two more bonds for him. After Webster's departure Byron found himself obliged to pay them. He wrote to Kinnaird:

> Ten years ago I lent him a thousand pounds on bond, on condition that he would not go to the *Jews* – He took the money and went to the Jews – Hanson has his bond – and there is ten years interest due upon it. – – I have never dunned him – but I think he might at least have paid some of the interest.
>
> (Byron to Douglas Kinnaird, 1 December 1822)[9]

> [I have laid up my Schooner in the Arsenal – (which stops that expense of wages &tc.) reduced my establishment – sold some horses – ... thereby keeping five – instead of ten – and I wish if possible – to live as simply as need be – for some years – though not sordidly.[10]
>
> (Byron to Douglas Kinnaird, Genoa, 28 December 1822)

The demands on his purse were unceasing and he was growing irritated by them. Three weeks after his arrival at Genoa he had written to John Murray on behalf of a 'poor Woman ... who is or was an author of yours – as she says ... the poor Soul's husband has died ... but instead of addressing the Bishop or Mr Wilberforce – she hath recourse to that proscribed – Atheistical – syllogistical – phlogistical person – *mysen* – as they say in Notts. – It is strange enough – but the rascaille English who calumniate me in every direction ... whenever they are in great distress – recur to me for assistance ... and as far as in my power – have tried to repay good for evil ... her situation and her wishes (not unreasonable however) require more than can be advanced by an individual like myself – for I have many claims of the kind ... and also some

448

remnants of *debts* to pay in England ... Can the "Literary fund" do nothing for her? by your interest ... can you get any of her books published?'[11]

(Byron to John Murray, Genoa, 31 December 1822)

Byron sent the woman three hundred francs. He was considering buying annuities for himself and Augusta and he wrote to Augusta suggesting that she should bring her family (including George) abroad where they could live comfortably on a much smaller outlay than in England. He offered to provide a house for the Leighs at Nice which was not far from Genoa. If they wished, he would move with the Gambas to Nice. Teresa would have separate apartments in his house so if Augusta came to call she would not be obliged to meet his mistress.

Writing to Sir Timothy Shelley on Mary's behalf had been embarrassing enough. Now Webster persuaded him to write to Lady Frances (who was living separately from him with her children) and ask her to forgive her husband and come home. He told a new friend:

This produced a long ... State paper from the Lady – full of the most extraordinary charges against your admirer – and invoking discussions – in which I had no wish to enter – I have therefore written to both parties to decline interfering further in so delicate a matter.[12]

(Byron to Lady Hardy, Genoa, 28 M[arc]h 1823)

Byron had recently acquired this new and charming correspondent – the wife of Admiral Hardy (Nelson's Hardy). She had met Byron briefly in 1814 and was a distant family connection. Lady Hardy was an intelligent woman in whom he could confide and he was amused to find that Webster was pursuing her with a clumsy and unwanted courtship.

Byron wrote her long letters in the easy, teasing manner of his letters to Lady Melbourne, addressing her as 'My dear Coz'. He warned her, 'Do *not defend me* – my Coz – it will never do – you will only make *yourself* enemies – and a pretty woman will always have enough.'[13] (Byron to Lady Hardy, Genoa, 17 May 1823)

Byron sent Kinnaird from Genoa further cantos of *Don Juan*, *The Age of Bronze* and another verse-tale, *The Island*. He had threatened to take a turn to Naples and write a fifth and sixth canto of *Childe Harold*. Instead he sent his hero, Don Juan, to England.

'... if they had let me alone – I probably should not have continued beyond the five first – as it is – there shall be such a poem – as has not been since Ariosto – in length – in satire – in imagery – and in what I please.[14] (Byron to Douglas Kinnaird, Genoa, 31 March 1823)

He was pleased to hear from a young man who worked at Galignani that the editions of *Don Juan* were by far the most popular of his poems in Paris.

He was planning for *The Liberal* and wrote to Hunt:

My dear H [there had been occasions when he had written 'My dear Leigh] ... *Don't fag* yourself too much – but take care of your health – as I have sent (with The Age of Bronze) what will be sufficient with the English and Italian Pulci for about eighty or a hundred pages of the next Number – you can send ... a little on your own – [& let] your home friends pull a little for the present ... Will you tell Mrs Shelley that the *Compass* – turned out *not* to have been our late friend S[helley]'s but to have always belonged to the other vessel – or I would have sent it – but there are some of his books here which I will look out and send.[15]

(Byron to Leigh Hunt, Genoa, 16 January 1823)

He wrote to Kinnaird, through whom he was trying to gather all the funds he could devote to the Greek cause:

If I go up into the Levant – I shall, want all the credit you can muster for me – ... I should think that you might sell my *ten* Cantos – you had a thousand offered for the *seven* – which is not a fair offer – but with the adjunct of the three new ones – and the four Cantos of The Island – and the permanent copyright of the poems (already published) to be collected into volumes – I think you might get a decent value for the whole. – Firstly – if I go up – there is some risk of not returning – and in this case – my *latest* works would have some value merely as *such* ... Murray *ought* to pay something for 'Werner'. I have made enquiries and find that at *Paris* at least – the sale of *four hundred* copies of a work – pays its *expences* – now M[urray] sold six thousand by his own account – then how can he have lost?[16]

(Byron to Douglas Kinnaird, 19 April 1823)

He tried continually to represent to his friends in London the merits of *Don Juan* and told Kinnaird firmly, 'I mean it for a poetical T[ristram] Shandy – or Montaigne's Essays with a story for a hinge.'[17]

450

Now Byron was delighted to meet young Henry Fox, son of Lord Holland, in Genoa.

> I left him a pretty mild boy, without a neckcloth, in a jacket, and in delicate health, seven long years agone, at the period of mine eclipse ... I always liked that boy – perhaps in part from some resemblance in the less fortunate part of our destinies – I mean, to avoid mistakes, his lameness. But there is this difference, that *he* appears a halting angel, who has tripped against a star; whilst I am the *Diable Boiteux*.[18]
>
> (Byron to Thomas Moore, Genoa, 2 April 1823)

In that April friends of Moore and Kinnaird arrived in Genoa for a two months' stay – the Earl and Countess of Blessington with their constant companion, a handsome young Frenchman, the Count d'Orsay. Byron described Lady Blessington to Lady Hardy:

> Miledi is the Miledi of whom Lawrence, made a picture that set all London raving ... As they were friends of Moore's and have been very civil to me – I could not easily (in my usual way) escape being occasionally with them – especially as they are Equestrians – and I met them frequently on my rides about Genoa. – But this has plunged me into a pit of domestic troubles – for 'la mia Dama' Me. La Contesse G – was seized with a furious fit of Italian jealousy – and was as unreasonable and perverse as can well be imagined. – God He knows – she paid me too great a compliment – for what little communication I held with this new Goddess of Discord – was literally literary – and besides that I have long come to years of discretion – and would much rather fall into the Sea than in Love, any day of the week.[19]
>
> (Byron to Lady Hardy, Genoa, 17 May 1823)

Lady Blessington was writing a book about her travels, *The Idler in Italy*, in which Byron was to figure. Long after his death when she was in financial difficulties she produced a record of her conversations with Byron which have been judged as unreliable as Medwin. It seems likely that she was disappointed, having hoped that Byron would fall in love with her. She asked him for a poem which proved equally disappointing. He liked her and admired her beauty but he was busy with plans for Greece. In order to justify the later book she was forced to pretend to having seen him regularly and known him far better than was the case. She would have been mortified by a second letter he wrote to Lady Hardy who had told him some gossip about the lady:

451

To return to our Irish Aspasia – I did not know that she had been *Post-mistress* of Cahir – but I had heard that she had been a mistress of some kind or other before she espoused the Earl of B[lessingto]n. – Her slight acquaintance with me was of the most decorous description – the poor woman seemed devoured with Ennui.[20]

(Byron to Lady Hardy, Genoa, 10 June 1823)

He regarded Lord Blessington with a similar irony: 'Mountjoy seems very good-natured, but is much tamed, since I recollect him in all the glory of gems and snuff-boxes, and uniforms, and theatricals, and speeches in our house – "I mean, of peers".'[21]

In *The Idler in Italy* Lady Blessington insisted that Byron was much maligned. Having written gushingly on arrival in Genoa, 'And am I indeed in the same town with Byron! And tomorrow I may, perhaps, behold him!'[22] She described him thus:

The Epicurean follies of Byron's youth, indulged in but for a brief period, will be falsely attributed to his maturity. [This perceptive judgement is applicable to some accounts of Byron even today] The most meagre fare … few hours devoted to sleep, and continual literary occupation, with a near total seclusion from society. That noble but pallid brow, on which deep thought has left its ineffaceable traces – that almost shadowy figure … are not those of a gross sensualist, but of an imaginative being, who has conquered the passions, or at least refused to minister to their indulgence. Such a triumph while yet in the flower of life, could only be achieved by a very superior mind.[23]

Other remarks Lady Blessington made about her new acquaintance were less flattering. She criticised his manners, his clothes, his appearance and his taste. She tried to give the impression that when the Blessingtons left Genoa Byron was devastated by their departure. Other witnesses claim that though tears were shed, they were shed by Lady Blessington and not by Byron.

The Countess wrote persuasively and many have been taken in. It has even been suggested that Byron was in awe of these new acquaintances who possessed a social ease and security he had never achieved. This is indeed 'imputing to his maturity' the uncertainties of his youth. This is the man welcomed at Holland House and Melbourne House, sought after by Walter Scott, Sheridan, Curran, Madame de Staël and all the notables of Milan, Venice and Ravenna, of whom Shelley wrote '… his conversation is a sort of intoxication, men are held by it as by a spell.'[24] It is inconceivable

452

that such a man would be overawed by a beautiful Irish woman of doubtful antecedents, her elderly husband and young companion, Count d'Orsay. Hobhouse described Byron's manner as 'commanding but not overawing' and claimed that he '... seemed always made for that company in which he found himself.'[25]

During his stay in Genoa Byron was preoccupied with more important matters. He discussed the Greek situation with travellers returning from the theatre of war and wrote to the London Greek Committee with a list of all 'the principal material wanted by the Greeks' and advice on 'the readiest mode of transmission.' He offered advice on the formation of a foreign brigade in *Greece*, '... an opinion – resulting rather from the melancholy experience of the brigades embarked in the Colombian Service – than from any experiment yet tried in Greece.' There should be officers of experience rather than '... raw British Soldiers – which latter are apt to be unruly and not very serviceable – in irregular warfare – by the side of foreigners.' Officers who had served in the Mediterranean would be best, as 'some knowledge of *Italian* is nearly indispensable.' They should be warned that it would be 'no party of pleasure' and that Greece was 'the country of all kinds of privations.'[26] (Byron to John Bowring, Genoa, 12 May 1823)

Byron was eager to take to Greece a horse he admired called Mameluke which belonged to Lady Blessington. He told the Earl: 'I fear that I can hardly afford more than two thousand francs for the steed in question ... and I suppose that will not suit you.'[27] Instead of taking the opportunity thus given her to withdraw from the transaction Lady Blessington sold the horse to Byron and later complained of his haggling over the price. Lord Blessington bought *The Bolivar* from Byron and then, unwittingly, revenged the unfortunate Baxter (still waiting after seven years for payment of the bill for the Napoleonic coach) by failing to settle the bill.

At the end of May Byron wrote at length to Henri Beyle (the writer, Stendhal). 'Beyle had described Walter Scott's character as 'little worthy of enthusiasm'. Byron told Beyle that '... of all men he [Scott] is the most *open*, the most *honourable*, the most amiable.'[28]

Trelawny had grown impatient of what he regarded as the 'dawdling life' in Genoa of a man who was writing all night and organising during the day. Lady Hardy now told Byron that Trelawny believed there was a coldness between himself and Byron. This

453

induced him to write a friendly letter inviting Trelawny to join him on the Greek adventure:

> My dear T. – You must have heard that I am going to Greece. Why do you not come to me? ... I did not write before, as I might have given you 'a journey for nothing; they all say I can be of use in Greece. I do not know how, nor do they; but at all events let us go. [29]
>
> (Byron to Edward John Trelawny, Genoa, 15 June 1823)

He wrote equally kindly to Captain Roberts, former captain of *The Bolivar*:

> My dear R. – We have already engaged a medical man – otherwise your friend would have been very welcome. – Trelawny is here – we sail on the 12th – I regret very much that you can't accompany us – but I hope that we shall all meet merrily some day or other either here or there.[30]
>
> (Byron to Captain Daniel Roberts, Genoa, 9 July 1823)

In the last weeks before he left Italy Byron received two presents which pleased him – a Mr Webb (one of those members of banking firms with whom Byron developed friendly and informal relations) sent him some raspberries, and Edward le Mesurier, an ex-naval man living in Italy, gave him a Newfoundland dog, which became almost as beloved as Boatswain and sailed with him for Greece.

30

THE ISLAND

The infant rapture still survived the boy,
And Loch-na-gar with Ida looked o'er Troy...[1]

In March 1823 Byron wrote to Kinnaird, 'In the mean time I send another poem in four cantos called "the Island &tc." – ... it is ... not in the same style with my former stories.'[2]

M.K. Joseph remarks that in *The Island* Byron returns to the heroic couplet but he has learned from the writing of *Don Juan* '...to improve in many ways on the old style.'[3]

For the story and background Byron went to Captain Bligh's account of the mutiny on the Bounty, but his chief inspiration was William Marriner's *Account of the Natives of the Tonga Islands* (1817) whose description of the scenery, costumes and people of the islands delighted him.

Arnold A. Schmidt points out that '*The Island* ... treats both captain and mutineers even-handedly ... three different points of view introduce readers to the three heroes and lead us to view events from the perspectives of Bligh [Captain of the Bounty], Christian [leader of the mutineers] and Torquil [the innocent] ... Christian ... presents himself as a tragic hero reminiscent of Satan in his bold, hopeless revolt against what he perceived as a tyrannical deity.'[4] He is tormented by guilt – not least for having implicated Torquil. The last Byronic hero, rather than face capture and return to England in irons, he throws himself from a cliff.

Torquil is the least guilty of the mutineers. He escapes retribution, saved by the South Sea girl, Neuha, who loves him.

Jerome McGann finds the poem autobiographical. The scenery is 'Byron's Greece in Polynesian trappings,' and 'the character of

Torquil becomes a focus for Byron's recollection of his youth in Scotland':[5]

VIII.

And who is he? the blue-eyed northern child
Of isles more known to man, but scarce less wild;
The fair-haired offspring of the Hebrides,
Where roars the Pentland with its whirling seas;
Rocked in his cradle by the roaring wind,
The tempest-born in body and in mind,
His young eyes opening on the ocean-foam,
Had from that moment deemed the deep his home,
The giant comrade of his pensive moods,
The sharer of his craggy solitudes,[6]

In his Commentary on the poem Jerome McGann writes of the chief literary influence on *The Island*: the pastoral tradition of Theocritus and Virgil, which B's poem recalls in its presentation of a South Sea Arcadia. But he shows how Byron '... uses his romance of the islands as a lever to expose and criticize the spirit of European imperialism. In this respect the poem is a companion piece to *The Age [of Bronze]* – which, to all appearances, can seem so different.'[7]

Wilson Knight observes that '... both Shelley and Byron responded to the magic of islands.' He calls *The Island* Melvillean – 'I am thinking of *Typee*' – and discusses '... the young lovers, Torquil and Neuha ... islanded in idyllic seas' and how they escape '... by plunging deep ... and reach a mysterious submarine cavern ... where love may rule.'[8]

Michael Cooke's verdict is that:

... special attention is due *The Island*, with its serene passage between the threatening rock of social order and the treacherous pool of individual preference ... no attempt is made at a reconciliation. The facts stand: mutiny is abhorrent; so is its punishment.

In the simplicity of Byron's affection for the 'happy days' of Torquil and Neuha, his acknowledgement of Bligh's integrity as a champion of dutiful ways, and his growing acceptance of an ennobling severity in his treatment of himself, one recognizes a fertile continuation whose fruit was denied by the prophyllaxis of death. Byron, we know, died at the age of thirty-six. And it remains beguilingly poignant to reflect that he had once, not altogether playfully perhaps, imagined thirty-six as the age at which he would have embarked on the life of perfection.[9]

31

THE DEFORMED TRANSFORMED

This play begins with the mother of the hunchback, Arnold, addressing him:

Bertha: Out, hunchback!

Arnold: I was born so, mother!

Bertha: Out!
         Thou Incubus! Thou Nightmare! Of seven sons
         The sole abortion![1]

Arnold is on the point of suicide when he is offered by a mysterious stranger transformation into the likeness of one of many heroic figures. He chooses Achilles.

Shelley described *The Deformed Transformed* as a bad imitation of Faust.

Byron himself had written of it to John Hunt on 21 May 1823: 'I have also *two parts* completed of an odd sort of drama – but I doubt if I shall go on with it.'[2] It remained unfinished.

M.K. Joseph describes it as:

> ... a tantalising fragment and is usually underestimated ... under the stranger's tutelage a transformed hero, Arnold, is launched on ... a series of adventures on the grand scale. We are shown only the first of these, Arnold's participation in the Sack of Rome, a historical set piece tinged with the grim battlefield humour of *Don Juan* Cantos VII–VIII, and the inhuman ironies of Faust. It begins to evolve an image of Byron's characteristic vision – the admiration for heroic activity combined with mockery of power, wealth and warfare. But Byron ... left it incomplete, perhaps realizing that what he had to say could be better said in a continued *Don Juan*.[3]

457

Samuel Chew considered that the '...fighting scenes are exceptionally crude and quite unworthy of Byron.'[4]

G. Wilson Knight comes to the rescue:

> If Byron was, as we are often told, superstitious, his superstitions, like Shakespeare's, empower much of *his greatest poetry* [my italics]; as in his sense of a numinous past through *Childe Harold*, the ghosts on the beleaguered battlements of Rome in *The Deformed Transformed*; the Doge's communing with the ancestral dead on the eve of the Revolution in *Marino Faliero*; and the hero's nightmare contacts with his forbears in *Sardanapalus*.[5]

Wilson Knight discusses the choice Arnold makes when offered transformation by the Stranger, who is a sort of Mephistopheles:

> Arnold, to his credit, chooses Achilles. The choice corresponds to Byron's final aim and direction, rejecting pleasures and ambitions for a greater good. Achilles is shown as a reflection of Byron's best ... His vulnerable heel is remembered. He symbolizes the state of mind and soul in which Byron, after a deeply true and semi-marital relationship with Teresa Guiccioli, undertook, without ambition, his Greek campaign.[6]

Bernard Beatty takes a similarly positive view of the play:

> The thought in process in Byron's last poems – *The Island, The Deformed Transformed, Heaven and Earth* and the last cantos *of Don Juan* – is so ambitious in its scope, so exploratory, relentlessly paradoxical, and yet so openly reactivating the inherited modes of European thought and value, that only a critic like the late G. Wilson Knight could sustain the panache with which to salute and elucidate the mysterious obviousness of Byron's endeavour.[7]

Wilson Knight claims that '...in the self-reflection of *The Deformed Transformed* Byron pictured himself as renouncing claims to a Caesar's leadership and the semi-divine honours of a Demetrius Poliorcetes for the purer ideal of service to Greece, symbolised by a *mild* Achilles.[8]

32

JOURNEY TO GREECE

In *Don Juan*, Canto III, Byron had written his great lyric on the servitude of Greece:

1.

The Isles of Greece, the Isles of Greece!
  Where burning Sappho loved and sung,
Where grew the arts of War and Peace,
  Where Delos rose, and Phoebus sprung!
Eternal summer gilds them yet,
But all, except their Sun, is set.

2.

The Scian and the Teian muse,
  The Hero's harp, the Lover's lute,
Have found the fame your shores refuse:
  Their place of birth alone is mute
To sounds which echo further west
Than your Sires' 'Islands of the Blest.'

3.

The mountains look on Marathon –
  And Marathon looks on the sea;
And musing there an hour alone,
  I dreamed that Greece might still be free;
For standing on the Persians' grave,
I could not deem myself a slave.

4.

A King sate on the rocky brow
  Which looks o'er sea-born Salamis;
And ships, by thousands, lay below,

And men in nations; – all were his!
He counted them at break of day –
And, when the Sun set, where were they?

5.

And where are they? and where art thou,
  My Country? On thy voiceless shore
The heroic lay is tuneless now –
  The heroic bosom beats no more!
And must thy Lyre, so long divine,
Degenerate into hands like mine?

6.

'T is something, in the dearth of Fame,
  Though linked among a fettered race,
To feel at least a patriot's shame,
  Even as I sing, suffuse my face;
For what is left the poet here?
For Greeks a blush – for Greece a tear.

7.

Must *we* but weep o'er days more blest?
  Must *we* but blush? – Our fathers bled.
Earth! Render back from out thy breast
  A remnant of our Spartan dead!
Of the three hundred grant but three,
To make a new Thermopylæ!

8.

What, silent still? and silent all?
  Ah! no – the voices of the dead
Sound like a distant torrent's fall,
  And answer, ' Let one living head,
But one arise, – we come, we come!'
'T is but the living who are dumb.

9.

In vain – in vain: strike other chords;
  Fill high the cup with Samian wine!
Leave battles to the Turkish hordes,
  And shed the blood of Scio's vine!
Hark! rising to the ignoble call
How answers each bold Bacchanal!

10.

You have the Pyrrhic dance as yet,
  Where is the Pyrrhic phalanx gone?
Of two such lessons, why forget
  The nobler and the manlier one?
You have the letters Cadmus gave –
Think ye he meant them for a slave?

11.

Fill high the bowl with Samian wine!
  We will not think of themes like these!
It made Anacreon's song divine:
  He served – but served Polycrates –
A Tyrant; but our masters then
Were still, at least, our countrymen.

12.

The Tyrant of the Chersonese
  Was Freedom's best and bravest friend;
That tyrant was Miltiades!
  Oh! that the present hour would lend
Another despot of the kind!
Such chains as his were sure to bind.

13.

Fill high the bowl with Samian wine!
  On Suli's rock, and Parga's shore,
Exists the remnant of a line
  Such as the Doric mothers bore;
And there, perhaps, some seed is sown,
The Heracleidan blood might own.

14.

Trust not for freedom to the Franks –
  They have a king who buys and sells;
In native swords, and native ranks,
  The only hope of courage dwells;
But Turkish force, and Latin fraud,
Would break your shield, however broad.

15.

Fill high the bowl with Samian wine!
  Our virgins dance beneath the shade –
I see their glorious black eyes shine;
  But gazing on each glowing maid,

My own the burning tear-drop laves,
To think such breasts must suckle slaves.

16.

Place me on Sunium's marbled steep,
    Where nothing, save the waves and I,
May hear our mutual murmurs sweep;
    There, swan-like, let me sing and die:
A land of slaves shall ne'er be mine –
Dash down yon cup of Samian wine![1]

The first stirrings of revolt in Greece had galvanised the Philhellenes
although the situation was so fluid and so unpredictable that no
one outside Greece, and few of those who travelled there to join
in the struggle, knew exactly what was happening.

In March 1823 the Greek Committee had been formed in London
by John Bowring, a scholar, politician and businessman who had
travelled widely in Eastern Europe. Its purpose was to raise a loan
to help the Greeks win their freedom from the Turks. Hobhouse
suggested that Byron might travel to Greece to assess the situation
and Captain Edward Blaquiere called on Byron in Genoa as agent
for the Committee:

My dear Hobhouse/ – Since I wrote I have heard from Capt, B[laquiere]
he is at Rome – was refused passage through Naples and must go to Corfu
– by Ancona – please to state this to the committee. – They [( ]i.e. B.
and his companion[)] are anxious for me to go up there – and if I can –
I will. – I have in the mean time ordered about a hundred pounds Sterling
worth of powder – and some hospital supplies to be sent up to the seat
of the provisional Government. – I have had the enclosed letter from my
banker here (Mr Barry – the Agent of the house of Webb & Co. – and a
very good fellow) but he tells me that we can have a choice of Vessels at
any time at a more moderate rate. – Pray tell me what you think that I
should do – and please to request Douglas K[innair]d to have the goodness
(in case I go up) to let me have credits in the most convenient Italian or
Levant places – for the whole of my disposable funds – which ought to
be a tolerable sum – including the present year – and as all my monies
must pass through his hands – I suppose that he will not hesitate. – I
have not broken in upon anything of the present year – and have still
three thousand pounds of my income of 1822. – I wish that he could get
anything for the Don Juans (he has ten cantos in hand) and an eleventh
nearly ready (besides some other M.S.S.) my going up far and away –
would neutralize the bookselling hostility against me – as being likely to
be my latest work. – That and any arrangement about Rochdale – however

462

scanty in proportion to it's actual value – would enable me to go up with means that might be of some real service – or even whether I go or not – enable me to forward the views of the Committee and the Greek people.[2]
(To John Cam Hobhouse, 17 April 1823)

There has been much speculation over why Byron went to Greece. An Italian spy wrote: 'Lord Byron is gone to purchase adoration from the Greeks.'[3] Some assumed that he had tired of Countess Guiccioli and went to escape her overpowering adoration. Others believe he went to retrieve his reputation and the sale of his poems. Yet others that he went for glory. Charles Donelan advances a theory that 'The choice of Greece was the result of fantasy. The fantasist gradually becomes responsible for the person he or she already is in daydreams.[4]

It has recently been suggested that 'In Greece ... Byron pursued young men with impunity. One might even say that Byron died less for nationalism than for the idea of same-sex love ... Byron may have participated in the Greek struggle for independence as much to recover buried sexual impulses as to free Greece from Turkey.'[5]

There may be an element of truth in all these suggestions – except the first and last. Byron was certainly not naive enough to believe that even the whole sum of money in his possession could purchase adoration from anybody – he had not forgotten the weapons secretly returned to his cellars by the Carbonari of the Romagna at the first sign of danger during their abortive revolt. The extraordinary theory that, going to Greece in the knowledge, he might lose his life there, he was prepared to die not for Greek freedom but for Greek love seems misguided. Was there no beautiful and willing boy in all Italy? Many foreigners came to fight for modern Greece because, like Byron, they were fired by the ideals of classical Greece. Byron came to serve the Greek people. During his earlier pilgrimage he had learned to love both Greece and the Greek people. He was eager to help them win back their identity, their freedom and their honour. To this end he was prepared to serve in whatever capacity the Greeks required and was ready to leave Greece the moment her people no longer needed him. He gave advice and financial aid but he did not patronise or try to dominate the Greek leaders.

William St Clair observed that:

Byron, almost alone among the Philhellenes of the Greek War of
Independence, did not rely on an unspoken assumption of superiority
in knowledge and ability. He tried to inform himself about Greek
conditions.[6]

Those who dispute his enthusiasm for Greek freedom should
consider the consistency with which he supported those struggling
for freedom throughout his life: the frame-breakers (in parliament
and in poetry), the Irish (with contributions of money, a speech in
support of Catholic Emancipation based on visits to Parliament to
hear earlier debates on the subject and in his poem 'The Irish
Avatar'), the Dutch (he longed to visit Holland on the verge of
revolution to listen to 'the shout of a Free Dutchman'), the Africans
(he wished he owned Africa to sweep slavery away), the South
Americans (he rejected the idea of emigrating to a country whose
economy was based on slavery), Italy (he supported the Risorgimento
in action as well as in poetry), Greece (*Childe Harold's Pilgrimage*
Cantos I, and II, written as a young man his early twenties, call
on the Greeks to take up um and win their freedom).

No doubt Byron went to Greece with mixed motives but the
evidence appears to support the theory that his intention was, first
and foremost, to serve the Greek people.

The immediate cause of his setting off for Greece was Hobhouse's
letter, followed by Blaquiere's call at Genoa and his own election
as member of the Greek Committee in London. His involvement
with the Committee was, however, disappointing and he would
come to regret it. By the time he arrived in Greece Blaquiere,
having agreed to meet him there, had changed his mind and left
for England. He had written to Byron, too late, to warn him not
to come.

Byron's earlier letter to John Bowring shows that he was
disappointed at the lack of instructions from the Committee which
had asked him to travel as their representative:

Dear Sir – We sail on the 12th for Greece – I have had a letter from
Mr Blaquiere too long for present transcription but very satisfactory. –
The G[ree]k Government expects me without delay. – In conformlity
to the desire of Mr B. and other correspondents in Greece – I have to
suggest with all deference to the Committee – that a remittance of even
'ten thousand pounds only' (Mr B's expression) would be of the greatest
service to the G[ree]k Government at present. – I have also to recommend

strongly the attempt at a loan – for which there will be offered a sufficient security by deputies – now on their way to England. – In the mean time I hope that the Committee will be able to do something effectual. – For my own part – I mean to carry up in cash or credits – above eight and nearly nine thousand pounds sterling – which I am enabled to do by funds which I have in Italy – and Credits from England. – Of this sum I must necessarily reserve a portion for the subsistence of my-self and Suite. – The rest I am willing to apply in the manner which seems most likely to be useful to the cause – having of course some guarantee or assurance that it will not be misapplied to any individual speculation.

If I remain in Greece – which will mainly depend upon the presumed probable utility of my presence there – and the opinion of the Greeks themselves as to it's propriety – in short – if I am welcome to them – I shall continue during my residence at least to apply such portions of my income present and future as may forward the object – that is to say – what I can spare for that purpose. – Privations – I can – or at least could once bear – abstinence I am accustomed to – and as to fatigue – I was once a tolerable traveller – what I may be now – I cannot tell – but I will try. – I await the commands of the Committee – address to Genoa – the letters will be forwarded to me – wherever I may be – by my bankers Messrs Webb and Barry. – It would have given me pleasure to have had some more defined instructions before I went – but these of course rest at the option of the Committee. – I have the honour to be

(Byron to John Bowring, 7 July 1823)

Byron persuaded Teresa that he must visit Greece to find out what was happening there and assured her that he would return to her before long. In the meantime the release of her father from prison appeared to solve the problem of where she was to go. Count Gamba was freed on condition that his daughter would leave Lord Byron and go back to live in her father's house. Deeply distressed, she bade her lover farewell and when the *Hercules* was driven back to port by storms she had already set out on the journey in the hope of joining her father. Byron and his party picnicked under a tree in the beautiful gardens of the Villa Lombellina with Mr Barry, his banker. Next day they embarked once more. The party consisted of Byron, Pietro Gamba and Trelawny, a Greek Prince who had asked for passage home and a young Doctor Bruno (who spent the first few days on board in terror since someone had told him that if Byron became angry with him over the slightest fault he would be fed to the dogs who were kept for this purpose).

Fletcher was naturally on board and so were Tita Falcieri, Lega Zambelli and five other servants, including an amiable young black man called Benjamin Lewis. There were five horses and several dogs.

On the 13 July the *Hercules* was loaded. The next day there was no wind so she could not sail. On the 15th *Hercules* sailed but suffered storm damage and returned to Genoa. They finally set off on the 16 July. At Leghorn they picked up supplies and gave passage to a young Philhellene, James Hamilton Browne, and a Greek called Captain Vitali.

Sailing through the straits of Messina they passed within sight of Elba, Corsica and the Liparian Islands. The original plan was to land at Zante but James Hamilton Browne persuaded Byron to head for Cephalonia since he knew that the British Military Resident, Sir Charles Napier, was a convinced Philhellene. The *Hercules* entered the harbour of Argostoli on 3 August 1823.

33

BYRON IN CEPHALONIA

I did not come here to join a faction but a nation.[1]

James Kennedy describes the sensation aroused among both Greeks and English by the arrival of the brig *Hercules* in the harbour of Argostoli:

> The former were eager to behold a wealthy English nobleman, and a celebrated poet ... on his way to join their country to add the whole weight of his name, influence, talents and fortune to the cause of freedom. The latter felt a still greater curiosity to behold a countryman not less interesting by his unrivalled talents than by his faults and misfortunes, but, above all, the daily rumours of his misanthropy, profligacy and infidelity, and by the warfare which he had so long carried on against many of the most distinguished literary characters, as well as against the government and religion of his native country. He was viewed by us all as an object of wonder and astonishment, and as one whose talents, character and sentiments separated him, as it were, from the rest of mankind. All alike were anxious to view his person and watch his proceedings.[2]

This blatant curiosity may explain why Byron elected to stay on board the *Hercules* at Argostoli for the next month.

James Hamilton Browne gives an account of arrangements on board the *Hercules*:

> During the voyage his Lordship was attentively occupied in reading and making notes upon Swift's works...
>
> His Lordship dined by himself, early, at about twelve o'clock, and his dinner generally consisted of fresh vegetables only ... and an immense quantity of red pickled cabbage, after which he ate a great

deal of cheese; during dinner he drank cider, afterwards generally ale and hock. A more unwholesome manner of living, in my opinion, in the Mediterranean, and in the month of July, could scarcely have been adopted...

Captain Scott ... used to give Lord Byron good advice, counselling him to engage the *Hercules* to carry him back to England, and not go amongst the Greeks with so much good money, who would only cut his throat for it... 'Why, my Lord, with your fortune and fame, you ought to be sitting in the House of Lords, and defending the right side of the question, as your friends Mr Hobhouse and Sir Frances Burdett are, in the Commons, instead of roaming over the world.'

The young man went on:

His Lordship, in the midst of the greatest mirth and jollity, used frequently to have his eyes suffused with tears, arising, I have no doubt, from some painful recollections. On these occasions he used always to rise and retire to the privacy of his cabin...[3]

Browne tells us that:

On the passage to Cephalonia Byron chiefly read the writings of Dean Swift. He also made it a constant rule to peruse every day one or more of the Essays of Montaigne. This practice he said he had pursued for a long time adding that more general knowledge and useful information are to be derived from an intimate acquaintance with that diverting author than by a long and continuous course of study.[4]

A passage from Montaigne may have reinforced the romantic aspect of Byron's complicated attitudes to war:

No occupation [writes Montaigne] is as enjoyable as soldiering, – an occupation both noble in its practice (since valour is the mightiest, most magnanimous and proudest of the virtues) and noble in its purpose ... You enjoy the comradeship of so many men who are noble, young and active, the daily sight of so many sublime dramas, the freedom of straightforward fellowship as well as a manly, informal mode of life, the diversions of hundreds of different activities, the heart-stirring sound of martial music which fills your ears and inflames your soul, as well as the honour of this activity, its very pains and hardships.[5]

But although Montaigne admired the courage and self sacrifice of the soldier he had no illusions about the motives of some of those engaged in a just war:

468

...we must not (as we do every day) give the name of duty to an inward bitter harshness born of self-interested passion, nor that of courage to malicious and treacherous dealings. What they call zeal is their propensity to wickedness and violence: it is not the cause which sets them ablaze but self-interest: they stoke up war, not because it is just but because it is war.[6]

As we have seen, Byron could be equally sceptical in his attitude to war. He felt compelled to engage in the Greek war (when he was asked to do so by the London Greek Committee) because it was a war of liberation. A war to relieve oppression of a people was a just war even though it might entail acts of barbarity on either side. During his time in Greece he did everything in his power to prevent such acts of barbarity.

We cannot tell whether Byron ever consciously put any of Montaigne's notions into practice but we know he was reading the *Essays* on his way to Greece. They must have been particularly interesting and useful to him on his last voyage because he was going to war and would soon be negotiating with Greeks and Turks, commanding Suliotes, dealing with squabbling factions, with questions of supply, with unruly soldiers and frightened civilians. Montaigne had experience of warfare and wrote about the problems of command. He had held office and wrote of the intricacies of diplomacy. He wrote of the hideously violent Civil Wars of Religion which swirled around his seat of Montaigne, sometimes threatening to overwhelm it. He wrote of cruelty and treachery and made subtle distinctions which Byron would instantly have grasped. 'Any honourable person,' wrote Montaigne, 'prefers to sully his honour than to sully his conscience.'[7] He dealt with the conflict between private morality and public necessity. One cannot imagine a more useful book for a tyro commander with a conscience to take to war.

There was much to be done on Byron's arrival in Cephalonia. Browne remarks:

Lord Byron had a marked predilection in favour of the Albanians and Suliotes, in consequence of the affection shown towards him, in illness, by two of the former, on his first visit to Greece, and his either having been assisted after, or saved from, shipwreck by some of the latter. This induced him to take those whom he found at Cephalonia into pay, although their demands and the constant altercations which they gave rise to, might have convinced him of their want of patriotism, and that they were only endeavouring to extort what money they could from him.[8]

Captain Scott said that if it were not for his respect for his Lordship he would not have allowed a single Suliote to enter his vessel, calling them '... those murderous-looking villains in sheepskins.'

Byron knew that he could not use the *Hercules* for transporting himself and his entourage to the mainland. Captain Scott said firmly that he could take on the hazard only if Byron would insure him for the loss of the ship in case it was confiscated by the Turks with all its contents. So Byron let Scott sail away and moved into a cottage '... in a very pretty village between the mountains and the sea – waiting what Napoleon calls "the march of events".'[9]

George Finlay, later historian of Greece but then a young man fresh from studies in Germany, arrived in Cephalonia soon after this and related:

> I met Lord Byron for the first time at Metaxata in Cephalonia. I found his Lordship had ridden out with Count Gamba ... was shown his only public room, which was small and scantily furnished in the plainest manner. One table was covered for dinner, another and a chair were strewed with books, and many were ranged in order on the floor. I found the greater part of Walter Scott's novels, Mitford's History of Greece, Sismondi's Italian Republics and an English translation of Pausanillo.[10]

Finlay praised Byron's conduct in Greece and, particularly, his behaviour towards the Greeks. Byron's attitude to the Greek campaign (as reported by William Parry) is admirable in its lack of hubris and its down-to-earth commonsense:

> I am here to act against the external enemies of Greece and will not take part with any faction in the country. We who come here to fight for Greece have no right to meddle with its internal affairs or dictate to the people or government.[11]

He also made clear that he had no antagonism towards the Turks:

> I have no enmity to the Turks individually. They are quite as good as the Greeks. I am displeased to hear them called barbarians. They are charitable to the poor and very humane to animals.[12]

470

George Finlay writes that Byron did not overlook the vices of the Greek leaders, but at the same time, he did not underrate the virtues of the people.

Byron himself, as reported by Parry, declared:

> No system of government in any part of Greece can be permanent which does not leave in the hands of the peasantry the chief part of the political power. They are warmly attached to their country and they are the best portion of the people.[13]

However, he was well aware of the complexities of the situation in Greece and recognised the delicacy of the choices before him:

> We must not suppose under our name of Greeks an entire, united and single people kept apart from all others by strongly marked geographical or moral distinctions. On the contrary. Those who are now contending for freedom are a mixed race of various tribes of men having apparent interests and different opinions. Many of them differ from and hate each other more even than they differ from and hate the Turks.[14]

This helps to clarify the difficulties experienced by the Greek leaders, which are set out by David Brewer in his book on the Greek War of Independence. In the early days of the war Ipsilantis's failure in Moldavia could partly be ascribed to '...the multiple manoeuvres of the supposed supporters ... the slippery allegiance of the captains – the uncertain adherence of the allies.'[15] Brewer points out that Kolokotronis described how almost impossible it was to lead an army composed of Greeks: 'If Wellington had given me an army of 40,000 I could have governed it; but if five hundred Greeks had been given him to lead he could not have governed them for one hour.'[16]

Another problem, which particularly affected the attitude of the foreigners in Greece, was the hideous massacres perpetrated by both Greeks and Turks. 'The mind-set which dehumanises one's opponents is as old as war itself, and the Greeks and Turks were no strangers to it.'[17]

Thomas Gordon, a Scottish former military man who had been a strong supporter of Greek Independence, was horrified by the massacre of the Turks at Tripolitza. This contributed to his decision to return home to Scotland. For several years he had nothing to do with the war beyond the offering of good advice.

In spite of these horrors, idealistic young men from all over the world flocked to the help of the Greeks. Byron's arrival in Greece was to bring in more and more, who continued to come, in spite of the dissensions among the Greeks which led to two civil wars. Brewer comments that: 'Perhaps only in the foreign reaction to the Spanish Civil War of the 1930s has there been such a sharp contrast between the cold abstention of govenments and the passionate involvement of individuals.'[18]

Byron wrote to Teresa from Metaxata:

> Here are arrived – English – German – Greeks – all kinds of people in short – proceeding to or coming from Greece – and all with something to say to me – so that every day – I have to receive them here or visit them in Argostoli.[19]

He explained to his sister the choices that lay before him: 'Oh Plato, what a task for a Philosopher!'[20]

He always insisted that he would have no concealment about the difficulties of the situation in Greece: 'I shall stay out as long as I can – and do all I can for these Greeks; – but I cannot exaggerate – they must expect only the truth from me both of – and to them.'[21] Nor does he mince words in his communications to Mavrocordato who seems to him, since the heroic death in action of the leader, Marco Botzaris (which happened, disappointingly, only days after his own arrival at Argostoli), '... the only *Washington* or *Kosciusko* ... among the Greeks'[22]:

> ... many officers are waiting only for a report from me to come to the aid of Greece, but in the present circumstances I would regard it a culpable trick to entice them to come – where not only does so much discord reign, but where there seems to be such great jealousy of foreigners.
>
> (Byron to Mavrocordato, November 1823)

And later:

> Most Excellent Prince, ...
> Greece now faces these three courses – to win her liberty, to become a Colony of the sovereigns of Europe, or to become a Turkish province. – Now she can choose one of the three – but civil war cannot lead to anything but the last two...[24]

472

Byron warns the Greek Government that:

> ...all hope of a loan will be lost, any assistance from abroad will be suspended and the great Powers ... will cut short all your noble hopes...
>
> Allow me to add ... I want what is good for Greece and nothing else: I will do everything in my power to insure this: But I do not consent, nor will I ever consent to permit the Public or private English citizens ever to be deluded about the true state of things in Greece. The rest depends on you, Gentlemen. You have fought gloriously...[25]
>
> (Byron to the General Government of Greece, 30 November 1823)

Soon after the arrival of the *Hercules* at Argostoli, Sir Charles Napier returned to the island and welcomed Byron and his party, inviting them to dine and meeting Byron almost daily to discuss plans for future action. Byron soon decided that Napier was the man to lead the fight against the Turks: '...a better or a braver man is not easily to be found.'[26] They became friends though Byron is said to have sometimes smiled at the enthusiasm of Sir Charles, pointing out where the soldier's ardour appeared to mislead his judgement. Napier was a friend of Mavrocordato and when Colonel Stanhope arrived from London to share with Byron the conduct of the war under the guidance of the London Greek Committee the two soldiers also became friends. Stanhope's relationship with Byron was more complicated.

Besides occupying himself with matters of state Byron had more mundane tasks to which he must attend. He had been kindly welcomed and entertained by the officers of the 8th Regiment (King's) of Foot, which was stationed on the island. He often rode out with Colonel Duffie, second-in-command of the Regiment and wrote to him to ask for the services of the Regimental smith 'to shoe my horses...'[27]

He took the trouble to write to a Captain Hill who was in charge of various logistical matters:

> ...our new lady of the laundry sends her daughter *alone* among my serving-men, one half of whom are pox'd ... If her parents do not want to make her a w——e and a thief they had better employ another messenger – for the poor girl seems half a child and to merit a better fate.[28]

The Suliotes were soon paid off and supplied with arms so that

473

they might remove themselves to the Mainland, joining their compatriots there.

Byron worried about the health of his daughter, having heard of an illness she had recently suffered. He wrote to Augusta for news of Ada and in one of his letters to his sister he adds diffidently:

> If you think this epistle or any part of it worth transmitting to Ly B[yron] you can send her a copy – as I suppose – unless she is become I know not what – she cannot be altogether indifferent to my 'whereabouts' and *what*abouts.[29]

Byron has been criticised for lingering at Metaxata and refusing to throw in his lot at this stage with one or other of the Greek factions, and has been compared unfavourably with Trelawny, especially by Trelawny, who, on leaving Cephalonia with James Hamilton Browne soon after they arrived there to travel to the Mainland, precipitately joined the treacherous and unreliable Greek chieftain, Odysseus, and was of no further use in the cause of Greek Independence.

William Parry points out that, in hesitating to commit himself at this early stage, Byron was alive to the risk of increasing the dissensions of the Greek leaders while Trelawny felt no such responsibility.

David Brewer defends Byron's decision to remain at Metaxata:

> Byron's months at Kephalonia have often been represented as a time of dithering and indecision ... [Trelawny wrote] 'I well knew that once on shore, Byron would fall back on his old routine of dawdling habits – plotting, planning, shilly-shallying, and doing nothing.' ... But this approach does Byron an injustice. Mesolonghi became a possible destination only with the prospect of Mavrocordatos' arrival there; if Byron had moved before that, he would have had to go to the Peloponnese (as he nearly did) and, as he wrote to Bowring ... Had I *gone sooner they would have forced me into one party or the other.*'[30]

Andrew Nicholson describes, in his admirable review of Stephen Minta's *On a Voiceless Shore*, the account of Byron's activities in Greece given by the author: 'Byron passed that time cautiously, patiently, diplomatically; spreading what humanity and justice he could, easing distress, listening; and all the while steadily gaining the confidence and trust of those whose cause he had come out to serve and of his colleagues who had come to join him.'[31]

One episode which shows Byron easing distress occurred during his visit with some of his party to Ithaca where they were kindly entertained by Captain Knox, the British Resident, and his family. Finding a family of girls with their mother in great distress he had them removed to Cephalonia and gave them a house and money to obtain their subsistence. Soon the two sons of the family came to share their good fortune. Loukas Chalandritsanos became an object of love for Byron.

Raymond Mills believes that this brief visit to Ithaca is important in assessing Byron's state of health in the last months of his life:

> The return journey took a week and involved a good deal of physical hardship, long rides on mule-back on very bad roads under a blazing sun, much walking and climbing, and sleeping in his cloak with the rest of the party in one cottage room. Byron had received a blow on the head from an overhanging branch on a steep mule track which literally stunned him.
>
> On the return journey to Cephalonia Byron was in an open boat under a hot sun. They arrived at Santa Euphemia in the afternoon, and in the evening he was welcomed by the Abbot of the monastery. Byron was tired and angry and lashed himself into a rage. While the Abbot of the monastery was giving an address Byron seized a lamp and cried 'My head is burning, will no-one relieve me from the presence of this pestilential madman? ...' and darted from the room. The Abbot and Dr Bruno tried to calm him. He refused all medicine and stamped and tore his bedding like a maniac. He finally took Dr Bruno's 'benedette pillule' ... lay down and went to sleep. The next morning Byron could hardly give credit to his own frantic conduct, and was exceedingly courteous to the Abbot on leaving.

Raymond Mills' diagnosis of this attack is that '... it may have been due to sunstroke which can cause unreasonable behaviour such as was described.'[32]

Byron was under tremendous pressure throughout this period from the various factions who were clamouring for him to join them. Kolokotronis insisted that he should attend the National Assembly at Salamis. Mavrocordato asked him to come to Hydra. The governor of Mesolonghi summoned him urgently to join him there.

Byron himself was extremely patient with Greeks, putting their unreliability down to the effect of years of subservience to their conquerors. He was convinced that winning their freedom would eventually transform their character for the better.

He had decided to set off for Tripolitza when James Hamilton Browne returned from the Mainland accompanied by the Greek deputies who were on their way to London to negotiate the loan. Browne brought with him a letter for Byron from Mavrocordato informing him that Western Greece was now the point of danger and asking for a loan of £4,000 to enable him to set sail for Mesolonghi with the Greek squadron at Hydra.

Byron cancelled his journey to Tripolitza and set about organising credits for Mavrocordato and planning his own voyage to join the Greek leader at Mesolonghi. The 'march of events' was now to take him, as he thought, to war.

34

BYRON AT MESOLONGHI

Mavrcordato's letter says that my presence will 'electrify the troops' so I am going to 'electrify the Suliotes'...

Byron hired two vessels for the journey to Mesolonghi – a swift, light *mistico* for himself, Dr Bruno, Fletcher, Loukas Chalandritsanos and his favourite dog, Lyon (the Newfoundland he had received as a gift from a stranger), and a bombard for Pietro Gamba which was much larger and slower and had room for the rest of the servants, the horses, guns and other supplies.

David Brewer found that 'This eventful journey showed Byron at his hardy and insouciant best.'[1] Byron gave up his cabin to Fletcher who was ill. '..we had bad weather almost always – though not contrary – slept on deck in the wet generally – ... but never was in better health ... – so much so that I actually bathed for quarter of an hour in the evening on the fourth inst. in the sea – (to kill the fleas and others) and was all the better for it.'[2]

In order to mislead the Turks should they fail to run the blockade successfully each boat was provided with false papers giving their destination as the Island of Kalanos fifty miles from Mesolonghi, and the purpose of the journey as a hunting expedition.

As they sailed in company the sailors began to sing patriotic songs and Byron sang with them. During the night the boats were separated. In the morning Byron and his party watched in dismay as the bombard was seized by a Turkish warship. He imagined they would have to 'take a turn at the Turks'[3] to get the boat out from Patras.

Gamba was interrogated but happily the Turkish captain recognised the Greek captain as a man who had once saved his life and the

477

grateful enemy eventually allowed ship, crew, animals, weapons and supplies to go free.

Gamba arrived at Mesolonghi a day before Byron. The *mistico* came upon another Turkish ship lurking near its destination and fled. Putting into shore further up the coast Byron landed Loukas with a letter to be taken to Mesolonghi asking for an escort. He then made for Dragomestre, fifty miles from Mesolonghi, and there was picked up by Greek gunboats. After two near-shipwrecks they finally arrived at Mesolonghi on 3 January, to be met by Pietro Gamba whose eyes filled with tears when he saw that Byron was safe.

Byron knew how important a moment this was – his arrival to join the elected representative of Greece and his troops, such as they were. From the experience of his former travels in Greece and Albania, Byron had learned the necessity of ceremonial dress and bearing for those who wished to achieve anything in Eastern Europe. He had designed Homeric helmets for himself and Pietro (which look absurd to modern eyes but resemble those worn by many officers in the armies of the period). The helmets were not suitable for this occasion. Byron came ashore in a brave scarlet uniform. He was welcomed by a large crowd of citizens with cheering, wild music and salvos of gunfire. Prince Mavrocordato and all the important administrators and military men in the town, as well as the clergy, came to receive him.

Colonel Stanhope was already installed on the first floor of the house of which Byron and his party were to occupy the second floor. The Suliotes occupied the ground floor.

In his review of Stephen Minta's book on Byron and Greece (*On a Voiceless Shore*), Andrew Nicholson claims that Minta's account '... can but silence the slightest murmur aspersing Byron's effective and disinterested commitment to the Greek cause ... Here is the vigorous, far-seeing, practical administrator, occupied with the daily, frequently routine, mundane and ordinary but necessary business of running a town in the throes of war ... putting affairs into some sort of order – doing the necessary.'[4]

In these efforts Colonel Stanhope, far from being helpful, caused Byron anxiety and irritation. George Finlay explains that '... the typographical Colonel, as Lord Byron sarcastically termed him, seemed to think that newspapers would be more effective in driving back the Ottoman armies than well-drilled troops and military tactics.'[5]

Byron himself protested that '... Stanhope wanted to establish posts and mail-carts among a people who have no food ... I cannot comprehend the use of printing presses to a people who do not read – Here the Committee have sent supplies of maps, I suppose, that I may teach the young mountaineers geography. Here are bugle-horns without bugle-men, and it is a chance if we can find anybody in Greece to blow them. Books are sent to a people who want guns.[6]

Finlay describes the difference between the two men:

> Order was, in his [Byron's] opinion, the first step to liberty. The Earl of Harrington [Colonel Stanhope] talked as if he considered Lord Byron's desire for order a proof of his indifference to liberty. Lord Byron was, however, a far wiser counsellor than the Colonel, and, had he lived, must have done much to arrest the factious madness and shameless expenditure which rendered the English loans the prize and the aliment of two civil wars.[7]

Finlay explains how Byron, who had been eager for the arrival of the Greek loan, became disillusioned as he began to understand the attitude of many Greeks to the loan:

> A mist fell from Lord Byron's eyes. He began to express doubts whether the circumstances had authorized him to recommend the Greek loan to his friends in England. He was struck by the fact that a majority of the Moreot captains and primates opposed pledging the confiscated Turkish property as a security to the lenders. He feared that the proceeds of a loan might be misspent by one party, and the loan itself disowned by another. Bowring and the bankers, he said, would secure their commissions and their gains, but he feared that many honest English families might lose their money by his Philhellenism.[8]

Byron had acquired an unlikely confidant to whom he communicated some of these worries. The Greek Committee had sent to Mesolonghi in early February a Firemaster, William Parry, six artificers and supplies for the setting up of a brigade of artillery. Byron wrote from Mesolonghi to Charles Hancock:

> I have been interrupted by the arrival of Parry and afterwards by the return of Hesketh who has not brought an answer to my epistles which rather surprises me. – You will write soon I suppose. Parry seems a fine rough subject – but will hardly be ready for the field these three weeks; – he and I will (I think) be able to draw together – at least *I*

479

will not interfere with or contradict him in his own department, he complains grievously of the mercantile and en*thusymusy* (as Braham pronounces enthusiasm) part of the Committee – but greatly praises Gordon and Hume, – Gordon *would* have given three or four thousand pounds and come out himself – but Bowring or somebody else disgusted him – and thus they have spoiled part of their subscription and cramped their operations. – Parry says Blaquiere is a humbug; – to which I say nothing. – He sorely laments the printing and civilizing expenses – and wishes that there was not a Sunday school in the world – or *any* school *here* at present save and except always an academy for Artilleryship. – He complained also of the Cold – a little to my surprise – firstly because there being no chimneys – I have used myself to do without other warmth than the animal heat and one's Cloak – in these parts – and secondly because I would as soon have expected to hear a Volcano sneeze – as a Fire-master (who is to burn a whole fleet–) exclaim against the atmosphere. – I fully expected that his very approach would have scorched the town like the burning glasses of Archimedes. – Well – it seems that I am to be Commander in Chief – and the post is by no means a sinecure – for we are not what Major Sturgeon calls 'a Set of the most amicable officers' whether we shall have 'a boxing bout between Captain Sheers and the Colonel' I cannot tell – but between Suliote Chiefs – German Barons – English Volunteers – and adventurers of all Nations – we are likely to form as goodly an allied army – as ever quarrelled beneath the Same banner.–[9]

(Byron to Charles Hancock, 7 February 1824)

Charles Hancock was Byron's banker in Cephalonia. Being one of Byron's bankers must have been an enjoyable experience. He wrote equally lively letters to Samuel Barff who was managing his affairs in Zante and to Charles Barry who was his banker in Genoa. Byron seems to have had a genius for friendship, with bankers as well as bookmen, for he opens his heart to these men of affairs, confiding in them, with his usual complete lack of discretion, and winning their friendship in return.

He explained to Hancock why he had been invited to take command in Western Greece: '... firstly – because they will sooner listen to a foreigner than one of their own people – out of native jealousies – secondly, because the Turks will sooner treat or capitulate ... with a Frank than a Greek ... and thirdly, – because nobody else seems disposed to take the responsibility.'[10] (Byron to Charles Hancock, Mesolonghi, 5 February 1824)

Parry perceived at once that Lord Byron and Colonel Stanhope 'did not row in the same boat.' Rough diamond he may have been

480

but he had intelligence and a sensibility which helped him to understand Byron's difficulties.

Lord Byron, he wrote, '... acted strictly in conjunction with the Greek government and with its representative in Western Greece, Prince Mavrocordato. Colonel Stanhope acted in conjunction with nobody, and in opposition to the government. His own thoughts and wishes and theories were the only rules he consulted. Hence the disputes about the medicines and about the printing press, the newspapers etc., etc., on all which subjects Byron did but second the views of the Greek government.'

Parry saw farther than most into the motives and characters of those thrown together at Mesolonghi. Of Byron he wrote, 'He was more a mental being, if I may use this phrase, than any man I ever saw. He lived on thought more than on food.'[11] Parry deplored the fact that Byron's courage, which endeared him even to the wild Suliotes, his generosity and his humanity was later forgotten, and he was censured by '... heartless and pretended friends who were quite unable to appreciate all the nobleness of his nature.'[12]

Here Parry is referring to the practical steps Byron took during his time in Greece to lessen the inhumanity of the combatants towards each other. He sent four Turkish prisoners to the Turkish commander at Patras:

Highness – A ship with some of my friends and servants on board was brought under the turrets of a Turkish frigate. It was then released on the order of Your Highness. I thank you, not for having released the ship – since it had a neutral flag and was under English protection, so that no one had the right to detain it – but for having treated my friends with the utmost courtesy – while they were at your disposition – In the hope of performing an action not displeasing to Your Highness I have asked the Greek Government here to place four Mussulman prisoners in my hands. – I now release them to Your Highness in recompense, as far as is possible, for your Courtesy. – They are sent without conditions – but if the circumstances could win a place in your memory I would only beg Your Highness to treat with humanity any Greek who may be (captured?) or fall into the hands of the Mussulmans – Since the horrors of war are sufficient in themselves without adding cold-blooded ruthlessness on either side. –[13]

(Byron to Jussuf Pasha, 23 January 1824)

He later sent twenty-four Turks to Mr Mayer at Prevesa:

481

Sir, – Coming to Greece, one of my principal objects was to alleviate as much as possible the miseries incident to a warfare so cruel as the present. When the dictates of humanity are in question, I know no – difference between Turks and Greeks. It is enough to know that those who want assistance are men, in order to claim the pity and protection of the meanest pretender to humane feelings. I have found here twenty-four Turks, including women and children, who have long pined in distress, far from the means of support and the consolations of their home. The Goverment has consigned them to me: I transmit them to Prevesa, whither they desire to be sent. I hope you will not object to take care that they may be restored to a place of safety, and that the Governor of your town may accept of my present. The best recompense I can hope would be to find – that I had inspired the Ottoman commander with the same sentiments towards those unhappy Greeks who may hereafter fall into their hands.[14]

(Byron to Mr Mayer, 21 February 1824)

Bernard Beatty discusses this attitude of Byron to warfare in an article deploring the terrorist attack on New York on 11 September 2001:

In his last days fighting for a renewal of civilisation in Greece, he is most careful to use the resources of the customary imagination for the purposes of war (I am thinking of his famous helmet) but he is equally careful not to allow his imagination to be taken over by simplifying, hate-filled images of the enemy nor by images of cleansing and purification. The Turks never became a 'Satan' for him just as, though sympathetic to the Carbonari, he yet tried to save the life of the commandant shot by them. Byron was never a fanatic but well understood the logic of fanaticism as well as its self-contradictions.[15]

The article is entitled 'And thus the peopled city grieves' and its author quotes from a stanza he considers one of the most moving in *Don Juan*:

> ... and human lives are lavished everywhere,
> As the year closing whirls the scarlet leaves
>   When the stript forest bows to the bleak air
> And groans, and thus the peopled city grieves,
>   Shorn of its best and loveliest and left bare.

Bernard Beatty comments: 'Byron grieves with grieving cities and is consistently appalled by those acts which lavish human lives for whatever cause.'[16]

482

Not surprisingly, Byron was particularly concerned with the rule of law and wrote to the British Resident at Zante:

> It would also be very much for the benefit of both sides if they could be induced to conduct themselves with some regard to the laws of War – or any laws whatsoever.[17]
>
> (Byron to Sir Frederick Stoven, Mesolonghi, 8 March 1824)

There were moments of enjoyment during the time at Mesolonghi, such as the visit to nearby Anatoliko when, in January, Byron, Prince Mavrocordato, Gamba, Stanhope and Bruno dined with the Metropolitan and all the chiefs, and primates. Byron was welcomed as a hero with noisy cannonades. As the party was approaching Anatoliko by sea this proved a dangerous moment since one of the cannon balls passed within three yards of the approaching guests. Byron found the Metropolitan the merriest of the party.

Another episode which gave Byron great pleasure took place during one of his daily rides. Parry reports that he returned one day from a long ride with a curd cheese and some honey which had been given to him by a peasant woman with a fine family who came out of her house to give him the gift and refused to take any payment for it. Parry describes Byron's pleasure at receiving such kindness. He sent Parry with a gift for the woman and told him, 'The peasantry are by far the most kind, humane and honest part of the population; they redeem the character of their countrymen.'

Parry then relates that:

> Lord Byron then sat down to his cheese and insisted on our partaking of his fare. A bottle of porter was sent for and broached that we might join Byron in drinking health and happiness to the kind family which had procured him so great a pleasure.[8]

Very different emotions were felt by Byron when he discovered that the supplies sent by the London Greek Committee had been left on the beach to be ruined by the torrential rain which was turning all Mesolonghi into a mud bath:

> I caught cold yesterday with swearing too much in the rain at the Greeks – who would not lend a hand in landing the Committee stores and nearly spoiled our combustibles; – but I turned out in person and made such a row as set them in motion – blaspheming at them all from

the Government downwards – till they actually did *some* part of what they ought to have done several days before.[19]

(Byron to Charles Hancock, Mesolonghi, 5 February 1824)

It is not surprising that, in a moment of disillusion, Byron said to Gamba, 'I begin to fear that I have done nothing but lose time, money, patience and health.'

The worst disappointment was perhaps the behaviour of the Suliotes of whom, remembering his youthful experiences, Byron retained romantic illusions soon to be dispelled. Moore comments on his meetings with the Suliotes during his first visit to Greece and Albania:

> At Salona, a solitary place on the Gulf of Salona, he once passed three days, lodged in a small, miserable barrack. Here he lived the whole time, familiarly, among the soldiers; and a picture of the singular scene which their evenings presented – of these wild, half-bandit warriors, seated round the young poet, and examining with savage admiration his fine Manton guns and English sword – might be contrasted but too touchingly, with another and later picture of the same poet dying as a chieftain in the same land, with Suliotes for his guards, and all Greece for his mourners.[20]

The first picture is probably accurate. The second is certainly not. Although the Suliotes were drilled and disciplined up to a point by Byron and Parry (Byron submitting to being drilled with the troops), and acted as escort when Byron rode out, running beside him and, according to Parry, keeping up with the horses, for these 'murderous looking villains in sheepskins' were taller than the Greeks and extremely athletic, their chief aim was to extort as much money as they could from Byron. They had no conception of what Greek liberty might entail. They demanded that one hundred out of their number (of about four hundred) should be raised to a higher rank simply to extort higher rates of pay. When Byron and Mavrocordato planned a march to invest Lepanto (which was in a weak state at that point and might have been overcome with relative ease) the Suliotes flatly refused to march 'against stone walls'. They mutinied on more than one occasion. On 19 February one of them was refused entrance by the guards at Byron's house and in the ensuing scuffle a Lieutenant Sass who was a Scandinavian member of Byron's brigade, was fatally wounded.

The townspeople were terrified of the Suliotes who threatened to murder all the foreigners. Calm was restored only by Byron's coolness and authority. He summoned the Suliote commanders and offered them a month's pay to take themselves off. He wrote a note on the Suliotes for Mavrocordato:

> Having tried in vain at every expense – considerable trouble – and some danger to unite the Suliotes for the good of Greece – and their own – I have come to the following resolution. – I will have nothing more to do with the Suliotes – they may go to the Turks or – the devil ... they may cut me into more pieces than they have dissensions among them, sooner than change my resolution.

Byron sent this note to Mavrocordato on 15 February, adding the words, 'For the rest, I hold my means and person at the disposal of the Greek nation the same as before.'[21]

The murder of Lieutenant Sass terrified Parry's six mechanics and, on Stanhope's admitting to them that their safety could not be guaranteed, they left.

Byron wrote to Samuel Barff at Zante:

> Parry will write to you himself on the subject of the artificers' wages, but with all due allowance for their situation, I cannot see a great deal to pity in their circumstances. They were well paid, housed and fed, expenses granted of every kind, and they marched off at the first alarm.[22]
>
> (Byron to Samuel Barff, Mesolonghi, 26 March 1824)

However, Byron took the trouble of arranging a passage home for the men.

He had written to John Murray of other events:

> On Tuesday a Turkish brig of war ran on shore – on Wednesday – great preparations being made to attack her though protected by her Consorts – The Turks burned her and retired to Patras ... On Saturday we had the smartest shock of an earthquake which I remember (and I have felt thirty ... at different periods – they are common in the Mediterranean) and the whole army discharged their arms ... it was a rare scene altogether – and on Sunday we heard that the Vizir is come down to Larissa with one hundred and odd thousand men.[23]
>
> (Byron to John Murray, Mesolonghi, 25 January 1824)

In the midst of all these events Byron conceived the strange plan of adopting a little Muslim girl and possibly even sending her to Lady Byron to be a companion for Ada. The plan fell through when the mother changed her mind about the prospect of being parted from her daughter.

On 13 March it was rumoured that plague had broken out in the town.

News from home had to be dealt with. Kinnaird gave Byron the verdict of the Court of King's Bench on *The Vision of Judgment*. He replied, 'We must pay the expenses and the fine...'[24]

The officers of the foreign brigade caused endless difficulties. The Prussian Officers were determined to administer a flogging to a soldier who was found guilty of theft. But Byron was adamant: 'I positively prohibited anything of the kind. The man was handed over to the Police Office to be dealt with by Civil Law. On the same day one of the officers challenged two others. I had the parties put under arrest until the affair could be accommodated.[25] (Byron to Douglas Kinnaird, 30 March 1824)

When a Prussian Officer was accused by the family on whom he had been billeted of terrorising them by his conduct, Byron wrote to him:

> You ought to recollect that entering into the auxiliary Greek corps, now under my orders, at your sole request and positive desire, you incurred the obligation of obeying the laws of the country, as well as those of the service.[26]

Byron wrote to John Bowring:

> I do wish seriously to impress upon the Committee – either *not* to send out officers of any description – or to provide for their maintenance. – I am at this moment paying nearly *thirty officers* of whom five and twenty would not have bread to eat (in Greece that is), if I did not.[27]
> (Byron to John Bowring, Mesolonghi, 30 March 1824)

He had already told Samuel Barff:

> There is an imperious necessity for some national fund, and that speedily; otherwise what is to be done? The Auxiliary Corps of about two hundred men, paid by me, are, I believe, the sole regularly and properly furnished with the money due to them weekly, and the officers monthly. It is true that the Greek Government give them rations; but we have had three mutinies owing to the badness of the bread, which neither native, nor stranger could masticate (nor dogs either).[28]
> (Byron to Samuel Barff, Mesolonghi, 26 March 1824)

On 30 March he wrote to Douglas Kinnaird:

– The Greek Cause up to this present writing hath cost me of mine
own monies about thirty thousand Spanish dollars *advanced*, without
counting my own contingent expenses of any kind. It is true, however,
that everything would have been at a standstill in Missolonghi if I had
not done so. Part of this money, the £4,000 advanced and guaranteed
by the Greek deputies is, or ought to be, repaid. To this you will look,
but I shall still spend it in the Cause.[29]
(Byron to Douglas Kinnaird, Mesolonghi, 30 March 1824)

On 19 March he had found himself dealing with the problems
caused by Colonel Stanhope's obsession with setting up newspapers
for the Greeks. He wrote to Barff:

...from the very first I foretold to Colonel Stanhope and to P[rince]
Mavrocordato that a Greek Newspaper (or indeed any other) in the
present state of Greece – might – and probably *would* lead to much
mischief and misconstruction – unless under *some* restrictions – nor
have I ever had anything to do with either – as a Writer – or otherwise,
except as a pecuniary contributor to their support on the outset, which
I could not refuse to the earnest request of the Projectors ... – [Meyer,
the Editor] is the Author of an article against Monarchy – of which he
may have the advantage and fame – but they (the Editors) will get
themselves into a scrape if they don't take care.[30]
(Byron to Samuel Barff, Mesolonghi, 19 March 1824)

Byron suppressed the twentieth number of the *Greek Chronicle*
because it included a violent attack on the Austrian Monarchy. The
Greeks required the aid of the Powers, most of which were
monarchies.

Byron also wrote to the *Greek Chronicle* defending the reputation
of a Philhellene who had been attacked in its columns:

Sirs – I have read for the first time yesterday an article in the Greek
Chronicle – denouncing the Danish Baron A[dam] F[riedel] – who is
not here to respond – I do not know if this is just but it does not
appear to me to be generous ... he has served the Government and the
Nation and they have thanked him for his services – they have been
his most zealous defenders. I do not know the B.A.F. as a compatriot
and scarcely as a person – but he is alone – a foreigner – oppressed –
and now far away – and for these reasons I take up his defence – until
I see evidence that would discredit him. – If after all he is an adventurer

487

worthy of being denounced in a public paper – which pretends to the most liberal sentiments – I have nothing more to say.[31]

(Byron to the *Greek Chronicle*, Mesolonghi, 23 March 1824)

Byron was well aware of the trickery and misrepresentation practised by some of the Philhellenes: 'If Friedel is no Baron he is no worse than others: – Bellier de Launay, a dismissed Prussian petty officer who pretended to be a Colonel and a Marquis; Baron Kolbe who was certainly not a Baron; Dr Meyer, a pharmacist who pretended to be a physician.'[32]

35

IMPLORA PACE

*'I found too such a pretty epitaph in the Certosa
Cimitery – or rather two – one was*

> Martini Luigi
> Implora pace.

The other –

> Lucrezia Picini
> "Implora eternal quiete."

*That was all – but it appears to me that these two and
three words comprise and compress all that can be said on
the subject – and then in Italian they are absolute Music.
– They contain doubt – hope – and humility – nothing can
be more pathetic than the "implora" and the modesty of
the request – they have had enough of life – they want
nothing but rest – they implore it – and "eternal quieta" –
it is like a Greek inscription in some good old Heathen
"City of the dead". – Pray – if I am shovelled into the
Lido Church-yard – in your time – let me have the "implora
pace" and nothing else for my epitaph – I never met with
any antient or modern that pleased me a tenth part so
much.'*[1]

All the difficulties which arose at Mesolonghi Byron seems to have
dealt with calmly and effectively. He was suffering at the time

489

from strong disappointment, having fallen in love with young Loukas Chalandritsanos who did not return his love. The last poem Byron wrote shows that it was unwillingly that he gave in to so inappropriate a preoccupation at this crucial moment. He fell in love with Loukas simply because the boy was there: 'My heart always alights on the nearest perch.'

Each stanza of this last poem refers to an experience undergone by Byron in the last adventurous months of his life:

[LOVE AND DEATH.]

1.

I WATCHED thee when the foe was at our side,
    Ready to strike at him – or thee and me.
Were safety hopeless – rather than divide
    Aught with one loved save love and liberty.

2.

I watched thee on the breakers, when the rock
    Received our prow and all was storm and fear,
And bade thee cling to me through every shock;
    This arm would be thy bark, or breast thy bier.

3.

I watched thee when the fever glazed thine eyes,
    Yielding my couch and stretched me on the ground
When overworn with watching, ne'er to rise
    From thence if thou an early grave hadst found.

4.

The earthquake came, and rocked the quivering wall,
    And men and nature reeled as if with wine.
Whom did I seek around the tottering hall?
    For thee. Whose safety first provide for? Thine.

5.

And when convulsive throes denied my breath
    The faintest utterance to my fading thought,
To thee – to thee – e'en in the gasp of death
    My spirit turned, oh! oftener than it ought.

6.

Thus much and more; and yet thou lov'st me not,
    And never wilt! Love dwells not in our will.
Nor can I blame thee, though it be my lot

490

To strongly, wrongly, vainly love thee still.[2]

An earlier poem, written on 22 January 1824, his thirty-sixth birthday, had been an exhortation to himself to give up thoughts of love and think only of Greece and its heroic struggle for freedom. David Brewer produces evidence of Greek heroism, pointing out that there were, from the outset 'gleams of the heroic idealism that was to attract so many foreign Philhellenes to the cause.'[3] He relates how a young officer of the Sacred Battalion (which was slaughtered during the early revolt on the Danube) wrote of marching with his bare feet cut to pieces and living on wild fruit: 'But my life is a delight ... for the first time at the head of free men ... who give me the sweet name of brother.'[4] This was the spirit which brought so many Philhellenes to Greece.

When Ibrahim Pasha ordered the Egyptian troops he had brought into the Peloponnese to destroy the trees – olive, fig and mulberry – David Brewer tells us that Kolokotronis replied, '...you cannot dig up and carry off the earth which nourished them ... Never hope that you will make our earth your own.' He adds: 'It was this spirit which had animated the Greeks at their best throughout the war and the many difficulties, some self-imposed, that they had endured. They might now be dependent on others for success, but it was their own tenacity which had kept the flame of freedom alight for six years, until more powerful allies came to their aid.'[5]

But this help came later. By then Byron was dead.

1.

'T is time this heart should be unmoved,
  Since others it hath ceased to move:
Yet, though I cannot be beloved,
  Still let me love!

2.

My days are in the yellow leaf;
  The flowers and fruits of Love are gone;
The worm, the canker, and the grief
  Are mine alone!

3.

The fire that on my bosom preys
  Is lone as some Volcanic isle;

491

No torch is kindled at its blaze –
    A funeral pile.

4.

The hope, the fear, the jealous care,
    The exalted portion of the pain
And power of love, I cannot share,
    But wear the chain.

5.

But 't is not *thus* – and 't is not *here* –
    Such thoughts should shake my soul, nor now,
Where Glory decks the hero's bier,
    Or binds his brow.

6.

The Sword, the Banner, and the Field,
    Glory and Greece, around me see!
The Spartan, borne upon his shield,
    Was not more free.

7.

Awake! (not Greece – she is awake)
    Awake, my spirit! Think through whom
Thy life-blood tracks its parent lake.
    And then strike home!

8.

Tread those reviving passions down,
    Unworthy manhood! – unto thee
Indifferent should the smile or frown
    Of Beauty be.

9.

If thou regret'st thy youth, *why live?*
    The land of honourable death
Is here: – up to the Field, and give
    Away thy breath!

10.

Seek out – less often sought than found –
    A soldier's grave, for thee the best;
Then look around, and choose thy ground,
    And take thy Rest.[6]

In February Byron fell into the arms of his companions in a fit which appeared to be epileptic. In a valuable article on 'The Last Illness of Lord Byron', Raymond Mills suggests the possibility that the fit '... may have been post-traumatic following the blow on the head which he received when crossing the island of Ithaca.'[7]

On the next day the doctors insisted on bleeding Byron, but they applied the leeches too close to the temporal artery and had great difficulty in stopping the flow of blood. His recovery was slow and though he was soon out riding again he suffered from weakness and depression and occasional episodes of vertigo.

During these last weeks of his life Bryon had other preoccupations besides Loukas. He was pleased at receiving good news of Ada's health from Augusta and told his sister that this news and other letters from England '... were of great comfort, and I wanted some – having been recently unwell – but am now much better – so that you need not be alarmed.'[8]

Among the letters which arrived for Byron on 9 April was one from Hobhouse offering him high praise:

Nothing can be more serviceable to the Cause than all you have done – Everybody is more than pleased and content. – As for myself, I only trust that the great sacrifices which you have made may contribute (which I have no doubt they will) to the final success of the great cause – This will indeed be doing something worth living for – and will make your name and character stand far above those of any contemporay.[9]

This letter must have consoled Byron for a tactless, earlier letter from Moore which mentioned rumours in London that, far from joining in the hardships of the Greek soldiers, he was lingering in Cephalonia and writing further Cantos of *Don Juan*. Moore was devastated after Byron's death to find how his own last letter to his friend had wounded Byron.

Hearing of Byron's sudden illness, Samuel Barff offered him his country house at Zante and invited him to withdraw from Mesolonghi for a period of recuperation. Byron was grateful for the offer – '... but I cannot quit Greece while there is a Chance of my being of any (even *supposed*) utility ... I am at the same time aware of the difficulties – and dissensions – and defects of the Greeks themselves – but allowances must be made for them by all reasonable people.'[10] (Byron to Samuel Barff, Mesolonghi, 10 March 1824)

Moore would have been even more unhappy if he had known

that Byron had refused the invitation from Samuel Barff to recuperate for a while at his house at Zante. Byron's pride would have revolted from such a withdrawal, knowing that it would give credibility to the rumours Moore had mentioned. So Moore's tactlessness may have contributed to Byron's death.

On 22 March he was writing to Barff again, informing him that it seemed possible that the Greek deputies had at last obtained the loan from London:

> In a few days – Prince Mavrocordato and myself – with a considerable escort intend to proceed to Salona at the request of Ulysses and the Chiefs of Eastern Greece – to concert if possible a plan of Union between Western and Eastern Greece – and to take measures offensive and defensive for the ensuing Campaign ... Excuse haste. – It is late – and I have been several hours on horseback – in a country so miry after the rains – that every hundred yards brings you to a brook or a ditch – of whose depth – width – colour – and contents – both my horses and their riders have brought away many tokens.[11]
>
> (Byron to Samuel Barff, Mesolonghi, 22 March 1824)

The conditions described in this letter were soon to make the journey to Salona impossible, all the roads being flooded.

On 17 March Byron wrote his last letter to Teresa – a short note added to a letter written to her by her brother, Pierino:

> My dearest T. – the Spring is come – I have seen a Swallow today – and it was time ... We are all very well, which will I hope keep up your hopes and Spirits ... Salute Corta and his lady – and Papa and Olimpia, and Giulia and Laurina and believe me – dearest T.T.A.A. – in E.[12]
>
> (Byron to Teresa Guiccioli, Mesolonghi, 17 March 1824)

Byron was reluctant to add to Teresa's misery by mentioning his illness but on 10 March he had written to Dr James Kennedy admitting that he was not sanguine about his health. Kennedy was a young clergyman who had tried in Cephalonia to convert him to Methodism; Byron and some of his officer friends would foregather every so often to discuss religion with Kennedy. Some of those present commented that Byron seemed more familiar with the Bible than Kennedy, but he listened patiently. Now he wrote:

> My Dear Doctor, – I have to thank you for your two very kind letters,

both received at the same time, and one long after its date. I am not unaware of the precarious state of my health, nor am, nor have been, deceived on that subject. But it is proper that I should remain in Greece; and it were better to die doing something than nothing. My presence here has been supposed so far useful as to have prevented confusion from becoming worse confounded, at least for the present. Should I become, or be deemed useless or superfluous, I am ready to retire; but in the interim I am not to consider personal consequences; the rest is in the hands of Providence, – as indeed are all things. I shall, however, observe your instructions, and indeed did so, as far as regards abstinence, for some time past...[13]

(To James Kennedy, Mesolonghi, 14 March 1824)

In spite of the weather Byron persisted in his daily rides. On the ninth of April he and his companions were soaked to the skin when out riding and chilled to the bone as they returned home in an open boat. That evening Byron fell ill of a fever with rheumatic pains. He insisted on riding again the next day and by the eleventh was so ill that Parry made arrangements to take him by boat to Zante. By the 13th when the boat was ready to sail, the sirocco had made the weather too stormy for them to set out.

Young Doctor Bruno, not long out of the University of Genoa, was extremely nervous about the reponsibility he bore for the treatment of so famous a patient, whose survival seemed essential for the welfare of Greece. He called in a colleague who had travelled to the aid of the Greeks under the aegis of the London Greek Committee. Dr Julius Millingen had studied medicine at Edinburgh but was not much more experienced than Bruno.

From the beginning, Byron resisted every effort to bleed him until they threatened him with brain damage. He then gave in. According to Raymond Mills these inexperienced and panicky young doctors took 2.5 litres of blood from the patient over the next twenty-four hours and he calculates that this amounted to 43% of his total blood volume. 'According to Professor John Cash of the Scottish Blood Transfusion Service, this loss would cause hypovolaemia, i.e. an abnormally decreased volume of fluid which would have been enough to kill him.'[14]

According to Raymond Mills Byron's fever could have been caused by any one of a number of conditions. Mesolonghi was a breeding place for parasites which cause malaria (mosquitoes being active from March to April). Another danger was the tick-borne

Mediterranean fever transmitted by the common dog tick. Byron spent much time playing with his Newfoundland dog, Lyon. The house in which he lived was not particularly salubrious since it had no drains and slops were tossed into the lagoon.

Raymond Mills concludes that, while we shall never know what the fever was which brought on the last illness:

'On the basis of the evidence it would seem probable that over-bleeding should be regarded as the proximate cause of death, together with an infection, probably Mediterranean fever. Whether Byron would have survived if the massive bleedings, purgings and blisterings had not been carried out can only be conjectured ... Had Byron been left well and truly alone by the doctors, the outcome may well have been different.'[15]

David Brewer points out that ... three other possibilities which have been suggested – syphilis, uraemic poisoning and cerebral malaria – are ruled out for a single reason – they are all relentlessly progressive whereas Byron was physically active and mentally alert for long periods between earlier attacks and for periods during his final fatal illness.[16]

The circumstances of Byron's death were detailed by Parry:

His habitation was weather-tight, but that was nearly all the comfort his deplorable room afforded. He was my protector and benefactor, and I could not see him, whom I knew to have been so differently brought up, thus perishing, far from his home, far from the comforts due to his rank and situation, far too from every fond and affectionate heart; without a feeling of deep sorrow ... The persistent *sirroco* was blowing a hurricane, and the rain was falling with almost tropical violence. In our apartment was the calm of approaching death.[17]

Parry and Tita were the only ones among Byron's companions with the courage to watch by his bedside. Fletcher and Gamba were overcome with grief.

At first no-one believed Byron's illness to be dangerous. By the time this was understood he was unable to utter any coherent messages for Augusta, Lady Byron, his daughter, his friends. Accounts of the course of his illness differ; even Millingen and Bruno producing conflicting stories. It is clear that he became delirious and suffered pain, headaches and fits of shivering.

News of the gravity of Byron's condition spread throughout Mesolonghi and the people were asked to maintain silence near

496

the house where he lay. On Easter Sunday, 18 April, Parry was asked to march the soldiers outside the boundaries of the town where they could celebrate Easter in their usual way by letting off firearms without disturbing Byron.

At 6.00 p.m. on that day Byron said, 'I want to sleep now.' He never woke again. At 6.15 p.m. on 19 April he opened his eyes, closed them, and died.

Parry wrote: 'At the very time Lord Byron died there was one of the most awful thunderstorms I ever witnessed. The lightning was terrific. The Greeks, who are very superstitious ... immediately exclaimed "The great man is gone".'

Patrick Leigh Fermor describes the effect of Byron's death on the Greek nation:

The news of his death as it spread through the dismal lanes of Mesolonghi in that rainy and thundery dusk, scattered consternation. His name, famous already, soared like a rocket into the Greek firmament and lodged there as a fixed star whose radiance grows brighter as the years pass. 'O Vyron', 'Lordos Vyronos' ... is Greek property now. Thousands of children are baptised by his name and his face is as familiar as any hero's in ancient or modern Greece – Every English traveller, however humble or unimpressive, and whether he wants it or not, is the beneficiary of some reflected fragment of this glory.[18]

36

'OUR SECOND ENGLISH EPIC'

It is in a way, Byron's A la Recherche du Temps Perdu.[1]
Anne Barton

'And if I laugh at any mortal thing,
'Tis that I may not weep;'[2]
(From *Don Juan*, Canto IV)

Don Juan has been described as Byron's *Remembrance of Things Past*. So perhaps an account of his masterpiece belongs here at the end of this book, witness to what the world lost when Byron died leaving the poem unfinished.

It was written during the following periods as set out by Jerome McGann in Volume V of the *Complete Poetical Works*:

Cantos I and II (1818–19)
Cantos III to V (1821)

(Teresa Guiccioli then persuaded Byron to abandon the poem, but later relented.)

Cantos VI to VIII (1823)
Cantos IX to XI (1823)
Cantos XII to XIV (1823)
Cantos XV to XVI (1824)
Canto XVII was written in 1823

Perhaps the most revealing remark made by Byron on the subject of *Don Juan* is his explanation, in a letter to Douglas Kinnaird (April 1823) that 'I mean it for a poetical Tristram Shandy, or

499

Montaigne's *Essays* with a story for a hinge.'[3] This comparison by Byron is extraordinarily interesting as a pointer to his intentions in writing *Don Juan*. He clearly sees it, like the *Essays*, as a compendium of wisdom and practical advice for living, as well as matter for laughter, wit and satire, although, as with Montaigne, the writer is not preaching to others, but addressing himself.

Byron's remarks about the poem, both in letters to his friends and in the work itself, are illuminating:

I have finished the First Canto (a long one of about 180 octaves) of a poem in the manner of *Beppo*. It is called *Don Juan*.[4]
(To Thomas Moore, Venice, 19 September 1818)

CC.
My poem's epic, and is meant to be
    Divided in twelve books; each book containing,
With Love, and War, a heavy gale at sea,
    A list of ships, and captains, and kings reigning,
New characters; the episodes are three:
    A panoramic view of Hell's in training,
After the style of Virgil and of Homer,
So that my name of Epic's no misnomer.

CCI.
All these things will be specified in time,
    With strict regard to Aristotle's rules,
The *Vade Mecum* of the true sublime,
    Which makes so many poets, and some fools:
Prose poets like blank-verse, I'm fond of rhyme,
    Good workmen never quarrel with their tools;
I've got new mythological machinery,
And very handsome supernatural scenery.[5]

*   *   *

I.
O LOVE! O Glory! what are ye who fly
    Around us ever, rarely to alight?
There's not a meteor in the polar sky
    Of such transcendent and more fleeting flight.
Chill, and chained to cold earth, we lift on high
    Our eyes in search of either lovely light;
A thousand and a thousand colours they
Assume, then leave us on our freezing way.

500

II.

And such as they are, such my present tale is,
    A nondescript and ever-varying rhyme,
A versified Aurora Borealis,
    Which flashes o'er a waste and icy clime.
When we know what all are, we must bewail us,
    But ne'ertheless I hope it is no crime
To laugh at *all* things – for I wish to know
What, after *all*, are *all* things – but a *show?*[6]

(*Don Juan*, Canto I)

Byron was hurt when Gifford, Crabbe, Kinnaird, Murray – and even Hobhouse – protested that *Don Juan* was immoral. He wrote sharply to John Murray:

I have written to you several letters – some with additions – & some upon the subject of the poem itself which my cursed puritanical committee have protested against publishing – but we will circumvent them on that point in the end. I have not yet begun to copy out the second Canto – which is finished; – from natural laziness – and the discouragement of the milk & water they have thrown upon the first. – I say all this to them as to you – that is for *you* to say to *them* – for I will have nothing underhand. – If they had told me the poetry was bad – I would have acquiesced – but they say the contrary – & then talk to me about morality – the first time I ever heard the word from any body who was not a rascal that used it for a purpose. – I maintain that it is the most moral of poems – but if people won't discover the moral that is their fault not mine. – I have already written to beg that in any case you will print *fifty* for private distribution. I will send you the list of persons to whom it is to be sent afterwards. –[7]

(Venice, 1 February 1819)

Byron requested Douglas Kinnaird to advise Murray how to circumvent the pirate editions which were now in the habit of appearing almost as soon as his works were published:

I have nearly completed three more Cantos of D. Juan – which will perhaps be ready by November or sooner. – If Murray publishes them he ought to print at the same time very small and cheap editions of the same price and size as the pirates' to anticipate and neutralize them – Pray tell him so.[8]

(To Douglas Kinnaird, Pisa, 24 July 1822)

Byron's fame was such that booksellers, printers and copyists were vying with each other to produce pirate editions and direct some of the wealth each new poem generated, into their own pockets. Byron was clearly aware of this but he either did not know or did not care that the worst of the pirates was Cawthorn, the publisher of *English Bards and Scotch Reviewers*. William St Clair reveals how Cawthorn enriched himself at Byron's expense:

[Byron] refused Cawthorn permission to print a fifth edition [of *English Bards*] and ordered the poem to be suppressed. The price of second-hand copies soared. Manuscript copies written by professional copyists appeared on the market, carefully reproducing the title-page, the preface, and, even the printers' imprint in expensive morocco notebooks. When an Irish publisher put on sale a printed pirated edition Cawthorn took legal proceedings to have him stopped. But the real pirate was Cawthorn himself. Denied permission to print a fifth edition he went on printing third and fourth editions. About twenty such fakes have been identified, all claiming on the title-page to have been issued in 1810 or 1811 but all manufactured from paper on which the manufacturing dates of 1812, 1815, 1816, 1817 and 1819 are visible in the watermark. Cawthorn probably sold twenty thousand more copies of *English Bards* than he was allowed to by his contracts, all without payment to the author.[9]

Later Byron decided to leave John Murray and to have his works published by John Hunt. Some parts of *Don Juan* were so outspoken that Anne Barton observes that it was less surprising that Murray refused to publish than that John Hunt dared to do so. Murray told Byron that he would not publish Cantos IX and X '...if you gave me your title, estates and genius.' Byron took up the defence of *Don Juan* in the Preface of Cantos VI, VII and VIII:

With regard to the objections which have been made on another score to the already published cantos of this poem, I shall content myself with two quotations from Voltaire:- '*La pudeur s'est enfuite des coeurs, et s'est refugiée sur les lèvres.*' ... '*Plus les moeurs sont dépravés, plus les expressions deviennent mesurées, on croit regagner en language ce qu'on a perdu en vertu.*'

'Nowadays we only pay lip service to decency. The more shamelessly we behave, the more circumspect are we in what we say, deluding ourselves that we can win back with empty words the virtue we have abandoned.'

This is the real fact, as applicable to the degraded and hypocritical mass which leavens the present English generation, and is the only answer they deserve. The hackneyed and lavished title of Blasphemer

502

– which, with Radical, Liberal, Jacobin, Reformer, etc., are the changes which the hirelings are daily ringing in the ears of those who will listen – should be welcome to all who recollect on *whom* it was originally bestowed. Socrates and Jesus Christ were put to death publicly as *blasphemers*, and so have been and may be many who dare to oppose the most notorious abuses of the name of God and the mind of man. But persecution is not refutation, nor even triumph: the 'wretched infidel,' as he is called, is probably happier in his prison than the proudest of his assailants. With his opinions I have nothing to do – they may be right or wrong – but he has suffered for them, and that very suffering for conscience' sake will make more proselytes to deism than the example of heterodox Prelates to Christianity, suicidal statesmen to oppression, or overpensioned homicides to the impious alliance which insults the world with the name of 'Holy!' I have no wish to trample on the dishonoured or the dead; but it would be well if the adherents to the classes from whence these persons sprung should abate a little of the *cant* which is the crying sin of this double-dealing and false-speaking time of selfish spoilers, and – but enough for the present.[10]

In November 1822 *The Examiner* (which was also published by John Hunt) came out with a blistering attack on the critics of *Don Juan*:

A Letter called Canting Slander addressed to the Reverend W.B. Colyer.

No work of modern days has been so cried out against as immoral and indecent as *Don Juan* and you see the consequences; – the critics one and all shake their heads at it, grave old gentlemen turn up their eyes and sigh out a lamentation over the depravity of the age; all ladies of character blush at its very mention; no writer has been found hardy enough to hint at a word in defence or palliation – yet, lamentable to relate, everybody reads it. Twenty thousand copies of the cheap editions have been sold, fifteen of which may be safely placed to the account of such prudent moralists as you and the vice suppressors and such solemn critics as those of *My Grandmother's Review*. You cavil at the jokes and irony of *Don Juan* as if you had found them in a sermon. But what right have you to comment on a satirical poem as if the author intended a sermon on the whole duty of man?

[Byron took much the same attitude when he refused to alter 'impious passages' in *Cain* at the request of John Murray, protesting that he could not make Lucifer talk like the Bishop of Lincoln.]

503

...the puritans and the hypocrites are seriously aiming to make their fellow creatures as miserable and desponding in this world as they say most of us will be in the next; while the object of Lord Byron and the wits is to add to our stock of innocent laughter and amusement and to help to make us merry and wise.[11]

Don Juan did not rival *Childe Harold* in popularity with sentimental young women but brought Byron fan-mail which amused him:

I have also had a love letter from *Pimlico* from a lady whom I never saw in my life – but who hath fallen in love with me for having written *Don Juan!* – I suppose that she is either mad or *nau*[ghty]. – do you remember *Constantia and Echo* – and *la Swissesse* – and all my other inamorate – when I was 'gentle and juvenile – curly and gay'.[12]

(To Augusta Leigh, Albaro, Genoa, 7 November 1822)

He wrote to Douglas Kinnaird:

...as to Don Juan – confess – confess – you dog and be candid – that it is the sublime of that there sort of writing – it may be bawdy – but is it not good English? – It may be profligate – but – is it not *life* – Could any man have written it – who has not lived in the world? – and tooled in a post-chaise? in a hackney coach? in a Gondola? against a wall? in a court carriage? in a vis à vis? – on a table? – and under it?[13]

He told Richard Hoppner:

There has been an eleventh commandment to the women not to read it – and what is still more extraordinary they seem not to have broken it. – But that can be of little import to them poor things – for the reading or non-reading a book – will never keep down a single petticoat.[14]

(29 October 1819)

Countess Guiccioli was shocked on reading *Don Juan* and Byron explained the reason:

The truth is that *it is too true* – and the women hate everything which strips off the tinsel of *Sentiment* – & they are right – or it would rob them of their weapons. – I never knew a woman who did not hate *De Grammont's memoirs* – for the same reason. – Even Lady Oxford used to abuse them.[15]

(To John Murray, Ravenna, 12 October 1820)

Shelley was overwhelmed with admiration: 'He has read to me one of the unpublished cantos of Don Juan which is astonishingly fine – it sets him not above but far above all the poets of the day: every word has the stamp of immortality.'[16] (To Mary Shelley, 10 August 1821)

And again:

It is a poem totally of its own species and my wonder and delight at the grace of the composition no less than the free and grand vigour of the conception of it perpetually increase – nothing has ever been written like it in English – nor – will there be; without carrying upon it the mark of a secondary and borrowed light.[17]

(To Byron, 21 October 1821)

J.G. Lockhart praised *Don Juan* in an anonymous *Letter to Lord Byron* published in *John Bull* (April/May 1821):

Your *Don Juan* again, is written strongly, lasciviously, fiercely, laughingly – every body sees in a moment that nobody could have written it but a man of the first order both in genius and in dissipation; – a real master of all his tools – a profligate, pernicious, irresistable, charming Devil...

... the charming *style* of *Don Juan*, which is entirely and inimitably your own – the sweet, fiery, rapid, easy – beautifully easy, anti-humbug style of *Don Juan*. Ten stanzas of it are worth all your *Manfred* – and yet your *Manfred* is a noble poem too in its way;...

In my humble opinion, there is very little in the literature of the present day that will really stand the test of half a century, except the *Scotch* novels of Sir Walter Scott and *Don Juan. They* will do so because they are written with perfect facility and nature – because their materials are all drawn from nature – in other words, because they are neither made up of cant, like Wordsworth and Shelley, nor of humbug like *Childe Harold*...[18]

The following extracts are sufficient to illustrate the merits of this remarkable achievement.

From Canto XI – the 'Ubi sunt' passage:

LXXVI.
'Where is the World?' cries Young, 'at *eighty*' – 'Where
  The World in which a man was born?' Alas!
Where is the world of *eight* years past? '*T was there* –
  I look for it – 't is gone, a globe of glass!
Cracked, shivered, vanished, scarcely gazed on, ere

505

A silent change dissolves the glittering mass.
Statesmen, Chiefs, Orators, Queens, Patriots, Kings,
And Dandies – all are gone on the Wind's wings.

LXXVII.

Where is Napoleon the Grand? God knows!
  Where little Castlereagh? The devil can tell!
Where Grattan, Curran, Sheridan – all those
  Who bound the Bar or Senate in their spell?
Where is the unhappy Queen, with all her woes?
  And where the Daughter, whom the Isles love well?
Where are those martyred saints the Five per Cents?
And where – oh, where the devil are the Rents?

LXXVIII.

Where's Brummell? Dished. Where's Long
  Pole Wellesley? Diddled.
Where's Whitbread? Romilly? Where's.
  George the Third?
Where is his will? (That's not so soon unriddled.)
  And where is 'Fum' the Fourth, our 'royal bird'?
Gone down, it seems, to Scotland to be fiddled
  Unto by Sawney's violin, we have, heard:
'Caw me, caw thee' – for six months hath been hatching,
This scene of royal itch and loyal scratching.

LXXIX.

Where is Lord This? And where my Lady That?
  The Honourable Mistresses and Misses?
Some laid aside like an old Opera hat,
  Married, unmarried, and remarried: (this is
An evolution oft performed of late).
  Where are the Dublin shouts – and London hisses?
Where are the Grenvilles? Turned as usual. Where
My friends the Whigs? Exactly where they were.

LXXX.

Where are the Lady Carolines and Franceses?
  Divorced or doing thereanent. Ye annals
So brilliant, where the list of routs and dances is, –
  Thou Morning Post, sole record of the panels
Broken in carriages, and all the phantasies
  Of fashion, – say what streams now fill those channels?
Some die, some fly, some languish on the Continent,
Because the times have hardly left them *one* tenant.

LXXXI.

Some who once set their caps at cautious dukes,
   Have taken up at length with younger brothers:
Some heiresses have bit at sharpers' hooks:
   Some maids have been made wives, some merely mothers:
Others have lost their fresh and fairy looks:
   In short, the list of alterations bothers.
There's little strange in this, but something strange is
The unusual quickness of these common changes.

LXXXII.

Talk not of seventy years as age; in seven
   I have seen more changes, down from monarchs to
The humblest individuals under Heaven,
   Than might suffice a moderate century through.
I knew that nought was lasting, but now even
   Change grows too changeable, without being new:
Nought's permanent among the human race,
Except the Whigs *not* getting into place.

LXXXIII.

I have seen Napoleon, who seemed quite a Jupiter,
   Shrink to a Saturn. I have seen a Duke
(No matter which) turn politician stupider,
   If that can well be, than his wooden look.
But it is time that I should hoist my 'blue Peter,'
   And sail for a new theme: – I have seen – and shook
To see it – the King hissed, and then caressed;
But don't pretend to settle which was best.

LXXXIV.

I have seen the Landholders without a rap –
   I have seen Joanna Southcote – I have seen
The House of Commons turned to a tax-trap –
   I have seen that sad affair of the late Queen
I have seen crowns worn instead of a fool's cap –
   I have seen a Congress doing all that's mean –
I have seen some nations, like o'erloaded asses,
Kick off their burthens – meaning the high classes.

LXXXV.

I have seen small poets, and great prosers, and
   Interminable – *not eternal* – speakers –
I have seen the funds at war with house and land –
   I have seen the country gentlemen turn squeakers –

507

I have seen the people ridden o'er like sand
　By slaves on horseback – I have seen malt liquors
Exchanged for 'thin potations' by John Bull –
I have seen John half detect himself a fool. –

LXXXVI.

But *'carpe diem,'* Juan, *'carpe, carpe!'*
　To-morrow sees another race as gay
And transient, and devoured by the same harpy.
　'Life's a poor player,' – then 'play out the play,
Ye villains!' and above all keep a sharp eye
　Much less on what you do than what you say:
Be hypocritical, be cautious, be
Not what you *seem,* but always what you *see.*[19]

From Canto I:

CCXII.

'Non ego hoc ferrem calidus juventà
　Consule Planco,' Horace said, and so
Say I; by which quotation there is meant a
　Hint that some six or seven good years ago
(Long ere I dreamt of dating from the Brenta)
　I was most ready to return a blow,
And would not brook at all this sort of thing
In my hot youth – when George the Third was King.

CCXIII.

But now at thirty years my hair is grey –
　(I wonder what it will be like at forty?
I thought of a peruke the other day –)
　My heart is not much greener; and, in short, I
Have squandered my whole summer while 't was May,
　And feel no more the spirit to retort; I
Have spent my life, both interest and principal,
And deem not, what I deemed – my soul invincible.

CCXIV.

No more – no more – Oh! never more on me
　The freshness of the heart can fall like dew,
Which out of all the lovely things we see
　Extracts emotions beautiful and new,
Hived in our bosoms like the bag o' the bee.
　Think'st thou the honey with those objects grew?
Alas! 't was not in them, but in thy power
To double even the sweetness of a flower.

508

CCXV.

No more – no more – Oh! never more, my heart,
    Canst thou be my sole world, my universe!
Once all in all, but now a thing apart,
    Thou canst not be my blessing or my curse:
The illusion's gone for ever, and thou art
    Insensible, I trust, but none the worse,
And in thy stead I've got a deal of judgment,
Though Heaven knows how it ever found a lodgment.

CCXVI.

My days of love are over; me no more
    The charms of maid, wife, and still less of widow,
Can make the fool of which they made before, –
    In short, I must not lead the life I did do;
The credulous hope of mutual minds is o'er,
    The copious use of claret is forbid too,
So for a good old-gentlemanly vice,
I think I must take up with avarice.

CCXVII.

Ambition was my idol, which was broken
    Before the shrines of Sorrow, and of Pleasure;
And the two last have left me many a token
    O'er which reflection may be made at leisure:
Now, like Friar Bacon's Brazen Head, I've spoken,
    'Time is, Time was, Time's past:' – a chymic treasure
Is glittering Youth, which I have spent betimes –
My heart in passion, and my head on rhymes.

*   *   *

CCXX.

But I, being fond of true philosophy,
    Say very often to myself, 'Alas!
All things that have been born were born to die,
    And flesh (which Death mows down to hay) is grass'
You've passed your youth not so unpleasantly,
    And if you had it o'er again – 't would pass –
So thank your stars that matters are no worse,
And read your Bible, sir, and mind your purse.'[20]

From Canto I – unincorporated stanza:

I WOULD to Heaven that I were so much clay,
    As I am blood, bone, marrow, passion, feeling –

509

Because at least the past were passed away,
    And for the future – (but I write this reeling,
Having got drunk exceedingly to-day,
    So that I seem to stand upon the ceiling)
I say – the future is a serious matter –
And so – for God's sake – hock and soda-water![21]

From Canto II:

IV

Well – well; the World must turn upon its axis,
    And all Mankind turn with it, heads or tails,
And live and die, make love and pay our taxes,
    And as the veering wind shifts, shift our sails;
The King commands us, and the Doctor quacks us,
    The Priest instructs, and so our life exhales,
A little breath, love, wine, ambition, fame,
Fighting, devotion, dust, – perhaps a name.[22]

From Canto VII:

III.

They accuse me – *Me* – the present writer of
    The present poem – of – I know not what –
A tendency to under-rate and scoff
    At human power and virtue, and all that;
And this they say in language rather rough.
    Good God! I wonder what they would be at!
I say no more than hath been said in Dante's
Verse, and by Solomon and by Cervantes;

IV.

By Swift, by Machiavel, by Rochefoucault,
    By Fénélon, by Luther, and by Plato;
By Tillotson, and Wesley, and Rousseau,
    Who knew this life was not worth a potato.
'T is not their fault, nor mine, if this be so, –
    For my part, I pretend not to be Cato,
Nor even Diogenes. – We live and die,
But which is best, *you* know no more than I.

V.

Socrates said, our only knowledge was
    'To know that nothing could be known;' a pleasant
Science enough, which levels to an ass

Each man of wisdom, future, past, or present.
Newton (that proverb of the mind), alas!
    Declared, with all his grand discoveries recent,
That he himself felt only 'like a youth
Picking up shells by the great ocean – Truth.'

VI.

Ecclesiastes said, 'that all is vanity' –
    Most modern preachers say the same, or show it
By their examples of true Christianity:
    In short, all know, or very soon may know it;
And in this scene of all-confessed inanity,
    By Saint, by Sage, by Preacher, and by Poet,
Must I restrain me, through the fear of strife,
From holding up the nothingness of Life?[23]

From Canto VIII:

LXXXVIII.

The bayonet pierces and the sabre cleaves,
    And human lives are lavished everywhere,
As the year closing whirls the scarlet leaves
    When the stripped forest bows to the bleak air,
And groans; and thus the peopled city grieves,
    Shorn of its best and loveliest, and left bare;
But still it falls in vast and awful splinters,
As oaks blown down with all their thousand winters.[24]

From Canto X:

XXV.

And Death, the Sovereign's Sovereign, though the great
    Gracchus of all mortality, who levels,
With his *Agrarian* laws, the high estate
    Of him who feasts, and fights, and roars, and revels,
To one small grass-grown patch (which must await
    Corruption for its crop) with the poor devils
Who never had a foot of land till now, –
Death's a reformer – all men must allow.[25]

*   *   *

LXXXII,

A mighty mass of brick, and smoke, and shipping,
    Dirty and dusky, but as wide as eye
Could reach, with here and there a sail just skipping

511

In sight, then lost amidst the forestry
Of masts; a wilderness of steeples peeping
   On tiptoe through their sea-coal canopy;
A huge, dun Cupola, like a foolscap crown
On a fool's head – and there is London Town![26]

From Canto XIII:

LXVIII.

Steel Barons, molten the next generation
   To silken rows of gay and gartered Earls,
Glanced from the walls in goodly preservation;
   And lady Marys blooming into girls,
With fair long locks, had also kept their station:
   And Countesses mature in robes and pearls:
Also some beauties of Sir Peter Lely,
Whose drapery hints we may admire them freely.

LXIX.

Judges in very formidable ermine
   Were there, with brows that did not much invite
The accused to think their lordships would determine
   His cause by leaning much from might to right:
Bishops, who had not left a single sermon;
   Attorneys-general, awful to the sight,
As hinting more (unless our judgments warp us)
Of the 'Star Chamber' than of 'Habeas Corpus.'[27]

From Canto XIV:

C.

But great things spring from little: – Would you think,
   That in our youth, as dangerous a passion
As e'er brought Man and Woman to the brink
   Of ruin, rose from such a slight occasion,
As few would ever dream could form the link
   Of such a sentimental situation?
You'll never guess, I'll bet you millions, milliards –
It all sprung from a harmless game at billiards.

CI.

'T is strange, – but true; for Truth is always strange –
   Stranger than fiction: it it could be told,
How much would novels gain by the exchange!
   How differently the World would men behold!

512

How oft would Vice and Virtue places change!
   The new world would be nothing to the old,
If some Columbus of the moral seas
Would show mankind their Souls' antipodes.

CII.

What 'antres vast and deserts idle,' then,
   Would be discovered in the human soul!
What icebergs in the hearts of mighty men,
   With self-love in the centre as their Pole!
What Anthropophagi are nine of ten
   Of those who hold the kingdoms in control!
Were things but only called by their right name,
Cæsar himself would be ashamed of Fame.[28]

From Canto XV:

LX.

I say, in my slight way I may proceed
   To play upon the surface of Humanity.
I write the World, nor care if the World read,
   At least for this I cannot spare its vanity.
My Muse hath bred, and still perhaps may breed
   More foes by this same scroll: when I began it, I
Thought that it might turn out so – *now* I *know* it,
But still I am, or was, a pretty poet.[29]

LXXIII.

The simple olives, best allies of wine,
   Must I pass over in my bill of fare?
I must, although a favourite *plat* of mine
   In Spain, and Lucca, Athens, everywhere:
On them and bread 't was oft my luck to dine –
   The grass my table-cloth, in open air,
On Sunium or Hymettus, like Diogenes,
Of whom half my philosophy the progeny is.[30]

XCIX.

Between two worlds Life hovers like a star,
   'Twixt Night and Morn, upon the horizon's verge.
How little do we know that which we are!
   How less what we may be! The eternal surge
Of Time and Tide rolls on and bears afar
   Our bubbles; as the old burst, new emerge,
Lashed from the foam of ages; while the graves
Of Empires heave but like some passing waves.[31]

From Canto I:

CXXXIII.

Man's a phenomenon, one knows not what,
   And wonderful beyond all wondrous measure;
'T is pity though, in this sublime world, that
   Pleasure's a sin, and sometimes Sin's a pleasure;
Few mortals know what end they would be at,
   But whether Glory, Power, or Love, or Treasure,
The path is through perplexing ways, and when
The goal is gained, we die, you know – and then –

CXXXIV.

What then? – I do not know, no more do you –
And so goodnight.

Notes

1. *Don Juan* and its Narrator

Readers who come upon Don Juan unawares may be surprised to find that he is not the Don Juan of legend. Anne Barton enlarges on this:

> In establishing this fictional Spanish libertine, murderer and blasphemer as the hero of his poem, Byron clearly intended to tease the prigs. He perplexed them further by presenting a Don Juan who is gentle and tender-hearted, and although amorous, forever being seduced by the women rather than seducing, with none of the traits of his treacherous archetype.[1]

Anne Barton also clarifies the vexed question of the narrator:

> Byron's stance as narrator, simultaneously creator and commentator on his own creation, digressive, ruminative and wryly comic, owes much throughout to Fielding's stage-management of *Tom Jones* – another work counter-poising a naive, uncomplicated protagonist with a sophisticated, sceptical and ultimately dominant authorial presence.[2]
>
> There are various differing accounts of the narrator of which Jonathan Gross gives a brief survey.[3] His own account describes the narrator as 'gay', choosing the word as 'connoting a way of life, rather than a form of sexual practice whereas "homosexual" refers solely to a form of sexual practice.'[4]

Though Byron's narrator is clearly bi-sexual – having had affairs with women in the past – I use the term 'gay' to foreground his homo-eroticism, which precipitates some of the poem's most subversive moments. By referring to Byron's narrator as 'gay', I do not mean to imply that his sexual character is fixed. Byron's narrator changes his tone and style throughout the poem's seventeen cantos, for Byron's friends urged him to abandon the narrator's lascivious asides and autobiographical references that characterized the first cantos.[5]

This is to give too much weight to the remonstrances of Hobhouse, Kinnaird, Moore and Murray. Apart from a temporary wavering – in making the remainder of the early cantos less lascivious and improper, Byron resisted their demands: 'You shan't make canticles of my cantos. I will have none of your damned cutting and slashing.[6]

It is, as Professor Trueblood observed, Teresa Guiccioli who is responsible for the more serious tone of the later cantos. It was by her decree that Byron gave up *Don Juan* after the first cantos and it was her persuasion that moved him to change the tone of his poem when she gave him permission to resume it. Trueblood believed that insufficient acknowledgement had been given to the influence wielded by the Countess Guiccioli over *Don Juan.*[7]

I believe that Jonathan Gross's reading, illuminating as it is in many respects, pins the narrator down and makes him too specific. The narrator's language and his *double entendres* have frequent homo-erotic references, but they have heterosexual references too, as well as philosophical references and political references and every other sort of reference to the reality and the anomalies, the pains and pleasures of human existence. One must question the usefulness of calling the narrator 'gay' while admitting that his sexual character is not fixed. Surely the persona of the narrator is as many-faceted as Byron himself, and this is what constitutes the extraordinarily complex, all-embracing impact of the poem. 'All of life is in it.'[8]

M.K. Joseph explains how the narrator-device allows the 'epic satire' more scope for self-consciousness, which becomes part of the very technique of the poem. The result is 'a poem about itself': and the poem, and literature generally, must count among the poem's major themes.[9]

2. *Don Juan* as Literary Criticism

Jerome McGann explains:

Byron began *Don Juan* ... as a critique of the most significant poetic movements of his time. Too often critics have read Byron's attacks upon Wordsworth and Southey and the others, as mere personal invective, not to be seriously considered for its intellectual content. I believe this attitude is badly mistaken, and that the vexed question about the form of *Don Juan* is closely related to Byron's critical ideas about contemporary poetry ... Byron had heard Coleridge's lectures on Shakespeare, he read the *Biographia*, he knew Wordsworth's 'Prefaces', and he was familiar with Keats's early poetic manifesto 'Sleep and Poetry', where Keats rashly attacked Byron's Augustan hero. He was, in short, thoroughly familiar with contemporary aesthetic theory, not only from his own reading, but from his frequent intercourse with persons like Hunt, Shelley, and Mme de Staël.[10]

M.K. Joseph refers to the:

'... series of passages which reflect on contemporary literature and Byron's place in it. There is the sustained campaign against the Lakers, beginning with the brisk attack on Southey in the suppressed Dedication, and sustained in the "poetical commandments", and the invocation of the "shades of Pope and Dryden". The turncoat bard who sings for Juan and Haidée is a kind of super-Southey, "an eastern anti-Jacobin", and serves to introduce a quick burlesque summary of contemporary poetic styles. And Juan's encounter with English literary society and its "ten thousand living authors" prompts a survey of the present state of things.'[11]

Some of these stanzas are outrageous and some extremely witty:

CCXXII.
'Go, little Book, from this my solitude!
    I cast thee on the waters – go thy ways!
And if, as I believe, thy vein be good,
    The World will find thee after many days.'
When Southey's read, and Wordsworth understood,
    I can't help putting in my claim to praise –
The four first rhymes are Southey's every line:
For God's sake, reader! take them not for mine.[12]

McGann observes that 'Byron was never more brilliantly witty, for the first four lines are indeed, word for word, from Southey's ridiculous *Lay of the Laureate*.[13]

3. The 'Indecency' of *Don Juan*

Byron denied that Don Juan was indecent:

... [It] is as free as La Fontaine, & bitter in politics – too – the damned cant and Toryism of the day may make Murray pause ... [It did make

516

Murray pause, but Byron went on...] when I say *free* – I mean that freedom – which Ariosto – and Voltaire – Pulci – Biardo – Berni – all the best Italian & French – as well as Pope & Prior amongst the English – permitted themselves; – but no improper words or phrases; – merely some situations – which are taken from life.[14]

Anne Barton points out that some of Byron's friends saw indecencies in the poem where none existed:

In pointless indecency he had no interest at all. Byron enjoys teasing the reader, but his innuendoes, like most of the jokes in the poem, have a serious purpose. They form part of his war on hypocrisy and cant, demonstrating how false the innocence of his 'chaste reader' really is.[15]

There is very little in *Don Juan* that would be regarded as shocking in the twenty-first century. In the early nineteenth it was regarded as deeply shocking that, as Anne Barton observes, *Don Juan* insists '... from the beginning upon the naturalness, in women as well as men, of sexual desire, and upon the unhappy consequences of society's attempts to stifle it, or to regard marriage as its only outlet.'[16]

William St Clair remarks how one of the characters in Thackeray's *The Book of Snobs* carries *Don Juan* about with him. He tries to seduce a 'baronne' and claims that he only did so '... because he was given to understand by Lord Byron's *Don Juan* that making love was a very correct, healthy thing.'[17]

Anne Barton goes on to remark how dismaying to English readers in Byron's day were the stanzas on Ismail: 'Byron's merciless assault on imperialism, militarism, heroes, glory and the concern for men of rank while ordinary soldiers die unheeded ... Most of the attitudes informing the Ismail cantos now seem so transparently right.'[18]

Professor Trueblood compares the attitude of Byron, Shelley and the early Wordsworth to war with '... that of the leading British poets of the First World War – Graves, Gibson, Sassoon, Owen, and others, who portray war in all its barbarity, senselessness and futility.'[19]

In both these respects Byron is far removed from his contemporaries. He is a thoroughly modern poet. *Don Juan* was castigated by many contemporary critics. J.G. Lockhart questioned their honesty: 'Furious paragraph after furious paragraph is written against a book of which the whole knot would have been happy to club their brains together to write one stanza.'[20]

Professor Trueblood criticised contemporary reviewers for the language they used when writing of *Don Juan*: ' "gross", "grovelling", "bestial" and "degrading debauchery"; "filth" ' ... 'It is no wonder that the reviewers "refused to exemplify" such "obscenities" with quotations from the poem; to do so was impossible, for they do not exist.'[21]

'O'Doherty' in *Blackwood's Magazine* on Cantos IX, X, XI asked:

Is it more obscene than *Tom Jones*? – Is it *more* blasphemous than Voltaire's novels? In point of fact it is not within fifty miles of either of them; and as to obscenity – there is more of that in the pious Richardson's pious *Pamela* than in all the novels and poems that have been written since.[22]

4. The Bewilderment of Some Nineteenth Century Readers of *Don Juan*

In comparison with fellow-writers of his own period, Byron was cavalier in his treatment of his readers. Jane Stabler observes that, '...while popular contemporaries such as Walter Scott, Felicia Hemans, William Wordsworth and L.E.L. [Letitia Elizabeth London] perfected reassuring modes of readerly address, Byron's relationship with his public was marked by abrupt transitions and discontinuities.'[23]

Charles Donelan emphasises, by reference to some remarks by Proust, the demands made on those readers of *Don Juan* who wish to 'engage in the adventure of Byron's art':

> ...Byron engages in the 'task of creating one's true life', which Proust, one of the few guides equal to the adventure of Byron's art, identifies as 'a most tempting prospect', but one that requires 'courage of many kinds', including the courage, of one's emotions, 'for, above all, it means the abrogation of one's dearest illusions. It means giving up one's belief in the objectivity of what one has oneself elaborated.'
>
> (Marcel Proust, *Remembrance of Things Past*, trans. Kilmartin and Moncrieff, New York, Random House, 1981, Vol. 111)

Donelan adds his own comment: 'Being mistaken, for Proust as for Byron, is the first step in being correct.'[24]

5. A Recently Published Account of the Language Used by Byron in *Don Juan* by Richard Cronin

'I write the world' is Byron's proud boast (XV, 60) and he supports the claim by admitting into his poem all the words that the world uses – 14,439 according to the compilers of the concordance to the poem, a figure which indicates that *Don Juan* makes use of a more copious vocabulary than that employed in the entire poetic output of any of his contemporaries famous enough to have had their vocabularies computed.

Most obviously he writes the world by incorporating fragments of the world's languages: much Latin and some Greek, a good deal of French, some Italian, the odd Spanish phrase, a snatch of German. Even when he is unfamiliar with a language, as, for example, Turkish or Russian, he gathers traces of it from the travellers and historians that he has read.'[25]

Professor Cronin quotes Byron on the subject of gin:

> 'Where juniper expresses its best juice,
>   The poor man's sparkling substitute for riches.
> Senates and sages have condemned its use –
>   But to deny the mob a cordial, which is
> Too often all the clothing, meat or fuel
> Good government has left them, seems but cruel.

Adding:

> Byron is an opponent of prohibition, not just governmental attempts to price gin out of the reach of the poor, but the attempts of literary legislators to remove from poetry references to gin or black drop or champagne or claret or hock or soda water or even the 'pot of beer', the memory of which is enough to make an expatriate Englishman weep.'[26]

Cronin also points out Byron's extraordinary proficiency in the use of professional 'rigmaroles' – for example ... 'medical jargon, the jargon of picture-dealing, of fox-hunting, of the ring, of newspapers, naval jargon, the bitchy jargon of the green room, the diplomatic phrase and thieves' cant.'[27]

37

THE GREAT ENIGMA OF THE REALMS OF RHYME

...every page should confute, refute, and utterly abjure its predecessor.[1]

Unlike Goethe and Wordsworth, Byron refused to play the role of the sublime poet. When they were in Rome together Hobhouse persuaded him to sit for the sculptor Thorwaldsen, who announced his intention of placing a laurel wreath on the brow of the completed bust. Byron categorically rejected the idea and told Hobhouse:

> ... I won't have my head garnished like a Xmas pie with Holly – or a Cod's head and Fennel – or whatever the damned weed is they strew round it. – I wonder you should want me to be such a mountebank.
>
> (Byron to John Cam Hobhouse, [La Mira], 20 June 1817)

It may be that it was the idea of being a poet rather than a hero to which he objected in this context. The fact remains that Byron was regarded all over the world as worthy of the laurel wreath and he says himself that he hopes to have his history intertwined with that of his language.

The *Literary Gazette* had compared him with Dante:

> Both poets possess the same intensity of passion and force of thought, the same neglect of grace, the same reiteration of stroke upon stroke which produces in the aggregate the effect of sublimity, and the same power of conveying all that is horrible and grand through the medium of emotion rather than description.[3]

521

Theodore Redpath's helpful summing up of his own account of the contemporary reviews of Byron, Keats and Shelley, shows that Byron was judged to have out-stripped his fellow poets in many respects:

> Byron's work was praised incomparably more on aesthetic grounds than that of either of the other two poets. It was praised often time and again, for energy, power, spirit, freedom, boldness of thought and expression, for felicity of diction, and, indeed, prodigious mastery of language, for versatility of style, for accuracy of description, for strength of feeling, for searching knowledge of human nature, for range of sensibility, for dignity, for pathos, for tenderness, for fire, for originality, for grandeur, for wit, for power to amuse, for ease and command of versification, even for the fascination of the egotism and scorn. Byron was thought and felt to be a great creative force (which indeed he was). His genius was scarcely ever put in doubt, even by those who utterly execrated the uses he made of it.[4]

The painter Delacroix wrote that he was inspired by Byron's poetry '...to spread good fat paint thickly onto a brown or red canvas'. Certain books and certain engravings never failed to inspire him and these included 'Dante, Lamartine, Byron, Michelangelo.'[5]

Yet this poet who so inspired others was himself filled with doubts. One cannot ignore the 'mobility', the perplexities and the contradictions which distance Byron from Milton, Goethe and Wordsworth and which make him the great enigma 'of the realms of rhyme' besides being their 'grand Napoleon'.[6]

He writes:

> God knows what contradictions [this] may contain. If I am sincere with myself (but I fear one lies more to oneself than to anyone else), every page should confute, refute and utterly abjure its predecessor.[7]
>
> (Journal, 6 December 1814)

This seems not only modern, but distinctly post-modern. 'A lie', he tells us, 'is but the truth in masquerade'.[8] This central tenacious adherence to the contradictoriness of things marks Byron and is the main reason why he is admired or patronised. Many recent critics have tried to catch this diversity and sense of paradox which is everywhere in his verse and personality. For instance, Jerome McGann says of him 'that Gide's famous remark – "Je ne suis jamais, je deviens", could not be more appropriately applied than to the last Canto of *Childe Harold's Pilgrimage*.'[9]

And of the whole of that poem Vincent Newey observes that:

...a central problem of the poem to which generations of readers have set their minds: is the Pilgrim a fiction, or is he the author's real, living and suffering self? There is, of course, no answer, for the real Byron is ... invisible and fathomless, shrouded as well as expressed by his creation.[10]

Brian Nellist remarks of the *Oriental Tales* that there is almost no action in them, '...instead, action is dissolved into lyric modes, description, elegy, reflection, memory –'.[11] In the Tales, 'Byron is, as it were, composing Goldberg variations on the theme of the *Liebestod*'[12] (reminding us of Hazlitt's 'flowers strewn over the face of death'.) But Brian Nellist points out what Hazlitt missed: that there is in the tales 'a strong morality of consequence.'[13] The vitality, even the wisdom of Byron, consists not only in his sense of diversity and contrariety but also in his puzzled sense that opposite things may turn into one another or disclose deep connections.

Byron died in Greece suspecting that he had wasted his time there and would succeed in achieving nothing of value for the Greek cause. Yet David Brewer informs us that in Greece '...Byron is revered as no other foreigner and very few Greeks, and, like a Homeric hero, is accorded an honorific standard epithet...' translated as '...a great and good man.'[14]

When she became engaged to Lord Byron Annabella Milbanke proclaimed to her friends that he was the best of men – kind to his servants, generous to the poor and always ready to console the unhappy. Less than two years later, she had convinced herself that there was no secret good even at the bottom of his heart. Balanced views of Byron are hard to find. You tend to be either against or for him.

Sir Walter Scott, one of the more balanced of Byron's admirers, had deplored the foolish contempt for public opinion which had contributed to the general misunderstanding of the character of a man of 'real goodness of heart and the kindest and best feelings.'[15]

E.M. Butler tried to explain this absence of balance in response to Byron by suggesting that:

[Byron] had no mind to play the lion after his disaster and rarely (if ever) uttered the lion's roar. The 'puissant and splendid personality'

523

displayed in his works was so well cloaked by frivolity and persiflage in daily life that it escaped the notice of the Medwins, the Hunts, the Lady Blessingtons and the Trelawnys of this world.[16]

But although there were many who rushed into print after Byron's death to flaunt their own egos or augment their own bank balances, and others who were as prejudiced as the Reverend John Styles (who, as we have remarked, had preached a sermon in Holland Chapel, Kennington, describing Byron as a 'denaturalised human being who, having drained the cup of sin to its bitterest dregs, is resolved to show that he is no longer human, even in his frailties, but a cool, unconcerned fiend...')[17] there were tributes to Byron after his death from people unaffected by superstition, prejudice, literary ambition, greed, affectation or envy. One of the most heartfelt came from James Hogg, the Ettrick shepherd:

I canna bide to think that Byron's dead. There's a powerful mind swallowed up somewhere – Gone! and gone so young! – and maybe on the very threshold of his truest glory, both as a man and as a poet. It makes me wae; wae to think o't.[18]

ABBREVIATIONS

CPW
Lord Byron, The Complete Poetical Works, ed. Jerome J. McGann (Oxford at the Clarendon Press, 1980–93).

PWB
The Poetical Works of Lord Byron, revised Edn, ed. Ernest Hartley Coleridge (London: John Murray, 1903), 7 volumes.

BLJ
Byron's Letters and Journals, ed. Leslie A. Marchand (London: John Murray, 1973–97), 13 volumes.

Prothero
The Works of Lord Byron: The Letters and Journals, ed. Rowland E. Prothero (London: John Murray, 1898), 6 volumes.

Moore
Moore, Thomas, *Letters and Journals of Lord Byron with Notices of His Life* (London: John Murray, 1832; repr. 1932).

Recollections
Lord Broughton
Recollections of a Long Life: Lord Broughton, ed. Lady Dorchester [his daughter] (London: John Murray, 1902), 2 volumes.

REFERENCES – PART ONE

Epigraph

1. Byron's Letter to John Murray Esqre, 1821. Prothero Vol. V, p. 559.
2. *Byron the Poet* by M.K. Joseph, Victor Gollancz, London 1964, pp. 93–4. Reproduced by kind permission of the Orion Publishing Group.
3. *Byron the Erotic Liberal* by Jonathan David Gross, Rowman and Littlefield, 2001, p. 8. By kind permission of Rowman and Littlefield.

Introduction

1. *The Byron Journal* 2003, 'Byron in Our Time', by John Clubbe
2. *Gorky Park* by Martin Cruz Smith, William Collins, London, 1981
3. BLJ Vol. 9, p. 11

Preface

1. *Byron: Romantic Paradox* by William J. Calvert, Chapel Hill, The University of North Carolina Press, 1935, p. 67

Scotland

1. PWB Vol. VI, p. 405 / CPW Vol. V, p. 442
2. Ibid., p. 405 / CPW Vol. V, p. 442
3. BLJ Vol. 7, p. 212
4. BLJ Vol. 8, p. 73
5. BLJ Vol. 7, p. 204
6. Moore, p. 7
7. PWB Vol. VI, p. 382 / CPW Vol. V, p. 416

8. BLJ Vol. 1, p. 136
9. Moore, p. 46
10. PWB Vol. VI, p. 51 / CPW Vol. V, pp. 50, 51
11. Moore, p. 9
12. Moore, p. 9 n.1
13. Moore, p. 8
14. BLJ Vol. 2, p. 89
15. Ibid., p. 136
16. PWB Vol. VI, p. 401 / CPW Vol. V, p. 438

Notes

1. *The Byron Journal*, 1989, 'The Temptations of a Biographer' by William St Clair
2. *Byron and Thomas Moore, A Literary Friendship* by Jeffery Vail, Johns Hopkins University Press, Baltimore & London, 2001, p. 81

Newstead Abbey

1. PWB Vol. VI, p. 498 / CPW Vol. V, p. 498
2. Moore, p. 5
3. Ibid., p. 7
4. Ibid., p. 10
5. Ibid., p. 10
6. BLJ Vol. 1, pp. 39, 40
7. Moore, p. 23
8. PWB Vol. 1, p. 95 / CPW Vol. 1, p. 165
9. BLJ Vol. 9, p. 40

Harrow

1. BLJ Vol. 1, p. 42
2. Moore, p. 19
3. *The Byron Journal 1989*, 'Byron's Harrow' by C.J. Tyerman
4. BLJ Vol. 1, p. 42
5. 'Byron's Harrow', op. cit.
6. Moore, p. 19
7. 'Byron's Harrow', op. cit.
8. *Abbotsford and Newstead Abbey* by Washington Irving, George Bell & Sons, London, 1878, p. 88
9. Ibid., p. 89
10. BLJ Vol. 1, p. 46/7
11. Ibid., p. 43

12. Ibid., p. 43
13. BLJ Vol. 1, p. 54
14. *The Making of the Poets: Byron and Shelley in Their Time* by Ian Gilmour, Chatto and Windus, London, 2002, p. 88 (copyright © 2002 by Ian Gilmour)
15. PWB Vol. 1, pp 128/129 / CPW Vol. 1, pp. 51, 52
16. BLJ Vol. 7, p. 117
17. BLJ Vol. 10, p. 68
18. *Lord Byron at Harrow School, Speaking Out, Talking Back, Acting Up, Bowing Out* by Paul Elledge, Johns Hopkins University Press, Baltimore and London, 2000, p. 137
19. *Lord Byron's Strength: Romantic Writing and Commercial Society* by Jerome Christensen, Johns Hopkins University Press, Baltimore and London, 1993, p. 54
20. BLJ Vol. 1, p. 44
21. BLJ Vol. 10, p. 208
22. BLJ Vol. 1, p. 46
23. Ibid., p. 52
24. Ibid., p. 45
25. Ibid., p. 52
26. Ibid., p. 56
27. Ibid., p. 59
28. Ibid., p. 61
29. Ibid., p. 55
30. Ibid., p. 66
31. 'Byron's Harrow', op. cit.
32. Ibid.
33. PWB Vol. 1, p. 87 / CPW Vol. 1, p. 160
34. BLJ Vol. 1, p. 49
35. BLJ Vol. 3, p. 242
36. *The Wit and Wisdom of the Rev. Sydney Smith*, Longman's Green And Co., London, 1869, p. 2
37. BLJ Vol. 1, p. 53
38. PWB Vol. 1, p. 91 n. / CPW Vol. 1, p. 172
39. PWB Vol. 1, p. 96 / CPW Vol. 1, p. 166
40. *Lord Byron: The Complete Miscellaneous Prose*, edited by Andrew Nicholson, Oxford University Press, 1991, p. 6

Southwell and Cambridge

1. BLJ Vol. 1, p. 95
2. Prothero Vol. 1, p. 110
3. Ibid., p. 109 n.
4. BLJ Vol. 1, p. 80

5. Ibid., p. 81
6. BLJ Vol. 1, p. 89
7. *Lord Byron at Harrow School*, op. cit., pp. 136/7
8. BLJ Vol. 1, p. 113
9. BLJ Vol. 3, p. 44
10. BLJ Vol. 2, p. 47
11. BLJ Vol. 1, pp. 117/18
12. BLJ Vol. 8, p. 24
13. *Byron and Shakespeare* by G. Wilson Knight, Barnes & Noble Inc, New York, 1966, p. 28
14. *Lord Byron's Strength*, op. cit., p. 61
15. PWB Vol. 111, p. 33 'To Thyrza' / CPW Vol. 2, p. 347
16. *Lord Byron at Harrow School*, op. cit., p. 204
17. *Byron the Erotic Liberal* by Jonathan David Gross, Rowman and Littlefield, Lanham, Boulder, New York, Oxford, 2001, p. 3
18. BLJ Vol. 1, p. 123
19. Ibid., p. 124
20. PWB Vol. 1, pp. 213/216 / CPW Vol. 2, pp. 19, 22
21. BLJ Vol. 1, pp. 130/131
22. Ibid., p. 105

Notes

1. *Byron and the Limits of Fiction*, edited by Bernard Beatty and Vincent Newey, Liverpool University Press, 1988, 'Lyric Presence in Byron from the Tales to *Don Juan*' by Brian Nellist, p. 44
2. *The Blind Man Traces the Circle. On the Patterns and Philosophy of Byron's Poetry* by Michael G. Cooke, Princeton University Press, Princeton, 1969, pp. 11/12/13

The Newly Published Poet

1. PWB Vol. 1, p. 300 / CPW Vol. 2, p. 230
2. BLJ Vol. 7, p. 50
3. *The Spirit of the Age or Contemporary Portraits* by William Hazlitt, Oxford University Press, 1935, p. 188 (first published 1825)
4. *The Letters of Sydney Smith*, edited by Nowell C. Smith, Oxford at the Clarendon Press, 1953, Vol. 1, p. 152
5. *The Monthly Review*, November 1807
6. BLJ Vol. 1, p. 26
7. Ibid., p. 162
8. *The Eclectic Review*, February 1808
9. Prothero, Vol. 1, p. 183 n.1
10. Moore, p. 80

11. PWB Vol. 1, p. 341 / CPW Vol. 1, p. 246
12. Ibid., p. 320 / CPW Vol. 1, p. 238
13. Ibid., p. 328 / CPW Vol. 1, p. 241
14. Ibid., p. 315 / CPW Vol. 1, p. 236
15. Ibid., p. 338 / CPW Vol. 1, p. 245
16. Ibid., p. 335 / CPW Vol. 1, p. 245
17. Ibid., p. 352 / CPW Vol. 1, p. 251
18. Ibid., p. 354 / CPW Vol. 5, p. 252
19. Moore, p. 81
20. BLJ Vol. 3, p. 224
21. BLJ Vol. 4, p. 68
22. Ibid., p. 74
23. *Spirit of the Age*, op. cit., pp. 99, 100
24. PWB Vol. VII, p. 46 / CPW Vol. IV, p. 125

Return to Newstead

1. PWB Vol. 1, p. 124 / CPW Vol. 1, p. 215
2. BLJ Vol. 1, pp. 134, 135
3. Ibid., p. 158
4. Ibid., p. 127
5. PWB Vol. 1, p. 263 / CPW Vol. 1, p. 215
6. Prothero Vol. 1, p. 154 n.
7. *Byron the Erotic Liberal*, op. cit., p. 10
8. BLJ Vol. 8, p. 146
9. *Abbotsford and Newstead*, op. cit., p. 78
10. *Recollections Lord Broughton*, op. cit., Vol. II, p. 231
11. BLJ Vol. 1, p. 174
12. Ibid., p. 176
13. *A Publisher and his Friends, Memoir and Correspondence of the late John Murray*, Samuel Smiles, John Murray, London, 1891, Vol. 1, pp. 353/354

The Pilgrimage

1. BLJ Vol. 4, p. 152
2. BLJ Vol. 1, p. 203
3. Ibid., p. 206
4. BLJ Vol. 2, p. 259
5. *The Making of the Poets*, op. cit., p. 179
6. BLJ Vol. 1, p. 207
7. *Byron the Erotic Liberal*, op. cit., p. 137
8. BLJ Vol. 1, p. 208

9. Ibid., p. 210
10. Ibid., pp. 215/216
11. Ibid., pp. 219/222
12. PWB Vol. II, p. 118 / CPW Vol. II, p. 54
13. Moore, p. 84
14. BLJ Vol. 2, p. 243
15. PWB Vol. II, pp. XXI/XXIV
16. BLJ Vol. 1, p. 225
17. Ibid., pp. 226/229
18. Prothero Vol. 1, p. 269 n.
19. BLJ Vol. 1, p. 234
20. Ibid., p. 237/239
21. BLJ Vol. 4, p. 152
22. BLJ Vol. 1, p. 256
23. BLJ Vol. 2, p. 8
24. Ibid., p. 28
25. BLJ Vol. 1, p. 241
26. PWB Vol. II, p. 121 / CPW Vol. 1, p. 55
27. Ibid., p. 18
28. BLJ Vol. 2, p. 49
29. PWB Vol. III, p. 15 / CPW Vol. 1, p. 280
30. BLJ Vol. 2, p. 35
31. *Byron and Goethe: Analysis of a Passion* by E.M. Butler, Bowes and Bowes, London, 1956, p. 40
32. Ibid., p. 14
33. BLJ Vol. 2, p. 29
34. Ibid., p. 31
35. BLJ Vol. 2, p. 46
36. BLJ Vol. 1, p. 232
37. Ibid., p. 243
38. BLJ Vol. 2, p. 25
39. Ibid., p. 34
40. Ibid., p. 57
41. Ibid., p. 66
42. Ibid., p. 51
43. Ibid., p. 68
44. Ibid., p. 81
45. *Byron the Erotic Liberal*, op. cit., pp. 133/134
46. BLJ Vol. 2, p. 93
47. Ibid., p. 68

Note

1. BLJ Vol. 4, p. 152

532

The Maiden Speech

1. *The Making of the Poets*, op. cit., p. 261
2. BLJ Vol. 2, p. 86
3. Ibid., p. 159
4. John Mortimer's Introduction to *Bright Darkness* by Anne Fleming, Nottingham Court Press, London, 1984
5. BLJ Vol. 2, p. 165
6. Prothero Vol. II, p. 430
7. John Mortimer, op. cit.
8. Prothero Vol. II, p. 428
9. BLJ Vol. 9, p. 16
10. Ibid., p. 17
11. PWB Vol. VII, pp. 13/14 / CPW Vol. III, p. 9
12. *The Spirit of the Age*, Hazlitt, op. cit., p. 185
13. BLJ Vol. 2, p. 91
14. BLJ Vol. 3, p. 55
15. *The Spirit of the Age*, op. cit., p. 236
16. BLJ Vol. 9, p. 30
17. Ibid., p. 20
18. PWB Vol. IV, p. 557 / CPW Vol. III, p. 8
19. Prothero, Vol. II, p. 432
20. Ibid., p. 435
21. Ibid., p. 400
22. Ibid., p. 441
23. Ibid., p. 441

Childe Harold's Pilgrimage

1. *Edinburgh Review*, May, 1812
2. *John Bull's Letter to Lord Byron* by J.G. Lockhart, edited by Alan Lang, University of Oklahoma Press, 1947, p. 93
3. PWB Vol. 1, pp. 380/381 / CPW Vol. 1, p. 262
4. BLJ Vol. 2, p. 91
5. Ibid., p. 75
6. Ibid., pp. 90/91
7. Ibid., p. 92
8. *The Spirit of the Age*, op. cit., p. 96
9. *The London Magazine*, January, 1821
10. PWB Vol. II, p. 151 / CPW Vol. II, p. 69
11. Ibid., pp. 49/50 / CPW Vol. II, pp. 25, 26
12. *Lord Byron's Strength*, op. cit., p. 71
13. PWB Vol. II, pp. 48/49 / CPW Vol. II, pp. 24, 25
14. Ibid., p. 39 / CPW Vol. II, p. 20

15. Ibid., p. 77
16. *Letters of Sydney Smith*, op. cit., p. 150
17. PWB Vol. II, pp. 109/110 / CPW Vol. II, p. 49
18. Ibid., p. 191 (Byron's note)
19. *Journey through Albania*, Hobhouse, Vol. I, p. 347
20. BLJ Vol. 2, p. 66 n.6
21. PWB Vol. II, p. 26 / CPW Vol. II, p. 13
22. Ibid., pp. 155/157 / CPW Vol. II, pp. 72, 73
23. Ibid., p. 131 / CPW Vol. II, p. 60
24. Ibid., pp. 126/127 / CPW Vol. II, p. 57
25. Ibid., p. 159 / CPW Vol. II, pp. 73, 74
26. Prothero Vol. II, p. 130 n.
27. PWB Vol. II, pp. 103/105 / CPW Vol. II, pp. 46, 47

Notes

1. *Byron the Poet* by M.K. Joseph, Victor Gollancz, a division of the Orion Publishing Group, London, 1964, p. 27
2. PWB Vol. II, pp. 115–6 / CPW Vol. II, p. 25
3. BLJ Vol. 4, p. 324
4. *The Letters of William and Dorothy Wordsworth, Vol. III, The Middle Years*, edited by Ernest de Selincourt, Oxford at the Clarendon Press, 1970, p. 579
5. *The Byron Journal*, 2003, 'Byron and Wordsworth' by Philip Shaw
6. *Fiery Dust, Byron's Poetical Development* by Jerome J. McGann, University of Chicago Press, Chicago and London, 1968, p. 65. © 1968 by the University of Chicago. All rights reserved.
7. BLJ Vol. 3, p. 58
8. *Lord Elgin and the Marbles* by William St Clair, Oxford University Press, 1967, paperback edition 1983, p. 194 n.

Whig Ladies

1. PWB Vol. VI, p. 560 / CPW Vol. V, p. 605
2. *The Reminiscences and Recollections of Captain Gronow*, Bodley Head, London, 1964, p. 114
3. *A Regency Chapter* by E. Colburn Mayne, Macmillan and Co., London, 1939, p. 238
4. *Letters of Harriet, Countess Granville*, edited by F. Leweson Gower, Longmans Green & Co, London, 1894, Vol. 1, p. 151
5. Ibid., p. 222
6. Ibid., pp. 15/16
7. Ibid., p. 16
8. Ibid., p. 87

9. Ibid., p. 21
10. Ibid., p. 17
11. Ibid., p. 199
12. Ibid., p. 169
13. Ibid., p. 192
14. Prothero Vol. II, p. 120
15. PWB Vol. VI, p. 473 / CPW Vol. V, p. 514
16. *Byron's 'Corbeau Blanc' The Life and Letters of Lady Melbourne*, edited by Jonathan David Gross, Rice University Press, 1997, pp. 54, 3, 33, 35, 349
17. *The Young Melbourne* by David Cecil, Constable, London, 1939, p. 215
18. *Byron's 'Corbeau Blanc'*, op. cit., p. 26
19. BLJ Vol. 3, p. 240
20. PWB Vol. VI, p. 560 / CPW Vol. V, p. 605
21. *Letters of Harriet Countess Granville*, op. cit., Vol. 1, p. 79
22. *The Spirit of the Age*, op. cit., pp. 253, 258
23. Moore, p. 163
24. Letters of Countess Granville, op. cit., p. 200
25. Gronow, op. cit., p. 43
26. *Studies in Literature* by Sir Arthur Quiller-Couch, Cambridge University Press, 1943, p. 12
27. PWB Vol. V, pp. 569/570 / CPW Vol. VII, pp. 18, 19, 20
28. BLJ Vol. 3, p. 70
29. BLJ Vol. 9, p. 23
30. Gronow, op. cit., p. 255
31. *The Young Melbourne*, op. cit., p. 152
32. *Byron the Poet*, op. cit., p. 176
33. BLJ Vol. 6, p. 237
34. BLJ Vol. 2, p. 170
35. Ibid., p. 177
36. Ibid., p. 203
37. Ibid., p. 188
38. Ibid., p. 200
39. Ibid., p. 209
40. Ibid., p. 195
41. *Journal of the Conversations of Lord Byron during a Residence with His Lordship in Pisa in the Years 1821 and 1822* by Thomas Medwin, Galignani, Paris, 1824, Vol. 1, p. 32
42. PWB Vol. III, pp. 59/60 / CPW Vol. III, p. 84
43. BLJ Vol. 2, p. 239
44. PWB Vol. II, pp. 12/13 / CPW Vol. II, p. 7
45. BLJ Vol. 3, p. 36
46. BLJ Vol. 2, p. 198
47. Ibid., p. 242
48. PWB Vol. VII, p. 15 / CPW Vol. III, pp. 31, 32
49. BLJ Vol. 3, p. 65

Love and Friendship

1. BLJ Vol. 3, p. 215
2. Ibid., p. 7
3. BLJ Vol. 4, p. 19
4. *Maria Edgeworth and her Circle, In the Days of Buonaparte and Bourbon* by Constance Hill, The Bodley Head, London, MCMX, pp. 128/129
5. BLJ Vol. 3, p. 244
6. Prothero Vol. 11, p. 384
7. *The Life and Letters of Anne Isabella, Lady Noel Byron*, Constable, London, 1929, p. 213
8. BLJ Vol. 3, p. 209
9. Ibid., p. 45
10. Ibid., p. 50
11. Ibid., p. 212
12. Ibid., p. 68
13. Ibid., p.87
14. *Life and Letters of Lady Byron*, op. cit., p. 165
15. BLJ Vol. 3, p. 72
16. *The Letters of Sydney Smith*, op. cit., Vol. 1, p. 238
17. BLJ Vol. 3, p. 76
18. Ibid., p. 77
19. *Journal of the Conversations of Lord Byron Noted During a Residence with His Lordship at Pisa in the years 1821 and 1822* by Thomas Medwin, A. and W. Galignani, Paris, 1824, Vol. 1, p. 33
20. BLJ Vol. 2, p. 243
21. BLJ Vol. 3, p. 120
22. Ibid., p. 124/125
23. Ibid., p. 128
24. Ibid., p. 135
25. Ibid., p. 135
26. Ibid., pp. 137/38
27. Ibid., p. 143
28. Ibid., pp. 146/147
29. Ibid., p. 151
30. Ibid., p. 155
31. PWB Vol. III, pp. 410/411 / CPW Vol. III, pp. 319, 320
32. BLJ Vol. 5, p. 28, n.1
33. BLJ Vol. 3, p. 246
34. Moore, op. cit., p. 229, n.1
35. Ibid., op. cit., p. 74
36. BLJ Vol. 3, p. 109
37. Moore, op. cit., pp. 180/81
38. PWB Vol. III, pp. 435/436 / CPW Vol. III, pp. 88, 89
39. BLJ Vol. 3, p. 173

40. Ibid., pp. 207/8
41. BLJ Vol. 9, p. 15
42. PWB Vol. IV, p. 73 / CPW Vol. IV, pp. 20, 21
43. BLJ Vol. 3, p. 233
44. BLJ Vol. 6, pp. 47/48
45. BLJ Vol. 3, p. 229
46. Ibid., p. 206
47. Ibid., p. 218
48. BLJ Vol. 4, p. 171

Byron, Moore and the Oriental Tales

1. PWB Vol. III, p. 137 / CPW Vol. III, pp. 75-76
2. Ibid., p. 73 / CPW Vol. III, p. 39
3. Ibid., p. 225
4. Ibid., p. 90
5. *Lord Byron's Strength*, op. cit., p. 99
6. PWB Vol. III, pp. 88/89 / CPW Vol. III, p. 42
7. BLJ Vol. 3, p. 141
8. BLJ Vol. 3, p. 230
9. BLJ Vol. 4, p. 28
10. *The Edinburgh Review*, July, 1813
11. *The Satirist*, July, 1813
12. *Painter of Passion. The Journal of Eugene Delacroix*, Phaidon Press Ltd for the Folio Society, London, 1995, p. 35
13. *The Spirit of the Age*, op. cit., p. 98
14. *The Critical Review*, 1814, RRB: 2: 628–29
15. *The Edinburgh Review*, April, 1814
15. *The British Critic*, March 1814
16. *A Publisher and his Friends*, op. cit., p. 357
18. BLJ Vol. 4, p. 77
19. Ibid., p. 77
20. *The Literary Relationship of Lord Byron and Thomas Moore*, Johns Hopkins University Press, Baltimore and London 2001, p. 194
21. BLJ Vol. 3, p. 245
22. *Letters of Countess Granville*, op. cit., 24 September, 1817
23. PWB Vol. III, pp. 234/5 / CPW Vol. III, pp. 157, 158
24. Ibid., p. 270 / CPW Vol. III, p. 190
25. BLJ Vol. 2, p. 181
26. BLJ Vol. 3, p. 208
27. The 'Opening Lines to Lara' do not appear in the early Coleridge edition of the Poetical Works. In my copy of Volume VII I found a newspaper cutting of this version of the lines printed in a letter to the Editor deploring their omission. CPW Vol. III, pp. 256, 257

28. PWB Vol. III, p. 336
29. *The Literary Relationship of Lord Byron and Thomas Moore*, op. cit., p. 193
30. PWB Vol. VII, p. 46
31. *The Literary Relationship of Lord Byron and Thomas Moore*, op. cit., pp. 101/102

Notes

1. *Byron and the Dynamics of Metaphor* by W. Paul Elledge, Vanderbilt University Press, Nashville, Tennessee, 1968, p. 16
2. Ibid., p. 17, n.13
3. *Fiery Dust*, op. cit., p. 162
4. Ibid., p. 145
5. *Byron the Poet*, op. cit., p. 55
6. *Mapping Male Sexuality in Nineteenth Century England*, edited by Jay Losey and William D. Brewer, Associated University Presses, London 2000, p. 70
7. PWB Vol. III, pp. 91–2 / CPW Vol. III, pp. 43, 44

Shock Tactics

1. Moore, p. 158
2. Prothero Vol. II, p. 429
3. BLJ Vol. 2, p. 260
4. BLJ Vol. 8, p. 27
5. Prothero Vol. II, p. 445
6. PWB Vol. VI, p. 478 / CPW Vol. V, p. 520
7. *The Creevey Papers* by Thomas Creevey, edited by John Gore, BT Batsford Ltd, 1963, p. 51
8. Ibid., p. 28
9. Ibid., p. 90
10. PWB Vol. III, pp. 45/46 / CPW Vol. III, p. 10
11. BLJ Vol. 4, p. 51
12. PWB Vol. IV, p. 548 / CPW Vol. IV, p. 242
13. BLJ Vol. 4, p. 53
14. BLJ Vol. 3, pp. 210, 256/257
15. PWB Vol. III, pp. 305, 309, 314 / CPW Vol. III, pp. 259, 262, 265, 266
16. BLJ Vol. 4, p. 298
17. *The Romantic Movement in English Poetry* by Arthur Symons, Constable, London, 1909, p. 256
18. *Letters of Sydney Smith*, op. cit., p. 244
19. *Wellington – The Years of the Sword* by Elizabeth Longford, Weidenfeld and Nicolson, a division of the Orion Publishing Group, London, 1969. One-volume edition, 1922, p. 225

20. *Byron the Erotic Liberal*, op. cit., p. 9
21. Ibid., p. 6
22. *A History of Western Philosophy* by Bertrand Russell, Routledge, London, 2000 (first published 1946), p. 718
23. *The Last Days of Lord Byron* by William Parry, Galignani, Paris, 1826, p. 7
24. BLJ Vol. 9, p. 41
25. BLJ Vol. 7, p. 80
26. *The Making of the English Working Class* by E.P. Thompson, Victor Gollancz, London, 1963, p. 5
27. BLJ Vol. 6, p. 226
28. BLJ Vol. 9, p. 49

Hebrew Melodies

1. PWB Vol. IV, pp. 95/96 / CPW Vol. IV, p. 64
2. *The Byron Journal*, 1999, 'Byron and Nathan: A Musical Collaboration' by Graham Pont
3. *Fugitive Pieces and Reminiscences of Lord Byron* by Isaac Nathan, London, 1829, p. 2
4. *The Byron Journal*, 1999, op. cit.
5. *Fugitive Pieces*, op. cit., p. viii
6. PWB Vol. III, pp. 381/382 / CPW Vol. III, pp. 288, 289
7. Ibid., pp. 404/405 / CPW Vol. III, pp. 309, 310
8. *Byron and Shakespeare* by G. Wilson Knight, Barnes and Noble, New York, 1960, pp. 14/15
9. PWB Vol. III, pp. 382/383 / CPW Vol. III, pp. 289, 290
10. *The Blind Man Traces the Circle*, op. cit., p. 29 n.30
11. *Fugitive Pieces*, op. cit., p. 24
12. *The Literary Relationship of Lord Byron and Thomas Moore*, op. cit., p. 92
13. *Byron and Shakespeare*, op. cit., p. 207

Augusta

1. BLJ Vol. 10, p. 208
2. *Augusta Leigh* by Michael and Melissa Bakewell, Chatto and Windus, London, 2002, p. 77
3. BLJ Vol. 4, p. 112
4. *Augusta Leigh*, op. cit., p. 17
5. Ibid., p. 77
6. Ibid., p. 103
7. BLJ Vol. 4, p. 19

8. BLJ Vol. 4, p. 21
9. Diary of Frances Lady Shelley, edited by Richard Edgcumbe, John Murray, London, 1912, pp. 52/53
10. BLJ Vol. 4, p. 11
11. Ibid., p. 25
12. Ibid., p. 25
13. BLJ Vol. 4, p. 36
14. Ibid., p. 44
15. Ibid., p. 46
16. Ibid., p. 40
17. Ibid., p. 110
18. BLJ Vol. 4, p. 50
19. *Byron and Shakespeare*, op. cit., p. 236
20. PWB Vol. III, p. 413 / CPW Vol. III, pp. 269, 270
21. BLJ Vol. 4, p. 49
22. Ibid., p. 54
23. Ibid., p. 69
24. Ibid., p. 56
25. Ibid., p. 57
26. Ibid., p. 84
27. Ibid., p. 53
28. Ibid., p. 61
29. Ibid., p. 75
30. Ibid., p. 101
31. Ibid., p. 101
32. Ibid., p. 130

Notes

1. BLJ Vol. 4, p. 104
2. *Augusta Leigh*, op. cit., p. 111

Childe Harold and the Princess of Parallelograms

1. BLJ Vol. 3, p. 227
2. BLJ Vol. 5, p. 44
3. BLJ Vol. 3, p. 108
4. Lady Tamworth to Judith Milbanke, 4 February 1812, *Lovelace Papers*, reproduced by kind permission of Pollinger Ltd and the Earl of Lytton
5. *The Life and Letters of Anne Isabella, Lady Noel Byron*, op. cit., p. 222
6. BLJ Vol. 3, p. 108
7. BLJ Vol. 2, p. 251
8. Ibid., p. 195

9. Ibid., p. 208
10. Annabella to Lady Gosford, 8 October 1814, *Lovelace Papers*, reproduced by kind permission of Pollinger Ltd and the Earl of Lytton
11. BLJ Vol. 4, p. 228
12. Ibid., p. 264
13. Ibid., p. 231
14. Ibid., p. 232
15. Ibid., p. 234
16. *Conversations of Lord Byron with the Countess of Blessington*, R. Bentley, for H. Colburn, 1834
17. BLJ Vol. 2, p. 195
18. *Recollections Lord Broughton*, op. cit., Vol. 1, p. 191
19. Ibid., p. 196

The Marriage

1. BLJ Vol. 4, p. 175
2. *Life and Letters of Lady Byron*, op. cit., p. 23
3. *Correspondence and Table Talk, Benjamin Robert Haydon*, Chatto and Windus, London, 1876, Vol. 2, p. 370

Annabella Through the Looking Glass

All letters from the *Lovelace Papers* are reproduced by kind permission of Pollinger Ltd and Lord Lytton.

1. *Annabella to her mother, March 1816, Lovelace Papers*
2. *Recollections Lord Broughton*, op. cit., Vol. II, p. 283
3. *Literary Life of William Harness*, L'Estrange, London, 1871, pp. 35/36
4. *Recollections Lord Broughton*, op. cit., Vol. II, p. 283
5. Ibid., pp. 278/279
6. Ibid., p. 265
7. Statement given by Annabella to her mother, 18 January 1816, *Lovelace Papers*
8. Ibid.
9. *Recollections Lord Broughton*, op. cit., Vol. II, pp. 252/253
10. BLJ Vol. 5, p. 63
11. *Recollections Lord Broughton*, op. cit., p. 260
12. Ibid., Vol. II, p. 207
13. *Lord Byron's Strength*, op. cit., p. 84
14. Annabella to her mother 21 January 1816, *Lovelace Papers*
15. BLJ Supplementary Volume, p. 79
16. Annabella to her mother, 4 March 1816, *Lovelace Papers*

17. Medwin, op. cit., p. 35
18. *Vindication of Lord Byron*, Alfred Austin, Chapman and Hall, London, 1869, p. 6
19. *Vindication of Lord Byron*, op. cit., pp. 5/6
20. *Recollections Lord Broughton*, Vol. 11, p. 280
21. Ibid., p. 280
22. Ibid., p. 263
23. PWB Vol. IV, pp. 64/65
24. Annabella to her mother, 8 September 1815, *Lovelace Papers*
25. BLJ Vol. 6, p. 181
26. Annabella to Byron, 3 September 1813, *Lovelace Papers*
27. Annabella to Dr Lushington, 11 February 1816, *Lovelace Papers*
28. Annabella to her mother, 12 April 1816, *Lovelace Papers*
29. Annabella to F.W. Robertson, 12 April 1851, *Lovelace Papers*
30. Augusta to Hodgson, 5 March 1816, *Lovelace Papers*

Byron for his Own Defence

1. BLJ Supplementary Volume, p. 79
2. BLJ Vol. 5, p. 22
3. BLJ Vol. 6, p. 150
4. BLJ Vol. 5, p. 26/27
5. *Recollections Lord Broughton* Vol. 11, p. 277
6. BLJ Vol. 5, p. 256
7. *Recollections Lord Broughton* Vol. 11, p. 280
8. BLJ Vol. 5, p. 25
9. BLJ Vol. 3, p. 249
10. BLJ Vol. 5, p. 223
11. Ibid., p. 225
12. *The Two Duchesses* by Vere Foster (Blackie 1898)
13. Ibid., p. 413
14. BLJ Vol. 5, p. 54
15. *Blackwoods*, July, 1869
16. *Macmillan's Magazine*, September, 1869
17. *Tinsley's Magazine*, October, 1869
18. *Vindication of Lord Byron*, op. cit., p. 13
19. BLJ Vol. 8, p. 146
20. BLJ Vol. 9, p. 24

The Separation Poems

1. BLJ Vol. 5, p. 63
2. PWB Vol. III, pp. 540/542 / CPW Vol. III, pp. 382, 383

3. Ibid., pp. 537/540 / CPW Vol. III, pp. 380, 381, 382
4. *Lord Byron's Strength*, op. cit., p. 87
5. Ibid., p. 152
6. Moore, p. 302
7. David V. Erdman, '"Fare Thee Well": Byron's Last Days in England', *Shelley and his Circle*, Cambridge MA: Harvard University Press, 1970, Vol. IV, p. 645
8. Ibid., p. 645
9. *The Champion*, April 1816
10. PWB Vol. III, p. 63/65 / CPW Vol. III, pp. 43, 44
11. BLJ Vol. 5, p. 93
12. PWB Vol. II, pp. 419/421 / CPW Vol. III, pp. 164, 165
13. *My Dearest Augusta* by Peter Gunn, Bodley Head, London, 1969, p. 149
14. *Recollections Lord Broughton*, Vol. II, Appendix p. 352. The Hon. Mrs Leigh to Mr Hobhouse, St James's Palace, 3 January, 1816
15. PWB Vol. III, pp. 544/546 / CPW Vol. III, pp. 386, 387, 388

Notes

1. CPW Vol. III, Commentary, p. 490.

Last Days in London

1. BLJ Vol. 5, p. 228
2. Ibid., p. 25
3. Augusta Leigh to Lady Byron, 18 January 1860, *The Lovelace Papers*, reproduced by kind permission of Pollinger Ltd & the Earl of Lytton
4. BLJ Vol. 5, p. 16
5. Ibid., p. 19
6. Ibid., p. 32
7. Ibid., pp. 35/36
8. Ibid., p. 31
9. Ibid., p. 39
10. Ibid., p. 40
11. *Recollections Lord Broughton*, Vol. II, p. 269
12. *Croker Papers 1805–57*, J. Wilson Croker, edited by Bernard Pool, Batsford, London, 1967, p. 56
13. *Diary of a Lady in Waiting* by Lady Charlotte Bury, edited by A. Francis Steuart, London, John Lane, The Bodley Head, MCMVIII Vol. II, p. 280
14. Ibid.
15. David V. Erdman, '"Fare Thee Well": Byron's Last Days in England', *Shelley and his Circle*, Cambridge MA: Harvard University Press, 1970, Vol. IV, p. 643

16. BLJ Vol. 5, p. 162
17. PWB Vol. III, pp. 17/19
18. BLJ Vol. 8, p. 28
19. *The Clairmont Correspondence* Vol. 1, 1808–1834, edited by Marion Kingston Stocking, Johns Hopkins University Press, Baltimore and London, 1995, p. 36
20. *Journals of Claire Clairmont*, edited by Marion Kingston Stocking, Harvard University Press, Cambridge, Massachusetts, 1968, p. 183
21. The Journal of Sir Walter Scott, edited by W.E.K. Anderson, Canongate, 1988, p. 53
22. BLJ Vol. 8, p. 13
23. BLJ Vol. 9, p. 87
24. *The Literary Relationship of Lord Byron and Thomas Moore*, op. cit., pp. 101/102
25. BLJ Vol. II, p. 85
26. BLJ Vol. 5, p. 67
27. Ibid., p. 66
28. Ibid., p. 67
29. Ibid., p. 68
30. *Recollections Lord Broughton*, Vol. II, p. 334
31. BLJ Vol. 5, p. 70
32. BLJ Vol. 5, p. 70
33. BLJ Vol. 5, p. 70
34. *Recollections Lord Broughton*, Vol. 1, p. 335
35. Ibid., Vol. 1, pp. 335/336

Notes

1. PWB Vol. IV, pp. 46, 47
2. *The Byron Journal*, 1998, ' "Churchill's Grave": A Line of Separation' by David Woodhouse
3. PWB Vol. IV, pp. 45, 48
4. *The Byron Journal*, 1998, op. cit.

Poet into Exile

1. *Byron and Goethe. Analysis of a Passion* by E.M. Butler, Bowes and Bowes, London, 1956, p. 14
2. *The Blind Man Traces the Circle*, op. cit., p. 182
3. *Byron and Shakespeare*, op. cit., p. 15
4. PWB Vol. II, p. 216
5. PWB Vol. IV, p. 174
6. *Nottingham Byron Lecture*, 1969, Professor Philip Collins. By kind permission of Professor Collins

7. *The Wit and Wisdom of Sydney Smith*, op. cit., p. 2
8. 'Lord Byron's Works Viewed in Connection with Christianity and the Obligations of Social Life'. A sermon preached in Holland Chapel, Kennington by the Revd. John Styles. Prothero Vol. VI, p. 9
9. PWB Vol. IV, pp. 48/51

REFERENCES – PART TWO

Journey to Geneva

1. PWB Vol. II, p. 218 / CPW Vol. II, pp. 77–8
2. *The Byron Journal*, 1991, '1816: Switzerland and the Revival of the "Grand Tour"' by Ernest Giddey
3. Ibid.
4. Ibid.
5. BLJ Vol. 5, p. 187
6. Prothero, Vol. 3, p. 330 n.
7. PWB Vol. II, pp. 225–7 / CPW Vol. II, pp. 82–4
8. Ibid., pp. 228–30 / CPW Vol. II, pp. 84–5
9. Ibid., pp. 233–4 / CPW Vol. II, p. 87
10. *Studies in Literature, Second Series* by Sir Arthur Quiller-Couch (Cambridge University Press, 1943), p. 15
11. PWB Vol. II, pp. 248–50 / CPW Vol. II, pp. 96–7
12. BLJ Vol. 5, p. 72
13. Ibid., p. 75
14. Ibid., p. 79
15. *Letters of John Murray to Lord Byron* edited by Andrew Nicholson (Liverpool University Press, 2007), p. 163, Letter 87 & n. 1, n. 2
16. BLJ Vol 5, p. 80
17. Ibid., p. 80

A Sunless Summer

1. PWB Vol. III, p. 424 / CPW Vol. III, p. 285
2. PWB Vol. II, p. 220 / CPW Vol. II, p. 79
3. Ibid., p. 237 / CPW Vol. II, p. 237
4. PWB Vol. IV, pp. 40–1 / CPW Vol. IV, p. 29
5. Ibid., p. 52 / CPW Vol. IV, p. 30

6. *The Byron Journal*, 1991, 'The Tempest-toss'd Summer of 1816: Mary Shelley's *Frankenstein*' by John Clubbe
7. PWB Vol. IV, pp. 42–5 / CPW Vol. IV, pp. 40–43
8. PWB Vol. III, pp. 544–5 / CPW Vol. III, p. 386
9. PWB Vol. II, p. 262 / CPW Vol. II, p. 104
10. BLJ Vol. 9, p. 119
11. BLJ Vol. 10, p. 69
12. BLJ Vol. 5, p. 107
13. PWB, Vol. IV, p. 53 / CPW Vol. IV, p. 16
14. PWB, Vol. IV, p. 7 / CPW Vol. IV, p. 3
15. Ibid., p. 7 / CPW Vol. IV, p. 3
16. *Quarterly Review*, October 1816, Review of *Childe Harold's Pilgrimage, Canto III* and *The Prisoner of Chillon*, by Walter Scott
17. BLJ Vol. 5, p. 92
18. Ibid., p. 118
19. *Letters of John Murray to Lord Byron*, op. cit., p. 238 n. 12
20. BLJ Vol. 5, p. 86
21. Ibid., p. 86
22. Ibid., p. 92
23. Ibid., pp. 104–5

Notes

1. *Fiery Dust: Byron's Poetical Development* by Jerome J. McGann (University of Chicago Press, 1968), p. 167
2. *Byron and the Dynamics of Metaphor* by W. Paul Elledge (Vanderbilt University Press, 1968), p. 46
3. BLJ Vol 5, p. 87
4. *The Reading Nation in the Romantic Period* by William St Clair (Cambridge University Press, 2004), p. 259
5. *Liberty and Poetic Licence: New Essays on Byron* edited by Bernard Beatty and Charles Robinson (Liverpool University Press, 2005), Introduction

Ada

1. PWB Vol. II, p. 215 / CPW Vol. II, p. 76
2. Ibid., pp. 215–6 / CPW Vol. II, pp. 76–7
3. Ibid., pp. 287–9 / CPW Vol. II, pp. 118–9
4. BLJ Vol. 5, p. 113
5. Ibid., pp. 109–10
6. Ibid., p. 180
7. BLJ Vol. 6, p. 256
8. BLJ Vol. 7, p. 196

9. *John Bull*, April 1821, 'Letter to Lord Byron' (by J.G. Lockhart) [*John Bull's Letter to Lord Byron* edited by Alan Lang Strout (University of Oklahoma Press, 1947)]
10. BLJ Vol. 8, p. 145

Childe Harold's Pilgrimage Canto III

1. *The Reading Nation in the Romantic Period*, op. cit., p. 198
2. BLJ Vol. 5, p. 159
3. BLJ Vol. 5, p. 165
4. Recollections Lord Broughton, Vol. 2, p. 11
5. *Fiery Dust*, op. cit., pp. 78–9
6. PWB Vol. II, pp. 216–18 & 220 / CPW Vol. II, p. 77
7. Moore, p. 317
8. *PWB, Vol. II,* pp. 261–4 / CPW Vol. II, pp. 103–5
9. *The Letters of William and Dorothy Wordsworth* edited by Ernest de Selincourt (Clarendon Press, 1970), Vol. III 'The Middle Years', p. 394
10. *Byron and the Dynamics of Metaphor*, op. cit., p. 40 n.
11. Ibid., p. 39
12. *The Dramas of Lord Byron: A Critical Study* by Samuel C. Chew (Russell & Russell, 1964), p. 113
13. *Byron the Poet* by Michael K. Joseph (Victor Gollancz, 1964), p. 80
14. PWB Vol. II, p. 269 / CPW Vol. II, p. 208
15. Ibid., p. 273 / CPW Vol. II, p. 110
16. *Byron the Poet*, op. cit., p. 77
17. *Fiery Dust*, op. cit., p. 120

Notes

1. *Studies in Literature*, op. cit., p. 14
2. *The Blind Man Traces the Circle: On the Patterns and Philosophy of Byron's Poetry* by Michael G. Cooke (Princeton University Press, 1969), p. 88
3. *Byron the Poet*, op. cit., pp. 78 & 82

Manfred

1. BLJ Vol. 5, p. 194
2. Ibid., pp. 101–2
3. PWB Vol. IV, p. 85 / CPW Vol. IV, p. 53
4. Ibid., pp. 133–4 / CPW Vol. IV, p. 100
5. Ibid., p. 104 / CPW Vol. IV, p. 72
6. Ibid., p. 114 / CPW Vol. IV, p. 82

7. Ibid., p. 86 / CPW Vol. IV, p. 53
8. Ibid., p. 106 / CPW Vol. IV, p. 74
9. Ibid., p. 98 / CPW Vol. IV, p. 66
10. CPW Vol. IV, p. 467, Commentary
11. *Byron and the Dynamics of Metaphor*, op. cit., p. 184
12. PWB Vol. IV, p. 99 / CPW Vol. IV, p. 68
13. Ibid., p. 106 / CPW Vol. IV, p. 74
14. Ibid., p. 106 / CPW Vol. IV, p. 74
15. Ibid., p. 118 / CPW Vol. IV, p. 86
16. Ibid., p. 126 / CPW Vol. IV, p. 93
17. Ibid., p. 135 / CPW Vol. IV, p. 101
18. Ibid., p. 136 / CPW Vol. IV, p. 102
19. *Edinburgh Review*, August 1817, Review of *Manfred*, by Francis Jeffrey

Notes

1. *The Dramas of Lord Byron*, op. cit., pp. 82–4
2. *The Blind Man Traces the Circle*, op. cit., p. 64

Augusta Lost

1. From the 'opening lines' to *Lara*
2. Prothero, Vol. 3, p. 366 n.
3. PWB Vol. IV, p. 56 / CPW Vol. IV, p. 35
4. BLJ Vol. 5, p. 95
5. Ibid., pp. 88–9
6. Ibid., p. 96
7. PWB Vol. IV, pp. 57–62 / CPW Vol. IV, pp. 35–40
8. BLJ Vol. 5, p. 119
9. BLJ Vol. 6, pp. 129–30
10. Ibid., p. 185
11. Ibid., p. 223

Venice

1. PWB Vol. II, pp. 327–8 & 330 / CPW Vol. II, pp. 124–5
2. BLJ Vol. 5, p. 121
3. Ibid., p. 116
4. Ibid. p. 119
5. Ibid., p. 119
6. Ibid., p. 124
7. Ibid., p. 120
8. Ibid., p. 126

9. *The Byron Journal*, 1987, 'The Venetian Climate of *Don Juan*' by Peter Graham
10. BLJ Vol. 5, p. 129
11. PWB Vol. IV, p. 162 / CPW Vol. IV, p. 132
12. Ibid., p. 1 / CPW Vol. IV, p. 143
13. *The Flowering of Byron's Genius* by Paul Graham Trueblood (Russell & Russell, 1962), p. 2
14. BLJ Vol. 5, p. 130
15. Ibid., pp. 146–7
16. Ibid., p. 151
17. Ibid., p. 135
18. Ibid., p. 155
19. Ibid., p. 160
20. Ibid., p. 188
21. Ibid., p. 189
22. Ibid., p. 141
23. Ibid., p. 170
24. Ibid., p. 171
25. Ibid., p. 200
26. Ibid., p. 200
27. Ibid., p. 255
28. Ibid., p. 164
29. PWB Vol. VII, pp. 47–50 / CPW Vol. IV, p. 126–8
30. BLJ Vol. 5, p. 208
31. *Letters of John Murray to Lord Byron*, op. cit., p. 229
32. Ibid., p. 230, n. 6
33. Ibid., p. 190
34. Ibid., pp. 241–2
35. PWB Vol. IV, p. 538 / CPW Vol. IV, p. 109

Childe Harold's Pilgrimage, Canto IV

1. BLJ Vol. 5, p. 196
2. Ibid., p. 218
3. *Blackwood's Edinburgh Magazine*, November 1817
4. *Fiery Dust*, op. cit., p. 49
5. PWB Vol. IV, p. 144 / CPW Vol. IV, p. 117
6. BLJ Vol. 5, p. 222
7. Ibid., p. 253
8. PWB Vol. II, p. 402 / CPW Vol. IV, p. 157
9. BLJ Vol. 5, p. 221
10. Ibid., p. 233
11. *Byron the Poet*, op. cit., p. 86
12. PWB Vol. II, pp. 388–90 / CPW Vol. II, pp. 150–1

13. Ibid., pp. 419–21 / CPW Vol. II, pp. 164–5
14. Ibid., pp. 457–61 / CPW Vol. II, pp. 184–6
15. Ibid., pp. 462–3 / CPW Vol. II, p. 186
16. *Constable's Edinburgh Magazine*, May 1818
17. *Edinburgh Review*, June 1818
18. BLJ Vol. 5, p. 263
19. PWB Vol. II, p. 430 / CPW Vol. II, p. 170

Notes

1. *Byron the Poet*, op. cit., p. 126
2. *The Blind Man Traces the Circle*, op. cit., p. 126
3. *Fiery Dust*, op. cit., pp. 48–9
4. Ibid., p. 138

Beppo

1. PWB Vol. IV, p. 187 / CPW Vol. IV, p. 144
2. *Byron and the Limits of Fiction*, edited by Bernard Beatty and Vincent Newey (Liverpool University Press, 1988), '*Beppo*: the Liberation of Fiction' by J. Drummond Bone, p. 97
3. *The Blind Man Traces the Circle*, op. cit., pp. 159, 161
4. PWB Vol. IV, p. 164 / CPW Vol. IV, p. 134
5. Ibid., p. 187 / CPW Vol. IV, p. 157
6. Ibid., p. 187 / CPW Vol. IV, p. 157
7. *Byron and the Limits of Fiction*, op. cit., p. 124
8. PWB Vol. IV, p. 189 / CPW Vol. IV, p. 160
9. Ibid., pp. 171–2 / CPW Vol. IV, p. 141
10. Ibid., pp. 174–5 / CPW Vol. IV, p. 144
11. *Literary Gazette*, March 1818
12. *Edinburgh Review*, February 1818
13. *British Review*, May 1818
14. *John Bull*, April 1821, 'Letter to Lord Byron', op. cit.

Allegra in Venice

1. BLJ Vol. 6, p. 150
2. Ibid., p. 7
3. Ibid., p. 41
4. Ibid., p. 62
5. *Julian and Maddalo* by Percy Bysshe Shelley, Preface
6. Ibid.
7. BLJ Vol. 6, p. 69

8. Ibid., p. 70
9. Ibid., p. 238
10. Ibid., p. 150
11. Ibid., p. 223

Teresa

1. PWB Vol. IV, p. 241 / CPW Vol. IV, p. 213
2. BLJ Vol. 6, pp. 107–8
3. PWB Vol. IV, p. 547 / CPW Vol. IV, p. 212
4. *The Last Attachment* by Iris Origo (Jonathan Cape & John Murray, 1949), p. 72
5. PWB Vol. VI, pp. 178–9 & 181 / CPW Vol. V, pp. 197–9
6. *The Last Attachment*, op. cit., p. 95
7. Ibid., p. 96
8. BLJ Vol. 6, p. 180
9. BLJ Vol. 9, p. 68
10. BLJ Vol. 6, p. 242
11. Ibid., p. 245
12. Ibid., pp. 255–6

The Prophecy of Dante

1. PWB Vol. IV, pp. 270–1 / CPW Vol. IV, p. 234
2. *Dante the Maker* by William Anderson (Routledge & Kegan Paul, 1980), p. 71
3. Ibid., pp. 3–4 & 6
4. 'Byron and Goethe' by Guiseppe Mazzini, *The Morning Chronicle*, September, 1839
5. PWB Vol. IV, p. 243 / CPW Vol. IV, p. 236. Byron's Preface.
6. CPW Vol. IV, p. 500, Commentary
7. BLJ Vol. 7, p. 59
8. Ibid., p. 115
9. Ibid., p. 158
10. *Medwin's Revised Life of Shelley*, Ed. H. Buxton Forman, Oxford University Press, 1913, p. 149
11. PWB Vol. IV, p. 272 / CPW Vol. IV, p. 236
12. *The Last Attachment*, op. cit., p. 303
13. *Edinburgh Review*, July 1820
14. *Letters of Percy Bysshe Shelley*, edited by F.L. Jones (Clarendon Press, 1964), Vol. II, p. 347
15. *Medwin's Revised Life of Shelley*, op. cit., p. 335, 336

16. *My Recollections of Lord Byron* by Teresa Guiccioli, London, Richard Bentley, 1869, p.249
17. *The Byron Journal*, 1979, 'Bamming and Humming' by William St Clair
18. BLJ Vol. 8, Ravenna Journal, p. 39

Mazeppa

1. PWB Vol. IV, p. 220 / CPW Vol. IV, p. 185
2. BLJ Vol. 6, p. 71
3. Ibid., p. 88
4. *Byron the Poet*, op. cit., p. 40
5. Ibid., p. 54
6. *Fiery Dust*, op. cit., p. 180
7. PWB Vol. IV, p. 215 / CPW Vol. IV, p. 181

Ravenna and Filetto

1. BLJ Vol. 7, p. 24
2 Ibid., p. 35
3. Ibid., p. 80
4. Ibid., p. 167
5. *The Last Attachment*, op. cit., p. 191
6. BLJ Vol. 7, p. 185
7. PWB Vol. VI, p. 120 / CPW Vol. V, pp. 130–1
8. BLJ Vol. 7, p. 144
9. BLJ Vol. 7, p. 134
10. BLJ Vol. 3, p. 253
11. PWB Vol. VI, p. 513 / CPW Vol. V, p. 556
12. BLJ Vol. 8, pp. 97–8
13. *Letters of Percy Bysshe Shelley*, op. cit., Vol. II, p. 283
14. Ibid., p. 309

The First Venetian Play: *Marino Faliero*

1. PWB Vol. V, pp. 335–6 / CPW Vol. IV, p. 363 (Preface to *Marino Faliero*)
2. *The Byron Journal*, 1977, 'A Comparison of *Marino Faliero* with Otway's *Venice Preserv'd*' by John D. Jump
3. *Fiery Dust*, op. cit., p. 227
4. *The Byron Journal*, 1977, 'A Comparison...', op. cit.
5. *Byron the Poet*, op. cit., p. 113

6. PWB Vol. III, p. 407 / CPW Vol. IV, p. 382
7. Ibid., p. 351 / CPW Vol. IV, p. 314
8. *The Byron Journal*, 1977, 'A Comparison...', op. cit.
9. *The Dramas of Lord Byron*, op. cit., p. 92
10. *Fiery Dust*, op. cit., p. 208
11. PWB Vol. IV, p. 335 / CPW Vol. IV, p. 303 / Preface

Hobhouse, Byron, Cato Street and Queen Caroline

1. BLJ Vol. 6, p. 93
2. *British Critic*, 1820
3. *Letters of John Murray to Lord Byron*, op. cit., p. 308 n. 14
4. Ibid., p. 289
5. Ibid., p. 289, n. 1
6. Ibid., p. 305
7. *The Byron Journal*, 2003, 'Hobhouse, Cato Street and *Marino Faliero*' by John Gardner
8. BLJ Vol. 6, p. 88
9. Ibid., p. 93
10. *Byron's Bulldog: Letters of John Cam Hobhouse to Lord Byron* edited by Peter W. Graham (Ohio State University Press, 1984), p. 302
11. Ibid., p. 310
12. Ibid., p. 304
13. Ibid., p. 311
14. PWB Vol. VI, p. 236 / CPW Vol. V, p. 260

The Second Venetian Play: *The Two Foscari*

1. *The Byron Journal*, 2001, 'Natural Law and the State in *The Two Foscari*' by Gordon Spence
2. *Fiery Dust*, op. cit., p. 227
3. BLJ Vol. 8, p. 218
4. PWB Vol. V, p. 149 / CPW Vol. VI, p. 160
5. Ibid., p. 140 / CPW Vol. VI, p. 150

Notes

1. *The Blind Man Traces the Circle*, op. cit., p. 183
2. Ibid., p. 184

Politics in Ravenna

1. CPW Vol. VII, p. 12, Commentary. See passage on war profiteers, pp. 113, 114
2. PWB Vol. V, pp. 560 & 564 / CPW Vol. VII, pp. 13–15
3. *The Mind of Napoleon: A Selection from his Written and Spoken Words* edited and translated by J. Christopher Herold (Columbia University Press, 1961; paperback edn.), p. 176
4. PWB Vol. VI, pp. 7–8 / CPW Vol. V, pp. 6–7, Dedication to *Don Juan*
5. BLJ Vol 8, Ravenna Journal, p. 39
6. Ibid., p. 84
7. Ibid., p. 79
8. Ibid., p. 84
9. Ibid., Ravenna Journal, p. 18
10. Ibid., p. 47
11. Ibid., p. 49
12. Ibid., p. 105
13. *The Byron Journal*, 2001, 'Two New Letters from Byron's Stay in Ravenna' by Andrea Casadio
14. Ibid.
15. Ibid.
16. BLJ Vol. 8, p. 142
17. *The Byron Journal*, 2001, 'Two New Letters...', op. cit.
18. Ibid.
19. Ibid.
20. BLJ Vol. 9, p. 53

The Bowles Controversy

1. BLJ Vol. 7, p. 217
2. Prothero, Vol. 5, pp. 539–41
3. Ibid., p. 560
4. *Blackwood's Edinburgh Magazine*, May 1821

Sardanapalus

1. PWB Vol. V, p. 20 / CPW Vol. I, p. 131
2. *The Dramas of Lord Byron*, op. cit., p. 113
3. Ibid., p. 113
4. Ibid., p. 109
5. *Byron the Poet*, op. cit., p. 116
6. *Byron and the Limits of Fiction*, op. cit., 'The Orientalism of Byron's *Giaour*' by Marilyn Butler, p. 94

7. PWB Vol. V, p. 21 / CPW, Vol. VI, p. 21
8. Ibid., p. 25 / CPW Vol. VI, p. 30
9. Ibid., p. 27 / CPW Vol. VI, p. 27
10. *Letters of Percy Bysshe Shelley*, op. cit., Vol. II, p. 283
11. PWB Vol. V, p. 32 / CPW Vol. VI, p. 38

Notes

1. *Byron and the Dynamics of Metaphor*, op. cit., pp. 125–6
2. *Byron the Poet*, op. cit., p. 116
3. *Byron and Shakespeare* by G. Wilson Knight (Barnes & Noble, 1966), p. 335
4. Ibid., p. 225
5. Ibid., p. 202

Pisa

1. *The Last Attachment*, op. cit., p. 292
2. BLJ Vol. 9, p. 64
3. Ibid., p. 74
4. Ibid., pp. 104–5
5. *The Last Attachment*, op. cit., p. 145
6. Ibid., p. 293
7. Moore, p. 566
8. BLJ Vol. 9, p. 106
9. Ibid., p. 127
10. Ibid., p. 108
11. Ibid., p. 108
12. Ibid., p. 103
13. Ibid., p. 123
14. *Letters of John Murray to Lord Byron*, op. cit., p. 434, Interim note
15. BLJ Vol. 9, p. 122
16. Ibid., p. 78
17. *The Last Attachment*, op. cit., p. 305

Cain

1. Recollections Lord Broughton, Vol. 2, p. 173
2. *Letters of Thomas Moore* edited by Wilfred S. Dowden (Clarendon Press, 1964), Vol. II 1818–1847, p. 494
3. *Letters of Sir Walter Scott* edited by H.J.C. Grierson, assisted by Davidson Cook, W. M. Parker and others (Constable, 1932–37), Vol. VII, pp. 37–8

4. Prothero, Vol. 5, pp. 477–8, n. 1 (Lady Granville to Lady G. Morpeth, 1 January 1822)
5. Ibid., p. 478 [*Autobiography, letters and literary remains of Mrs Piozzi* edited by A. Hayward (London, 1861), Vol. II, p. 447]
6. *Letters of Sir Walter Scott*, op. cit., pp. 37–8
7. BLJ Vol. 9, p. 60
8. Ibid., p. 61
9. PWB Vol. V, p. 218 / CPW Vol. VI, p. 236
10. Ibid., p. 219 / CPW Vol. VI, p. 237
11. BLJ Vol. 9, pp. 53–4
12. PWB Vol. V, p. 236 / CPW Vol. VI, p. 255
13. Ibid., p. 262 / CPW Vol. VI, p. 282
14. Bernard Beatty, in conversation with the author
15. BLJ Vol. 9, p. 103
16. *Letters of Percy Bysshe Shelley*, op. cit., Vol. II, [p. 388] (Shelley to Gisborne, 26 January 1822)
17. *Byron and Goethe: The Analysis of a Passion* by E.M. Butler (Bowes & Bowes, 1956), p. 95
18. Ibid., p. 184
19. PWB Vol. V, p. 275 / CPW Vol. VI, p. 295
20. Bernard Beatty, in conversation with the author

Notes

1. *Méditations Poétiques* by Alphonse de Lamartine (Hachette, 1922), p. 27, 'L'homme à Lord Byron'
2. BLJ Vol. 7, p. 127
3. *Méditations Poétiques*, op. cit., p. 322, n. 5
4. *History of Western Philosophy* by Bertrand Russell (Routledge, 2000), pp. 716–21

Heaven and Earth

1. BLJ Vol. 9, p. 81
2. Ibid., p. 59
3. Ibid., p. 136
4. BLJ Vol. 10, p. 22
5. *London Literary Gazette*, 4 January 1823
6. *Monthly Magazine and British Register*, February 1823
7. Ibid.
8. CPW Vol. VI, p. 682, Commentary
9. BLJ Vol. 10, p. 105
10. Ibid., p. 137
11. *Byron and Goethe*, op. cit., p. 185

12. *Fiery Dust*, op. cit., p. 263
13. *Eve's Children* edited by Gerard P. Luttikhuizen (Brill, 2003), pp. 143–54, 'Milk and Blood, Heredity and Choice: Byron's Readings of Genesis' by Bernard Beatty
14. PWB Vol. V, p. 294 / CPW Vol. VI, p. 355

A Most Lovable Child

1. Prothero, Vol. 5, p. 501, Appendix I
2. *Letters of Percy Bysshe Shelley*, op. cit., pp. 397
3. Prothero, Vol. 5, p. 498, Appendix I
4. *The Last Attachment*, op. cit., p. 360
5. Ibid., p. 362
6. *Letters of Percy Bysshe Shelley*, op. cit., p. 416
7. Ibid., p. 420
8. *The Last Attachment*, op. cit., p. 311
9. BLJ Vol. 9, pp. 163–4
10. BLJ Vol. 10, p. 54
11. *The Last Attachment*, op. cit., pp. 363
12. *Conversations of Lord Byron with the Countess of Blessington* (London, 1834), H. Colburn, p. 72

The End of a Friendship: Byron and John Murray

1. *Letters of John Murray to Lord Byron*, op. cit., p. 444
2. Ibid., pp. 458–9
3. Ibid., pp. 442–3
4. Ibid., p. 449
5. Ibid., p. 446
6. Ibid., p. 410
7. Ibid., p. 467
8. Ibid., p. 466 [BLJ Vol. 11, pp. 123–5]

Werner

1. *Byron Tonight: A Poet's Plays on the Nineteenth Century Stage* by Margaret J. Howell (Springwood Books, 1982), p. 148
2. *Byron and Shakespeare*, op. cit. pp. 183–4
3. *Byron the Poet*, op. cit., p. 111
4. *Byron Tonight*, op. cit., p. 146
5. CPW Vol. VI, p. 695, Commentary

6. Ibid., p. 510
7. *The Dramas of Lord Byron*, op. cit., pp. 143–4
8. *Fiery Dust*, op. cit., p. 227
9. *Byron the Poet*, op. cit., p. 111
10. PWB Vol. V, p. 328
11. *Byron and Shakespeare*, op. cit., p. 184

Montenero

1. *The Last Attachment*, op. cit., p. 346
2. BLJ Vol. 9, pp. 162–3
3. Ibid., p. 185
4. Ibid., p. 197
5. *The Last Attachment*, op. cit., p. 373
6. Ibid., p. 376
7. BLJ Vol. 9, p. 211

The Vision of Judgment

1. PWB Vol. IV, p. 483, Preface / CPW Vol. VI, p. 310
2. *The Spirit of the Age: or, Contemporary Portraits* by William Hazlitt (Oxford University Press, 1935, 'The World's Classics' series), pp. 109–10
3. PWB Vol. IV, p. 483, Preface / CPW Vol. VI, p. 310
4. Ibid., pp. 499, 516, 518 & 520–5 / CPW Vol. VI, pp. 323–4 & 339–45
5. BLJ Vol. 9, p. 100
6. *Constable's Edinburgh Magazine*, November 1822
7. *Bright Darkness: Byron's Poetry in the Context of his Life and Times* by Anne Fleming (Nottingham Court Press, 1983), Preface [by John Mortimer]
8. *The Works of Lord Byron* (John & Henry L. Hunt, 1824), Vol. VI, pp. 187–90, Appendix
9. *Blackwood's Edinburgh Magazine*, December 1824

Notes

1. *Byron the Poet*, op. cit., p. 136
2. *Byron and the Limits of Fiction*, op. cit., 'Fiction's Limit and Eden's Door' by Bernard Beatty, p. 9
3. Ibid., 'The Orientalism of Byron's *Giaour*' by Marilyn Butler, p. 85

Genoa

1. BLJ Vol. 10, p. 77
2. Ibid., p. 11
3. Ibid., p. 11
4. *Letters of Percy Bysshe Shelley*, op. cit. Vol. II, p. 685
5. BLJ Vol. 10, p. 32
6. Ibid., p. 34
7. Ibid., p. 205
8. Ibid., p. 105
9. Ibid., p. 48
10. Ibid., p. 60
11. Ibid., pp. 22–3
12. Ibid., p. 129
13. Ibid., p. 173
14. Ibid., p. 132
15. Ibid., p. 83
16. Ibid., p. 153
17. Ibid., p. 150
18. Ibid., p. 136
19. Ibid., pp. 174–5
20. Ibid., p. 197
21. Ibid., p. 137
22. *The Idler in Italy* by Marguerite, Countess of Blessington (Henry Colburn, 1839–40), Vol. II, p. 39
23. Ibid., Vol. II, pp. 38–9
24. *Julian and Maddalo* by Percy Bysshe Shelley, Preface
25. *The Times*, May 1824 [Hobhouse on Byron]
26. BLJ Vol. 10, pp. 169–70
27. Ibid., p. 183
28. Ibid., p. 189
29. Ibid., p. 199
30. Ibid., p. 211

The Island

1. PWB Vol. V, p. 609 / CPW, Vol. VII, p. 44
2. BLJ Vol. 10, p. 117
3. *Byron the Poet*, op. cit., p. 62
4. *The Byron Journal*, 2004, 'Bligh, Christian, Murray and Napoleon: Byronic Mutiny from London to the South Seas' by Arnold A. Schmidt
5. CPW Vol. VII, p. 134, Commentary
6. PWB, Vol. V, pp. 605–6 / CPW Vol. VII, p. 40
7. CPW Vol. VII, p. 134, Commentary

8. *Byron and Shakespeare*, op. cit., pp. 292–3
9. *The Blind Man Traces the Circle*, op. cit., pp. 211–13

The Deformed Transformed

1. PWB Vol. V, pp. 477–8 / CPW Vol. VI, p. 517
2. BLJ Vol. 10, p. 182
3. *Byron the Poet*, op. cit., p. 126
4. *The Dramas of Lord Byron*, op. cit., p. 148
5. *Byron and Shakespeare*, op. cit., p. 80
6. Ibid., p. 156
7. *Byron and the Limits of Fiction*, op. cit., p. 26
8. *Byron and Shakespeare*, op. cit., p. 324

Journey to Greece

1. PWB Vol. VI, pp. 169–72 / CPW Vol. V, pp. 188–92
2. BLJ Vol. 10, p. 151
3. *The Last Attachment*, op. cit., p. 324 (quotation from the diary of the Italian spy, Torelli)
4. *Romanticism and Male Fantasy in Byron's Don Juan: A Marketable Vice* by Charles Donelan (Macmillan, 2000), p. 177
5. *Byron the Erotic Liberal* by Jonathan David Gross (Rowman & Littlefield, 2001), pp. 144 & 148
6. *That Greece Might Still Be Free: The Philhellenes in the War of Independence* by William St Clair (Oxford University Press, 1972), p. 167
7. BLJ Vol. 10, p. 210

Byron in Cephalonia

1. BLJ Vol. 11, p. 32
2. *Conversations on Religion with Lord Byron and Others Held in Cephalonia,* by James Kennedy (John Murray, 1830), p. 3
3. *Voyage from Leghorn to Cephalonia with Lord Byron,* James Hamilton Browne, Blackwood's XXXV (January 1834)
4. Ibid.,
5. *Complete Essays* by Michel de Montaigne, edited and translated by M.A. Screech (Penguin Classics, 1991), p. 1244
6. Ibid., p. 895
7. Ibid., p. 717

8. *Voyage from Leghorn to Cephalonia*, op. cit.
9. BLJ Vol. 11, p. 22
10. *History of the Greek Revolution* by George Finlay (Zeno, 1971), p. 208
11. *The Last Days of Lord Byron*, William Parry (A & W Galignani, 1826), p. 139
12. Ibid., pp. 140–1
13. Ibid., p. 133
14. Ibid., pp. 128–9
15. *The Flame of Freedom: The Greek War of Independence 1821–33* by David Brewer (John Murray, 2001), p. 60
16. Ibid., p. 65
17. Ibid., p. 121
18. Ibid., p. 135
19. BLJ Vol. 11, p. 66
20. Ibid., p. 45
21. Ibid., p. 17
22. Ibid., p. 44
23. Ibid., p. 39
24. Ibid., p. 71
25. Ibid., pp. 69–70
26. Ibid., p. 73
27. Ibid., p. 51
28. Ibid., p. 48
29. Ibid., p. 45
30. *The Flame of Freedom*, op. cit., p. 203
31. *The Byron Journal*, 2000, Review by Andrew Nicholson of *On a Voiceless Shore: Byron in Greece* by Stephen Minta (New York: Harold Holt & Co., 1998)
32. *The Byron Journal, 2000*, 'The Last Illness of Lord Byron' by Raymond Mills

Byron at Mesolonghi

1. *The Flame of Freedom*, op. cit., p. 205
2. BLJ Vol. 11, p. 92
3. Ibid., p. 87
4. *The Byron Journal*, 2000, Review by Andrew Nicholson..., op. cit.
5. *History of the Greek Revolution*, op. cit., p. 327
6. *The Last Days of Lord Byron*, op. cit., pp. 144–5
7. *History of the Greek Revolution*, op. cit., p. 327
8. Ibid., p. 317
9. BLJ Vol. 11, p. 108
10. Ibid., p. 107
11. *The Last Days of Lord Byron*, op. cit., p. 188

12. Ibid., p. 88
13. BLJ Vol. 11, p. 98
14. Ibid., p. 118
15. *The Byron Journal*, 2002, 'And Thus the Peopled City Grieves', by Bernard Beatty
16. Ibid.
17. BLJ Vol. 11, p. 129
18. *The Last Days of Lord Byron*, op. cit., pp. 124–5
19. BLJ Vol. 11, p. 145
20. Moore, p. 99
21. BLJ Vol. 11, p. 111, 112
22. Ibid., p. 142
23. Ibid., p. 124
24. Ibid., p. 135
25. Ibid., p. 145
26. Ibid., p. 150
27. Ibid., p. 146
28. Ibid., p. 144
29. Ibid., p. 139
30. BLJ Supplementary Volume, p. 83
31. Ibid., p. 84
32. Ibid., p. 84

Implora Pace

1. BLJ Vol. 6, p. 147
2. PWB Vol. VII, pp. 84–5 / CPW Vol. VII, p. 81
3. *The Flame of Freedom*, op. cit., p. 61
4. Ibid., p. 61
5. Ibid., p. 328
6. PWB Vol. VII, pp. 86–8 / CPW Vol. VII, p. 79
7. *The Byron Journal*, 2000, 'The Last Illness...', op. cit.
8. BLJ Vol. 11, p. 121
9. *Byron's Bulldog*, op. cit., p. 352
10. BLJ Vol. 11, p. 131
11. Ibid., pp. 140–1
12. Ibid., p. 137
13. Ibid., p. 126
14. *The Byron Journal*, 2000, 'The Last Illness...', op. cit.
15. Ibid.
16. David Brewer, in conversation with the author
17. *The Last Days of Lord Byron*, op. cit., p. 98
18. *Roumeli: Travels in Northern Greece* by Patrick Leigh Fermor (John Murray, 1966) p. 172

'Our Second English Epic'

1. *Byron: 'Don Juan'* by Anne Barton (Cambridge University Press, 1992), p. 7
2. PWB Vol. VI, p. 184 / CPW Vol. V, p. 204
3. BLJ Vol. 10, p. 150
4. BLJ Vol. 6, p. 67
5. PWB Vol. VI, p. 73 / CPW Vol V, p. 73
6. Ibid., p. 302 / CPW Vol. V, p. 337
7. BLJ Vol. 6, p. 99
8. BLJ Vol. 9, p. 187
9. *The Reading Nation in the Romantic Period*, op. cit., pp. 163–4
10. PWB Vol. VI, pp. 266–7 / CPW Vol. V, pp. 296–7
11. *The Examiner*, November 1832
12. BLJ Vol. 10, p. 29
13. BLJ Vol. 6, p. 232
14. Ibid., p. 237
15. BLJ Vol. 7, p. 202
16. *Letters of Percy Bysshe Shelley*, op. cit., Vol. II, p. 323
17. Ibid., pp. 397–8
18. *John Bull*, April 1821, 'Letter to Lord Byron', op. cit.
19. PWB Vol. VI, pp. 450–3 / CPW Vol. V, pp. 488–91
20. Ibid., pp. 77–79 / CPW Vol. V, pp. 77–9
21. Ibid., p. 2 / CPW Vol. V, p. 88
22. Ibid., p. 82 / CPW Vol. V, p. 337
23. Ibid., pp. 302–4 / CPW Vol. V, p. 337
24. Ibid., p. 357 / CPW Vol. V, p. 391
25. Ibid., p. 407 / CPW Vol. V, p. 444
26. Ibid., p. 425 / CPW Vol. V, p. 462
27. Ibid., p. 501 / CPW Vol. V, pp. 544–6
28. Ibid., pp. 542–3 / CPW Vol. V, p. 588
29. Ibid., p. 562 / CPW Vol. V, p. 606
30. Ibid., p. 564 / CPW Vol. V, p. 610
31. Ibid., p. 571 / CPW Vol. V, pp. 617–8
32. Ibid., p. 51 / CPW Vol. V, p. 51

Notes

1. *Don Juan* and its Narrator

1. *Byron: 'Don Juan'*, op. cit., p. 3
2. Ibid., p. 72
3. *Byron the Erotic Liberal*, op. cit., p. 135
4. Ibid., p. 130
5. Ibid., p. 130

6. BLJ Vol. 6, p. 105
7. *The Flowering of Byron's Genius*, op. cit., p. 6
8. Vladimir Markuzan, in conversation with the author
9. *Byron the Poet*, op. cit., p. 252

2. *Don Juan* as Literary Criticism

10. *Don Juan in Context* by Jerome J. McGann (John Murray, 1976), p. 107
11. *Byron the Poet*, op. cit., p. 252
12. PWB Vol. VI, p. 80 / CPW Vol. V, p. 80
13. *Don Juan in Context* by Jerome J McGann (John Murray, 1976), p. 78

3. The 'Indecency' of *Don Juan*

14. BLJ Vol. 6, pp. 76–7
15. *Byron: 'Don Juan'*, op. cit., p. 83
16. Ibid., p. 27
17. *The Reading Nation in the Romantic Period*, op. cit., p. 410
18. *Byron: 'Don Juan'*, op. cit., p. 58
19. *The Flowering of Byron's Genius*, op. cit., p. 153
20. *John Bull*, April 1821, 'Letter to Lord Byron', op. cit.
21. *The Flowering of Byron's Genius*, op. cit., p. 74
22. *Blackwood's Edinburgh Magazine*, September 1823

4. The Bewilderment of Some Nineteenth Century Readers of *Don Juan*

23. *Byron, Poetics and History*, [Cambridge Studies in Romanticism] by Jane Stabler (Cambridge University Press, 2002) p. 3
24. *Romanticism and Male Fantasy in Byron's Don Juan: A Marketable Vice* by Charles Donelan (Palgrave Macmillan, 2000) p. 139

5. A recently published account of the language used by Byron in *Don Juan*, by Richard Cronin

25. *Romanticism and Religion from William Cowper to Wallace Stevens* edited by Gavin Hopps and Jane Stabler (Ashgate, 2006), 'Words and the Word: the Diction of Don Juan' by Richard Cronin, p. 139
26. Ibid., pp. 140, 141
27. Ibid., p. 144

The Great Enigma of the Realms of Rhyme

1. BLJ Vol. 3, p. 233
2. BLJ Vol. 5, p. 243
3. *London Literary Gazette*, March 1817
4. *The Young Romantics and Critical Opinion*, 1807–1824 by Theodore Redpath (Harrap, 1973), p. 174
5. *Painter of Passion: The Journal of Eugène Delacroix* selected and edited by Hubert Wellington, translated by Lucy Norton (Folio Society, 1995), p. 27
6. PWB Vol. VI, p. 444 / CPW Vol. VII, p. 482
7. BLJ Vol. 3, p. 233
8. PWB Vol. VI, p. 438 / CPW Vol. V, p. 476
9. *Fiery Dust*, op. cit., p. 49
10. *Byron and the Limits of Fiction*, op. cit., 'Authoring the Self: *Childe Harold* III and IV' by Vincent Newey, p. 185
11. Ibid., 'Lyric Presence in Byron from the Tales to *Don Juan*' by Brian Nellist, p. 49
12. Ibid., p. 47
13. Ibid, p. 51
14. *The Flame of Freedom*, op. cit., p. 219
15. Prothero, Vol. 3, p. 3 (Sir Walter Scott to John Murray, December 1821)
16. *Byron and Goethe*, op. cit., p. 14
17. 'Lord Byron's Works Viewed in Connection with Christianity and the Obligations of Social Life', a sermon preached in Holland Chapel, Kennington, by the Revd. John Styles (Prothero Vol. VI, p. 9)
18. *Blackwood's Edinburgh Magazine*, June 1824

BIBLIOGRAPHY

Byron: Works

The Works of Lord Byron (London: John & Henry L. Hunt, 1824) 8 volumes projected [only vols. 5–7 published].

The Works of Lord Byron: The Letters and Journals, Ed. Rowland E. Prothero (London: John Murray, 1898), 6 volumes.

The Poetical Works of Lord Byron, revised Edn., Ed. Ernest Hartley Coleridge (London: John Murray, 1903) 7 volumes.

Byron's Letters and Journals, Ed. Leslie A. Marchand (London: John Murray, 1973–97) 13 volumes.

Lord Byron, The Complete Poetical Works, Ed. Jerome J. McGann (Oxford: Clarendon Press, 1980–93) 7 volumes.

Lord Byron: The Complete Miscellaneous Prose, Ed. Andrew Nicholson (Oxford: Clarendon Press, 1991)

Byron, Life

Medwin, Thomas, *Journal of the Conversations of Lord Byron: noted during a residence with His Lordship at Pisa in the years 1821 and 1822* (Paris: A. & W. Galignani, 1824)

Nathan, Isaac, *Fugitive Pieces and Reminiscences of Lord Byron* (London: Whittaker, Treacher & Co., 1829)

Moore, Thomas, *Letters and Journals of Lord Byron with Notices of His Life* (London: John Murray, 1832; repr. 1932)

Conversations of Lord Byron with the Countess of Blessington (London: Richard Bentley for Henry Colburn, 1834)

Austin, Alfred, *The Vindication of Lord Byron* (London: Chapman & Hall, 1869)

Guiccioli, Teresa, *My Recollections of Lord Byron* (London: Richard Bentley, 1869) 2 volumes.

Stowe, Harriet Beecher, *The Vindication of Lady Byron* (London: 1869)

Irving, Washington, *Abbotsford and Newstead* (London: George Bell & Sons, 1878)

To Lord Byron: Feminine Profiles, Ed. George Parton and Peter Quennell (London: John Murray, 1939)

Origo, Iris, *The Last Attachment* (London: Jonathan Cape & John Murray, 1949)

His Very Self and Voice: Collected Conversations of Lord Byron, Ed. Ernest J. Lovell Jr (New York: Macmillan Co., 1954)

Marchand, Leslie A., *Byron: A Biography* (New York: Knopf, 1957) 3 volumes.

Moore, Doris Langley, *The Late Lord Byron* (London: John Murray, 1961)

Moore, Doris Langley, *Lord Byron: Accounts Rendered* (London: John Murray, 1974)

Chapman, John S., *Byron and the Honourable Augusta Leigh* (New Haven & London: Yale University Press, 1975)

Marchand, Leslie A., *Byron: A Portrait* (London: John Murray, 1971)

Crompton, Louis, *Byron and Greek Love* (London: Faber and Faber, 1985)

Foot, Michael, *The Politics of Paradise: A Vindication of Byron* (London: Collins, 1988)

Elledge, W. Paul, *Lord Byron at Harrow School: Speaking Out, Talking Back, Acting Up, Bowing Out* (Baltimore & London: John Hopkins University Press, 2000)

Beckett, John, with Aley, Sheila, *Byron and Newstead: The Aristocrat and the Abbey* (Newark: University of Delaware Press, & London: Associated University Presses, 2001)

Vail, Jeffery W, *The Literary Relationship of Byron and Thomas Moore* (Baltimore: Johns Hopkins University Press, 2001)

Gilmour, Ian, *The Making of the Poets: Byron and Shelley in their Time* (London: Chatto & Windus, 2002)

Guiccioli, Teresa, *Vie de Lord Byron en Italie*, Trans. Michael Rees as *Lord Byron's Life in Italy*, Ed. Peter Cochran (Newark: University of Delaware Press, 2005)

Byron in Greece

Gamba, Pietro, *A Narrative of Lord Byron's Last Journey to Greece* (Paris: A. & W. Galignani, 1825)

Parry, William, *The Last Days of Lord Byron, to which are added Reminiscences of Lord Byron, contained in letters addressed to L. Stanhope* (Paris: A. & W. Galignani, 1826)

Kennedy, James, *Conversations on Religion with Lord Byron and Others Held in Cephalonia* (London: John Murray, 1830)

Finlay, George, *History of the Greek Revolution* (London: Zeno Publishers, 1971) [A reprint of vols. VI & VII of the author's *History of Greece* (Edinburgh: W. Blackwood, 1851).]

St Clair, William, *That Greece Might Still Be Free: The Philhellenes in the War of Independence* (London & New York: Oxford University Press, 1972)

Minta, Stephen, *On a Voiceless Shore: Byron in Greece* (New York: Harold Holt & Co., 1998)

Brewer, David, *The Flame of Freedom: The Greek War of Independence 1821–33* (London: John Murray, 2001)

Letters

Letters of Harriet, Countess Granville, Ed. F. Leveson-Gower (London: Longmans, Green & Co., 1894) 2 volumes

Letters of Sir Walter Scott, Ed. H.J.C. Grierson, assisted by Davidson Cook, W. M. Parker and others (London: Constable, 1932–37)

Letters of Sydney Smith, Ed. Nowell C. Smith (Oxford: Clarendon Press, 1953) 2 volumes

Letters of Thomas Moore, Ed. Wilfred S. Dowden (Oxford: Clarendon Press, 1964) 2 volumes [consecutive pagination: Vol. 1, 1793–1818, 466 pp; Vol. 2, 1818–1847, 467–989 pp]

Clairmont, Clara Mary Jane, *Journals of Claire Clairmont*, Ed. Marion Kingston Stocking (Cambridge, Massachusetts: Harvard University Press, 1968)

Letters of Percy Bysshe Shelley, Vol. II, Ed. F.L. Jones (Oxford: Clarendon Press, 1964)

Letters of William and Dorothy Wordsworth, Vol. III, The Middle Years, Ed. Ernest de Selincourt (Oxford: Clarendon Press, 1970)

Byron's Bulldog: Letters of John Cam Hobhouse to Lord Byron, Ed. Peter W. Graham (Columbus: Ohio State University Press, 1984)

Byron's 'Corbeau Blanc': The Life and Letters of Lady Melbourne, Ed. Jonathan David Gross (Houston, Texas: Rice University Press, 1997)

The Clairmont Correspondence, Vol. I, 1808–1834, Ed. Marion Kingston Stocking (Baltimore & London: Johns Hopkins University Press, 1995)

Letters of John Murray to Lord Byron edited by Andrew Nicholson (Liverpool University Press, 2007)

Biographies

L'Estrange, Alfred Guy Kingham, *The Literary Life of the Rev. William Harness, Vicar of All Saints, Knightsbridge, and Prebendary of St Paul's* (London: Hurst & Blackett, 1871)

Smiles, Samuel, *A Publisher and his Friends: A Memoir and Correspondence of the late John Murray* (London: John Murray, 1891) 2 volumes.

The Two Duchesses: Georgiana, Duchess of Devonshire, Elizabeth, Duchess

of Devonshire. Family correspondence, 1777–1859, Ed. Vere Foster (London: Blackie & Son, 1898)

Medwin, Thomas, *The Life of Percy Bysshe Shelley*, new Edn. with introduction and commentary by H. Buxton Forman (London: Humphrey Milford, 1913)

Recollections of a Long Life: Lord Broughton, Ed. Lady Dorchester [his daughter] (London: John Murray, 1902) 2 volumes.

Mayne, Ethel Colburne, *The Life and Letters of Anne Isabella, Lady Noel Byron* (London: Constable, 1929)

Sadleir, Michael, *Blessington-D'Orsay: A Biography of Marguerite, Countess of Blessington and Alfred Count d'Orsay, a Masquerade* (London: Constable, 1933)

Cecil, David, *The Young Melbourne* (London: Constable, 1939)

Lady Bessborough and Her Family Circle, Ed. the Earl of Bessborough, in collaboration with A. Aspinall (London: John Murray, 1940)

Butler, E.M., *Byron and Goethe: The Analysis of a Passion* (London: Bowes & Bowes, 1956)

Herold, Christopher J., *Mistress to an Age: Madame de Staël* (London: Hamish Hamilton, 1959)

Elwin, Malcolm, *Lord Byron's Wife* (London: Macdonald, 1962)

Gunn, Peter, *My Dearest Augusta* (London: The Bodley Head, 1968)

Reid, Loren H., *Charles James Fox: A Man for the People* (London & Harlow: Longmans, 1969)

Holmes, Richard, *Shelley: The Pursuit* (London: Weidenfeld & Nicolson, 1974)

Burnett, T.A.J., *The Rise and Fall of a Regency Dandy: The Life and Times of Scrope Berdmore Davies* (London: John Murray, 1981)

Hinde, Wendy, *Castlereagh* (London: Collins, 1981)

Boyes, Megan, *Queen of a Fantastic Realm*, [A Biography of Mary Ann Chaworth, 1785–1832] (Derby: M. Boyes, 1986)

The Journal of Sir Walter Scott, Ed. W.E.K. Anderson (Edinburgh: Canongate, 1988)

Boyes, Megan, *Love Without Wings: the story of the unique relationship between Elizabeth Bridget Pigot of Southwell and the young poet, Lord Byron* (Derby: M. Boyes, 1988)

Holmes, Richard, *Coleridge: Early Visions* (London: Hodder & Stoughton, 1989)

St Clair, William, *The Godwins and the Shelleys: The Biography of a Family* (London: Faber & Faber, 1989)

Boyes, Megan, *My Amiable Mama: The Biography of Mrs Catherine Byron, the mother of the poet George Gordon, 6th Lord Byron* (Derby: M. Boyes, 1991)

Storey, Mark, *Robert Southey: A Life* (Oxford: Oxford University Press, 1997)

Foreman, Amanda, *Georgiana, Duchess of Devonshire* (London: Harper Collins, 1998)

Holmes, Richard, *Coleridge: Darker Reflections* (London: Harper Collins, 1998)

Bakewell, Michael and Melissa, *Augusta Leigh* (London: Chatto & Windus, 2000)

Normington, Susan, *Lady Caroline Lamb* (London: House of Stratus, 2001)

Douglas, Paul, *Lady Caroline Lamb* (Basingstoke: Palgrave Macmillan, 2004)

Literary Background

Hazlitt, William, *The Spirit of the Age: or, Contemporary Portraits* (London: Henry Colburn, 1825) [also in 'The World's Classics' series, Oxford University Press, 1935]

Haydon, Benjamin Robert, *Correspondence and Table Talk* (London: Chatto & Windus, 1876) 2 volumes

Symons, Arthur, *The Romantic Movement in English Poetry* (London: Constable, 1909)

Quiller-Couch, Sir Arthur, *Studies in Literature, Second Series* (Cambridge: Cambridge University Press, 1934)

Praz, Mario, *The Romantic Agony*, 2nd Edn, Trans. Angus Davidson (London: Oxford University Press, 1951)

Shelley and his Circle, 1773–1882, being an edition of the manuscripts in the Carl H. Pforzheimer Library, Ed. Kenneth Neill Cameron and Donald Henry Reiman (Cambridge, Massachusetts: Harvard University Press, 1961–86) 8 volumes

Byron: The Critical Heritage, Ed. Andrew Rutherford (London: Routledge & Kegan Paul, 1970)

Redpath, Theodore, *The Young Romantics and Critical Opinion, 1807–1824* (London: Harrap, 1973)

English Romantic Poets: Modern Essays in Criticism, 2nd Edn, Ed. M.H. Abrams (London: Oxford University Press, 1975)

Christiansen, Rupert, *Romantic Affinities: Portraits from an Age, 1780–1830* (London: The Bodley Head, 1988)

Schock, Peter A., *Romantic Satanism: Myth and the Historical Moment in Blake, Shelley and Byron* (Basingstoke: Palgrave Macmillan, 2003)

Cavaliero, Roderick, *Italia Romantica: English Romantics and Italian Freedom* (London & New York: I.B. Tauris, 2005)

Political and Social Background

Bury, Charlotte Campbell, Lady, *The Diary of a Lady in Waiting*, Ed. A. Francis Stuart (London: The Bodley Head, 1908), 2 volumes

Hill, Constance, *Maria Edgeworth and her Circle in the days of Buonaparte and Bourbon* (London & New York: John Lane, 1910)

In Whig Society: 1775–1818 ... the hitherto unpublished correspondence of Elizabeth, Viscountess Melbourne, and Emily Lamb, Countess Cowper, afterwards Viscountess Palmerston, compiled Mabell, Countess Airlie (London: Hodder & Stoughton, 1921)

Mayne, Ethel Colburn, *A Regency Chapter: Lady Bessborough and her Friendships* (London: Macmillan & Co., 1939)

The Mind of Napoleon: A Selection from his Written and Spoken Words, Ed. & trans. J. Christopher Herold (New York: Columbia University Press, 1955)

Briggs, Asa, *The Age of Improvement* (London: Longman, 1959)

Nicolson, Harold, *The Congress of Vienna* (London: Methuen, 1961)

Creevey, Thomas, *The Creevey Papers*, Revised Edn, Ed. John Gore (London: Batsford, 1963)

Gronow, R.H., *The Reminiscences and Recollections of Captain Gronow*, Abridged John Raymond (London: The Bodley Head, 1964)

Ayling, S.E. *The Georgian Century: 1714–1837* (London: Harrap, 1966)

Croker, J. Wilson, *The Croker Papers, 1808–1857*, New & abridged Edn, Ed. Bernard Pool (London: Batsford, 1967)

Longford, Elizabeth, *Wellington, Vol. I. The Years of the Sword* (London: Weidenfeld & Nicolson, 1969) [Abridged edition, incorporating *Vol. 2: Pillar of State*, published in one volume as *Wellington*, 1992]

Mitchell, L.G., *Charles James Fox and the Disintegration of the Whig Party, 1782–1794* (London: Oxford University Press, 1971)

Wardroper, John, *Kings, Lords and Wicked Libellers: Satire and Protest, 1760–1837* (London: John Murray, 1973)

Emsley, Clive, *British Society and the French Wars, 1793–1815* (London: Macmillan, 1979)

Gash, Norman, *Aristocracy and People, Britain 1815–1865* (London: Edward Arnold, 1979)

Butler, Marilyn, *Romantics, Rebels and Reactionaries: English Literature and its Background, 1760–1830* (Oxford: Oxford University Press, 1981)

Byron's Political and Cultural Influence in Nineteenth Century Europe: A Symposium, Ed. Paul Graham Trueblood (London: Macmillan, 1981)

Christie, Ian, *Wars and Revolutions: Britain 1760–1815* (London: Edward Arnold, 1982)

Porter, Roy, *English Society in the Eighteenth Century* (London: Allen Lane, 1982)

Mapping Male Sexuality: Nineteenth Century England, Ed. Jay Losey and William D. Brewer (London: Associated University Presses, 2000)

Miscellaneous

Hobhouse, John Cam, *A Journey through Albania, and other provinces of Turkey in Europe, and Asia, to Constantinople during the years 1809 and 1810* (London: John Cawthom, 1813) 2 volumes

Blessington, Marguerite, Countess of, *The Idler in Italy* (London: Henry Colburn, 1839–40) 3 volumes.

Smith, Sydney, *The Wit and Wisdom of The Rev. Sydney Smith: a selection of the most memorable passages in his Writings and Conversation* (London: Longmans, Green & Co., 1869)

Shelley, Frances, Lady: *The Diary of Frances, Lady Shelley, edited by her grandson Richard Edgcumbe, Vol. 1, 1787–1817* (London: John Murray, 1912)

Russell, Bertrand, *History of Western Philosophy* (London: George Allen & Unwin, 1946; London: Routledge, 2000)

Thompson, E.P., *The Making of the English Working Class* (London: Victor Gollancz, 1963)

Fermor, Patrick Leigh, *Roumeli: Travels in Northern Greece* (London: John Murray, 1966)

St Clair, William, Lord Elgin and the Marbles (London: Oxford University Press, 1967) [Pbk Edn 1983]

Anderson, William, *Dante the Maker* (London: Routledge & Kegan Paul, 1980)

Howell, Margaret J., *Byron Tonight: A Poet's Plays on the Nineteenth Century Stage* (Windlesham, Surrey: Springwood Books, 1982)

Montaigne, Michel de, *Complete Essays*, Ed. & trans. by M.A. Screech (London: Allen Lane, Penguin Classics, 1991), p. 1244

Painter of Passion: The Journal of Eugène Delacroix, Selected and Ed. Hubert Wellington, Trans. Lucy Norton (London: Folio Society, 1995)

Mapping Lives: The Uses of Biography, Ed. Peter France and William St Clair [British Academy Centenary Monograph] (Oxford: Oxford University Press, 2002)

Cheeke, Stephen, *Byron and Place: History, Translation, Nostalgia* (Basingstoke: Palgrave Macmillan, 2003)

St Clair, William, *The Reading Nation in the Romantic Period* (Cambridge: Cambridge University Press, 2004)

Liberty and Poetic Licence: New Essays on Byron, Ed. Bernard Beatty and Charles Robinson (Liverpool: Liverpool University Press, 2005)

Romanticism and Religion from William Cowper to Wallace Stevens, ed. Gavin Hopps and Jane Stabler, Ashgate 2006

Criticism

Symons, Arthur, *The Romantic Movement in English Poetry* (London: Constable, 1909)

Calvert, William J., *Byron: Romantic Paradox* (Chapel Hill: University of North Carolina Press, 1935)

John Bull's Letter to Lord Byron. Ed. Alan Lang Strout (Norman: University of Oklahoma Press, 1947)

Trueblood, Paul G., *The Flowering of Byron's Genius: Studies in Byron's Don Juan* (New York: Russell & Russell, 1962)

Chew, Samuel C., *The Dramas of Lord Byron: A Critical Study* (New York: Russell & Russell, 1964)

Joseph, Michael K., *Byron the Poet* (London: Victor Gollancz, 1964)

Knight, G. Wilson, *Byron and Shakespeare* (New York: Barnes & Noble, 1966)

Elledge, W. Paul, *Byron and the Dynamics of Metaphor* (Nashville: Vanderbilt University Press, 1968)

McGann, Jerome J., *Fiery Dust: Byron's Poetical Development* (Chicago & London: University of Chicago Press, 1968)

Cooke, Michael G., *The Blind Man Traces the Circle: On the Patterns and Philosophy of Byron's Poetry* (Princeton, New Jersey: Princeton University Press, 1969)

McGann, Jerome J., *Don Juan in Context* (London: John Murray, 1976)

Vassallo, Peter, *Byron: The Italian Literary Influence* (London: Macmillan, 1984)

Beatty, Bernard, *Byron's Don Juan* (Totowa, New Jersey: Barnes & Noble, 1985)

Byron and the Limits of Fiction, Ed. Bernard Beatty and Vincent Newey, [Liverpool English Texts and Studies] (Liverpool: Liverpool University Press, 1988)

Graham, Peter W., *Don Juan and Regency England* (Charlottesville: University of Virginia Press, 1990)

Barton, Anne, *Byron, 'Don Juan'* (Cambridge: Cambridge University Press, 1992)

Christensen, Jerome, *Lord Byron's Strength: Romantic Writing and Commercial Society* (Baltimore & London: Johns Hopkins University Press, 1993)

Donelan, Charles, *Romanticism and Male Fantasy in Byron's Don Juan: A Marketable Vice* (Basingstoke: Palgrave Macmillan, 2000)

Gross, Jonathan David, *Byron the Erotic Liberal* (New York & Oxford: Rowman & Littlefield, 2001)

Stabler, Jane, *Byron, Poetics and History* [Cambridge Studies in Romanticism] (Cambridge, U.K. & New York: Cambridge University Press, 2002)

Beatty, Bernard, 'Milk and Blood, Heredity and Choice: Byron's Readings of Genesis' in *Eve's Children*, Ed. Gerard P. Luttikhuizen (Leiden & Boston, Massachusetts: Brill, 2003)

Cronin, Richard, 'Words and the Word: the Diction of *Don Juan*' in *Romanticism and Religion from William Cowper to Wallace Stevens*, Ed. Gavin Hopps and Jane Stabler (Aldershot: Ashgate, 2006)

From: *The Byron Journal*

1977 Jump, John D., 'A Comparison of *Marino Faliero* and Otway's *Venice Preserv'd*'
1979 St Clair, William, 'Bamming and Humming'
1987 Graham, Peter, 'The Venetian Climate of *Don Juan*'
1989 St Clair, William, 'The Temptations of a Biographer'
1989 Tyerman, C.J., 'Byron's Harrow'
1991 Clubbe, John, 'The Tempest-toss'd Summer of 1816: Mary Shelley's *Frankenstein*'
1991 Giddey, Ernest, '1816: Switzerland and the Revival of the "Grand Tour"'
1996 Spence, Gordon, 'Byron's Polynesian Fantasy'
1998 Woodhouse, David, ' "Churchill's Grave": A Line of Separation'
1999 Pont, Graham, 'Byron and Nathan: A Musical Collaboration'
2000 Mills, Raymond, 'The Last Illness of Lord Byron'
2001 Casadio, Andrea, 'Two New Letters from Byron's stay in Ravenna'
2001 Spence, Gordon, 'Natural Law and the State in *The Two Foscari*'
2002 Beatty, Bernard, 'And Thus the Peopled City Grieves'
2003 Clubbe, John, 'Byron in Our Time'
2003 Gardner, John, 'Hobhouse, Cato Street and *Marino Faliero*'
2003 Shaw, Philip, 'Wordsworth and Byron'
2004 No. 1 Schmidt, Arnold A., 'Bligh, Christian, Murray and Napoleon: Byronic Mutiny from London to the South Seas'

ACKNOWLEDGEMENTS TO WRITERS AND PUBLISHERS

My apologies are due to Jerome McGann. Although I have been able to quote from his invaluable critical works, most notably in my second volume, circumstances have obliged me to change from his edition of the poems of Byron to the earlier Coleridge edition. However, I have made sure that every stanza quoted in the book is numbered for those who wish to consult the McGann edition.

Innumerable fine books on Byron, his life and his poetry have been published over the years by John Murray. All I have ever written on Byron is informed by the works of such writers as Professor Marchand and Mrs Langley Moore. In this volume I have used the Coleridge edition of the poetry and the Marchand edition of the Letters and Journals, both published by John Murray.

My thanks are due to the following for permission to quote:

Sir John Mortimer for allowing me to quote from his introduction to *Bright Darkness* by Anne Fleming, Nottingham Court Press, London 1984.

Professor Philip Collins for permission to quote from his Nottingham Byron Lecture, 1969.

Pollinger Ltd and the Earl of Lytton for brief extracts from letters to be found among the *Lovelace Papers*.

Liverpool University Press for extracts from:

Byron and the Limits of Fiction, 1968, edited by Bernard Beatty and Vincent Newey.

Liberty and Poetic Licence; New Essays on Byron, ed. Bernard Beatty and Charles Robinson, 2006.

The Letters of John Murray to Lord Byron, ed. Andrew Nicholson, 2007.

University of Chicago Press for quotations from *Fiery Dust: Byron's Poetical Development* by Jerome J. McGann © 1968 by the University of Chicago. All rights reserved.

Johns Hopkins University Press for extracts from:

Elledge, Paul, *Lord Byron at Harrow School: Speaking Out, Talking Back, Acting Up, Bowing Out*, pp. 28, 40, 44, 50. © 2000 The Johns Hopkins University Press. Reprinted with permission of the Johns Hopkins University Press.

Vail, Jeffery W., *The Literary Relationship of Lord Byron and Thomas Moore*, pp. 156, 160, 161, 162, 185. © The Johns Hopkins University Press. Reprinted with permission of The Johns Hopkins University Press.

Christensen, Jerome, *Lord Byron's Strength. Romantic Writing and Commercial Society*, pp. 28, 48, 44, 103, 153, 218, 238. © 1993 The Johns Hopkins University Press. Reprinted with permission of The Johns Hopkins University Press.

Stocking, Marion Kingston, ed., *The Clairmont Correspondence*, pp. 225, 164. © 1995 The Johns Hopkins University Press. Reprinted with permission of The Johns Hopkins University Press.

Oxford University Press for extracts from:

The Complete Poetical Works of Byron – Commentary (1980), edited by McGann, Jerome. By permission of Oxford University Press.

The Letters of William and Dorothy Wordsworth. The Middle Years (1970), edited by de Selincourt, Ernest de. By Permission of Oxford University Press.

The Letters of Sydney Smith (1953) by Smith, Sydney, edited by Smith, Nowell C. By permission of Oxford University Press.

The Spirit of the Age WC57 (1953) by Hazlitt, William. By permission of Oxford University Press.

That Greece Might Still be Free: The Philhellenes in the War of Independence, William St Clair, 1972. By permission of Oxford University Press.

The Orion Publishing Group Ltd for extracts from:

Byron the Poet by M.K. Joseph, Victor Gollancz, 1964, an imprint of the Orion Publishing Group.

Wellington: The Years of the Sword by Elizabeth Longford, Weidenfeld and Nicolson, 1969, a division of the Orion Publishing Group Ltd.

The Random House Group Ltd for extracts from:

The Making of the Poets: Byron and Shelley in Their Time by Ian Gilmour, published by Chatto and Windus. Reprinted by permission of The Random

House Group Ltd and of Gillon Aitken Associates Ltd. Copyright © 2002 by Ian Gilmour.

Augusta Leigh by Michael and Melissa Bakewell, published by Chatto and Windus, 2000. Reprinted by permission of The Random House Group Ltd.

My Dearest Augusta by Peter Gunn, published by Bodley Head, 1969. Reprinted by permission of The Random House Group Ltd.

Taylor and Francis for extracts from:

Byron and Shakespeare by G. Wilson Knight, Barnes and Noble, New York, 1960, pp. 14/15, 235, 15.

A History of Western Philosophy by Bertrand Russell, Routledge, London, 2000, p. 718.

Dante the Maker by William Anderson, Routledge and Kegan Paul, 1980.

The Rowman and Littlefield Publishing Group, Lanham, Boulder, New York, Oxford for extracts from *Byron the Erotic Liberal* by Jonathan David Gross, 2001.

Vanderbilt University Press, Nashville, Tennessee, for extracts from *Byron and the Dynamics of Metaphor* by Paul Elledge, 1968.

Cambridge University Press for extracts from:

Studies in Literature by Sir Arthur Quiller-Couch, London, 1943

The Reading Nation in the Romantic Period by William St Clair, 2004.

Byron: Don Juan by Anne Barton, 1992.

Byron, Poetics and History by Jane Stabler, 2002.

Constable and Robinson for an extract from *The Young Melbourne* by Lord David Cecil, Constable, 1943.

Harvard University Press for an extract reprinted by permission of the publishers from *The Journals of Claire Clairmont*, edited by Marion Kingston Stocking, Cambridge, Mass., Harvard University Press. Copyright © 1968 by the President and Fellows of Harvard College and for extracts from *Shelley and his Circle 1773–1882, being an edition of the manuscripts in the Carl Pforzheimer Library*, ed. Kenneth Neill Cameron and David Henry Reiman (Cambridge, Mass., Harvard University Press, 1961–86, 8 volumes).

BJ Batsford for extracts from:

The Creevey Papers by Thomas Creevey, edited by John Gore, 1963

The Croker Papers by J. Wilson Croker, edited by Bernard Pool, 1967

581

Columbia University Press for an extract from *The Mind of Napoleon*, ed. and translated by J. Christopher Herold, 1961.

Ashgate for extracts from:

Romanticism and Religion from William Cowper to Wallace Stevens, ed. Gavin Hopps and Jane Stabler, 2006.

The Nineteenth Century Series, general editors, Vincent Newey, Professor of English and Joanne Shattock, Director of the Victoria Centre of Studies at the University of Leiecester.

Ohio State University Press for extracts from *Byron's Bulldog: The Letters of John Cam Hobhouse to Lord Byron*, ed. Peter W. Graham, 1984.

John Murray for extracts from:

The Flame of Freedom: the Greek War of Independence by David Brewer, London, 2001.

Don Juan in Context by Jerome J. McGann, 1976.

Palgrave Macmillan for extracts from *Romanticism and Male Fantasy in Byron's Don Juan: A Marketable Vice* by Charles Donelan, 2000.

Benedetta Origo with gratitude for kindly giving permission for quotations from *The Last Attachment* by Iris Origo, Jonathan Cape and John Murray, 1949.

Every effort has been made to track down all holders of copyright material quoted in *Byron the Maker*. If there is anyone who has not been acknowledged here we would be pleased to hear from them so that we can rectify the omission.

INDEX

Byron, Catherine (*continued*)
at mercy of husband's creditors, 5;
Gight Castle sold, 5; follows husband
to France, 6; nurses step-daughter,
Augusta, through illness and brings
home to Grandmother, Lady
Holdernesse, 6; Byron born London, 6;
move to Aberdeen, 6; Mrs Byron 'quite
a Democrat', 7; sells belongings and
moves to Newstead Abbey with child
when he succeeds to title and lands, 12;
hires John Hanson, lawyer, to manage
the boys' affairs, 16; disapproved of by
Dr Glennie, schoolmaster, 18;
dismisses May Gray, 19; move to
Southwell, 37; drawn to Lord Grey de
Ruthyn, tenant of Newstead Abbey,
who has alienated her son, 37; alarmed
at Byron's extravagance, 39; patronised
by Byron, 41; collects son's reviews,
51; Byron says she is to live at
Newstead when he goes to Europe, 61;
worries about welfare of Byron's
creditors, 64; attends Infirmary Ball
with Byron and Hobhouse, 64; letters
from Byron from his travels, 70, 73, 74,
78, 81, 82; she dies at Newstead, 82;
Byron contests scurrilous allegations
against her *The Scourge*, 83
Byron, George Anson, 7th Baron, 179,
185, 200, 201, 212, 234
Byron, George Gordon, 6th Baron
appearance: on dieting, becomes 'a
regular Apollo', 37, 42
deformity: 7, 9, 43
education: Bodsy Bowers School,
Aberdeen, 7; Grammar School,
Aberdeen, 8; Dr Glennie's Academy,
Dulwich, 18; Harrow School, 20, 21–35
finances: extravagance with large
Cambridge allowance, 39; tries to
persuade Augusta to guarantee a loan
and refuses her offer of a loan herself,
40; in hands of money lenders, 40; Mrs
Massingherd go-between and
guarantor, 40; raises travel money for
self and Hobhouse, 64; leaves England
without settling debts, 66; extravagance
threatens Newstead, 66; learns

Rochdale unsold and debts unpaid, 76;
resigned to poverty, 82; generosity to
Augusta, 179; prospective purchaser of
Newstead, Mr Claughton, 128; quixotic
loan to James Wedderburn Webster,
131; Claughton pays £5000 on account,
Byron clears some debts for George
Leigh and lends Hodgson £1000 to
enable him to marry, 177; Claughton
relinquishes purchase and deposit, so
Byron repays rest of Scrope Davies
loan, 184; plans generous settlement for
bride, Annabella Milbanke, 185; sale of
Newstead falls through, offers to
release from engagement, 192;
creditors descend on move into
Piccadilly Terrace, 196; bailiff moves
in, 197; death of Lord Wentworth
brings more creditors but money goes
to Milbanke, now Noels, 196; financial
offer from Annabella over separation
greatest insult for Byron, 234;
discussion of Wentworth legacy and
marriage settlement income, 234, 235;
Byron agrees legal arbitration and
signs separation papers, 235; bailiffs
descend on Piccadilly Terrace, 241;
failure of lawsuit over Rochdale
property, 361; must economise to settle
English debts and raise money for
Greece, 448; instructs Kinnaird to do
so, 450; arranges legacy of £5,000 for
Allegra, aged five, 339; anxious, as
must be prepared to support Augusta
and her children if necessary and,
possibly, even the Gambas, 402;
Wentworth income comes in, 401; by
March 1824 Greek cause has cost him
30,000 Spanish dollars excluding his
personal expenses; £4,000 loan should
be repaid but he will still use it for
Greece, 487
friendships: verdict of Aberdeen
schoolmates, 15/16; young friends at
Harrow, 23, 25; Elizabeth Pigot, 38, 39,
45, 46, 47, 58, 59, 60; John Pigot, 38,
39, 83; meeting with Charles Skinner
Matthews, John Cam Hobhouse, Scrope
Berdmore Davies, Douglas Kinnaird at

Byron, George Gordon, 6th Baron
  (continued)
  Cambridge, 61; Lady Byron's
  disapproval of friends, 63; Charles
  Dallas, 65; on death of mother,
  Matthews and Wingfield, Byron sends
  for Scrope Davies, 83; epigraph on
  social gluttony, 125; first meeting
  Thomas Moore, Samuel Rogers and
  Thomas Campbell, 91; family affection
  for half-sister, Augusta Byron, 29; Lady
  Frances Shelley on relationship with
  Augusta, 178; Lord and Lady Holland,
  82, 109; Lady Melbourne, 120–122,
  126, 134, 159, 177, 179, 182–184, 186,
  190, 195, 202, 209; Mme de Stael, 125,
  126, 127; Richard Brinsley Sheridan,
  137, 138; Leigh Hunt, 182; James
  Hogg, the Ettrick Shepherd, 183; Byron
  recommends Hobhouse as friend to
  Lady Holland, 183; Caroline, Princess
  of Wales, 236; John Murray, kindest
  correspondent, 267, 276; gift of
  poems of Casti from Pryse Gordon,
  268; visits Mme de Staël, 275;
  disillusioned Coleridge, 275; new
  friendship with Shelley, 273; Hobhouse
  and Scrope Davies arrive, 276; Shelley
  doses with Wordsworth physic, 287;
  Byron tries to help Polidori, 315; new
  friend Hoppner, 336; swimming contest
  with friends, 336; Shelley at Palazzo
  Mocenigo, 337; ride together at Lido,
  337; Hanson and son arrive, 339;
  Thomas Moore arrives, 346; Byron
  encourages Hobhouse in political
  career, 371; Hobhouse persuades Byron
  to omit cruel joke about Queen
  Caroline from *Don Juan*, 372; meets
  Pietro Gamba, 383, meeting with
  Samuel Rogers, 389; Shelley persuades
  Byron to come to Pisa, 389; Byron's
  bankers become his friends and
  confidants, 480; Byron tells Moore not
  to alter *Loves of the Angels* to appease
  critics, 'Forbid it, Ireland!', 414;
  Byron's last letter to Murray, 422;
  meets and sees through Trelawny, 427;
  Leigh Hunt arrives, 430; installed with
  family at Casa Lanfranchi, 430; visit of
  Earl of Clare, 429; Byron joins in
  search for Shelley, 431; attends
  cremation at Viareggio, 431; Problems
  with the Hunts, 432; Hobhouse visits
  briefly and Byron tells him he should
  never go, 432; new friend Lady Hardy,
  449; Blessingtons arrive, 451; Byron
  writes to Stendhal defending character
  of Sir Walter Scott, 455; letter to
  Greece from Hobhouse with high praise
  for Byron's actions there, 493;
  disappointed in reactions of friends to
  Don Juan, 501; Scott on his character,
  523; tribute of James Hogg, 524
  homosexual tendencies: discussed by
  Ian Gilmour, 26, Paul Elledge, 26, 27,
  28, Jerome Christensen, 28; theory
  Byron exclusively homosexual and not
  bi-sexual, 28; incident with Lord Grey
  de Ruthyn, 26, 28, 37; John Edleston,
  26, 44; mistaken belief Edleston taken
  up for indecency and its effects, 45;
  Thyrza cycle, lines from, 83, 86; death
  of Edleston, 86; Eustathius Gregorious,
  78; boys at Capuchin monastery, 29;
  Nicolo Giraud, 79; Byron's boasts of
  sexual prowess with boys in Greece,
  79; uses code for buggery, 79; Loukas
  Chalandritsanos becomes an object of
  love for Byron, 475; 'Love and Death',
  490; poem on his 36th birthday, 491, 492
  in love: Mary Duff, 10; Mary
  Chaworth, 24, 25, 64; Southwell
  beauties, 38; Lady Caroline Lamb,
  115–123; Lady Oxford, 119–123; Lady
  Frances Webster, 129–134; Augusta
  Leigh, 175–186; Augusta remains
  Byron's great love, he sends her flowers
  from Coblenz, 266; Marianna Segati,
  313; Margarita Cogni, 338; Teresa
  Guiccioli, 341; Loukas
  Chalandritsanos, 490
  poetry: extracts 'Childish
  Recollections', 19; 'Damaetas', 26;
  from 'Childish Recollections', 32; from
  Thyrza cycle for Edleston, 44; from 'To
  a Knot of Ungenerous Critics', 46;
  quotations from *English Bards and*

Byron, George Gordon, 6th Baron
(continued)
Scotch Reviewers, 53, 54, 55; repents of
satire, 55/56; itinerary and timing of
Childe Harold's Pilgrimage, 98–103;
Byron re-writes Cantos I and II, Childe
Harold's Pilgrimage, 83, 84, 86,
95–106; also Hints from Horace, 85;
Byron claims the air of Greece made
him a poet, 85; 'Ode to the Framers of
the Frame Bill', 89, 90; mention of
English Bards and Scotch Reviewers,
91, 95; Don Juan, 97; lines linked to
Lady Melbourne in Don Juan, 110;
lines on women and fame in Don Juan,
111; lines on rent from The Age of
Bronze, 113–115; lines from 'The
Monody on the Death of Sheridan',
137; The Giaour, 141–143, 150, 151;
The Bride of Abydos, 143, 147; lines
from The Corsair, 143–144, 146; Lara,
Parisina, Siege of Corinth, 144; The
Curse of Minerva, 145, 146; Lara, 147,
148; 'My Boat is on the Shore', a
tribute to Thomas Moore, 148, 149;
The Corsair, 149; Byron's poetry
inspires revolutionaries, 150–151; lines
on the Prince Regent from Don Juan,
157; from 'Ode to Napoleon
Bonaparte', 161; 'Weep, daughter of a
royal line', 158; sonnet to the Prince
Regent, now George IV, 159; Hebrew
Melodies, 166–173; lines on music,
Manfred, 167; 'She walks in Beauty',
169; 'Destruction of Sennacherib', 169,
170; 'The Harp the Minstrel Monarch
swept', 171; 'I speak not, I trace not, I
breathe not, thy name', 181; from
'Lines on Hearing that Lady Byron was
ill', 206; 'The Separation Poems',
219–229; 'Stanzas for Music', 237,
238; 'Churchill's Grave', 242, 243;
'Prometheus', 247, 248; Childe
Harold's Pilgrimage Canto III, 263,
264, 265; 'Darkness', 270, 271, 272;
Childe Harold's Pilgrimage Canto III,
279, 280, 286, 287, 287, 288, 289, 290;
Manfred, 293, 294, 295, 296; 'Though
the Day of My Destiny's Over', 299,
300; 'Epistle to Augusta', 302–304;
Child Harold's Pilgrimage Canto IV,
309, 320, 321, 322, 323, 324, 325, 326;
Beppo, 329, 330, 331, 332, 333;
'Epistle from Mr Murray to Dr
Polidori', 315–317; 'So We'll Go No
More a-Roving', 318; from Dedication
to the Prophecy of Dante, 341; from
'Stanzas to the Po', 342; from Prophecy
of Dante, 349; from Marino Faliero,
366, 367; from Don Juan, Canto V,
372; from Mazeppa, 355, 356; from
The Two Foscari, 376; from The Age of
Bronze, 380, 381; from the Dedication
to Don Juan, 382, 383; from
Sardanapalus, 394, 395, 396; from
Cain, 409; from Heaven and Earth,
415; from The Vision of Judgment,
436–440; from The Island, 456; from
Don Juan, Canto III, 'The Isles of
Greece', 459–462; from 'Lines
Composed on My 36th Birthday',
491–492; From Don Juan, 500,
505–514, 516

contemporary criticism of poems:
Hours of Idleness: Antiquarian
   Review and Magazine, December
   1807, The Satirist, January 1808,
   The Monthly Monitor, 51, The
   Eclectic Review, 57, Hazlitt, 58
Childe Harold's Pilgrimage, I
   and II: J.G. Lockhart, 97, Hazlitt,
   97, John Scott, 97, Edward Daniel
   Clarke, 103, The Edinburgh
   Review, 143, 144, The British
   Review, 143, The Satirist, 143
The Corsair: Hazlitt, 143, The
   Critical Review, 143, 144, The
   Edinburgh Review, 144, 194
The Siege of Corinth: Gifford, 144
Manfred: Edinburgh Review, Jeffrey,
   297
Canto IV, Childe Harold's
   Pilgrimage: Constable's
   Edinburgh Magazine, 325,
   Quarterly Review (Sir Walter
   Scott), 325
Edinburgh Review (John Wilson),
   325

modern criticism of poems
(continued)
Vision of Judgment: M.K. Joseph,
443, Bernard Beatty, 443, Marilyn
Butler, 444
The Island: M.K. Joseph, 455,
Arnold A. Schmidt, 455, Jerome
McGann, 455, 456, G. Wilson
Knight, 456, Michael Cooke, 456
The Deformed Transformed: M.K.
Joseph, 457, G. Wilson Knight,
458, Bernard Beatty, 458
Don Juan: Anne Barton, 499, 514,
515, 517, Paul Trueblood, 515,
517, M.K. Joseph, 515, 516,
Jonathan Gross, 515, Jerome
McGann, 516, Jane Stabler, 518,
Charles Donelan, 518, Marcel
Proust (quoted by Charles
Donelan), 518, Richard Cronin,
518, 519
politics: influence of Aberdeen on
political views, 7; Mrs Byron 'quite a
Democrat', 18; prospect of
parliamentary career, 22; Greece
instilled love of freedom, 85; maiden
speech on death penalty for frame-
breakers, 87; explains views on this to
Lord Holland, 87, 88; castigates
parliament for attitude to 'the mob', 88;
own account of the speech, 88, 89;
'Ode to the Framers of the Frame Bill',
89, 90; London newspapers and
workers' reform clubs, 91; Catholic
Emancipation, 92, 93; Convention of
Cintra, 99; views on Spanish nobility
versus Spanish people, 99; tirade
against war-profiteers *Age of Bronze*,
113–115; Mme de Staël on freedom in
England for Byron to abuse
government, 125; Byron's poetry
inspires revolutionaries, Philhellenes
and the founders of Solidarity in
Poland, 150; Charles James Fox, 153;
Derbyshire rising, 154; Cato Street
conspiracy, 154; safer to be a felon than
a radical, 154; presents Major
Cartwright's petition for parliamentary
reform, 155; Foxite whigs, 156; stanzas
on Prince of Wales as young man, 157;
insult to Prince Regent of 'Lines to a
Lady weeping', 158; furore over poem,
158, 159, 182; distress over fall and
unheroic role of Napoleon Bonaparte,
159, 160; lines from 'Ode to Napoleon
Bonaparte', 161; outrage caused by
poems purporting to be 'from the
French', 162; description by Jonathan
Gross of 'the principles of whiggery',
163; mistaken view of Bertrand Russell
that Byron was 'almost a fascist', 163;
Byron on Freedom for Greeks and other
nations, 164; he praises Mirabeau and
La Fayette and condemns cruelty of
Marat and Robespierre, 164; E.P.
Thompson on Hunt and Cobbett, 164;
Byron decides only a Republic will do,
165
(see 'War' and 'Romagna' for politics
in exile)
religion: puzzling over it as a child, 11;
denies nothing but doubts everything,
34; lack of religious instruction at
Harrow, 35; abhors religion but
reverences God, 35; writes of religion
to Annabella Milbanke, 130; Catholic
Emancipation, 93, 94
servants: Joe Murray, 16, 18, 135;
Robert Rushton, 67/68; William
Fletcher, 67, 68, 74, 78, 81; Mrs Mule,
134; Susan Vaughan, 86; Nanny Smith,
62, 63; Mary Chaworth's old nurse, 24;
May Gray, 10, 12, 17, 19; Byron
remonstrates with Lady Byron for
refusing Mrs Fletcher a reference
thereby denying her the means of
earning her bread, 208; asks Hobhouse
to arrange references for coachman and
footman who must not suffer from his
forgetfulness, 267; Fletcher sobbing
beside Byron's bed when ill at La Mira,
347; Allegra looked after by a nurse
and two maids, 360; defence of Tita
Falcieri over altercation with soldier,
will not dismiss him unless the matter
goes before a court since the fortune,
life and honour of his servant is at risk,
387

war: 'Byron's Blacks', 8; better ways to benefit mankind than shooting them at Waterloo, 11; remonstrates with Edward Long for going to war, 43; and with Hobhouse for joining the militia, 77; 'detestation of licensed murder', 85; in *Childe Harold* exhorts the Greeks to 'throw off their bondage', 97; anti-war lines from *Childe Harold*, 98; 'sublime war reportage with Goya-esque caricature', 98; fall of Napoleon, 157; Timon of Athens, 397, 398, Napoleon justified or not, 398; Alcibiades, 398; Montaigne on war, 468, 469; speculation over his reasons for joining in the Greek war, 463; poem on 36th birthday, 491, 492; desire to serve the Greek people, 464; Risorgimento, 350, 367, 391; Mazzini on Byron 350; *Sardanapalus* anti-war statement, 393–98; *The Island*, 456; *The Deformed Transformed*, 458; *Greek Project* thoughts turning to Greece, 406; discusses situation and advises London Greek Committee, 453; almost alone in not patronising the Greeks, 464; Philhellenes follow Byron to Greece, 472; Byron doesn't mince words in dealing with Mavrocordato, 472; arrival of Sir Charles Napier, 473; criticised by Trelawny for staying at Metaxata but this the only wise course at this stage, 474; patience with Greeks, 475; cancels Tripolitza to join Mavrocordato at Mesolonghi, 476; voyage to Mesolonghi, 477, 478; welcome there, 478; problems with Colonel Stanhope, 478, 479; Finlay says Byron a far wiser counsellor than Stanhope, 479; Byron fears British families who contributed to the Greek loan may lose their money by his Philhellenism in absence of guarantee but bankers will get their commissions, 479; arrival of William Parry, 479; gift from Greek peasant woman, 483; dismisses Suliotes, 485; heroic conduct of Greeks, 491; death in Greece and transformation into a Greek hero, 497

Deplorable behaviour by Byron: high notions of rank as a boy, 18; insufferable letter to mother, 32; outrageous behaviour to Dr Butler at Harrow, 33; adolescent rebellious behaviour at Southwell, 39; cutting a dash at Cambridge, 39; episode of contemptuous attitude to Hanson as part of this, 40; extravagance at Cambridge to impress, 39, 40; tries to persuade Augusta to guarantee a loan for him while at Cambridge, 40; persuades landlady, Mrs Massingbird, to act as security for loan, she becomes go-between with moneylenders, 40; patronising attitude to his mother at this time, 41; gets a maid at Newstead pregnant (provides for her financially), 62; revenges himself on Lord Carlisle for House of Lords snub by comments in *English Bards and Scotch Reviewers*, 55; leaves people to whom he owes money unpaid when leaves England, expecting, but not knowing, that Rochdale would be sold to pay them, 64; demand for precedence at Constantinople, 84; dilatoriness in visiting home of his bride to be, 190, and in travelling to Seaham for the wedding, 192; resorts to alcohol and laudanum over arrival of bailiffs during marriage, 197; affair with actress during marriage, 197; weakness, as a young man, for dramatic and tragic extravagance, 199; one instance (of which there is reliable evidence) of angry behaviour to his pregnant wife, 201; confesses to Hobhouse neglect and unkind behaviour to his wife, 212; 'The Sketch', a violent attack on a female servant, 220; 'Fare Thee Well' verses, later, Teresa Guiccioli scolds him, as she finds them not worthy of him, 225; unkind joke about Queen Caroline intended for *Don Juan*, 372, 373; strong attack on the lawyer, Romilly, after his death, 383; attack on Castlereagh, 382, 383

Travels in Exile: irritated by inquisitive tourists from England, 261; settles at Villa Diodati near Geneva, 268; visits Chillon, 273; Vevay, Clarens, Lausanne, 274; Bernese Oberland, 276; Ouchy, 300; Milan, Vicenza, Verona, 310; settles in Venice, 310; to Rome, 319; summer at La Mira, 329; Ferrara, 319; Arqua, 319, 345; Ravenna, 343; Bologna, 345; Pisa, 309; Montenero, 427; Genoa, 454, Argostoli, 466; at Cephalonia, 467; Mesolonghi, 477; Ithaca, 475

Generosity: kind letter of advice to nervous new author, 57; asks Hodgson to review the publication, 57; raises money to enable Hobhouse to travel with him to Greece, 64; lends money to Wedderburn Webster, 131; sends news to Lord Carlisle that his son died at Waterloo without prolonged suffering as he had believed, 241; asks Murray to help Polidori make his way, 315; recommends Leigh Hunt as an author, to Murray, 317; gives Shelleys use of rented Villa at Este so Claire can be with Allegra, 337; brings Dr Aglietti from Venice to Ravenna to treat Teresa, 344; makes present of his *Memoirs* to Moore (in financial trouble), 346; gives regularly to beggars in the Ravenna woods, 358; rents a house in the country for Allegra during heatwave in Ravenna, 360; offers to support Teresa, 361; puts Allegra in expensive convent, 362; when Murray in danger of prosecution for *Cain*, offers to refund copyright and come to England to stand trial, 403; persuades Murray to publish *Commentary* by Taaffe, 403; offers money to rescue man accused of sacrilege from being burned to death, 404; agrees to fit out part of his house for the Hunt family and sends Hunt £250 for the journey, 428; gives Hunt copyright of *Vision of Judgment*, 430; writes to Sir Timothy Shelley on behalf of Mary, 446; and to John Murray on behalf of a previous author of his, a woman who has lost her husband and seeks help, 448; sends the woman 300 francs, 449; offers to provide a home for the Leighs at Nice, 449; when Lady Hardy tells him Trelawny suspects a coldness between them, writes kindly invitation for him to come with him to Greece, 454; warns laundry woman in Greece not to send her young daughter alone among his serving men as she is a mere child and deserves a better fate, 473; rescues Chalandritsanos women from poverty in Ithaca, Loukas comes to share the house provided in Cephalonia, 475; sends 4 Turks to commander at Patras in hope that he will be equally merciful to Greek prisoners, 481; sends 24 Turks to Governor at Prevesa to rescue from distress, 482; insists on paying fine for John Hunt over decision of Court of King's Bench over *Vision of Judgment*, 486

Byron, Sir John, 1st Baron, 3
Byron, Captain John, 'Mad Jack', Byron's father, 6, 29, 30, 175
Byron, Admiral John, 'Foulweather Jack', 13
Byron, William, 5th Baron, 'The Wicked Lord', 12, 13, 16

Campbell, Thornas, 91, 138
Candide, Voltaire, 291
Canning, George, 137, 236, 237
Carbonari, 383, 384, 463, 482
Carlile, Richard, 408
Carlisle, Frederick Howard, 5th Earl of, 18, 20, 30, 31, 39, 55, 76, 115, 117, 177
Carlyle, Thomas, 298
Caroline, Princess of Wales, later Queen, 236, 372, 373
Cartwright, Major John, 154, 155
Casa Magni, 418, 427, 430, 431
Casa Saluzzo, 445
Casti, Ciambattista, *Animali Parlanti*, 268
Castle of Chillon, 273
Castlereagh, Robert Stewart, Viscount, 93, 163, 236, 379, 382, 383

Galt, John, 106
Gamba, (Ghiselli) Count Ruggiero, 346, 357, 359, 360, 362, 379, 388, 389, 400, 429, 465
Gamba, Pietro, 383, 386, 388, 389, 400, 404, 429, 430, 432, 465, 477, 478, 483, 484, 496
Genoa, 445–454
George III, 435, 440, 441, 442, 443
George IV, 110, 156, 157, 158, 159, 176, 182, 237, 394
Ghigi, Pellegrino, 417
Gibbon, Edward, 273, 274, 291, 327
Gide, André, 327, 522
Gifford, William, 50, 52, 90, 144, 285, 422, 501
Giorgione, 311
Giraud, Niccolo, 79, 181
Glenarvon, 315
Glennie, Dr, 18
Godwin, William, 232
Goethe, Johann Wolfgang von, 245, 274, 297, 298, 410, 415, 521
Gordon, Jane, Duchess of, 47
Gordon, Mrs Pryse Lockhart, 262, 263
Gordon, Pryse Lockhart, 262, 263, 268
Gordon, Thomas, 471
Goya, Francisco, José, 98
Grand Canal, Venice, 336, 337
Granville, Harriet, Countess of, née Cavendish, 107, 108, 109, 111, 112, 145, 186, 396, 407, 408
Gray, May, 10, 19
Greek Chronicle, 487, 488
Gregorious, Eustathius, 78
Grey de Ruthyn, Henry Edward Gould, 19th Baron, 27, 28, 37
Guiccioli, Count Alessandro, 341, 343, 346, 347, 357, 359, 360, 362
Guiccioli, Countess Teresa, née Gamba, 341, 343, 344, 345, 346, 347, 352, 357, 360, 361, 363, 389, 395, 396, 400, 401, 428, 430, 465, 472, 494, 504, 515

Hancock, Charles, 479, 480
Hanson, John, 16, 17, 18, 19, 20, 21, 22, 25, 40, 41, 53, 63, 65, 73, 76, 184, 185, 202, 241, 281, 338, 339

Hardy, Anne Louise Emily, Lady, née Berkeley, 449, 451, 452
Harley, Lady Charlotte, 120, 121
Harness, Revd William, 23, 86, 199
Hatchard, Bookseller, 57, 52
Hazlitt William, 57, 58, 91, 111, 112, 143, 435, 523
The Hercules, 465, 466, 468, 470, 473
Histoire de Charles XII, Voltaire, 356
Hobhouse, John Cam, later Baron Broughton de Gifford: detests Byron on sight, 34; travels with Byron, 45; introduced to Byron, 49; remarks on Byron's distress at review in *Edinburgh Review*; in Brighton with Byron, 60; discusses Greek love possibilities on trip to Greece, 68; sails from Falmouth with Byron, 69; with Byron in Athens, 74, letters from Byron on boys in Athens, 80; approves removal of Elgin Marbles to London, 100; Byron invites Hobhouse to travel once more with him, 139; Byron recommends Hobhouse as friend to Lady Holland, 182; Hobhouse remarks on Byron's lack of discretion, 191; accompanies to Seaham for wedding, 192; relays claims about reasons for separation, 200; tells how Lady Noel tried to bully Ann Fletcher into changing her testimony, 204; advises Annabella to return to Byron, 208; tells Byron horrific rumour that Byron asked his wife in labour if the baby was dead, 213; agrees to destruction of the *Memoirs*, 215; Augusta learns to value him as faithful friend to Byron, 228; he and Byron drunk at Piccadilly Terrace, 231, 232; discusses prosecuting Milbankes for conspiracy, 234; constant visitor to Byron, 238; moves into Piccadilly Terrace, 241; sees Byron off at Dover, 241, 242; Byron relies on Hobhouse for practical help, 268; invites him to Villa Diodati, 276; sad poem about distant friends includes Hobhouse, 269; arrives in Switzerland, 276; puzzled by *Canto III*, 268; travels to Venice with Byron, 310; writes notes for *Canto IV*, 326;

Mazzini, Giuseppe, 350
Mealey, Owen, 25, 37
Meditations Poétiques, Lamartine, 411
Medwin, Thomas, 352, 353, 400
Melbourne, Elizabeth, Viscountess, née Milbanke, 130–34, 177, 179, 182–94, 186, 191, 195, 196, 202, 209
Memoirs, Byron, 198, 215, 346
Mengaldo, Angelo, 336
Mesolonghi, 477–97
Milan, 310
Milbanke, Judith, Lady, later Noel, 89, 189, 219, 234, 281, 401
Milbanke, Sir Ralph, later Noel, 185, 189, 192, 219, 234, 281
Millingen, Dr Julius, 495
Milton, John, 294, 304, 392, 522
Mirabeau, Honoré Gabriel, Comte de, 164
Moldavia, 406, 471
Montaigne, Michel de, *Essays*, 450, 468, 469
Monti, Vicenzo, 310
Moore, Thomas: judged it difficult to distinguish real from fanciful in Byron's life, x; regards precociousness in love sign of artistic soul, 10; Moore biography praised by William St Clair, 12; and Jeffery Vail, 13; Moore on Byron's childhood, 15, 16, 17; John Pigot tells Moore no spark of malice in Byron, 38; believes Byron left England in melancholy mood, 67; he and Byron become fast friends, 92; Moore finds Lady Frances Webster vain and cold-blooded, 133; writes of Byron's tendency to fun and laughter, 135; Byron writes to Moore from Venice in defence of Sheridan's memory, 138; Byron dedicates *The Corsair* to Moore, 141; denigrates his *Oriental Tales* to Moore, 144; Moore knows this young man is Caesar among poets, 145; Byron and Moore share audience, 148; tribute of farewell song for Moore, 148, 149; Moore and Byron merits argued in *Java Gazette*, 155; Moore saw Byron listening to his *Irish Melodies* with

tears in his eyes, 167; Moore and Byron share liking for melancholy poetry and helping the downtrodden, 172; Byron describes to Moore his love for Augusta as 'a new scrape', not a crime, 180; Moore and Byron in London during Summer of the Sovereigns, 184, Byron tells Moore cannot cast any blame on Lady Byron during the marriage, 187; Moore reluctantly agrees destruction of the *Memoirs*, 215; discusses 'Fare Thee Well' with Byron, 223; kind letter from Moore, 233, Rogers describes Byron's sadness at being far from Moore, 239; message for Moore from Venice, 240; Moore finds traces of Shelley and Wordsworth in *Canto III* of *Childe Harold's Pilgrimage*, 287; Moore arrives in Venice, 345; meets Teresa but stays at Palazzo Mocenigo, 346; Hobhouse angry at gift of Byron's *Memoirs* to Moore, 346; Moore's view of Castlereagh, 382; Byron asks Moore to help get Taaffe's *Commentary* published, 403; Moore's admiration for *Cain*, 407; Moore's *Loves of the Angels* comes out soon after *Heaven and Earth*, 414; tactless letter from Moore to Byron in Greece, 493
Morning Chronicle, 89, 91, 153
Mortimer, John, 441
Mule, Mrs, 134
Murray, Joe, 16, 62, 67, 70, 135
Murray, John, 50, 66, 85, 96, 125, 179, 211, 232, 267, 268, 273, 275, 280, 282, 285, 293, 299, 300, 312, 313, 315, 317, 318, 319, 320, 321, 326, 346, 351, 355, 358, 366, 379, 389, 391, 399, 402, 403, 413, 421, 422, 446, 448, 501, 503, 515, 516
Musters, Jack, 64, 77

Napier, Sir Charles, 473
Nathan, Isaac, 168, 170, 171, 172
Newgate Prison, 370, 371
Newstead Abbey, 3, 12, 13, 15, 16, 24, 25, 27, 28, 34, 37, 59, 60, 61, 62, 65, 66, 81, 82, 86, 96, 128, 140, 177, 178, 179, 185, 189, 192, 193, 226, 241, 339

597